ENCYCLOPEDIA OF LONG-TERM FINANCING AND CAPITAL MANAGEMENT

Also by the author:

Long-Term Financing—1961
Profit Goals and Capital Management—1968
Earnings per Share and Management Decisions—1971

ENCYCLOPEDIA OF LONG-TERM FINANCING AND CAPITAL MANAGEMENT

John F. Childs

Prentice-Hall, Inc. Englewood Cliffs, New Jersey

Prentice-Hall International, Inc., *London*
Prentice-Hall of Australia, Pty. Ltd., *Sydney*
Prentice-Hall of Canada, Ltd., *Toronto*
Prentice-Hall of India Private Ltd., *New Delhi*
Prentice-Hall of Japan, Inc., *Tokyo*

Library of Congress Cataloging in Publication Data

Childs, John Farnsworth.
Encyclopedia of long-term financing and capital management.

Includes index.
1. Corporations--Finance. 2. Capital investments.
I. Title.
HG4011.C54 658.1'5'03 75-20333
ISBN 0-13-276113-0

Printed in the United States of America

Dedication

I dedicated my books to my daughter. As time went by things changed:

My first book: "To Susan, my wonderful ten-year-old daughter, whose strong feeling about this book was that it took too much of Dad's time."

My second book: "This book I also dedicate to her but things have changed. At 16 she is so interested in her horse, that it is less important how Dad spends his time—but she is still just as much fun."

My third book: "I also dedicate this one to her. I am pleased that she did the illustrations in this book."

She is now about to become an art teacher, which talent I can't claim came from me. May whatever she does bring her enduring pleasure.

About the Author

The author is widely known in the field of finance as an advisor, lecturer and writer on all phases of corporate finance for all types of corporations. He has worked in Wall Street for over 40 years, initially as a financial analyst with an investment banking firm. Subsequently, he joined a major New York bank where he spent his time largely in the area of long-term corporate financial policy and capital management. He was a Senior Vice-President in charge of the bank's Corporate Services Division, which included the Corporate Financial Counseling Department.

He is now a Senior Officer of a leading investment banking firm.

His book *Long-Term Financing* achieved 12 printings and acceptance as one of the most practical books in its field. He also is author of *Profit Goals and Capital Management* and *Earnings per Share and Management Decisions*, all three books having been published by Prentice-Hall, Inc. In addition, he has written numerous articles on various financial subjects.

Mr. Childs lectures regularly throughout the country before financial, accounting and management associations and institutes. The financial seminars he originated for senior executives of industrial companies, banks and utility companies earned a unique reputation for their practical approach to finance.

A director of the Florida Power Corporation (1968-1975), and past director of both the Atomic Industrial Forum and the American Management Association, the author has been an active member of the New York Society of Security Analysts, at one time filling the position of Secretary and Chairman of the Program Committee.

Mr. Childs earned his M.B.A. Degree from the Harvard Graduate School of Business and his LL.B. from Fordham University. He is a member of the New York Bar.

Author's Introduction—The Book's Plan

The purpose of this encyclopedic work is to gather in one place the many subjects which corporate executives will need for planning and decision making in finance and capital investment for their companies. It should show you how to plan your financing, raise needed capital, handle relations with investors and put capital to work successfully.

This book updates and expands the material included in my three earlier books and adds much new material.

Though encyclopedic in length and detailed coverage, the book is purposely written in easy, readable language and style to show that finance need not be as mysterious as some people would have you believe.

The Book's Plan

The book is divided into two parts. Financing or raising capital is covered in Part I; putting capital to work in a meaningful way is covered in Part II.

Plan for Part I

In the first chapter, we will see how finance and capital management fits into our economic system.

One of the aims of the book will be to assist a company in financial planning.

There are three fundamental steps in financial planning:

1. Determine the proper make-up of long term capital.
2. Establish a dividend policy—whether none, low or high.
3. Make a five-year forecast with specific securities to be sold each year to raise capital.

Since the first step requires the determination of the make-up of long term capital, we will begin with this subject in Chapter 2.

In Chapter 3, we will cover dividend policy since this is the next logical step in financial planning.

Because we will use specific types of securities in a financial plan, we will discuss the various types of securities in Chapter 4. In Chapter 5 we will consider the possible corporate setups for financing, such as a separate finance subsidiary. Then we will be ready to illustrate how to lay out a financial plan in Chapter 6. We will have answered many questions in Part I such as:

How much long term debt can a company use?
What types of securities should be sold?
Can the formation of a subsidiary aid in financing?
When should financing be done?
Should dividends be sacrificed to provide funds for capital investment?
What dividend payout policy should be followed?
How does one set up a financing plan?
To what extent should short term financing be used?
What is the best corporate setup for financing?
Where do the funds come from?

The above will get us a long way on the road to financing for a company, but there is, of course, much more to the subject of finance. Therefore, there will be many other questions which will also have to be answered in the other six chapters in Part I, such as:

How should securities be sold?
Should an investment banker be used to assist in the financing?
How should he be chosen?
What part should he play?
How much should he be paid?
At what price can securities be sold?
What may be the best market for your outstanding securities?
How do security analysts look at your securities?
Who makes up the financial community?
Who are the investors to cultivate?
What program should be used to cultivate investors?
When and how should the rating agencies be contacted?

We will finish Part I with a chapter on bank financing which requires special treatment.

Plan for Part II

When a company finances an expansion or an acquisition, it is preparing to put capital to work. One follows the other, and there is a natural relationship between the two, but financing and putting capital to work are separate subjects and require separate decisions. We will discuss putting capital to work in this part.

We will start off in Chapter 14 with an explanation of how earnings per share increase since this is of such obvious interest. In Chapter 15, we will explain in as simple a way as possible the fact that all capital has a cost, and that a company must understand the importance of covering all costs, including the capital costs, for a successful expansion. We will show how to set a profit goal.

To make a decision for go or no-go for expansion requires that the profitability of a project, in terms of return on capital, be calculated correctly. This we will cover in Chapter 16. We will also cover the mysteries of acquisition pricing in this chapter.

Once the capital has been raised and put to work, management should monitor the results. In Chapter 17 we will discuss setting standards for division performance.

In the final Chapter, 18, we will complete the cycle of finance and capital management and discuss how an investor gets a fair return and what this means for the price of your stock. Everything has to tie together, from the investor supplying the money, to the company putting it to work, to the investor receiving a fair return.

The Importance of Principles

There are basic principles of finance and capital management just as there are principles of economics. They are the starting point for decision making. They will give you something solid to hang your hat on. Throughout the book, we will be developing principles; this is an important feature of the book.

John F. Childs

ACKNOWLEDGMENTS

Joe Tenicki for his help throughout the book. While he was working on the book, he continuously worried about the possibility of getting blamed if there were any errors, no matter who made them. As a matter of fact, the more he mentioned it the better the idea sounded.

"Chi Chi" Rodriguez, my wonderful secretary, for all the help she has been in business and with the book. There were times when she acted as though I had been married to her for 20 years, without the benefit of a honeymoon, but she always ended up with super work and good cheer.

J.F.C.

TABLE OF CONTENTS

PART ONE

Financing

CHAPTER 1

Purpose of Finance and Capital Management

Our Economic System

Finance plays a vital service role in our economic system. In order to see where finance fits, let's take a quick look at how our economic system works. Our economic system should operate to raise the standard of living of our nation by producing the most goods and services possible that can be sold at prices which will cover all costs. In the process, the elements of production—including labor and capital—should be paid fairly.

Our economic system is characterized by:

Private capital ownership—capital owned either directly or indirectly by the individual.

Incentive—profits act as the incentive and as a reward for management and capital. Also, profits are the "carrot" to guide management in capital decision making. Wages and salaries are based on the ability to produce.

Competition—competition protects the consumers by driving prices down to cover all costs, including at least the cost-of-capital, or, in other words, sufficient profit to satisfy investors in the competitive capital market.

Freedom of choice—for the consumers, workers and investors.

There are two other economic systems in the world today regardless of the name under which they may parade:

Socialism—with capital owned by the government and labor rewarded on the basis of the ability to produce.

Communism—with capital owned by the government and labor rewarded on the basis of need.

There is no place in this book to discuss the merits and failings of the three systems, but socialism and communism do differ markedly from our system in the ownership of capital, incentive and freedom of choice.

The Goal for a Company

The primary goal for a company, in the atmosphere of our free enterprise system, is to satisfy the consumer's needs and in so doing make a profit. This is the most fundamental *principle.* It was succinctly stated in an article "Put Profit in Its Place":[1]

> The primary purpose of——business is to satisfy the needs of the consumer . . .
>
> Capital is essential for the business process because it lowers the cost of satisfying our consumer's needs, so we must earn a rate of profit sufficient to attract the necessary capital to our business. Capital is necessary for our business and profit is necessary for our business. But to say that profit is our purpose is no more correct than to say wages are the purpose of our business. Profit, then, is a means, a very necessary means, to accomplish our purpose.

The test of whether the goods and services are needed is whether they stand up in the face of competition so that consumers are willing to pay prices sufficient to cover all costs, including good wages and a fair return to investors.

A company which can do something better for the consumers than its competitors, should make a true profit above all costs, since the consumers, with freedom of choice, will eagerly buy the company's products.

Purpose of Profits

We have already pointed out the purpose of profits, but we can summarize it here as a *principle* in terms of its three functions:

1. A reward to the providers of capital.
2. An incentive.
3. A guide in capital decision making.

[1]"Put Profit in Its Place," by John Adams, Jr., *Harvard Business Review,* March-April 1973. Copyright by the President and Fellows of Harvard University.

Purpose of Finance

The purpose of finance in our economic system is to provide companies with capital to assist in the production of goods and services. This requires a regular and orderly transfer of the savings of our nation from investors, who are the savers. In the process investors should be rewarded fairly.

The idea of "regular and orderly transfer of savings," is an integral part of finance. The regular flow of the savings into production is necessary for the smooth working of our economy. All people connected with finance—those in Wall Street, those investing funds and those handling finance in companies—should aid this regular flow. Unfortunately, some people, both inside and outside of corporations, take a relatively selfish approach to finance regardless of the consequences to our economy. Particularly during a boom period, they seem to think of finance as having an end in itself, as a "money-making machine." As a result, there is unsound financing with booms and busts. This inhibits the regular and orderly flow of capital.

Savings flow into corporations through the sale of securities. There are two basic types of securities—long term debt and common equity, as shown under long term capital in the simple balance sheet of a typical industrial company in Exhibit 1-1. Retained earnings, which go into common equity are forced savings which management decides to retain rather than pay out in dividends.

Current liabilities provide capital through accounts payable, short term bank loans, etc., but they are not the major capital source which involves long term financing.

Thus, we can put into a *principle* the purpose of finance:

> To transfer the savings of our nation in an orderly fashion into production so as to produce more goods and services and reward the investors fairly.

Exhibit 1-1

FLOW OF SAVINGS INTO A COMPANY

Balance Sheet

Assets		*Liabilities*			
Current Assets	$100	Current Liabilities		$ 50	
Plant, Net	50	Long Term Capital			
		Debt	$25		Savings
		Common Equity	$75		flow
		Total		$100	in here
Total	$150	Total		$150	

Purpose of Capital Management

The purpose of capital management is another basic *principle:*

> To direct the flow of capital and manage it so as to produce goods and services which, when sold at competitive prices, will provide sufficient income over the life of the investment to more than cover all costs, including a fair return to investors.

Today, the success of your company depends to a great extent on correct decisions on capital management. They are vital to:

> Your stockholders—because of the direct effect on profits through the return realized on the capital.
>
> All companies in an industry—because over-expansion by one company will hurt prices in the entire industry and have a corresponding effect on profits.
>
> Our entire economy—because capital directed where it is not needed means production of the wrong goods and a resulting reduction in our standard of living. Furthermore, if excessive expansion occurs in a prosperous period, it will accentuate the business cycle and the unemployment problem.

Total capital of all U.S. Corporations[2] is the staggering amount of $1.5 trillion; it represents about $25,000 per employee.

A company which handles capital poorly may be doomed to mediocrity or failure.

Long vs. Short Range View— For Whom Is Management Working?

Another important point, which we will be stressing throughout the book, is to take into account the long range view.

Management has many responsibilities, one of which, as stated above, is to reward the stockholders, the owners, fairly; stockholders are rewarded through dividends and market appreciation of their stock. Many financing and capital investment policies may benefit stockholders in the short run but not the long run. Yet, there are pressures on management to take a short range point of view and the short range view is generally the easiest.

Stockholders can take a different view than management. Stockholders always buy a

---

[2]Figures for year end 1973. Total debt and employees from *Survey of Current Business,* June 1974; common equity at market from *Annual Total Flows of Funds and Year End Assets and Liabilities,* Board of Governors of the Federal Reserve System, August 1974.

stock with the idea that it is going up; otherwise, they would not buy it. When they buy a stock, they may hope to be a long range investor and desire long term gains. However, investors can change from long range to short range at will, and, if things go sour, they can either sit tight and hope for an improvement or they can sell out and take their loss. They have fluidity of capital.

A company, on the other hand, does not have fluidity of capital, it cannot readily dispose of its assets and liquidate, nor quickly improve its financial position. A company will have stockholders when its earnings and the market price of its stock are going up and down. And when adversity is encountered, it may not be able to take a passive attitude and sit tight until its stock improves: it may have to raise capital, it may have to meet debt maturities, it may have to pay dividends, etc.

Management cannot ignore the short range effects of its decisions because of the temporary effect it has on its stockholders, but, above all, it must weigh the long range effect. Concentrating on the short range alone can result in anything from poor results to disaster for a company's stockholders which it will have as long as it stays in business through good years and bad.

Thus, in financing and capital management decisions, we have the *principle:*

> The short run effect should not be disregarded, but primary emphasis should be placed on what is good for the continuous, whole body of stockholders in the long run.

Throughout the book, we will point out examples to explain the significance of this principle.

CHAPTER 2

Capital Structure–Long Term Debt vs. Equity

In planning to raise capital, a company must first establish a financial policy to determine how much long term debt it should have in its capital structure. This must precede a decision as to the type of securities to sell and the timing of the sales. It is the most important financial decision a company makes. In this chapter we will be concerned with this fundamental question of the division of long term capital between debt and equity. It is not easy because there is no obvious answer.

Sources of Corporate Funds

There are four principal sources of corporate funds.

1. Revenues—cash generated from revenues through depreciation or other non-cash expenses in the income statement, and earnings retained after dividends.
2. Conversion of assets.
3. Short term borrowings.
4. Sale of long term securities.

This is illustrated in Exhibit 2-1.

The first three sources are relatively limited:

1. The ability of a company to generate funds from future revenues depends on the size of non-cash items such as depreciation and the company's earnings and dividend policy. The amount from this source is uncertain; it will vary with earnings and may decrease radically with poor earnings.
2. Conversion of assets is not a ready source. A company generally does not hold large amounts of cash reserves as part of its assets. It cannot readily sell fixed assets to obtain funds.
3. A company's short term borrowings may be limited to borrowings which can be paid off seasonally. If it uses short term borrowings which cannot be paid off seasonally, it will probably be dependent on the sale of long term securities to pay them off.

These three sources of funds have to be taken into account in financial planning. However, the wide open door that a company

Exhibit 2-1

SOURCES OF CORPORATE FUNDS

Income Statement

Sales	$200	
Operating expenses	169	
Depreciation	10	← Non-cash expenses → 1. Revenues
Interest	1	
Taxes	10	
Total	$190	
Net Income	$ 10	
Common dividends	5	
Retained earnings	$ 5	← Retained earnings → 1. Revenues

Balance Sheet

	Assets					
2. Conversion of assets →	Current assets	$100	Current liabilities		$ 50	← 3. Short term borrowings
	Plant, net	50	Long term capital			
			Debt	$20		
			Common	80		
			Total		$100	← 4. Sale of long term securities
	Total	$150	Total		$150	

should be able to count on to obtain funds is the fourth source:

4. That is, its ability to sell long term securities. If it has this ability, it will be free to meet maturing obligations and pursue expansion projects as they may arise. This is the key to a company's financial strength. It emphasizes the importance of management making a correct decision with regard to the make-up of long term capital.

Long Term Capital

In the brief balance sheet previously summarized in Exhibit 1-1, the two basic types of securities in the long term capital were as follows:

	Amount	*Percent*
Long Term Capital		
Debt	$ 25	25%
Common equity	75	75
Total	$100	100%

Long term debt may be referred to as funded debt. Sometimes the debt in long term capital is expressed as a ratio of debt to equity. In the above figures this would be 1 to 3, or, as a percentage, 33% ($25 debt ÷ $75 common equity). Throughout the book we will use the ratio of debt to the total of debt and equity, or 25% as shown above. The different ways the amount of debt may be expressed are shown in Exhibit 2-2.

For analytical purposes, long term debt includes:

Debt such as notes, debentures, mortgage bonds, with maturity longer than one year.

For accounting purposes, debt with a maturity of less than one year is included in current liabilities. It is referred to as floating debt. However, for analytical purposes, debt with a maturity of less than a year, such as short term bank loans, which are not seasonal and not cleaned up annually, should be included with long term debt regardless of the stated maturity. This is long term capital with a short maturity.

Leases of a financial nature should be capitalized and included with long term debt.

Convertible debt should also be included with long term debt, but may be shown as a separate item.

Equity includes:

Principally common stock, but preferred and convertible preferred stocks are a form of equity. Preferred stocks may be shown as a separate item.

Exhibit 2-2

THE DIFFERENT WAYS IN WHICH DEBT RATIO MAY BE EXPRESSED

(Used throughout the book) Long Term Capital				
Debt	*Common Equity*	*Total*	*Debt as % of Common Equity*	*Ratio Debt to Common Equity*
20%	80%	100%	25%	1 for 4
25	75	100	33 1/3	1 for 3
33 1/3	66 2/3	100	50	1 for 2
50	50	100	100	1 for 1
66 2/3	33 1/3	100	200	2 for 1
75	25	100	300	3 for 1
80	20	100	400	4 for 1
83 1/3	16 2/3	100	500	5 for 1
90	10	100	900	9 for 1

However, for our analysis in this chapter, we will not distinguish between the various forms of equity. Preferred will be covered in Chapter 4, Types of Securities.

In Appendix 2-A at the end of this chapter is a detailed discussion of how to analyze the long term capital of a company.

Goals for Long-Term Capital Determination

In determining the amount of debt a company should have in its long term capital, management should have the following goals:

1. Assure the company's ability to raise capital at all times. This means during both favorable and unfavorable conditions when the company's earnings are poor and security markets are adverse.
2. Assure the company's ability to raise capital at all times without straining its credit.
3. Raise capital under all conditions at the least cost so that the company can meet competitive prices and produce a satisfactory return to the stockholders in the long run.

   This calls for the use of debt to the extent appropriate, because the cost of debt is low compared with equity securities and interest is deductible for tax purposes. However, debt should not be increased to the point that the company is forced to:

   a) Pay high rates for senior capital.
   b) Include unduly restrictive terms in senior securities.
   c) Pay excessive rates on junior securities or include costly kickers in the form of incentive securities such as convertibles and warrants.
   d) Sell common stock when the price is depressed.

   We will consider the effect of the capital structure mix on cost-of-capital in this chapter in general terms. We will review it in more detail in Part II, Chapter 15.
4. Assure that dividends will not have to be cut for financial reasons.
5. Have a good quality common stock—not a yo-yo stock—which will have regular gradual increases in earnings per share from plowback of earnings, and, with a stable price-earnings ratio, will provide long range price appreciation.

Leverage—The Use of Debt

Any security senior to common equity provides leverage, but leverage is generally thought of in terms of debt. Leverage is also referred to as trading on the equity; it appears both in the balance sheet and income statement.

In the balance sheet, the amount of debt relative to the amount of equity determines the amount of debt claims to assets ahead of the common.

In the income statement, the amount of debt affects the size of the interest charges senior to the earnings for the common. The rate of interest also affects the size of the interest charges. Thus, as regards the income statement, leverage is affected by both the amount of debt and the interest rate. For example, a company with 40% debt and a 4% interest rate will have the same leverage effect in the income statement as a company with 20% debt and an 8% interest rate. In viewing leverage, both the amount and rate must be considered.

Leverage Appeal to Investors

The appeal of leverage to an investor is as follows: If you can make an investment of \$100 and earn 20% annually before taxes and have a 50% tax rate you will make \$10 annually after taxes—see Exhibit 2-3, Part I. However, if in addition to your \$100, you use leverage and borrow \$100 at an 8% interest rate and earn 20% before taxes on the \$200, you will make \$16 on your \$100 after paying interest and taxes at a 50% rate. These figures are shown in Exhibit 2-3, Part II.

Thus, you may make more money and a higher rate on your investment by the use of leverage. This, however, is not all the story. Let's see what would happen if earnings decreased.

If in the example in Exhibit 2-3, Part I and II, the return before taxes on the total investment fell to 10%, your income would be $5 without leverage and $6 with leverage.

If earnings fell further, you would be worse off with leverage. If the earnings before taxes fell to a 4% return on your investment in Exhibit 2-3, Part I, you would get $2, but if they fell to 4% on the $200 in Exhibit 2-3, Part II, the income on your $100 would be $0.

If a real bad year occurred and there were no earnings, you would have a loss of $8 with the leverage situation.

These figures are summarized in Exhibit 2-3, Part III.

The effect of leverage for an individual making a direct investment, as shown above, can be readily translated in terms of earnings per share from the point of view of the common stockholder. They are shown in Exhibit 2-4, Parts I, II and III.

So far we have discussed the effect of leverage on the amount· of earnings for the

Exhibit 2-3

LEVERAGE EXAMPLE FOR INDIVIDUAL

PART I

NO LEVERAGE

		Your Annual Income			
		Before Tax		After Tax (50% Rate)	
		Rate	Amount	Rate	Amount
Total Investment	$100	20%	$20		
Loan	0		0		
Your Investment	$100	20%	$20	10%	$10

PART II

LEVERAGE

		Your Annual Income			
		Before Tax		After Tax (50% Rate)	
		Rate	Amount	Rate	Amount
Total Investment	$200	20%	$40		
Loan	100	8	8		
Your Investment	$100	32%	$32	16%	$16

PART III

SUMMARY OF EFFECT OF NO LEVERAGE VS. LEVERAGE

	Your Annual Income After Tax	
Return on Total Investment Before Tax	No Leverage	Leverage
20%	$10	$16
10	5	6
4	2	0
0	0	Loss 8

Exhibit 2-4

LEVERAGE EXAMPLE FOR COMPANY

PART I

NO LEVERAGE

Debt	0	0%
Common (1 share)	$100	100
Total	$100	100%

Income before interest and taxes (20% return on total capital)	$20
Interest	0
	$20
Taxes—50% rate	$10
Net income	$10
Earnings per share—1 share	$10

PART II

LEVERAGE

Debt	$100	50%
Common (1 share)	100	50
Total	$200	100%

Income before interest and taxes (20% return on total capital)	$40
Interest—8%	8
	$32
Taxes—50% rate	16
Income for common	$16
Earnings per share—1 share	$16

PART III

SUMMARY OF EFFECT OF NO LEVERAGE VS. LEVERAGE

Return on Total Capital Before Interest & Taxes	Earnings per Share Common	
	No Leverage	Leverage
20%	$10	$16
10	5	6
4	2	0
0	0	Loss 8

common, but not the effect on the quality and value of the earnings.

The value of earnings to you as an investor depends on the extent of the risk. If earnings were riskless like interest on a government bond, you would be willing to accept a low return. As the risk increases, you want a progressively higher return. Leverage adds risk. While the return on your leveraged investment is higher when earnings are favorable, the return will be lower when earnings are poor. Because of the added risk, you should not value the leveraged earnings as highly as earnings which are non-leveraged.

What value you may place on the earnings will depend on your assessment of the risk. Under certain circumstances, it is not inconceivable, if the leverage were excessive, that you might put a lesser value on the greater earnings than on a smaller amount of non-leveraged earnings. When earnings are going up, some investors may consider leverage an advantage because they expect to sell their stock before earnings turn down. On the other hand, when earnings turn down, the more the leverage, the more investors will consider it a disadvantage.

Leverage Appeal to Management

Management should look at leverage from the point of view of its stockholders, since management works for its stockholders. However, management can't look at it from the point of view of any one stockholder who can sell his stock; it must consider that a company will have stockholders when the market price of its stock is going down as well as up.

In spite of the fact that management should take a long range view, management tends to be overly attracted to leverage for the following reasons:

1. Interest on debt is lower than the required return on common stock.
2. Interest is tax deductible.
3. It avoids immediate dilution from issuing new shares. Management tends to focus on current earnings per share and fears temporary dilution of earnings per share from the sale of common stock.
4. Leverage boosts earnings per share when earnings are increasing.
5. Almost universally, management feels that the stock of their company is underpriced and that there will be an increase in earnings per share or in the price-earnings ratio. If common financing is postponed, a better price will be obtained.
6. Management is sensitive to the reaction of financial analysts who make the market in their stock, and analysts generally make it known to management that they will shy away from the stock of a company which plans to issue more common. Analysts like leverage because it pushes up earnings per share. Remember, investors have fluidity of capital.
7. Management fails to accept the fact that dilution from the sale of common stock may be only temporary and earnings per share may increase after the sale of common when the money has been put to work. If common stock is sold above book value and the return on the new investment is the same or greater than on the existing capital, earnings per share will increase. We will explain this statement fully in a subsequent chapter.

   Furthermore, management may fail to realize that sale of common increases the company's ability to sell debt subsequently, whereas sale of debt decreases the ability of the company to use it in the future.
8. Investment bankers know management's attraction for debt and are hesitant to recommend the use of common stock and lose the business. Furthermore, if a company's common stock represents a problem to market, investment bankers may prefer to sell a senior security.

In their desire to finance with debt, management may take one of three attitudes:

1. They may contend that they only believe in the reasonable use of debt, but their idea of what is reasonable may in fact be excessive.
2. One more time—by this is meant that management realizes that the excessive use of debt is a danger but that the outlook for their company is good; therefore, common financing can be put off until the next financing when it can be done at a better price.
3. Leverage is good because it increases earnings per share, and management should use all the debt it can obtain.

If a company's earnings always go up and it could readily sell common stock at any time, the high leverage approach would be perfectly satisfactory. Under those conditions, if a company had too much debt it could always sell common. However, management is playing Russian Roulette to make plans on the basis of such an assumption.

Test of Financial Policy— Unforeseeable Adversity

The test of financial policy comes when a company runs into bad earnings and a stock market unreceptive to new equity capital. The key to a company's ability to raise capital at all times and under all conditions, is its ability to sell debt. Debt can practically always be sold if a company keeps its capital structure in order without too much leverage when the company's earnings are satisfactory.

An adverse period cannot be foreseen by management because of the inability to forecast more than a limited number of years ahead with any degree of certainty. A company may encounter one or more of four difficulties:

1. Economy problems including recession and inflation.
2. Security market crisis.
3. Industry problems.
4. Company problems.

A company should allow for the possibility of any one or more of these things happening some time in the unforeseeable future.

Inflexibility of Capital Structure

Any fool can go into debt to increase leverage and it can be done very easily and quickly, but capital structure is flexible in only one direction; it is hard to get out of debt.

A company can correct its debt ratio by reducing debt and building up equity with retained earnings or sale of common stock. Retained earnings are generally small in relation to the total capital, so it takes a long time to build up equity from this source. Selling common stock to pay off debt generally results in immediate real dilution, because there is only the savings in interest charges from the reduced debt, and this represents relatively little in terms of earnings per share on the new shares.

Investors require a long record of good earnings and sound financing after a company's credit has been strained before they will accept the improvement. They want proof that management will continue to follow a sound policy. It may take from five to ten years to correct a poor financial position and gain acceptance. This is a long, tedious and costly process and may restrict a company's ability to grow.

Risk of Business Affects Amount of Debt

There are three basic risks in a company:

1. The risk of the business itself. For example, an industrial company will be more risky than an electric utility company.
2. A financial risk which is added by management by increasing the debt ratio too far. As debt is added past a certain point, the quality of all the securities of a company become speculative and consequently an element of risk is added. This results in an increase in the cost of debt and also an increase in the return the common stockholder wants. Since the common is junior to the debt, it too must have risk added to it. Thus, the overall cost of capital is increased.
3. A credibility gap or investor relations risk, when management does not tell the truth or fails to give out adequate information.

Risk of a business is assessed in terms of the amplitude of variations likely to occur in its earnings. Management cannot change the risk of a business unless it changes the business itself. This is not to say that the characteristics of a business may not change over time. However, at any one time, the risk will depend on the nature of the business.

The extent of risk may be revealed in the past earnings, but this is not necessarily so. There may be inherent risks due to the nature of the business which have not shown up in past earnings. Unrecorded potential risk must be determined from a study of all the factors of the business which may affect risk, such as the make-up of sales, potential competition, expenses which may increase, technical problems, obsolescence, etc. For example, suppose that a company manufacturing auto parts and selling all its output to one automobile company has had an excellent earnings record for ten years. Past earnings would tend to indicate little risk. But the risk might be very substantial because of the dependence on one customer.

Most large companies have sufficient stability to use debt up to a certain point without adding a significant financial risk. Management should establish a financial policy which will use leverage up to the point that a financial risk is not added. How much debt can be added without adding a financial risk depends on the risk of the business. From industry to industry the risk may vary widely and affect the use of debt as shown in Exhibit 2-5. Also, there may be differences in risk for companies within an industry so that the appropriate debt ratio will vary from company to company.

Principles of finance are generally the same for all types of companies; their application will differ depending on the nature of the business as it affects risk and special financing needs.

The question we are seeking to answer is: How can you establish a policy for your company's long term capital which will use leverage properly and achieve the five goals for long term capital determination? These are:

1. Ability to raise capital at all times.
2. Ability to raise capital without straining credit.
3. Raise capital at the lowest cost.
4. Assure no dividend cuts for financial reasons.
5. Have a good quality common stock.

In other words, how much debt can a company use without adding a financial risk and maintain financial flexibility? Is 20% right or should it be higher or lower? The answer is not easy because there are no ready pegs on which to hang your hat.

Quality of Securities—Key to Long-Term Capital Determination

An individual's ability to obtain capital and the terms and price he will have to pay depend on his earnings, his assets and the amount to which he has gone into hock. Has he got a good steady salary? Does he borrow sensibly? Is he in hock up to his ears? These questions might be put in another way: Is his financial position excellent, fair or poor quality?

The same idea applies to a company in determining the amount of debt it should have—what should be the quality of its securities?

The quality of securities determines the company's ability to sell securities and the terms and price at which they can be sold. A company with good quality securities will be able to do some form of financing even under adverse conditions; it will have financial flexibility.

We first think of quality in terms of a company's debt securities. But the quality of a company's debt affects the quality of the equity since the equity is in a junior position. It is impossible to have a high grade equity and a low quality debt.

In extremes, we might think of a company's debt being of such good quality that it is as good as a government bond—in other words, no one would question its quality. At the other extreme would be a company with very poor credit so that there was concern about the company's ability to pay its interest and principal. Between these two extremes are various gradations of quality ranging from good to fair, to somewhat speculative.

Exhibit 2-5

DEBT RATIOS FOR VARIOUS TYPES OF BUSINESSES

	All Manufacturing Companies*	Electric Utility Companies**	Finance Companies***
Long Term Capital			
Debt	25%	53%	86%
Preferred and common equity	75	47	14
Total	100%	100%	100%
Times fixed charges earned before taxes†	9.0	2.8	1.7
Cash flow as percent of long term debt	41%	12%	–
Return on total long term†† capital after taxes	11.3%	7.8%	7.4%
Return on common equity after taxes	12.4%	10.8%	10.4%

Quarterly Financial Report for Manufacturing Corporations–4th Quarter, 1973. Federal Trade Commission–Securities and Exchange Commission. This report covers the 12 months ended December 1973. Included in the figures are all manufacturing corporations except newspapers.

**Privately Owned Electric Utilities–*Edison Electric Institute Statistical Year Book,* 1974 Edition.

***Average of Commercial Credit Company and Dial Financial Corporation December 31, 1973. Senior debt rated A.

†Includes all interest payments, debt discount and expense and other miscellaneous charges.

††Return is after taxes but before interest on long term debt.

In order to talk about quality, it is handy to have symbols for the various grades. We could use 1st, 2nd, 3rd, etc, or A, B, C, etc. Better yet, we have a ready-made rating system which we can use since Moody's Investors Service, Standard & Poor's Corporation and Fitch Investors Service rate the various grades of bonds with symbols such as AAA, AA, A, BBB, BB, etc. Our fundamental concern is with the factors affecting quality and not with the ratings per se.

Some people are critical of these ratings. They claim that they are not accurate and that a company should not be a slave to ratings, because the rating agencies are only an isolated part of the financial scene. However, a company cannot avoid having its financial position being thought of in terms of the quality rating for its bonds. A company may sell a bond privately and thus avoid a rating, because only publicly offered bonds are rated. However, financial experts looking at the company will evaluate its debt in much the same way as a rating agency analyst and will undoubtedly think of the quality of the company's securities in terms of the bond rating. Bond ratings are not just something assigned by the rating agencies as an isolated part of finance; they are a part of the universal language of finance. Bond ratings are also an indication of the quality of a company's common stock. The common stock could not be of high quality if the senior securities of the same company are considered speculative. The symbols used by the three rating agencies, starting with the best quality, are as follows:

Moody's	Standard	Fitch
Aaa	AAA	AAA
Aa	AA	AA
A	A	A
Baa	BBB	BBB
Ba	BB	BB
etc.	etc.	etc.

Excerpts from the definition of the ratings by Moody's which typifies their quality are as follows:

Aaa ". . . the best quality . . . 'gilt edge' . . ."
Aa ". . . high quality by all standards . . ."
A ". . . higher medium grade . . . elements may be present which suggest a susceptibility to impairment some time in the future."
Baa ". . . lower medium grade . . . lack outstanding investment characteristics, and, in fact, have speculative characteristics as well."
Ba ". . . their future cannot be considered as well assured . . . not well safeguarded during both good and bad times . . ."

What quality rating should a company try to achieve in establishing a financial policy? In order to achieve the five goals we have suggested, it would have to have good quality.

BB is definitely eliminated. Bonds rated BB have an uncertain future. Investors will require a relatively high interest rate and during any adversity will undoubtedly require kickers. Under adverse conditions a company with a BB rating on its senior debt might have serious difficulty in raising capital and might not even be able to raise capital at all. It may have to cut its dividend.

BBB is one step better and under ordinary conditions a company with such a rating can finance, but bonds with that quality do contain speculative elements and are not high grade.

Therefore, we are left with three ratings which would satisfy our goals: AAA, AA, and A.

A company with AAA credit is the creme de la creme. It has all kinds of financial strength and borrowing reserve. It would weather any storm. For this reason the rating agencies reserve the AAA rating for a few very choice, large companies. There are approximately 45 companies with debt rated AAA by Standard & Poor's, of which 16 are industrials. The stocks of such companies are the bluest of blue chip.

As far as financial policy is concerned, the few industrial AAA companies may wish to remain in that category. Is it stronger than necessary? This is debatable. However, AAA does put a company in an unassailable financial position. Furthermore, companies in this category are generally very large, and when they offer securities the amounts are large. The AAA rating puts them in good position to appeal to a broad group of investors to absorb large security offerings.

AA is excellent quality. A company with AA rating only fails to be AAA because it has some characteristics which prevent it from being perfect. Only very large companies receive an AA rating. In this category Moody's shows approximately 139 companies, most of which are electric utilities, and 44 are industrials.

Very large, stable types of companies can achieve an AA rating and have a reasonable portion of their long term capital in the form of debt. A company of this type would be in a strong position to fulfill the five goals we have suggested for capital structure determination. Therefore, we suggest that such a company would do well to have AA as its measure of quality.

Most companies, particularly in the industrial field, can only have their bonds rated A and have an opportunity to use a reasonable amount of debt. They might not be able to be an AA even with minor amount of debt. Thus, their borrowing ability would be highly restricted by trying to do better than A. They will have to settle for A as their goal.

Standard & Poor's rates a total of $140.4 billion of corporate bonds which includes practically all publicly held issues. The ratings on these bonds show that most companies are in the three top categories as follows:

	% of Principal Amount	% of Number of Issues
AAA, AA or A	83%	77%

The details are shown in Exhibit 2-6. In determining the number of issues, each separate series of a bond was counted as one. There would be an increase in the amount and number of bonds in the better grades if convertible bonds were excluded. Convertible bonds generally receive a low rating because they are in a junior position and have a weak indenture.

The use of debt quality for capital structure determination is summarized in Exhibit 2-7.

Before we leave this section, a word about companies which have no debt whatsoever, even though they could have some debt with a good quality rating. On the basis of the above discussion it would appear that a company with only common is being overly conservative, but it is difficult to criticize them too severely. They have a built-in reserve which may come in handy. It is certainly worth something. It may be an advantage in this highly competitive world wherein companies may find themselves in trouble, and may need to resort to large borrowings in a hurry. They could maintain their dividend come hell or high water. In a sense, it may be said that their stocks have some of the investment attributes of senior securities. Most companies in this position are companies which have not needed to sell securities to raise outside capital. If they did need outside capital, it would be uneconomical not to use debt.

Financial Flexibility—Borrowing Reserve and Financial Insurance

A company with well-rated debt has financial strength because it has financial flexibility. We can use two terms to describe financial flexibility: borrowing reserve and financial insurance.

Borrowing reserve refers to a company's ability to increase debt without losing its bond rating. In all rating categories, there is a moderate range of debt which will permit a company to qualify. And a company can vary from its average debt ratio within certain limits for a limited period of time without losing its bond rating.

Financial insurance refers to the maintenance of adequate quality so that if a company's bond rating slips it will still have respectability. AAA and AA provide strong financial insurance. A grade doesn't provide real financial insurance, because if the bond rating slips from A, it falls into the BBB category. BBB obviously provides no financial insurance.

Quality Translated into Debt Ratio

Having determined the bond rating you desire for your non-convertible debt, which will assure your ability to meet your financial goals, the next step is to translate that rating into a ratio of long term debt to total long term capital.

The procedure to follow is to make a statistical comparison with similar companies which have bonds with ratings. This will include a study of all the financial ratios which are used to depict the quality of the bonds for that type of company.

The two most fundamental ratios are long term debt as a percent of long term capital, and the number of times interest charges are earned. It is *primarily earnings, their amount, volatility and dangers of decrease which make for quality of a bond. Therefore, the number of times interest is earned will weigh most heavily in the study.* A company with low debt in relation to assets may have a good looking balance sheet, but if the assets are poor earners, its borrowing capacity will be limited. With regard to a company's assets, their nature, in terms of liquidity, may be important. Other things being equal, a com-

Exhibit 2-6

DISTRIBUTION OF PUBLICLY OFFERED CORPORATE BONDS
RATED BY STANDARD & POOR'S*
(As of September 30, 1972)

	Public Utilities 2,588 Issues $82.8 Billion Principal Amount		Industrials 695 Issues $36 Billion Principal Amount	
	% of Principal Amount	% of Number of Issues	% of Principal Amount	% of Number of Issues
AAA	31%	13%	16%	6%
AA	34	36	23	16
A	25	36	35	38
BBB	8	12	14	21
BB and lower	2	3	12	19
	100%	100%	100%	100%

	Finance** 296 Issues $15.2 Billion Principal Amount		Transportation 299 Issues $6.4 Billion Principal Amount	
	% of Principal Amount	% of Number of Issues	% of Principal Amount	% of Number of Issues
AAA	13%	13%	5%	8%
AA	41	29	9	8
A	34	35	20	20
BBB	7	14	16	14
BB and lower	5	9	50	50
	100%	100%	100%	100%

	Total 3,878 Issues $140.4 Billion Principal Amount	
	% of Principal Amount	% of Number of Issues
AAA	24%	12%
AA	31	30
A	28	35
BBB	10	14
BB and lower	7	9
	100%	100%

**The Anatomy of the Secondary Market in Corporate Bonds,* Salomon Brothers.

**Within the finance sector 85 issues representing $3.4 billion are not rated by S & P or Moody's. Fitch rates 37 of these issues AAA, 30 AA, 4 A, 1 CCC, and 13 remain not rated. These Fitch ratings are reflected in the table.

Exhibit 2-7

SUMMARY OF DEBT QUALITY FOR CAPITAL STRUCTURE DETERMINATION

Bond Rating	
AAA	Unquestionable financial strength. Only a few companies can obtain this rating.
AA	High quality. Provides real financial strength. Only very large companies can obtain this rating and be able to use a significant amount of debt. For such companies this rating is worth shooting for. Provides financial insurance.
A	Fair quality. This is the best rating that most companies, particularly, industrials, can achieve. It is weak on financial insurance.
BBB	Inadequate quality.
BB	Poor quality.

pany with a large part of its assets consisting of a special type of plant and equipment, which is not readily salable, is less attractive to a lender than a company with a liquid type of asset which could be disposed of at a price close to book value. The more liquid assets would put the company and the debt holder in a more flexible position if the company ran into trouble and some assets had to be used to reduce liabilities.

To bring out the financial strength fully, other ratios will be needed. The nature of the business will affect the type of ratios. For example, for oil companies, the number of barrels of reserves per $1,000 of funded debt will be significant.

The ratios themselves are just the starting point. You should make a study of all the factors which affect the company's earning power and variability. This will include a review of the company's balance sheet and income statements, both present and historical. Assets and earnings may be over- or understated and all information which will throw light on this situation should be taken into account in viewing the significance of the ratios.

It may be important to study the figures and facts about a company at and prior to the time when the company's bonds first received their rating or when there was a change in the rating. This will give a clue as to the ratios the rating agencies looked at when they reviewed the company for rating purposes. Subsequently, the company's debt may have increased or decreased and earnings may have improved or deteriorated. The rating agencies do review bond ratings and change them when there is an indication that the financial strength of the company has changed, but there may be a lag in the change in rating from the time when the ratios change. Therefore, the ratios subsequent to the time when the bonds were originally rated may be misleading. A comparison of companies with rated bonds is referred to as a statistical stack-up. It will look something like the data in Exhibit 2-8.

Once the figures have been gathered, the ratios calculated and the companies studied so that the figures can be reviewed in the light of all facts affecting the financial strength of the companies, then judgment has to be applied. The figures themselves do not tell all the story—the application of judgment is most important.

The rating agencies, though operating entirely independently, generally arrive at the same rating. Because there are differences at times, it is advisable to show the ratings of the three rating agencies.

The task of making a study to determine how much long term debt a company can have to achieve a certain rating, can be accomplished with a reasonable amount of work and with fair precision, if a comparison can be made with a number of companies in the same business with rated bonds. However, if a company is unique and there are no companies directly comparable with rated debt, the task becomes far more difficult. In such a situation, it is helpful first to try to decide in what broad category of business the company

Exhibit 2-8

EXAMPLE OF STATISTICAL STACK-UP WITH BOND RATINGS
FOR DEBT POLICY CONSIDERATIONS

	Company in Question	Company A	Company B	Company C
Date				
Long Term Capital				
Debentures	%	%	%	%
Convertible Debentures				
Preferred				
Common Equity (Less Intangibles)				
Total	100%	100%	100%	100%
Bond Ratings–Senior Debt				
Moody's				
Standard & Poor's				
Fitch				
Bond Ratings–Junior Debt				
Moody's				
Standard & Poor's				
Fitch				
Times Total Interest Charges Earned				
Before Taxes				
After Taxes				
Return on Long Term Capital After Taxes				
Sales by Principal Categories %				
Net Tangible Assets as % of Long Term Debt				
Cash Flow as % of Long Term Debt				

(This is an example of a few of the ratios that might be used. Some industrials may require special ratios to best show the financial quality of the debt.)

fits as regards the nature of the risk involved. Does it approximate a typical industrial company, or is it more in the area of a merchandising business, or a finance company, etc.? This type of approach will help to bring the picture into focus. After that, all the statistical help from at least reasonably comparable companies that have rated bonds should be used.

Maximum Debt Ratio–With Good Credit

In our approach to establishing a debt ratio as a key for financial planning, we have talked about average debt ratio. An average presupposes fluctuations below and above the average.

We have stressed the tendency of management to favor debt and avoid selling common stock like the plague. If a company's debt ratio is at the average and a company needs to raise outside capital, management will naturally turn to debt. There is nothing wrong with this reasoning but what is wrong is where it leads. If, subsequently more outside capital is needed, the urge will be to use debt again. There is no signal to warn that the company has gotten too far away from the average.

Therefore, as an additional key for financial planning, it is necessary to define the maximum debt ratio. The maximum debt ratio should act as a red light which will alert management to the need for equity and prevent a drift too far in the wrong direction.

There is no need to establish a minimum debt ratio; it represents no problem in financial planning.

Bond buyers and the rating agencies don't expect a company to hew to the average debt ratio at all times. How far away from the average can the maximum extend and for how long? This has to be within limits so as to maintain the quality rating that has been established as the company's goal. The extent of variation will depend on the ability of the company to get back to the average and how long it will take.

A company can correct a debt ratio by reducing its debt and building up its equity. A company's ability to get back to the average will depend on various factors.

The size of the cash flow resulting from non-cash expenses in the income statement, such as depreciation and the amount of earnings available after dividends.

Capital requirements which will use up internally generated cash and require outside financing.

The company's ability to sell common at a reasonable price.

An example of an industry which cannot have much variation from the average, say 5% (average debt 50%–maximum 55%), is the electric utility industry. It has small depreciation, a moderate return on its common, a high dividend payout and large demands for capital. Contrast this with an airline which has large depreciation. Capital demands may be large, but they tend to come in waves and can be postponed in an emergency.

Some bond analysts use a ratio of cash flow as a percent of debt. This only shows part of the picture of a company's ability to reduce debt from a maximum to an average, but it does give some indication.

The maximum we have talked about is a maximum with good credit and is not to be confused with the maximum the company can borrow. The maximum the company can borrow will result in a debt ratio which will produce poor quality credit.

Thus, an average debt ratio and a maximum debt ratio which will provide a good quality debt are essential tools for financial planning. And the difference between the average debt ratio and maximum debt ratio provides what we have described as borrowing reserve.

Breaking Up a Company for Debt Ratio Determination

For most companies, debt capacity is determined by looking at the company as a whole. For example, the assets of most manufacturing companies consist of plant and current assets, including receivables which are not interest bearing. The plant and receivables are an integral part of the whole operation. Nothing would be gained by breaking up the company into parts and deciding how much mortgage debt the plant could carry and how much could be borrowed on the receivables.

There are a few exceptions when the parts of the company are really divisible. For example, a department store is in three businesses: receivables financing, real estate and merchandising. The receivables are interest bearing and could be segregated in a separate finance company. With good earnings, it might carry 85% debt with an A rating on its senior debt. The real estate is fairly general purpose and could be placed in a separate company and might be mortgaged up to 65% and the debt have good quality. With good earnings, the remaining merchandising business might carry some long term debt. These ratios could then be weighted by the assets involved to arrive at an overall debt ratio. This might result in an overall debt ratio for a department store, with leases capitalized, of 55% and still have good quality. Looked at on a consolidated basis, without breaking it up into parts, 55% debt would appear to be high when compared with an electric company, which might have 50% debt. Of course, the principal reason for the difference is the interest bearing receivables of the department store which can carry a high debt ratio.

Small Companies—Use Bond Rating Approach Indirectly

Size of company affects the risk in the eyes of investors. Size is important because a small company is generally more vulnerable to factors affecting sales and expenses. It may be less diversified. A small company may not have the strength to withstand a prolonged strike. Management tends to be dependent on a single person or a few key people; depth of management may be lacking.

What is small depends to some extent on the nature of the business. An automobile company with $100 million sales would be very small; whereas, most industrial companies with sales of this amount would be approaching the large category. In general, the dividing line is $100 million of sales or total assets, whichever is larger. For an industrial company, the sales figure would be larger; for a utility, the asset figure would be larger. Since the risk is greater for small companies, bond ratings are affected by size. Bond ratings of companies in some industries may even be affected because of size for a company with assets or sales of $100 million.

Small companies will receive low bond ratings even though they have a small amount of debt. They will have to pay higher interest rates than a large company regardless of their debt ratio. Relying on bond ratings as a guide to debt ratio would restrict a small company's use of debt. Therefore, we cannot use bond ratings directly in establishing an average and maximum debt ratio for a small company.

This may seem illogical and that we are abandoning our basic approach of quality. Not so, we still will use quality, but think in terms of the rating the company would receive if it were large. It should establish an average and maximum debt ratio on this basis. For example, if we shot for an A rating assuming the company were large, it would produce what might be termed a fair credit standing for the small company. The ratios would be sufficiently in line so that buyers of debt would feel comfortable and commercial bankers would not hesitate to lend short term funds.

If a small company has its long term debt privately held by institutional investors, it should have close contact with the institutions and know how they feel about the company's credit. Are the institutions anxious to loan more money? Are they squeamish about its present loan? What is the maximum the institutions would lend the company? This last question refers to the maximum the company could borrow, not the maximum to provide good credit. A company with the maximum debt it could borrow would have poor credit; it would have no borrowing reserve. A company should plan to keep its maximum debt ratio below the maximum it could borrow. Thus, a small company, in determining its capital structure policy, should supplement a statistical and debt quality approach with a good understanding of how its sources of capital feel about its position.

Privately Owned Companies

A privately owned company, unlike a publicly owned company, is not dependent on the volatility of the stock market and on being able to present a good earnings picture for its common stock to public investors. The limited number of owners of a privately owned company base their opinions on their intimate knowledge of the company. The slow acceptance of improved credit standing by stockholders, which occurs in a publicly owned company, does not exist in a privately held company; owners of a private company are close enough to the picture to evaluate the situation without the wait-and-see approach of an outsider. Therefore, a privately owned company may be able to have a high debt ratio and be more flexible than a publicly owned company, providing, of course, the owners have more of their own money to dump in if adverse circumstances are encountered.

On the other hand, if the owners have no extra capital, a privately owned company is less flexible than a publicly owned company. Then its only source of capital is through debt financing, and, if its capital needs are large, it may get into debt up to the hilt rather quickly. Then it will have no other source of capital. Of course, a privately owned company may seek to raise common equity capital from outsiders, but this means dilution of their ownership and it presupposes that the stock will be attractive to public investors. If the owners of a privately owned company have no extra capital to put in, they should plan carefully to sell stock to the public when earnings are favorable and stock can be sold. As another alternative, sale of the whole company to another company should be weighed. The owners should not wait to make either of these decisions until earnings are poor because then they will be forced to sell at a disadvantage.

Thus, each privately owned company is a special situation depending on: its financial strength, its need for outside capital, the financial position and desires of its owners, the willingness of its owners to let in outsiders, its attractiveness to outside common stock investors and finally its salability to another company.

If a privately owned company intends to go public in the near future, or a few years hence, it should do financial planning as though it were publicly held in order to prepare itself for the day it comes out of its shell. It will be judged on its past financials and it cannot go back and change them when the company decides to go public.

Adherence to Proper Financial Policy not Always Possible

When a new company is started, the investors who put in the seed money may not have enough capital to provide adequate equity. Furthermore, they may be willing to take the risk of high debt ratio. A mature company may run into difficulties and lose its rating so that its financial position becomes weak. There are many companies with BBB- and BB-rated debt.

While such situations are not ideal, a company cannot abandon ship and do no financing if it needs capital. It will have to do the best it can under the circumstances. However, management should have a plan to gradually reach the proper goal. If it has no plan it will drift and run a good chance of getting into financial trouble unless it is lucky. The plan should be made known to investors; this in itself will have a salutary effect.

There is a matter of balance in taking steps to improve a poor capital structure. Improvement means more equity and less debt. A gradual pace will prevent too much immediate dilution from common financing and will fit the pattern of investors' gradual acceptance.

False Approaches to Debt vs. Equity

You may hear other approaches to the question of the use of debt vs. equity. We summarize three below:

Spread in Yield Between Bond Ratings

There is a superficial approach to financial policy which says that there is relatively little spread in the cost differential between Aa, A and BBB bonds, and the added debt which can be obtained with BBB bonds more than offsets the small added cost.

The spread in yield between ratings widens as the ratings decrease in quality. It will vary from time to time depending upon market conditions. During times when interest rates are increasing, the spread tends to open up like an accordion. The spreads may not be too significant in a favorable bond market, but they may be material in a financial crunch.

The interest rate cost differential for new industrial issues between an "Aa"-rated and "A"-rated straight bond issue and between an "Aa" and a "Baa" issue are shown in Exhibit 2-9, Part I.

The effect of higher interest costs becomes apparent when the added financing costs are expressed in additional dollar costs over the life of an issue. Exhibit 2-9, Part II shows these added costs for a $50 million bond issue maturing in 25 years, assuming no sinking fund requirements. The costly aspect of a poor credit rating is, of course, startling when the additional interest cost is large as was the case in 1974. For example, when the interest cost spread between Aa- and Baa-rated issues is 2.00%, the total additional cash interest payment in the illustration, was $25 million, or, in other words, averaged $1 million per year before taxes and half a million annually, assuming a 50% tax rate. These are substantial additional burdens to bear, especially for corporations that must meet the competitive challenge of high-rated firms.

However, the added interest cost is only a small part of the disadvantage of loss of rating For a particular company, as debt is increased, the quality of the debt decreases, but more important, the quality of the junior securities and the common decrease and their costs arise. Thus, the addition of debt past the point of good credit may increase the overall cost-of-capital in the long run.

Furthermore, as we have explained throughout this chapter, there are many other more important considerations in determining long range financial policy which favor a company having a good quality rating for its debt.

Exhibit 2-9

INTEREST RATE SPREAD BETWEEN BOND RATINGS FOR
NEW STRAIGHT LONG INDUSTRIAL BONDS*

PART I

INTEREST COST SPREAD**

	A vs. Aa		Baa vs. Aa	
Years	High	Average	High	Average
1971	+0.45	+0.27	+1.25	+0.95
1972	+0.25	+0.18	+0.75	+0.61
1973	+0.25	+0.18	+0.95	+0.65
1974 (First 8 mos.)	+0.65	+0.33	+1.90	+0.70

PART II

ADDITIONAL INTEREST COST PAID OUT OVER LIFE OF A $50 MILLION
BOND DUE IN 25 YEARS WITH NO SINKING FUND

Incremental Coupon Rate	Additional Interest Cost
+0.05%	$ 625,000
+0.10	1,250,000
+0.20	2,500,000
+0.25	3,125,000
+0.50	6,250,000
+0.75	9,375,000
+1.00	12,500,000
+2.00	25,000,000

*Unpublished statistical data from Salomon Brothers, 1 New York Plaza, New York City.
**The high spreads in each year were based on monthly averages.

Net Cost of Debt vs. Earnings-Price Ratio for Common

In deciding on whether to finance with debt of common stock, you may run into the idea that you should compare the cost of debt with the cost of common on the following basis:

> Interest cost of debt, after allowing for tax savings of interest, versus the earnings-price percentage for the common.

For example, assume that a company's stock sells at 20 times earnings, then the earnings-price percentage is 5%. In such a situation, it is sometimes contended that the common cost is 5% and that the company could raise capital on a cheaper cost basis if it could sell debt with an interest rate of less than 10% with a 50% tax rate. If such a company sold debt with an interest rate of 9%, the cost after a 50% tax rate would be 4.5%. Thus, the net interest cost of debt of 4.5% is less than the earnings-price ratio of 5%. It may be suggested that debt should be sold rather than common.

There is nothing wrong with the figures, but there is much wrong with the comparison as a method for making a decision as to whether to use debt or common. Furthermore, the terminology is wrong as far as common stock is concerned because the earnings-price percentage is not the common cost;[1] the common cost is not based on the relationship of current earnings to market price but on investors' expectations of earnings. And evidence points to the fact that the common cost has probably never been below 10% after taxes for any type of company. It should be obvious that a company can always sell debt securities at a lower cost than the common cost; debt comes before the common stock and the common stock must have a greater risk. With the greater risk, the common stockholders would expect a higher return than the debt investors. To put it another way, interest is a fixed dollar cost, whereas the earnings for the common will be expected by investors to increase substantially above the interest rate on the company's bonds, otherwise the market price of the stock would fall.

Therefore, the comparison is wrong as far as the cost of the two types of securities is concerned and it is a superficial basis on which to make a financial policy decision.

Cash Flow

Another false approach to the use of debt is the cash flow school. This school suggests that cash flow is the basis of determining debt capacity. The reason this sounds so plausible, is that cash flow can be used for debt repayment.

This theory is unsound for a number of reasons. Cash flow shows the ability of a company to pay debt but not necessarily its ability to raise new capital. A company with a good cash flow because of large non-cash items such as high depreciation, will not have financial strength if it does not have good earnings. Such a company is more of a liquidating proposition and lenders do not want to do business with that type of company. A company, to have a good future, must have the ability to earn. It is earning power not cash flow which carries the most weight in determining the quality of securities. Without earnings, a company will eventually be unable to raise common equity, and a strong equity is one of the bases for financial strength. Furthermore, the cash flow approach does not work for certain types of companies. For example, cash flow could not be used to determine debt capacity of a bank. A bank is overloaded with cash or equivalent. Nor could cash flow be used to determine the debt capacity of an electric utility. An electric utility has practically no cash flow relative to its capital requirements. Its bonds generally have no sinking fund and must be refunded at maturity. Its stability of earnings in the past

---

[1]It approximates the common cost only in the unusual situation wherein the company's current earnings are the same as investors' expectations of the company's future earnings. This is a situation in which investors expect no growth in earnings per share.

have permitted it to use a large amount of debt which is repaid at maturity with another debt issue.

We are not suggesting that cash flow can be disregarded in determining debt capacity. Quite the contrary; it is a factor to consider, and in some industries it may be important. But earning power is dominant. Cash flow may be more important in determining the spread between the average and maximum debt ratio.

Debt Ratios and Coverages for Industrial Companies by Bond Ratings

Now we will look at some actual figures. We will use the companies included in Moody's Bond Indexes for Aaa, Aa, A and Baa. The data for the industrial companies are shown in Exhibit 2-10.

The variations in the figures for the same rating for each company in the Exhibit indicate there are many other factors that affect a rating such as:

1. The figures are spot at a particular time and not averages over a number of years. The single year may represent low or high earnings and temporary low or high debt. Averages are more representative.
2. There may have been changes in the figures from the time the bonds were rated.
3. The figures are based on company reports without any adjustment for intangibles, etc.

Exhibit 2-10

DEBT RATIO AND FIXED CHARGE COVERAGE FOR BONDS IN MOODY'S INDUSTRIAL BOND INDEX
(Figures as Reported in Moody's Manual)

1973

Company Name	Debt as a % of Total Capitalization		Times Charges Earned Before Taxes	
–Aaa–				
Proctor & Gamble Co.	12%		31.9	
Kraftco Corp.	15		23.3	
Texaco	18		15.2	
Mobil Oil Corp.	16		22.1	
Sears Roebuck	16		5.4	
Standard Oil (Cal.)	15		20.3	
Exxon	16		21.9	
Western Electric	24		11.4	
General Electric	21		8.9	
Gulf Oil Corp.	22		17.1	
Average		18		17.8
–Aa–				
Corning-Glass Works	19		4.6	
H.J. Heinz	25		6.6	
American Cyanamid	21		13.8	
Atlantic Richfield	24		8.2	
Reynolds Tobacco	24		13.2	
Bethlehem Steel	23		10.2	
Consolidated Foods	26		11.7	
Abbot Laboratories	23		8.4	

Exhibit 2-10 (Cont'd.)

1973

Company Name	Debt as a % of Total Capitalization		Times Charges Earned Before Taxes	
Shell Oil	25		8.5	
Nabisco	39		6.1	
Average		25		9.1
–A–				
Armstrong Cork	17		14.1	
Safeway Stores	16		14.3	
Woolworth	24		4.1	
Eaton Corp.	34		8.7	
Cities Service	29		5.3	
Stauffer Chemical	31		8.0	
Standard Brands	33		6.3	
Owens-Illinois	36		5.0	
Weyerhauser	28		10.7	
Dow Chemical	44		5.4	
Average		29		8.2
–Baa–				
Rockwell Intl. Corp.	26		9.2	
Tenneco Corp.	37		3.3	
Mack Trucks	47		7.7	
B.F. Goodrich	35		3.8	
Lone Star Industries	36		4.7	
Norton Simon	28		10.8	
American Metal Climax	34		6.6	
Food Fair Stores, Inc.	49		1.6	
U.S. Plywood-Champ. Papers	43		5.9	
Pennzoil	53		3.2	
Average		39		5.7

4. They do not include other elements of long term debt such as leases which should be capitalized. Leases are particularly important for companies in retailing.
5. They only represent two ratios, and many others should be considered in determining a bond rating.
6. There is no information regarding the background and nature of each company's business. Some of the companies have hidden assets in the form of natural resources such as oil, minerals and timber.

However, the figures do show that as the debt increases and coverages fall, the quality tends to decline as shown by the average figures.

	Debt as a % of Long Term Capital	Times Interest Charges Earned Before Taxes
Aaa	18%	18
Aa	25	9
A	29	8
Baa	39	6

Summary

In summary, the aim in financial policy should be to make it possible for a company to raise whatever capital is needed so it can pursue any capital investments management deems appropriate. It should be able to finance at its own choosing and not be forced into the sale of long term securities at the mercy of security markets at rates and terms dictated by security buyers. And it should provide an attractive investment to investors over the long run, in both good and bad years.

Debt is cheaper than other types of securities and interest is deductible for tax purposes. While leverage works for you on the upswing, it may work against you on the downswing. Leverage itself is not bad; our

Exhibit 2-11

OUTLINE OF LONG TERM CAPITAL DETERMINATION

Goals

1. Always be able to raise capital.
2. Raise capital without straining credit.
3. Raise capital at the lowest cost in the long run.
4. Never have to cut dividend for financial reasons.
5. Have a good quality and not a yo-yo stock.

Limitations

The effect of financial policy should be tested in the short run, but the period further ahead is more important in making a final decision.

Company Forecast

Years

1	2	3	4	5	6	7	8	9	10	etc.
		?	?	?						

After five years the outlook for a company is unforeseeable. More capital may be needed and debt may mature in this period. Equity securities are outstanding indefinitely. Four possible difficulties may arise.

1. Economy problems—recession and inflation.
2. Security market crisis.
3. Industry problems.
4. Company problems.

Policy

Debt used properly is good. Use debt up to the point that financial flexibility will be preserved and a financial risk will not be added. Long term capital is easily changed in only one direction—the debt ratio can be easily increased, but corrected only with difficulty. A company should determine an average and maximum debt ratio policy as a basis for financial planning so that its nonconvertible debt will be rated no lower than A, and preferably AA if circumstances permit.

economy is based on the use of debt by both companies and individuals. The important point is to use leverage properly; that is, as the essence of sound financial policy; use it within a range which will be to a company's benefit over the long run even if adversity is experienced. This requires a rating on non-convertible debt no lower than A grade, and preferably AA if a company is large and strong enough to permit it adequate access to the debt market. The ideas covered in this chapter are outlined in Exhibit 2-11.

Your financial policies should play a tune which will be pleasant to stockholders' ears even over the discordant chords of bad times. You should never have to dance to the tune of the senior security holders.

APPENDIX 2-A

LONG TERM CAPITAL ANALYSIS

For complete analysis purposes, long term capital should be broken down in detail, with securities shown in order of their seniority with their rating, if any.

LONG TERM CAPITAL				INCOME STATEMENT			
Balance Sheet				Income Statement			
Finance leases capitalized	$			Interest component on finance lease payments	$**		
Mortgage bonds	$			Interest	$		
Debentures	$			Interest	$		
Short term debt continuously renewed	$			Interest	$		
Convertible debentures	$			Interest	$		
Income bonds	$			Interest	$		
Total long term debt		$		Total interest		$	
Preferred	$			Dividends	$		
Convertible preferred	$			Dividends	$		
Total preferred		$		Total preferred dividends		$	
Total senior securities			$	Total charges on senior securities			$
Common Equity (Common Book Value)*			$	Net Income Available for Common Equity			$
Long Term Capital			$	Return			$

*Less intangibles.

**Lease payments include two parts: principal and interest. In the income statement we are only including the interest component to make it comparable with interest on debt.

Any debt which is directly or indirectly guaranteed should be added to long term debt. An indirect guarantee may appear in the form of a contract to provide sufficient income to service the debt, or a guarantee to keep working capital at a specified level. In determining the burden of this guaranteed debt, the nature of the guarantee must be analyzed as well as the strength of the primary obligor. If the obligor has high credit, which is usually not the case or the guarantee would not be needed, then the guarantee might not be a burden on the company making the guarantee. This will require an examination of all the facts.

Convertible preferred stocks issued in connection with mergers may be placed on the balance sheet at nominal values which are not at all comparable with their dividend rate. They should be restated at their liquidating value and the common equity reduced accordingly.

Common equity includes the stated or par value, capital surplus and earned surplus. Common equity should be reduced by the amount of intangibles on the asset side such as goodwill. It is essential that intangibles be deducted in order to make capital structure ratios comparable between companies. If one company had no intangibles and another had a large amount of intangibles, a comparison of long term capital would be meaningless. It may be contended that the goodwill represents the excess price a company paid for another company because of the earning potential of the acquired company. In such a situation, this would show up in reported earnings or in earning prospects. Goodwill which does not show up either in present or future earnings is worthless. And sound analysis will not lose sight of it in the income statement analysis.

Percentages should be shown for totals of each of the items which are on an equal basis. For example, various forms of debt may place different restrictions and burdens on the company. Applying this idea to the above figures would result in the following:

Mortgage bonds	%		
Finance leases capitalized	%		
Secured debt		%	
Debentures	%		
Short term debt continuously renewed	%		
Unsecured debt		%	
Total senior debt			%
Convertible debentures			%
Income bonds			%
Long term debt			%
Preferred	%		
Convertible preferred	%		
Total preferreds			%
Total senior securities			%
Common equity (common book value) less intangibles			%
Long term capital			%

The percentages must be viewed in the light of the balance sheet figures of the assets—whether they are significantly over- or under-valued. If assets are over-valued due to inadequate depreciation or obsolescence, the common equity ratio will be over-stated. On the other hand, it may be understated—a lumber company may own land bought many years ago at low prices, an oil company may have extensive oil reserves not recorded on its books, etc.

Some analysts use common equity at market value rather than book value. It may be interesting as one ratio to look at, but it has disadvantages: the percentages are subject to variation due to market fluctuations and it reflects market appraisal of future earnings' prospects as estimated by common stock investors. An appraisal of the company's earnings would better be handled by an analysis of the income statement.

The *return on long term capital after taxes (to investor rate)* is calculated as follows:

All Interest Charges Applicable to Long Term Debt or Equivalent (At Full Rate with no Tax Adjustment), Preferred Dividends and Net Income Available for Common Equity

---

Total Long Term Capital, Less Intangibles

This shows the return on a to-investor-rate basis; that is, the total return that goes to the holders of long term capital as we have defined it for analytical purposes.

The *return on common equity* is calculated as follows:

$$\frac{\text{Net Income Available for Common Equity After Interest, Taxes and Preferred Dividends}}{\text{Common Book Value, Less Intangibles}}$$

An analysis of the long term capital of a company with subsidiaries becomes more complicated because of the subsidiary debt, subsidiary preferred and minority interest.

If the top company and all subsidiaries operate as a unit so that the top company will be responsible for the liabilities of the subsidiaries, then the consolidated balance sheet best represents the long term capital picture. For analysis purposes, the long term capital should be shown with subsidiary obligations and minority interest ahead of the parent company obligations as follows:

- Subsidiary
  - Debt
  - Preferred
- Minority Interest
- Parent Company
  - Debt
  - Preferred
  - Common

The same type of breakdown should be made for the consolidated income statement. The minority interest comes ahead of all parent company securities, because it represents a drain on earnings ahead of all securities of the top company. A complete analysis will require a detailed breakdown of all long term capital between the different layers of debt and preferred of the subsidiaries as well as the parent company.

Even if a company with subsidiaries is operated as a single unity, it may be necessary for a complete understanding of the long term capital position to study the long term capital of the subsidiaries separately. This becomes particularly true when the nature of their businesses differ widely. For example, if a manufacturing company owned a finance company, a bank and an insurance company, the consolidated long term capital would be relatively meaningless.

If a company with subsidiaries operates the system so that each subsidiary stands on its own and will not be supported financially by the parent, then it is necessary to study each subsidiary separately. For example, if one of the subsidiaries is heavily in debt and loses money, it detracts from the consolidated figures. If this losing subsidiary has to stand on its own, it can be taken out of the picture entirely in order to see what the picture looks like with the good parts remaining. However, managements sometimes give lip service to the idea of each subsidiary standing on its own, but if put to the test and the poor subsidiary runs into financial difficulty, they will use the financial strength of the system to save it.

CHAPTER 3

Dividend Policy

Dividend Importance

Dividends are an important financial policy decision and a major part of financial planning for three reasons:

1. Dividends are a part of stockholders' return, the other part being market appreciation.
2. Dividends affect the budget since they represent an outflow of cash and affect the amount of cash available for corporate purposes such as capital investment.
3. Dividends reduce the amount of earned surplus and thus the amount of common equity, and consequently the percent of debt to total long term capital.

Cash dividends are one of the few items in the budget almost entirely variable at the discretion of management, or perhaps we should say at the discretion of the board of directors. You might wonder why the qualification. Dividends are declared by the board of directors, but management must recommend a dividend policy to the board to be passed on by them.

Some companies stick to their past dividend policy primarily because they have become accustomed to it. Some companies avoid paying out adequate dividends because of fear that they may have to cut them in the future. Some companies hesitate to pay cash dividends because they need the money for expansion purposes. None of these are sound reasons for a dividend policy. We will suggest a comprehensive picture of dividend policy with the advantages and disadvantages from various angles.

Which Comes First, Stockholders' Interest or Company's Need for Cash?

The first question that may be raised is whether either the stockholders' interest in dividends or the company's need for cash and earned surplus takes priority. There should be no conflict, because what is good for the company should be tested in terms of what is best for the common stockholders in the long run.

There are three types of needs for funds which may or may not restrict dividend payments, having in mind the benefit to stockholders, as follows:

1. Basic corporate needs, for a financially weak company which cannot raise outside capital, for such purposes as:
   Maturing debt,
   Maintenance of a minimum working capital position,
   Capital investment in order to save its existing investment.

   Sacrificing dividends for a financially weak company will hurt stockholders through loss of cash dividends and adverse market action of the stock. However, when a company has its back to the wall, stockholders might be hurt more in the long run if the company did not take such action.
2. Profitable expansion when outside capital cannot be raised.

   Aside from any problems of saving old

investment, if a company has profitable opportunities for expansion which it is unable to finance, a nice question is raised as to whether a company should ignore stockholders' wishes for dividends and conserve cash for such expansion. If it would improve the position of the existing stockholders by more than offsetting any harm from limiting cash dividend payments, such a policy would be appropriate. The return on investment would have to be very attractive in order to justify such action.

3. Profitable expansion or other needs for outside capital when capital can be raised satisfactorily.

   The need for outside capital should not weigh heavily in determining dividend policy if a company can finance on a satisfactory basis. Then the funds which are not supplied by cash generated internally should be raised through the sale of securities. In this situation, dividend policy comes first and should not be made dependent upon expansion requirements. Most well-run companies should be in this position.

Some managements may contend that dividends should not be paid when there is need for common equity because retaining earnings builds up common equity without incurring financing costs. This is not sound reasoning. The amount of common equity which can be obtained by retaining earnings is relatively small. Furthermore, the stockholders get the dividends, and if they want to increase their investment they can buy outstanding stock or new stock when it is offered. There is no loss to the stockholders as far as the money paid out is concerned, because it goes to the owners. All that is lost as far as the stockholders are concerned is financing costs to raise new common equity money and this is small. This can be explained by some figures for a company which starts out with common equity, earnings and dividends as shown in Exhibit 3-1, Part I.

The company needs $7,500,000 of common equity money for expansion on which it expects to earn 10%. It can obtain $5 million from retained earnings without disturbing its dividend policy. It is considering the possibility of reducing its dividend from $5 to $2.50 per share, in order to obtain an additional $2,500,000 from retained earnings rather than sell 25,000 shares at $100. By so doing, it would save financing costs on that $2,500,000 as contrasted with raising it by the sale of common stock. For our present purpose, accept a figure for financing costs of 5% of the sale price of the stock, which would amount to $125,000 for $2,500,000 of new common stock. This sounds like a lot of money, but we are interested in the effect of the extra $125,000 financing costs on the earnings per share for entire common stock outstanding. Financing costs reduce the net proceeds the company receives. This would mean that the company would have to sell about 1,250 more shares to cover the $125,000 and produce the same total $2,500,000.

Since earnings per share are based on total number of shares outstanding, the effect on earnings per share would be negligible or only $0.012 ($125,000 ÷ 1,026,250 shares) as shown in Exhibit 3-1, Part II. If the company repeated the process for ten years rather than cut the dividend, it would only reduce earnings per share $0.12. This is insignificant compared with the possible effect of the cut in dividend on the market price.

The above discussion is not to suggest at this point, whether a company should pay any dividends, and if so how much. It is merely to state the place that dividend policy occupies in decision making.

To summarize, if a company is weak financially, dividends may have to be sacrificed regardless of the consequences; if it is strong financially, dividend policy comes before cash needs and cash needs should be satisfied by financing.

Desires of Individual Stockholders

In considering stockholders' interests, it is not what one individual stockholder wants, or

Exhibit 3-1

EFFECT OF PROVIDING CAPITAL BY SALE OF COMMON RATHER THAN REDUCING DIVIDENDS

PART I

POSITION OF COMPANY WITH EXISTING DIVIDEND POLICY

Common equity book value	$100,000,000
Number of shares outstanding	1,000,000
Income available for common	$ 10,000,000
Common dividends	$ 5,000,000
Retained earnings	$ 5,000,000
Book value per share	$ 100
Market price per share	$ 100
Earnings per share	$ 10
Dividends per share	$ 5
Dividend payout ratio	50%
Return earned on common equity	10%

PART II

EFFECT ON EARNINGS PER SHARE FROM SALE OF COMMON STOCK TO PROVIDE CAPITAL RATHER THAN REDUCE DIVIDEND

New shares to raise $2,500,000 by sale of new stock at $100 per share	25,000
New shares to cover 5% financing costs or $125,000	1,250
Shares previously outstanding	1,000,000
Total shares after financing	1,026,250
Previous earnings	$ 10,000,000
Additional earnings on $2,500,000 at 10%	250,000
Total	$ 10,250,000
New earnings per share	$9.988

a few; their interests may be opposite to those of the stockholders owning the majority of the stock. If some stockholders wish to sell their stock, they might desire an excessive increase in dividends in order to obtain the cash before they sell, or in order to increase the market price temporarily. This might adversely affect the company in the future and be detrimental to those who continue to hold.

Management should not ignore any stockholders' communications, but it should beware of taking a few stockholders' letters as an indication of what the stockholders owning a majority of the stock want on such a subject as dividends. Those who write represent the opinion of the vocal stockholders.

At times, even the majority of stockholders may want the company to take immediate action which would be harmful over the long run. This raises a nice question of what the company should do if it considers the stockholders' wishes and carries out "true" corporate democracy. Here management must accept the fact that there is a turnover in the stockholder list, and that it has an obligation to follow sound policies for the continuing group of stockholders. With this in mind, management should resist unsound suggestions on the part of stockholders and explain the reasons for management's action.

Should a Company Pay Any Dividends?—Growth Rate of Earnings per Share from Plowback

Now that we have covered some hang-ups in determining dividend policy, let's start our discussion about the amount of dividends to pay by raising the question of whether a company should pay any dividends whatsoever. We will first, give you all possible reasons for not paying dividends and then show you why this reasoning is unsound.

If no dividends are paid, the money is retained by the company which can be used for reinvestment. If the company earns on the new investment, earnings will increase and investors will benefit from an increase in market appreciation of the common.

The way retained earnings build up capital, earnings and market appreciation of the stock is illustrated in Exhibit 3-2, Part I. The growth rates are due to the increase in investment from retaining 50% of the earnings and putting them to work at the same 10% rate on the original investment. The $5 retained in the first year is reinvested at 10% to produce $0.50 more earnings per share, resulting in a 5% increase. As long as the return on the equity investment and dividend payout ratio stay the same, the growth rates will be constant. They can be obtained from the formula as in Exhibit 3-2, Part II. It should be emphasized that the rate of return on the new investment is what determines the growth rate from retained earnings. Of course, a change in earnings on past investment will affect earnings per share, but this is aside from the effect of plowback.

To further illustrate the formula in Part II, it is applied to various rates of return and payouts in Part III.

To the extent that a company retains earnings, investors do not get dividends. But, as we have illustrated, the retained earnings build up earnings per share, which, in turn, result in market appreciation equal to the growth rate in earnings per share if the price-earnings ratio remains constant.

It would make no difference to stockholders whether a company paid dividends or reinvested them in assets under the following circumstances:

1. The price-earnings ratio is not affected by dividends.
2. Stockholders could reinvest dividends without paying any brokerage fee, and earn on the reinvested dividends the same percent return as the company could earn on retained earnings. And the resulting earnings are worth the same price-earnings ratio as the company's earnings.
3. The company would reinvest the retained earnings above the cost-of-capital.
4. There is no difference in the tax rate paid by stockholders for regular income or capital gains.
5. The stockholders have no personal, legal or accounting reason to care whether they got dividends or market appreciation.
6. The stockholders can supplement their income by sale of stock without paying any brokerage fee.

Some Investors Want Dividends

While the above reasoning sounds logical, it leads to the wrong conclusion for the following reasons:

1. Other things being equal, dividends are more valuable to stockholders than prospects of an equal amount of market appreciation because there is risk in market appreciation. Dividends are a bird in

Exhibit 3-2

GROWTH RATE IN EARNINGS PER SHARE FROM PLOWBACK

PART I

ILLUSTRATION

CONSTANT RATE OF RETURN ON BEGINNING BOOK VALUE, DIVIDEND PAYOUT RATIO AND PRICE-EARNINGS RATIO

Year	Common Stock Book Value per Share	Return on Beginning Book Value	Earnings per Share Common Stock	Dividend Payout Ratio	Dividends per Share	Retained Earnings per Share	Price-Earnings Ratio	Market Price per Share
1	$100.00	10%	$10.00	50%	$5.00	$5.00	15	$150.00
2	105.00	10	10.50	50	5.25	5.25	15	157.50
3	110.25	10	11.025	50	5.5125	5.5125	15	165.375

Growth Rate—Earnings per Share —5%
" " —Dividends per Share — "
—Book Value per Share — "
—Market Price per Share— "

PART II

FORMULA

% Earned on Beginning Book Value		% of Earnings Retained		Growth Rate in Earnings per Share, Dividends per Share and Book Value per Share
% Earned on Beginning Book Value	X	100%–% of Earnings Paid Out	=	"

Figures from Part I:

10%	X	50% (50% paid out)	=	5%

PART III

GROWTH RATES IN EARNINGS PER SHARE FROM PLOWBACK FROM VARIOUS RATES OF RETURN AND PAYOUTS

% Earned on Beginning Book Value	X	% of Earnings Retained	=	% Growth Rate
10%	X	30% (70% paid out)	=	3%
15	X	50% (50% paid out)	=	7.5%
20	X	70% (30% paid out)	=	14%

the hand, while market appreciation depends on the company's ability to put the capital to work at an adequate return and the market to translate the increase in earnings into market appreciation.

2. The views of investors vary widely as regards their desire for dividends and market appreciation.
   (a) Some investors won't buy stocks that don't pay dividends.
   (b) Some investors cannot legally buy common stocks unless they have a dividend record. For example, common stocks to be eligible for investment by New York savings banks, must, among other things, have paid cash dividends on their common stock in each year for a period of ten years next preceding the date of investment.
   (c) Some investors cannot consider income from dividends and market appreciation as interchangeable. Laws govern the handling of dividends and market appreciation in trust funds between the life beneficiary and the remainder man. Dividends go to the life beneficiary and market appreciation to the remainder man. The trustee will wish to choose investments which will be fair to both and would be interested in stocks paying dividends in order to give some return to the life beneficiary.
   (d) Some institutional investors cannot, for accounting or legal reasons, treat dividends and market appreciation as interchangeable.
   (e) Many investors do not like to treat dividends and market appreciation as interchangeable. They want to keep their investment and not have to sell part in order to get income.
   (f) Investors vary widely as to their tax advantage of dividend income vs. capital gains from market appreciation. Individuals in the lower income tax brackets do not get any advantage from capital gains. And there is a wide variation in institutional investors' interest in the tax treatment of dividends vs. market appreciation. Corporations get an 85% dividend tax credit. Mutual insurance companies pay a relatively low income tax rate. Some institutional investors are tax exempt.
3. Dividends may put a floor on the market price of a stock when earnings are adverse and the yield becomes significant. When a stock is selling at a high price-earnings ratio and a low yield, this advantage of a dividend may seem quite remote. But if a company runs into trouble so that the market price of the stock sinks, a high yield tends to prevent stockholders from selling and may attract investors who feel that the dividend gives them an attractive return as well as protection against further decline. If the company has to offer common stock under such circumstances, the dividend may be the difference between success and failure. For example, the yield on electric utility stocks was around 3.00% in the early 1960's and 4.75% in the late 1960's. Utility stocks lost favor in the 1970's, at a time when the companies had to raise large amounts of capital through sale of securities, including common stock. The yields increased to over 10% for many companies. This was about equivalent to the yield on a good grade bond. The success of common stock sales for many electric companies was dependent primarily on the attractive yield.
4. Dividends may add stability to the market price of a stock because dividends should fluctuate less than earnings.
5. If dividend policy affects the market price, then stockholders benefit when the company sells new stock because of the better price the company receives. This improves existing stockholders' book value. Earnings per share increase if new stock is sold above book value, and the company is able to earn at least the same return on the new book value as on the existing.

Thus, there is a wide range of interest in dividends on the part of both individual and institutional investors, and it does make a difference to some investors whether earnings are paid out or retained for certain types of companies.

In view of the interest of some investors in dividends, how do you make a decision regarding the appropriate policy for your company?

The Goal—Attract Greatest Number of Stockholders

In order to determine a dividend policy for your company, what should be your goal? The goal should be to establish a policy which will appeal to the greatest number of stockholders over the long run. By enhancing the demand for your stock, you improve the market price and do most for your stockholders in terms of total return from dividends and market appreciation. When you sell new stock, you will receive the best price.

Occasionally, you may hear the management of a company say, "Dividend policy should be established which will attract the type of investors the company wants." This is putting the cart before the horse. Such a policy would not necessarily result in the greatest benefit to stockholders in the long run, because it might cut down on the long range total demand for the stock.

The type of company itself, regardless of the dividend policy, will have much to do with the type of investors which it attracts. A new speculative company will tend to attract investors who are willing to take a large risk and want capital gains exclusively. Such investors tend to be in the high income tax bracket. Dividends would be an annoyance to them.

A strong, well-established company with a high return on common can do more for stockholders by retaining a high percentage of earnings. It can probably reinvest the money at a better rate than its common stockholders could do if earnings were paid out in dividends. Furthermore, retention of a large part of the earnings will result in a fast growth in earnings per share from the effect of plowback and a high price-earnings ratio adding to market appreciation. Such a company will tend to attract investors who want some dividends, but have most interest in market appreciation. This calls for a low payout.

A stable type of company which does not have an opportunity to invest its capital at a high rate of return will tend to attract investors who are more interested in income from dividends. A higher payout fits such a company best.

Therefore, in order to achieve the goals we have suggested, dividend policy should be established to fit the type of company in view of the type of investors who will naturally be attracted to it. You cannot change the nature of your company with dividend policy.

Thus, a dividend policy should be established which will complement and strengthen investors' natural interest in the company in the long run.

Correlation Between Price-Earnings Ratio and Dividend Payout Ratio

In order to determine the most appropriate dividend policy for a company, it would be ideal if a large sample could be obtained of exactly similar companies but with different dividend payout policies. Then a correlation table could be developed which would show the payout ratio which would produce the highest price-earnings ratio. This cannot be done for two reasons:

1. It is difficult to obtain a broad sample of companies which are sufficiently similar except for dividend policy so that the effect of dividend policy alone can be determined. So many other factors affect the price-earnings ratio, such as differences in sales, expenses, outlook for earnings, etc.
2. It is future earnings as expected by investors which affects the common stock market price and not current earnings. Therefore, in developing such a correlation table, the relationship of

market price to future earnings as estimated by investors should be used rather than a price-earnings ratio based on current earnings. As a practical matter, it would be impossible to obtain a representative cross section of prospective earnings as estimated by investors to use for this purpose.

What Have Other Similar Companies Done?

For background information, it may be of interest to study the policies other similar companies in your industry follow. But this does not necessarily mean that their policies are correct. They might or might not be, and the figures should be viewed with this in mind.

A high or low payout ratio for a company in any one year may not be indicative of a company's policy. It may be the result of unusually low or high earnings. To get a clue as to a company's payout policy, the results should be studied over at least a five-year period, as well as all the circumstances surrounding the company, such as the level of the company's earnings, the company's financial strength, availability of profitable investment projects, etc.

In studying what other companies have done, it may be interesting to observe the effect on the market price of a stock when the dividend increase was made. However, the market effect of a dividend increase may not be discernible for three reasons:

1. The market may anticipate the dividend increase so that at the time of the increase the market action may already have been spent.
2. A dividend increase may cause a market action due to investors interpreting the increase as an indication of a favorable outlook for the company's earnings. Investors are aware that the directors must consider a company's prospects when deciding on dividend policy.
3. Other factors may affect the stock at the time of the increase so as to negate or over-shadow the effect of the dividend increase.

Two Questions—Amount and Type

Now that we are getting to the point of suggesting a method of deciding on cash dividend policy, there are two major questions that have to be determined:

1. The amount, if any, as measured by the percentage of earnings paid out.
2. The type of payment—regular, extra, variable, etc.

The type and amount are to a degree interdependent; type will have an effect on amount.

Selection of Dividend Payout Percentage by Process of Elimination Through Judgment

Since a statistical approach cannot be used to determine dividend policy, it is necessary to rely on judgment, by establishing a policy which will complement and reinforce the natural appeal of investors for a particular company. Dividend policy cannot be determined with a great degree of precision and need not be. All that is necessary is to establish a payout policy within reasonable limits.

Given below are five basic cash dividend policies[1] in terms of percentage payout. Brief comments indicate the types of companies which they might fit the best.

1. 0%

   For a company with speculative characteristics which will only attract investors who are primarily seeking capital gains.

2. Nominal—5%

   For a company in a transition period from the type with no cash dividend to a more stable type of company starting to pay dividends on a gradual basis in order to build a record. Such a nominal dividend will not mean much to stockholders, and it will have little

---

[1]The Federal tax code (Internal Revenue Code, Section 531) penalizes any undue withholding of dividends under certain circumstances, but there is nothing in the discussion in this book that suggests evasion of this statute.

effect on market price. However, the purpose is to build a dividend record to satisfy investors in the future who are attracted to a company which has a sustained dividend record.

3. Low—25%

   For a company with a sound capital structure and a high quality common stock which generates a high return such as 15%. It will produce an 11 1/4% (75% retained earnings x 15% return on common book value) growth rate in earnings per share from plowback. It is unlikely that the company's stockholders could reinvest the dividends at as high a rate as 15%. Furthermore, such a company can do more for investors with a low payout because the high growth rate will produce a high price-earnings ratio. In order for this to happen, the company must have new capital investment opportunities which will provide a high return, otherwise the high growth rate in earnings per share from the low payout will not occur.

   For a company with a high return on capital, a high growth rate and a high price-earnings ratio, the yield to the investor based on market price will be relatively small. Therefore, it may be asked whether the dividend has any effect on price? There are various reasons why it may have some effect. It may attract investors who would not buy the stock if it paid no dividends. A steady upward dividend pattern gives confidence to investors. If the company runs into trouble, the dividend will eventually act as a stabilizing influence as the market price declines. Furthermore, while the yield may be low based on the current dividend related to market price, investors may look ahead to dividend increases and anticipate a satisfactory yield on their original investment. For example, a stock selling at $100 and paying a $3 dividend would yield 3%. If the dividend increases 10% a year for five years it would be $4.83 and the yield on the original investment would be 4.83%. It may be illogical for investors to look at yield in this manner. They should consider the yield based on the current market price and not the historical price they paid for it. However, individual investors do look at it this way and even institutional investors consider the yield on their original investment.

   A company with a high return on common equity due to leverage should have a low payout for another reason: the earnings are vulnerable to a decline.

4. Average—50%

   For a typical large industrial company earning 12% on the beginning common book value, providing a 6% growth rate from plowback and a fairly generous dividend. Because of the variability of earnings of a typical industrial company, a higher payout might make the dividend vulnerable to being cut.

5. High—65%

   For a stable type of company like a large utility or a large money center bank which cannot earn a high return on its common book value but does have stability of earnings and therefore can offer a generous dividend without fear of cutting it. This will appeal to the broad group of investors who want a high return.

In order to determine the dividend policy for a particular company proceed as follows:

1. Consider what the company has to offer stockholders and what type of stockholders might naturally be attracted to the company regardless of dividend policy.
2. By the process of elimination decide which of the five policies would most nearly fit the company, in view of its nature and the type of stockholders who would naturally be attracted to it.

Other Views of Payout Ratio

It is interesting to view the effect on the payout ratio of an increase in the return on common equity if the dividend is kept at a set percentage of common book value. We will give two examples to illustrate this idea.

For a company which should have a 50% payout with a return on common book value of 10%, the dividend would represent 5% of common book value. If the dividend is kept at 5% of common book as the return on common book value increases, the payout would fall as shown in Exhibit 3-3, Part I.

For a company which should have a 65% payout with a return on common book value of 10%, the dividend would represent 6.5% of common book value. If the dividend is kept at 6.5% of common book value, as the return on common book value increases the payout would fall as shown in Exhibit 3-3, Part II.

The figures in these two exhibits suggest that if a company starts out with the correct payout ratio when it earns about 10%, and keeps the dividend at a constant percent of book value, the payout ratio will automatically adjust itself downward as the company's return on common book value increases and the benefit from plowback increases. This is another way of looking at your dividend policy.

This approach has some significance as regards the yield to the investor at the market price of the stock. If the market price of your stock is equal to the common book value per share, then the dividend as a percent of common book value would equal the yield of the dividend on the market price for the investor. You can carry this thought a step further by asking yourself what would be a fair total return for an investor in your stock from both dividend yield and market appre-

Exhibit 3-3

DIVIDEND ESTABLISHED AS A PERCENT OF BOOK VALUE WITH A MODERATE RETURN ON BOOK VALUE WILL RESULT IN LOWER PAYOUT AS RETURN INCREASES

PART I

DIVIDEND ESTABLISHED SO THAT YIELD ON BEGINNING COMMON BOOK VALUE IS 5%. SUBSEQUENT INCREASE IN RETURN ON COMMON BOOK VALUE LOWERS PAYOUT

Year	Beginning Common Book Value	Return on Beginning Common Book Value	Earnings per Share	Dividend Payout Ratio	Dividend	Dividend Yield on Beginning Common Book Value
1	$100.00	10%	$10.00	50%	$5.00	5.00%
2	105.00	15	15.75	33	5.25	"
3	115.50	20	23.10	25	5.78	"

PART II

DIVIDEND ESTABLISHED SO THAT YIELD ON BEGINNING COMMON BOOK VALUE IS 6.5%. SUBSEQUENT INCREASE IN RETURN ON COMMON BOOK VALUE LOWERS PAYOUT

Year	Beginning Common Book Value	Return on Beginning Common Book Value	Earnings per Share	Dividend Payout Ratio	Dividend	Dividend Yield on Beginning Common Book Value
1	$100.00	10%	$10.00	65%	$6.50	6.5%
2	103.50	15	15.53	43	6.73	"
3	112.30	20	22.46	33	7.31	"

ciation. Since you will already have the dividend yield if the market price equals the common book value, then by subtraction you can get the market appreciation which must occur for an investor to get the fair return which you have deemed appropriate. Of course, hopefully your stock would be above book value, so this approach is limited in its significance. We will discuss in detail the relationship of the market price of your stock and the return to the investor in the last chapter.

Why Not Pay Out All Earnings in Dividends?

We have discussed the question of not paying any dividends and shown that such a policy would not be appropriate for many companies. How about the other extreme of paying out all earnings in dividends? There are three reasons why this would not be beneficial.

1. The amount of the payment would depend entirely on earnings each year so that investors could not count on it. Therefore, it would not have a stabilizing effect on the market price of the stock.
2. It would kill all growth of earnings per share from plowback.
3. Creditors might be unhappy because there would be no build-up of common equity through retained earnings.

Additional Factors to Consider in Determining Payout Policy

Since the payout policy depends on earnings, the company should consider the earnings from various angles.

1. Is the company earning a high return on capital which may decrease in the future? What would be the payout related to earnings based on an earnings rate on total capital that can be maintained over the long run? What is the minimum rate that would have to be earned on total capital in order just to earn the dividend?
2. What have been the reasons for the growth rate in earnings per share? What will be the sustainable growth rate in earnings per share which can justify a long range growth rate in dividends.
3. Does the company contemplate common stock financing which will temporarily reduce earnings per share. For example, if a company issues one new share for each ten existing shares, the total shares outstanding will be increased by 10% and earnings will be immediately reduced approximately by this amount. If a company had a 50% payout ratio before the issue, it would be increased to 55%. Of course, this is only a temporary effect because earnings should increase when the money is put to work.
4. Is the company financially strong so that it can maintain the dividend even if it was not earned? Has the company a large amount of senior securities in the capital structure? Other things being equal, the more senior securities the greater will be the variability of the earnings for the common equity, since the earnings are farther out on the limb. This is shown in Exhibit 3-4. Preferred stock is used rather than debt for illustrative purposes, as it eliminates the problem of interest being deductible for tax purposes; the same principle applies for all types of senior obligations.

   Both companies earn 10% on total long term capital. Company X, which only has common equity, earns 10% on common equity. Because of leverage, Company Y earns 14% on common equity. Company Y has the preferred dividends to pay as well as the common; combined, they total \$6,500,000, which represents 65% of the income available. It is a heavier burden on earnings than the common dividends for Company X. To put it another way, if Company X's earnings were cut in half, to \$5 million, the dividend would still be earned. On the other hand, a cut of \$5 million for Company Y would leave only \$2 million after preferred dividends to pay the \$3,500,000 of common dividends.

Exhibit 3-4

EFFECT OF LEVERAGE ON DIVIDEND PAYOUT

	No Leverage Company X	Leverage Company Y
Long Term Capital		
Preferred		$ 50,000,000
Common Equity	$100,000,000	50,000,000
Total	$100,000,000	$100,000,000
Earnings	$ 10,000,000	$ 10,000,000
Preferred Dividends		3,000,000
Balance for Common	$ 10,000,000	$ 7,000,000
Common Dividends	$ 5,000,000	$ 3,500,000
Return on Long Term Capital After Taxes	10%	10%
Return on Common Equity	10%	14%
Payout Ratio for Common Dividends	50%	50%
Payout Ratio for Common & Preferred Dividends		65%

Therefore, in observing any particular company's ratio, the company's capital structure must be kept in mind.

Type of Dividend—Pattern Is All-Important

Past dividends are over the dam when investors buy a stock; they are concerned with what they may get in the future. However, past dividends are important to the extent that they give a clue about the future. For this reason, the past pattern is very important.

A policy of paying out the same percentage of earnings each year would result in dividends varying with earnings. This would not help to stabilize the market price of a company's stock; predictions about dividends would have as much uncertainty as predictions about earnings. The percentage paid out should be based on trended earnings over a number of years in the future so that the dividend will follow a regular pattern and have some certainty.

Shown in Exhibit 3-5 are the various types of dividends.

A *(I) Regular* dividend with no increase is a reflection on the company's inability to earn an adequate return on the retained earnings. The retained portion of the earnings remains in the company and the stockholders' equity increases to the extent of such retained earnings. A company should earn on the added investment—which should result in increased earnings per share and an increase in dividends.

If we combine regularity or certainty as well as an increasing dividend, then the most desirable type of dividend is *(II) Regular Increasing Regularly.* By increasing regularly, we mean regular percentage increases and not regular amounts. If the earnings showed a regular percentage increase, the payout would decrease if the dividend was increased a constant dollar amount. However, in order for a pattern to be effective, it must be believed by investors, because they cannot use it for projecting into the future unless the past pattern is plausible.

Exhibit 3-5

EXAMPLES OF TYPES OF DIVIDEND PAYMENTS

	1st Year by Quarters				2nd Year by Quarters			
	1st	2nd	3rd	4th	1st	2nd	3rd	4th
I. Regular	10¢	10¢	10¢	10¢	10¢	10¢	10¢	10¢
II. Regular increasing regularly	10¢	10¢	10¢	12¢	12¢	12¢	12¢	14¢
III. Regular increasing irregularly	10¢	10¢	11¢	11¢	12¢	12¢	14¢	14¢
IV. Regular with irregular extra	10¢	10¢	10¢	10¢	10¢	10¢	10¢	10¢
				4¢ extra				2¢ extra
V. Regular with regular extra	10¢	10¢	10¢	10¢	10¢	10¢	10¢	10¢
				3¢ extra				3¢ extra
VI. Variable	10¢	5¢	5¢	12¢	10¢	14¢	10¢	5¢

Since earnings vary instead of increasing regularly, the best that can be achieved by most companies is a *(III) Regular Increasing Irregularly* when earnings increase. An effort should be made to achieve the ideal pattern as nearly as possible.

Let's go to our next two types involving extras–*(IV) Regular with Irregular Extra,* and *(V) Regular with Regular Extra.* The irregular extra is not expected to be repeated. It can be used when a company has unusually good earnings and cannot invest retained earnings at an adequate return. The market price of the company's stock will not be permanently affected to any material extent by this type of extra. Thus, the stockholders will only be temporarily benefited.

The regular extra is expected to be repeated if conditions warrant. If a company is uncertain whether a higher regular rate can be maintained, it could start out with a regular extra but make it clear that it will be paid only if conditions warrant. It can be correctly argued that the market will not give the same effect to a regular extra as it will to a similar regular dividend, due to the uncertainty involved. How much the market will discount the regular extra compared with a similar amount of regular will depend on the prospects of the extra being continued. The advantage of the regular extra lies in the fact that it may permit some companies to pay out a higher percentage, yet not be in the embarrassing position of having to tamper with its regular rate if adverse conditions develop.

If a company's earnings are relatively stable, the company should not be overly timid and declare an extra which could justifiably be rolled into the regular rate.

Now we come to the final category–*(VI) Variable.* If a company is in a cyclical business and one which is quite risky, so that earnings per share are highly erratic, then the company has two alternatives.

1. A variable dividend.

   This will not be too effective to increase the market price of the stock because investors will not be able to count on it. However, if the company is a type which will attract investors who want some cash income, it may be better than not paying any dividend.
2. A low payout regular dividend with year-end extras.

   This would be preferable because it would at least give investors a part of the dividend they could count on.

Since pattern is so important, sharp, irregular increases defeat the purpose. If a company's character changes with regard to its earnings stability, and if its ability to earn so that the nature of the investors attracted to it changes, it will wish to change its dividend policy. An increase in the amount paid out should be done gradually to present a good pattern. When a decrease in payout is desired, it is best, if possible, to achieve results by slowing down the dividend increases as compared with the earnings increase. Then the payout ratio will gradually fall.

Company with Excess Cash

Warning! If you do not expect to earn at least your cost-of-capital on new projects, you have no justification whatsoever for retaining earnings on the grounds that the company needs money for plant expansion. While a strong cash position is good to maintain, a company should not hold huge amounts of cash just on the vague assumption that sometime, somehow it might be handy to have. On the other hand, a company which is expanding should not hesitate to keep cash available for any reasonable prospect for expansion.

A company with excess cash has various possibilities:

1. If the senior securities are too high and they can be retired on reasonable terms, cash can be used for this purpose.
2. It can pay an extra dividend at the end of the year in order to distribute cash. Or have a high regular dividend payout policy, if the company can't find enough high return projects and expects to continuously generate extra cash. You will find some companies which have a high return on common book value with a relatively high payout policy for this reason. For a company with a high return on common book value, the price-earnings ratio will probably be so high that the dividend yield is very low. However, since the company can't use the cash, the high dividend does something for the stockholders and it adds character to the common stock.
3. Repurchase of the company's stock in the market. This is a rather lengthy subject and we will cover it at the end of this chapter.

Examples of Dividend Policies

An example of a well-established company with a sound capital structure which has a high return on common and fits category Low 25% is shown in Exhibit 3-6. The average payout was 25%. The growth rate in earnings per share averaged 21.3%. The growth rate from plowback alone averaged 12.8% (17.0% x 75%). The increase in return on beginning book value of 5.8% accounted for most of the other increases in earnings.

The dividend record for a typical industrial company with a moderate return on common and fits category Average 50% is shown in Exhibit 3-7. The average payout was 51%. The growth rate in earnings per share averaged 7.8%. The growth rate from plowback alone was 5.9% (12.0% x 49%). The other principal reason for the increase in earnings per share was the increase in return on equity which averaged 2.9%.

Exhibit 3-8 shows the figures for a company which represents a relatively stable type of business earning a moderate return and approximately fits the category High 65%. The average payout was 69%. The growth rate in earnings per share average 5.7%. The growth rate from plowback alone was 3.6% (11.7% x 31%). The increase in return on common book value accounted for 0.7% of the earnings growth, and the balance came primarily from the sale of common stock above book value.

Survey of Stockholders as to Their Interest in Dividends

Should a company ask its stockholders what cash dividends they want? They own the company, so why not ask them?

As a matter of fact, if we were concerned only with companies which are privately owned and had no public stockholders, dividend policy would not be an issue. The owners would tell management how much of the earnings they wanted in dividends and how much should be plowed back.

Exhibit 3-6

EXAMPLE OF DIVIDEND PAYOUT–LOW 25%
A LARGE INDUSTRIAL COMPANY WITH A HIGH QUALITY COMMON
AND A HIGH RETURN ON COMMON BOOK VALUE

	Earnings per Share				Return on Beginning Common Equity	
Year	Amount	Yr. to Yr. % Change	Dividends per Share	Payout Ratio	Percent	Yr. to Yr. % Change
10	$2.59	20.5%	$0.52 1/2	20%	19.8%	3.1%
9	2.15	18.1	0.44 2/3	21	19.2	2.1
8	1.82	20.5	0.43	24	18.8	5.0
7	1.51	18.9	0.34	23	17.9	(11.4)
6	1.27	39.6	0.28 1/3	22	20.2	21.7
5	0.91	19.7	0.21 2/3	24	16.6	5.7
4	0.76	13.4	0.20 1/2	27	15.7	4.7
3	0.67	17.5	0.18 1/3	27	15.0	5.6
2	0.57	23.9	0.16	28	14.2	15.5
1	0.46	21.1	0.13 1/3	29	12.3	--
Average		21.3		25	17.0	5.8

Exhibit 3-7

EXAMPLE OF DIVIDEND PAYOUT–AVERAGE 50%
A LARGE INDUSTRIAL COMPANY WITH HIGH QUALITY COMMON STOCK
AND MODERATE RETURN ON COMMON BOOK VALUE

	Earnings per Share				Return on Beginning Common Equity	
Year	Amount	Yr. to Yr. % Change	Dividends per Share	Payout Ratio	Percent	Yr. to Yr. % Change
10	$2.51	(21.6)%	$1.60	64%	9.7%	(23.0)%
9	3.20	0.6	1.53	48	12.6	(8.7)
8	3.18	7.8	1.47	46	13.8	0.7
7	2.95	6.5	1.37	46	13.7	(0.7)
6	2.77	9.1	1.32	48	13.8	0.7
5	2.54	18.7	1.17	46	13.7	11.4
4	2.14	20.9	.98	46	12.3	20.6
3	1.77	23.8	.89	50	10.2	20.0
2	1.43	(1.4)	.87	61	8.5	1.2
1	1.45	13.3	.80	55	8.4	6.3
Average		7.8		51	12.0	2.9

Even for a company which is publicly owned, it would be easy to decide on the amount of payout, provided your stockholders were well versed in finance and you knew what they wanted.

However, a survey of opinions of the small uninformed investors regarding their desires for dividends would be relatively meaningless. They know so little about the financial consequences of dividend policy that they would not know how to answer for their own benefit. The answers to even a simple question such as—Do you want cash dividends or market appreciation?—might not be of much value. Some uninformed investors might automatically answer: "Of course, we want all the dividends we can get." Therefore, a company could probably not gain much assistance from contacting its uninformed stockholders.

Rather than relying on uninformed stockholders' opinions on dividend policy, it might be helpful if a company could classify its uninformed stockholders on the basis of a size of income and tax bracket, but such information is, of course, not readily available.

If a company did try to survey its uninformed stockholders, here are some of the questions it might ask:

Some helpful information about dividend policy might be obtained from informed institutional holders of a company's stock. They should know their interest in dividends vs. market appreciation. For this reason, management should know the type of institutional investors that hold its stock. When the opportunity presents itself, management should not hesitate to ask these informed stockholders the extent of their interest in dividends. However, it should look at the answers from the point of view of the institutional holders that it will attract over the long run. At times, there may be a temporary surge of interest in a company's stock by some institutions because of the market price or the immediate outlook for the company. It is not such temporary interest that should be weighed by the company for long range dividend policy information. Also keep in mind that when an institutional investor gives you an answer on dividend policy, he may be talking in terms of his immediate interest and not the best policy for stockholders over the long run.

It is not advisable to ask financial analysts with brokerage firms about dividend policy. They tend to be biased against dividends. They are primarily interested in short or near

Did you purchase the stock on your own analysis or was it recommended to you by someone?

On my own __________
Recommended to me by broker __________
banker __________
other __________

What is your age?
What is your income?
Are you interested in cash dividends or would you rather have the company pay no dividends and put the money to work to increase the market price of your stock?

Want some dividends __________
Would rather forego dividends in favor of market appreciation __________

If you had a choice between cash dividends or an equal amount of increase in the price of your stock, which would you take?

Cash dividends __________
Equal amount of increase in price of stock __________

Exhibit 3-8

EXAMPLE OF DIVIDEND PAYOUT–HIGH 65%
A RELATIVELY STABLE TYPE OF COMPANY WITH A HIGH QUALITY COMMON STOCK

	Earnings per Share				Return on Beginning Common Equity	
Year	Amount	Yr. to Yr. % Change	Dividends per Share	Payout Ratio	Percent	Yr. to Yr. % Change
10	$1.88	19.7%	$1.40	75%	10.7%	13.8%
9	1.57	(23.0)	1.40	89	9.4	(27.1)
8	2.05	7.3	1.40	68	12.9	3.2
7	1.91	3.2	1.30	68	12.5	(1.6)
6	1.85	7.6	1.20	65	12.7	1.6
5	1.72	3.6	1.10	64	12.5	(2.3)
4	1.66	12.2	1.00	60	12.8	8.5
3	1.48	11.3	.95	64	11.8	7.2
2	1.33	5.6	.90	68	11.0	0.9
1	1.26	9.6	.85	67	10.9	2.8
Average		5.7		69	11.7	0.7

term market appreciation; this is the way they get their reputation. If you are going to talk to financial analysts, go to the ones working with institutions which are managing funds.

Investment Banker's Advice for a New Company Going Public

When a company goes public for the first time, the investment banker may urge a dividend policy on a company in order to assist in the sale of the stock. The first public offering is important, but management should decide on what is a proper long range dividend policy for the company. Then it should weigh the advantages of the policy suggested by the investment banker and its effect on the new offering vs. the best policy for the company over the long run.

Additional Questions

In deciding on the actual dividend payment, various additional questions arise:

When to increase the dividend.
Cutting dividends.
Calculation of the payout ratio.
Dates of payments and fractional payments.
Need for earned surplus.
Information about dividend policy.

When to Make an Increase

Dividends can be increased at any meeting of the board of directors, but generally, earnings permitting, a board will review the matter at the same meeting each year–the dividend meeting. If changes have been made in the past at a certain dividend date, investors get to expect a decision to be made at that time. If it is passed over to a future meeting, investors may interpret the failure of the increase as bad news and sell their stock. Therefore, it may be well to review dividend policy once each year at the same board meeting. This is not to suggest that it would be earth shaking to postpone a dividend increase for a quarter if there were good reasons to do so.

At which board meeting should the dividend be reviewed? We have already said that dividends should be based on trended earnings and not the same percentage payout of each year's earnings. However, a company will wish to weigh the current year's earnings in making any change. If management is sure of its forecast earnings for the year, it can make an increase in the first quarter. If the company's earnings are very volatile, it may wish to have the dividend meeting later in the year when the full year's earnings are more certain.

The quarter you increase the dividend affects the amount of cash paid out during the year. If you increase the rate in the first quarter, more cash will be paid out than if it is increased in the third quarter. At the end of the year, the new annual rate will be the same with either method. We think there is some advantage in making an increase in the first quarter so that the annual payments are the same as four times the quarterly payments. This is illustrated in Exhibit 3-9.

Should you increase the dividend just prior to or during a common stock offering? It has been done and there is nothing against it, but unless it occurs as part of a regular pattern of dividend increases, it could upset the pattern. Furthermore, it might be viewed by investors as being done just to influence the market price because of the offering. In that event, it might not have the desired beneficial effect.

Cutting Dividends

If dividends have the purpose we have suggested, then cutting dividends is bound to have adverse effects.

1. Investors suffer an immediate cash loss which makes them place a lower evaluation on the stock as far as dividend income is concerned.

Exhibit 3-9

EFFECT OF TIMING OF QUARTERLY DIVIDEND INCREASE ON ANNUAL RATE

PART I

INCREASE IN FIRST QUARTER

Year	Quarter 1st	2nd	3rd	4th	Dividends Paid in Year	Annual Rate at New Quarterly Rate
1	50¢	50¢	50¢	50¢	$2.00	$2.00
2	60	60	60	60	2.40	2.40
3	70	70	70	70	2.80	2.80

PART II

INCREASE IN THIRD QUARTER

Year	Quarter 1st	2nd	3rd	4th	Dividends Paid in Year	Annual Rate at New Quarterly Rate
1	50¢	50¢	50¢	50¢	$2.00	$2.00
2	50	50	60	60	2.20	2.40
3	60	60	70	70	2.60	2.80

2. Investors are fearful of what a dividend cut may signal. They may worry about what is wrong with the outlook for the company which made it necessary for management to cut the dividend.
3. It hurts the historical dividend pattern which investors study. They may ask, if the company cut in the past, will they cut again in the future? It will tend to undermine their faith rather than build it.

Therefore, a company which has satisfactory financial strength should try hard not to cut a dividend. It should not fear a high payout percentage as earnings decrease, and it should not hesitate to dip into earned surplus. It should not hesitate to borrow money to pay dividends if it is strong financially.

For example, a company made statements akin to the following: "We have established a regular 50¢ quarterly dividend and will attempt to maintain that base dividend." As a result of this and other statements by the management which were all made in good faith, investors were led to believe that the 50¢ quarterly rate would be maintained, come what may. Unfortunately, the management had not followed a sound financial policy and had underestimated the variability of the earnings. Here is approximately what happened.

Year	Earnings per Share	Dividends per Share	Dividend Payout Ratio
1	$3.60	$2.00	56%
2	4.00	2.25 (25¢ extra)	56
3	1.00	1.50	150

When the dividend was cut because of the company's weak financial position, there was a strong reaction against the company by the stockholders.

A historic dividend action which shook an industry and Wall Street was the elimination by Consolidated Edison of its common dividend in the first quarter of 1974. The stock sold at $18 the day before the announcement. On the basis of the $1.80 annual dividend rate, the yield was 10%. This was more than the yields on other electric utilities, which were around 8 1/2%, because Con Ed had been experiencing poor earnings. However, the stock price was being held up by the dividend and the street did not expect the cut.

This action clobbered the stockholders. The day on which the dividend was eliminated the stock fell to $12–a 33% drop in price–and subsequently sold down to $6.

With the cut, the company may have eliminated its ability to sell common, and raised questions about its ability to sell senior securities.

Reaching back in history to the great depression in the 1930's, we find an unusual example of a well-known company which maintained its dividend even though it was not earned for four years. We refer to American Telephone and Telegraph Co., figures for which are shown in Exhibit 3-10.

Exhibit 3-10

AMERICAN TELEPHONE AND TELEGRAPH COMPANY DIVIDEND RECORD DURING THE GREAT DEPRESSION

Year	Earnings per Share (Consolidated)	Dividends per Share	% Dividend Payout
1936	$9.90	$9.00	91%
1935	7.14	"	126
1934	5.94	"	151
1933	5.40	"	167
1932	5.94	"	152
1931	9.54	"	93

The company knew that its earnings were overly depressed compared with any reasonable norm and it was in a strong financial position. By having the fortitude to maintain the dividend, it did much for its stockholders during these years and the effect on the market price of the stock was felt for many years in the future.

A company's creditors tend to look at dividends as disadvantageous to them because dividends result in an outflow of cash. If a company is weak financially, this is a reasonable concern. However, creditors should understand that in the long run a company's ability to raise common equity capital is an important factor affecting its financial strength. Therefore, they should appreciate the importance of trying to maintain dividends even if earnings fall off. And a company should resist unsound requests by creditors to cut dividends.

Thus, a dividend should only be cut under two circumstances:

1. If a company is in a real financial bind.
2. If a company's payout is so excessively high for the type of company that it would take too long to lower the payout by waiting until earnings increased.

When a company establishes a dividend policy, it should lay out the expected dividend pattern five years ahead based on forecast earnings. Of course, there will have to be changes as earnings change. In order to visualize the problem of maintaining the dividend, a calculation should be made which shows the return needed to be earned on common book value just to maintain the dividend. For example, if a company has a common book value of $100 and is earning 12% on book value, the earnings per share would be $12. If it pays out 50% of earnings in dividends the dividend would be $6. The dividend represents a return on common book value of 6%, so that earnings could fall to that rate on common book value and still have the dividend just earned.

Calculation of Dividend Payout Ratio

We have used the term dividend payout ratio thus far in the chapter as dividends divided by earnings. It is not a ratio but is expressed as a percentage. We will now discuss the ratio more precisely and show how best to calculate it.

We are interested in the percent of earnings actually paid out in common dividends.

To obtain this figure easily, divide the total annual dividends paid to the common stockholders by the total corresponding annual earnings available to pay the dividends after all expenses, taxes, interest and dividends on preferred stock.

$$\text{Dividend Payout Ratio} = \frac{\text{Annual dividends paid to common stockholders}}{\text{Corresponding annual earnings available to pay dividends after all expenses, taxes, interest and dividends on preferred stock.}}$$

You may wish to calculate the ratio by excluding extraordinary and non-recurring items from earnings in order to study the relationship of dividends to regular earnings.

If the number of shares of common stock do not change during the period, the same figure can be obtained by dividing annual dividends per share for the common stock by the corresponding annual earnings per share.

$$\text{Dividend Payout Ratio} = \frac{\text{Annual dividends per share common}}{\text{Corresponding annual earnings per share common}}$$

However, if the number of shares change during the period due to sale of new common, conversion of a convertible issue or issuance of more shares in a stock dividend or stock split, the per share basis of calculation will not produce the same results as obtained by using the total figures. This is illustrated in Exhibit 3-11.

If the shares increase due to conversion of a convertible debenture or convertible preferred, analysts may calculate the ratio on a pro-forma basis as though conversion took place at the beginning of the year. This would require eliminating the net after tax interest payments on the convertibles and assuming common dividends were paid for the full year.

If the quarterly dividend rate changes during the year, some analysts may calculate the payout ratio on a per share basis using the new quarterly rate as though it were in effect for a full year. This will show what the

Exhibit 3-11

ILLUSTRATION OF EFFECT OF ISSUANCE OF COMMON STOCK
ON CALCULATION OF DIVIDEND PAYOUT RATIO

	Total	Per Share
Year 1		
Shares outstanding	100	
Annual earnings	$100	$1.00
Annual dividends	$ 40	$0.40 (10¢ per quarter)
Dividend payout ratio	40%	40%
Year 2		
Shares outstanding at beginning of year	100	
Shares issued after 2nd quarterly dividend payment	10	
Shares outstanding at end of year	110	
Average number of shares	105	
Annual earnings	$100	$0.909 On year end total shares (110) $0.952 On average number of shares (105)
Annual dividends	$ 42	$0.40 (10¢ per quarter)
Dividend payout ratio based on:		
Total dividends and earnings	42%	
Year end shares		44%
Average number of shares		42%

pro-forma payout would be at the new rate. This would, of course, produce a higher payout, and not give effect to possible earnings increases that might occur in the coming year.

This discussion is really making a simple situation rather complicated because generally the resulting differences are not significant, but you should understand the effect of the different ways to calculate the dividend payout ratio, and that the use of annual total unadjusted figures rather than per share figures will do the job the easiest.

Dates of Payments and Fractional Payments

Most companies pay dividends quarterly. There are a few which pay them monthly, semiannually and annually. From the stockholders' point of view, income spread out quarterly would be preferable to payments semiannually or annually. This is not a major issue, but if a company's dividend is sufficient in amount to appeal to stockholders, it would seem wise to adopt a quarterly dividend policy to meet their interests better. Dividend payments do require expense on the part of the company and any further refinement to payments monthly would not be sufficiently advantageous to stockholders to justify the extra cost. If the amount of the dividend is small, it may be necessary to pay it semiannually.

A company which has preferred stock outstanding may wish to have those payments on the same dates as the common so that the directors can declare both at the same time. On the other hand, if they are staggered, they would provide a more even drain on cash.

Payments in fractional cents are no obstacle. For a company which pays $2.25 annually, the quarterly rate is 56 1/4¢. One way to handle the fraction is to pay the total amount due each stockholder on the basis of the next highest cent.

Need for Earned Surplus

If current earnings are not sufficient to cover dividend payments, then past accumulated earned surplus will have to be used. Seldom does the lack of earned surplus hinder a company's ability to pay dividends, unless a company has experienced serious difficulties and has had to use up earned surplus for large write-offs of assets. Usually the inability to pay dividends arises from lack of current earnings and the need to conserve cash.

There is no clear-cut answer to the amount of earned surplus that is needed to assure dividend payments. Earned surplus should be sufficient to take care of dividends when earnings are inadequate, as well as providing for special deductions for various corporate purposes. Earned surplus may be eroded as a result of write-off of worthless assets, or other accounting adjustments. When new shares are offered, the earned surplus per share will decrease in proportion to the new number of shares. Stock dividends require a transfer of earned surplus.

The amount of earned surplus may come to the fore when a company does some debt financing. Purchasers of the debt may require the company to freeze some of the earned surplus against use for dividend payments. The purpose of this restriction is to prevent a company from dissipating its cash through excessive dividend payments. The severity of the restriction will depend on the lenders' appraisal of the strength of the company's credit, and the extent of the danger that the company might be hurt by excessive payments. A typical type of freeze permits dividends to be paid only out of earnings accruing after the debt is issued, plus a certain amount of earned surplus previously accumulated. Generally, this restriction is not a serious matter, but a company should guard against being too limited. Actually, a lender would have no reason to restrict a company too severely unless the company was in poor financial condition. It is to the advantage of a lender to keep the common stock attractive so that the new common can be sold and thus add to the protection of the senior securities.

If a company has a large amount of preferred stock outstanding, there is more reason to watch earned surplus, because there is more need to continue preferred dividend payments even if not earned.

How large the earned surplus needs to be to take care of dividend payments will depend on the particular company, especially with regard to erosion through write-offs, expected common financing, stock dividends, debt restrictions, etc.

Can earned surplus be too large? Not from a financial point of view. A company may, however, prefer not to show a large earned surplus for some public relations reason. If so, it would be a simple matter to transfer some of it to capital surplus through one means or another.

In the electric utility field, where the prospect of erosion of surplus through write-offs does not seem to be a major problem, a rule of thumb is sometimes used as follows: earned surplus should be about three times dividend requirements. Earned surplus for the electric utility industry[2] is close to this figure; earned surplus is about four times preferred and common dividends.

Figures for industrial companies are not indicative of what they require, because undoubtedly most of them have far more than needed for dividend purposes. For example, for all manufacturing companies,[3] earned surplus is about 13 times the preferred and common dividend requirements.

The above comments refer to the matter of earned surplus from the point of view of

[2]"Privately Owned Electric Utilities," *Edison Electric Institute Statistical Yearbook,* 1973 Edition.

[3]*Quarterly Financial Report for Manufacturing Corporations*–4th Quarter, 1973. Federal Trade Commission, Securities and Exchange Commission. Included in the figures are all manufacturing corporations except newspapers.

dividend purposes alone. As previously emphasized, it would be expected that as earnings are retained, the earned surplus would build up to provide growth in the stockholders' investment.

Information About Dividend Policy

Dividends are dear to stockholders' hearts. They tend to be resentful when dividends are reduced, although the managements may have no alternative due to circumstances outside their control. The resentment may arise from the secrecy with which dividend policy is guarded. In some annual reports only a brief comment is made about dividends, and yet they are one of the first things stockholders look for.

Admittedly, there are limitations concerning what can be said about dividend payments. At least, there should be a clear statement in the annual report of what was paid each quarter and the total for the year, and also for the previous year. If there was a change in the quarterly rate, it calls for an explanation. At the time of the change, it is important that the press and financial services receive a complete story. If, in the previous year, there had been a change in the quarterly rate, a comment about it should be repeated in the annual report. Further, there seems to be room for a discussion of some of the factors which affected the decision regarding dividend payments and the relationship between the payments and earnings. A general statement about the company's policy in terms of percentage payout of average earnings would be well worthwhile.

Many companies include in their annual reports financial statistics for a period of ten years. This should show dividend payments by years with the percentage of payout and a footnote explaining the method of calculating the payout. A brief story regarding the changes in the past and the reasons would be of interest. If dividend payments are affected by restrictions imposed by regulatory authorities or senior securities, this should be carefully explained, particularly if it might have any immediate effect on payments.

The question of talking about future dividend payments is a debatable one. Most companies will shy away from such a policy, and certainly no one can criticize them for doing so. For a company with relatively stable earnings, something might be said in carefully guarded language. An example of a well-worded statement follows:

> Regular quarterly dividends of 50¢ per share were paid on the common stock aggregating $2 per share for the fiscal year, which represents a cash distribution of approximately 70% of earnings available for the common shares, thus continuing the policy of liberal distribution of dividends on the common stock.
>
> Subsequent to the close of the business last year, at a regular meeting of the board, the quarterly dividend was increased from 50¢ to 55¢ per share payable December 15. In the opinion of the management, past and prospective earnings justify this increase in dividend rate, and it is expected that such increase can be maintained with a fair margin on the increased number of shares to be outstanding following completion of the common stock financing this year.

Dividend Reinvestment

Some companies in recent years have offered their stockholders the right to reinvest their dividends in the company's common stock. The company, through a bank as its agent, buys the stock at the market price for those requesting dividend reinvestment. Because the bank buys the stock in volume for all participants, stockholders may save up to 50% in brokerage fees. There is also a small service charge of about 5% of the transaction with a maximum of $2.50 for the services of the bank. The stockholders do have to pay income taxes on the dividends reinvested as though it were part of regular income.

Dividend reinvestment apparently is for the little guy with 100 shares or less who wants to maximize his investment at minimum cost. Retired people living off income would not be interested nor would institutions which will wish to direct reinvestment of their funds themselves.

Dividend reinvestment results may give a clue as to the stockholders' interest in dividends or capital gains. If a large number of stockholders want dividend reinvestment, it may suggest that the company's cash payout is too high for the type of company. The record to date indicates that the amount of dividend reinvestment is small. In 1974, about 160 companies on the New York Stock Exchange had dividend reinvestment plans. How many stockholders participated varied from company to company, but apparently the number of stockholders participating is less than 10% and the amount of stock represented by these stockholders would be still smaller.

For a company which needs new common equity, it may be more advantageous for the company to have the right to issue new stock at the market price rather than buying it in the market in order to provide stock for the dividend reinvestment. However, this involves the problem of keeping a prospectus up to date. This is only worthwhile for a company which has such a large expansion program that it can use new common stock continuously. Some utilities have used this approach for dividend reinvestment. Since the company issues the stock directly, the issuing cost is very small and much less than the brokerage fee to buy stock in the market. Therefore, utilities issuing new stock do not charge a brokerage fee for dividend reinvestment, and may absorb the service charge because it would be less than the company would have to pay investment bankers to raise new capital. It is interesting that issuing new stock so that the brokerage fee is eliminated seems to double the interest of investors in dividend reinvestment. A few utilities have even given stockholders the right to purchase a small amount of stock in addition to the amount of dividend. This would permit a small investor to buy one share of the stock from a broker in order to become a stockholder, and then get the chance to buy additional stock without paying a brokerage fee.

American Telephone and Telegraph, which needs gigantic amounts of common, has such a plan. Without paying any brokerage fee, stockholders have the option of:

Reinvesting their dividends,
Continuing to receive their dividends and making a $3,000 investment in the stock each quarter, or
Reinvesting their dividends and up to $3,000 per quarter.

Stockholders representing 15% of the share owners, reinvested 12% of the dividends in 1974.

Some companies feel that it is unfair to their stockholders to absorb the cost of handling a dividend reinvestment program which only benefits a small number of stockholders. If a company issued new stock rather than bought it in the market, this objection is eliminated, because the company gets new capital at a lower cost than it could through a new offering and paying an underwriter's compensation.

A company should be careful not to permit stockholders to buy new stock directly from the company on a continuous basis to the extent that it would adversely affect the purchases of stock on the market and thus its quoted market price.

STOCK DIVIDENDS

Now we come to the subject of stock dividends, which are dividends paid in shares of stock.

To distinguish a stock dividend from a stock split, the New York Stock Exchange has an arbitrary rule that the issuance of 24% of stock or less is a stock dividend and 25% or more is a stock split.

You can skip this explanation of stock dividends completely if you will accept the fact that they are a waste of time. In fact, they might be said to be as useless as the way a little girl tried to get a longer blanket: she cut one end off and sewed it on the other end. However, there is some value in being well versed in the subject because you may have to answer questions on the subject at your stockholders' annual meeting, in letters from your stockholders, from a member of your board of directors who is not knowledgeable in finance, etc.

If you don't look stock dividends squarely in the eye, they may appear to have some real merit. We will use as simple an example as possible to show the effect of stock dividends on your company and stockholders.

Explanation of Stock Dividends

A company has 100 shares outstanding and declares a 10% stock dividend so that the shares outstanding are increased to 110. Each holder of ten shares receives one new share for nothing. A holder of less than ten shares will receive a fraction of a new share. The question of how to handle the fractional shares is a matter of mechanics. It must be done properly because it will affect your stockholder relations, but this is not a major problem to handle.

The total annual earnings, dividends and common book value do not change as shown below.

	Before	After 10% Stock Dividend
Total earnings	$ 100	$ 100
Total dividends	$ 50	$ 50
Total common book value	$1,000	$1,000

Since a stock dividend adds nothing of value to the company there should be no change in the price-earnings ratio:

	Before	After 10% Stock Dividend
Price-earnings ratio	10	10

The per share figures decrease in proportion to the increase in the number of shares:

	Before	After 10% Stock Dividend
Per share earnings	$ 1.00	$ 0.91
Per share dividends	$ 0.50	$ 0.45
Per share book value	$100.00	$90.91

Since the price-earnings ratio has not increased, the market price decreases in proportion to the increase in number of shares:

	Before	After 10% Stock Dividend
Per share market price	$10	$9.09

While the per share market price decreases, there is no change in the total market price:

	Before	After 10% Stock Dividend
Total market price	$1,000	$1,000

These figures are summarized in Exhibit 3-12.

The company's ability to provide a return to its stockholders in terms of cash dividends and market appreciation has not changed in any respect. The company received nothing for the new shares. Then what did happen? Merely the creation of more pieces of paper worth proportionately less per share with the total market price the same. Erroneous thinking regarding stock dividends arises from a failure to understand the "paper" nature of the transaction—more paper worth less per unit.

One thing that may cause misunderstanding regarding stock dividends is the fact that a company generally keeps the cash dividend rate the same when it declares a stock dividend. This changes the picture. With a 10% stock dividend and no proportionate decrease in the cash dividend rate per share, the

Exhibit 3-12

EFFECT OF STOCK DIVIDEND SHOWING WHAT CHANGES AND WHAT DOESN'T CHANGE

	Before	After 10% Stock Dividend
Change		
Total shares	100	110
No change		
Total earnings	$ 100	$ 100
Total dividends	$ 50	$ 50
Total book value	$1,000	$1,000
Price-earnings ratio	10	10
Change		
Per share earnings	$ 1.00	$ 0.91
Per share dividends	$ 0.50	$ 0.45
Per share book value	$100.00	$ 90.91
Per share market price	$ 10	$ 9.09
No change		
Total market price	$1,000	$1,000

amount of cash the company pays out in dividends increases. The stockholders who hold their stock dividend get 10% more cash. The stockholders who sell their stock dividend get the same total cash dividends on their remaining stock. To apply this to our example, the figures would be as follows:

	Before	After 10% Stock Dividend
Per share dividends	$ 0.50	$ 0.50
Total dividends	$50.00	$55.00

The amount of cash paid out in dividends increased from $50 to $55. If the dividend rate per share is kept the same after the stock dividend and the stock is the type that sells on a yield basis, it is possible that the market price would not decline in proportion to the stock dividend. This may be interpreted as being due to the stock dividend. It is, in fact, due to the increase in the total cash dividends paid.

The company could have accomplished the same thing without using a stock dividend by increasing the cash dividend per share 10% from 50¢ to 55¢. This would result in the following:

	Before	After 10% Cash Dividend Increase if No Stock Dividend Paid
Per share dividends	$ 0.50	$ 0.55
Total dividends	$50.00	$55.00

The total effect on the market price would be the same and the stockholders would be just as well off.

In other words, if the cash dividend rate is kept the same, a stock dividend does cause a change—the company pays out more cash and the stockholders receive more. This, however, is not the result of the stock dividend itself but a decision on the part of the company to change its cash payment; the company could just as well have increased the cash rate on existing shares.

Stripped of any auxiliary effect, a stock dividend is still strictly a paper transaction.

Calculation of Yield for Stock Dividends

Before we proceed, we should explain how to figure yield when a stock dividend is declared. The yield for a stock is the relationship of the price per share to the annual cash dividend per share. If a stock pays 50¢ in dividends per share in a year and the price of the stock is $10 per share, the yield is 5%.

Some confusion may occur when a company pays a stock dividend. We will use two companies—S and A—which have the same dividend and yield at the start.

$$\text{Yield—Company S} = \frac{\text{Dividends per Share—\$0.50}}{\text{Market Price per Share—\$10}} = 5\%$$

$$\text{Yield—Company A} = \frac{\text{Dividends per Share—\$0.50}}{\text{Market Price per Share—\$10}} = 5\%$$

At the end of the first year, after all cash dividends have been paid, Company S announces that its cash dividend will be kept at 50¢ per share but that a 10% stock dividend will be paid.

Company A announces that its cash dividend will be increased 10% to 55¢ per share.

What is the prospective yield for each company?

$$\text{Prospective Yield—Company S} = \frac{\text{\$0.50 plus \$0.05}}{\text{Market Price per Share \$10}} = 5.5\%$$

The $0.05 is the cash dividend that will be received next year on the 1/10 of a share of stock dividend which is still attached to the share of stock of Company S before it goes ex-stock dividend.

$$\text{Prospective Yield—Company A} = \frac{\text{\$0.55}}{\text{Market Price per Share \$10}} = 5.5\%$$

Just after Company S goes ex-stock dividend, here is the picture for each company if the market price of Company S does not decline after the stock dividend and Company A's price increases 10% because of the increase in cash dividend.

$$\text{Prospective Yield for Company S on Original Share of Stock} = \frac{\text{\$0.50}}{\text{Market Price per Share Ex-Stock Dividend \$10}} = 5\%$$

$$\text{On 1/10 of New Share Received as Stock Dividend} = \frac{\text{\$0.05}}{\text{Market Price per 1/10 New Share \$1}} = 5\%$$

$$\text{Prospective Yield for Company A} = \frac{\text{\$0.55}}{\text{Market Price per Share \$11}} = 5\%$$

Why all these figures to explain a simple subject like yield? We haven't yet pointed out the confusion that may arise with a stock dividend. It is sometimes erroneously contended that the yield for Company S with the stock dividend should be figured not by including the cash dividend which will be received on the stock dividend, but by including the market value of the stock dividend itself. This, of course, is fallacious reasoning, as the above figures for Companies S and A show. The market value of the stock dividend is part of the stockholder capital. If he sells it, he is selling some of his capital on which he would pay capital gains. Yield must be based on cash dividends alone. If a company pays no cash dividend and only pays a stock dividend, there will be no yield.

Disadvantages of Stock Dividends

Some of the disadvantages of stock dividends may be summarized as follows:

1) An expense is incurred in issuing stock dividends, because of the paper work involved. This expense is not deductible for tax purposes. For a small company the expense may be negligible, but for a company with a large stockholder list, the expense is significant and may amount to about 1¢ per share of the stock outstanding. For a company with 5 million shares outstanding the non-tax deductible expense for a 10% stock dividend might be $50,000.
2) It messes up a company's financial record. A company should wish to report a sustained increase in dividends and earnings per share. Stock dividends dull the increases. Adjustments can be made for prior years to give effect to the stock dividend, but the picture is neater if such adjustments don't have to be made.
3) They are an annoyance to many investors. Institutional investors may see nothing to be gained from the added paper handling. An institution which supervises the investments of a large number of individuals will not only have a lot of paper work to do, but also may have to communicate with the individual holders in order to inform them of the stock dividend. It may even have to request approval for the action to be taken.

   Stock dividends cannot be treated as cash income in certain trust accounts, because they have been ruled by some state courts to be a part of capital. Therefore, a trustee would not be interested in buying a stock paying stock dividends if income were desired.

Why Are Some Managements Captivated by Stock Dividends?

If stock dividends accomplish nothing, why then do some people think that they have a purpose? Let's look at the various reasons advanced in their favor.

1) They give stockholders a choice: those who don't need cash can hang on to it; those who need cash can sell it—all things to all people. Until you analyze it, this argument sounds very enticing.

   What do the stockholders who hang on to their stock dividend gain? Precisely, nothing! They have no more after than before. And yet the company incurs an expense which is not tax deductible. For those stockholders, the expense is wasted.

   For the stockholders who sell their stock dividends, it is claimed there is a tax advantage over a cash dividend, because a stock dividend is taxable on a capital gains basis. The size of the stockholder's income will determine the savings in taxes from capital gains vs. regular income. Generally, it is the small stockholders with low income who are the ones with a need to supplement their cash income by selling stock dividends. They would be the least benefited by the capital gains advantage. Furthermore, if a stockholder wishes to supplement his cash income by sale of some of his principal, he can do so without the stock dividend, merely by the sale of some of his original holdings.

   Perhaps the small stockholders cannot divide up their holdings easily in order to sell off part. A stock dividend provides a convenient mechanical means for a stockholder to sell a small portion of his principal. It would appear that if this argument is to hold, a majority of the stockholders should desire a stock dividend for this purpose. Otherwise, the company would be incurring the expense to satisfy a few stockholders. For this reason, it is important to know how much of the stock dividend is sold by a company's stockholders. One company that adopted a stock dividend found that stockholders owning only a small percentage of its stock sold the stock dividend. Could it possibly justify the expense of such a policy for holders of a small amount of stock?

When a stock dividend is sold by a stockholder, the stockholder has to pay the brokerage fee. For example, a holder of 40 shares who received a stock dividend of 5% would receive two shares. If the stock sold for $25 he would receive $50. If the stock were listed on the New York Stock Exchange, he might have to pay a brokerage commission of approximately $6, or 12%, in addition to other miscellaneous charges.

These costs to the stockholders who sell may be reduced by some effort and expense on the part of the company. A company can work out a means to handle the sale for stockholders wishing to sell. One company devised the idea of sending out a return post card with the stock dividend notice so that a stockholder could indicate whether he wanted to receive the stock dividend, round out his fractional shares or have the company sell it. The company then pooled all the stockholders' requests and sold the shares in one transaction through an underwriting house. The cash was remitted to the individual stockholders. The pooled stock involves the expense of registration with the Securities and Exchange Commission. To the extent that the expenses of sale of stock dividends are charged directly to those who sell, it should not be considered as any disadvantage to the other stockholders. However, when the company handles the sale, it is a company expense and all stockholders bear the expense indirectly. This is unfair because it is a charge to many who get no benefit.

It should not be overlooked that if a large number of stockholders sell their stock dividend, it may cause a depressing effect on the market price of the stock. Therefore, it is incorrect to reason that a stock dividend benefits both groups of stockholders. The expense incurred is only for the benefit of those who sell. If the number of stockholders who sell their stock dividend are large, showing that many stockholders want cash, then the company should review its cash dividend policy and perhaps consider increasing it.

2) Stock dividends can be used as a substitute for cash dividends and thus the company can conserve cash and avoid the high cost of equity financing.

A major company with large demands for funds for construction purposes was paying a quarterly dividend of 40¢ per share. In order to conserve cash, it decided to pay one quarterly cash dividend of 40¢ and substitute three stock dividends for the other three quarters, which would each have a market price of 40¢. In order to make it easy for those stockholders who desired cash, the company would sell the stock dividends and remit the cash at no cost to the stockholders. It sounded like a great idea, but it didn't turn out that way; all hell broke loose when the company announced the plan. The stock immediately took a sharp drop, and many institutional and individual investors contacted the company to vent their displeasure. As a consequence, the company had to abandon the idea. Other companies have had similar reactions when they tried to replace a cash dividend with a stock dividend.

It is not just a question of whether the company gets the advantage of retained earnings rather than the expense of selling new common stock. The question is what cash dividend is best to help maintain the best market price of the stock so that when the company finances it will get the best price?

3) Some stockholders like them. A sophisticated financial executive of a large company got talked into a 2% stock dividend. He felt that the stockholders liked them and that stock dividends permitted the conservation of cash. One of the statements he made to a critic of his action was:

> "You just don't understand. I have received a number of letters from stockholders saying how they liked the stock dividend. In fact, a lady

> wrote to say that she couldn't have paid for her appendix operation unless she had had the stock dividends."

It was rather sad to hear an otherwise logical, intelligent executive use such foolish reasoning to justify his actions. If he wanted to level with the lady, he might have written back:

> Dear Ms:
>
> I am glad you were able to pay for your operation with the stock dividends. However, we feel badly that your investment in your company has decreased as a result of the sale of your stock dividends.

Some companies have relied on surveys of stockholders to justify the use of stock dividends. A survey of small stockholders who purchased stocks which paid stock dividends is a biased one. Perhaps, they liked stock dividends in the first place or they would not have been attracted to these stocks. What about stockholders who bought stocks of companies that didn't pay stock dividends?

In the survey, it would be important to frame certain preliminary questions in order to determine whether the stockholder surveyed understood the import of a stock dividend. There is a vast difference between the reply of a stockholder who understands and one who does not. Obviously, there are a large number of stockholders in the latter category. A company executive who says it makes no difference whether stockholders understand the significance of a stock dividend, as long as they like it, would seem to be basing his decision on superficial reasoning. How many other actions could be justified on the same grounds?

In such a survey, the alternative to paying a stock dividend should be presented. Why wouldn't stockholders tend to seize upon a stock dividend as being "better than nothing," although we have no proof that it is better than nothing. If a company planned to pay a regular stock dividend with a fixed cash rate, then the alternative without a stock dividend would be a gradual increase in the cash dividend. A questionnaire should be so worded as to provide for the latter alternative and not merely a fixed cash rate, which would obviously be misleading.

The final decision must be based on the percentage of stock represented by holders who like stock dividends, because control of the company is on that basis, as it should be. For this reason, large institutional holdings are important.

In weighing the so-called psychological value of stock dividends, it should also be remembered that stockholders like to see growth in their stock. Continuous payment of stock dividends will correspondingly restrict growth in earnings per share. If stockholders fail to take this into account in their comparison of such a stock with one which has not paid a stock dividend, there may be a psychological disadvantage.

What seems most important is that a company should not rely upon a show of stockholder preference by itself as a crutch for adopting such a policy. It costs a company money to issue stock dividends. Therefore, a company should have concrete reasons for their use which will actually benefit the holders of a majority of the stock in a tangible manner.

4) They increase the market price. You will run into a few managements who actually believe this to be true in spite of the fact that you can't create value out of thin air or rather more paper. They will try to tell you a convincing story about how the market price of their stock benefited from the payment of stock dividends. They are so intrigued with their stock dividend, that they fail to appreciate that their stock might have gone up anyway for various other reasons:

    Investors believed the company's earnings will increase.

Enthusiasm developed for the company's stock so that the demand for the stock increased.

The company kept the cash dividend rate the same so that cash payout increased when a stock dividend was paid.

The whole market improved and the company's stock with it.

Only if all of these other reasons which might have affected the market price are eliminated can it be concluded that the stock dividend caused the market price of the stock to increase.

Stock dividends make their appearance with advancing earnings and during a bull market; it is not surprising to find some people automatically associating stock dividends with an increase in the price of their stock.

Numerous studies[4] have been made regarding the effect of stock dividends on market price, and they have concluded that there is no permanent effect.

You cannot pick yourself up by your boot straps. The most that occurs is a slight market flurry around the time of the payment which is caused by brokers stimulating customer action in order to generate brokerage commissions.

If stock dividends do permanently increase the market price of a company's stock to such an extent as to offset the expenses involved and annoyance to some stockholders, how many companies should declare a stock dividend? Every single company!

5) Increases the number of shares. Is increasing the number of shares any reason for a company to declare a stock dividend? Possibly in a few isolated situations. If a company wants to list on an exchange and does not have enough shares outstanding, and also the market price of the stock is too low to declare a stock split, it may have to declare a stock dividend. However, it probably should think twice before it rushed to list if it was that small.

6) Hides a cash dividend increase. If a company does not wish to increase the cash dividend rate per share for some public relations reason, it may use a stock dividend as a device to increase the cash paid out and keep the rate the same.

7) A way to capitalize earned surplus. If a company has a large earned surplus, it may wish to change some of it to capital surplus or stated value of common for public relations reasons. Many banks are limited to the amount they can lend to one borrower to a percentage of the bank's capital stock and capital surplus. Therefore, in order to increase their lending limit, they will wish to make transfers from their undivided profit accounts. In order to accomplish this they may use a stock dividend.

No uniform method has been established for the accounting treatment of a stock dividend, but the New York Stock Exchange requires listed companies to have "transferred from earned surplus to the permanent capitalization of the company (represented by the capital stock and capital surplus accounts) an amount equal to the fair value of such shares. While it is impractical to define 'fair value' exactly, it should closely approximate the current share market price adjusted to reflect issuance of the additional shares."[5]

It may be unnecessary for a company to use a stock dividend in order to transfer earned surplus to capital surplus or stated value of common. It may be possible to make the transfer by an action of the board of directors or by some other corporate action. The company should investigate the feasibility of more readily handling this matter.

If a company does contemplate declaring a stock dividend, it should

---

[4] "Evaluation of a Stock Dividend," by C. Austin Barker, *Harvard Business Review,* July-August 1958.

[5] New York Stock Exchange Company Manual A1235, July 21, 1935.

examine the effect it may have on earned surplus. There should be enough earned surplus to make possible the transfer accompanying the stock dividend, and there also should be enough remaining so that the cash dividend policy will not be impaired.

8) May be the only type of dividends possible—a way out for directors and management.

If a company has senior obligations outstanding, their terms may limit the earned surplus available for payment of cash dividends on the common stock. Stock dividends generally are excepted from such restrictions, for the obvious reason that they do not in themselves deplete a company's assets. Therefore, if a company runs into a period of bad earnings and does not have adequate free earned surplus, stock dividends may be the only type that a company can issue.

In other words they are better than nothing. If you can't pay a cash dividend, throw the stockholders a fish in the form of a stock dividend. Nonsense, they cost money and mess up the earnings record.

Companies Using Stock Dividends

The percent of companies listed on the New York Exchange that declared stock dividends over a ten-year period is shown in Exhibit 3-13.

Conclusion on Stock Dividends

In concluding this section on stock dividends, we must return to the problem of the cash dividend. A company has to face the question of whether it would be better off if its stockholders received a different cash dividend. Remember, a company has to decide on a dividend policy which will produce the best market price over the long run. A company should not proceed to stock dividends as an excuse for avoiding an appropriate cash dividend. If stock dividends are considered, the decision should be based on a thorough evaluation of each of the points discussed above.

Exhibit 3-13

COMPANIES LISTED ON THE NEW YORK STOCK EXCHANGE WHICH PAID A STOCK DIVIDEND. INCREASE IN NUMBER OF SHARES OF LESS THAN 25%

	Percent of Total Number of Listed Companies
1973	7%
1972	8
1971	6
1970	8
1969	9
1968	9
1967	11
1966	12
1965	12
1964	12

In making your analysis, it might be well to study what happens when companies eliminate a stock dividend, and their reasons. If stock dividends are so beneficial, it would appear that eliminating them would produce adverse results. Mere opinions by managements either favoring or against stock dividends should not be used as a basis for making a decision. However, the following brief summary of the comments made by the officer of a company which eliminated them is of interest because of the reasons for the decision:

To halt constant dilution which was taking place. The regular small stock dividend was not being recognized in the price of the stock by the investors as being worth any more than a corresponding percentage increase in the cash dividends.

The payment of the stock dividend was of itself rather expensive, and because fractional shares were paid in cash, it did not save as much money as it appeared to save. The point was finally reached where additional equity was required because of the magnitude of the expansion program, and it was decided to issue Convertible Preferred. Continuance of stock dividends would dilute this conversion price on a

> Convertible Preferred thereby increasing dilution. The conversion price of a convertible is generally protected against dilution from stock splits and stock dividends.
>
> Many complaints were received from trusts and investment funds of the headaches caused by small common stock dividends. They did not like the bookkeeping or the necessity of selling small blocks of stock to maintain income. Many people felt that the cash dividend should be increased.
>
> Since discontinuing the stock dividend, practically no complaints were received from existing stockholders.

If you do decide to use stock dividends and believe in the principle of keeping your stockholders fully informed about subjects close to their hearts, you might wish to include an explanation in your annual report. Give the reasons for such action, the alternative if you had not taken such a step and the results as to the number of shares represented by stockholders who sold or retained the stock dividend. Stockholders would need that information if they were to communicate with you on the subject.

Our final conclusion on stock dividends requires us to recall the story we told at the beginning of this subject about the little girl who wanted a longer blanket, so she cut one end off and sewed it on the other end.

STOCK SPLITS

A stock split is not a dividend and therefore does not belong in this chapter, but it is so much like a stock dividend that it can logically follow that discussion. As we have said, the New York Stock Exchange has an arbitrary rule that generally the issuance of 24% stock or less is a stock dividend and 25% or more is a stock split. This indicates the close association between the two. A stock split in itself, like a stock dividend, is a pure paper transaction, and practically all of the discussion on stock dividends applies to stock splits. In order to avoid repetition, our discussion of stock splits presupposes that you have read the previous section on stock dividends.

Accounting Treatment

Besides size, the principal difference between a stock split and a stock dividend is the accounting treatment. When there is a stock split, earned surplus is unaffected. The only change on the balance sheet is the par or stated value of the stock, which remains the same in total but is reduced per unit according to the number of shares increased.

Example

As an example, we can use a 2-for-1 stock split for a company which has 100 shares outstanding, earns $4 per share, pays $2 per share in cash dividends and has a market price of $60. The figures are summarized in Exhibit 3-14.

If the cash dividend rate is reduced to correspond with the increase in number of shares, as in the exhibit, then the total cash income to stockholders will be the same. Each stockholder will have twice as many shares, with each share worth one-half as much, but in total the same.

Only if the cash dividend rate is kept at the same rate on the new shares as the old, or is not decreased proportionately to the stock split, will the stockholders receive more dividend income. Under these circumstances there might be a permanent increase in the market price of the stock, but this would be due to the dividend increase and not the stock split itself.

Why a Stock Split?

If stock dividends are generally worse than nothing, why should a company split its stock? When a company splits its stock there is a tendency for the number of stockholders to increase.[6] The broadened ownership may make for a better market and facilitate sale of new common stock when needed.

---

[6]"Stock Splits in a Bull Market," by C. Austin Barker, *Harvard Business Review,* May-June 1957.

Exhibit 3-14

EFFECT OF STOCK SPLIT

	Before	After 2-for-1 Split
Earnings Available for Common	$400	$400
Shares Outstanding	100	200
Earnings per Share	$4.00	$2.00
Dividends per Share (Assuming a Reduction to Correspond to the Stock Split)	$2.00	$1.00
Payout Ratio	50%	50%
Total Dividends Paid	$200	$200
Market Price of Stock	$ 60	$ 30
Price-Earnings Ratio	15 times	15 times
Dividend Yield	3.3%	3.3%

Popular Price Range

There exists what is known as a popular price range for common stocks, somewhere between $20 and $50 per share. People seem to like to buy stocks in 100-share lots. Shares traded on the New York Stock Exchange in 100-share units or multiples thereof are generally known as round lots; less than 100 shares is an odd lot.[7] If the price per share is too high, the purchase of 100 shares or a multiple thereof would require a large amount of capital.

Exhibit 3-15 gives the New York Stock Exchange round-lot share volume by price groups. The greatest volume is in the $20 to $29 7/8 price group. This does not necessarily indicate the most popular price range, because the number of outstanding shares are not equal in each group.

It is unwise to split a stock so that its price is too low. A stock which gets below $10 per share may be considered by some investors as belonging in the "cat and dog" class. This is primarily a matter of psychology, but nevertheless it is unwise to over-split so that the market price of the stock may fall into that class. If the price of a stock gets too low, it may make new common financing more costly. The underwriters' compensation includes an allowance for a selling concession which is higher for a low-priced stock. And with a rights offering, a low-priced stock would result in a low rights value.

Factors to consider when making a split in order not to over-split are:

1. The level of the whole stock market.
2. The demand for stocks for your type of company.
3. The earnings level of your company.
4. The price-earnings ratio of your stock.

You have to weigh the effect that a decrease in these factors would have on the price of your stock after the split and the possibility of their occurring.

May Not Always Increase Number of Stockholders

We should note that you can't always count on a stock split increasing the number of stockholders. If institutional buyers are hungry for a stock, there may be a decrease in holders as some little holders sell some of

[7] Some shares are traded in ten-share units which is then the measure for a round lot.

their shares after a split and the large holders buy. This might occur particularly for a small company when certain large holders are anxious to gain control. A split would not loosen up stock in the hands of the large holders, and if it loosened up stock in the hands of the small holders, their stock would be grabbed up by those seeking control.

Exhibit 3-15

NEW YORK STOCK EXCHANGE
ROUND-LOT SHARE VOLUME BY PRICE GROUPS
Three-Year Average 1970-1972

Price Group	Round-Lot Share Volume Traded
Under $10	7%
$ 10-19 7/8	22
20-29 7/8	25
30-39 7/8	17
40-49 7/8	12
50-59 7/8	6
60-99 7/8	8
100 & over	3
TOTAL	100%

Volume of Stock Splits

Stock splits tend to increase during a bull market because more stocks are in a price range which make splits possible. The percent of companies listed on the New York Stock Exchange that split in the last ten years is shown in Exhibit 3-16.

Size of Stock Splits

If you intend to split, you should make it as simple as possible so your stockholders can immediately calculate the effect on earnings and dividends per share. For this reason, a 2 for 1 is much to be desired. There seems to be little reason for a 3 for 2 or 4 for 3, etc. Such odd splits may be done by managements who get itchy to show some action for their stockholders. It is preferable to let your stock go to a higher price before splitting so you can use a 2 for 1. A breakdown by size of splits in the last ten years by companies listed on the New York Stock Exchange is shown in Exhibit 3-17.

How often you can split will depend on the growth rate of your earnings per share and market appreciation of your stock. For example, if your earnings grow at a 6% rate and the market price of your stock appreciates accordingly, it would double in 12 years, so you might have a 2-for-1 split every 12 years.

Exhibit 3-16

COMPANIES LISTED ON THE NEW YORK STOCK EXCHANGE WHICH SPLIT THEIR STOCK

	% of Number of Companies
1973	5%
1972	8
1971	5
1970	3
1969	11
1968	12
1967	7
1966	11
1965	9
1964	8

Exhibit 3-17

SIZE OF SPLITS BY COMPANIES LISTED IN THE NEW YORK STOCK EXCHANGE AVERAGE FOR 1964-1973

Size of Split	Number of Splits per Year
25% to 49%	6
50% to 99%	20
2 for 1 to 2 1/2 for 1	71
3 for 1 to 3 1/2 for 1	7
4 for 1	.4
Over 4 for 1	.6
	105

Coordinate with Dividend Increase

When you split, you might coordinate it with the time you will increase the cash dividend per share. This will give a good market flavor at the time of the split and attract added interest.

Effect on Brokerage Commissions

You should not overlook the effect of a stock split on broker commissions that your stockholders will have to pay when they buy and sell. An example of the effect of a split on commissions for stócks listed on the New York Stock Exchange is shown in Exhibit 3-18. When an odd lot investor becomes a round lot investor as the result of a split, there is some decrease in commission. If an investor continues in the odd lot class after the split, his commission will increase somewhat. An investor who was in the round lot class before the split will pay higher brokerage commissions after. Therefore, splitting a stock may increase brokerage commissions; brokers naturally favor splits.

Stock Splits Not a Big Issue

There is no need to go overboard on the matter of stock splits and the popular price range. Many companies with stocks which have sold above that range for many years have been popular with investors. The price ranges in the first half of 1974 for the ten companies listed on the New York Exchange with the largest number of stockholders are shown in Exhibit 3-19.

As a matter of fact, it may be suggested that a lot more fuss and feathers is made over stock splits than is justified. However, if your stock does sell at a relatively high price, you may wish to consider a split.

Reverse Splits

If your stock is selling in the very low price range of a few dollars a share, you may wish to reverse split. The low price would make it difficult to offer new stock.

Management and stockholders may consider a reverse split an unpopular action because it indicates past failure. Theoretically,

Exhibit 3-18

EFFECT OF 2-FOR-1 STOCK SPLIT ON NEW YORK STOCK EXCHANGE
MINIMUM COMMISSIONS TO BUY AND SELL (EFFECTIVE SEPT. 25, 1973)

Column	I Odd Lot Before Split	II Round Lot After Split	III Odd Lot Before Split	IV Odd Lot After Split	V Round Lot Before Split	VI Round Lot After Split
Total Market Value	$3,000	$3,000	$3,000	$3,000	$3,000	$3,000
Market Price	$ 60	$ 30	$ 100	$ 50	$ 30	$ 15
Number of Shares	50	100	30	60	100	200
Total Brokerage Commission	$51.70	$53.90	$51.70	$51.70	$53.90	$67.10
Extra Cost for Odd Lot*	6.25	--	3.75	7.50	--	--
Total Charge	$57.95	$53.90	$55.45	$59.20	$53.90	$67.10
Total Charge as % of Total Value	1.93%	1.80%	1.85%	1.97%	1.80%	2.24%

*In figuring total charge to buy an odd lot, $1/8 per share is added on to the price.

Exhibit 3-19

PRICE RANGE OF TEN COMPANIES ON THE NEW YORK STOCK EXCHANGE WITH THE LARGEST NUMBER OF STOCKHOLDERS*

Company	Common Stockholders*	Average of Price Range 1974 First Six Months
American Tel. & Tel.	2,934,000	53 – 41 3/4
General Motors	1,283,000	55 1/2– 40 1/2
Exxon Corp.	725,000	99 3/4– 67 3/4
International Business Machine	557,000	254 –196 1/4
General Electric	537,000	65 – 42 1/2
General Telephone & Electronics	430,000	26 5/8– 19
Ford Motor	341,000	54 3/8– 39 3/8
Gulf Oil	333,000	25 1/4– 18 5/8
Texaco, Inc.	310,000	32 7/8– 23 1/2
Consolidated Edison	308,000	21 1/2– 6

**New York Stock Exchange Fact Book, 1974.*

the effect on the market price from the reverse split itself should only be temporary.

If your stock gets so low that it sells for $1 or $2, a reverse split may present a problem. In such a situation, earnings per share may be only nominal and the market price may not bear any reasonable relationship to earnings per share. A sizeable reverse split would be called for, but after the split the stock might sell at a more realistic price-earnings ratio and not increase in market price per share in proportion to the split. For example, if a company earned 5¢ per share and had a market price of $1, the price-earnings ratio would be 20 times. This might be an unreasonably high price-earnings ratio in view of the type of stock. A 1-for-20 reverse split would increase the earnings per share to $1. The stock then might sell at a price-earnings ratio of ten times, which would mean a market price of $10. If a stockholder had 200 shares before the reverse split, the total market value would be $200. After the 1-for-20 reverse split, the stockholder would have ten shares worth $100. This would make stockholders unhappy. This is due to the fact that the market quote of $1 before the split was in effect nominal and not too significant. Stockholders would not necessarily understand this. However, a reverse split in such a situation is necessary in order for the company to get its feet on the ground with a meaningful common stock price. Thus, the company may have to swallow a bitter pill.

REPURCHASE OF COMMON STOCK

Since repurchase of stock may be an alternative to paying cash dividends, we will cover this as the last subject on dividend policy. When the stock market takes a dive and managements see their stocks selling at what they believe are bargain prices, they may get the urge to repurchase stock. Some managements become almost desperate to get their stock prices up by providing a demand for their stock in the market and increasing earnings per share by reducing the number of shares outstanding.

A company may obtain funds for this purpose from various sources:

1. Cash.
2. Short term borrowings.
3. Long term borrowings.
4. Exchange for other securities.
5. Sale of part of business.

On the surface, stock repurchase may seem like a logical thing to do. But, whether such a policy makes sense depends on many factors. In the first place, while it may appear to have a beneficial effect on the market price of a stock, it is really like trying to pick yourself up by the boot straps. And it may even have a negative connotation. The way a company gets a good price-earnings ratio is by putting capital to work to expand the company and earn a high return on the capital. Stock repurchase actually shrinks the company and is an admission that the company can't find attractive capital investments.

Repurchase of stock should not be looked at as an isolated decision. It affects the leverage of the company if there are senior securities outstanding. It should be considered in relation to the effect on the company's financial goals and five-year financial plan. It is self-defeating if a company with too high a debt ratio repurchases its stock because common equity is reduced by the total market price of the stock acquired. It should, under those circumstances, decrease the debt instead of the common. And to issue more debt to raise money to repurchase common is even more ridiculous. If a company has a small floating supply of stock, repurchase of stock will aggravate the situation.

The reasons why a company may wish to repurchase its stock are as follows:

1. For stock options, stock bonus plans or employee stock purchase plans.
2. To meet conversion of convertibles, or exercise of warrants or for stock dividends.
3. For acquisitions—resulting in cash acquisitions.
4. To shrink the business after sale of property.
5. To eliminate small stockholders who only have a few shares and are costly to service.
6. To increase earnings per share.
7. To save cash dividend payments.
8. To provide a demand for the stock in the market.
9. As a good investment, it is cheap.
10. To prevent a raid.
11. To increase control in hands of insiders.

Sometimes companies do not like to reveal the true reason why they repurchased their stock, so they use a catch-all statement: for general corporate purposes.

If the market price of a company's stock is depressed and if the company has need for shares for such purposes as stock options, to meet conversion of convertibles, or for acquisition purposes, then, providing the company's debt ratio is satisfactory, it may be appropriate for a company to repurchase its stock. If a company has a low debt ratio and it needs stock for acquisition purposes, it even may be appropriate for a company to borrow money so that it can repurchase its stock.

However, such legitimate reasons are a far cry from repurchase for such reasons as pushing up the price of the stock, because management thinks the stock is cheap, or to save cash dividends, etc.

Three examples of the different circumstances under which stock purchase was considered may help to make the discussion more concrete:

> *Company A,* very large and with strong financial position with bonds rated AA, had some extra cash which it would not need for three years. It already had all the shares it needed for stock options, etc. Its stock was only moderately depressed. In three years it expected to need large sums for expansion. This company correctly decided to keep the cash in temporary investment. In view of the large expansion plans in the future, investors should consider this excess cash as a source of strength.

Company B had a low debt ratio and no foreseeable large capital expenditures. It had excess cash and its five-year plan showed strong cash generation. Its stock was quite depressed and it needed stock for stock options. Clearly, this company should repurchase stock for its stock options.

Company C was weak financially with too high a debt ratio. Its stock was depressed and the president wanted to borrow money to repurchase its stock in order to improve its market price. This is an obvious case of a boot-strap operation which would be self defeating.

If a management is manipulative minded, they will be attracted to such an idea as stock repurchase and they will not listen to reason. For more mature managements, stock repurchase is not something that should be entered into lightly. It should only be done if sound reasons can be advanced. A company should consider other uses for excess cash:

1. Reduce senior securities.
2. Extra dividend, or if a continuous flow of extra cash appears likely, increase the regular dividend.

Management should decide which will benefit stockholders most in the long run. If a company does decide to launch a program of stock repurchase, it will have four ways it might be accomplished:

1. Open market through broker or brokers. It is preferable to work with one broker in order to avoid pushing up the market.
2. Block trades. This may be done by letting the principal block trading firms know that you are interested in hearing about large blocks.
3. Private transaction from some large stockholders.
4. Tender offer, used primarily when a large amount of stock will be repurchased.

Which method a company chooses will depend on the size of the repurchase, the nature of the market for the stock and what method will be most fair to all your stockholders.

A company is in a delicate position when it repurchases its own stock. If the market price of the stock subsequently goes up, those investors who sold their stock may feel that they were "horn swaggled." Or if stock is repurchased in a private transaction from a few large stockholders, the remaining stockholders might be more than unhappy if the stock subsequently "fell out of bed."

In order to protect stockholders, there are definite procedures that must be complied with, and a company should be guided by a lawyer who is thoroughly familiar with the securities laws. Some of the considerations which may come into play, depending on the nature of the company, the size of the transaction and how it is handled, are:

1. Making known the company's intention to acquire stock.
2. Insider information which should be revealed prior to and during the repurchase.
3. Regulations on each transaction such as size.
4. The price that may be paid in the market in relation to the last quotation.
5. Reporting to the Exchanges and Securities and Exchange Commission.
6. The need to register the transaction if it involves new securities.
7. State laws that may come into play.
8. Limitations in any loan agreement or bond indenture.
9. The accounting treatment, depending on whether the stock is kept alive in the treasury or is cancelled.
10. Purchase or sale by a director or officer during repurchase.
11. Reissuance of treasury stock, which is treated like brand new stock and requires registration.
12. The limitations on the use of repurchased stock for acquisitions as it affects pooling of interests. Very broadly, for pooling, the stock must be held in the treasury for at least two years.

If a company does consider stock repurchase, one of the vital questions is whether it is cheap or a good buy. Many companies have repurchased stock at prices which the managements considered rock bottom, only to watch the stock subsequently plummet. This is embarrassing to say the least and very hard to explain to remaining stockholders. This possibility cannot be avoided but a company should take a long, hard look at the price.

Merely the fact that earnings per share will be increased is no basis for saying that repurchase is a good investment. Whether current earnings per share will be increased will depend on the earnings-price ratio of the stock repurchased and the source of the funds used to repurchase the stock. If cash is used, earnings per share will increase regardless of the earnings-price ratio, if the company is earning anything. If short-term liquid assets are sold, whether earnings per share will be increased will depend on the earnings on the short term investment compared with the earnings-price ratio of the stock.

Of course, the effect on earnings per share should be considered, but in making a decision as to whether a stock is a good investment, the stock should be looked at totally separate from the source of funds which is used to make the repurchase.

One way to look at the price is as though the company were an investor. The company makes a forecast of future earnings. How does the price look in relation to those future earnings in terms of return on investment? Will it represent good investment which will produce a high return to an investor from dividends and market appreciation? Since managements' forecasts are so unreliable, it must be appreciated that this approach is fraught with danger. The company should also look at certain fundamentals such as the relationship of the market price to book value per share, the present return on book value in relation to the long range return and the prospects for a higher return in the future.

Another way to look at it is on the basis of the principles of cost-of-capital. This requires an appraisal by management of the relationship of the market price to the company's estimate of future earning power. If such a relationship provides a return greater than would be required by investors, the stock is underpriced. In other words, the stock is underpriced if investors' expectations of future earnings power are less than the company's estimate.

We can summarize our thoughts on stock repurchase as follows:

1. It is perfectly sound when used for a specific purpose as in the first three reasons given above for stock repurchase, providing it fits in with a company's financial goals and the stock is a "good investment."
2. It is perfectly sound when used for the fourth reason given above when a company has an excessive amount of cash, providing it already has gotten its debt ratio in line, it sees no use for the cash and the stock price represents a good investment. This is a corporate liquidating situation. In such a situation, a company should consider whether dividend payments would be more beneficial to stockholders.
3. Most expanding companies will need all the equity they can get to provide a base for selling debt.
4. When used principally to boost the stock price or increase earnings per share, it indicates the management is stock manipulative minded; it is a sign of poor management.
5. Managements universally are poor judges of a proper price for their stock. They almost always think it is underpriced.
6. Repurchase of stock in order to eliminate the cost of servicing small stockholders is a special situation, and we will finish up this chapter by considering it under a separate heading.

Repurchase of Stock to Eliminate Small Stock Holdings

Some companies, for various reasons, have developed a large number of stockholders who hold a small number of shares. For example, 50% of the stockholders of one major corporation owned only 3% of its shares.

It may be costly for a company to service small holders compared with the benefit the holders receive.

If a stockholder owned ten shares of a stock selling for $10, his total investment would only represent $100. If the company paid a 50¢ dividend, the stockholder would only receive $5 per year. And if the company earned $1 per share, his total interest in the earnings of the company would only be $10.

If the stockholder wanted to sell his ten shares, the brokerage commission would be approximately $12. Thus, the stockholder might just sit with his small holding rather than get rid of it.

The annual cost for the company to service this stockholder might be approximately as follows:

Cost to pay dividend	$1.35
Cost to maintain records	$2.85

Some companies have taken steps to try to eliminate small stockholders.

Before taking such a step, a company should consider the long range effect. If a stockholder is eliminated, particularly with the urging of the company, it is quite likely that he would not have any further interest in the company. However, as long as he continues to be a small holder, there is always the possibility that he might represent potential market support for the stock by buying some additional shares, and he might be a candidate to purchase a new offering of common stock. It would be difficult to gauge this potential benefit. A review of the stockholder list over a period of time might give some clue as to whether some of the small stockholders were stepping up their holdings.

If having weighed this possible disadvantage, a company decides to go ahead with the idea, there are two principal questions which it has to answer:

1. What size holdings should be eliminated?
2. What technique should be used?

As to the size of the holdings which might be eliminated, the market price of the stock would obviously weigh heavily. If a stock sold at $10 per share, then ten shares would represent a total investment of $100; whereas, if a stock sold for $100, it would only take one share to represent a total investment of $100. The size of holding to be eliminated should be related to the cost to service compared with the benefit the stockholders receive.

The question of technique used revolves around the incentive offered and the general approach.

The incentive used is generally an offer by the company to purchase the shares at the market price without any brokerage fee. Some companies have offered to pay a fixed price or the market price, whichever is higher. This might be disadvantageous to the company if the stock took a sharp drop. It would not appear that a company could offer too much incentive, because it should bear some relationship to the cost to service such stockholders.

The results that companies have experienced which have tried this operation vary widely. It is hard to account for the wide differences. It may be due to various factors, such as: the method the company used, the general securities market at the time, the nature of the stockholder list, the outlook for the company, etc.

The results of five companies that tried it are summarized below:

Company A offered to repurchase shares over an eight-year period to shareholders owning ten shares or less. The plan was presented in the quarterly report to shareholders and offered these shareholders the option of selling their shares at the previous day's closing market price. The company absorbed all brokerage fees. During the repurchase offer, the market price ranged from $25-$40. The operation turned out to be insignificant; an average of only 500 shares were repurchased each year. They in turn were sold to employees in lots of 100, resulting in about five transactions per year.

Company B offered to purchase all shares of holders of 25 shares or less for a period of 17 days at the market price plus a premium of 50¢, and for 24 more days at a premium of 25¢. The stock was around $20 per share at the time of the offer.

The company made the offers directly to the owners who would not have to pay any brokerage fee. The offer was also made to brokers who might be holding some stock for beneficial owners. The company paid brokers for any out-of-pocket expenses.

Shares received were held in the treasury. The offer was not considered successful. Furthermore, new shareholders continued to buy the stock in small lots.

Company C offered to repurchase shares from shareholders of nine or less shares at the prevailing market price, which ranged from $21-$23, without incurring brokerage fees. A special letter was sent to the shareholders describing the repurchase plan. The offer was considered successful in reducing the number of small shareholders.

Company D developed a large number of small stockholders because another company which owned 20% of Company D's stock paid a dividend to its stockholders in the form of Company D's stock. This resulted in 9,000 additional new stockholders with 5,000 owning three shares or less.

The first offer was for a period of one month to shareholders with 14 shares or less at $15.25 per share. This was a 25¢ premium over the market price at the beginning of the offer. The stockholders did not have to pay any brokerage fee. The company paid the transfer tax. The offer was quite successful with more than half of the shareowners and shares eliminated, as shown below:

	Shareowners	Shares
Holding 14 shares or less	69%	3%
Percent of 14 shares or less eliminated	57%	65%

The company made another offer two years later for a period of one month and five days to shareholders of 24 shares or less at $18 per share. This was a 50¢ premium over the market price at the beginning of the offer. The company paid the transfer tax. The stockholders did not have to pay any brokerage fee. The company was also successful with about one-third of the shareholders and shares in this category eliminated, as shown below:

	Shareowners	Shares
Holding 24 shares or less	55%	2%
Percent of 24 shares or less eliminated	36%	37%

Company E made two offers to repurchase shares from holders of 25 shares or less. In both cases brokerage fees were absorbed by the company. The offers were presented in a special letter to the shareholders. Approximately 25% of the shareholders were eligible. The first offer, which was made at the prevailing market price, was considered to be far more successful than the second offer. The second offer was at a fixed price, and fluctuation in market price upset the plan. Prior to both offers, the company had 11,000 shareholders—they now have 4,000.

Rather than offer to repurchase the shares of small stockholders, a company might take a more positive attitude. It might offer to pay brokerage fees if small stockholders would increase their holdings. As an alternative, it could also offer stockholders the opportunity to sell their stock. In the explanation to stockholders, the purpose should be made clear and any intention that the company is recommending purchase or sale of the stock should be carefully avoided. This method would require a prospectus.

Thus, in conclusion, a company should not try to eliminate small stockholdings without weighing the possible disadvantages of losing these people as potential larger holders. And if it did decide to go ahead, it might prefer to use a positive approach and give them an opportunity to step up their holdings rather than just ask them to sell.

CHAPTER 4

Types of Securities and Security Features

In the second chapter, on capital structure, securities were divided into debt and equity. There are numerous kinds of securities within these classifications. Since we are approaching the point of setting up a financing program, we will have to be more specific. This chapter will sort out the principal media of financing, some of which are not strictly securities. Also, it will cover some ideas about the principal terms.

Where feasible, advantages and disadvantages of types of securities will be listed. Much of the material will be presented in outline form. Three controversial media are lease financing, warrants and convertibles. They are treated in more detail because of their complexity.

Undoubtedly, you realize that the chapter will not give you a description of every possible security, or all the terms that might be included in a particular security. The many terms can be varied in so many ways as to create an almost infinite shading of securities. Furthermore, the terms of a single bond issue alone may require more space than this chapter.

The purpose of the chapter is to give you a bird's-eye view, in order to help you sit back and view the financing media in broad perspective so as to make a sound choice. This chapter has a lot of material; you may only be interested in part of it. You can pick out what you want by referring to the headings.

If you have ever had a chance to listen to the many varieties of opinions of the financial community on types of security to use, it should be clear that, in the last analysis, you must rely on your own judgment. Whatever your choice, you will wish to have a good answer to why and why not, for possible alternatives.

Aims of Company and the Investor

There are two parties ultimately involved in a security transaction, the company and the investor. An investment banker may intervene as the intermediate purchaser before the security is distributed to the investor. Also, in a debt issue there may be a trustee whose function is to hold title to property and see that the provisions of the security are met for all the holders.

Whether or not the investor purchases directly from the company or through an investment banker, each party, the company and ultimately the investor, is attempting to obtain the most for his money in a very competitive market. For senior issues, the investor wants as much income as possible and terms which will provide as much security of principal as possible. The company wants to pay as little as possible and have what might be called loose terms. It wants freedom of action regarding use of assets and sale of other securities to raise capital.

During negotiations for the sale of a security, it is to be expected that neither party may seem entirely reasonable to the other since the company and the investor are seeking the best deal for themselves. However, it should be far from a cat-and-dog fight. There should be an appreciation by both parties of the justification of a common sense balance.

The company should not agree to unnecessary limiting provisions, particularly those which will hobble it in the future. Nevertheless, it should accept the fact that many provisions are highly necessary for the investor and it should be willing to accept them. This particularly applies to those provisions which the company should realize are mutually beneficial. Some provisions work to the company's advantage, although they may not seem to do so. For example, a sinking fund helps restore a company's credit by debt reduction.

Certain investors may take the approach that the more restrictive provisions they can get, the better. This is not practiced by the majority of far-seeing, large institutional investors. They should have as much interest as the company itself in keeping the company flexible and able to finance, so that it will remain financially healthy. If both parties know what they are doing, each gets what he pays for.

No instrument of a long-term security will fully protect it unless the enterprise continues to be successful. Within this limitation, what is the investor in senior securities trying to achieve by the terms?

In the first place, he wants to be sure of payment of income and principal. Payment of principal of a debt security can come only from cash generated by operations in one way or another, or refinancing, or liquidation of assets. If refinancing has to be relied upon for repayment of a debt obligation, there may be an added uncertainty where the maturity is far in the future.

Secondly, he will wish to have the quality and market price maintained in case he decides to sell the security before maturity. The following comment by a representative of a large institution emphasizes this point: "My firm recently had a 10% market loss in its investment in the bonds of a company when the bond rating was lowered a notch due to adverse developments. The loss amounted to millions of dollars. Therefore, we do have a direct interest in the maintenance of a company's credit."

Types of Securities

There have been some atrocious examples of companies messing up their nest with a horrendous variety of securities. In the 1920's the electric utility holding companies tried all types of financing. One of the real lulus was the Associated Gas and Electric System. A summary of the securities included in the various layers of holding companies was as follows:

Debentures—with various seniority.

Convertible debentures—some issues convertible into common, some into preferred, some into debt and some into two types of securities. Some convertibles converted at the company's option. Some convertibles had warrants permanently attached and some had detachable warrants.

Convertible investment certificates.

Allotment certificates.
Preferred stocks.
Preference stock.
Optional stock purchase warrants.
Class A stock.
Class B stock.
Common stock.

This type of financing worked in the 1920's boom but the holding companies collapsed in the 1930's. And it took years and much expense to straighten the mess out.

The conglomerates played the same financial games in the 1960's as the utilities did in the 1920's, but perhaps to a lesser degree. The conglomerates likewise prospered in the boom, but many of them clobbered their stockholders when the boom ended. And the management should go down in corporate history as financial manipulators and not corporate managers—a sorry blight on our free enterprise system.

In dividing up the capital structure pie between the various security holders, a company has just so much earnings and assets. It cannot add to the pie by adding different kinds of securities. There is no free lunch—what one security holder gets must be subtracted from another. If you push your finger into a balloon, its effect must show up somewhere, and the same idea applies to securities and their terms. Some financial experts pride themselves on their ability to design special types of securities that on the surface appear to be very intriguing. However, if such securities are analyzed in depth, it may become apparent that their long range effect will be adverse.

Why then are there so many varieties of securities? There must be, of course, some common stock. It represents the ownership and has the major risk. The reason for the great variety of securities: to fit the nature and needs of different types of companies and the different desires of investors at a particular time. Special characteristics of some companies call for special securities. One type of security with all its features will fit some investors' needs, another type will appeal to others, depending on existing circumstances. A variety of securities permits a company to call on the various pools of capital and raise capital on the cheapest basis. However, a company should strive to keep a simple capital structure with as few uncomplicated securities as possible.

You will wish to compare the cost and terms of one security with another. When you do, you will come up with some erroneous results if you do not correctly distinguish the security by the three broad types. You will be comparing oranges and apples without recognizing their differences. Any kind of debt is quite different from either of the equities—preferred and common—and within the equity family, preferred is different from common. Preferred is a senior security, and comes ahead of common, but preferred is an equity and protects debt.

We will start out with a brief explanation of three types of securities:

1. *Debt*—a form of obligation requiring payment of principal and interest or the equivalent until the principal is repaid. The payments may be combined together as in a lease, but no matter how stated, these two parts are present. If they are not paid, rights accrue to the holder of the obligation regarding either one or both of the following: the enforcement of a claim to the general funds of the company ahead of equity securities; the enforcement of a claim to specific property or income pledged as collateral.
2. *Preferred stock*—in all respects junior to debt obligations. Non-payment will not permit enforcement of debt type of claim. Within the limits provided in the preferred stock terms, the company can issue debt ahead of the preferred. It provides protection for debt. When there is non-payment of dividends for a certain period, some of the common stock privileges may accrue to the preferred stock. The important point with regard to pre-

ferred is that it is an equity and not a form of debt.

3. *Common stock*—represents the ownership. It takes the ultimate risk, and comes after all senior securities.

In our discussion of the media of financing, we will start with some explanation and definitions and then proceed from the most towards the least secure. Convertible securities and warrants may seem out of place as far as security is concerned. The reason for the order as shown below will be apparent as we go along.

- Debt Securities
  - Secured
    - Mortgage financing for real estate
    - Mortgage bonds
    - Equipment trust certificates
    - Lease financing
    - Industrial revenue bonds
    - Pollution control bonds
  - Unsecured
    - Debentures
    - Long term notes
    - Term bank loans
    - Income debentures
  - Floating Rate Notes
  - Single Payment Bonds—Example of an analysis of the cost of a special type of senior security and its effect on a company
  - Preferred Stocks
  - Convertible Securities
  - Warrants
  - Class A Convertible Stock
  - Common Stock

In selecting a particular security for your company, the points which you may need to consider are:

1. Its cost—meaning yield to maturity for debt and current yield for preferred. You will find these yields explained in Chapter 8, "Selling Senior Securities." To get cost to the company you should take into account the financing costs.
2. The terms—which should be looked upon as part of the cost.
3. The strategic position, as to assets and earnings, that the claim for payments of principal and income may occupy in relation to existing securities and possible future issues.
4. The immediate effects of the security on the other securities in the capital structure.
5. The effects of the security on future financing.
6. The expense of the instrument, such as a mortgage, to create and service the issue.

General Comments About Terms

Some of the terms of senior securities are included for the purpose of maintaining a company's credit standing. They are the bare minimum boundary lines which buyers of securities will accept. They may be expressed in terms of financial ratios. One astute buyer of securities suggested that such indenture terms are one of four credit standards, the other three being:

> *Limitations as to quality established by investors* to satisfy their requirements, arrived at through security analysis of all the ratios and factors affecting the quality of a company's securities.
>
> *Ratings by Fitch, Moody's and Standard*—the credit ratings assigned a security by these three agencies, arrived at through security analysis.
>
> *State laws defining the legality of securities for investment by certain institutional investors*—the bare minimum boundary lines for a security just to qualify for investment by such institutions.

In evaluating terms, have in mind what you are attempting to achieve for the protection of the investor and compare them with standards of good credit. The extent and complexity of the restrictive terms depend on the credit standing of a company, the nature of the business and the type of security. New ventures by companies with no previous record may necessitate more detailed provisions. Terms may be affected by money market conditions, and by regulation for types of companies which are subject thereto.

Unfortunately, most terms of securities are expressed in a complicated way. This is due partly to the nature of the animal. The wording is an endeavor to encompass all conditions that might arise over a period of many years. They must be so worded that they cannot be misinterpreted to permit the company to wander astray later on, under changed circumstances not presently apparent. The situation is compounded where an old existing instrument for a security has been added to and modified over a period of years with subsequent financing.

Complication is due partly to the fact that the persons who draft the instruments may not be willing to take the time to unravel the mess to make it easily understood. At the time a security is sold, everyone is rushing to meet a deadline and the only aim is to complete the paper work. The form it takes is secondary. Complication should not be the aim. It adds to the difficulty of understanding on the part of the investor. Simplicity in securities is worth a try.

When deciding on what terms to include in your security, it will be helpful to make an analysis of all the terms of securities of a similar nature recently offered by comparable companies. You probably have to rely on public offerings because very little information is available on private sales. Refer to prospectuses for some of the principal features, but probably you will wish to obtain more comprehensive information about some offerings. It will be found in registration statements, original Listing Statements, Forms 10K, indentures, etc. Just as a reminder when you are considering the terms, some do's and don'ts follow:

Don't consider that just because a term has been included in a certain way in the past that it has to be repeated, especially if it is unsound. If the market or buyers require your repeating such a term, you have to do so. There are styles in finance which are hard to combat. However if they do not correctly serve a function, you should not hesitate to try to change them.

Do look upon terms of your securities as very important. They may turn out to be a tight noose around your company's neck, if you failed to think of all their possible effects under different circumstances when you set them up. Your company must be able to run its affairs so as to have flexibility within the iron fence imposed by the terms. Evaluate each of them as though they applied under trying conditions, including the maturity of debt and even the default provisions which may seem quite remote.

Do understand that sound terms should be good for you as well as for the investors. Try to express them so that they are reasonably intelligible. In this connection, choose a lawyer who is an expert in this field and can think in terms of economics rather than in a purely legal framework, and who also has a sincere interest in making his writing understandable. Give him time to achieve this goal.

DEBT SECURITIES

Before we start on specific types of debt issues, we will discuss some ideas which might be helpful in understanding them, and some provisions which apply to most types. If you have had some experience in this field, you can skip the items which are old hat to you.

Definitions

Funded Debt

Funded debt, which is the type of debt we will be talking about, refers to debt with a maturity longer than one year. The other type of debt is current, short-term or floating debt, with a maturity of a year or less and included in current liabilities.

Bond

A bond is a certificate stating the amount of debt that the particular bond evidences. The legend or wording on the bond includes a few terms and refers to the indenture, which is a separate legal document giving the complete terms of the bond issue. A bond must be properly dressed up—fully engraved or printed on steel-engraved borders.

Indenture

The word indenture is defined in the dictionary as an agreement in writing, or a formal document. It is likewise given broad meaning in the Trust Indenture Act. There the term is stated to mean "any mortgage, deed of trust, trust or other indenture, or similar instrument or agreement . . . under which securities are outstanding or to be issued." A provision in an indenture is known as a covenant, which means a contract, a promise, a pledge.

Trustee

It would be impractical for each holder of a bond issue which is held by a number of investors to have to see that all the terms of the indenture are fulfilled by the company. In order to solve this problem, a trustee may be appointed who acts for all bondholders. When there is a trustee, the indenture is a contract between the issuing corporation and the trustee. The holders of the bonds have a right to participate in the indenture, and it is administered by the trustee for the benefit of the bondholders. There may be more than one trustee, but there need not be. The Trust Indenture Act requires that at least one trustee shall be a corporation authorized by law to exercise corporate trust powers and be subject to regulation.

Mortgage Bond

A bond may be secured by a mortgage. Such a bond has assets pledged as a security and has a lien on those assets. A mortgage bond may require three documents: the bond, the indenture giving the terms of the issue and the mortgage which covers the pledged property. The latter two may be combined.

Debenture Bond

A debenture bond is an unsecured bond, and therefore there are only two documents: the bond and the indenture.

Coupon and Registered Bonds

A bond can be a coupon bond, a registered bond or registered as to principal with coupons.

A coupon bond has coupons attached to it—one for each date on which interest is due. The holder sends the appropriate coupon to the paying agent and a check is remitted for the interest. Also, coupons may be collected through banks in much the same fashion as a check. This is how the picture of the wealthy man clipping coupons originated. Coupon bonds are generally in $1,000 denominations, or a few multiples thereof. It is a bearer instrument and as such is negotiable and transferable without any registrar intervening. Anyone can collect the interest by sending in the coupon when due. A coupon bond may be registered, but it need not be. If it is registered, then the bond itself is non-negotiable, although the coupons will remain so.

A fully registered bond does not have coupons attached, but contains a statement of the rate of interest and dates when due. It is non-negotiable. When such a bond is sold by one investor to another, it must be sent to the registrar for the bonds—who keeps track of the owner and his address and sends the interest to the person in whose name the bonds are registered. Transfer of a registered bond is handled in a similar way as transfer of a share of stock. When a bond is traded, the registrar gives a single bond to the buyer, generally in multiples of $1,000, representing in one piece the total principal amount of bonds he owns.

The usual practice in the past was to provide two forms of bonds for a single issue. For example, bonds might be in the form of coupon bonds in the denominations of $1,000 with coupons attached, and in fully registered form in denominations of $1,000 or any multiples thereof. These two forms are interchangeable as provided in the indenture, upon payment of a small charge, which usually does not exceed $2 per certificate. However, a company usually will make such exchanges without charge in order to convenience original purchasers of a new issue, and may do so subsequently as a matter of policy.

The small investors may prefer coupon bonds because they are easily transferable without going through a registrar, and some people may prefer them in order to hide their ownership. Institutional investors with large holdings prefer registered bonds because it reduces the amount of paper that has to be in safekeeping.

Today, most corporate bonds are in fully registered form. There is a small continuing expense for the company with registered bonds because of the transfer fees when bonds are bought and sold; however, this expense is more than offset by the fact that the company has an up-to-date list of its bondholders in case it is necessary to contact them. Trying to find holders of coupon bondholders is a laborious task.

Price of a Bond

Since bonds may be in different denominations, their prices are expressed as percentages of principal amount. A price of 100 means 100% of the principal amount, whatever the denomination. This is in contrast to the price of a stock, which is expressed in dollars per share.

Note

A less formal type of indebtedness is a note. It may be secured. Like a bond, it briefly states the amount owed, the interest rate and the maturity. As with a bond, there will be a more lengthy document, known as the loan agreement, which spells out the provisions of the loan. It corresponds to the indenture for a bond, except that the loan agreement is a contract between the lender and the borrowing corporation rather than with the trustee, who therefore may be eliminated.

Trust Indenture Act of 1939

The Trust Indenture Act of 1939, which is administered by the Securities and Exchange Commission, was passed for the purpose of protecting bondholders from the dangers of inadequate indentures and unqualified trustees. The need for the Act became apparent in the depression of the 1930's when there were so many business failures and resulting financial reorganizations. The Trust Indenture Act attempts to insure that the trustee will be qualified, be independent, be subject to penalties for failure to act, etc. An indenture is qualified by including therein such provisions as are required by the Trust Indenture Act. It does not attempt to define the standards required to maintain sound credit.

Debt Provisions

The provisions of debt securities have to cover a multitude of ideas. Their extent will depend on the nature of the security. Some of them may be put in the following three categories:

1. *The terms of the issue,* such as the interest rate, maturity, sinking funds, redemption provisions, etc.
2. *The protection provisions,* which assure payment of principal and interest, and maintenance of the quality.
3. *The default provisions,* which define what constitutes a default and the rights of the security holders when a default occurs.

We will be concerned with some of the terms in the first two categories. This is not to minimize the importance of the default provisions. If inadequate thought is given to them when they are drawn, they can cause serious trouble if the company runs into difficulty. As previously stated, they should be written as if default was just around the corner.

We will now discuss some of the terms which apply to most types of debt issues.

Maturity, Sinking Fund and Serial Issues

Maturity

First, how long should the maturity of your bonds be—ten years, 20 years, 30 years, 50 years, or even perpetual?

Examples can be found of practically all possible maturities. Generally, the question is not a major problem, because the maturity for a particular type of company tends to follow the pattern which has been set by other similar new issues. However, the question is far from academic and a company should have a good reason for choosing whatever maturity is decided upon. Sinking fund is so closely related to maturity that we will treat it along with maturity.

Other things being equal, companies unconsciously seem to favor long maturities, since that will give them the use of the money for as long a period as possible. Also, they thereby postpone the trouble and expense of refinancing the maturity. Some financial experts, in fact, urge such a policy. However, merely lengthening the maturity for such reasons alone may not be the best course to follow.

There are two considerations in deciding on the maturity. They are the character of the company and the condition of the bond market.

The nature of some companies is such that they should not attempt to issue bonds with long maturities. One very good reason is that investors would not purchase them. Examples of such situations occur where there is a wasting asset, or where a company is dependent on contracts for sale of a product for a limited period. A company in a risky type of business or one with poor credit may be in a similar position. In other words, the maturity must be within the period that the company has prospects of assured income. A company is only asking for trouble if it attempts to drag out the maturity longer than is economically reasonable.

On the other hand, for a company which is capable of selling a long maturity, there may be reasons why it should not consider a short maturity. If a company has a heavy construction program and maturing debt issues in the near future, it would be compounding its financing problem by using a short maturity.

The condition of the market for debt securities at the time of the proposed security sale, particularly the cost expressed as yield for different maturities, also affects the maturity. A company will wish to consider the differences in yield within the maturity range which the company's character will permit. The yield pattern will vary with maturity from time to time, depending on the demand and supply for short and long term funds. Generally, interest rates are lower for the shorter maturities of equal quality, but the slope of the curve varies considerably. At times, the reverse has occurred, and short term rates have been higher.

A company can get a general idea of the effect of maturity on interest rates by first referring to the yields on U.S. Government bonds with different maturities. This information is readily available in chart form in the monthly bulletin of the United States Treasury.[1] An example of yields taken from charts contained in the bulletin is shown in Exhibit 4-1 for two dates when the yield pattern was quite different. These yields[2] represent the rates on the highest type of credit.

Yields on corporate bonds would naturally be higher. Furthermore, the pattern might be somewhat different. As the quality of corporates falls, the spread would tend to be greater for the longer maturities, because of the greater uncertainty of payment for the weaker issues. In order to get some idea of the pattern for corporate bonds, you may refer to

---

[1] *The Treasury Bulletin,* Superintendent of Documents, U.S. Government Printing Office, Washington, D.C. 20402. Subscription per year $43.30 domestic, $54.15 foreign. Single copy varies.

[2] When a Treasury issue is above the call price, the yield is figured to the first call date.

Exhibit 4-1

EFFECT OF MATURITY ON BOND YIELDS

YIELDS ON U.S. TREASURY ISSUES
AS READ FROM YIELD CURVE*

Maturity in Years	September 30, 1974	September 30, 1964
1	8.2%	3.90%
2	8.1	3.95
3	8.1	3.98
4	8.1	4.02
5	8.1	4.05
6	8.2	4.08
7	8.0	4.10
8	7.9	4.12
9	7.9	4.16
10	7.9	4.18
11	8.0	4.19
12	8.0	4.19
13	8.1	4.20
14	8.2	4.20
15	8.3	4.20
16	8.4	4.20
17	8.4	4.20
18	8.4	4.20
19	8.5	4.20
20	8.5	4.20
21	8.5	4.20
22	8.5	4.20
23	8.5	4.19
24	8.5	4.19
25	8.5	4.19

**Treasury Bulletin,* October 1974, and October 1964, United States Treasury Department.

data on outstanding non-convertible corporate bonds with different maturities and the same credit rating as the company in question. Care must be taken for the possible effect on the yield of a sinking fund, the call price if the issue sells above call and the size of the interest coupon. As will be pointed out in Chapter 8, on selling senior securities, the yields on outstanding bonds will not give the rate at which a new issue can be sold, but it will give some idea of the effect of different maturities on yield. Of greater significance are the offering yields on recent new issues of corporate bonds of similar quality with different maturities. It may be impossible to obtain an adequate sample of new corporate bond issues with different maturities and comparable quality. Then you will have to rely on the data suggested above and on the advice of an investment banker, who should be able to make an educated estimate because of his closeness to the market.

Thus, the final decision as to the maturity of a debt issue will depend on the nature of the company's business and its future demand for capital, and the interest rate differential on the various maturities. It will also depend on what happens to interest rates in the future, but that is an unknown quantity at the time the decision has to be made. It might be poor economy to try to take advantage of the lower interest rates for a short maturity and then get caught at maturity in a poor securities market when the company is already burdened with other financing. We will stress throughout the book, that you should not rely on an excessive amount of short term securities during favorable conditions and thus use up the short term borrowing reserve. In other words, keep the short term debt door open.

The condition of the bond market in 1974, which forced all but the best credits to sell bonds with a short maturity, resulted in many companies having to issue debt which did not fit their financial needs.

Gradual Repayment

Having decided on the longest maturity consistent with the nature of the company, the next question will be whether there should be a gradual repayment schedule prior to maturity. Actually, this matter cannot be disassociated from the maturity question.

The pattern of the debt reduction—when it starts, the annual payments and total amount—should be tailor-made to each company. A repayment schedule prior to maturity reduces the burden of final payment at a time relatively far off when it cannot be known what the company's financial strength will be.

It should at least be sufficient to reduce the debt to a reasonable level in line with future potential risks. If a company's credit is weak, the repayment schedule may have as its purpose to gradually improve the company's debt ratio. A company with a wasting asset would be expected by investors to provide for gradual repayment.

Some companies have a tendency to fight the inclusion of prior repayment programs in their debt issues, feeling that they are a disadvantage and a form of cost. They are, of course, a drain on cash, and insofar as additional financing is required to repay them, they will necessitate financing costs. However, on the plus side, it should be recognized that they, in most instances, reduce the interest cost, and also they do improve a company's credit position as time goes on. Furthermore, a satisfactory schedule may reduce the severity of the restrictive provisions. The reduction in debt gradually decreases the burden of payment on the company and, correspondingly, the investor's risk of non-payment. In other words, it is a provision which, if viewed objectively, has real advantages.

Tunnel Sinking Fund

When a series of bonds of equal security are issued under one indenture, each series will have a separate sinking fund. There have been instances in which the sinking fund of one series may be satisfied with bonds of another series. This permits a company to use the series of bonds with the highest interest rate to satisfy the sinking fund for all the series. This is known as a tunnel sinking fund—a high interest rate bond is tunneled to a low interest rate bond to satisfy sinking fund requirements, through call at the sinking fund call price or by purchase in the market. Bond purchasers do not like this type of provision, particularly when new bonds are sold during a period of high interest rates. Whether you can include it or not will depend on conditions in the bond market.

Sinking Fund vs. Serial Payments

Should your debt reduction be through a sinking fund or serial maturity? A serial maturity has the advantage of reducing the average maturity of the debt for the purposes of yield calculations by the investor. If interest rates are lower for shorter maturities, the company will derive a greater advantage in a lower average rate with serial maturities than it might from a sinking fund. The reason for this is as follows: a reduction in debt by a sinking fund is handled by calling bonds by lot or purchase in the open market. No one holder of the bonds knows whether he will have his bonds called. Therefore, in calculating the yield, each bondholder must assume that he will have to wait until final maturity, with only a possibility that he will be paid before then. On the other hand, the holder of serial bonds has a definite payment schedule.

This is not to say that an investor will not look at the average maturity of a sinking fund bond, but he may give it little weight as far as the effect on yield is concerned, unless he owns the whole issue, or is otherwise assured of pro-rate call for the sinking fund.

The company should figure the yield to the average maturity because it correctly represents the maturity which the company faces. Average maturity calculation is explained in Chapter 8.

A sinking fund may have an advantage as far as the company is concerned over a serial issue. If interest rates increase and bond prices fall, the company may be better able to purchase the bonds in the market at a discount in order to satisfy the sinking fund and thus save money. Its ability to purchase the bonds at a discount will depend upon the future pattern of bond prices and how the bonds are held. The wider the distribution of bondholders, the better the company's position to purchase bonds for sinking fund.

If a company sells bonds privately, it should consider carefully whether it will be blocked from ever buying bonds at a discount for sinking fund purposes. Then, in effect, a sinking fund bond is the same as a serial bond.

If the number of investors in a private offering are large, the company may be able to shop around and get some investors to let bonds go for sinking fund at some discount from the sinking fund call price, which would be a higher price than the investors could get from sale in the market.

In a serial issue, the interest coupon may be the same for all maturities, with different offering prices for the different maturities to satisfy yield requirements of the market, or the offering price may be the same with the interest coupon varying. Serial maturities have been used largely in equipment trust certificates for railroads, but seldom for industrials. This does not mean that their pros and cons should not be weighed whenever offering debt. Some problem may be encountered in listing a serial bond on the New York Stock Exchange, because of the requirement of separate application and quotation for each maturity. However, listing of a debt issue may not be of sufficient importance for this to be a major obstacle.

Examples of many varieties of sinking funds can be found. The date when the sinking fund starts may be delayed for a number of years. The amount may be equal annually or varying on different bases. The amount may be dependent on earnings or production; in the case of a wasting asset, it might be a certain number of cents per barrel or ton. However, the most common is a fixed annual principal amount.

There may be optional amounts. A company may have the right to double sinking fund payments. This is an advantage if the company generates extra cash. The company can extinguish the additional amount of bonds at the sinking fund call price which is lower than the regular call price.

While sinking funds do have some advantages, they also may get a company into financial difficulty when too heavy. This, of course, is generally a sign of too much debt in the first place.

Most industrial company bonds have sinking funds. The risk factor is such that investors require it. In the past, mortgage bonds of electric utility companies generally have not had fixed sinking funds requiring debt reduction. For such companies, the sinking funds were small because of the nature of their business and in most instances could be satisfied by putting up new property. This keeps up the security beyond the debt. For example, if the issuance of new mortgage bonds is limited to 65% of net property additions, an equivalent amount of property can be used to satisfy the sinking fund. In other words, for each $100 of new property, the company will get a $65 credit for sinking fund. This has an advantage for such a company in that, as expansion continues, existing bonds do not have to be paid off. This type of sinking fund is applicable only to companies which have special characteristics and, in addition, a high credit standing.

Bonds purchased to satisfy sinking fund requirements usually can be tendered by the company to the trustee at 100 in lieu of cash. They may be acquired by purchase in the open market or through tenders, or in some instances through negotiation, if an issue was sold at private sale. If not so available, then the bonds may be called by lot at the sinking fund call price.

By studying debt issues of companies like your own, you can obtain an idea of the general pattern of serial maturities, sinking funds and final maturities. This will be a good starting point. You should then evaluate the situation for your company on the basis of the two considerations discussed above—the nature of the company and its financing requirements and the pattern of interest rates for different maturities.

As an example of how there may be radical departures from the norm in maturities and sinking funds, we will refer to examples of two bonds issued many years ago.

When interest rates were low in the early 1950's, a few well-known industrial companies sold bonds privately with a 100-year maturity to a few large institutional investors. There was an interesting additional provision. There was an optional provision permitting a change in the maturity after a few years. For example, one such loan carried an interest rate of 3 3/4% for 100 years. Both the lending institutions and the company had the right to change the maturity eight years after it was issued into a 25-year loan with a 100% sinking fund of equal annual payments, starting five years hence. If such a request were made, the interest was to be reduced to 3 1/2%. The lending institutions took advantage of this option. You may wonder why. The answer is due to the fact that interest rates had increased substantially to above 5%. It was the appraisal of the lending institutions that rates would continue high, and as the loan was repaid through the sinking fund at 100, they would be able to reinvest the money at a higher rate. From the point of view of financial policy, the companies issuing such debt would have had to assume the short maturity when it was issued, since the option was with the investors. That was the way it actually worked out. It may be noted that, had this been a public offering rather than a private sale, the company might have been able to purchase bonds in the open market at substantial discounts for sinking fund purposes.

Another piece of financing which was an example of a maturity out of the pattern for similar types of issues was a large issue of debentures sold by an electric company in 1949. The company subsequently sold other similar issues. At the time, the pattern for maturities of long term debt by similar types of companies was 25 or 30 years. The interest rate on the debenture issue we refer to was 3% and the final maturity 50 years. A 2% cash sinking fund was provided, to retire an equal amount each year so that the entire issue would be taken care of by maturity. This bond was offered publicly. Thereafter, the company was able to realize substantial savings through purchase of bonds for sinking fund in the market when interest rates increased and the bonds fell in price to below 50. This was entirely due to a change in interest rates and not to the quality of the issue.

These two examples are presented merely for purposes of showing how it may be possible to step out of the general pattern. However, before a company considers such a radical departure it should evaluate carefully how such an issue might work out at various times in the future if interest rates stayed the same, went up or down and the company's needs for capital increased or decreased.

Redemption Provisions

A debt issue generally has two sets of prices at which it can be paid off before maturity.

One provision applies if the company is forced to reduce debt in compliance with the terms of the indenture, such as for sinking fund purposes. It is referred to as the sinking fund call or special redemption provision. The other call is referred to as the regular or optional redemption provision and may be used at the company's option.

Sinking Fund or Special Redemption Provision

Reduction of debt for sinking fund is for the purpose of assuring repayment of principal. It is for the benefit of the investor. Therefore, the investor should be willing to permit redemptions for this purpose with no penalty to the company. Generally, the call price starts at the issue price or 100, whichever is higher. If the issue is sold below 100 the sinking fund call price is 100. Because of the nature of this call price, it is a disadvantage for a company to sell a bond at below 100.

If bonds are sold at a premium above 100, then naturally the sinking fund call price should start at that premium because an investor wouldn't wish to obtain less than the money he put up. When the sinking fund call price is above 100 because the bond is sold at a premium, the sinking fund call price is gradually reduced each year to 100 at maturity. The call price decreases on the basis of a constant yield to maturity at which the bonds were offered. If you are not familiar with figuring the yield to maturity for a bond, it is explained in Chapter 8.

A simple example is as follows: A ten-year bond is sold at 101.43 with a 7% interest coupon. The yield to maturity at a price of 101.43 is 6.80%. The redemption price for sinking fund purposes will start at 101.43. Thereafter, the redemption prices are fixed at values corresponding to a 6.80% yield for a 7% bond for the terms remaining to maturity. They would be as shown in Column III of Exhibit 4-2. The figures were taken directly from Bond Value Tables.

When a new issue is sold, it is necessary to await the offering price in order to calculate the sinking fund and also the regular redemption prices. This is one of the rush jobs that takes place at the time a bid is opened at competitive bidding.

There may be other provisions in an indenture requiring payment of the debt before maturity, such as from the proceeds of the sale of property. Such a requirement, if obligatory, should also provide for redemption at the sinking fund call price.

An example of the effect of sinking fund call price is as follows:

One investor offered to buy an entire debenture issue in a private sale at a price of 100 and an interest rate of 5%. The maturity was to be ten years with an equal annual sinking fund which would pay off the entire issue in ten years. Another investor offered a price of 100 and an interest rate of 4 3/4%. At first, the borrowing company was happy with the second offer because it was able to save 1/4% interest. However, there was a catch. The investor who offered the 5% rate established a sinking fund call price of 100, as would be expected. Here is where the catch came in. The second investor had in mind imposing a sinking fund call price of 101 1/2. Since the issue would all be held by one investor, the company had no chance of buying bonds back in the market. Therefore, each year the company would have to pay 4 3/4% interest and 1 1/2% penalty for retiring part of the bonds for sinking fund. This was approximately equivalent to selling the bonds at 98 1/2 with a 4 3/4% interest rate and a sinking fund call at 100. That would mean a yield to maturity of 5.06% based on the average life of the issue. The company would have been worse off if it had accepted the 4 3/4% rate with the higher sinking fund call price. To determine an exact comparison of costs for these two propositions, the after tax cost should be calculated on a discounted cash flow basis.

Purchase of Bonds for Sinking Fund

If the market price for a company's bonds is below the sinking fund call price, a com-

Exhibit 4-2

REDEMPTION PRICES FOR SINKING FUND FOR BOND WITH 7% INTEREST COUPON, SOLD AT 101.43
REDEMPTION PRICE DECREASES ON BASIS OF CONSTANT YIELD FOR REMAINING LIFE

Column	I	II	III	IV	V
	Price at Which Bond Was Sold	Remaining Time to Maturity	Interest Coupon	Redemption Price for Sinking Fund	Yield to Maturity
	101.43	10	7%	101.43	6.80%
		9	"	101.33	"
		8	"	101.22	"
		7	"	101.10	"
		6	"	100.97	"
		5	"	100.84	"
		4	"	100.69	"
		3	"	100.53	"
		2	"	100.37	"
		1	"	100.19	"
		0	"	100.00	"

pany can purchase bonds in the market in order to satisfy the sinking fund. How far ahead the company should anticipate sinking fund requirements will depend on a number of factors.

To illustrate the necessary calculations and judgments in making purchases of bonds for sinking fund purposes, we will use the following assumptions:

Bond—5% coupon with 25 years remaining to maturity.
Call price for sinking fund purposes—100.
Yield to maturity for completely similar bonds in a free market unaffected by the special demand for sinking fund—8%.

With a yield of 8% in a free market the bonds would sell for 67.78. However, since the market knows that the company has to purchase bonds for sinking fund purposes, the market price has been pushed up to 70. Thus, you would have to pay a premium over what the bonds were worth of 2.22.

The company needs some bonds for sinking fund purposes which it will have to obtain by calling them at 100 unless it decides to purchase the bonds at 70. By purchasing them it saves 30 compared to calling them. This is a very simple situation and requires no calculations or judgment. The only thing the company has to do is be sure it buys the bonds in the market at the best price.

The company also needs bonds for sinking fund purposes for the remaining 25 years to maturity. A decision has to be made as to whether to buy bonds now and hold them to use to satisfy sinking fund requirements in the future or wait and try to purchase them subsequently. The decision is not a simple one. The company has to make up its mind as to what price it should pay at present and how many bonds it should acquire.

Yield to maturity takes into account the interest coupon and the fact that the holder receives 100 at maturity. As a consequence, a bond selling at a discount increases in price as the number of years to maturity decreases, providing the yield remains constant. As the bonds come close to maturity, the yield might decrease because of the shorter maturity, but in our example the bonds are still long term and the few years difference in maturity would probably not decrease the yield sufficiently enough to affect our calculations. The bond with the 5% interest coupon used in our example would have the following prices with an 8% yield in the free market:

Beginning Year	Remaining Years to Maturity	Price with 8% Yield
1	25	67.78
2	24	68.21
3	23	68.67
4	22	69.18
5	21	69.72
6	20	70.31

Now we have to make a comparison between two calculations:

1. What it costs to acquire bonds today to satisfy sinking fund requirements in future years.
2. An estimate of what it might cost to acquire the bonds in future years.

We then compare these two calculations in order to decide whether we should acquire the bonds today.

If we consider purchasing bonds at the beginning of year 1 for sinking fund requirements at beginning of year 2, we have to consider two factors:

1. The cost of money for one year, because no matter where we get the funds the cost of that capital must be taken into account. For this purpose, it is proper to assume that the funds will be supplied by short term borrowings, and we will use a rate of 7%.
2. If we purchase bonds at the beginning of year 1 which we will use for sinking fund purposes at beginning of year 2, we will not have to pay the $5 in bond interest at the beginning of year 2.

   We should note at this point, that in order to simplify our calculations, we will assume all interest payments are made on an annual basis.

Our calculations would therefore be as follows:

Market price of bonds today (Premium 2.22 over free market for bonds)	$70.00
Tax on discount ($30) at which bonds are purchased, assuming a 50% tax rate. Assumed to be payable today.[3]	15.00
7% rate of interest on short term loan used to acquire the bonds and pay tax, paid at end of year–3.5% net after 50% tax rate.[4]	2.98
Total cost to acquire bonds at beginning of year 1 for sinking fund at beginning of year 2.	$87.98

In order to help decide whether to purchase bonds this year for next year's sinking fund requirements, we now have to make our second calculation which is the price at which the bonds might be purchased at the beginning of year 2.

The price in future years will be affected by two things:

1. The premium you might have to pay over the free market value of the bonds.
2. The prospects for a change in interest rates which will affect the price.

Let's assume that the premium and interest rates stay the same. Then the calculations for our second estimate as to what we might pay at the beginning of year 2 would be as follows:

Price of bond at beginning of year 2 with 8% yield in free market	$68.21
Premium	2.22

[3]To avoid over-complicating the example, the most direct tax treatment was employed. The company has the option of treating the gain on the reacquired bonds as a reduction of the asset which was financed with the proceeds of the bonds. This would reduce the future annual depreciation for tax purposes and increase future tax payments. Thus, instead of paying the tax immediately it would pay it over a period of years. This deferral of taxes would give the company the temporary use of funds.

[4]Assumed to include all costs such as compensating balances.

Market price of bonds	$70.43
Tax on discount ($29.57) at which bonds are purchased at 50% tax rate	14.79
	85.22
Interest on bonds for one year after 50% tax	2.50
Total cost to retire bonds at the beginning of year 2	$87.72

On the basis of the above figures, we estimate that to retire bonds today to use one year hence would cost $87.98. And we estimate that the cost to retire bonds at the beginning of year 2 will be $87.72. Therefore, on the basis of these figures alone, we should wait until next year.

However, for our conclusion, we are relying on estimates and should make other estimates to see what might happen. Such estimates can be compiled in a table as shown in Exhibit 4-3. Column III shows what it would cost today in order to purchase bonds for sinking fund purposes. Columns IV, V and VI show what it might cost, with different interest rate changes, if you waited and purchased the bonds when the need arose. From the exhibit, it can be seen that it would be better to wait if interest rates stayed the same or increased. If they decreased to 7%, it would be better to purchase the bonds today.

In order for you to decide on your purchases for sinking fund, you will do well to go through the calculations as we have suggested based on rates which apply to your situation. However, as a practical matter, the final decision will depend largely on your estimate of the premium you will have to pay in future years and whether interest rates will decrease.

For preferred stock which has a mandatory sinking fund, the same principles apply, but the calculations will be somewhat different because of the difference in the tax treatment for the various items.

Regular or Optional Redemption Provision

Now we turn to the regular call provision. Its purpose is to permit the company to eliminate the issue in whole or in part at its option, if future conditions make it advisable to do so. However, the company must pay a premium if it exercises this option since this is a privilege and not an obligation.

It has been suggested that investors are perhaps inconsistent in requiring a sinking fund and thus making a company reduce the debt, yet at the same time requiring a premium if the company retires more than the sinking fund amount. Actually there is no inconsistency. The purpose of the sinking fund is to assure sound credit and payment of principal. On the other hand, the purpose of the regular call premium is to prevent the company from refunding bonds, which are considered appropriate from a credit angle, at a lower interest rate, without compensation to the investor for the trouble he incurred in advancing the money.

There are two questions involved in the regular call feature: its size and the pattern of the decrease. There, of course, need not be a decrease, but if not, then, in effect, the penalty becomes greater as the maturity decreases with the passage of time, due to the nature of bond yields.

The pattern for a regular call price for a non-serial bond is different from one with serial maturities. The serial bond generally will have lower call prices for the shorter maturities. This again is due to the nature of bond yields. In a serial issue, there is generally the requirement that retirements be made in order of longest maturity. Henceforth, we will be discussing the redemption provisions for a non-serial bond.

As to the amount of the premium for a non-serial bond, one approach is to start with a penalty of one year's interest. In other

Exhibit 4-3

CASH COST TO PURCHASE BONDS FOR SINKING FUND

Assuming: 50% Tax Rate, 7% Short Term Borrowing Rate and 2.22 Premium

Column	I	II	III	IV	V	VI
				Cost to Purchase Bonds in Future Years		
	Remaining Years to Maturity	Number of Years Before Sinking Fund Is Due	Cost to Purchase Bonds Today for Future Sinking Fund Payments	No Change in Interest Rates	Long Term Interest Rates Fall to 7%	Long Term Interest Rates Rise to 9%
	25	0	$85.00	--	--	--
	24	1	87.98*	$87.72**	$ 92.07	$84.08
	23	2	91.06	90.54	94.85	86.91
	22	3	94.24	93.47	97.74	89.86
	21	4	97.54	96.51	100.74	92.93

*Includes:

1	Market price of bonds today.	$70.00
2	Tax on discount at which bonds are purchased, assuming a 50% tax rate. Assumed to be payable today.	15.00
3	7% rate of interest on short term loan funds used to acquire the bonds and pay tax, paid at end of year–3.5% net after 50% tax rate.	2.98
4	Total cost to acquire bonds at beginning of year 1 for sinking fund at beginning of year 2.	$87.98

**Includes:

1	Price of bond at beginning of year 2 with 8% yield in free market.	$68.21
2	Premium.	2.22
3	Market price of bond.	70.43
4	Tax on discount at which bonds are purchased at 50% tax rate.	14.79
5	Interest on bonds for one year after 50% tax.	2.50
6	Total cost to retire bonds at beginning of year 2.	$87.72

words, if the company decides to call the bonds, it must pay one year's extra interest. This must be added to the premium, if any, at which the bonds are sold above 100. For example, if a bond is sold at 102 with a 7% interest coupon, the call price might be 109 for the first year. If a bond is sold below 100, the coupon is added to 100; with a 7% interest coupon, the call price would be 107. The call price may be sweetened by adding one or two additional points.

A pattern which is widely used is to reduce the call price an equal amount each year so that it reaches 100 a few years prior to maturity for a bond with a long maturity. This gives the company an opportunity to anticipate the maturity a few years in advance without a penalty. It would seem to make more sense to have it decrease on the same basis as for the sinking fund redemption, which is on a constant yield basis. Some institutional investors purchasing bonds at private sale may demand this, but the custom is not that way on public issues. In analyzing call prices, whatever pattern is used, a company should figure the yield at each call price for the term remaining to maturity.

Non-Refundable Provision

In the 1940's, interest rates were very low. As a result, companies called their existing debt, which had previously been issued with high interest rates, and refunded it with new low interest rate issues. This was very disturbing to the large institutional investors having a substantial part of their funds invested in such issues. It meant a sizeable reduction in their income. Having been badly stung by this process once, they were in no mood to have it repeated again when they purchased new issues during the period of rising interest rates starting in the 1950's. In order to protect themselves as funds for investment became scarce and they were better able to impose terms more favorable to them, they insisted that a non-refundable provision be tacked on to the regular call feature. It prevented refunding the bonds for five years, for ten years or even for the life of the issue, with another debt issue at a lower yield than that at which the bonds were originally sold. Thus, they blocked the company's option to take their investment away from them for a certain number of years if interest rates should decrease in the near future.

This was viewed as a rather highhanded approach by some borrowing corporations. They felt that it was being unfair. This feeling does not seem to be justified. If the money situation is such that investors can obtain a non-refundable provision as part of their price, they should be free to do so; it is quite understandable why they would try.

It may be noted that some regulatory authorities with jurisdiction over some companies are opposed to non-refundable provisions as a matter of policy. In some instances, if a company does not include such a feature, a somewhat higher original call provision may be used to sweeten up an issue in a period of tight money by having the call price higher than the interest coupon.

A non-refundable provision should be distinguished from a non-call. The former is only for the purpose of preventing redemption to save interest through issuing another bond at a lower interest rate. It does permit redemption at regular call prices if the issue must be eliminated in connection with a merger, consolidation, etc. This preserves flexibility for a company. A complete non-call will prevent redemption for any purpose and should be avoided.

One company which had a large financing program sold an issue of common and used the proceeds to call a senior security which had a provision restricting it from being refunded with the proceeds from another senior issue having a lower rate. The investors holding the senior issue yelled foul play, contending that very shortly the company would sell more senior securities, thus bringing the debt ratio up to the previous level and that the company could not contend that the true purpose of the common issue was for refunding purposes. This case is being litigated and undoubtedly will result in tighter wording of non-refundable provisions.

Non-Refundable for Five vs. Ten Years

Depending on the market situation, when a company sells a bond or preferred stock, it may have the choice of accepting a ten-year non-refundable provision in a private sale, or paying a higher interest or dividend rate and obtaining a five-year non-refundable provision in a public offering.

By accepting the ten-year non-refundable provision, the company may obtain a lower interest or dividend rate, but it loses the possible opportunity to refund the issue at the end of five years if rates decrease.

In making a decision as to which method to choose, the company has to compare the extra cost of the five-year non-refundable with the possible savings which the company might achieve by refunding the issue at the end of five years if rates decrease.

In order to make a judgment, it is necessary to calculate how far rates would have to decrease at the end of five years in order to just absorb the higher rate that has to be paid for the five-year non-refundable provision.

The calculations have to take into consideration the financing costs which are different for a public and a private financing. And calculations have to be made after giving effect to any item which is deductible for tax purposes, which is particularly important in the case of a bond.

To show how to make the calculations, we will use a non-sinking fund preferred stock.

We will use the figures as a basis for our calculations as shown in Exhibit 4-4.

We will give our conclusions before we give you proof. We will show that for there to be no difference between the alternatives in Exhibit 4-5, the company would have to be able to refund the five-year non-refundable preferred, which was issued with a yield of 9.00% to investors, with a similar preferred stock at a yield to investors of 6.97% as follows:

Dividend rate	$ 7.06
Price to investor	101.30
Underwriters' commission	1.00
Financing expense	0.30
Price to company	100.00
Yield to investors	6.97%
Cost to company	7.06%

Thus, rates for such a preferred stock would have to decrease more than 2.03% in order for there to be an advantage for the five-year non-refundable if the company had to pay a 0.44% higher yield for the five-year non-refundable as compared with the ten-year non-refundable. The calculations to prove this conclusion are shown in Exhibit 4-5. We have assumed call prices for the two issues as shown in Exhibit 4-4. They are 106 at the end of five years for the five-year non-refundable, and 105.22 at the end of ten years for the ten-year non-refundable. These call premiums are not deductible for tax purposes.

In the calculations, we have assumed that the market holds level so that both issues can be refunded at the 6.97% rate to investors at the end of their respective non-refundable periods.

Thus, the final decision as to whether the company should sell the five- rather than the ten-year non-refundable depends on whether management feels that the yield which investors will pay for the preferred stock will decrease below 6.97% at the end of five years. The exhibit shows how the calculations must be made in order to give management the basis on which it can make a judgment.

The exhibit does not include all the facts that might occur. The results will depend on the course of rates five and ten years ahead. For example, if rates decreased from the end of the fifth year up to the tenth year, but increased thereafter so that no refunding could be done at the end of the tenth year, the five-year refunding provision would be worth substantially more. And this possibility has to carry weight in favor of the public offering.

The same type of calculations should be made for bonds, but the tax treatment of various items are different and yields will have to be based on yields to maturity. The interest, call premium, underwriters fee and financing expense are deductible for tax purposes and would therefore be carried at their net after tax cost.

Conditional Call

One more point should be added in connection with the call feature. The company must issue a notice of call, usually not more than 45 nor less than 30 days prior to the day on which the bonds are to be redeemed. If a refunding is being done, the company may have to raise the necessary money before it issues the call, as it might be in default if it fails to get the money after the call has been issued. This results in payment of interest on both issues during the notice period. This may

Exhibit 4-4

ASSUMED FIGURES USED IN EXHIBIT 4-5 TO ILLUSTRATE
A COMPARISON OF COSTS OF A FIVE-YEAR VS. A TEN-YEAR
NON-REFUNDABLE PROVISION FOR A PREFERRED STOCK

	Public Sale 5-Year Non-Refundable	Private Sale 10-Year Non-Refundable
Dividend rate	$ 9.12	$ 8.68
Price to investor	101.30	100.35
Underwriter's fee or commission	1.00	0.30
Financing expenses	0.30	0.05
Price to company	100.00	100.00
Yield to investors	9.00%	8.65%
Cost to company	9.12%	8.68%
Call price at end of 5 years	106.00	
" " " " " 10 "		105.22

Exhibit 4-5

CALCULATION OF BREAKEVEN POINT FOR A FIVE-YEAR VS. TEN-YEAR
NON-REFUNDABLE PROVISION

Extent to Which Rates Must Fall at the End of Five Years
to Absorb a 0.44% Higher Rate for the Five-Year Non-Refundable

Year	5-Year Non-Refundable Public Offering. Cost to Company	10-Year Non-Refundable Private Sale. Cost to Company	Advantage of Public Offering	Column III Discounted with 12% Over-All Cost-of-Capital Rate
1	9.12%	8.68%	–0.44	– .3929
2	"	"	"	– .3508
3	"	"	"	– .3132
4	"	"	"	– .2796
5	"	"	"	– .2497
Call price	6.00	0.00	–6.00	–3.405
6 New issue	7.06	8.68	+1.62	.8207
7	"	"	"	.7328
8	"	"	"	.6543
9	"	"	"	.5842
10	"	"	"	.5216
Call price		105.22	+5.22	1.681
				0.000

be eliminated by having the call provision include a conditional call feature, the call to be effective only if the company is able to raise the money. Thus, the company does not take the risk of default, if it waits to raise the money, until after issuing the notice, and then fails to do so.

Call Prices and Pricing of New Debt Issues

Call prices came into play in pricing new debt issues. The call premium at the time an issue is sold is the difference between the call price and the price at which the issue is sold; it is the penalty the company pays in order to extinguish the issue in relation to what the investors paid. If a bond is sold at 100 and the regular call price is 108, the call premium is 8 points. If the same bond is sold for 98, the call premium is 10 points.

To show the significance of the call prices and pricing a new issue, we will use as an example, a 25-year bond with an 8% interest coupon which is sold at 97.99 to yield 8.19% to maturity. The sinking fund call will be 100 since the sinking fund call is the price at which the bond is sold, but never below 100. The regular call price might be 108 which is 100 plus the 8% interest coupon.

The call premiums for the new bond offering would be as follows:

Sinking fund call premium = Call price 100 - Offering price 97.99 = 2.01 points.
Regular call premium = Call price 108 - Offering price 97.99 = 10.01 points.

The effect of the offering price on the cost to call is illustrated in Exhibit 4-6. In both parts the bond has a maturity of 25 years. In Part I, the bond is offered with an 8% coupon at a price of 97.99 to yield 8.19%. Since the bond is sold at a discount, the sinking fund call price would be 100, and the regular call price for the first year would be 108, based on adding the interest coupon of 8% to 100. In relation to the offering price of 97.99, the premium for the sinking fund call price would be 2.05% for the first year, and the premium for the regular call price would be 10.22%.

In Part II, the bond is offered at a price of 100.63 with an 8 1/4% coupon to provide the same yield of 8.19% as the bond in Part I. Since the bond is sold at a premium, the sinking fund call price for the first year would be the offering price of 100.63, and the regular call price for the first year would be 108.88, based on adding the interest coupon of 8 1/4% to the offering price of 100.63. In relation to the offering price of 100.63, the premium in the first year for the sinking fund call price would be 0.00%, and for the first year the premium for the regular call price would be 8.25 points or 8.2% of the offering price.

Because of the effect on the call premiums, a new bond issue should be sold at 100 or a small premium rather than at a discount. Sometimes new bond issues are priced at a slight discount in order to sweeten up the issue for investors in terms of better call premiums. If a company does sell a bond at a discount, it should be aware of the adverse effect on the call premium.

The factors that prevent a company from selling a bond with the same yield to maturity but with a high interest coupon and at a high price over 100 are: 1. The high coupon looks bad on the balance sheet. 2. When bonds are called, the call price has to be written off out of earnings. And a high coupon results in a high call price because the coupon is generally added to the offering price to get the regular call price.

Protective Provisions

Now we turn to protective provisions. In broad terms, the means of protection, as viewed by the investor, may take one of the following forms or maybe a combination thereof:

1. *A lien in one way or another on a readily salable asset which can be used for obtaining payment, if the company fails to pay.* A lien on automobiles would be in this category. They are readily marketable at a price. A margin of protection must be maintained to take care

Exhibit 4-6

EFFECT OF OFFERING PRICE OF A BOND ON THE COST TO CALL

$10,000,000 Issue–25-Year Maturity

PART I

BOND SOLD BELOW 100

	Sinking Fund Call	Regular Call
Coupon	8%	8%
Offering price to public	97.99	97.99
Yield to maturity at offering price	8.19%	8.19%
Call price	100.00	108.00 1st yr.
Cost to call as a percent of offering price	2.05%	10.22%
Total amount of issue at offering price	$10,000,000	$10,000,000
Number of $100 units sold	102,051	102,051
Total cost to call	10,205,100	11,021,508
Call premium	$ 205,100	$ 1,021,508

PART II

BOND SOLD ABOVE 100

	Sinking Fund Call	Regular Call
Coupon	8 1/4%	8 1/4%
Offering price to public	100.63	100.63
Yield to maturity at offering price to public	8.19%	8.19%
Call price	100.63 1st yr.	108.82 1st yr.
Cost to call as a percent of offering price	0.00%	8.2%
Total amount of issue at offering price	$10,000,000	$10,000,000
Number of $100 units sold	99,374	99,374
Total cost to call	$10,000,000	$10,819,841
Call premium	0.00	819,841

of the danger of a price decline if sale is necessary.

2. *A lien in one way or another on an asset which may not be readily salable, but which can be taken away from the borrowing company and which is so important to its operations that the company will have to continue payment in order to operate.* A railroad equipment trust certificate with a lien on railroad cars is in this category. During adverse conditions, there might not be a market for the railroad cards, but the railroad cannot operate without them and even might pay this obligation before payment of debt which has a mortgage on the roadbed. The company must have a sufficient equity in the property to assure that there will be an incentive to pay the charges on the senior obligation under adverse conditions.
3. *A lien on an asset which is an integral part of the assets of a company and could not be removed, and which is primarily of value as used by the company itself.* A lien on such property is principally of value to the investor through the assurance that it gives of a senior position over other debt issues. This type of asset is typified by the

roadbed of a railroad or the plant of a specialized manufacturing company.

4. *A lien in one way or another on a flow of income to the company from some assured source, with a sufficient margin to cover the risk of decline in the flow.*
5. *A general obligation of the company with no specific lien, but with provisions protecting the position of the security by preventing assets and earnings from being pledged to other debt.* This is what is known as a negative pledge covenant. Also the issue will be protected against the issuance of an excessive additional amount of debt with an equal position.

From the above, it can be seen that the two extremes in protective provisions are: reliance solely on lien vs. reliance on a general obligation with no lien.

Where reliance is solely on a lien, it provides a means of repayment if there is a default, or provides inducement for the company to continue payment. A lien also provides protection of senior position.

At the other extreme, with a general obligation, the investor will have to require provisions which will protect his position in relation to other securities and assets, and also keep the company from becoming too weak financially. Even where there is a lien these provisions also will probably be included.

The nature of the company and its assets may determine the type of obligation that can be used. In some instances a lien is just not workable.

Where a lien can be used, it may be said that there are two schools of thought regarding how the investor may achieve protection. One emphasizes the importance of a mortgage or lien position, although it alone may not assure repayment; the other school believes in provisions for the maintenance of the financial health of the enterprise. In the opinion of one large institutional investor, the added provisions in mortgage bonds since 1940 have been more in the direction of the second school; that is, to protect the credit of the company in addition to having a lien. And this seems more in line with common sense. The plant of many corporations, unless it is of a very general nature, only has real value as it is used to create earnings by the owning company. If the earnings cannot be maintained, the bondholder does not obtain much advantage through foreclosure and possession or sale. Furthermore, the long procedure necessary to realize on the property is most painful. Therefore, the indenture in a mortgage bond today will look toward keeping the debt within reasonable limits so that even poor earnings will make service possible, and with provisions which will tend to keep the credit strong. Such provisions as coverage requirements and maintenance of working capital are in line with this idea. In fact, even some of the provisions which are strictly of a mortgage nature may be evaluated as to how they may force the company to maintain a sound credit. This, of course, does not mean that unsecured bondholders will be disinterested in maintenance of the property in good condition. That is an essential part of protection of assets even if not mortgaged.

From the company's point of view, the type of protection provided should be analyzed in terms of its possible effect on the interest rate the company will have to pay, on flexibility of financing and on other factors previously mentioned. The company should consider what exceptions may be made to the property mortgaged to facilitate practical operations of the company.

The relationship of a security to the earnings or assets to which the holder looks for protection may be direct or through a lease or dummy corporation. No matter what the veil, the investor is interested in the substance. The more indirect his position, the higher may be the interest rate, because each additional contract may add some risk. There is always the possibility that some flaw may develop in a contract and be challenged if there is financial failure.

The senior security holder will wish to assure that a margin of protection is maintained in either specific earnings or assets or in all earnings and assets. Therefore, he will wish to be certain that there is no dissipation in whatever he relies upon for the protection, and many of the provisions of a security will be for the purpose of preventing such dissipation.

At this point, you may wish to visualize how there may be a dissipation of earnings and assets. This can arise only through transactions ultimately affecting the balance sheet or income statement. The terms of a bond may not be expressed this way, but the brief outlines shown in Exhibit 4-7, based on the effect on the financial statements, may help you understand why so many contingencies have to be guarded against.

The investor will have to weigh the need to guard against all of these possibilities. The company should recognize such a need, but it should be careful that the terms will permit it freedom of action within the limits required to protect the investor.

Since all possible contingencies cannot be seen, a provision is included permitting modification of the terms. Usually, for a bond, the consent of the holders of 66 2/3% of the bonds must be obtained for the modification of any important provision. This does not apply to the interest rate and maturity, which, in respect of any bond, cannot be changed without consent of the holder of such a bond.

VARIETIES OF DEBT

The greatest variety in type of securities occurs among debt issues. This is because there are many means used to protect the investor as regards assets and earnings, and to establish the position of the debt in relation to existing and potential securities in the capital structure. For example, a mortgage gives the holder a lien on certain property; debentures and notes have no lien, but are a general obligation; equipment trust certificates have a lien on a special type of asset; lease financing gives title to the investor; etc. We will cover briefly the principal types of debt issues in broad terms, proceeding from secured to unsecured.

Mortgage Financing for Real Estate

The most basic type of secured debt financing is that of a real estate mortgage. In effect, it is similar to a mortgage loan on a residence. For large corporations, it is limited to situations in which money can be raised from a few large institutional investors, since it is not suitable for a public offering. Only two instruments are required—that describing the borrowings and terms, and the mortgage itself. There is no indenture to be administered by a trustee. Types of companies which institutional investors may be willing to finance with this medium are stores, hotels, theatres, garages, warehouses, office buildings, factories, etc. The property on which the mortgage is made has a market value, affording protection to the lending institution through the possibility of sale if there is a default. In order to afford a margin of protection, the investor will wish to restrict the amount of the financing to a certain percentage of the value of the property. Most fiduciaries are permitted by law to lend only up to 66 2/3% (75% for some institutions) of the appraised value. The mortgage will apply to a specific piece of real estate. As far as that property is concerned, it will be closed-end; that is, limited in amount to the original issue. Since it is the property to which the lenders look for security, there will be no general restrictions on the company's over-all financial policies. There will be ample provisions, of course, covering maintenance of the specific property in good condition, and so forth, and the repayment schedule will assure a continuing margin of value above the amount of the mortgage. The advantages and disadvantages are summarized in Exhibit 4-8.

Mortgage Bonds

Mortgage bonds are different in form from a real estate type of mortgage in that the mortgage on the property is held by a trustee for the benefit of bondholders. The mortgage generally will cover the entire properties of a

Exhibit 4-7

DISSIPATION OF PROTECTION FOR SENIOR SECURITIES

PART I

INCOME STATEMENT

Above the line (expense items which are before income available for payments to investors):

Excessive salaries or other expenses which sap earnings. This also may occur when the management owns a sales or purchasing company and thus exacts tribute from the company, which it is supposed to be running for the stockholders—highly unethical.

Incurrence of fixed payments, such as lease rentals or other payments akin to debt.

Overstatement of earnings due to low depreciation or maintenance.

Below the line:

Excessive dividend payments.

PART II

BALANCE SHEET

Assets

Transfer outside the company in one way or another such as through sale, lease, etc., so that the position of a security may be adversely affected.

Transfer to a subsidiary without adequate compensation, or so that the position of a security is hurt.

Acquisition of an inferior asset for which a good asset is given up, or an excessive obligation is incurred.

Purchase of assets at an excessive price. This may occur when management abuses its trust by purchase of an asset and then resells it to the corporation at a profit.

Pledge to another security.

Use for payment or repurchase of another junior security of the company.

Decrease in working capital below a reasonable level, necessary to carry on operations.

Inadequate insurance.

Failure to maintain in condition.

Failure to pay taxes and assessments.

Failure to defend title to property.

Excessive law suits not properly defended.

Loss of special franchises or patents.

Loss of corporate entity.

Liabilities

Incurrence of other obligations senior to or with an equal lien, through sale of securities, or which arise in a merger, consolidation or acquisition.

Reduction of equity protection by paying dividends out of past accumulated earned surplus, or repurchase of junior securities out of company funds.

Sale of equity to insiders at unreasonably low price.

Exhibit 4-8

MORTGAGE FINANCING FOR REAL ESTATE

Advantages	*Disadvantages*
1. The expense of a trustee is eliminated.	1. The amount of money that can be raised will be limited to a percentage of the appraised value of the property.
2. It has the inherent advantages of a private sale, such as speed of arrangement, reduction of financing expense, possible change in terms through negotiations with a few investors.	2. As far as the specific property is concerned, it may not be available for use in securing other debt obligations.
3. There may be no terms restricting the company's general financial policies.	3. It is limited to situations in which institutional investors are interested in making such loans and the transaction can be handled as a private sale and not a public offering.
4. It does not have an after-acquired clause attaching to other separate projects of a company.	4. It has the inherent disadvantages of a private sale. For example, the reduction in debt must be made at the sinking fund call price; the possibility of purchase in open market at a discount is nonexistent. The investor is in a strong bargaining position and may require a higher interest rate than might be obtained with some other form of debt financing. For further information on private sale of securities see Chapter 8.

company rather than just a specific building, but it need not do so. There is an indenture which describes the terms of the bonds and which is administered by the trustee. This form of secured financing permits more investors to be included and permits the possibility of a public offering. Concerning the theory of protection for investors, we now run into the two schools of thought as to how the protection may be achieved—through limitation of indebtedness to a certain percentage of the property, or primarily through additional terms regarding earnings covenants, etc. As has been previously indicated, today the two schools are intermingled.

The form of the mortgage will depend on the state or states in which the property is located, since the state laws will govern.

If a company has widespread properties which are changing rapidly, a mortgage may be cumbersome to handle, because the lien must be recorded in all the counties in which the properties are located. This is a routine matter, but it can run into real money when the property is located in many counties.

Some companies have property which just does not lend itself to being mortgaged; others own properties suitable for this form of financing. Typical of the latter are the electric utilities with very large tangible assets which are expanded in a regular manner; most of them use mortgage bonds as their principal form of debt financing. In the case of a utility, the mortgage primarily provides a means for assuring seniority of claim. Such property could not be sold to provide cash for payment if there was a default.

It is interesting to note in the utility field that the subsidiaries of American Telephone and Telegraph Company have not used mortgage bonds.

In the past, the railroads relied heavily on mortgage bonds when they were built. Many of these mortgages were closed-end divisional liens, and they made almost an insoluble mess of debt issues. In reorganization and subsequent refinancing, the divisional liens were eliminated wherever possible and turned into a general mortgage.

In the industrial field, mortgage bonds are used by some companies which have large fixed assets.

Why should a company use a mortgage bond if it is so cumbersome? There may be three reasons:

1) In certain situations, investors may feel that they need the added protection and will not do the financing any other way.
2) A mortgage bond may add to the security for the investors, and as a result this may mean a lower rate of interest. In some special situations a mortgage bond may have some influence on the bond rating, as compared with a debenture with weak terms.
3) It may give a company more freedom to put out another junior form of debt, such as a debenture.

Since the investor has an underlying position as a result of the mortgage, the provisions limiting junior debt may be less strict. If there were no mortgage bonds, and only debentures and a junior debt issue were desired, it might be necessary to issue a subordinated debenture with quite an inferior credit position.

If you look at a textbook on finance, you may find many pages devoted to a long list of different types of mortgage bonds, each one with a high-sounding name and a detailed description of what it represents. It may look like a great maze, but if you study them, it should be quickly apparent that they are just a variation of a general mortgage bond. Some of the types are as follows:

Purchase Money Mortgage—to provide funds for an acquisition and secured by a mortgage on that property.

General and Refunding—to provide funds to pay off a maturing issue or refund an existing issue and also provide funds for other purposes.

Divisional Bonds—secured by a lien on a part of a company's property, most prevalent in railroads.

Terminal Bonds—specifically a mortgage on the terminal of a railroad owned by a separate company which receives its income from the roads using the terminal.

Mortgage and Collateral Trust Bonds—secured by property plus securities as additional collateral, and called by the latter term when only securities are involved, such as in the case of a holding company. Except in special situations, they are little used today. A debenture bond can generally serve as well, with adequate protective provisions. The only added feature which the collateral trust bond affords is the hypothecation of the collateral with a trustee, in order to add to the safety factor and provide for its sale if there is a default. Under some circumstances, this form of security may be a necessity, or it may produce a lower rate of interest.

Examples of all the types of secured bonds mentioned above and many others are in existence today, but most were issued years ago. At present, new issues of mortgage bonds tend to have a first or general open mortgage on all the property of a company, although there are exceptions. Mergers and consolidations may complicate the picture. There may be a second mortgage. However, the more complicated the debt structure, the less flexibility is available in future financing. Unless there is a very special situation justifying a policy of complexity or unless it is a matter of dire necessity, it should be avoided.

A mortgage bond as designed today will generally be open-end. This permits the issuance of additional bonds up to a certain percentage of new property additions, provided certain tests as to the company's financial strength are met. These will be discussed later. A closed-end mortgage, which will permit no new bonds with a similar lien to be issued, may place a company in a financial bind. It means that any new debt associated with the same asset will have to be in a junior position.

A limited open-end mortgage, wherein new bonds can be issued up to a certain stipulated amount, may turn out to be disadvantageous if the company grows at a greater rate than expected. If a company has a good credit standing, it should have no trouble keeping a mortgage open-end. Of course, a company with poor credit or a new venture may have to accept a closed mortgage.

A mortgage will generally include an after-acquired property clause, so that subsequent additions come under the mortgage. This is not objectionable, provided new bonds can be issued up to a certain percentage of new property so that as additions are made, there will be property available to use as a basis for new bonds.

In some instances, when a new mortgage bond is first issued, further bonds are limited to a portion of the cost only of subsequent property additions. This means that if the original issue is small in relation to original amount of property, the ability to issue bonds

Exhibit 4-9

OUTLINE OF CERTAIN PROVISIONS
IN MORTGAGE BOND INDENTURE

I. To Create, Maintain, Protect and Account for the Trust Estate.
   A. Created by deed of trust which conveys title to all property to the Trustee for the protection of bondholders.
   B. Lien will extend to all "after-acquired" property, which must be subjected specifically, perhaps by supplemental indenture or additional recordings or both.
   C. Property may be released only upon substitution of like property or the deposit with Trustee of cash equal to fair value, upon application, unless property is no longer used or useful and certificate can state: no detriment to bondholders to abandon.
   D. Property no longer used or useful must promptly be classified as retired.
   E. Property must be maintained in first-class working order and condition; expense related to standards of expenditure for maintenance and performance, policed by right of bondholder to inspect and enforce correction of any deficiencies found.
   F. Property must be adequately insured with proceeds payable to Trustee, subject to withdrawal to reimburse company for restoration or rebuilding.

II. To Preserve the Lien Position of the Bondholder.
   A. Property descriptions must be adequate to establish the lien, and no equal or prior liens may exist or be created to secure any debt except that additional bonds may be issued under the Indenture.
   B. No defects may exist in title; all attacks upon realty title or franchises must be defended.
   C. Additional property may be acquired subject either to no liens at all, or to only very limited prior liens which must be circumscribed and often quickly extinguished.
      1. Leases existing at date of an acquisition may be treated as a disallowed encumbrance of title.
      2. See also Sales, Consolidations and Mergers in item IV on next page.
   D. Taxes must be paid when due unless contested in good faith, and workmen's and materialmen's liens equally must not be permitted to arise.
   E. Except within limits, no subsidiary may issue debt or equity securities to anyone other than the company.

III. To Maintain the Financial Integrity of the Enterprise.
   A. Company must maintain corporate existence and must comply with requirements of regulatory authorities, if any.
   B. Additional bonds may be issued only upon the basis provided in the Indenture, which will specify, at least:
      1. Property base shall be net additions to the Trust Estate; i.e., gross additions less retirements to the date of application.
      2. Minimum acceptable earnings for a period recently past as related to the requirements of the total debt including that proposed to be issued.
   C. Company shall prevent defaults under prior liens and in respect of all other indebtedness.
   D. Accounts must be maintained in accordance with sound accounting practice.

Exhibit 4-9 (Cont'd.)

E. Equity cannot be reduced voluntarily; all distributions thereon must be made out of earnings accumulated after a date proximate to the date of the bonds, computed after adequate reservation for depreciation or after deducting depreciation and maintenance expense in amounts not less than a fixed standard.

F. Investments in, or advances to other companies may be prohibited or, if allowed, must be restricted:

1. Subsidiaries–limited in amount. Securities must be pledged with Trustee (refer also to II, E). No third party interest.
2. Controlled companies–more limited in amount than subsidiaries, except to the extent that earnings otherwise available for dividends may be invested, pledge may be required.
3. Earnings computations for dividends of parent may take account of dividends received only to the extent earned, and must take account of losses incurred.

IV. To Provide for Sales, Consolidations and Mergers.

A. Lien must be protected as first lien on property subject to mortgage immediately prior to transaction. Liens securing debts of other company may not be extended to mortgage property.

B. Surviving company must, by supplemental indenture, assume all obligations and restrictions of the Indenture.

in the future will be held down by this initial freeze. Whether a company can avoid such a freeze will again depend on its credit standing.

An outline of certain provisions that may appear in a mortgage bond indenture are shown in Exhibit 4-9:

We will now discuss the principal provisions which may be included to protect the credit standing of a mortgage bond:

1. *The aggregate amount which may be issued under the indenture.* This ranges from the closed-end issue, to the completely open-end, with some specified aggregate in the intermediate position. If the other provisions requiring adequate earnings, etc., are sufficiently tight to protect the credit position for the investor, a company should not need to submit to severe limitation as to aggregate amount.
2. *Amount of new bonds in relation to new property additions.* Bonds may be allowed to be issued up to a certain percent of net property additions, depending on the nature of the company. Net property must take into account retirement, replacements and depreciation. Provision may be made for the issuance of bonds against the deposit of cash with the Trustee, which can be drawn down as sufficient property constructed to comply with the percentage of net property additions. This makes it possible for a company to sell bonds in contemplation of property additions.
3. *Amount of equal and prior lien debt, including proposed financing, limited to a percentage of some balance sheet item or items.* Examples can be found of many different ways to express this relationship. For example, in some instances total assets have been used as the denominator. Another and perhaps the most logical approach is to express the relationship to the amount of equity, both common and preferred. It is the equity which provides protection for the debt.

   It might be expressed by saying that equity had to be 200% of equal or prior liens, which would mean that, if there were no junior debt, the debt ratio to total capitalization would be limited to 33 1/3%. For legal reasons, this relationship may be found expressed in many ways. In order to determine its significance from the point of view of financial policy, it should be analyzed in terms of capital structure ratios.

   In order to prevent the debt in question from being pushed out on the limb, there almost certainly will be a provision limiting the aggregate amount of prior lien debt which may be incurred or guaranteed. Merger, consolidation or sale of properties could have an effect on the prior position of a security, and provision may place some limitation on such actions.

4. *Interest on equal and prior lien debt, including the proposed financing, covered a certain number of times by earnings in a recent period.* This provision may be expressed in many different ways. It undoubtedly will provide for the inclusion of lease payments along with the interest charges. It is a most important provision from the company's point of view. Its possible limitation of further debt issues should be analyzed in terms of poor earnings, to insure maintaining leeway for borrowing reserve.

   If a company's debt requires heavy sinking funds because of wasting assets or for some other reason, there may be an additional provision as regards coverage of debt service—that is, interest and sinking fund payments—by cash generated through earnings available for that purpose. This should be tested in a similar way as coverage of interest charges in order to provide borrowing reserve.

5. There may be a covenant that *net working capital or current ratio must be maintained at a certain level.* For example, current assets might be required to be maintained at two or two and a half times current liabilities; or net working capital—that is, current assets less current liabilities—may be required to be maintained at a certain dollar level.

   You may feel that such a provision might hinder rather than help a company if it got in a financial bind, because it could not use its current assets for an emergency. The purpose is threefold: to prevent a company from letting its working capital get so low that its operations will be hurt; to prevent a company from relying on current borrowings, on a permanent basis, which are, in effect, long-term obligations and to prevent a company from being just a shell if it runs into trouble so that there is nothing left to rehabilitate.

6. *Restriction on dividend payments.* This provision will take the form of a freeze of either all or some of past accumulated earned surplus. It will include a restriction on the use of funds for the repurchase of a company's stock so that the equity protection will not be decreased.

The importance and extent of each of these six provisions will depend on the nature of the company. They are the principal ones which may restrict a company's flexibility and should be carefully tested in order to appreciate their effect under adverse conditions, having in mind the importance of keeping debt within satisfactory limits so that "borrowing reserve" will still be available.

The advantages and disadvantages of mortgage bonds in general are shown in Exhibit 4-10.

Examples of a few of the provisions contained in the indenture of one actual mortgage bond are shown in Exhibit 4-11. They are so summarized for easy reading, but they may not represent the true legal import as they apply to the actual issue. They are merely presented to give an idea of their scope. This is an example of a new series of bonds being issued under an old instrument which has relatively liberal provisions regarding the issuance of additional debt. Because of the company's reputation, it could sell bonds publicly without tightening the indenture.

Equipment Trust Certificates

Equipment obligations are, in effect, a chattel mortgage on specific units of equipment. If a company is dependent on the equipment for its operation, such as a railroad is on freight cars and motive power, or an airline is on planes, the obligation places the lender in a senior position. Assuming the company could not operate without certain equipment, it could not, as a practical matter, permit a default on obligations secured by such equipment, since loss of the equipment to the company's operations would further aggravate the situation. Moreover, in connection with equipment trust certificates publicly sold, the company usually makes an initial payment of approximately 20% towards the cost of the equipment. Naturally, therefore,

Exhibit 4-10

MORTGAGE BONDS	
Advantages	*Disadvantages*
1. As contrasted with a real estate type of mortgage financing, which must be sold privately, mortgage bonds make possible a public offering of securities. This may result in some advantages. 2. May result in a lower rate of interest. 3. May be the only basis on which investors will buy a particular company's debt securities. 4. There may be less restrictive provisions in issuance of a junior form of debt such as a debenture. This may make possible a second debt issue such as a debenture without designating it as a subordinated debenture, which would be necessary if the senior form of debt was a debenture. 5. It may make possible the sale of the issue to certain institutional investors which are limited by law to investing in issues secured by a mortgage under certain circumstances.	1. Handling of assets on which mortgage applies may be cumbersome. Recording the mortgage in each county where property is located requires added expense. 2. The multiplicity of security instruments involves some expense. 3. May add to the difficulty of the merger, consolidation or sale, etc. There may be a problem of working out a surviving mortgage when two companies, each with mortgage debt, are merged.

the user has an economic incentive to continue payments to protect this equity. Equipment trust obligations are repayable on a serial basis generally at a faster rate than the equipment is depreciated; so there will be satisfactory equity position throughout the life of the loan.

It is essential that the lien on the equipment be free from all other liens. If a company has no other mortgage debt outstanding, there is no problem. Title to the equipment is, as a rule, transferred to a trustee or agent to secure equipment certificates. The certificates are then sold in the market to provide the user with funds.

If a company has a mortgage bond outstanding with an after-acquired property clause attaching to new purchases of property, then one of two methods must be used in order to keep the title to the equipment separate:

1. The property is sold to the user by the manufacturer on a conditional sales basis, with or without an initial down payment. Title is retained by the manufacturer, who passes it on to an agent. The agent acts in behalf of the lenders who supply funds for paying the manufacturer. The agent receives serial payments from the user to provide funds to cover the payments on the certificates. At times lending institutions act as their own agents. Upon final payment, title passes to the user. This is known as the Conditional Sale Agreement method, and most often the financing is for the full cost of the equipment and is privately arranged.
2. Title to the equipment is passed to a trustee by the manufacturer. The equipment is leased to the user, with the lease payments sufficient to take care of the initial down payment, serial payments, interest, etc. Certificates issued by the trustee are sold in the market through investment bankers to provide the funds to pay the manufacturer. Upon final payment, title passes to the user. This may be referred to as the Philadelphia plan and is the one most frequently used today.

Under each of the plans, the user agrees: to keep the equipment in proper condition,

Exhibit 4-11

CERTAIN PROVISIONS CONTAINED IN MORTGAGE BOND INDENTURE

	Industrial company—$75,000,000. Issue price 99 5/8, coupon 8 7/8%, maturity 25 years. Bond rating: Moody's A, Standard AA.
Form	Fully registered in denominations of $1,000 and multiples thereof.
Lien	One of a series of bonds issued under a mortgage dated in 1928 which represents a general mortgage on the company's properties.
Redeemable	In amounts of not less than $2,000,000, on 30 days' notice at 108.50 for the first year and decreasing thereafter to 100 five years prior to maturity. Non-refundable for 10 years at a lower interest rate.
Sinking Fund	Starting after 6 years at equal annual amounts, so as to retire the entire issue by maturity. The company, at its option, can double the sinking fund payments in any one year, but if this option is not exercised in any year, it is not carried forward.
Limitations on Additional Debt	Additional bonds may be issued up to 75% of capital expenditures, provided consolidated earnings available for interest charges, on an average for the last three years, are equal to 1 1/2 times interest charges on funded debt.
Restriction on Dividends	The company can pay common dividends out of earned surplus accumulated for the last 16 years, plus $50,000,000 of earned surplus accumulated prior thereto, after deducting dividends paid on the preferred stock.

insure it, pay taxes, pay for any claims which may arise as a result of its use, provide necessary evidences of the trustee's ownership, etc. This type of financing, as it exists today, is made possible by provisions in laws affecting the companies which rely on it, such as the Interstate Commerce Commission Act for railroads and bus companies, the Admiralty Act for steamship and barge companies, and the Transportation and Airport Act for airlines. If there is a default, these laws give the trustee or holders of equipment obligations the right to enforce their lien on the property and seize it, wherever it is located. This enhances the position of the security holder. The advantages and disadvantages of equipment trust certificates are summarized in Exhibit 4-12.

Lease Financing

Some misconceptions and controversy seem to persist about leasing. And it is difficult to calculate the true cost of a lease.

A lease may take one of two forms:

1. A lease of property or equipment from a lessor.
2. Original ownership of property or equipment and sale to a party, the lessor, who leases it back. This is known as a sale and leaseback.

The lessor is the investor for financing purposes. In some instances, there may be a dummy company to hold the property as a mechanism of financing. A third party may be brought in as the investor by means of an assignment.[5]

Some types of leases only include financing charges which cover principal and interest. They are known as *net leases.* The company using the property has to maintain, insure, pay taxes, be responsible for law suits, etc. Other types of leases may include payments to the lessor for one or more of these or other items; they are known as *gross leases.* It is necessary to weigh the financial and the non-

[5] A owns a piece of land. B, an oil company, wants a service station on the land. B builds the service station and sells it to A for a note from A for the full amount of the building. A now owns the land and the building and has a note outstanding to B.

A leases the land and building to B and pledges part of the lease payments from B to take care of the note. B now finances the building cost by selling A's note to C. C has the credit of A and B behind the note, because A has pledged part of the lease payments from B. When the note is paid off, A owns the building free and clear.

Exhibit 4-12

EQUIPMENT TRUST CERTIFICATES

Advantages	*Disadvantages*
1. May represent the only means of financing available to a company which has a poor credit standing. 2. Because of the strong security position, the interest rate may be lower than could be obtained by other means of financing.	1. The paydown is rapid and new financing is generally required for additional equipment. If a company's credit is strong, it might be less burdensome and expensive to use a more permanent form of financing which will provide a pool of funds to buy equipment.

financial considerations separately, and also to analyze each point under them separately.[6]

The form of the lease does not greatly affect the principles which we will now discuss.

In some instances, a company does not have a choice as to whether or not to lease. With respect to financial policy, we are primarily interested in those leases which may be handled by an alternate method of financing, and we will only consider the financial charges in a lease. When a choice exists, a company should analyze the alternative financing methods and correctly compare their costs and advantages and disadvantages.

Our discussion will proceed as follows:

1. We will explain the nature of leasing with very simple examples.
2. Then with some changes in the examples, we will explain how to analyze the cost of a lease.
3. Finally, we will review the significance of leasing and its advantages and disadvantages.

[6]A partial check list of factors to consider in leasing equipment, as suggested by a representative of a leasing company, is as follows:

1. Lowest possible rates, interest and fees; 2. Advance knowledge of costs and expenses; 3. The right to specify types of equipment meeting your requirements; 4. The right to specify replacement frequency; 5. Delivery of equipment within the area of need; 6. In the case of maintained equipment, full monthly accounting of all charges; 7. Depreciation period acceptable to the Internal Revenue Service; 8. Consultation at no additional charge; 9. Buying and selling at no extra fee; 10. The right to 100% of any profit on trade-in or other disposition; 11. A plan tailored to your needs.

A Simple Example—Lease vs. Ownership and Bond Financing

For explanatory purposes, we will start with as simple a net lease as possible. Your company needs $10 million of equipment which is expected to have a ten-year life. An investor, the lessor, suggests that he provide you the equipment and keep the title, but lease it to you on the following terms:

10-year lease,
$1,490,000 equal annual payments,
All maintenance, insurance and taxes to be borne by you,
At the end of 10 years you have the option to buy the property for $1,500,000, or renew the lease for $120,000 per year for 10 additional years.

Since the building is expected to have a life for only ten years, the lessor will wish to get back his $10 million investment in that period and also interest on the money he has put up. The $1,490,000 annual rental payments are designed to cover repayment of the $10 million and also an interest rate of 8%. The two parts of the lease payments are shown in Exhibit 4-13. The interest payments are larger at the beginning of the period because there is more principal on which to pay interest. This is the typical pattern for the two components of lease payments with equal annual total payments.

Before accepting the proposition, you decide to consider other ways to obtain the equipment. Your credit is good so you could raise the $10 million by the sale of a debenture bond and purchase the equipment. The bond would have the following terms:

8% interest rate,
10-year maturity,
Equal annual sinking fund of $1,000,000 a year to pay off the entire principal by maturity,
Regular call price starting at 108 and gradually reducing to 100 at the end of 10 years.

Exhibit 4-13

LEASE PAYMENTS FOR TEN-YEAR LEASE WITH 8% INTEREST RATE
(000's omitted)

Column	I	II	III
Year	Principal Payments	Interest	Total Lease Payments
1	$ 690	800	1,490
2	745	745	1,490
3	805	685	1,490
4	869	621	1,490
5	939	551	1,490
6	1,014	476	1,490
7	1,095	395	1,490
8	1,183	307	1,490
9	1,277	213	1,490
10	1,379	111	1,490
Total	10,000	4,900	14,900

The payments under the bond deal would be as shown in Exhibit 4-14.

These two propositions are comparable from the point of view of the type of obligation. The company must make fixed payments of both principal and interest for the lease and bond; if it fails to make payments on either, it will be in default.

As we have designed the lease and the bond, they are not exactly comparable on the basis of the timing of principal payments. The sinking fund payments for the bond are equal annually. For this reason the total amount of interest is slightly larger for the lease.

There are other areas of difference:

1. With bond financing and ownership, the company owns the property at the end of ten years. With leasing, the company has to pay $1,500,000 to get the property, or renew the lease for another ten years at $120,000 per year. If the renewal rental is low in relation to other comparable space available when the lease is renewed, the lease then may be an asset. However, whatever the renewal rental charge, it would be in addition to what the company would have had to pay had it done straight debt financing and owned the plant. The property belongs to the lessor at the expiration of the lease.
2. In the lease, the full rental payments are deductible for tax purposes. With bond financing and ownership, interest and depreciation are deductible for tax purposes. Accelerated depreciation results in greater tax deductions in the early years than the lease payments. This is shown in Exhibit 4-15. For illustrative purposes, we have depreciated the property

Exhibit 4-14

BOND PAYMENTS FOR TEN-YEAR 8% BOND WITH EQUAL ANNUAL SINKING FUND TO PAY OFF ENTIRE ISSUE IN TEN YEARS
(000's omitted)

Column	I	II	III
Year	Sinking Fund Payments	Interest	Total Bond Payments
1	$ 1,000	800	1,800
2	1,000	720	1,720
3	1,000	640	1,640
4	1,000	560	1,560
5	1,000	480	1,480
6	1,000	400	1,400
7	1,000	320	1,320
8	1,000	240	1,240
9	1,000	160	1,160
10	1,000	80	1,080
Total	$10,000	4,400	14,400

Exhibit 4-15

TAX DEDUCTIONS FOR LEASING VS. BOND FINANCING.
BOND SINKING FUND SAME AS LEASE PRINCIPAL PAYMENTS
(000's omitted)

Column	I	II	III	IV	V
		Bond Financing			
Year	Total Lease Payments	Depreciation Double Declining Balance	Interest*	Total	Difference in Tax Deductions Column IV– Column I
1	1,490	2,000	800	2,800	1,310
2	1,490	1,600	745	2,345	855
3	1,490	1,280	685	1,965	475
4	1,490	1,024	621	1,645	155
5	1,490	819	551	1,370	-120
6	1,490	655	476	1,132	-358
7	1,490	655	395	1,050	-440
8	1,490	655	307	963	-527
9	1,490	655	213	868	-622
10	1,490	655	111	766	-724
Total	14,900	10,000	4,900	14,900	0.0

*The interest payments for the bond in this exhibit are different from the interest payments in Exhibit 4-14, because the sinking fund payments in Exhibit 4-14 were equal annually. In Exhibit 4-15, the sinking fund payments for the bond are the same as the principal payments in the lease.

on the basis that there would be no residual value at the end of ten years. Thus, the company will have to pay the same total amount of taxes with either method, but the timing of the payments will be postponed longer with bond financing and ownership. As a consequence, the company will get the use of the deferred tax money for a certain period. We have not included an allowance for an investment tax credit which would reduce taxes in the first year if the equipment were owned and financed with bonds. This would result in a decrease in depreciation for tax purposes in subsequent years. In order to make the two methods strictly comparable in this exhibit, we have set up the sinking fund on the bond the same as the principal payments under the lease.

A correct analysis of all the costs of leasing vs. bond financing and ownership must take into account the factors we have discussed and has to be done on a discounted cash flow basis to give effect to the present value of money. This can be done by hand but is rather laborious, and there are computer programs which can quickly make the calculations.

Since the use of tax benefits is a primary reason for leasing, it is important that the lease be a true lease so that the Internal Revenue Service will approve. For this reason, it is well to get IRS approval before the papers are signed. The IRS is mainly interested in having the party who gets the tax benefits be the real owner of the property. Lawyers have developed numerous tests which determine whether the IRS will consider it to be a true lease. Important in this test is that the option price approximate the fair market price when the option may be exercised. One possible test is that the residual value at the expiration of the lease should be at least 15% of original cost.

If IRS should decide that it is not a true lease, it would become a conditional sale and the lessor could not claim the tax benefits.

Up until now we have been trying to get across the concept that a lease is a form of debt. The tables which we used for illustrative purposes showed an 8% interest rate for both bond financing and leasing. We have said that to get the true cost of a lease, we have to allow for such factors as loss of residual value and the time value of money.

Now we will illustrate how to make a cost analysis of a lease. Instead of an 8% interest rate for the lease, we will use 6%. Generally, the implicit interest rate in a lease is less than the interest rate in a bond. Now, our approach will be to calculate the true cost of a lease by determining the rate at which a company could afford to finance with a bond and come out even, under the following assumptions:

1. The bond rate 8%.
2. Implicit interest rate in lease 6%.
3. Equal debt service payments for principal and interest combined.
4. $10 million original amount of equipment.
5. Residual value $1,500,000.
6. Tax at 50% rate.
7. Overall cost-of-capital rate 12%.
8. No allowance made for any renewal option.

Exhibits 4-16 and 4-17 show the after-tax cash flows of ownership with bond financing and leasing.

Exhibit 4-18 shows the difference in after-tax cash flows discounted at 12%. It shows a net present value benefiting ownership by $137,000. By computer calculation, it can be shown that the company could afford to do bond financing at an interest rate as high as 8.8% and be as well off with ownership as with leasing.

Exhibit 4-19 shows the after-tax present value of the residual value to be $322,000. This is lost under the leasing arrangement.

Therefore, the cost of leasing is $459,000 more than the cost of bond financing. On this basis, it can be calculated that the company could afford to do bond financing at an interest rate as high as 10.6% and be as well off with ownership as leasing. If we allowed for the investment tax credit at the end of year one, the rate would be 14%.

Thus, the way to determine the cost of lease financing is to compare it with a similar debt instrument with a specific interest rate and determine the net after-tax cash benefit or cost. Then determine the rate at which debt financing could be done so that ownership with debt financing would be equivalent to leasing. Allowance must be made for residual value, tax effects and the time value of money. On this basis, the effective rate for a lease is generally more costly than an equivalent debt financing. In addition, a lease is less flexible than ownership and bond financing for the following reasons:

1. The bonds can be called if the company wants to undo the financing. In general, finance leases are non-cancellable. If it wants to eliminate the lease, it will have to bargain with the lessor and be at his mercy as to the premium to be paid.
2. With bond financing, the company has more complete control of the property. It may be freer to alter, improve or sell it. A lease may include other restrictions, such as a provision preventing a company from building branches which might compete with the leased property.
3. If a lease does not provide for the lessor to obtain the property at a price after the expiration of the lease or the renewal period, a company may find itself in an embarrassing position without the property—in the case of real estate, it may have no place to live. Some department stores ran into this trouble in the past.

Exhibit 4-16

OWNERSHIP WITH BOND FINANCING—AFTER-TAX CASH OUTFLOW
(000's omitted)

Column	I	II	III	IV	V	VI	VII
Year	Loan Payment. Principal and Interest	Interest @ 8.0%	Depreciation Double Declining Balance Method	Total Tax Deductions	Tax Rate	Tax Savings	After-Tax Cash Outflow
1	$ 1,490	$ 800	$2,000	$ 2,800	.50	$1,400	$ 90
2	"	744	1,600	2,344	"	1,172	318
3	"	685	1,280	1,965	"	983	507
4	"	620	1,025	1,645	"	822	668
5	"	551	820	1,371	"	686	804
6	"	476	655	1,131	"	565	925
7	"	395	655	1,050	"	525	965
8	"	307	655	962	"	481	1,009
9	"	212	655	867	"	434	1,056
10	"	110	155	265	"	132	1,358
Total	$14,900	$4,900	$9,500	$14,400		$7,200	$7,700

Exhibit 4-17

LEASING-AFTER-TAX CASH OUTFLOW
(000's omitted)

Column	I	II	III	IV
		Tax Savings		
Year	Lease Payments	Tax Rate	Tax Savings	After-Tax Cash Outflow
1	$ 1,360	.50	$ 680	$ 680
2	"	"	"	"
3	"	"	"	"
4	"	"	"	"
5	"	"	"	"
6	"	"	"	"
7	"	"	"	"
8	"	"	"	"
9	"	"	"	"
10	"	"	"	"
Total	$13,600		$6,800	$6,800

Exhibit 4-18

PRESENT VALUE OF DIFFERENTIAL IN AFTER-TAX CASH OUTFLOW—LEASE VS. OWNERSHIP
(000's omitted)

Column	I	II	III	IV	V
Year	After-Tax Cash Outflow Under Lease	After-Tax Cash Outflow Under Ownership	Difference	Present Value Factor @ 12%	Net Present Value of Difference
1	$ 680	$ 90	$ 590	.893	$ 527
2	"	318	362	.797	289
3	"	507	173	.712	123
4	"	668	12	.636	8
5	"	804	(124)	.567	(70)
6	"	925	(245)	.507	(124)
7	"	965	(285)	.452	(129)
8	"	1,009	(329)	.404	(133)
9	"	1,056	(376)	.361	(136)
10	"	1,358	(678)	.322	(218)
Total	$6,800	$7,700	$(900)		$ 137

Exhibit 4-19

LOSS OF RESIDUAL VALUE WITH LEASING
(000's omitted)

Column	I	II	III	IV	V	VI
		Tax on Sale				
Year	Estimated Disposal Value	Selling Price	Tax Basis	Gain on Sale	Tax Rate	Tax on Gain
10	$1,500	$1,500	$500	$1,000	.50	$500

Column	VII	VIII	IX
	After-Tax Proceeds	Present Value Factor	Present Value of After-Tax Proceeds
10	$1,000	.322	$322

Misconceptions and Controversy

At the start, we said that there has been some misconceptions and controversy regarding leasing. The problem of understanding leasing seems to center on three points:

1. There is a tendency to slough off a complete analysis of all the elements and effects of a lease. We have already tried to answer this point by showing how it is necessary to make a complete analysis of a lease.
2. Two simple but patent misconceptions as to what lease financing may accomplish: (a) A company can raise money from real estate or other property for use in its regular operations, such as for inventory, which is a fast turnover type of asset as compared with the type that is leased. (b) Leasing in itself will take a company out of the business of handling the type of asset it leases. For example, some companies have said that they leased in order to get out of the real estate business.
3. Some disagreement as to what lease financing represents; that is, whether or not it is a form of debt.

So that we will be talking about the same thing, we will use a simple example of a sale and leaseback to explain the two misconceptions mentioned above under point 2. Company A owns a building worth $10 million which will wear out in ten years. It transfers ownership by sale to an investor for $10 million. The investor immediately leases it back to the original owner for $1 million a year plus the equivalent of interest for a period of years. As a result, the company occupies the building but no longer owns it; in its place, it now has $10 million to use as it sees fit. It pays back the money with the equivalent of interest over the period of years during which it is allowed to use the building under the lease. These transactions are summarized in Exhibit 4-20.

The same thing could have been accomplished by financing without resort to leasing. The company could have arranged the sale of a debt security to the investor for $10 million with payments of interest and principal over the life of the building. The company would get the same $10 million to use as it saw fit, and it could pay it back at the rate of $1 million per year over a period of years plus an amount of interest. At the end, it would have clear title to the property and could continue to use it without any further payments.

We will now use this example to dispel the two misconceptions listed under the second point.

2(a). A company can raise money from real estate or other property for use in its regular operations.

In our example, the company did not raise any more money by lease financing than it could have by debt financing. It would have received $10 million in each case. This is so ridiculously simple that it is hard to see how anyone could be confused about it, yet some people seem to have the idea that lease financing produces funds out of nowhere. In lease financing, you give up an asset which could otherwise be used as a basis for some other medium of financing. While no obligation is recorded on the liability side of the balance sheet in a lease arrangement, the company takes on a fixed charge equivalent to that for another type of debt financing. Lease financing is merely one means of raising capital.

If part of the assets of a company are removed and interest charges and depreciation are replaced with rental charges, some ratios such as turnover of capital may look tremendously improved, but this is merely due to a change in the figures included in the denominator. This is more of an accounting change than any change in substance.

2(b). A company can concentrate on its operations rather than be in the real estate business.

This is unsound; the company still uses the building just as if it were

Exhibit 4-20

SALE AND LEASEBACK

Company A, Lessee	*Investor, Lessor*
Building is owned by company at start.	Investor gets title and pays the sale price.
Company gives up title and gets $10,000,000 from sale.	Investor receives $1,000,000 per year plus an amount equivalent to interest.
Building is leased back to company, which pays lease charges.	At the expiration of the lease, the investor owns the building.
Company uses the building without change, during the life of the lease.	
At the expiration of the lease, the company no longer has any right to the building.	

owned. As far as use is concerned, there is no change whatever. None of the supposed disadvantages of ownership is eliminated by the mere act of lease financing itself. If anyone thinks that he is getting out of the real estate business merely by the process of leasing, he should realize that the problem of price and terms of a lease are just as much a part of obtaining real estate as buying it outright. Furthermore, in a net lease all the burdens of ownership, maintenance, insurance, taxes, operation, etc., continue to be borne by the lessee.

It makes no difference as far as the above two points are concerned whether the property or equipment was originally owned, then sold and leased back, or whether it was leased in the first instance. The results are the same.

Now we will proceed to point three and explain further why leasing should be considered to be just another form of debt financing.

1. A lease is an obligation to pay a fixed amount annually. If not paid, the property under lease will be lost to the company regardless of the wishes of the common stockholder. The lessor has a claim—a valid, legally enforceable claim for the full lease except in bankruptcy. The claims of the investor in the lease are far superior to those of either a preferred or common stockholder. Lease financing has one characteristic which makes it somewhat akin to a mortgage type of financing. In a mortgage, the investor has a hold on the property, and in most forms of mortgages, a defeasible title is transferred to the lender or the trustee until payment. In lease financing all title is given up.
2. Some people suggest that a lease is dissimilar from a debt claim because statutory limitations generally restrict a lease claim, if the trustee terminates the lease, to a maximum of one year's rent in bankruptcy and three years' rent in reorganization. However, when a default occurs, the company loses the property. This could not occur if a lease had the characteristics of any form of equity. Furthermore, non-payment of a lease may lead to bankruptcy just as any other liability.
3. Rent is said to be an operating expense and not a financial fixed charge such as interest, and there are other operating expenses equally as fixed or burdensome as a lease rental. However, many operating expenses are not long-term obligations as is a lease. Flexibility is generally lacking in lease payments as far as minimum charges are concerned. Furthermore, if we compare one company with another, we would wish to compare one type of operating expense with another of like character; the same idea applies to financing costs. The charges for a lease are comparable with debt and not

with any type of expense or any payments on equity.

Some laws affecting investors require them to measure a company's credit by treating lease rentals as a fixed charge. Even if the law did not so provide, any astute investor would do so.

No matter how you slice it, a lease is an obligation to pay a fixed amount, more similar to a form of debt than equity, and it is therefore with other media of debt financing that the cost should be compared.

Cost Analysis Review

In Chapter 15, "Cost-of-Capital–Profit Goals," it is explained that the profit goal must be based on a composite cost of all long term capital, because we are seeking a rate which will be applied on the asset side of the balance sheet. However, in comparing the cost rates of securities we are not concerned with the composite cost. We are working with the liability side of the balance sheet and must compare the rates of similar types of securities.

We have already explained why the financial costs of a lease should be compared with debt financing and how to make the comparison. We will now summarize the calculation:

1. The net financial charges on a lease must be compared with the alternative of debt financing, with the final maturity and the repayment schedule on the debt financing the same as the lease.
2. Allowance must be made for the loss of residual value, or any payment or rent renewal which will have to be made in order to get title to the property or keep on using it.
3. Allowance must be made for the tax effect of leasing vs. ownership.

The result, readily handled with a computer program, can best be expressed by arriving at an answer in terms of the rate that could be paid with debt financing and ownership of the property, and be equal to the effective rate on the lease.

Generally, the effective interest cost of a lease is higher than for straight debt financing.[7] If a leasing company provides the capital, it has to make a spread over the rates at which it borrows to pay its expenses and make a profit.

There are some other costs which may be considered as a part of financing costs. There may be a finder's fee, if an agent arranges the lease. This is comparable to the investment banker's commission in a security sale. If there is a third party in a lease deal, there may be an additional fee which is rolled into the rental charge. In lease financing as well as security financing, there may be a commitment fee if the money is not to be used immediately.

You will do well to start out on the assumption that lease financing is more expensive than straight debt financing, unless there is some unusual tax situation. Therefore, generally, there must be some other reason to use leasing than the financing costs alone.

Burden of Lease Financing vs. Debt Financing

Is there less apparent debt burden with a lease than with equivalent debt? How do investors evaluate a lease vs. a debt obligation in assessing the effect on the balance sheet and income statement? Can a company carry more debt by using lease financing?

One of the tests for debt quality is the percentage that it represents of total capital structure. Since lease financing does not appear on the balance sheet, it may not be considered by some investors as being as burdensome as an equivalent amount of debt. This may be an advantage of lease financing. However, it would not be expected that most

[7]For example, a representative of an equipment leasing company has stated that its effective interest rate is about 2% over the rate at which a company could borrow directly. It is that company's contention that it can more than make up the extra financing cost by better buying and selling equipment. It has been stated that the effective interest charge alone for a long term lease might be 1/2% more than an equivalent bond rate.

experienced, highly skilled, large institutional investors would make any real distinction. The reason for the distinction in the past by some investors may have been due to the difficulty of analyzing leases from the information reported by companies. It is reasonable to expect that investors will require more and more complete information on leases. Some people contend that complete revelation of facts requires the company to show the capitalized equivalent of leases, and some companies follow this policy.[8]

Certainly, if a company believes in the principle of keeping investors fully informed, it will wish to report lease obligations so that the investor can make whatever calculations he chooses to assist in his analysis. If a lease is a net lease—that is, with no payments except for principal and interest—a footnote to the income statement giving the annual charges and the maturity of the lease will make it possible for an investor to arrive at an approximate capitalized amount. For example, the capitalization multipliers to apply to annual level lease rentals with various implied interest rates are as shown in Exhibit 4-21. If a lease has a minimum fixed annual payment and may increase with an increase in sales, the capitalization ratio is only applied to the fixed minimum rental.

If leases include items other than capital charges, and it is in the nature of a financial lease, the footnote should separate these capital charges on an approximate basis. A company may find that failure to provide complete disclosure may work to its disadvantage, because some investors may apply a capitalization ratio to the entire charges ranging from eight to ten times.

Some financial analysts may not capitalize leases in their balance sheet analysis, but will evaluate them in their analysis of the income statement. They may figure coverage by adding the full lease payments to interest charges. The resulting coverage will be a hybrid, because the lease payments include principal payments as well as interest. It would be preferable to do a complete financial analysis and capitalize leases in the balance sheet and figure coverage of charges by including only the interest component of a lease with other interest charges. In a prospectus, the Securities and Exchange Commission requires companies to include one-third of lease rentals in fixed charges in figuring coverage.

A small amount of leases, which represent less than 5% of total long term capital when capitalized, may be disregarded by investors. However, if the amount increases, the total will be treated as debt, including the 5%. Some investors may not bother to capitalize even large leases. For these reasons, it may be possible to get away with a slightly greater debt burden by leasing.

While this idea of hiding debt through lease financing may be some advantage in favor of lease financing today, it would seem to be a questionable one for a company to use as its basic reason for leasing. Such an advantage depends on investors' failure to do a complete analysis. A company should not try to take advantage of the lease method of financing by failing to reveal adequate information. That is totally out of step with the idea of a sound investor relations program. This is also a problem for the accountants in the certification of financial statements and full disclosure.

Required reporting for leases will have an effect on how much a lessee can do in trying to hide leases so that they may not be treated as an equivalent amount of debt. The Securities and Exchange Commission requires significant[9] finance leases to be disclosed in a footnote to financial statements as follows:

1. The present value of future commitments and the implicit interest rate in the lease.

[8]The Financial Accounting Standards Board is now considering how leases should be reported, and their decision should be available in 1975.

[9]Includes finance leases which cover 75% or more of the asset's life, or which recovers the lessor's cost, and if the present value is more than 5% of the company's capitalization and the impact on net income is more than 3%.

Exhibit 4-21

LEASING CAPITALIZATION RATIOS*

To Capitalize the Monthly Lease Rental, Multiply the Annual Rental by the Appropriate Capitalization Ratio.*

Final Maturity of Original Lease in Yrs., Before Renewal	6% Interest	8% Interest	10% Interest
1	1.0	1.0	.9
2	1.9	1.8	1.8
3	2.7	2.7	2.6
4	3.5	3.4	3.3
5	4.3	4.1	3.9
6	5.0	4.8	4.5
7	5.7	5.3	5.0
8	6.3	5.9	5.5
9	6.9	6.4	5.9
10	7.5	6.9	6.3
11	8.0	7.3	6.7
12	8.5	7.7	7.0
13	9.0	8.1	7.3
14	9.5	8.4	7.5
15	9.9	8.7	7.8
16	10.3	9.0	8.0
17	10.6	9.3	8.2
18	11.0	9.5	8.3
19	11.3	9.7	8.5
20	11.6	10.0	8.6

*For example, if the lease rentals were $1,000,000 annually, payable on equal monthly installments and the interest component of the lease was 6% with the lease maturing in 20 years, multiply by 11.6 to get an equivalent principal of $11,600,000.

The figures in the table can be calculated from tables giving the present value of periodic payments of $1 at a certain interest rate over a period of years.

2. The effect on net income if the asset were owned.

It is suggested that because it may be possible to have a little more debt with leasing rather than with straight debt financing that the cost of lease financing should be given credit for the small amount of common equity which can be eliminated. In other words, with straight debt financing, a little more common equity would be required. And in calculating the financing cost of leasing vs. debt financing and ownership, the comparison should penalize debt financing and ownership with the added common. This is a poor way to handle the situation. It is better to compare like with like; that is, lease financing on the basis of judgment with the slightly larger amount of debt that might be obtained. Again we, of course, would object to this idea of increasing debt by hiding it from your owners.

In the above discussion, it should be emphasized that we are talking about leasing which is financial in nature and which, as an alternative, can be handled with straight debt financing. Some leases are of an operating nature and can appropriately be accounted for in operating expenses.

Other Reasons for Leasing

Since lease financing is generally more expensive than straight debt financing, the use of lease financing must be based on non-financial factors. The following are reasons other than financial:

1. Equipment may be available only on a lease basis.
2. Property or equipment may only be needed for a brief period.
3. The lessee may wish to return the equipment for a more advanced model and prefer to have the lessor assume the responsibility for resale of the equipment. Obsolescence can't be avoided; the lessee will have to pay for it. But the lessor may be in a better position to resell the property.
4. A retail store which wishes to open a branch in a large building and occupy only a small part would probably not wish to go to the trouble of financing the whole building. The same idea may apply in a shopping center.
5. A company may find that lease financing is the only means by which it can obtain capital because of poor credit standing. Under such circumstances, the investor will charge a high overall effective rate and expect to get benefits from the residual value of the property. A lease of salable equipment may put the investor in a more secure position so that he could recover his investment if the company went broke, or the investor's position may be so strategic that the company would wish to pay his obligation above others.
6. In government contract work, lease payments may be allowed as a cost, in a cost plus contract. Thus, leasing of equipment, etc., may make it possible for a company to be assured more readily of getting back its capital cost. By leasing equipment with leases tailored to the term of the contract, the company can charge off the full cost of the equipment to the government. If it were owned, the equipment would have to be depreciated over its normal life.
7. If a company's profits are poor, a company might not be able to take advantage of the tax benefits of ownership and fast depreciation. If an investor has a higher tax bracket than the lessee, tax benefits may result to the lessor. The cost of leasing may be less than the cost with debt financing and ownership if the lessor will share some of the tax benefits with the lessee.
8. The lessee may want certain services performed by the lessor and the lessor would not provide them with ownership.
9. A short lease will produce a lower equivalent amount of debt when leases are capitalized. The capitalizing multiple depends on the interest rate and the length of maturity.
10. In some instances, sale and leaseback may be used for the purpose of realizing a capital gain or loss. When property has changed in value, it may be reappraised and then transferred to a subsidiary. The property may by leased back and the lease used as a basis for debt financing by the subsidiary. This provides a way to accomplish a write-up or -down, and at the same time a medium of financing.

Leveraged Lease

The term leveraged lease is really a sales term rather than a correct description. Company X wants to lease some property. Company A is set up to own the property and lease it to Company X. Company A's credit depends almost entirely on the lease payments by Company X. On the basis of these lease payments, Company A does debt financing up to a high percent of the total cost of the property, say 80%. The 20% common stock of Company A is owned by an investor who is independent of Company X. The common stock investor gets the tax advantage of the depreciation of the property, and he also gets all the other advantages of a lessor such as residual value.

This is an expensive form of lease financing because the lease payments have to go to support not only debt but some common equity. It would be better for Company X to do business with an investor who would supply the lease on the basis of 100% debt financing. The reasons for a leveraged lease are:

1. The credit of Company X may not be adequate to support debt up to the full amount of the lease.
2. It may be necessary to bring in a common stock investor with a high tax bracket who can take advantage of tax depreciation that the company can't use and thus attain an overall lower rate.

Unless one of these reasons are present a straight lease would be cheaper, assuming the lessor could get all the tax benefits. One potential lessee had a number of leveraged lease proposals. In his situation there were no tax benefits from leasing. The lessee was concerned with the rate at which the lessors would borrow, and he requested that each proposal be based on a 9 1/2% borrowing rate for the lessor's debt. He then wanted to know what interest rate was calculated in the lease payments. One showed an implicit effective interest rate in the lease of 6.8%. None of this information would really do him any good, and, in fact, it might only confuse him.

What he really should have been seeking was the equivalent borrowing rate at which he could have owned the property and financed it 100% with debt. A complete analysis on this basis, taking into account all factors which would make it comparable with straight debt financing, showed that he could have done straight debt financing and owned the property even if he had paid an interest rate of 15%. This does not take into account other costs such as brokers' commission and other expenses. You can be sure leasing companies and brokers would not give you this figure. However, you need it before making a decision whether to lease.

Conclusion

The following gives a brief conclusion regarding lease financing:

Correct analysis of leases which are of a financial nature involves calculations over the life of the lease. The financing charges must first be separated from any charges for non-financial services. Then, the cost of leasing must be analyzed by comparison with a like debt financing, taking into account all elements of cost. On the basis of financing costs alone, lease financing is generally more costly than other types of debt financing.

While the question of lease financing in the first instance is one of costs, judgment must be applied in many other respects and questions answered such as: Are there reasons for leasing other than costs? Will a lease or ownership be more flexible? Can you and should you try to gain by leasing rather than straight debt financing because leasing does not appear on the balance sheet? Can you, in good conscience and in duty to your security holders, fail to give complete disclosure about leases? That is a good point on which to leave this type of financing.

Tax Exempt Revenue Bond Financing—Industrial and Pollution Control

A method of financing facilities of private companies through tax-exempt revenue bonds has existed for some time. Their original purpose was to induce private companies to build plants in depressed areas. Under this arrangement, private companies build facilities which are owned by an entity of a state or local government. The facilities are leased to the private company. The tax-exempt bonds are to provide financing for the facilities. The lease payments by the private company provide for payment for interest and principal on the debt. The credit depends entirely on the credit of the company leasing the facilities without reliance on the credit of the political entity.

This method of financing was ultimately abused. Some large companies financed major facilities by this method. The law was subsequently changed so that so-called industrial revenue financing was limited to a facility whose total cost during the three years before and three years after completion does not exceed $5 million.

Pollution control tax-exempt revenue bond financing is an extension of tax-exempt industrial revenue bond financing. It came into being in 1971. In order to comply for tax exemption, the bonds must meet certain tests such as:

- They must be for the purpose of complying with air or water regulations of the state in which they are located—the facilities would not have been built except for this purpose. They cannot increase the present production.
- The facilities are for recycling purposes.
- The state entity should exist before the project is started.

States must have statutes which permit this type of financing.

Such financing is generally treated as an installment sale for Federal tax purposes. Therefore, the company can treat the property as though it were owned. The investment tax credit and depreciation can be taken by the company. And the interest part of the lease payments can be deducted for tax purposes. The company can purchase the properties at the end of the lease for a nominal amount. Such an arrangement would require that the lease be capitalized and put on the balance sheet.

However, the financing can be arranged on a true lease basis for financial reporting and indenture restriction purposes. Special circumstances would be required to justify such a treatment. This might occur if the company using the facilities was not paying taxes and could not use the facilities for tax purposes, and an investor could be brought in who could use the tax benefits.

The principal advantage of this type of financing is that, because of the tax-exempt feature, it may result in a lower interest rate of up to 2% as compared with the interest rate on the company's own bonds. Also, it may tap a new source of debt funds for corporate purposes. It is exempt from regulation of the Securities and Exchange Commission.

Setting the issue up so that it complies with the state statutes and so that the interest will be tax exempt requires the services of a lawyer who is thoroughly familiar with all the regulations. And an IRS ruling should be obtained before the company decides to go ahead.

Debentures

Many industrial companies use debentures as their principal form of funded debt. The indenture for a debenture is of necessity an extensive document, as is a mortgage indenture exclusive of the provisions covering the mortgage itself. If a debenture is sold publicly, it will have to include provisions required by the Trust Indenture Act of 1939. It will cover such items as the form and denominations of the bond; definitions, registration and transfers; long lists of covenants; redemption provisions, sinking fund provisions; remedies in event of default; provisions regarding the trustee and his duties; effect of merger, consolidation, transfer or lease; supplemental indentures; debenture holders' lists and reports by the company and trustee; etc. Much of the voluminous material is "boiler plate," but must be included. The important parts are the provisions affecting the credit.

A well-drawn indenture for an unsecured debt can generally place the investor in almost as strong a position as a mortgage indenture through various protective covenants covering maintenance of assets and handling of them in event of merger, sale, etc., and by restriction on the sale of additional debentures unless credit ratios afford adequate protection to the holders, etc. The types of provisions that might be included were discussed under mortgage bonds. Since a debenture does not have a lien on property, there will have to be a provision preventing other issues from grabbing the property, unless the debentures are equally secured. This is referred to as a negative pledge clause. Furthermore, provisions as to the effect of liens and dissipation of assets in event of merger, consolidation or sale will have to be tightly drawn.

When an original debenture is formed, the indenture can be drawn so as to permit subsequent issues under the same indenture by means of a supplemental indenture. This will save money and effort over the alternative of an entirely new indenture. However, it calls for care and foresight in the drawing of the original indenture. Provided the terms of the original debenture issue will permit it, a junior debenture may be issued and even a junior to the junior issue. However, it would certainly be advisable to avoid such financing except in a dire emergency.

Given in Exhibit 4-22 in outline form are advantages and disadvantages of three possible situations in which debentures may be used.

Three things to keep in mind with regard to debentures might be summarized as follows:

1. They should not be used if they restrict seriously the availability of unsecured bank credit.
2. The debenture slot should not be so used up as to prevent the employment of a convertible debenture in an emergency.
3. If mortgage bonds are the principal form of a company's debt, the debentures might be reserved for an emergency, so that additional debt could be issued temporarily with a heavy sinking fund and not disturb the credit rating of the principal form of debt.

Examples are given in Exhibit 4-23 of a few terms in the debentures of one company which used debentures as its senior debt security. The terms are not representative of the correct legal interpretation because they are summarized to assist the reader in visualizing their significance. This is an example of the open terms for a public offering which could not be obtained with a private sale.

Long Term Notes

In some instances, particularly in a private deal, notes may be used rather than a debenture. A note replaces the bond, and an agreement replaces the indenture. The terms are less elaborate than in a debenture bond offered publicly. A trustee is generally not used. Such a type of unsecured funded debt is most likely to occur when there is a private deal and only one or a very few investors.

It is, of course, possible for there to be a trustee in a note form of financing and a public sale just as in the case of a debenture, but then all the requirements of a debenture bond would have to be fulfilled, so that the difference would be in name only. A brief statement of the advantages and disadvantages are given in Exhibit 4-24.

Floating Rate Notes

In 1974 a rash of variable rate notes made their appearance. They were used primarily by bank holding companies but they even spread to the industrial field.

Their purpose was to tap a source of funds of individual investors, replace the dependence of the issuers on commercial paper or other short term forms of indebtedness, obtain a lower rate and perhaps extend the average maturity of its debt.

One of the principal ways small investors could save was to put their money in time deposits of thrift organizations. These organizations were held down on the rates they paid by regulation. For example, commercial banks were prevented from paying more than 5 1/2% on 90-day paper under regulation Q of the Federal Reserve System. With the floating rate notes carrying rates over 9%, they offered a substantial increase for small investors. The terms vary with different issues, but some of the features of floating rate notes were approximately as follows:

Interest Rate:

At a fixed rate for the first six months and then 1% above the "three-month

Exhibit 4-22

DEBENTURES IN PLACE OF MORTGAGE BONDS FOR SENIOR SECURITY

Advantages

1. May be no difference in rating or cost in most instances.
2. Eliminates the necessity to pledge property to secure the issue, and the ensuing expenses.
3. May be more flexible in merger or consolidation than a mortgage bond.

Disadvantages

1. May have some tight restrictive provisions.
2. If mortgage bonds are used for the senior obligation, then debentures may be used as a second form of debt financing. When debentures are the senior obligation, another layer of debt will have to be in the form of a junior debenture.

DEBENTURES IN ADDITION TO MORTGAGE BONDS

Advantages

1. Cheaper than preferred stock, but this is an incorrect comparison because preferred is a form of equity.
2. May be a necessary form of financing in an emergency, and might be reserved better for that purpose.

Disadvantages

1. Affects debt limit.
2. May restrict unsecured borrowing limits.
3. May prevent use of convertible debentures.
4. If it represents much over 7% of the total capital structure, it may reduce the rating in the mortgage bonds.
5. Generally requires heavy sinking fund.

SUBORDINATED OR SECOND DEBENTURES

Advantages

1. May have to be resorted to in an emergency, if other media of debt financing are prevented by restrictive provisions in the indenture, etc.
2. For special types of companies, such as finance companies, it may be an appropriate means of raising debt capital.

Disadvantages

1. The use of this type of security is generally an indication of financial weakness in an industrial company and should be avoided if possible.

interest yield" on U.S. Treasury bills. The rate varies every six months and is determined one month ahead of the time when the rate becomes effective. The 1% spread is within the range of the historical spread between Treasury tax bills and commercial paper.

Maturity:

Final maturity about 15 years. But after two years holders can demand payment every six months at 100 plus accrued interest. The payment demand must be made with 30 days' notice prior to the next six-month term.

Callable by Company:

Non-callable for ten years, then at 100 plus accrued interest.

Size of Offering:

Multiples of $1,000 with $5,000 as the initial purchase.

Listing:

The New York Stock Exchange.

When used by a bank, the Federal Reserve System would require the bank to carry reserves against them because of their optional short maturity. In a bank holding company, no reserves would have to be carried if the funds are used other than for bank purposes.

For capital base purposes in a bank, the maturity question is important. If they are considered to have a maturity of less than seven years, they will not be allowed as capital base securities.

Exhibit 4-23

CERTAIN PROVISIONS CONTAINED IN A DEBENTURE INDENTURE

Industrial Company—$75,000,000 Issue,
Price 100, Coupon 8.85%, Maturity 30 Years,
Bond Rating: Moody's A, Standard AA

Form	Fully registered in denominations of $1,000 and multiples thereof.
Redeemable	On 30 days' notice, at 108.85 for the first year and decreasing thereafter to 100 five years prior to maturity.
	Non-refundable for ten years at a lower interest rate.
	Redeemable for sinking fund purposes starting in ten years at 100.
Sinking Fund	Starting after ten years an equal amount each year so as to retire at least 90% of the issue by maturity.
	At the company's option, it may retire for sinking fund an equal additional amount each year, but if this option is not exercised in any year it is not carried forward.
Limit on Additional Debt	No limit on additional debt unsecured, or secured debt, as long as these and similar debentures are equally secured.
	Additional restrictions cover: creation of liens, sale of securities by subsidiaries, lease-back financing, merger and consolidation, etc.
Restrictions on Dividends	None
Modification of Indenture	With consent of 66 2/3% of principal amount, but does not apply to maturity, interest rate, reduction of principal amount, reduction of redemption premium or reduction of percentage requirement for consent.

Exhibit 4-24

LONG TERM NOTES

Advantage	*Disadvantage*
May eliminate the expense of a trustee, and some of the elaborate legal work of a debenture bond with all the appurtenances.	Largely limited to special situations where the investors have no particular interest in having the security in a form suitable for resale, and for which, in most instances, repayment is expected in a relatively short period.

The Maturity?

Whether the holders will wish to divest themselves of these notes will depend on whether:

1. They have need for funds.
2. They can find a more attractive investment.

Undoubtedly, some of the holders will need funds and there will be a gradual attrition.

The prospects of their being a more attractive debt medium of investment in 1974 was rather unlikely with interest rates above 9% and regulation of savings institutions still in force. However, this could be changed so that the picture might be radically different in the future. Furthermore, an improvement in the stock market would undoubtedly result in some of these funds being shifted to the stock market.

If the holders decide they want out of these notes, they will either sell or redeem them. If they sell them, they will remain outstanding. Whether they will sell them rather than redeem them depends on whether in selling them they can get more than 100 plus the brokerage commission. The brokerage commission for a sale of $5,000 of notes is about 50¢ per 100. It appears that the 1% spread of Treasury bills compared with commercial paper will not permit them to sell at a sufficient premium so that there will be assurance that they will be sold rather than redeemed. A larger spread than 1% would be uneconomical from the issuer's point of view. The attitude of the buyer towards the premium will depend on how long he expects to hold the note. If it is for only six months, even a small premium would eat into his return. A 9% yield would be reduced to an 8% yield by a 50¢ premium on a six-month basis. The longer he expects to hold it, the less the burden of the premium and the more likely he will sell them rather than redeem them.

Therefore, for financial planning purposes, floating rate notes with these types of terms should be considered as short term. It is pure conjecture, with a 1% spread, how much of them will remain outstanding for how long. Money market conditions at any time after the two-year holding period may encourage a large number of untimely redemptions, creating a cash crisis when the cost of refunding could be a disadvantage.

One company which issued these notes reserved the option to increase the spread. This might be used to increase the premium so that investors would sell rather than redeem them. However, it would take a large increase in spread to cause an increase in premium because of the six-month term after the two-year period. For example, a note selling at 100 with a 9% rate would have to have the rate increased to 10% in order to produce a 50¢ premium. Apparently, the primary reason for having the option to increase the spread was to guard against other companies subsequently selling notes with a higher rate and thus inducing holders to redeem the notes with the lower rate.

Term Bank Loans

Bank loans which mature after one year are known as term loans. If they are just over a year they may be, for all intents and purposes, the same as current loans. However, when banks have had excess funds, they have made loans for as long as ten years on a serial basis. The repayment schedule may include a balloon or large payment at the final maturity. The length of maturity that can be obtained will depend on the willingness of the banks to lend. Such loans are truly a part of funded debt. Other types of bank loans which fall in the category of term loans are commitments with the right to borrow over a period of time, with repayment to come within some such period as five years from the date of the agreement. There generally will be a fee of 1/4 to 1/2 of 1% on the unused portion of the commitment. A commitment may include a revolving feature, which permits the borrower to borrow, repay and borrow again within a specified time. The interest rate on a term loan will generally be at some premium over the prime rate. It may be fixed or vary with the prime rate. If the rate varies it may include a collar which establishes a maximum. An added cost of such loans, as compared with other types of loans from non-bank lenders, is the cost to carry the deposit account that will have to be kept as a compensating balance.

Term bank loans will generally require a loan agreement. The extent of the restrictions will depend on the company's credit standing. They are relatively flexible with respect to repayment prior to maturity, because banks are generally willing to permit repayment without any call penalty, as long as the proceeds for such purpose are not obtained from a loan from another bank.

If a company has a good credit standing and has carried good deposit balances, it is in a strong bargaining position in arranging such a loan, as compared to loans from other institutional investors. Because of the deposit account and other possible banking business, a bank will have a desire to please a customer. This element is not present with other types of lenders.

The danger in term bank loans lies largely in their excessive use to finance a long-term capital need with a relatively short maturity. When a term loan is arranged, a company should have clearly in mind how it will be repaid at maturity. It should consider whether it might not be better off doing long term financing in the first place.

Income Debentures

The interest on income debentures is paid only if earned, under certain circumstances, as is the case with preferred stock dividends; yet income debentures have the advantage over preferred stocks in that the interest is deductible for tax purposes, provided the terms are properly drawn. In other words, they appear to be similar in nature to preferred stock; yet they have the advantage of the interest being deductible for tax purposes. This has led to the suggestion that income debentures should be substituted for preferred stock.

On the surface, income debentures do seem to have the edge on preferred stock, but if you study the terms carefully, you will find that there are many hookers which give them many of the disadvantages of debt. They may affect borrowing reserve because of debt restrictions. Their terms are actually more onerous than those of preferred stock and thus are more of a burden as far as common stock is concerned. Some contain a provision to the effect that if the interest is ruled to be not deductible for tax purposes, it becomes fixed. They have a maturity in most instances.

Thus they should be included in the debt category and are by no means any panacea. You can't have your cake and eat it too. They should not be used under any circumstances unless every one of their provisions is carefully evaluated and weight is given to their effect on the principles of sound financial policy. It would seem that their use might be considered an exception rather than the rule. Their advantages and disadvantages are outlined in Exhibit 4-25.

Other Forms of Debt Financing

Capital may be raised with other forms of debt financing, some of which appear as unfunded debt, but, because of regular renewals, actually perform the function of providing long term capital. Included are such media as commercial paper, loans on warehouse receipts, receivable financing in its many forms, acceptance financing of goods in transit by a bank, etc. Some of these types of financing may meet the needs of a particular company.

Any valuable asset or regular source of income represents the basis for a possible medium of financing, but, of course, not necessarily an appropriate medium. A company should know about all of the various media of financing that might be available to it and should study them from all angles, in order to determine whether they offer any real advantage in the long run over more conventional forms of financing. Any special form of financing should not be allowed to obscure the essential nature of individual transactions.

Segregation of an asset in a subsidiary or in a dummy company with ownership outside of the company may represent a corporate maneuver tying in with a method of financing. As one example, a company having a large amount of receivables may set up a separate finance company; as another exam-

Exhibit 4-25

INCOME DEBENTURES	
Advantages	*Disadvantages*
1. Apparently similar advantages as preferred stock in that interest is paid only if earned. 2. If properly drawn, the interest is deductible for tax purposes. 3. If a company is in dire financial condition, it may be necessary to resort to this type of financing.	1. Restrictive provisions may be required by buyers of the security which give it all the disadvantages of debt, in that it affects "borrowing reserve" and "financial insurance." The restrictive provisions may be triggered if there is a default; this would not occur if a preferred dividend is postponed. The advantages may be only apparent, and a lower rate might be obtained on a straight debenture. 2. Principal and interest are a fixed obligation. Default is like any debt—not like a preferred. 3. May indicate a company's weak financial standing and inability to finance in a more conventional manner. 4. The purchasers would expect to get paid for their more junior position.

ple, a company may form a separate company to finance its real estate holdings and lease them from that company. If a separate company is formed for financing purposes, the transaction should be analyzed from the point of view of the asset that is given up and the obligation that is assumed. We will discuss corporate organization and financing in Chapter 5.

A short term medium of financing should not be regularly relied upon as a source of long term capital. Hiding of debt from the balance sheet should not be the primary basis for use of a special type of financing. All forms of debt financing should be viewed from the essential aspect of maintaining a strong capital structure.

Single Payment Bond—Example of an Analysis of the Cost of a Special Type of Senior Security and Its Effect on a Company

Note:

> As will be explained in the following discussion of the single payment bond, its principal advantage is based on the assumption that, for tax purposes, it will qualify as a discount bond.
>
> At the time this book went to press, no decision had been made by the Internal Revenue Service as to whether the deduction would be allowed. The following discussion should be read with this in mind. If the IRS rules against this treatment of interest for tax purposes, the bond will not fly as described below.

Special types of securities require careful analysis to determine their true cost and all aspects of their short and long range effect on the company. In determining the true cost, all tax effects must be allowed for and all calculations must take into account the time value of money by discounting.

As an example, we can refer to a special type of bond[10]—The Single Payment Bond.

[10]This bond was developed by Albert C. Barkwill, Ebasco Services Inc., and Thomas N. Hennigan, Smith Barney & Co., Inc. Most of the exhibits which are used in our explanation are developed by them. See article "The Single Payment Book: An Innovative Financing Technique," by Albert C. Barkwill, *Public Utilities Fortnightly,* Vol. 93, No. 10, May 9, 1974.

This bond is a special type. It may have limited use and is not of interest to most companies.

Its principal feature is that no interest payments are made during its life. Interest is accumulated on a compound basis, and would be paid in a lump sum at a maturity or call date.

The main advantage of a Single Payment Bond is that it has a tax advantage since it may qualify as a "discount bond." The tax advantage arises because interest costs must be amortized for income tax purposes on a straight-line basis rather than on an accrued basis. The value of this tax advantage increases with the length of maturity and as interest rates increase. The bonds would be sold to institutional investors, such as pension funds, which do not pay any income taxes so the amortization of interest on a straight line would be no disadvantage to the investors.

Since the bond would be a special type of bond, salable only to a special type of investor, it might lack liquidity. In order to increase the liquidity of the Single Payment Bond, it would have a conversion feature. After a five-year period of non-convertibility, the holder of a Single Payment Bond would have the option of exchanging this security with its principal and compound interest into the standard bond. The option to convert would not permit reconversion.

It appears that for a bond with an interest rate of 7.177%, there might be savings because of the tax advantage equivalent to as much as 0.763% on an after-tax basis. We will first consider the tax advantage. Then we will discuss the other advantages and disadvantages.

In order to understand the type of bond we are talking about, it is contrasted with a standard bond in Exhibit 4-26. In all our calculations, in order to simplify the picture, we will use the following basic assumptions:

Interest—7.177%. It will result in doubling principal and interest every ten years on a compound basis.
Compounding on an annual basis.
Tax rate—50%.

The standard bond would be sold for $100, and would pay $7.177 in interest each year. The $100 of principal would be repaid at maturity in ten years.

The Single Payment Bond would be sold for $100. It would not pay any interest, but both principal and interest of $200 would be paid at maturity at the end of ten years. The annual amount of interest would increase because the company would have to pay interest on the accumulated interest as well as on the principal. At the end of ten years the company would owe $200, of which $100 would be principal and $100 would be accumulated interest.

The single payment bond in Exhibit 4-26 is not strictly comparable with a $100 standard bond, because the compounding of interest for the single payment bond results in more debt for the company.

On the company's books, the annual interest payments would be recorded in the income statement. Rather than paying out the cash, the amount of the bond principal would be increased in the balance sheet. For example, at the end of year 1 the income statement would show interest expense $7.177 and the balance sheet would show bonds outstanding $107.177. At the end of year 2, the income statement would show interest expense $7.693 and the balance sheet would show bonds outstanding $114.870, etc.

For tax purposes the company could deduct interest on a straight line basis. Since total interest is $100, and the period of time is ten years, the annual interest deduction for income tax purposes would be $10 annually.

For the full ten years, the total interest reported in the income statement and deducted for income tax purposes would be the same. However, since the interest for tax purposes is higher in the first years, there is an advantage to the company because of the time value of money. This is shown in Exhibit 4-27.

Exhibit 4-26

TEN-YEAR SINGLE PAYMENT BOND COMPARED WITH A STANDARD BOND—INTEREST RATE 7.177%

PART I

INTEREST AND PRINCIPAL PAYMENTS

Column	I	II	III	IV	V
	Standard Bond		Single Payment Bond		
				Compound Interest Included in Single Payment	
Year	Principal	Interest	Principal and Interest	Annual	Cumulative
0	$100		$100		
1		$7.177	107.177	$ 7.177	$ 7.177
2		"	114.870	7.693	14.870
3		"	123.114	8.244	23.114
4		"	131.950	8.836	31.950
5		"	141.421	9.471	41.421
6		"	151.572	10.151	51.572
7		"	162.450	10.878	62.450
8		"	174.110	11.667	74.110
9		"	186.607	12.497	86.607
10	100	"	$200	13.393	100.000
		$71.77		$100.000	

PART II

SINGLE PAYMENT BOND

Column	I	II	III
	Interest Reported in Income Statement and for Tax Purposes		
Year	Reported in Income Statement	For Tax Purposes	Tax Deferral Column II Less Column I Times the Tax Rate
1	$ 7.177	$ 10.00	$1.412
2	7.693	"	1.154
3	8.244	"	0.877
4	8.836	"	0.582
5	9.471	"	0.265
6	10.151	"	–0.075
7	10.878	"	–0.439
8	11.667	"	–0.830
9	12.497	"	–1.248
10	13.393	"	–1.697
	100.000	100.00	0.000

Exhibit 4-27

SINGLE PAYMENT BOND BENEFITS FROM TAX DEFERRAL
RESULTING FROM LARGER INTEREST CHARGES
DEDUCTIBLE FOR TAX PURPOSES IN EARLIER YEARS

Column	I	II	III	IV
Year	Tax Deferral. Difference in Interest Payments Deducted for Tax Purposes and Interest Recorded in Company's Income Statement Times the Tax Rate	Discount Factors for Interest Rate 7.177%	Present Value of Annual Tax Deferral. Column I Multiplied by Column II	Cumulative Present Value of Tax Deferrals
1	$1.412	.933	$1.317	$1.317
2	1.154	.871	1.004	2.321
3	0.877	.812	0.713	3.034
4	0.582	.758	0.441	3.475
5	0.265	.707	0.187	3.662
6	-0.075	.660	–0.050	3.612
7	-0.439	.616	–0.270	3.342
8	-0.830	.574	–0.477	2.866
9	-1.248	.536	–0.669	2.197
10	-1.697	.500	–0.848	1.348
	0.000		$1.348	

Thus, while the company will pay the same amount of taxes in the ten years, by using equal interest payments for tax purposes, it will pay less taxes in early years and a greater amount in later years. Therefore, there is a tax benefit based on the time value of money of $1.348 for each $100.

In order to make a judgment as to whether the savings are significant, they should be translated into yield to maturity. This is done in Exhibit 4-28. The yield to maturity, giving effect to the tax savings, is calculated as follows:

1. The after-tax cash flows are determined. They include the $100 received from the sale of the bond, the annual tax savings and the principal payment at maturity.
2. A discount rate is then determined which will make the present value of the cash flows equal to zero. This rate is the effective yield to maturity on an after-tax basis.
3. The pre-tax yield is just the coupon rate if sold at par or as obtained from the bond tables if sold at discount or premium.
4. The reduction in after-tax interest cost is the difference between the standard bond net after-tax interest cost of 7.177/2 = 3.589 (50% tax rate) and the single payment bond effective after-tax cost 3.589 - 3.517 = .072%.

Referring back to Exhibit 4-27, it should be noted in Column IV that while there is always a net discounted tax benefit, it is greatest at the point just before the interest payments, for income statement purposes are greater than that which the company reports for tax purposes. This happens in year 5 and is a significant fact, because with a callable bond, the company could call the issue to make sure the tax benefits were maximized. However, in this connection allowance has to be made for the cost of the call premium. And there is an additional tax the company has to pay on the difference between the interest accrued for tax purposes and the interest accrued on the company's books when the bond is called, paid off at $100 or converted. In our example, as shown in Exhibit 4-26, the principal and interest amounted to $141.421 at the end of five years, of which $41.421 was interest. For tax purposes the company had deducted $50.000 ($10.000 x 5). A tax on the difference of $8.579 would require a tax payment of $4.289, the present value of which at 7.177% would be $3.033. This compares with the cumulative present value of tax deferrals as shown in Exhibit 4-27 for year 5 of $3.662. Thus, the savings would be $0.629, but this does not allow for the cost to call.

The tax deferral benefit from the Single Payment Bond is relatively small for a bond with a short maturity, but the benefit increases as the maturity increases. Therefore, let's look at a 30-year bond. In Exhibit 4-29 it is shown that the effective after-tax cost savings is .576%. In Exhibit 4-30 it is shown that the savings is increased to .763% if the bonds in Exhibit 4-29 are converted in the 17th year. If the bonds are called, there would be a reduction in the savings.

Now that we have gone through the calculations, let's consider the advantages and disadvantages of this type of bond from the investors' and issuing company's points of view.

First, the investor, the buyer of the bonds:

Advantages

1. The non-receipt of interest results in an immediate reinvestment at a fixed rate without a brokerage fee, which is call protected for five years.

Exhibit 4-28

AFTER-TAX CASH FLOW
TEN-YEAR BOND–7.177% COMPOUND INTEREST.
STRAIGHT LINE AMORTIZATION TO MATURITY

Column	I	II	III
Year	After-Tax Cash Flow	Discount Factor for 3.517% Effective After-Tax Interest Rate	Present Value
0	$+100.000	1.000	$+100.000
1	+ 5.000	.966	+ 4.830
2	+ 5.000	.933	+ 4.667
3	+ 5.000	.902	+ 4.507
4	+ 5.000	.871	+ 4.354
5	+ 5.000	.841	+ 4.206
6	+ 5.000	.813	+ 4.063
7	+ 5.000	.785	+ 3.925
8	+ 5.000	.758	+ 3.792
9	+ 5.000	.733	+ 3.663
10	+ 5.000	.708	+ 3.539
10	–200.000	.708	–141.546
			0.000

Interest Rate on Bond	7.177%
Effective Before-Tax Cost	7.177%
Effective After-Tax Cost	3.517%
Tax Rate	50%

Exhibit 4-29

AFTER-TAX CASH FLOW
30-YEAR BOND–7.177% COMPOUND INTEREST.
STRAIGHT LINE AMORTIZATION TO MATURITY

Column	I	II	III
Year	After-Tax Cash Flow	Discount Factor for Interest Rate After Tax 3.013%	Present Value
0	$+100.000	1.000	$+100.000
1	+ 11.666	.971	+ 11.325
2	"	.943	+ 10.994
3	"	.915	+ 10.672
4	"	.888	+ 10.360
5	"	.862	+ 10.057
6	"	.837	+ 9.763
7	"	.812	+ 9.477
8	"	.789	+ 9.200
9	"	.766	+ 8.931
10	"	.744	+ 8.669
11	"	.722	+ 8.416
12	"	.700	+ 8.170
13	"	.680	+ 7.931
14	"	.660	+ 7.699
15	"	.641	+ 7.473
16	"	.622	+ 7.255
17	"	.604	+ 7.042
18	"	.586	+ 6.836
19	"	.569	+ 6.636
20	"	.553	+ 6.442
21	"	.536	+ 6.254
22	"	.521	+ 6.071
23	"	.505	+ 5.893
24	"	.490	+ 5.721
25	"	.476	+ 5.553
26	"	.462	+ 5.391
27	"	.449	+ 5.233
28	"	.436	+ 5.080
29	"	.423	+ 4.931
30	"	.426	+ 4.787
30	–800.000	.426	–328.262
			0.000

Interest rate on bond	7.177%
Effective after-tax cost	3.013%
Tax rate	50%
Reduction in effective after-tax interest cost	
Standard bond effective after-tax cost	3.589%
Single payment bond effective after-tax cost	3.013
Savings	0.576%

Exhibit 4-30

AFTER-TAX CASH FLOW
30-YEAR BOND–7.177% COMPOUND INTEREST.
STRAIGHT LINE AMORTIZATION UNTIL CALL DATE
WITH NO CALL PENALTY CALCULATION

Column	I	II	III
Year	After-Tax Cash Flow	Discount Factor for Interest Rate 5.652% After Tax 2.826%	Present Value
0	\$+100.000	1.000	\$+100.000
1	+ 11.666*	.973	+ 11.346
2	"	.946	+ 11.034
3	"	.920	+ 10.731
4	"	.895	+ 10.436
5	"	.870	+ 10.149
6	"	.846	+ 9.870
7	"	.823	+ 9.599
8	"	.800	+ 9.335
9	"	.778	+ 9.079
10	"	.757	+ 8.829
11	"	.736	+ 8.586
12	"	.716	+ 8.350
13	"	.696	+ 8.121
14	"	.677	+ 7.898
15	"	.658	+ 7.681
16	"	.640	+ 7.470
17	"	.623	+ 7.264
17	– 85.883**	.623	– 53.476
17	–324.901***	.623	–202.302
			0.000

Interest on bond	7.177%
Effective after-tax cost	2.826%
Tax rate	50%
Reduction in effective after-tax interest cost	
Standard bond effective after-tax cost	3.589%
Single payment bond effective after-tax cost	2.826
Savings	0.763%

*+11.666, straight line amortization.

**-85.883, reversal of excess amortization. The interest as accrued on the income statement at 7.177% compounded amounts to \$224.901 at the end of 17 years. On the tax books the interest amounts to \$396.667 (\$23.333 x 17 years). The company has to pay a 50% tax on the difference (\$171.766) or \$85.883.

***The principal amount at the end of the 17th year is \$324.901. This, however, does not include the cost to call which would amount to \$10.453 pre-tax and \$5.277 after-tax.

2. May be able to get higher interest rates to reflect some of the seller's tax savings.

Disadvantages

1. There is no cash income.
2. Only investors who pay no taxes, such as pension funds, would be interested in this type of bond. Therefore, there is a limited market for the bond.
3. Since the bond would be callable after five years, the investor would only have assurances that reinvestment would last for that limited period.
4. It is a strange type of bond, and investment committee approval might be difficult. This may be largely cured by the conversion privilege but not completely.
5. This is a reverse sinking fund type of bond. Investors like a sinking fund because it reduces debt and strengthens the company's financial position. It gives investors another look at their money. This, however, is taken care of by the conversion feature. If investors felt that the company's credit was deteriorating, they could convert into a standard bond with a sinking fund.
6. If interest rates increase, the investors are stuck with the rate on reinvestment because they can't convert for five years.

The tax deferral is made possible by the non-tax paying nature of the investors who would buy the bond. Generally, when investors confer a savings on a company they expect to share in that savings. Also, because of the special type of security, investors would probably want a higher rate than on a standard bond.

Now, the issuing company's point of view:

Advantages

1. It produces a tax deferral and therefore a lower cost of capital.
2. It saves financing cost on new debt to the extent of the accrued interest which is equivalent to raising new debt capital.
3. If tax rates drop then deferring taxes in the beginning offers additional savings.

Disadvantages

1. Its use is strictly limited to a special type of company, such as electric utility, which expects continuous growth; otherwise, the debt would be an ever mounting burden.
2. It would have to be limited in amount by the rate at which the company is expected to grow. If growth eventually slowed down, the company would have to reduce this or other issues of debt in order to keep its capital structure in balance.
3. It has no sinking fund call features which permit debt reduction at the low sinking fund call price.
4. It may result in a single issue so large in the future that it will be difficult to refund. If the time of payment came when interest rates were adverse, the company would have to sell a large refunding issue at a high rate.
5. It may result in a conflict with an existing bond indenture:

   An indenture may limit issuance of additional bonds:

   1. Unless interest is covered a certain number of times.
   2. And to a certain percentage of property.

   If the increase in debt due to the single payment bond conflicted with these provisions, there would have to be an automatic conversion feature. An existing indenture would have a sinking fund. Therefore, if these bonds were issued under an existing indenture, it too would have to have a sinking fund. For an electric utility company, mortgage bond sinking funds can be satisfied with cash, bonds or property. Such a sinking fund would thus require sufficient property additions to satisfy the sinking fund. If it couldn't be satisfied in this manner then cash or bonds would have to be used.
6. If the company had to sell single payment bonds in the form of debentures

because it couldn't be issued under an existing mortgage indenture, the interest rate would be higher. Furthermore, it might limit the company's ability to use other unsecured indebtedness. And similarly, it might limit a company's ability to sell a convertible debenture.

7. The bonds will probably be sold privately, and there will be no open market for the bonds if the company wished to repurchase them unless the bonds are converted.
8. There would be no tax advantage to the stockholders if a commission required a company to flow through the tax advantage to the consumers. If a commission does not require flow-through, this can be changed by commission order.
9. The tax laws can be changed. This would not affect savings already realized and it might not affect future savings on bonds sold before a change in the tax laws. However, it could put a damper on new single payment bonds.
10. If the tax rate is increased in the future, deferring taxes is a disadvantage.

An investor who buys the bonds has to consider how long the bonds may remain outstanding. The life of the bonds affects one of the principal advantages from the investor's point of view—that is, the reinvestment of interest. And the company has to consider how long it may remain outstanding because it will affect whether or not a savings is realized and the size. Various reasons why the bonds might be terminated before final maturity are as follows:

1. Called by the company:
   a. If interest rates decrease.
   b. If the tax law changes.
2. Converted by the investors:
   a. If the investor wanted to sell the bonds.
   b. If interest rates increase.
   c. If the company's credit deteriorates.
3. Converted automatically if any indenture provision was violated.

Because of possible termination before final maturity, we should consider the savings to the company at various periods. The necessary data is included in Exhibit 4-31. In Column V, is the effective after-tax yield if the bonds are converted each year up to 17 years when the maximum benefit is obtained. Included in the calculations is the difference between the interest accrued and the interest used for tax purposes. In Column IV, is the effective after-tax yield if the bonds are called each year up to 30 years. In the calculations is included the cost to call the bonds and the tax which has to be paid on the difference between the interest accrued and the interest used for tax purposes. It is interesting to note that the optimum call year occurs in year 21. This shift is due to the addition of a call penalty.

Summary

The gross interest savings for a 30-year bond seems impressive. It is 0.763% in terms of yield to maturity on an after-tax basis if the bonds are converted in 17 years. However, when all factors surrounding the savings and the nature of the bond are considered, it may become far less attractive to the company.

1. The investors might want a greater yield than on a standard bond, possibly as much as 0.20% because of the special nature of the bond and the fact that the investors made possible the savings. Furthermore, investors would have to consider that the bonds might be called after five years so that any benefit they might gain from buying the bonds would be terminated.
2. If a utility company had to sell debentures instead of mortgage bonds the added yield might be as much as 0.20%. And if the company had mortgage bonds and debentures already outstanding, it might have to sell junior debentures in order to avoid a conflict with existing indentures.

Therefore, the possible savings could sink to less than .30% if the bonds remained

Exhibit 4-31

EFFECTIVE AFTER-TAX YIELD EACH YEAR IF THE BONDS ARE TERMINATED EACH YEAR BEFORE FINAL MATURITY 30 YEARS. INTEREST COUPON 7.177%. CALL PRICE STARTING AT 107.177 AND DECREASING TO 100.0 AT MATURITY.

Column	I	II	III	IV	V
			Cumulative	Yield	
Year	Principal Amount	Call Price	Diff. Between Int. Accrued on Books and Int. Used for Tax Purposes	Bonds Called Each Year	Bonds Converted Each Year
1	107.177	107.692	16.156	7.345%	3.589%
2	114.870	107.690	31.797	5.262	3.456
3	123.114	108.227	46.886	4.488	3.345
4	131.951	108.491	61.383	4.069	3.251
5	141.421	108.750	75.245	3.797	3.171
6	151.572	109.003	88.428	3.604	3.103
7	162.450	109.247	100.883	3.458	3.046
8	174.110	109.480	112.557	3.345	2.998
9	186.607	109.699	123.393	3.254	2.957
10	200.000	109.900	133.333	3.180	2.923
11	214.355	110.080	142.312	3.120	2.896
12	229.740	110.235	150.260	3.070	2.873
13	246.229	110.360	157.104	3.030	2.856
14	263.902	110.450	162.765	2.997	2.843
15	282.843	110.500	167.157	2.971	2.834
16	303.143	110.504	170.190	2.951	2.828
17	324.901	110.453	171.766	2.935	2.826
18	348.220	110.342	171.780	2.924	2.827
19	373.213	110.161	170.120	2.916	2.831
20	400.000	109.900	166.667	2.913	2.837
21	428.709	109.549	161.291	2.912	2.846
22	459.479	109.098	153.854	2.914	2.857
23	492.458	108.532	144.209	2.919	2.871
24	527.803	107.838	132.197	2.927	2.886
25	565.685	107.000	117.648	2.937	2.903
26	606.287	106.002	100.380	2.948	2.922
27	649.802	104.825	80.198	2.962	2.943
28	696.440	103.447	56.893	2.978	2.965
29	746.426	101.847	30.240	2.995	2.989
30	800.000	100.000	0.000	3.014	3.014

outstanding for 17 years. If the bonds were called prior to the time the maximum savings occurred, the company has to pay the call price and also if the bonds are called or converted, the company has to pay a tax on the difference between the interest used for tax purposes and accrued on the books. The final net effect of the bonds being extinguished before the year in which the maximum benefit occurred reduces the effective savings and it could turn into a loss.

Preferred Stock's Place in Capital Structure

At the start of this chapter we gave a brief explanation of three fundamental types of securities—debt, preferred and common. Now we will consider preferred stock, which is a part of equity.

Preferred stock is sometimes referred to as being "neither fish nor fowl," neither debt nor common, and therefore no good. Some people even refer to it as "bastard" security. When you hear a Financial Vice President talk that way, he is tying on to a glib phrase rather than putting on his thinking cap. All types of securities represent media through which to raise capital. Whether they serve the purpose depends on: (a) how they fit the capital structure based on general financial principles which we have discussed, (b) on all their respective provisions, and (c) on what basis they can be sold in the market.

Preferred stock has the advantage of not being a fixed obligation which will put the company in bankruptcy and it does not directly hurt borrowing reserve or financial insurance, two very important points in its favor. However, it does come ahead of common and if used inappropriately or to too great an extent even where it is appropriate, then it will impair the common stock with the ensuing disadvantages.

In deciding whether to use preferred, the basic question is whether it should in some degree be substituted for common. Do not fall into the wrong type of reasoning by trying to decide on the use of preferred stock rather than debt, or vice versa. Debt has an entirely different character from stock. First decide, as emphasized above, how much, if any, debt there should be. Then seek an answer to the possible use of preferred stock.

To show how a reverse of this procedure might cause confusion and lead to erroneous results, just consider the cost question alone which is fully explained in Chapter 15. Debt might cost 8%, which would be equivalent to 4% after an income tax rate of 50%. Assuming no change in the tax law as regards preferred dividends being deductible for tax purposes, then preferred stock might cost 9%. Common stock might cost 13% or more.

We shouldn't say that preferred costs more than twice the net cost of debt after taxes, therefore don't use it but consider debt instead; this is incorrect reasoning. The two securities are quite unlike. At this point, we already should have settled the debt question on the basis of all of the factors to weigh in determining the use of debt.

Now that we are at the preferred stock stage, we should compare it with common, since it is a form of equity and more nearly like common than debt. We should say that preferred stock might cost 30% less than common. The cost rate for the preferred, which is based on the dividend rate, is much less than the common cost, which is based on the expected earnings per share of common. After a company has decided how to divide long term capital between debt and equity, the question of whether preferred is appropriate requires an answer to the question: Will a moderate amount of preferred in place of common detract from the quality of the common in the long run?

For example, in the electric utility field it has been acceptable to have debt 50%, preferred up to 15% and common 35%, rather than 50% debt and 50% common equity. Up to 15% preferred does not seem to detract seriously from the quality of the common. Generally, industrial companies have used very little preferred. However, an industrial company which had 25% debt and 75% common, might consider substituting a small sliver of preferred for common as follows: Debt 25%, preferred 10% and common 65%. However, there is a catch. The principal markets for preferred stocks are institutions rather than individuals. Corporations which buy preferred stocks get an 85% dividend tax credit. Therefore, they will buy preferred stocks on a yield basis close to bonds of the same company. However, in order to attract institutional investors, the preferred must be good quality. The preferred stock of many industrials would not attract institutional demand.

Some companies which have had preferred have felt that it should be eliminated by debt financing because interest is cheaper than preferred dividends and is deductible for tax purposes. If the preferred is moderate in amount and has no objectional provisions it might be better to leave the preferred outstanding. It is a cheaper form of equity than common. Substituting debt for preferred should not be done if it pushes the debt ratio above the amount which will provide good quality.

We can conclude about the use of preferred by saying that it may be used as a small sliver in between debt and common, providing it is of such quality that it can be sold to institutions, and is not of such an amount that it will detract from the quality of the common.

Convertible preferred is another question, and will be discussed subsequently under convertible securities. Convertible preferred may be very useful for acquisition purposes.

The advantages and disadvantages of preferred stock are summarized in Exhibit 4-32.

One advantage not included in the exhibit is the fact that the issuance of preferred stock may result in the increasing of common equity. This may occur when a preferred stock is sold above the par value and the liquidating value is the same as par. The amount above par value is recorded in the company's books as capital surplus. Thus, the common equity is increased.

The provisions affecting preferred stock may be found in the company's charter, the by-laws, the stock certificate and in state laws, where the company is incorporated. For certain regulated industries, there may be restrictions regarding preferred stocks imposed by regulation. The New York Stock Exchange has something to say about such matters as voting rights for preferreds listed on that Exchange. The senior security provisions may affect the preferred.

A company may have just one preferred stock issue, or there may be classes running all the way from prior preferreds to those in a junior position which may be referred to as preference stock. For example, if a preferred stock is non-cumulative, gets very limited special rights if the dividends are not paid, is not preferred over the common stock in event of liquidation, then it is close to being a common stock. A preferred stock may include some of the privileges of a common stock, if it is a participating preferred; that is, if it also participates in additional dividends with the common as earnings increase. Today it would be relatively impossible for a company to get away with issuing a preferred stock in the nature of common. And a company should avoid the other extreme of issuing a preferred which is too restrictive. Of course, if a company's back is against the wall financially and its only means of financing is by means of a preferred, it may have to accept whatever terms the investors dictate.

Ideally, if a company does use preferred, it should have one class and attempt to establish terms so that the preferred is what its name implies. It should be in a truly senior position to the common, but without terms approaching a contractual nature so that noncompliance would put the holders in a position akin to that of debt holders. Preferred stockholders are interested in preventing dissipation of assets and earnings and therefore will desire protection against some of the points discussed under protective provisions for debt. Such protection will provide some maintenance of the quality of the preferred stockholders' investment.

As we explained, the regular or optional call provision for a bond is reduced an equal amount each year so that it reaches 100 prior to maturity. Since a preferred stock has no maturity, the regular call price may be reduced gradually until it reaches par after a certain number of years. The sinking fund call

Exhibit 4-32

PREFERRED STOCKS

Advantages	*Disadvantages*
1. It has no maturity unless a sinking fund is required by investors.	1. If too much preferred is used, it might hurt the common equity when adverse developments are encountered.
2. It preserves "borrowing reserve" and "financial insurance."	2. It may limit unsecured borrowing or long-term debt financing if provisions are too restrictive.
3. It is cheaper than common stock.	3. It may be necessary to include a purchase or sinking fund, which will drain cash.
4. Failure to meet its terms will not place the company in bankruptcy.	

is at the offering price or par if the preferred is offered below par.

Sinking Fund on Preferred

One of the disadvantages of a sinking preferred compared with a perpetual preferred is that the company has to pay the extra financing costs to sell new preferred to replace preferred paid off with sinking fund. This requires the payment of the financing costs to raise the new capital. In order to explain the disadvantage of a sinking fund from this point of view, we will assume that the preferred is sold to yield 7 1/2% and that financing costs, including the underwriters spread and the financing expenses, are 1.50%. We will further assume that the sinking fund starts with the sixth year and is 4% annually until the preferred is retired in 30 years. Each year the company sells new preferred to meet sinking fund payments. As a practical matter, issues of this small size would not be sold but it is appropriate as a basis for our calculations.

The financing costs for the sinking fund are shown in Exhibit 4-33 in Column II, and the present value of these costs are shown in Column IV. The total present value of the financing costs is 0.4658. Now we can translate this in terms of yield. If a 7 1/2% perpetual preferred is sold at $100, then giving effect to the extra financing reduces the proceeds of the offering to 99.534, which would mean a current cost of 7.54%. The difference in yield is only 0.04%. Thus, the sinking fund, from the financing cost angle, to pay off one issue, does not appear to be a significant disadvantage in financing.

In other words, a sinking fund merely shortens a maturity and requires an extra financing. However, such is not the entire picture in comparing a preferred stock with a sinking fund and one without a sinker. The preferred without the sinker has no maturity whatsoever. Therefore, when we introduce a sinking fund for a preferred stock, we are increasing the capital raising burden where none whatsoever existed. It is not just a question of shortening the maturity. Furthermore, in weighing the significance of a preferred with a sinking fund and one without, you have to consider the nature of the additional obligation to make sinking fund payments. While default provisions may vary with each preferred, these obligations represent a burden ahead of the common stock.

There may be a small advantage in having a sinking fund if rates decrease. As we have already explained, the regular call price is always higher than the sinking fund call. If rates decrease, when sinking fund payments have to be made, the lower call price is an advantage compared to refunding at the higher regular call price. Of course, sinking fund only permits a small amount to be refunded. If rates go up, then refinancing the sinking fund is a disadvantage.

Investors look upon a sinking fund as a factor which improves a company's credit,

Exhibit 4-33

MEASUREMENT OF COST OF SINKING FUND ON 7½% PREFERRED STOCK

Column	I	II	III	IV
Year	Sinking Fund Payment	Financing Cost for Sinking Fund Payment	Discount Factor for 7 1/2%	Financing Costs Discounted
1	– 0 –	– 0 –		
2	– 0 –	– 0 –		
3	– 0 –	– 0 –		
4	– 0 –	– 0 –		
5	– 0 –	– 0 –		
6	$4.00	$.06	.647961	.0388
7	4.00	.06	.602754	.0362
8	4.00	.06	.560702	.0336
9	4.00	.06	.521583	.0313
10	4.00	.06	.485193	.0291
11	4.00	.06	.451343	.0271
12	4.00	.06	.419854	.0252
13	4.00	.06	.390561	.0234
14	4.00	.06	.363313	.0218
15	4.00	.06	.337966	.0203
16	4.00	.06	.314386	.0189
17	4.00	.06	.292453	.0175
18	4.00	.06	.272049	.0163
19	4.00	.06	.253069	.0152
20	4.00	.06	.235413	.0141
21	4.00	.06	.218988	.0131
22	4.00	.06	.203710	.0122
23	4.00	.06	.189498	.0114
24	4.00	.06	.176277	.0106
25	4.00	.06	.163979	.0098
26	4.00	.06	.152538	.0092
27	4.00	.06	.141896	.0085
28	4.00	.06	.131997	.0079
29	4.00	.06	.122787	.0074
30	4.00	.06	.114221	.0069
Total present value of financing costs				.4658

because it acts as a discipline to management to reduce senior securities to keep a balanced capital structure. And it gives investors a look at their money so they can decide whether to go back in again.

A company should avoid a sinking fund on a preferred if possible. It should not use a preferred if the sinking fund is so heavy that it retires the issue in a short period such as seven years, except in unusual circumstances.

It is no real equity in such a situation.

We can summarize the advantages and disadvantages of a sinking fund on a preferred compared to a preferred with no sinking fund as follows:

Advantages:

1. May make preferred more salable and thus a better rate may be obtained.
2. If rates decrease, the lower sinking fund call is an advantage to refunding at the higher regular call price. But sinking fund payments are small in any one year so this is a minor advantage.
3. It may improve investors' attitude towards a company's credit.

Disadvantages:

1. An additional financing burden where none exists whatsoever, with a non-sinking fund preferred.
2. A small extra cost to refinance the sinking fund.
3. If rates go up, new financing to take care of the sinking fund payments will have to be done at a higher rate.
4. If the preferred is not replaced with new preferred as the old preferred is paid off, the company's equity is decreased.

Preferred Provisions

We will conclude our discussion about preferred stocks with a summary of some of the types of provisions that might be included. The provisions given in Exhibit 4-34 are taken from an issue which was offered publicly. They are summarized in order to assist the reader in obtaining a quick idea of their significance; for this reason, they are not all-inclusive and do not necessarily represent a correct legal interpretation of the specific provisions.

Tax Law Changes for Preferred

In 1974, the government proposed making dividends on preferred stocks deductible for tax purposes the same as interest. This would cause some reduction in the after-tax burden of preferred dividends. However, the general principles outlined above for the use of preferred stock still hold: after determining the proper debt ratio, it may be possible to use a sliver of preferred between the debt and the common; preferred should not be used to the extent that it will push the common too far out on a limb.

There used to be a rule of thumb that a good grade preferred stock would yield about 0.75% more than the yield on the bonds of the same company. For example, if bonds yielded 7.00%, preferred might yield 7.75%. However, as we have noted, a market developed for preferred stocks by investing institutions which were corporations and could receive an 85% tax credit on dividend income. This considerably increased the after-tax yield on preferred stocks for such institutions, and drove down the yield on good grade preferreds to about the same level as the bonds of the same company. For example, if an investing corporation, which had an effective tax rate of 50%, bought a 7% bond, the net after-tax yield would be 3.50%. If it bought a 7% preferred, it would pay no taxes on 85% of the 7% or on 5.95%. It would only pay taxes on 15% of the 7% or on 1.05%. At a 50% tax rate, the tax would only be 0.525%, so that the net after-tax effective yield would be 6.475%. This compares with the net after-tax yield for the bond of 3.50%. Of course, the end result depends on what tax bracket the corporation is in.

If dividends of preferreds are made deductible for income taxes, they will lose their advantage of being 85% tax free for corporate investors. This will mean that institutional investors will either lose interest in buying preferreds or they will expect to receive a considerably higher rate. Thus, the markets for preferred stocks will be upset by such a move.

A corporate investor, which bought a 7% preferred and received an after-tax income of 6.475% would have to buy a 12.95% preferred, if it had to pay a full 50% tax on the

Exhibit 4-34

CERTAIN PROVISIONS CONTAINED IN A PREFERRED STOCK

Electric Utility Company—$10,000,000. Issue price—$100, Dividend 11%.

To increase authorization of additional or prior preferred	Vote of 2/3 of this preferred.
Restrictions on dividends on stock junior to this preferred	No dividends on stock junior to this preferred unless all dividends paid on this preferred.
	Some additional restrictions on common dividends contained in a previously issued preferred stock. Dividend payments depend on certain capital structure ratios but they are not very restrictive.
Redeemable	On 30 day's notice, starting at $111 during first 10 years, at $106 during next 3 years, $103.50 during following 3 years and $101 thereafter. Not redeemable within first 10 years as part of any refunding operation involving an effective cost of money of less than 11%.
	For sinking fund purposes, redeemable at $100 after 5 years.
Purchase or sinking fund	After first 5 years a 5% per year sinking fund. An additional 5% may be applied at the company's option each year, but this option is not cumulative.
Liquidation rights	Voluntary—at regular redemption prices.
	Involuntary—at $100 per share.
Issuance of additional equal or prior preferred stock	Pro-forma coverage in a recent period, after taxes, of dividends on the cumulative preferred stock, senior stock and parity stock must be at least twice the dividend requirement for that period, and gross income must be at least one and one-half times the interest on long-term debt plus dividends on this and prior preferred.
	This and all equal or prior preferred cannot be more than 100% of common equity. If this test is not met, then there must be approval of two-thirds of the preferred.
Issuance of additional long term debt	No restrictions.
Voting rights	None, unless default on amount equivalent to four quarterly dividends on cumulative preferred stock. Then holders shall be entitled to elect a majority of the directors.
Charter alteration affecting preferred	Only if approved by 2/3 vote of this stock.
Sell (or lease) substantially all property	No restrictions.
Merge with an outside company	Only if approved by a majority of the stock.
Preemptive rights	None.
Subject to provisions of long term debt, existing charter provisions, state laws, etc.	All provisions of this preferred are subject to any such existing provisions.

dividend income, in order to receive the same net after-tax income.

For the issuing corporation, with a 50% tax rate, the net after-tax cost of a 12.95% preferred would be 6.475%.

Providing the tax change goes through, the market for preferreds would settle down somewhere in between the extremes we have suggested. The incremental effective tax rate of some corporate investors is below the 50% rate so that they would not be hit as hard by taxes as we assumed. And the higher yield on preferreds would attract individual investors so that the yield would tend to be pushed down.

We might conjecture that a company which could sell a 7% preferred before the tax change with a pre-tax cost of 14%, might be able to issue a 9% preferred with a pre-tax cost of 9%. The law might be changed so as to permit a company to have the choice of selling either a preferred with a tax deductible dividend or one without the tax deductible feature.

WARRANTS

What Is a Warrant?

A warrant is an engraved document giving the holder the right to purchase a security at a certain price for a certain period of time. Generally, the security to be purchased is common stock, but it need not be.

Warrants are used in the issuance of common stock through rights. Such warrants have a short life of about 20 days. The warrants we will be discussing now have a much longer life.

Intrinsic Value

An example of a simple warrant is as follows:

> Option for the holder to purchase one share of common stock at an exercise or option price of $90 per share for a period of ten years.

If the common stock sells for $100 per share, the warrant will have an intrinsic value of $10. The intrinsic value is the difference between the market price of the common and the exercise price.

Market price of common	$100
Warrant exercise price	90
Intrinsic value of warrants	$ 10

A warrant will always be worth its intrinsic value, since it represents the discount at which a holder can purchase common stock below the market price. Generally, a warrant will have a higher market price than its intrinsic value, because of its nature.

Nature of a Warrant

A warrant is a leverage type of security. It provides a greater potential percentage appreciation with an upward movement in the common stock price, and conversely a greater potential depreciation with a decrease in the common price. This is illustrated in Exhibit 4-35, assuming that a warrant is only worth its intrinsic value.

When the common in our example moves up 10%, the intrinsic value of the warrant appreciates 100%. When the common moves down 9%, the intrinsic value of the warrant depreciates 50%.

An analogy can be made between a warrant and buying a common stock on margin with a bank loan as shown in Exhibit 4-36. However, a warrant is a more convenient way to speculate in a common stock. It avoids the bother of arranging a bank loan, it saves the interest payments on the bank loan and margin requirements may limit the amount of bank loan that can be obtained. With a bank loan there is always a danger of the margin falling so low that more money will have to be put up. If the common stock falls below the amount of bank loan, a greater loss might result with a bank loan. With a warrant, the most that can be lost is the price of the warrant. The only advantage of buying com-

Exhibit 4-35

ILLUSTRATION OF LEVERAGED NATURE OF WARRANT ON BASIS OF INTRINSIC VALUE

Column	I	II	III	IV	V
	Common		Warrant		
Year	Market Price	Appreciation or Depreciation	Exercise Price	Intrinsic Value	Appreciation or Depreciation
0	$100		$90	$10	
1	110	+10%	"	20	+100%
2	100	– 9%	"	10	– 50%

Exhibit 4-36

ILLUSTRATION OF ANALOGY OF A WARRANT TO PURCHASING COMMON STOCK ON MARGIN WITH BANK LOAN

Excludes Expenses of Bank Loan, Etc. and Dividend Income from Common Stock

Column	I	II	III	IV	V
	Common		Purchase of Stock on Margin		
Year	Market Price	Appreciation or Depreciation	Bank Loan	Investor's Equity	Appreciation or Depreciation
0	$100		$90	$10	
1	110	+10%	"	20	+100%
2	100	– 9%	"	10	– 50%

mon stock on margin with a bank loan is that the holder gets the dividend; whereas, the warrant holder gets no dividend.

A warrant is also analogous to buying a call on a stock from a put-and-call broker. Generally, such calls are for a shorter duration than a warrant, but the idea is the same. If you were to buy a call at $90 on a stock selling for $100, you would naturally have to pay $10 for such a call, and in addition a premium to compensate the put-and-call broker for the risk that the common stock might go up in price and for his expenses and his profit.

Therefore, an investor, or rather a speculator, will pay a premium for a warrant over its intrinsic value, because it gives him a ready option or call on a common stock and a greater opportunity for appreciation than an investment in the common stock.

Method of Offering

Warrants are generally offered as part of a package with a senior security such as a debenture or preferred stock; they may be offered as a package with common stock. They may be offered separately.

Purpose

Warrants may have six general uses:

1. As part of a package with a security to add a kicker or incentive to make it possible to sell the security which otherwise might not be salable. They provide a speculative inducement.
2. As part of a package with a security, when it is not necessary to make the security salable, in order to give the appearance of obtaining a better price for the security. For example, an investment banker may suggest to a company that the interest rate on a debenture can be lowered from 8% to 6% if warrants are attached. Careful analysis is required in such a situation to determine the true nature of the transaction and whether there is any actual reduction in interest rate.
3. As a separate instrument to raise capital, though this is seldom done.
4. As an inducement in an acquisition or merger in addition to the principal means of payment, to satisfy the desires of some investors for the prospects of a speculative gain.
5. As a tool in reorganizations to satisfy certain parties.
6. It may even be used as a dividend payment.

Warrants are misused probably more times than they are used correctly, because they are not fully understood and because their short range benefit is emphasized to the exclusion of their long range disadvantages.

Terms

The terms of a warrant may vary widely and include some rather far out provisions. Some terms may be beneficial to the issuing company, others may be adverse. The terms will generally have an effect on the premium at which the warrant sells over its intrinsic value.

The principal terms are:

1. The exercise or option period.

   It may be long or short; it is generally not less than five years; it may be perpetual. If it is too short it will reduce the premium. If it is long, the company will be unable to tell whether it can use the capital which will result from exercise of the warrants at maturity. Furthermore, they may interfere with other financing which the company may wish to do in the future. Perpetual warrants are a headache, because the only way a company can get rid of them is to buy them back in the market. This may be difficult to do and relatively costly. Furthermore, they continuously weigh on the common stock because of their potential dilution effect. Generally, an exercise period of from five to ten years is reasonable.

   The right to exercise may be delayed. This will prevent any warrants from being exercised during the period of delay, but it would seem to accomplish little, since most warrants are not exercised until close to maturity. As long as there is a premium, more can be obtained by the holder of the warrant by selling it in the market rather than exercising it at the option price.
2. Type of security received upon exercise and number of shares or amount received.

   If it is exercisable into common, the number of shares received will be stated. Warrants may be exercisable into other types of securities.
3. The exercise or option price.

   This is the price the warrant holder must pay for the security into which the warrant is exercisable. At time of issuance, the exercise price may be set 10% to 20% above the market price of the security into which it is exercisable. If the exercise price is too far above the market price, the premium decreases.
4. Detachable from the security which it is offered.

   A warrant is generally detachable because if it remains attached to the security with which it is offered, the premium is decreased, because speculators in the warrants don't want to make the additional investment in the security.

There are many special terms which can be included in a warrant such as:

1. The exercise or option price may change at a specific date or dates. For example, if a common stock sells for $100, the first exercise price may be $115, and $130 after five years. This will tend to decrease the premium. If the market price is below $115 in five years, the only effect will be that the company will get a higher price when the warrants are exercised if the stock subsequently moves up above 130. If the stock sells above $115 before the exercise price increases to $130, the increase in the exercise price will tend to force exercise of the warrants.
2. They may be made callable at a certain time at a certain price, either the exercise price or higher. This in effect shortens the exercise period to the call date and tends to hold down the premiums.
3. The exercise price may be met with senior securities rather than cash. For example, if the exercise price is $100 and the holder can pay the $100 in cash or principal amount of bonds, it will be less expensive to the warrant holder if the company's bonds can be bought in the market at a discount. However, to the extent that the warrant holder gains, the company loses, unless it is able to get a correspondingly better price for the warrant at the time the warrant is offered.
4. They may be convertible into common. Such convertibility is usually not effective until after the exercise period. It would only be of value if the common stock price is below the exercise price. This prevents the holders from having the warrants become worthless at the end of the exercise period. However, it complicates the problem of determining the warrant price and the ultimate diluting effect.
5. There may be a flush-out provision. This gives the company the right to reduce the exercise price for a short period in order to induce the warrant holders to exercise. For example, if the exercise period was for 20 years and the exercise price was $100, the company could have the right to lower the exercise price to $90 at the end of five years for a 30-day period. This would induce the holders to exercise their option to take advantage of the lower exercise price. To be effective, the reduction must be more than the premium on the warrant.

Complicated provisions in warrants should generally be avoided. Warrants are hard enough for the investor to understand and price without adding complications. Furthermore, many of the complicated provisions tend to reduce the premium. A simple, detachable warrant with a moderate maturity, between five and ten years, and no other provisions, is preferable.

Pricing a Warrant

For our explanation of the market price of a warrant, we will assume that a warrant is exercisable into common stock rather than any other type of security. Determining the market price of a warrant is not easy, so we will look at it from various angles.

Thus far, we have said that a warrant will always be worth at least its intrinsic value, which is the difference between the common market price and the warrant exercise price. We have also said that a warrant will sell at a premium under certain circumstances because a warrant represents an easy way to speculate in a common stock on a leveraged basis. We can say the following about the premium:

1. The premium will be at the maximum in dollar amount when the market price of the common is the same as the warrant exercise price; that is, when the intrinsic value is zero. At this point the warrant holder has the greatest potential market appreciation if the market price of the common moves up. This is illustrated with the following figures:

Common		Warrant	
Year	Market Price	Exercise Price	Intrinsic Value
0	$ 90	$90	0
1	100	"	$10

As the common stock price moves away from the exercise price, either higher or lower, the dollar amount of the premium decreases.

2. The premium will decrease as the warrant approaches the end of the exercise period. It may start to decrease about two years before the end and will completely disappear when there is only a few months left. This is due to the fact that there is little time left for the common stock to move up in price and thus benefit the warrant holder.
3. If the market price of the common falls below the exercise price, a warrant will have a value, which will be all premium, based on the prospects that the common stock will rise above the exercise price in the future. A warrant will only be worthless if the common price gets so far below the exercise price that there is no hope that it will ever increase above the exercise price during the exercise period.

These facts are summarized in chart form in Exhibit 4-37. We show a large increase in the common stock price in a short period of time in order to illustrate the ideas in limited space. Part I of the exhibit shows how the intrinsic value is non-existent until the market price of the common exceeds the exercise value.

Part II shows how the entire market value of the warrant is premium as long as the common price is below the exercise price. The dollar value of the premium maximizes when the market price of the common equals the exercise price. As a quick rule of thumb, the premium may be between 25% and 40% of the common market price at this point. As we have pointed out, the dollar amount of premium is progressively smaller as the common market price gets further away from the exercise price. Also included in Part II are the lower and upper price limits which we will now explain.

Lower Limit

As we have said, a warrant may be worthless or sell for practically nothing if the market price of the common is so much below the warrant exercise price as to preclude any hopes that the common price will exceed the exercise price during the life of the warrant. When the common price is above the exercise price, the warrant will sell for at least the intrinsic value. Arbitrage would prevent the warrant market price from going lower.

Therefore, the lower limit of the price of a warrant is zero or the intrinsic value.

Upper Limit

Observations of the market price of warrants show that there will be no premium if the common price is four times the exercise price.[11] At this point, the market price of the warrant would be its intrinsic value, which would be three-quarters of the market price of the common. Assuming an exercise price of $90, these figures would be as follows:

Common market price (4 times exercise price)	$360
Warrant exercise price	$ 90
Premium	$ 0
Maximum warrant price—intrinsic value (3/4 of common market price)	$270

The reason that there is no premium when the common is four times the exercise price is due to the fact that the price of the warrant is so close to the price of the common stock that there would be little future prospects of a greater percentage gain in an investment in the warrant than the common stock. Furthermore, the holder of the common stock would

[11] See article, "The Relation of Price of a Warrant to the Price of Its Associated Stock," by John P. Shelton, *Financial Analysts Journal*, May-June, 1967.

Exhibit 4-37

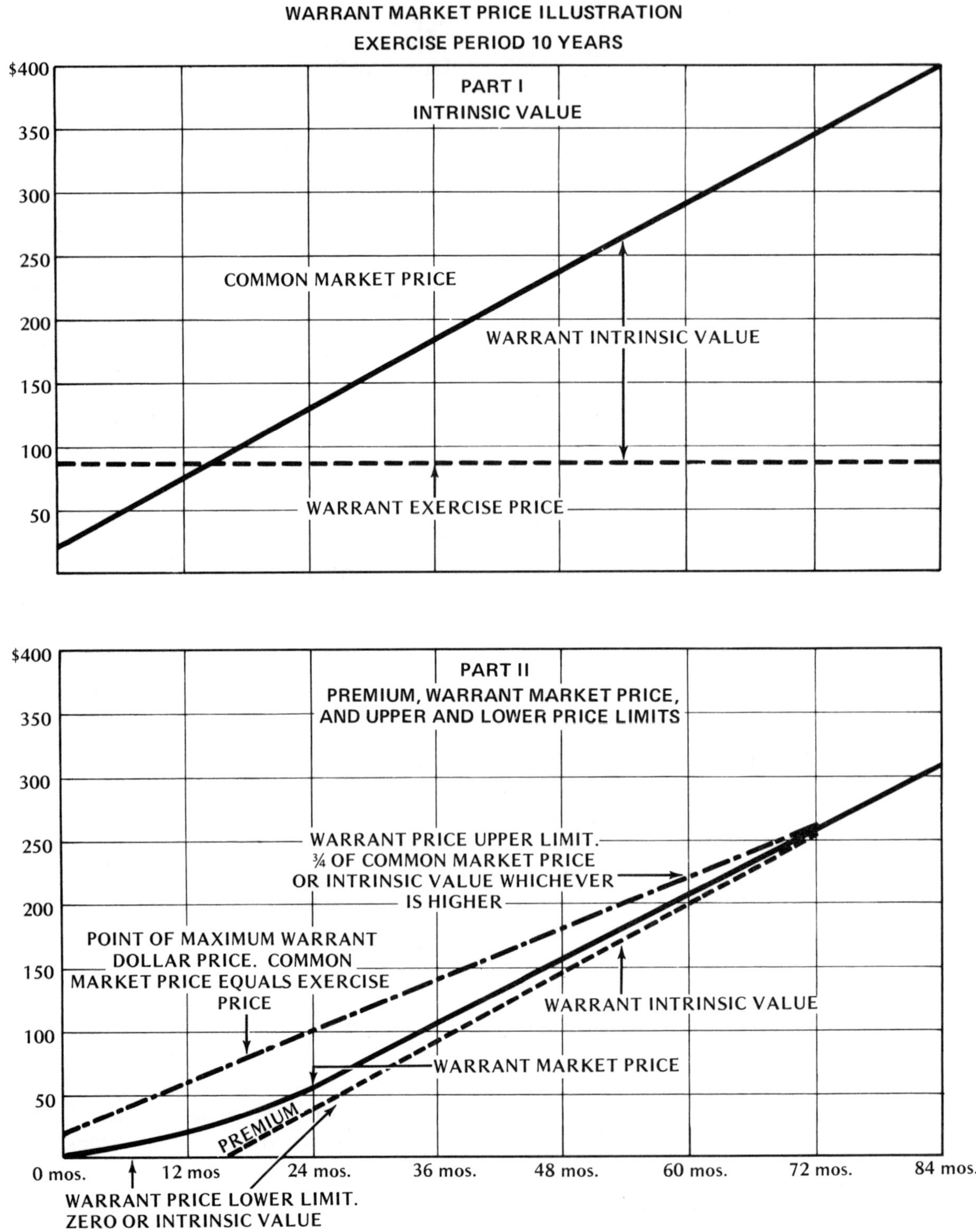
WARRANT MARKET PRICE ILLUSTRATION
EXERCISE PERIOD 10 YEARS
PART I
INTRINSIC VALUE
$400
350
300
250
200
150
100
50
COMMON MARKET PRICE
WARRANT INTRINSIC VALUE
WARRANT EXERCISE PRICE
PART II
PREMIUM, WARRANT MARKET PRICE, AND UPPER AND LOWER PRICE LIMITS
WARRANT PRICE UPPER LIMIT. ¾ OF COMMON MARKET PRICE OR INTRINSIC VALUE WHICHEVER IS HIGHER
POINT OF MAXIMUM WARRANT DOLLAR PRICE. COMMON MARKET PRICE EQUALS EXERCISE PRICE
WARRANT INTRINSIC VALUE
WARRANT MARKET PRICE
PREMIUM
0 mos.
12 mos
24 mos.
36 mos.
48 mos.
60 mos.
72 mos.
84 mos.
WARRANT PRICE LOWER LIMIT. ZERO OR INTRINSIC VALUE

get dividends if any were paid; whereas, the holder of the warrant would not get this benefit. Thus, there is no significant leverage advantage of a warrant at these levels.

It also follows that when the common stock is at any higher price than four times the exercise price, the maximum warrant price will be solely the intrinsic value. And then the maximum and minimum will be the same; that is, the intrinsic value.

What about the maximum price of a warrant if the common stock is below four times the warrant exercise price? If the maximum price is three-quarters of the common market price when the common is four times the exercise price, it has to follow that at any lower price, the maximum warrant price will still be three-quarters of the common market price because there will be no greater prospects of market appreciation in the warrant than the common. This is illustrated in the following figures:

Year	Common Market Price	Warrant: Exercise Price	Warrant: Intrinsic Value	Warrant: Maximum Premium	Warrant: Maximum Market Price. 3/4 of Common Price
0	$100	$90	$ 10	$65	$ 75
1	360*	"	270	0	270
% Increase	+360%				+360%

*Common market price 4 times exercise price.

In summary, the upper limit of a warrant price is three-quarters of common market price up to the point when the common is four times the exercise price. After that the maximum price is the intrinsic value and the same as the minimum value. A warrant only moves close to its maximum value when the market price of the common is high in relation to the exercise price.

As we have said, a warrant may be between 25% and 40% of the common market price when the premium is a maximum; that is, when the common market price equals the exercise price.

The above remarks about the price of a warrant with the upper and lower market limits are summarized in tabular form in Exhibit 4-38. The figures are as used in the previous exhibit in chart form.

How an Investor Might Look at the Price of a Warrant

An investor, in deciding on the price to pay for a warrant within the upper and lower limits, might proceed as follows:

1. Decide how long he may wish to hold the warrant.
2. Estimate the market price of the common at the end of the period.
3. Estimate the price at which the warrant would sell in the market at the end of the period.

   If it is the expiration date of the warrant, then the warrant market price would be the intrinsic value.
4. On the basis of the percent gain from appreciation desired by the investor on his investment in the warrant over the period, calculate the price that can be paid for the warrant at present.
5. Or make an estimate in reverse. Calculate what the warrant will have to sell for in the future to provide an adequate return in terms of appreciation from the present price. Then estimate what the stock would have to sell for in the future to justify the future warrant market price. Finally, decide whether it is reasonable to expect that the common might sell at that price.

How a Company Might Look at the Price of a Warrant

In evaluating the use of a warrant, there is a tendency for a company to compare the exercise price of a warrant with the price of

Exhibit 4-38

ILLUSTRATION OF MARKET PRICE OF WARRANT
WITH UPPER AND LOWER LIMITS
EXERCISE PERIOD–10 YEARS

Months	Common Market Price	Exercise Price	Intrinsic Value	Premium	Warrant Market Price	3/4 Common Market Price
0	23	90	--	5	5	17
6	50	"	--	10	10	38
12	77	"	--	20	20	58
18	104	"	14	20	34	78
24	130	"	40	15	55	98
36	185	"	95	10	105	139
48	240	"	150	5	155	180
72	347	"	257	0	257	260
84	400	"	310	0	310	300

Months	Lower Limit. Zero or Intrinsic Value	Warrant Market Price	Upper Limit. 3/4 of Common Market Price or Intrinsic Value, Whichever Is Higher
0	0	5	17
6	0	10	38
12	0	20	58
18	14	34	78
24	40	55	98
36	95	105	139
48	150	155	180
72	257	257	260
84	310	310	310

the common at the time that the warrant is offered. Since the exercise price is generally above the market price of the common when the warrant is sold, it may appear that a premium is obtained for the common stock. This is not a correct analysis, because the company does not issue common equity, it issues a warrant. It only gets the common equity when the warrant is exercised, which is generally not until it expires. The comparison of the exercise price with the common market price when the warrant is issued is only important because it is necessary to keep the exercise price reasonably close to the common market in order for the warrant to have value.

As far as the company is concerned, it is important to consider the time when the warrant expires. At that time, it can be calculated what the warrant holder may ultimately gain, and what the company may sacrifice in terms of discount from the common market price at which the company has to issue common to the warrant holder. In other words, by issuing warrants, the company is subsequently forced to issue common at a price which may be below the price at which it could sell stock in the market. The gain to the investor and sacrifice to the company are shown in Exhibit 4-39.

Part 1 gives the assumptions on which the exhibit is based.

Part 2 gives the investor's view or the return to the investor. An investor estimates that the common stock will appreciate at a rate of 8% per annum in ten years when the warrant expires. The stock would then be worth $108. Subtracting the warrant exercise price of $55 would give an intrinsic value of $53, which would be the same as the market price at the expiration of the warrant. The investor could afford to buy the warrant for $16 at year zero, and obtain a 13% compounded rate of return from appreciation in the warrant price.

With these same facts, there is shown in Part 3 the company's view or its sacrifice by issuing the warrant. At the expiration of the warrant in ten years, the company could have sold stock at $102 per share after allowing for a $6 financing expense. When the warrant holders would exercise their warrants in ten years, the company would only get $55, the exercise price. Therefore, the company sacrificed $47 by the use of a warrant. When the company sold the warrant, we have assumed that it received $16 less $1 financing expense, or $15. Comparing the net amount of $15 the company received at the time the warrant was sold with the $47 it sacrificed at the expiration, would result in a compound rate of 12%. It represents the cost of the warrant in terms of what the company sacrificed.

The difference between what the investor got and what the company sacrificed is due to the financing costs that would have to be incurred by the company.

Formula Approach

We have considered the value of a warrant from various angles. Now let's give further consideration to the market price. Many formulas have been developed to arrive at the market price of a warrant. They are based on a statistical analysis of a sample of market prices of existing warrants. An example of one of the formulas is given in Exhibit 4-40.

Some of the literature which describes this formula explains the principal factors which predominate in affecting the price of the warrants and which are taken into account in the formula. This formula provides a means of estimating the warrant price between the maximum and minimum prices described above. The factors it allows for are: (1) the time left before the warrant expires, (2) the yield on the common stock, and (3) whether the warrant is listed.

It is interesting to note that most formulas do not seem to allow for all factors which would logically affect the market prices of warrants. Some of the factors which would seem to have the most effect are:

1. The terms; that is, whether any terms might dampen the value of the warrants such as a short maturity.
2. The nearness of the market price of the common and the exercise price.
3. The nature of the common stock and its outlook; that is, whether it is stable or highly speculative and its future prospects. It may be contended that the effect of the outlook for the company is already expressed in the market price of the common stock, and that taking it into account separately would be double counting. This point has some validity but it does not appear to be entirely true. Take two companies with warrant provisions and stock prices exactly the same, but one of the companies has a stable and dull outlook and the other has

Exhibit 4-39

WARRANT RETURN TO INVESTOR AND SACRIFICE BY COMPANY

PART 1

ASSUMPTIONS

	At Time of Issue	At Expiration of Warrant
Year	0 1 2 3 4 5 6 7 8 9	10
Common market price	$50 —8% compound growth→	$108
Warrant exercise price	$55	55
Warrant market price	$16	53

PART 2

INVESTOR'S VIEW.
RETURN TO INVESTOR

Year 0 1 2 3 4 5 6 7 8 9 10

	Year 10	
	$108	Common market price
	$ 55	Warrant exercise price
	$ 53	Warrant market price

Warrant market price $16 —Return to Investor 13% Compound→ $ 53

PART 3

COMPANY'S VIEW.
SACRIFICE BY COMPANY

Year 0 1 2 3 4 5 6 7 8 9 10

	Year 10	
	$108	Common market price
	$ 6	Financing expense
	$102	Net proceeds received by company if it sold common
	$ 55	Warrant exercise price
	$ 47	Net proceeds company sacrificed

	Year 0
Warrant market price	$16
Financing expense	$ 1
Net proceeds received by company from sale of warrant	$15

$15 —Sacrifice by Company 12% Compound→ $ 47

bright prospects. The price of the latter's stock would sell at a higher price-earnings ratio, and it would seem that the warrant would also sell higher in relation to the price of the company's stock.

Exhibit 4-40

FORMULA FOR DETERMINING
WARRANT PRICE
DESIGNED BY JOHN P. SHELTON*

a. Maximum Value–3/4 price of common stock.
b. Minimum Value–Market price of common less exercise price for 1 share of stock or zero.
c. Most probable value

$$\left(\sqrt[4]{\frac{M}{72}}\right)(.47 \;-\; 4.25Y + .17L)$$

M = Months of remaining longevity

Y = Dividend expressed as a fraction of the market price of the common–For example $5 ÷ $100 = .05

L = 1 if listed on an exchange, 0 if not listed.

Multiply the result of this formula by the difference between the maximum and minimum values, to determine how much should be added to the minimum value to obtain an estimated value for a warrant exercisable into 1 share of common. If a warrant is exercisable into less or more than 1 share of common, adjust for this difference.

*"The Relation of the Price of a Warrant to the Price of Its Associated Stock," by John P. Shelton, *Financial Analysts Journal, May-June, 1965.*

Premium Affected by Relationship of Stock Price and Exercise Price

We have already noted that the dollar amount of the premium is largest when the common price is the same as the exercise price.

There is also a relationship between the size of the premium as a percent of the stock price and the stock price as a percent of the exercise price. In other words, there is a relationship between these two percentages:

Premium as % of Common Price	vs.	Common Prices as % of Exercise Price

Given a number of warrants with terms reasonably comparable, these relationships can be calculated and plotted. Shown in Exhibit 4-41 is a plot of a sample of warrants. Note how the premium is largest when the common market price is the same as the exercise price. The reasons why they do not fall in a more uniform pattern may be due to:

1. Different terms of the warrants.
2. Different market interest in the warrants as regards the outlook for the companies and their stocks.
3. Special market demand which throws the market off at any particular time.

Another Approach to Premium Related to Common Market Price

The term premium can be defined in another way as follows:

Premium (Redefined) = Warrant Market Price - Intrinsic Value

Intrinsic value is the difference between the common stock market price and the warrant exercise price. When the common market price is above the exercise price, the premium is the same as we have previously defined it. For example, if the warrant market price is $25, the common market price is $70 and the exercise price is $50, the warrant premium would be $5.

However, if the common market price is below the exercise price, we come up with a different premium based on the definition given above. For example, if the warrant market price is $5, the exercise price is $50 and the common market price is $30, the premium (redefined) would be $25 as follows:

Premium
(Redefined) = Warrant Market Price – Intrinsic Value
= Warrant Market Price – (Common Market Price – Exercise Price)
= $5 – ($30 – $50)
= 5 – (-20)
= 5 + 20
= $25

Thus, under premium (redefined), we subtract the intrinsic value from the warrant

Exhibit 4-41

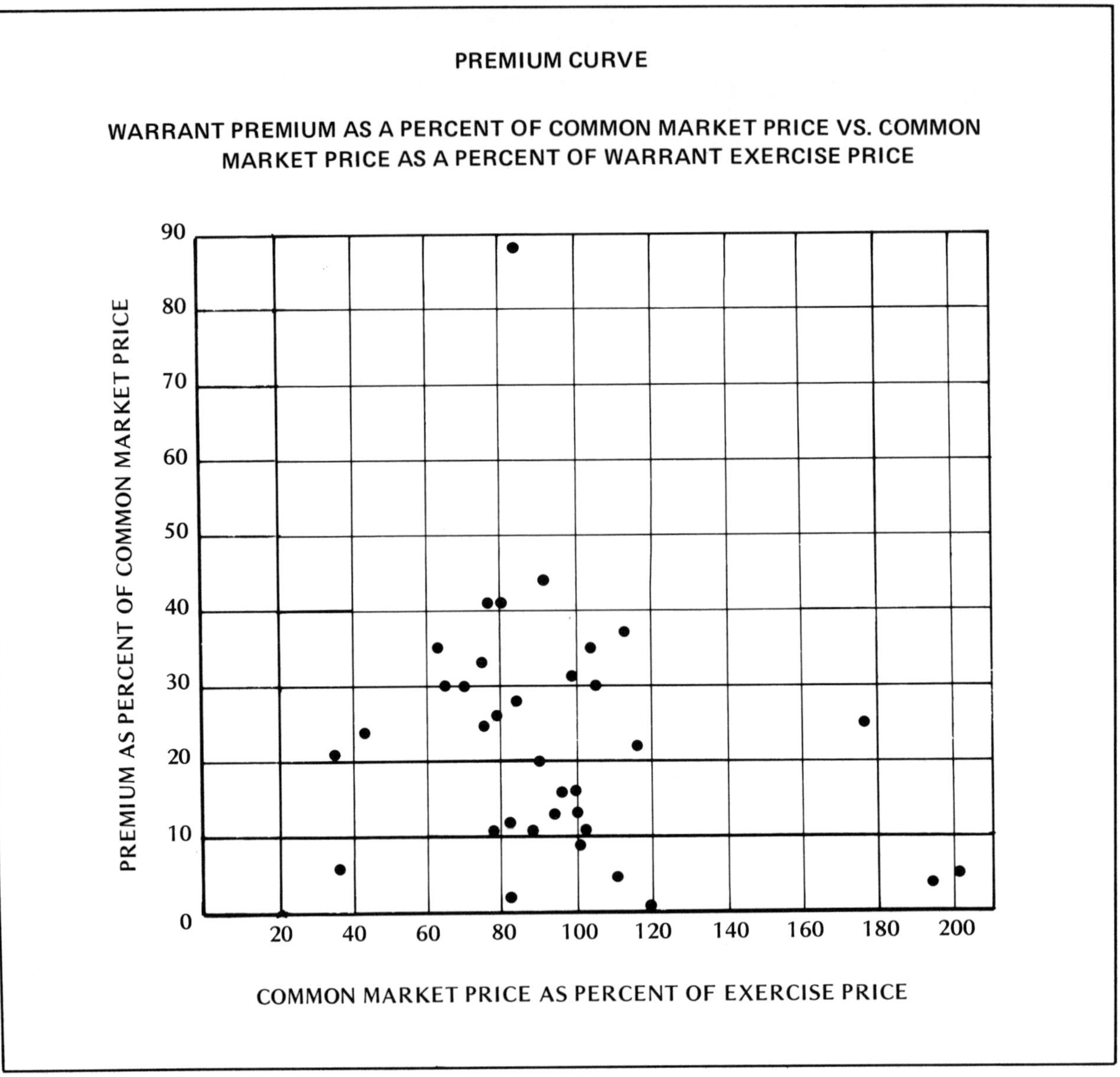

market price, when the intrinsic value is positive. When the common market price is below the exercise price, and the intrinsic value is negative, we add the intrinsic value to the warrant market price to get the premium (redefined).

This approach to premium compared with the common market price gives a chart which is easier to interpret. This is shown in Exhibit 4-42.

It may be noted that the two exhibits are the same when the common market price is 100% or more than the exercise price.

Pricing a Warrant

If you have the job of pricing a warrant, you will probably have to use various approaches, and consider the factors we have suggested above.

Exhibit 4-42

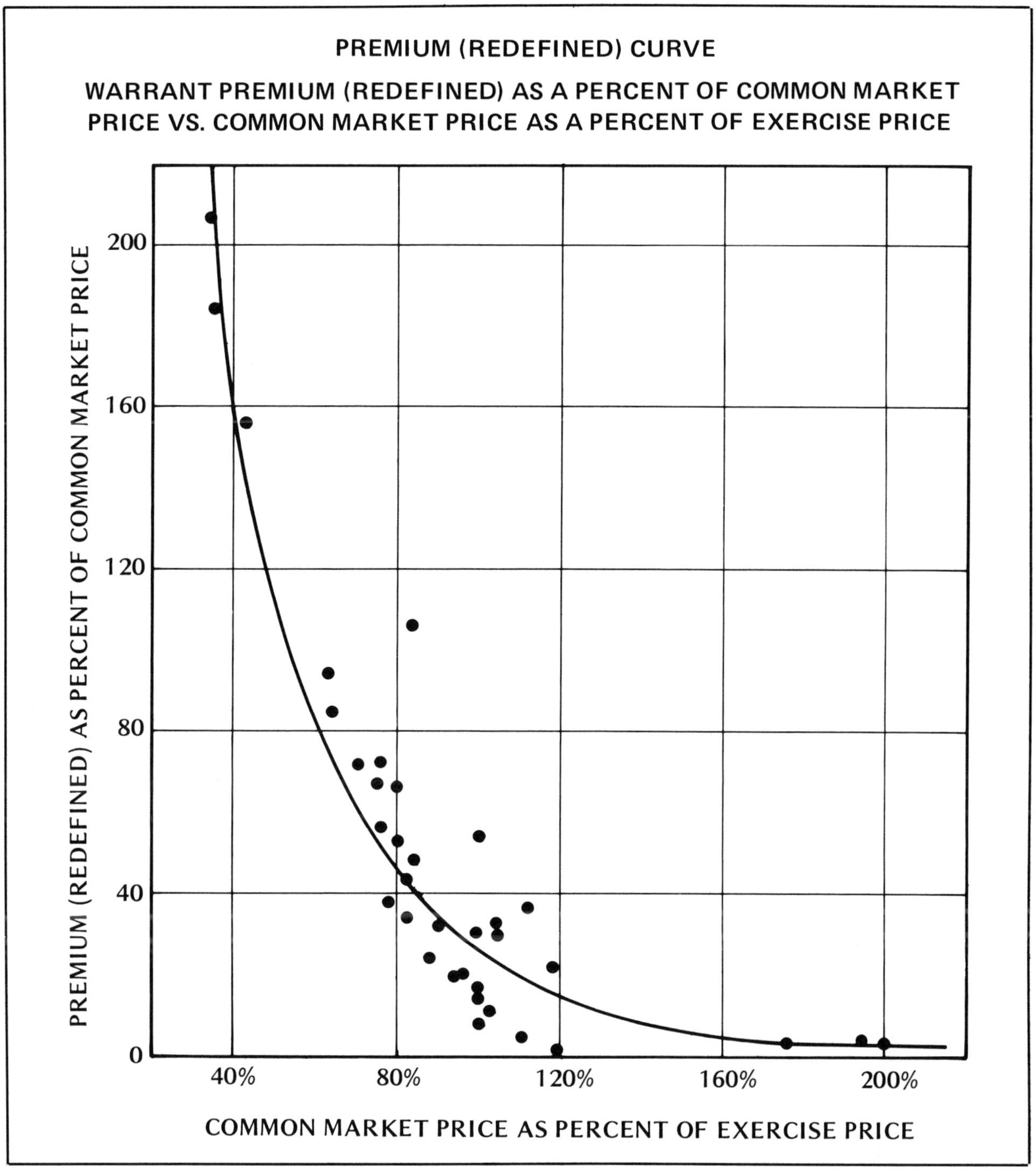

You can use the method shown in Exhibit 4-39. This involves the problem of first estimating the market price of the common at some time in the future and then working backwards and figuring out the current price of the warrant on the basis of an annual percentage return that an investor might be willing to accept. This method may produce too low a figure. Warrants tend to be overpriced in the market because of the limited supply.

You can apply one or more of the formulas such as the one shown in Exhibit 4-40.

You can obtain a sample of similar warrants and develop curves as shown in Exhibit 4-41 and Exhibit 4-42 and make an estimate from these curves. If you use this approach, be sure that the warrants are reasonably comparable to that of your company. As we have pointed out, factors which may affect the price are maturity if it is too close; special terms which may dampen the warrant price and nature of the company issuing the warrants.

With all possible available estimates, you can then make up your mind on the basis of judgment as to a reasonable price. Finally, you will probably have to check your conclusion with a person who regularly trades in warrants and can add the market feel to the picture.

Now we will look at the way they are treated in financial reporting and for tax purposes.

Financial Reporting for Warrants

When warrants are sold as a package with bonds, the balance sheet treatment can be explained with the following example:

A bond and warrant is sold for $100. The warrant when detached is worth $10. The assets and liabilities would be recorded as follows:

Assets		Liabilities	
Cash	$100	Bonds	$100
Bond discount	$ 10	Capital surplus	$ 10

The warrants are shown in a footnote. The bond discount is written off over the life of the bond the same as any bond discount. Therefore, there is no effect of a lower interest rate as a result of a warrant in the income statement. When the warrants are exercised, the cash account and common stock account are increased equally.

When warrants are sold as a package with preferred stock, no discount is shown.

When warrants are permanently attached to a security, they are not treated separately.

When warrants are sold separately, there are only two entries; cash and capital surplus, with the warrants shown in a footnote.

With regard to the effect on earnings per share, the company does not have to report diluted earnings per share if common shares resulting from the warrants and other securities affecting dilution are less than 3% of the outstanding stock.

If the total resulting dilution is larger than 3% but less than 20% (other rules apply for dilution over 20%), the effect of dilution from warrants depends on the price of the common stock and the exercise price of the warrant. The "treasury stock method" is used in reporting both the primary and fully diluted earnings per share:

1. When the common market price is below the warrant exercise price, no adjustment is made.
2. When the common market is above the exercise price, a calculation is made to determine the proceeds that would be received if all the warrants were exercised. This sum is then used to purchase common stock at the market price. The difference between the number of shares issued at the exercise price and the shares purchased are added to shares outstanding in calculating both primary and secondary earnings per share.

Tax Treatment of Warrants

When warrants are issued as a package with a bond, the company writes off the discount created by the warrants against income over the life of the bond. There is no write-off if warrants are issued with a preferred.

If the warrants expire unexercised, there may be a tax liability on the amount of money the company received at the time the warrant was issued.

The investor treats a warrant as a capital gain if held for six months. The discount on a bond represented by a warrant is taken in as ordinary income on a pro-rate annual basis if the discount falls within the rules for original issue discount.

By way of further background, before considering their use, let's look at an outline of the advantages and disadvantages of warrants from the company's point of view.

Warrant Advantages and Disadvantages for Company

Advantages

1. Assists in the sale of a security when a kicker is needed.
2. Used by venture capital type of company in order to give the investor a run for his money.
3. May seem tempting for acquisition purposes. May be helpful in reorganizations, etc.
4. May be over-priced in market due to the small supply of warrants.
5. May produce proceeds to company with no dilution if the common price falls below the exercise price at expiration of warrant. As we have said, there may be a tax liability.

Disadvantages

1. Warrants in themselves raise very little money in relation to the potential dilution. For example, if a company has outstanding 1 million shares of common stock which are selling for $30 per share, a 1-for-10 offering of 100,000 new shares would raise $3 million. If a warrant were issued which had the right to obtain 1 share of common at an exercise price of $35 per share, the warrant might be priced in the market for about $10. In order to raise $3 million immediately with warrants, it would require 1 million warrants, which would ultimately mean the issuance of 1 million common shares, or the equivalent of a 1-for-1 common offering. In other words, a warrant by itself is not a satisfactory way to raise capital.
2. Generally, warrants are non-callable and a company has no control over them. They are generally not exercised until they expire.
3. Whether the company will get common equity through exercise of the warrants depends on the common market price. This uncertainty makes financial planning difficult.
4. The company may not need common equity capital at the time the warrants are exercised.
5. The potential dilution will hang over the market and may have a depressing effect on the market price of the common, even though under the "treasury stock" method reported earnings per share may be little affected.
6. The senior security with a warrant may in effect be sold at a discount which will result in an adverse call premium even though the rate on the senior security is apparently lowered.
7. If common stock increases substantially, the company, in effect, has to issue common at an excessive discount at the expiration date.
8. It is a leveraged type of security, more leveraged than even common stock, and must have more risk. It is only logic that investors will require a higher return to compensate them for the added risk. For example, if investors wanted an 8% interest on a bond, they would want a higher return on common and a still higher return on a warrant. For this reason, it is a higher cost medium for raising capital than common stock.

Analysis of an Offering of a Package of a Senior Security with a Warrant

When a security is offered with a warrant, there are two ways to analyze the pros and cons of the offering:

1. As a package with the two securities combined.
2. With the security and warrant as separate financing instruments.

An investment banker will generally explain the effect with the two securities combined and tell an intriguing story about two advantages of the package:

1. The rate on the senior security is lowered.
2. Since the exercise price of the warrant is above the common market price at the time of the offering, a premium is obtained for the common.

Neither of these advantages are real.

To analyze the package, it is essential to study the two parts separately—the security and the warrant. Generally, the two become separate as soon as they are offered. To explain the importance of this approach, we will use as an example a preferred stock issued with a warrant as follows:

8% preferred ($100 par value) offered at $100 with one warrant, with the warrant having an exercise price of $50.
Call price of preferred starting at $108.
Common market at time of offering—$40.

The company could sell a straight preferred without a warrant attached at a 9.50% yield and with a call price starting at $110.

On the basis of these facts, the company apparently reduced the yield at which it would have to sell preferred from 9.50% to 8.00% by adding a warrant or a 1.50% savings in dividends per share. And it supposedly received a premium for the common since the exercise price of the warrant was $50 compared with the common market price of $40.

However, the fact is that the company in no way could possibly sell a preferred stock at less than a 9.50% yield. The dividend savings was due entirely to the warrant. Therefore, if we separate the preferred and warrant, the picture would be as follows:

8.00% preferred, market price separately	$ 84.50 to yield 9.50%[12]
Estimated warrant market price	15.50
Offering price of 8.80% preferred plus one warrant	$100.00

Again, the only reason the company was able to sell the preferred at a lower yield was due entirely to the warrant. Without the warrant, the yield on the 8.00% preferred would be 9.50%, the same rate at which it could have sold the preferred separately.

With a call price of $108, the 8.00% preferred stock would have a call premium of $23.50 (the difference between the market price at time of offering of $84.50 and the call price of $108). This is a very adverse call premium from the point of view of refunding if rates go lower. If the company were offering a preferred separately, it would not offer a preferred at such a discount; a senior security is never sold at a discount for this reason. Thus, the company would probably decide against the 8% discount preferred as a separate means of raising capital.

Would the company sell a warrant separately to raise capital? Probably not because it raises so little capital in relation to the potential dilution. This we previously discussed. Furthermore, when the preferred with the warrant was sold, the exercise price of the warrant was $10 above the market price of the common, but the test as to whether a premium for the common was obtained does not occur until the warrants are exercised. If, at the expiration of the warrants, the common market price is substantially above the exercise price, the company would be forced to give stock to the warrant holders at a discount.

Thus, the company did not really attain a lower yield on the preferred and it did not attain a premium for common stock. It would not sell either security separately as designed.

Preferred Stock with Warrant at a Premium Rather than at Par

If the company wished to sell a preferred with a warrant, it would have been better off

[12] Actually, a senior security sold at a discount will sell at a slightly higher price (lower yield) because investors have the advantage of a high call premium. For illustrative purposes, we will not make any allowance for this factor.

to have sold a 9.50% preferred with a starting call price of 109.50 with a warrant attached as follows:

9.50% preferred	$100.00
Warrant market price	15.50
Total	$115.50

Then the call premium would only have been $9.50 (call price $109.50 less the offering price $100). The company would merely sell less of the 9.50% preferred with a warrant and raise the same amount of money. The total dividend payments would be the same. In fact, 0.8665 of a share of this package would produce $100, and the cash dividend payments would be only slightly higher—$8.23.

Undoubtedly, once the company saw what was really happening, it would decide to sell the 9.50% preferred without a warrant (assuming the market was receptive) or abandon the financing for some other approach. At least you should not fool yourself into believing that through some sleight of hand you were able to sell a preferred at a yield of 8.00%, when without the warrant the yield would be 9.50%. And you should also realize that the premium for the common is another myth.

These same ideas are equally applicable to any package of a senior security with a warrant, such as a debenture with a warrant.

Common Stock with a Warrant

A company's common stock was selling below book value and at a poor price earnings ratio. An investment banker suggested that the company attach a warrant to the common so that a price above book value could be obtained. The package suggested by the investment banker was as follows:

1 share of common with 1 warrant which as a package would sell for $24.

The common alone was selling for $18. The warrant was to be exercised at $21. The warrant value alone was estimated to be worth about $6.

The fallacy of this package can be seen by taking it apart as we did above with the preferred and warrant.

The company did not receive a higher price for the common; it in no way could do so. The reason why it appeared to do so was because the warrant was added. The package was as follows:

1 share common	$18
1 Warrant	6
Package	$24

In other words, it did not avoid selling common at $18. Furthermore, its financial position was such that it had to sell common. Therefore, the only question left is whether it should also have sold the warrant. The warrant added an equal amount of potential dilution and only raised $6 compared with $18 for each share of common. The company could have raised an amount of money equal to that obtained by the warrant by selling one-third more shares of common. Furthermore, if the company prospered and its stock appreciated, it would be forced to let warrant holders exercise their warrants at $21 when the stock might be worth considerably more.

The company sensibly decided to sell the common separately without the warrants.

Privately Held Warrants

Thus far we have talked about warrants which had a public market. There has been some private placement financing of senior securities for privately owned companies with warrants included in order to get investors to do the deal. These warrants have to be looked at differently because there is no market in which the investor can obtain the benefit of the premium. The only way the investor can benefit from the warrants is to hold them until they expire and then get their intrinsic value. This is not to say that there would not be some premium, but it would be considerably less. There is no set formula to use to arrive at the value of such warrants. To the extent that arrangements are made to have the warrants and the stock marketable before the warrants expire could add to the premium.

An Example

We will use the package of warrants and debentures issued by AT&T in May 1970 as an example. The package was $1,569,327,000 of debentures with warrants attached which would exercise into $1,632,100,080 of common. The company attached warrants to the debentures as a matter of necessity. Its credit was excellent, but it was contended that the company could not have sold the large amount of debentures without adding a kicker to attract a sufficient number of investors. The package was as follows:

Debentures—interest coupon 8 3/4%—maturity 2,000 (30 years)—beginning call price 107.

Each $100 of debentures included two warrants.

1 warrant had the right to purchase 1 share of common at $52 per share. Exercise period of warrants expired in five years on May 15, 1975.

The package was offered to shareholders on a rights basis at $100. The market price of the package at the time of the offering was 116 3/4 to yield 7.35%. The debentures and warrants traded on a when-issued basis are as follows:

Debentures	98 1/2	—Yield to maturity 8.89%
2 Warrants	19	—(Price per warrant $9.50)
Total	117 1/2	

In order for the warrants to be worth the market price at the time they were offered, the common would have to sell for $67 per share at the time the warrants were exercised in order for a warrant holder to receive a minimal compound return of 10% over the life of the warrant. This is shown in Exhibit 4-43.

Now we will look at the warrants about halfway through their life on December 18, 1972. On that date, the warrants had a life of 2 1/2 years. Then the common stock sold for $51 3/4 and one warrant for $8 1/2. For one warrant to be worth this price without any return to the investor in the meantime, the stock would have to sell for $60 1/2 at the expiration of the warrants:

Common Market Price	$60 1/2
Exercise Price	52
Intrinsic Value at Expiration	$ 8 1/2

To give the investors a minimal 10% compound return, the warrant would have to have an intrinsic value of $10.80, and the common stock would have to sell for $62.80 at the end of the expiration period. This calculation is made on the same basis as in Exhibit 4-39.

Applying the formula in Exhibit 4-40 to pricing this warrant at December 18, 1972 would be as shown in Exhibit 4-44. While generally the premium of a warrant is not affected significantly by the expiration date until there is less than two years remaining life, the approaching maturity dampens this price from then on.

These figures for AT&T warrants indicate how the market may vary from the various approaches used to determine the price.

Conclusion

In outline form, we can conclude as follows:

1. Warrants attached to a senior security give the false appearance of a low rate on the senior security and a premium on the common at the time issued. Analyzed separately, it becomes apparent that there is no true reduction in the senior security rate, and if the package is at 100, the senior security will be sold at a discount with an adverse call premium.
2. Warrants by themselves raise relatively little money.
3. Regardless of their effect on reported earnings per share, their diluting effect will hang over the market and may depress the common.
4. Warrants at times may be over-priced because of the lack of supply.
5. The excessive use of complicated securities for short range expediency burdens a company's financial position and makes it hard for investors to understand. Con-

Exhibit 4-43

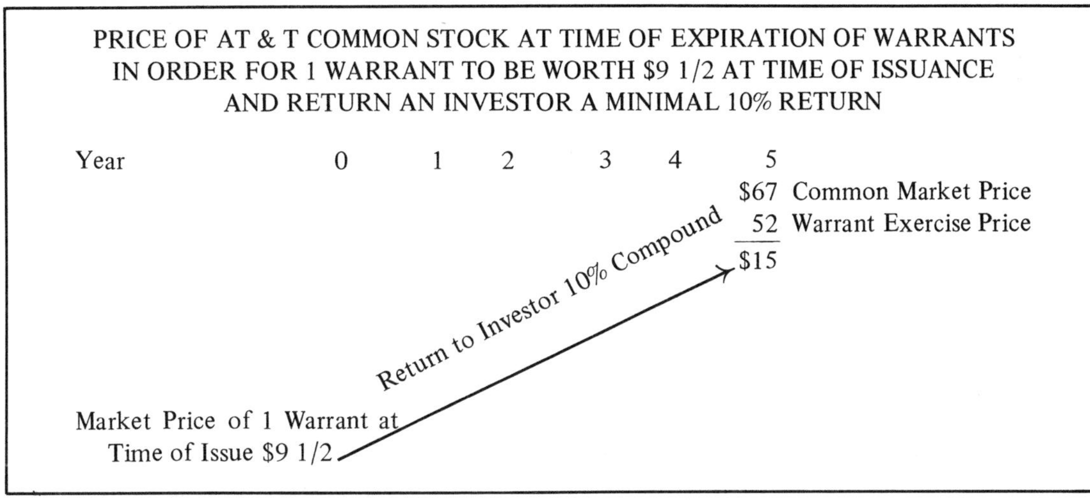

Exhibit 4-44

APPLICATION OF FORMULA IN EXHIBIT 4-40 TO PRICING
OF AT & T WARRANTS AT DECEMBER 18, 1972

a) Maximum value–3/4 price of common ($51 3/4) = $39

b) Minimum value–Market price of common ($51 3/4) less exercise price for 1 share of stock ($52) = 0

c) Most probable value

$$\left(\sqrt[4]{\frac{M}{72}}\right) \times (.47 - 4.25Y + .17L)$$

$$\left(\sqrt[4]{\frac{30}{72}}\right) \times (.47 - 4.25 \times .054 + .17 \times 1)$$

$$\left(\sqrt[4]{.4167}\right) \times (.47 - .22950 + .17)$$

$$(.8) \times .4105$$

$$.33$$

Difference between (a) maximum ($39) and (b) minimum ($0)	=	$39
Multiply difference ($39) by result of formula above (.33)	=	$13
Add result ($13) to minimum (0)	=	$13

sequently it is more costly to raise capital in the long run. When used, warrants should at least be kept simple, with relatively short maturity.

6. Warrants may have some special purposes in acquisitions and reorganizations.
7. Warrants may be helpful for raising capital for a company which has financing

problems and cannot sell a security without a kicker. *In general, they should be saved for this purpose.*

CONVERTIBLE SECURITIES

A convertible is a senior security containing a provision which permits the holder to convert, or in other words, exchange the security for another security, generally common stock. As an example, a debenture or preferred stock may be convertible into common.

A few of the features of a convertible preferred are shown in Exhibit 4-45. We will use this simple example to start our explanation. The same ideas apply to a convertible debenture; where there are differences we will point them out.

We have assumed that the credit of the company will permit the preferred to be worth $80 as a straight preferred stock without the conversion privilege, and that it would yield 8% with the $6.50 dividend.

The market price of the common is $80. Therefore, the convertible preferred will also be worth $80 based on the privilege to convert into one share of common stock.

As we have shown in the exhibit, the convertible preferred might sell in the market at $100 to yield 6.5%. Why would it sell at $20 more than it is worth either as a straight preferred or due to its convertibility?

Exhibit 4-45

A SIMPLE EXAMPLE OF A CONVERTIBLE PREFERRED

Dividend $6.50–Par value $100
Market price–$100 to yield 6.50%
Conversion price $100. Each share of convertible preferred, convertible into 1 share of common.
Price of common–$80

Yield at which company could sell a similar non-convertible preferred is 8%, and the price of such a non-convertible preferred with $6.50 dividend would be $80.

Thus:

Market price of convertible preferred	$100
Conversion value	80
Investment value	80
Premium	20

Terms

Before we give an answer to that question, we will define certain terms that are essential to use in a discussion of convertibles:

Conversion Ratio–Conversion Price

This tells how much common is obtained upon conversion. For a convertible preferred, we want to know how many shares of common are obtained for each share of convertible preferred. In our simple example, one share of convertible preferred is convertible into one share of common.

Confusion sometimes arises over the difference between conversion ratio and conversion price. Conversion price is usually nothing more than the amount of par or stated value of convertible preferred which can be exchanged for one share of common. It is another way of expressing the conversion ratio. To translate a conversion price to a conversion ratio, the par or stated value of the preferred is divided by its conversion price.

In our simple example, the conversion price is $100; that is, the amount of par value which can be exchanged for each share of common:

$$\frac{\$100 \text{ Par Value}}{\$100 \text{ Conversion Price}} = \text{1-for-1 conversion ratio}$$

If a convertible preferred has a par value of $100, and a conversion price of $50, the conversion ratio would be as follows:

$$\frac{\$100 \text{ Par Value}}{\$\ 50 \text{ Conversion Price}} = \text{2-for-1 conversion ratio}$$

For convertible debentures, we will wish to know how many shares of common will be received for each $100 of convertible debentures.

So, the conversion ratio for a convertible preferred is the shares of common received for each share of convertible preferred. For a convertible debenture, it is the shares of common received for each $100 principal amount of debentures.

Conversion Value—Value Based on the Common Stock

This is the value of the convertible based on the right to receive common stock. It is the conversion ratio multiplied by the market price for the common stock. If the common is selling for $80 as in our example and the conversion ratio is one share of common for each share of convertible preferred, the conversion value is $80.

Investment Value—Value Based on Straight Senior Security Value

This is the value of the convertible based on its status as a senior security alone without any conversion value. In other words, stripped of the conversion privilege, what is it worth? If a $6.50 convertible preferred would be worth $80 to yield 8% without the conversion privilege as a straight preferred alone, that would be its investment value. The yield obtained by dividing the market price into the dividend rate has to be sufficient to satisfy investors without the conversion feature.

For a convertible debenture, the investment value is the market price based on the yield to maturity which will satisfy investors without the conversion feature.

Investment value can be estimated with a fair degree of accuracy by a competent security analyst. The analyst first judges the quality by considering all relevant factors; he obtains a sample of other similar quality non-convertible securities to obtain the yield that the market would place on the issue without the conversion feature. With this yield related to the dividend rate or interest coupon, depending on whether it is a preferred or a debenture, he determines the investment value.

The investment value may vary over time as a result of a change in the quality of the issue due to a change in the company's financial strength, or as a result of a general market change in the level of yields on preferreds or bonds.

Market Price

This is the price the market places on a convertible because of its two features—its conversion value and investment value.

Before we started defining terms, we asked why the convertible preferred in our simple example should sell for $100 when the investment value and conversion value were each $80? The reason lies in the fact that the convertible gives an investor an opportunity to speculate in the common with protection on the downside if the common declined in price.

If the common stock price rose to $150, the convertible preferred would likewise rise because of its conversion value. However, if the common fell to $50 so that the conversion value was only worth $50, the convertible preferred would not fall below $80 since it is worth $80 on its investment value alone.

This opportunity to be protected from a decline in the common price by the investment value and yet be able to benefit from a rise in the common stock price causes the convertible to sell at a premium. So we need another definition.

Premium

This is the amount by which the market price of the convertible is above the higher of its conversion value or investment value. It represents the price an investor will pay for a call on the common when he has protection on the downside.

Premium is sometimes taken to mean the amount by which the market price of the convertible is above the conversion price. This interpretation carries with it the idea that the issuer has achieved something for nothing in terms of a better price for its common stock. However, where the market price of a convertible is substantially higher than its conversion price, the price primarily reflects the worth of the convertible as a straight preferred. For example, if the common stock price of our simple example was $50, the figures would be:

Convertible preferred par value—$100
Conversion price—$100
Conversion ratio—1-for-1
Common price—$50
Conversion value—$50
Investment value—$80
Convertible market price—$85
Premium—$5 or 6%

The premium is not the conversion price of $100 compared with the common market price of $50. The premium is $5 or 6%, the amount by which the market price of the convertible is above the investment value which is the higher of the conversion value and the investment value.

Size of Premium

One of the principal factors which affects the size of the premium is the nearness of the conversion value and the investment value. The closer together, the larger the premium. When they are equal the premium will be at a maximum.

If the conversion value is far above the investment value, the premium will be small because there will be little protection from a decline in the common price by the investment value.

If the conversion value is far below the investment value, the premium will also be small because there will be little chance that the common will move up far enough so that the convertible would appreciate above the investment value.

Thus, the premium depends on the ability to be protected from a decline in the common price, with the opportunity to benefit from a rise in the common price. Without the protection of the investment value on the downside there would be no premium.

The above points are illustrated in Exhibit 4-46.

Factors which affect the size of the premium are:

1. The closeness of the conversion value and investment value which we have just discussed.
2. The outlook for the common stock.

   Is it a dull stock without much prospects of growth or does it have real potential? The greater investors' hopes for the stock, the greater the premium.
3. The downside risk in the common.

   If it is a risky stock that might fall out of bed, there is more reason to pay a premium than for one that has little prospects of a decline. For example, a common stock which has an assured dividend and is selling on a yield basis might have little prospects for a decline.
4. The market demand and supply situation.

   There may be certain investors who are particularly anxious to buy convertibles because they provide some yield and protection on the downside.

   Certain corporations receive a dividend tax credit, so they would have a particular interest in convertible preferreds.

   Market limitations impair the demand and the premium. Convertible preferreds issued to acquire closely held companies are usually not marketable initially because SEC registration has not taken place. Further, restrictions against sale or conversion may be built into the terms of such an issue.

   Under certain circumstances, a convertible debenture may have a special demand because of the ability of investors to borrow more on a convertible than on common stock.
5. The yield differential between the common and the convertible.

   The size of the spread between the yield on the convertible and the common available through conversion will affect the premium. When the convertible is sold, the yield on the convertible may be larger than the yield on the common. This spread narrows over time with increases in the dividend rate on the common. When the yield on the common is larger than the yield on the

PREMIUM ILLUSTRATION FOR A CONVERTIBLE

$6.50 Convertible Preferred – Convertible Into 1 Share Common

C.V. – Conversion Value
I.V. – Investment Value
M.P. – Market Price
P – Premium By Which M.P. Exceeds the Larger of C.V. and I.V.

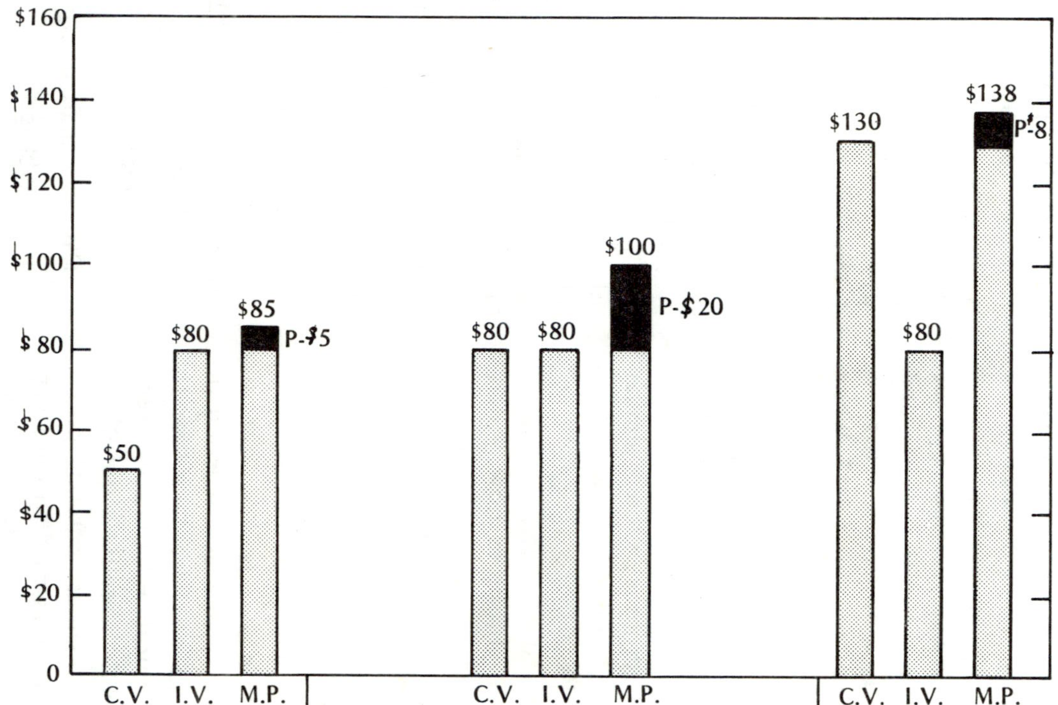

$\frac{IV}{CV} = \frac{\$80}{\$50} = 160\%$

Premium = $\frac{MP - IV}{IV} = \frac{\$5}{\$80} = 6\%$

$\frac{IV}{CV}$ or $\frac{CV}{IV} = 100\%$

Premium = $\frac{MP - IV}{IV}$ or $\frac{MP - CV}{CV} = \frac{\$20}{\$80} = 25\%$

$\frac{CV}{IV} = \frac{\$130}{\$80} = 160\%$

Premium = $\frac{MP - CV}{CV} = \frac{\$8}{\$130} = 6\%$

Exhibit 4-46

convertibles, there is less reason for investors to buy the convertible.

6. The provisions.
   The provisions may dampen or eliminate the premium if they limit the opportunity for the convertible to appreciate with a rise in the common stock price.

A premium is a result of all the factors we have mentioned. It is impossible to separate the various factors to show the effect of each. However, as we have said, the nearness of the conversion value and the investment value has a major effect. Statistical services provide current data on the conversion value and investment value of convertibles. There is shown a sample of data in Exhibit 4-47. When the conversion value is equal to the investment value the premium is the largest, and it tends to be minimal when either the conversion value and the investment value is twice the other. When you consider issuing a convertible, you will wish to develop a similar chart from data on convertibles which are comparable to your issue.

The exhibit indicates the problem of valuing a convertible. It shows how widely premiums can vary from issue to issue even when the same relationship exists between conversion value and investment value.

Misuse of Convertibles

Convertibles may be used to raise new capital, for acquisition purposes, in reorganizations, etc. For our principal discussion of convertibles, we will consider their use to raise new capital. Before we finish convertibles we will discuss their use for acquisitions.

There are fundamental misconceptions with regard to convertibles used to raise new capital. Convertibles are said to be advantageous because they produce:

> A lower dividend or interest rate than could be obtained on a straight senior security, and a premium for the common stock.

Investment bankers like to sell convertibles because they are easy to sell, and investment bankers can talk a company into using convertibles on the basis of these two points. This is a totally unsound approach; many convertibles are sold which never should be sold. Ultimately they do not convert, and the company does not get the common stock it needed. You may say, yes, but look at the lower dividend or interest rate the company received. Indeed it did, but the dividend or interest savings is not much consolation if the company has gotten in a financial jam as a result of too little equity and has suffered such consequences as having to cut its common dividend. The history of finance is strewn with companies which played this game and their stockholders came out the loser.

Why do we make these disparaging remarks about convertibles? To explain, let's go back to our simple example of the convertible preferred in Exhibit 4-45.

First, the company did not get a reduction in the rate on preferred stock. True, the yield on the convertible is 6.5% compared to a yield on a straight preferred of 8%, so the dividend was reduced 1.5%. However, why was it reduced? It was entirely due to the fact that the company offered an additional feature which was the call on the common that was included with the convertible. It was worth \$20. The yield on the preferred without this call on the common is still 8%. The company sold a \$6.50 preferred stock at \$80 to yield 8% and it also sold a call on its common stock for \$20. These figures are summarized below.

\$6.50 preferred to yield 8%	–\$ 80 (market price)
Call on 1 share of common at \$80–	20
Total Package	\$100

We covered warrants attached to a senior security before convertibles, because there is an analogy between a warrant being attached to a senior security and the call that a convertible gives on the common stock. In both instances, the yield on the senior security is not reduced by the warrant or convertible; the senior security is sold at a discount with

Exhibit 4-47

EFFECT OF CLOSENESS OF CONVERSION VALUE AND INVESTMENT VALUE ON SIZE OF PREMIUM

A SAMPLE OF CONVERTIBLE BONDS

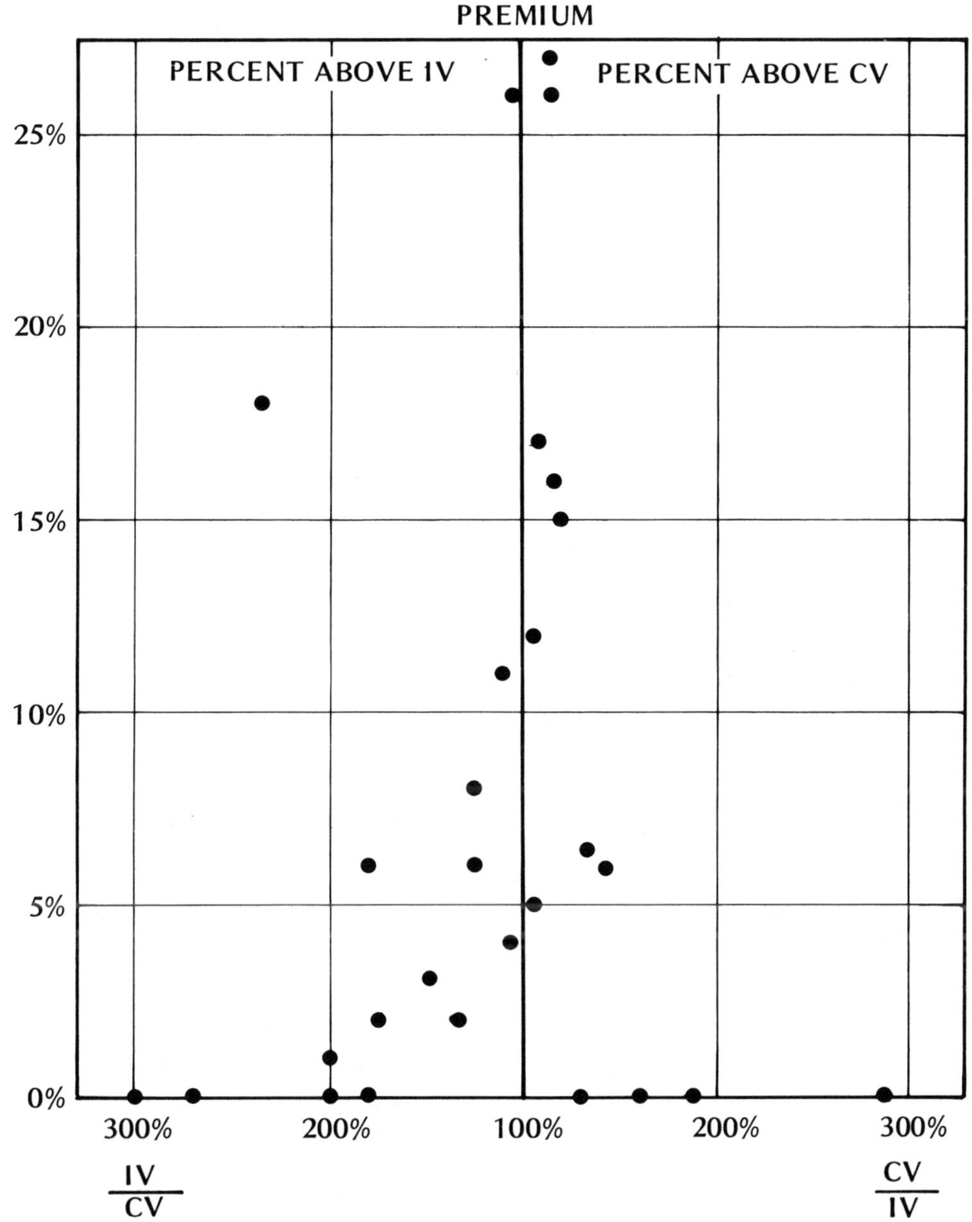

the same yield it would have standing alone. The discount is represented by the warrant, or by the call on the common for a convertible.

Secondly, the company did not get a premium for its common stock. True, in our example the market price of the common was $80 compared with the conversion price of $100. However, the company does not get common until conversion takes place, and the only test as to what price the company gets for its common occurs at that time. What it did get was a premium for a call on its common with some protection against a decline—quite a difference.

To explain with our example, the company's common stock is selling for $80. The company desires to have additional common stock in its capital structure, but feels that the common price is too low at present, and would like to obtain at least $100 per share. It sells a $6.50 convertible which is convertible into one share of common stock. The convertible is sold at $100. The company expects, because of improved earnings, that the stock will sell for somewhat over $100 within two years and that conversion will take place at that time. Let's view the picture at the end of the two years, assuming three different market prices for the common stock—$110, $90 and $150:

Stock at $110—conversion takes place as anticipated.

Stock at $90—no conversion occurs; the goal to get more common stock in the capital structure was not achieved, and the company is still stuck with the senior security.

Stock at $150—conversion occurs, but contrast the market price of the stock with the $100-per-share conversion price.

How could financing have been handled otherwise? One possible solution would have been to borrow the money from a bank for two years and then repay the bank loan with the sale of common. This is how it would have fared under these conditions with the three different assumed market prices for the stock:

With the stock at $110, the company would have been approximately as well off because it could have sold common at about $100 per share after all financing costs.

With the stock at $90 after two years, the company could get the necessary equity by selling stock at a reduced price, and not continue to be stuck with the convertible.

With the stock at $150, the company would be substantially better off, because it could obtain a much better price for the stock than it would have through conversion.

In other words, the company would have been as well or better off by avoiding a convertible under these assumed situations. Let's look a little further as to what happens if the common stock moves up fast, and compare the dividend savings from the convertible and the sacrifice of having to issue common at a discount at the time of conversion. This can be put into figures as in Exhibit 4-48.

For a true comparison, the figures should be discounted to a common time frame.

Let's look at it in another way as shown in Exhibit 4-49. Here we compare the sale of a convertible with an alternative of selling straight preferred and subsequently repurchasing it with the proceeds from the sale of common. If the common appreciates substantially it can be seen that the company loses with the convertible. The company saved $7.50 in dividends, but it lost the opportunity to get $12 more for its common stock, a net loss of $4.50. These figures should also be discounted to a common time frame for a true comparison.

Let's look at it by comparing it with a warrant. When the company sold the $6.50 convertible preferred, it got $100. Of that $100, $80 was for the straight preferred yielding 8%, and $20 was for the premium which represented a call on the common stock, with the common stock selling at $80 at the time of the offering. This is analogous to selling a $6.50 preferred at $100 with a warrant attached, with the warrant giving the holder the right to purchase one common share at $100.

Now let's look at it from the investor's point of view. If the common goes up 8% a year to $118 in five years and the convertible holder converts, he has lost $7.50 per share in dividends compared with the dividend on a

Exhibit 4-48

DIVIDEND SAVINGS FROM CONVERTIBLE VS. LOSS OF OPPORTUNITY TO SELL COMMON AT A HIGHER PRICE

Column	I	II	III	IV
Year	Dividend on Straight Preferred	Dividend on Convertible	Dividend Savings per Share of Convertible Preferred	Common Market Price
1	$8	$6.5	$1.5	$ 80
2		"	1.5	(8% compound increase)
3		"	1.5	
4		"	1.5	
5	Conversion takes place	"	1.5	$118
Total			$7.5	$ 38

Exhibit 4-49

CONVERTIBLE PREFERRED VS. NON-CONVERTIBLE PREFERRED AND REPAYMENT OF NON-CONVERTIBLE WITH COMMON SALE

Column	I	II	III	IV	V	VI
	Convertible Preferred		Non-Convertible Preferred			
Year	Market Price	Dividend	Market Price	Dividend	Dividend Savings	Common Market Price
1	$100	$6.5	$100	$8	$1.5	$ 80
2		6.5		8	1.5	(8% compound increase)
3		6.5		8	1.5	
4		6.5		8	1.5	$118
5		6.5		8	$7.5	

Sale of 1 share common	$118.00
Less financing costs	6.00
Net proceeds to company	$112.00
Repurchase of $8 preferred at market	100.00
	$ 12.00
Less dividend savings on convertible	7.50
Net loss from use of convertible	$ 4.50

straight preferred, and gained $18 because of the call on the common, a net gain of $10.50.

The reason we discussed convertibles from these various angles is to explain why there is a basic fallacy in the way in which convertibles, used to raise new capital, may be presented to a company. They are not "all this and heaven too" as is often ascribed to convertible securities. This is not to say that convertibles may not be very useful under some circumstances.

Purposes of Convertibles

In general, a convertible should not be used unless a company needs common stock. It would be foolish to incur the potential dilution in earnings per share if equity was not needed.

The various purposes of convertibles are outlined below.

1. *Necessity—the addition of the conversion feature to sweeten up a senior security which would otherwise be impossible to sell or difficult to sell at a reasonable price.* The investor is offered a fixed income obligation, with the additional bait of potentialities of appreciation through the conversion feature. Some investors go for such a security even though it is weak, provided there are real possibilities of appreciation. This purpose means an admission of financial weakness on the part of the company, but if capital is needed and this is the only way it can be obtained, the use of a convertible may be not only justified, but required.
2. *When the company has such an extensive financing program that the market will not readily absorb all the common that should be sold in order to keep the capital structure ratios in balance, and it would be unwise to postpone long term financing.* A convertible security used for this purpose will permit the capital to be raised by means of a long term security, and the capital structure will be strengthened as conversion takes place. In this situation, where common equity is definitely the goal, the conversion ratio should be attractive enough to assure conversion.

   There are a number of reasons why a large convertible issue may be more readily absorbed than a similar amount of common stock. At times, a convertible may be just what the doctor ordered as far as certain investors' desires are concerned. For example, some investors may not wish to buy a straight debenture or preferred stock, but at times might buy a convertible. Furthermore, some institutions might not be interested in a common stock, but would buy a senior security combining the common stock feature. In designing a convertible to meet such a market demand, it may be necessary to have in mind the special requirements of institutional investors. They may be restricted from buying common stocks, or a convertible issue, if it sells primarily on a parity basis of the common stock rather than on its worth as a senior security.

   At times, the greater amount that may be borrowed by investors from banks on a convertible debenture may be important in assisting in the sale. Banks may be willing to lend more money on a convertible than on a straight common stock, and they may be permitted to lend more by law.
3. *As a refunding medium for existing debt, to permit a gradual strengthening of the capital structure.* This is perhaps one of the least controversial uses. No additional harm is done to the capital structure if conversion doesn't take place, unless, of course, the existing debt had a large sinking fund or serial maturity and this is not included in the convertible. Of course, the possible effect on dilution of earnings per share must be carefully analyzed.
4. *When a company needs to add common stock to its capital structure, and the market price of the common stock is unreasonably depressed for one of the following reasons:*

   a. Poor earnings, which are expected to improve.

b. A seriously adverse stock market in general.
c. A large block of the company's stock overhanging the market and depressing the price unreasonably.

The conversion price will be set above the existing market price of the stock at the time of the sale. It will be expected that with an improvement in the market price, conversion will take place. Therefore, the conversion price should be set so as to assure conversion, even if the market price doesn't improve to the extent anticipated as a result of the natural optimism of the management.

This may be a good reason for the use of a convertible, but the advisability of other methods of financing should also be evaluated, such as temporary financing with a bank loan and then repayment through the sale of common. Caution should be used in relying on this purpose to justify a convertible, because most managements have a tendency to think their common stock price is too low no matter what the price.

5. *To permit a gradual dilution of earnings per share of common stock as conversion takes place rather than heavy dilution, which would result if all the common were sold at one time.* If common is needed, then the conversion price should be low so that conversion will be assured. This may result in a disadvantage in that a higher price might be obtained subsequently from the direct sale of common.

   This is not a very good reason for the use of a convertible. The effect of dilution may be anticipated by investors.
6. *If the market for either debt or preferred stock is poor and rates required to sell the securities are high, the addition of a conversion feature may be used to sweeten up the security in order to receive a lower rate of interest or dividends.* Use of a convertible for this purpose is debatable. It may be trying to slice the bacon too thin, and the company may end up with a convertible which never converts, or converts at the wrong time to cause dilution of earnings per share and thus pressure on the market price of the stock.
7. *To provide cheap money for a period while the convertible issue is outstanding, perhaps during a period when construction is taking place, and then to turn into the more costly type of security, common stock, at the end of the period, when earnings may materialize.* This also may be slicing the bacon too thin. There are other methods of handling such a situation, and they should be examined carefully. For example, a bank loan might be used temporarily prior to issuing common.
8. *As a mechanical aid in issuing common stock with lower financing costs, since the underwriting fees are less on a convertible than on a straight common issue, and the conversion price of the stock may be set closer to the market.* In view of all the other complications of a convertible, this reason alone is hardly a good one.
9. *Present common stockholders wish to delay temporarily the addition of more stockholders in order to preserve their control.* This is a special situation and one not likely to occur often.

In some situations, a convertible may be used to accomplish more than one of the purposes outlined above, but in deciding whether to use a convertible, each purpose should be analyzed by itself with its advantages and disadvantages. This should include an analysis of how a convertible will work out with various stock prices each year throughout the life of the convertible, and alternatives for raising the capital with their advantages and disadvantages at the various stock prices. If there are alternatives and they are compared correctly, one of them may prove more advantageous than a convertible issue.

Keep in mind that if a convertible doesn't convert as planned, the company may be saddled with a senior security which might not fit into the capital structure. Furthermore, a convertible tends to exert a depressing effect on the market for the common because of the potential dilution which will result when conversion does occur. If it converts at the wrong time, there may be a depressing effect on the market when the company would prefer that this not occur, as, for example, when more common is to be offered.

A company will do well to think of a convertible issue as an emergency type of security and save this slot in its capital structure for this purpose. It is a good form of reserve type of security. A simple rule to follow is that if a company needs common stock, the market is reasonably receptive and earnings are satisfactory, it should go ahead with the sale of common and not gamble with a convertible. Anyone who has had experience trying to forecast security prices will readily admit that it is very difficult to tell at what price a stock will sell in the future. The more a company needs common stock in its capitalization, the less chance it can take on using a convertible and being subject to whims of the stock market to determine whether conversion takes place. If a company can sell stock but wishes to use convertible debentures merely because the market won't afford a high price for the stock, that company should be thoroughly prepared to justify the position that it can stand the additional debt if no conversion takes place. A company with a very conservative capitalization is in a better position to play with a convertible for other than emergency purposes. It can better stand the additional senior securities if conversion does not occur.

In summary, as we have said, a company has three reserves:

1. Long term borrowing reserve.
2. Short term borrowing reserve.
3. Incentive securities, such as convertibles and senior securities with warrants.

Convertibles are thus a form of financial reserve and should be saved for that purpose.

Provisions of Convertibles

Many of the provisions will be similar to those included in a non-convertible. However, convertibles contain less restrictive provisions since they are expected to turn into common.

1. The conversion ratio. This is the most important term. We have already said that the conversion ratio is the number of shares of common which can be acquired by surrender of $100 principal amount of debentures or of a share of preferred stock. This provision will be fully protected against dilution.

   Low ratios are equivalent to high prices for the common, and vice versa. It can be so low that it will have no immediate value and the convertible will sell primarily on its value as a senior security. The ratio can range up to the point where the aggregate value of the common commanded at the current market is equal to the par value of the senior security, and on up so that the convertible's price is entirely dependent on the market price of the common. Where the conversion price is set will depend on the purpose or purposes to be achieved.

   The conversion ratio can contain complications. The convertible privilege may be made to change during the life of the issue and also be made to apply to only a part of the issue. For example, an issue of $16,677,000 convertible debentures was convertible at $60 principal amount of debentures for each share of common stock. The conversion price remained at that rate until $8 million of the debentures had been converted; then the rate changed to $66 2/3 principal amount for each share of common. This provision operated so that on the day that the amount converted reached $8 million, all the holders that sent in their bonds on that particular day prior to 3 p.m. received the same treatment, even though the total exceeded $8 million. This feature tends to force conversion without any action on the part of the company. Thus, if the common market price is above $60, and less than $8 million has been converted, the holders will wish to be among the first $8 million to convert rather than to be penalized by the higher conversion price.

From the company's point of view, a possible danger arises if the step-up turns out to be too high and conversion is blocked.

This change in the conversion price is what is known as a blackjack provision, so-called because it holds a penalty over the holders' heads to take action. If it is made to apply to only part of the debentures as above, investors may be in the dark in making their decisions as to whether or not to convert. It would be difficult for them to keep currently posted on the extent of conversion. This may result in some investor dissatisfaction.

A special type of conversion feature is fixed at a percentage below the market. For example, one convertible debenture was convertible at 80% of the market price of the common after two years. There was a minimum and maximum conversion price of $13.50 and $7. The stock was selling for about $9 when the issue was sold.

When you consider a complicated type of security such as convertibles with special provisions mentioned above, you should analyze:

a. The cost to the company at various intervals of time in the future and under various stock prices.
b. How the security would turn out under various stock prices; that is, whether it would convert by action of the investors or whether the company could call it.
c. The return that investors might receive for various time intervals and different stock prices.

A flashy security may turn out to have a bunch of bugs in it when carefully analyzed.

A few convertibles have been issued with special features designed to make them sell for an extended time at premiums over their conversion values so the holders will have an incentive not to convert. The main idea in issuing such convertible preferred stock is to create a security the issuer could use for a series of acquisitions over a period of years without having to change its terms to keep pace with increases in the dividend rate or the market price of the common.

One such stock was convertible share-for-share into common and was entitled in perpetuity to double the dividend on the common with a minimum of $2.40.

Another convertible preferred was entitled to cash dividends equal to those paid on the common and was also entitled to a somewhat complex stepped-up conversion feature. The net effect of the conversion privilege was to give the holder a compound annual growth rate of about 6% in the conversion value which terminated after 25 years.

These latter types of convertibles are considered participating convertible preferreds which are residual securities and affect reported primary earnings per share.

In view of the whims of the stock market, a fancily designed convertible may look good on paper, but it is hard for investors to understand, and how it will work out certainly will be in the laps of the gods. Nor does it appear that they can be relied on to command premiums which fully reflect what their issuers are giving up in dividends or convertibility.

2. There may be a delay in the start of the conversion privilege. Preventing an immediate conversion postpones possible dilution in earnings per share from conversions and may exert a stabilizing effect on the price of the common stock during such period. Also it may enhance the premium.

The conversion privilege may expire before maturity. One of the reasons for shortening the period is to encourage conversion at an early date. Such action might be justified on this basis, but again it assumes that the market price of the stock will, without fail, be sufficient to make conversion attractive. If this is not the case, then the primary objective is defeated and the longer conversion period would be better.

3. The type of conversion feature by which the holder has to pay some cash as well as surrender the convertible issue in order to exercise the conversion privilege. As an example, an issue may be convertible into one share of common stock for each $100 principal amount of debentures upon the payment of $50 in cash. Thus, as conversion takes place, the company is provided with additional funds. Such a feature may be best suited to a holding company with many subsidiaries which have a continuing large demand for funds over a period of many years.

   This is an attractive feature as far as selling the issue is concerned, in that less money has to be paid by the investor for the convertible when it is issued.

4. The call feature. It provides the means by which the company can force conversion, provided, of course, the conversion value of the issue appreciates above the call price. The call price is generally low. That does not work any hardship on investors because they can convert, and it places the company in a favorable position if it wishes to force conversion. However, if it is callable at a pricc low enough to force conversion, the convertible will not sell at any appreciable premium over its conversion value. On the other hand, high call prices and lengthy call protection contribute to the size of the premium.

   In an acquisition, the call price can be a significant negotiating point, since a high call price favors the holder and a low one the issuer.

   The call privilege may be delayed. Investors will thus have some time during which they can voluntarily convert before the company can force conversion. This may fit in with a blackjack provision. The call provision must include a notice period, but the conversion right may be suspended ten days prior to the date fixed for redemption. Thus, if the company decides to force conversion by issuing a call, it will know ten days before the final redemption date how much will have been converted, rather than being faced with continuing conversations right up to the redemption date, leaving to be determined at the last minute the amount that will have to be paid off.

   In an acquisition, the recipients of a convertible preferred usually have call protection for at least five years. This feature may be desirable to assure tax-free treatment of the transaction.

5. Characteristically, convertible debentures do not carry a sinking fund. Nevertheless, under some circumstances, particularly with a weak issue, a sinking fund may be justified, at least after the conversion period expires. For example, a regulatory authority suggested that for a company under its jurisdiction, a sinking fund should be included in a convertible, starting after the date that the conversion privilege expired, which was about ten years prior to maturity. The sinking fund was made equivalent to the savings resulting from the difference between the dividend requirements on the common stock and the interest payable on the debentures. Convertible preferreds are even less likely to have a sinking fund.

6. Liquidation rights for convertible preferred. The claim of the preferred senior to the common on corporate assets in liquidation is specified. Liquidating value can vary widely. In most cases, involuntary liquidating value is set close to the price at which the issue is designed to sell initially, while voluntary liquidating value will be set somewhat higher—often at the call price. Holders are generally entitled to accumulated dividends in either case.

7. Voting rights for convertible preferred. Convertible preferred shareholders generally vote with the common, especially when the preferred is an acquisition security designed for a tax-free transaction. The preferred usually has one vote per share, although there are a number of cases of fractional voting rights. In these instances, the fractional

vote is usually equal to the fraction of a share of common into which a share of preferred is convertible. The main points to consider here are voting control, and the possibility that an absurdly low voting privilege for the preferred relative to its value could affect the tax status of the exchange.

In addition to voting with the common, the preferred generally votes as a class to authorize a prior preferred or a change in the terms of the issue, or to approve a sale of major assets or merger of the company. A two-thirds vote is generally required. The preferred as a class will also be entitled to board representation if dividends are defaulted for a specified number of quarters. To qualify for a NYSE listing, the preferred must have the right to elect at least two directors if dividends are the equivalent of six quarterly payments in arrears.

8. Par value for convertible preferred. Par value is often avoided in favor of a low stated value. This eliminates certain legal and accounting problems which might otherwise arise. However, this can lead to distorted figures in the balance sheet. For example, if a convertible preferred is used for an acquisition, it may have a stated value much below the price of the acquisition and its liquidating value. The difference will appear in capital surplus. This results in an over-statement of the common equity and is very misleading. An explanation is required to be carried in the balance sheet or footnote showing the difference related to the liquidating value. However, this is hardly a proper way to handle the situation.

Calling a Convertible

If a company calls a convertible, the holder has the choice of converting or allowing the company to redeem them at the call price. If the conversion value is in excess of the call price, a holder would lose money if he did not convert. Thus, the company can force conversion.

A company should wait until the conversion value is well above the call price if it wishes to insure conversion when calling a convertible. Otherwise, a drop in the market price of the common might put the conversion value below the call price during the notice of redemption period. Then the company would be obliged to redeem the issue for cash. The necessary spread between conversion value and the call price to provide an adequate margin of safety depends largely on general market conditions and the volatility of the common.

Occasionally, a company may wish to call an issue when the conversion value is not far enough above to insure conversion. In this situation, an investment banker may be willing to underwrite the call for a fee. In an underwritten call, the investment banker agrees to buy the convertible at the call price and convert into common all shares presented for redemption. The investment banker will then sell the common.

Convertible Debentures or Convertible Preferred for New Money?

We have not as yet suggested whether you should use a convertible debenture or a convertible preferred for raising new capital. The convertible debenture has the obvious advantage that the interest rate would undoubtedly be lower than the dividend on a preferred, and interest results in income tax savings.

A company's capital structure and its future financing plans will be the major determinant as to which is used. If a company has too much debt already and no preferred stock, a convertible preferred may be the better one. On the other hand, if its debt picture is satisfactory, a convertible debenture will offer the advantages already mentioned. The other principal determinant in deciding whether to offer a convertible debenture or convertible preferred is the market receptivity. This will depend on the market at the time and the circumstances surrounding the company.

If a company's capital structure is overburdened with senior issues, it may be necessary to resort to junior convertibles in the form of second convertible debentures or second convertible preferreds. While necessity may demand that type of security, it would be hoped that a company would manage its financial policy so as to avoid such a step.

Size of Offering

The amount of a convertible offering will depend on:

1) The amount of capital required if it is for raising capital.
   The size of the acquisition if it is for an acquisition.
2) The ability of the company to support the senior charges on the convertible. If a company is being acquired, then the earnings from the new company should be included and may make a major difference.
3) The effect on the long-term capital structure.
4) How the convertible may affect the market for the outstanding common before it is converted.
5) The amount of common that will result upon conversion and how the capital structure and earnings per share will be affected.

There is a rule of thumb that a common offering which increases the shares of common stock 20% (one new share for each five outstanding) is a heavy offering. This would result in a 20% decrease in earnings per share from the added shares without allowing for any increase in earnings from the new capital. A 10% (one new share for each ten outstanding) increase in shares is considered moderate and a 5% (one new share for each 20 outstanding) increase is light. This same rule of thumb may be used for a convertible which provides new capital, by considering the amount of new common shares which would result from conversion. If a convertible is used for acquisition purposes, consideration must be given to the picture with the new company consolidated; this would add to the size of the offering which would be appropriate.

Amount of Convertible Preferred to Authorize

In order for a company to be in a position to issue convertible preferred, the stockholders must first authorize the stock.

How many shares should a management have authorized? There seems to be some apprehension on the part of management about the amount of stock to have authorized for fear that the stockholders and market will think that the management has intentions of issuing it all at one time. This fear is unfounded. Many companies have had large amounts authorized in order to have it on the shelf for the time when it may be needed. The authorization within reasonable limits makes no difference when the company is substantial and reputable. It may range up to 100% of the common shares outstanding.

Should a company wait until it needs to use convertible preferred to get authorization? It will probably put it off until then, but it is helpful to get it done ahead of time so that it will be prepared for any eventuality.

The number of shares to be issued, the dividend rate, the conversion rights and other features of each issue are left to the discretion of the company's directors at the time the stock is issued.

When convertible preferred is chosen as the security to use for an acquisition, an acquirer with a blank check authorization already in hand can close the deal without going to its stockholders if their approval is not required for the acquisition itself.

Of course, stockholder approval of an acquisition may well be required by the acquiring company's charter or bylaws, the statutes of the state in which it is incorporated or the rules of a stock exchange on which its securities may be listed.

What Causes Conversion?

There are four principal reasons for convertible holders to exchange their shares for common: arbitrage, a differential in yield in favor of the common, a change in conversion rights or a call.

Arbitrage: When the conversion value is so much higher than its investment value that premium has disappeared, imperfections in the market may cause the convertible to sell at a slight discount from its conversion value. Whenever this occurs, arbitrageurs will buy it, sell the common short simultaneously and then convert to cover their short sales at a profit.

Dividend differential: A favorable difference between the common dividend yield available through conversion and the convertible yield could induce some voluntary conversion. However, there is no single point where all holders will convert. They have to weigh not only the relative yields available to them, but also the relative risks of the securities. With or without conversion, the convertible holder will benefit from any market appreciation in the common. Therefore, an investor loses only the difference in yields by delaying conversion. If the protection against a decline in the common due to senior security is worth more to the investor than the difference in yields, he will not convert.

A change in conversion rights: Most convertibles have conversion rights at a fixed conversion ratio for the life of the issue. However, some convertibles lose their conversion rights after a specified date, which causes voluntary conversion as the date approaches if conversion value exceeds investment value. Some convertibles are subject to a stepped-down conversion ratio after a specified date, which may cause conversion depending on the size of the step-down and the premium on the convertible before and after the change.

Effect of Convertible on Price of Common

How do convertibles affect the market price of the common stock? This depends on a number of factors:

1) The effect on reported earnings per share.
2) The prospects for conversion depending on the nearness of the conversion price and market price of the common.
3) The effect of the convertible as a senior security on the position of the common stock and on the ability of the company to raise capital in the future—particularly if earnings decrease.
4) The effect of the convertible on the amount of retained earnings if not converted and if converted.

Reported Earnings per Share

"Accounting Bulletin No. 15" of the Accounting Principles Board defined how earnings per share should be reported on two bases for a company which has a convertible.

Primary Earnings

Primary earnings per share are calculated on a weighted average number of common shares outstanding. Shares of common which result from convertibles are included if the convertibles are common stock equivalents at the time they are issued. Convertibles are common stock equivalents if the yield is less than 66 2/3% of the bank prime rate. For example, if the bank prime rate is 6%, the yield on the convertibles would have to be less than 4% (66 2/3 x 6%).

Fully Diluted Earnings

In general, fully diluted earnings per share include the shares of common which will result from all convertibles being converted.

If the company earns more on the capital provided by the convertibles than the charges on the convertibles and the convertible is not a common stock equivalent, primary earnings per share are increased by the leverage effect of senior security position of the convertible. To this extent convertibles boost earnings per share. Fully diluted earnings per share, on the other hand, represent the earnings per share which would actually exist if conversion took place in any particular year. This is illustrated in Exhibit 4-50.

If the common price is sufficiently above the conversion price so that conversion may

Exhibit 4-50

EFFECT OF CONVERTIBLE ON EARNINGS PER SHARE ON COMMON

Shares of Common Outstanding–500,000

12,500 Shares of $6 Convertible Preferred Convertible into 50,000 Shares Common

Column	I	II	III	IV
		Conversion Takes Place in 6th Yr.		Conversion Takes Place in 1st Yr.
Year	Net Income Available for Common	Primary Earnings per Share	Fully Diluted Earnings per Share*	Earnings per Share*
1	$1,200,000	$2.40	$2.32	$2.32
2	1,260,000	2.52	2.43	2.43
3	1,324,000	2.61	2.54	2.54
4	1,391,000	2.78	2.67	2.67
5	1,463,000	2.93	2.81	2.81
6	1,538,000	2.93		2.93

*Dividends on the convertible preferred are added to net income available for common. This total is divided by the common shares outstanding plus the additional common shares resulting from conversion.

take place voluntarily or could be forced, primary earnings per share are really meaningless, and fully diluted earnings per share are more representative.

Only if there is little or no prospects of conversion should primary earnings per share have any significance.

Market's Reaction to Earnings per Share Before Conversion

Before conversion, there is a period during which the common stockholder appears to be better off because reported earnings per share are higher and grow at a slightly faster rate due to the leverage effect of the convertible. This is only temporary and will disappear when conversion takes place. But while the company's operations are improving, some investors, and in fact, the market, may take a short range view and disregard the ultimate effect of conversion on earnings per share. And the market may also disregard the possible effect of the convertible on the company's ability to finance and the adverse effect of the leverage when earnings decline.

Consequently, a company which issues a convertible may enjoy better prices for its common while the convertible is outstanding and its earnings are on the upswing.

However, there are several points a prospective issuer should consider before concluding that a market advantage, which has no rational basis, is sure to result. In the first place, competent analysts will consider the future claim on the common stock represented by a convertible security. Their evaluations will generally influence stock prices, and may often determine them. Secondly, most convertibles will ultimately convert. The issuing company which believes otherwise is betting against itself. Any over-pricing of the common in the meanwhile will be eliminated by conversion if not before.

Use of Convertible Preferreds in Acquisitions

Convertible preferreds have been used extensively for acquisitions for various reasons:

1. Pooling, when permitted, allowed an acquired company to be included in the

combined balance sheet on the basis of book figures without goodwill. This is no longer permitted with a convertible preferred, so goodwill will have to be shown and subsequently written off out of earnings. This change caused convertible preferreds to become much less popular.
2. The transaction permits the seller to avoid a capital gains tax if the stock is voting.
3. The convertible preferred gives the seller protection on the downside with a chance for appreciation on the upside.
4. The dividend can be designed to meet the requirements of the buyer for income, and without the seller altering its own common dividend policy which might be needed if common stock were used rather than convertible preferred.
5. It minimized immediate dilution of the earnings per share of the buyer's common.
6. Fewer shares of common will ultimately have to be issued if the convertible preferred is designed to have a premium. To illustrate, suppose an acquiring company's stock sells for $80 a share, and the price of the acquisition is $10 million. An acquisition using common would require 125,000 shares. Instead, a convertible preferred could be designed to sell at $100 with a conversion ratio of 1 for 1, producing a conversion value of $80. An issue of 100,000 shares would achieve the required $10 million market value and would eventually convert into only 100,000 shares of common.
7. The voting power of the selling company's stockholders can be minimized. This can be important on occasion, particularly if the seller is closely held. In the example used above to illustrate the minimization of dilution, a common-for-common acquisition would give the selling stockholders 125,000 votes at the outset. A convertible preferred with one vote per share would give the seller only 100,000 votes before conversion and 100,000 thereafter. The conversion ratio and the initial premium over conversion value are the key factors in this context. A convertible can be designed to further minimize the voting power where a convertible preferred may have one vote and be convertible into more than one common share.

Each one of these advantages must be weighed in considering the use of convertibles for an acquisition. Also, the impact of the convertible preferred on the buying company's future financial position is important. If the issue is too large it may put the common stock in a weak position. Careful study of the possible market consequences is in order if the use of a convertible preferred is considered for a major acquisition.

Designing an Issue

How a convertible is designed will depend on the purpose for which it is used. If it is for new money, the aim may be to attain the maximum premium. This may also be the aim when a convertible preferred may be used for an acquisition. However, there may be other aims, particularly when a security is to be used for an acquisition such as:

1. Satisfying the dividend desires of the selling company.
2. Minimizing the voting power of the common into which the convertible is converted.

We will suggest some steps that might be taken to design a convertible which will have a maximum premium. We will use as an example a convertible preferred:

1. Determine the yield at which the preferred could be sold as a straight preferred stock. For example, 8% yield as straight preferred.
2. Decide at what price range you wish the convertible preferred to sell—$25, $50 or $100, etc. For example, $100 public offering price.
3. Make an estimate of the premium at which the convertible will sell if the investment value and conversion value are the same. For example, 20% premium over investment value and conversion value when equal.
4. Establish the investment value so that the premium of 20% above the invest-

ment value will produce the public offering price:

$100	Public offering price
17	Premium 20%
$ 83	Investment value

5. Determine the dividend rate for the convertible which will produce an 8% yield for the straight preferred at a price of $83:

$$\frac{\text{Dividend}}{\$83} = 8\% \text{ yield for straight preferred}$$

$$\text{Dividend} = 8\% \times \$83$$
$$= \$6.60$$

6. Determine the conversion ratio which will make the conversion value equal to the investment value:

$$\text{Conversion ratio:} = \frac{\$83}{\$25} \quad \frac{\text{Conversion value}}{\text{Common market price}} = 3.3$$

($25 Common market price)

One share of convertible preferred is convertible in 3.3 shares common:

As a result we have a convertible preferred with a dividend rate of $6.60. One share of convertible preferred is convertible into 3.3 shares of common (common market price $25). The convertible will sell for $100 to yield 6.6% compared with the yield at which the company might sell a straight preferred of 8%.

If it is desired to have less dilution upon conversion, the conversion price would be below the investment value. The premium would be measured from the investment value and would be smaller. The dividend would have to be increased because of the smaller premium. For example:

$7 convertible preferred.

Market price of common $25.
Conversion ratio 2.5 shares common for each share of convertible preferred.
Conversion value $62.50.
Decide how much the investment value would have to be above the conversion value to produce a market price for the convertible preferred of 100.
Investment value $88 to yield 8% requires a $7 dividend.
Premium $12 or 13.7% (premium divided by investment value).

If it is desired to move the conversion price up so that there will be more chances of conversion, the ratio could be increased to 3.5 shares of common for each share of convertible preferred. Then the picture might be as follows:

$6.40 convertible preferred.

Market price of common $25.
Conversion ratio 3.5 shares of common for each share of convertible preferred.
Conversion value $88.
Decide how much the investment value could be below the conversion value to produce a market price for the convertible preferred of 100.
Investment value $80 to yield 8% requires $6.40 dividend.
Premium $12 or 13.7% (premium divided by conversion value).

A convertible can be designed to meet practically any one aim at a time; it cannot be designed to meet all aims at the same time because some are conflicting. The same principles apply to designing a convertible debenture as a convertible preferred.

Convertibles vs. Senior Security with a Warrant

As an incentive security a company may have a choice as to whether to use a convertible or a senior security with a warrant. Now that we have covered these two types of securities, we can compare them in outline form from the point of view of the issuing company. There would be some differences whether the two types are debentures or preferreds, but we will cover the points that might apply to both.

Advantages of a convertible security vs. a senior security with a warrant:

1. A convertible is callable and can be forced into common if the conversion value is sufficiently above the call price. Thus, the company's capital structure is

improved by eliminating the senior security. When a warrant is exercised, the senior security to which it was attached remains outstanding.

2. The chances are that a convertible will not affect reported primary earnings per share. A warrant may affect primary earnings per share. This is a matter of reported earnings per share and not necessarily how investors will look at it.
3. Disadvantages of a warrant:
   (a) Company does not know whether it will get the warrant money at time of exercise.
   (b) Company may not need the money and common when the warrant is exercised.
   (c) The senior security may have an adverse call premium.
   (d) A warrant is not callable.

Disadvantages of a convertible security vs. a senior security with a warrant:

1. There is more opportunity with the use of a warrant to limit the ultimate amount of common that may be issued.
2. A warrant may never be exercised and the company may obtain the warrant money at time of issuance without having to issue any common.
3. A warrant will probably have less effect on fully diluted earnings per share.
4. The discount represented by the warrant price when sold with a bond can be written off for tax purposes.
5. A warrant may be designed so that the exercise price can be met with senior securities as well as cash, so that senior securities may be extinguished.

In summary, a convertible senior security provides an incentive for the sale of the senior security and turns the senior security into common upon conversion. Thus, the company's capital structure is improved.

A warrant provides an incentive for the sale of a senior security and results in some additional common only when the warrants expire. An incentive can be added with less potential dilution, but the company has less control over the warrant and the senior security remains outstanding.

How Convertibles Are Offered

If the common stockholders have preemptive rights in respect of new issues of common, this privilege will generally extend to securities convertible into common stock. Otherwise, the company must make the choice whether to offer directly or through rights. In that decision, the same principles apply as for straight common stock, as discussed in Chapter 9 on Selling Common Stock.

Summary

Convertibles can be a misused security, if they are misunderstood. They are not magic and do not do many of the things attributed to them. If they are sold at the wrong time for the wrong purpose, they can become a burden on a company rather than a benefit and can turn out to be costly. Until converted, convertibles have a senior claim on earnings and are in a senior position as regards assets. Like any senior security, it can be over-used.

For raising new money, they generally should be reserved for the time when the company can't sell more debt and it can't sell common. Then convertible debentures may be a very handy security to have available.

For acquisition purposes, a convertible preferred may be helpful to meet the demands of the seller. In designing such a convertible, allowance must be given to the financial picture with the company combined. The convertible preferred should not be so large as to put the common stock of the buying company too far out on a limb until conversion takes place.

One thing convertibles will not do is allow the issuer to avoid dilution of common share earnings. The groundwork for dilution is laid when a convertible is first created rather than when conversion actually occurs. Convertibles may not even allow the issuer to "postpone" dilution. New financial reporting standards may well prompt an increasing number of investors to discount their estimates of the worth of a company's common share earnings as soon as the company issues a convertible.

Whichever type of incentive security is used, it should be fitted into the company's financing plan. And it should be realized that a considerable period of time is required before the curative results of such securities are felt in the balance sheet.

ODDBALL SECURITIES

A company has just so much earnings to offer to investors. By dividing up the flow of earnings to investors in a sensible fashion in order to appeal to the broad group of investors who may be interested in a company's earnings, will facilitate raising capital. Complications and razzle-dazzle may work in a boom. However, it may boomerang under adverse conditions and in the long run it will then lose investor interest and make financing more costly.

A company which is a moderate but steady earner can create speculative types of securities which may, because of the terms, appeal to some speculators. Thus, it will add a new group of investors to its fold. However, what it gives to the speculators must come out of the hide of the other investors. Furthermore, it may complicate its capital structure and may drive away more of the investors who will be its main source of capital.

As we have discussed, there is a place for incentive securities such as senior securities with warrants and convertibles, but they should be kept as simple as possible.

If we go back in financial history, we can find that practically every means of financing possible has been tried at one time or another. In spite of this fact, in every boom, new people enter finance and try to be the bright "boys who come up with 'new ideas'." They advance various types of exotic securities as a new panacea for capital raising. And management and investors are always looking for what they consider a free lunch. As the boom develops others follow the leaders and the cycle is begun. This happened in the 1960's when the "conglomerates" were playing the earnings-per-share game and trying to jazz up earnings per share by acquisitions with all kinds of securities. Investors were sucked in, and when the acquisition fever slowed down, the crash in the stock of many conglomerates followed to the detriment of investors and our economy.

Some of the unusual terms of convertibles and senior securities with warrants which we have mentioned can be put in the class of oddball securities. We will now explain an oddball security which stands by itself. It is a form of convertible.

Class A Convertible Stock

The principal feature of this stock is that it becomes automatically convertible in common at the end of 15 years. The dividend is not cumulative, but has preference over the company's common dividend. It is junior to the company's existing preferred stock.

The company which used this security got too heavily burdened with debt and it needed equity. In the prospectus, the reason stated for issuing the stock was to provide less dilution than raising the same amount of proceeds with the sale of common stock, in other words, it was issued in lieu of common. Data for the class A convertible and common stock are given in Exhibit 4-51.

The company might have received an 8.15% yield for a straight preference preferred. On this basis, the facts surrounding the Class A convertible stock were as follows:

Conversion value—$15.125
Investment value—$16.44
Offering price —$17.375
Premium —$ 0.935 (6%)

Thus, the premium received for the preferred was relatively small compared with a convertible preferred with more normal terms. Premium for a convertible is measured as a percent of the higher of the investment values, or the conversion value.

The company increased its dividend at an average annual rate of 3% in the past five years. If it increases the dividend in the future

Exhibit 4-51

CLASS A CONVERTIBLE STOCK DATA

Dividend $1.34—non-cumulative, preference over common dividend, junior to preferred dividend.
Liquidation—participates equally with common.
Voting rights—participates equally with common.
Non-callable
Convertible—into 1 share common for 15 years and then automatically converted into common.
Offering—500,000 shares at $17.375 to yield 7.7%.

COMMON STOCK DATA

Shares outstanding	2,161,932
Price	$15.125
Dividend	$ 1.12
Earnings per share	$ 1.38
Price-earnings ratio	10.9
Yield	7.4%
Book value per share	$13.00
Market value divided by book value	116%

at the same rate, the common dividend compared to the Class A convertible dividend would be as shown in Exhibit 4-52. On the basis of this estimate, an investor would have every reason to convert as soon as the common dividend exceeded the Class A convertible dividend in the eighth year.

The net proceeds from the sale of Class A convertible stock and the amount of common shares which the company would have to have sold to raise an equivalent amount of proceeds would be approximately as shown in Exhibit 4-53.

Giving effect to full conversion, the total number of common shares outstanding would be 2,661,932. If common had been offered, the total shares outstanding would have been 2,735,649, or only a negligible 2.8% more.

There is an additional total dividend cost with the Class A convertible rather than common for the first two years of about $37,663.[13] Because of the greater number of common shares that would have to be issued, the total dividend cost would start to be less in the third year for the Class A convertible.

For reporting purposes, primary earnings presumably would not be affected by the Class A convertible stock, but this is not altogether clear.[14] Fully diluted earnings per share would give effect to the potential added number of common shares. Regardless of how earnings per share will be reported, any alert analyst would calculate earnings per share assuming full conversion of this stock since it ultimately becomes common mandatorily.

It may be suggested that the company saved issuing 73,717 shares of common at a net proceeds price of $14.515 or a total of $1,070,000, and it only had to pay out a little more than $37,673 in dividends in the first two years. Or to put it another way, if the company issued the same number of Class A convertible shares as common shares, the proceeds would be as follows:

Class A convertible	$16.655 × 573,717 shares =	$9,555,257
Common	$14.515 × 573,717 shares =	8,327,502
Greater proceeds from Class A convertible		$1,227,755

The added dividend requirement on the Class A convertible for the first eight years before voluntary conversion might take place would be 80¢ per share or a total of $458,974 (573,717 shares x 80¢). In other words, it appears that the company would have gotten a net additional cash amount of $768,781 ($1,227,755 - $458,974).

These are the figures, but this alone is a superficial analysis. There is no magic in these figures: they had to come from somewhere. Class A convertible stock is not the same as common. If it is, then there is no doubt but that it would have to be included in calculation of primary earnings per share. The extra price that investors were willing to pay for the

[13] 500,000 Class A stock @ 1.34 for two years equals $1,340,000. 573,717 shares of common at $1.12 for first year and $1.15 for second year equals $1,302,337. The difference is $37,663.

[14] Opinion 15 of the Accounting Principles Board includes in common stock equivalents, contingent shares. Contingent shares are defined as shares to be issued in the future upon the mere passage of time. Such shares are included in calculation of primary earnings per share. It would appear that the Class A convertible might be considered contingent shares because they are automatically convertible.

Exhibit 4-52

DIVIDENDS ON COMMON AND CLASS A CONVERTIBLE STOCK

Year	Common	Class A Convertible	Difference	
1	$1.12	$1.34	$ .22	
2	1.15	↓	.19	
3	1.19		.15	
4	1.22		.12	
5	1.26		.08	
6	1.30		.04	
7	1.34		--	$ 0.80
8	1.38		(.04)	
9	1.42		(.08)	
10	1.46		(.12)	
11	1.51		(.17)	
12	1.56		(.22)	
13	1.60		(.26)	
14	1.65		(.31)	
15	1.70		(.36)	
				(1.56)
				(0.76)

Exhibit 4-53

CLASS A CONVERTIBLE STOCK FINANCING COMPARED WITH COMMON FINANCING TO PRODUCE SAME TOTAL NET PROCEEDS TO COMPANY

Column	I	II	III
	Common	Class A Convertible	Column I Less Column II
Price	$15.125	$17,375	
Financing costs	0.61	0.72	
Net proceeds	14.515	16.655	
Shares offered	573,717	500,000	73,717
Total net proceeds	$8,327,502	$8,327,500	
Total dividends 1st year	$ 642,563	$ 670,000	
Total shares outstanding			
Common	2,735,649	2,161,932	
Class A convertible		500,000	
Total	2,735,649	2,661,932	73,717

Class A convertible had to be due to the fact that the Class A convertible has a prior claim on dividends over the common stock. To that extent, the common is in a more leveraged position. Furthermore, it limits, to some extent, the company's ability to issue preferred or convertible preferred in the future, because the place for preferred is to some extent used up. It is not the same as though the company had issued common. But to isolate and statistically measure the effect of the Class A convertible on the common is impossible because so many other factors affect the price of the common. In the calculations above, we showed a net additional cash amount of $768,781 if the same amount of Class A convertible shares were issued. In terms of the total number of shares of common outstanding 2,475,649 (2,161,932 plus 573,717), the $768,781 only represents 28¢ per share of common. In other words, the Class A convertible would only have to decrease the common marketprice about 1/4 point as far as the total number of stockholders are concerned.

The non-callable provision of the Class A convertible is an unattractive feature because it leaves control of conversion entirely in the hands of the holders; the company cannot push the stock into common if it chose to do so when the common price goes above the conversion price.

The company had other alternatives: the sale of straight common, straight preferred, a regular convertible preferred or a combination. Without a thorough analysis of all the factors surrounding the situation, a solution should not be suggested. However, the effect on dilution and dividends of a combination of common and straight preferred would have been as follows in the first year:

	Proceeds
250,000 shares $1.45 straight preferred (yield to publiç 8.15%–net proceeds $16.655	$4,164,000
286,841 shares common (net proceeds to co. $14.515	4,163,502
Total	$8,327,502
	Dividends 1st Year
250,000 shares $1.45 preferred	$ 362,500
286,844 shares common $1.12 dividend	321,263
Total	$ 683,763

This would have cut the amount of common shares that ultimately would be issued in half.

In summary, the design of this stock appears to have been an attempt to gain some of the advantages of a convertible preferred and a common stock at the same time; it sits somewhere in between. However, it produced only a small premium and did not get a low dividend on the stock because it does not provide investors real protection on the downside. The Class A convertible stock is an example of much fuss and feathers over very little. It would appear that there was at least as good a solution in the form of more conventional securities.

Another version of this type of stock was considered by some electric utilities during 1970 when they were having difficulties selling common stock. Stocks of such companies were selling primarily on a yield basis. Some companies found themselves with a low payout ratio, and consequently their stocks were in an adverse position in the marketplace. At the time, there was a government price freeze on increasing dividends more than 4% annually. Some companies in that position concocted the idea of creating another class of common stock which would have a high dividend and could be used for raising new common at a better price. The new class of stock was to have a constant high dividend for a period of ten years, and then as the regular common dividend gradually increased so that it equalled the dividend in the new stock, the new class of stock would convert into the old stock.

The advantages of this new class of stock are:

1. It would permit the company to get a better price when it sold new stock.
2. The company would not have to sell as many new shares.
3. The lower dividend on the existing shares would provide more internal funds for expansion and reduce the amount of financing.

However, a company should be working for its stockholders. If it is so clear that stockholders wanted more dividends, then the company should have petitioned the price commission to permit it to increase the dividend on all its shares. And furthermore, the price of the new stock should only be greater than the old stock by the present value of the higher dividends paid on the new stock until it converts.

If a company contemplates listing on the New York Stock Exchange, it can't have two classes of stock outstanding in the hands of the general public. A company would be far better off at the start to avoid two classes of stock if it is possible to do so.

Common Stock

There can be classes of common stocks, similar to the situation for preferred stocks, with various shadings in voting privilege and preference as to earnings and rights to assets in liquidation.

A method used by some privately owned companies when they go public is to classify their stock into two different classes, A and B. The original owners who would retain a large amount of the stock may want no dividends because they are in a high tax bracket. In order to make the stock attractive to the public, a dividend may have to be included for the public stock. Therefore, two classes of stock are created, one with no dividends and one with dividends. Years ago, the owners would keep the voting power in their class of stock only. That day has passed, and each class would now have to vote equally.

The idea of two classes of stock in such a situation seems like a simple solution. However, it tends to complicate the financial picture, and, if a company expects to be a significant publicly owned company in the future, it would be better off having just one class of stock. At least, if there are two classes to start with, there should be a provision which will result in the conversion of one into the other after a certain limited length of time. Otherwise, if eventually you wish to eliminate one of the classes, you will have to pay a premium.

The basis on which to decide the best terms for common stock is different from that for senior securities, since the stockholders own the company. The primary test should be what is good for them over the long run. The problem can be viewed with these two premises in mind:

1. There should be fair distribution of powers among the stockholders themselves, on the basis of number of shares. The desires of the holders of the majority of the stock should be most influential, but the minority stockholders should be protected against abuses.
2. The stockholders' position should be protected against unsound and unresponsive management.

Under no circumstances should any provisions be included which will protect the management against the stockholders, except those stockholders who try to interfere with the operations of the company to the detriment of the other holders. Unfortunately, in some instances, managements appear to become detached from the reality of their job of working for the stockholders. Provisions which will allow such an attitude are, of course, unsound.

The powers of the corporation derive from the consent of the stockholders. However, many of the major factors affecting the common stockholders are a matter of financial policy, such as debt ratio, dividend policy, stock splits, listing vs. non-listing, keeping the stockholders fully informed, setting proper profit goals, etc. They cannot be covered in the common stock provisions. Furthermore, the provisions of the senior securities will have an important bearing on the position of the common stockholders, although their effect may not become significant until financial difficulties are encountered.

The specific provisions directly pertaining to the common stock may be found in the charter, the bylaws, the stock certificate, resolutions of the board of directors and the laws of the state in which the company is incorporated. If the company is regulated, government authorities may require certain standards, as may the stock exchanges for listed stocks.

We will mention only a few ideas about provisions for the common.

Par or No Par

Perhaps the first idea that might arise in your mind is whether common stock should be par or no par. The New York State transfer tax paid by the person who sells stock was formerly a factor affecting whether a stock should be no par or par, and the size of the par value. However, in January, 1959, the law was changed so that the tax is based on the value of the stock. How it is stated on the company's books has no effect.

Some state laws and regulatory authorities may require some companies to have a par value. And some states may impose a tax on the company based on the way the stock is carried on the books. Aside from these factors, par or no par is not a major consideration.

When new stock is sold which has a par value, it generally cannot be sold below par by state law. Therefore, if a company's stock has a par value, it should be low enough so that it will not hinder financing even under adverse circumstances. When you split your stock, you don't have to be worried about the reduction in the par value. If, after the split, it comes out to dollars and a fraction, you may wish to transfer enough surplus to make it an even dollar, just for balance sheet appearances.

Preemptive Rights

Some companies are required by the law of the state of incorporation to issue common stock and securities convertible into common to their stockholders through preemptive rights. Some companies not so required by law, may have such a provision in their charter. Others are free from any restriction, and management can make a choice. The other method of offering such securities is by direct sale to the public.

In Chapter 9, the question of offering stock through rights or by direct sale is fully discussed. How to analyze correctly which is better for your stockholders is explained. All surrounding circumstances will determine which is better, but such an analysis may show that in most instances the rights method is preferable. Nevertheless, as far as charter provisions are concerned, it might be better for a large, publicly owned company to have flexibility, so that it can follow whichever course seems more appropriate at the time. If a company is free to make a choice, the management should be responsive to stockholder interest in making such a decision.

Charter Changes

Statutes of the state of incorporation will establish the minimum standards for the vote required for charter and certain other changes. In any large corporation with a widespread stockholder list, there is a maximum vote that can be obtained which is hard to exceed on any proposal, no matter how important and uncontested. This is due to the fact that some companies have a certain percentage of stockholders who just don't vote. The size will depend on the nature of the stockholder list, etc. A vote of around 80% of the number of shares is high even under favorable circumstances. Therefore, a company may not wish to make the standards higher than the minimum required by statute.

SUMMARY: TYPES OF SECURITIES

Now that we have finished types of securities, let's put into a few words a principle or rather things to keep in mind:

1. In calculating cost, consider all tax effects over the life of the issue.

   Include all elements of cost such as residual value in a lease.

   Don't let costs be camouflaged, such as

the lowering of interest on a debenture by attaching a warrant.

Make calculations using the time value of money.

2. When comparing an issue with another, be sure you compare like with like, as for example leasing with debt.
3. Evaluate how the security may affect the company and the investors over the life of this issue under differing market conditions.
4. Consider how the terms may affect financial flexibility over the life of the issue.
5. Consider the accounting effects over the life of the issue.
6. Consider possible legal implications, such as how a security may affect the company's obligations to other security holders and the legality of the company's other securities for investments by institutions.
7. Consider how investors will treat the issue for security analysis and rating purposes.
8. Finally, if you think you have found a free lunch, look again.

CHAPTER 5

Corporate Organization and Financing

A company may hold assets either directly in the company itself, or in whole or in part in subsidiaries or affiliated companies. We will discuss the various types of corporate organization which may be used to raise capital.

In general, for a subsidiary to be consolidated for reporting purposes, ownership should be more than 50%. There are certain situations in which consolidation would not be appropriate even if ownership is more than 50%. With ownership between 20% and 50%, the investment is carried by the equity method. This means that the investment is carried on the balance sheet at original cost plus additional investment in undistributed earnings. The proportionate share of each year's earnings is shown in the income statement on a one-line basis. Below the 20% ownership level only dividend income is recorded. For tax purposes, ownership must be 80% in order to file a consolidated return.

Stockholders' and Debt Holders' View

The debt of the parent company generally establishes the credit standing of the corporate system. In determining the total amount of debt that the company and subsidiaries can handle, the debt ratio on a consolidated basis and the rating of the bonds the holding company governs are considered. This is illustrated in Exhibit 5-1.

The debt of the holding company will generally have a lower rating than subsidiary debt because the subsidiary debt is in a senior position, but there may be exceptions. The holding company debt can be put in a senior position by having the indenture prevent the issuance of any subsidiary debt.

A holding company system may not be as simple as in the exhibit. If a parent company owns two subsidiaries, one of which shows poor earnings and the other good earnings, the poor earner detracts from the good earner in a consolidated income statement. If the parent company is going to support the poor earning subsidiary, then the consolidated picture correctly shows the overall financial strength of the system. However, if the management has decided to let the poor earning subsidiary swim entirely on its own and not give it any financial support even if it goes under, then the consolidated picture understates the strength of the system. In such a situation, it would be appropriate for analytical purposes, to eliminate the losing subsidiary from the consolidated picture. However, a buyer of securities of the parent company would be skeptical about a management's statement that it is not going to save the losing subsidiary; the temptation is always there to try to save the sinking ship. Senior security holders of the parent company would want protective provisions to make sure that the weak subsidiary would not be a drain.

Where to Do Financing

In financial planning, an average and maximum debt ratio should be determined, either on a consolidated basis or by analyzing each of the subsidiaries separately and then determining a weighted average debt ratio for the system. To the extent that debt financing is done in the subsidiaries, it will decrease the amount that can be done in the parent company.

Where the financing is done depends on the credit of the various companies and the need and ability to move cash from one to the other.

For example, a holding company, which owns a number of small subsidiaries, may be able to raise capital on the best basis by doing all financing in the holding company with a provision in the indenture preventing any long-term debt financing in the subsidiaries. On the other hand, if the subsidiaries are large and can stand on their own, senior capital financing may be done in the subsidiaries alone. If a holding company system has both large and small subsidiaries, the senior security financing for the large subsidiaries can be done in those subsidiaries, and the senior security financing for the small companies in the holding company.

Exhibit 5-1

POSITION OF PARENT COMPANY AND SUBSIDIARY DEBT

	Parent Holding Company	Subsidiary 100% Owned	Consolidated			Bond Rating
Common equity	$70,000,000		$70,000,000		70%	
Bonds	10,000,000		10,000,000	10%		A
Preferred		$10,000,000	10,000,000	10	30	
Bonds		10,000,000	10,000,000	10		AA
Total			$100,000,000		100%	

If all debt financing is done in the holding company, the system has more freedom to move funds from one subsidiary to another, or upstream funds to the holding company and then downstream them to another subsidiary. The debt holder of the holding company will have less concern where the money goes as long as it stays in the system. However, if debt financing is done in each subsidiary, the debt holders of the subsidiaries will not want funds moved out of the subsidiaries so that their positions would be weakened.

On the other hand, if all debt is in the holding company rather than in separate subsidiaries, sale of a subsidiary might be more difficult. The holder of the holding company debt might not want an asset removed which protects his debt. In such a situation, the release of property clause in the indenture is particularly important.

More than one holding company weakens the quality of the securities at the top so that financing would be more costly.

Due to lack of financial planning, a holding company system may grow like topsy, with financing being done in the easiest fashion at the time. Ultimately, as the company grows larger, it may become apparent that the financial picture is a mess. Then it is too late because the bondholders will present a barrier to reorganization on a more logical basis. To avoid such a problem, requires financial planning with long range policies being established from the start for both the holding company and subsidiaries.

A holding company faced this interesting problem. Debt financing had been done by subsidiaries. They were small and the company wished to merge certain subsidiaries together to provide a more attractive financing media. They were grouped in three areas and the goal was to have one subsidiary serving each area. However, the debt holders of the subsidiaries would not go along unless the company gave them an increase in interest rate. A solution was suggested to set up three sub-holding companies to own the companies in the three areas and finance through the sub-holding companies. This is a possible solution, but not as good as merging the subsidiaries into three groups. Two layers of holding companies produce a complicated and costly financial structure. All factors considered in this case, it was probably preferable to confine future financing to the top holding company, close the indenture on the subsidiary debt so no new subsidiary debt could be issued and leave the small subsidiaries undisturbed until the debt matured. By so doing, however, any new debt in the holding company would be junior to existing subsidiary debt, and therefore it would be rated one notch lower.

Separate Subsidiary for Financing Purposes

Generally, a secured bond will have a higher rating and command a lower rate than unsecured debt. One way to put a bondholder in a senior position is to segregate certain assets in a separate subsidiary and issue bonds on that subsidiary. Such a move only makes sense if certain criteria are met:

1. The assets and their earnings must be of a nature which will satisfy creditors.
2. The company must be of sufficient size to give it strength and to make it worthwhile for investors to analyze the company.
3. It must stand primarily on its own feet and not have to rely on the parent company's credit, otherwise segregation accomplishes little financially.
4. The company must have sufficient common equity, commensurate with the nature of the business, to support senior obligations.
5. It must be possible to set aside the assets in a separate subsidiary without the debt of the parent company having any claim on those assets. While we said at the beginning of this chapter that with 50% or more ownership financial statements should be consolidated, there are exceptions if for better understanding there should be a separate subsidiary.

6. The parent company must continue to be a complete operating unit without the assets of the subsidiary.

In other words, it must be a separate entity with sufficient earnings to provide its own credit standing and not destroy the parent company's credit when the assets are segregated.

Providing these criteria are met, the company may be able to obtain a better rate on its subsidiary securities, or it may be able to obtain more overall debt with an equal credit rating.

It may sound illogical to say that the sum of the parts are greater than the whole. The reason why this may occur is as follows: If all assets are in one company and that company issues unsecured bonds, the bondholders are in an equal position with all other creditors as regards the company's assets. If certain assets can be segregated in a separate subsidiary and debt issued on that subsidiary, then those debtholders can look directly to those assets for their protection; they do not have to share equally with all other debtholders of the parent company. Obviously this would reduce the amount of debt the parent company could issue, but the overall amount of debt might be somewhat greater.

Typical of these types of situations are:

1. Captive finance companies.
2. Real estate subsidiaries.
3. A relatively small, financially weak company which produced and leased a large piece of equipment to a large company with good credit. This asset can be put in a separate subsidiary and leased to the customer. The lease rental income will then be the basis for debt financing.
4. Financing of foreign operations.

A Captive Finance Company as an Example

A company may wish to finance receivables or leases of the company's products in order to assist in sales or as an additional avenue of capital investment. If receivables are large enough so that a separate finance company can be set up which can stand on its own feet, financing may be assisted. Receivables should be in the neighborhood of $100 million or more.

Aside from the financing advantages, there may be additional advantages:

1. It may improve control over credit by providing a separate organization for appraisal of the credit risk. This removes the approval of credit risk a step further from sales pressure.
2. The parent company can appraise the finance business more clearly and measure its profitability better. It may tighten operating procedures.
3. Lenders will receive regular reports in a standard format.
4. Some analysts may disregard the debt of the non-consolidated finance subsidiary in analyzing the parent company.

There may be some additional expenses to set up and maintain a separate corporation. There may be some additional staff costs if employees are not permitted to work for both companies. There will be separate accounting and certified statements, but this might not be any greater than would be necessary if the company's receivables were merely segregated for financing purposes.

There are tax and legal problems which will have to be passed on by your tax experts and attorneys. There is no tax difference if the company files on a consolidated basis, but if it files separately there will be a question whether the receivables can be transferred to the financing company without tax liability, particularly if the parent is using the installment method of reporting for tax purposes. Other tax questions will have to be investigated. On the legal side, two companies may have to file to qualify to do business in various states, and the finance company must file to protect liens.

If financial reports are consolidated, some of the advantages of a separate subsidiary are lost. One line reporting with full earnings taken into the parent builds up the parent company's investment through retained earnings. The parent company can influence where profits are shown to some extent, but to make financing possible on an independent basis it should strive to earn a reasonable return on the finance company.

Lenders may prefer the company to restrict its business to that of its parent.

A captive finance company may have a working agreement with its parent. The extent of the working agreement depends on the size, nature of operations, diversification and risk of assets. It may take one or more forms:

1. An outright guarantee. This would have to be reported in the financial statement of the parent. It is generally confined to small companies with poor credit.
2. Maintenance of capital so that the debt is adequately protected.
3. Hold-back reserve agreement. Receivables are sold to the captive by the parent at less than their face value, with final payment by the finance subsidiary upon final collection.
4. Buy-back reserve agreement covering delinquent receivables. The parent agrees to buy all or part of receivables that are past due for a certain length of time.
5. Product buy-back agreement for repossessions when product is difficult to sell.

The working agreement may be included in the indenture for the long term debt of the finance company. The short term lenders may not have such control, but they may refuse to lend if the terms are not met. The extent to which a working agreement is needed has an important effect on the advantages which may be obtained on a separate finance subsidiary. A complete guarantee will eliminate, to a large extent, the financial advantages of a separate finance subsidiary.

The amount of debt a finance company can carry will depend on the type of company and all the factors surrounding it. Assuming satisfactory earnings, a rule of thumb for senior debt to capital base is 4 to 1. However, the common equity should not be below 15%, and, therefore, if there is a significant amount of subordinated debt, the ratio of senior debt to capital base would have to be lower than 4 to 1. Senior debt to be rated A may require senior debt, subordinated debt and common equity to be approximately as follows:

	Senior debt			
A	Long term debt	45%		
	Bank loans and			
	Commercial paper	35		
	Total			80%
	Capital base			four
BBB	Subordinated debt	(25%)	5	for
	Common equity	(75%)	15	one
	Total			20%
	Total			100%

Bank loans and commercial paper may be seasonal, rolled over and term. Working agreements are generally only included in term bank loans. For the commercial paper to be rated prime, the receivables should be $100 million or more, and the capital base a minimum of $15 million. There is a minimum interest coverage and the commercial paper must be covered 100% by lines of credit.

Direct placements with insurance companies may supply the long-term senior debt and unsubordinated debt. Public offerings of debt are limited to the very large companies. Sometimes the parent company supplies the subordinated debt.

The New York Insurance Law requires a minimum fixed charge coverage, before income tax, of 1.15 for insurance companies to buy the long term debt, providing a liquidity test is also met. It is somewhat amusing that the figure was lowered from 1.25 times in 1947 in order to accommodate certain large captive finance companies. Calculation of coverage figures is shown below.

			Rate	*Charge*
Senior debt	75%	(Before tax)	8%	6.00
Subordinated debt	10	" "	9	0.90
Common equity	15	(After tax)	12	1.80
Total	100%			8.70

Times interest charges earned after income taxes $= \frac{8.70}{6.90} = 1.26$

Times charges earned before income taxes $= \frac{10.50}{6.90} = 1.52$
(Assuming a 50% tax rate)

A Joint Project

Two independent companies may form a joint venture in which each company puts in a small amount of common equity and either directly or indirectly guarantees the company's debt. An indirect guarantee might consist of an agreement to take or pay for an amount of the company's product to provide sufficient income to pay principal and interest of the debt. This may be an appropriate way to handle such a joint project. However, each of the sponsoring companies will have to add the amount of debt of the joint company for which they are responsible to their own debt in calculating their capital structure ratios.

Tenancy in Common

A project can be developed by the technique of tenancy in common. The property is owned by more than one owner on an agreed percentage basis. A tenant in common may mortgage or finance his interest as he wishes, and he may sell it. Each tenant in common includes his share of assets of the project in his own balance sheet and his share of the operating expenses in his own income statement. The project itself has no income. Each participant may determine his own depreciation policies. Management of the project may be by one of the co-tenants on a contractual basis.

This type of ownership is not without its problems. There may be special legal problems. Sharing of expenses may result in disputes. If the plant is shut down for repairs, it may inconvenience one owner more than the other. In case disputes do arise, there should be incorporated in the contract buy-out terms.

Other Types of Corporate Organization for Financing

To make possible special types of financing, property may have to be segregated in a separate corporation or placed in custody of a trustee. A non-profit organization may be brought into the picture where a non-tax paying party is needed, or for other reasons. The purpose of this type of financing may be to solve problems such as:

Accounting
Tax
Credit
Legal
Regulatory

The important point in analyzing such types of financing is to see through the veil to the entity which is relied on for credit. The so-called advantage of keeping debt off the balance sheet is sometimes touted by bankers as one of the principal reasons for using special types of financing. In any form of debt financing someone has to be responsible for the credit, and whoever does should have the debt added to their capital structure for analytical purposes. It would appear that with all the "sophisticated" graduate schools, with the "enlightened" era of accounting and with careful government regulation, such a statement would be unnecessary, but that, unfortunately, is not the fact.

For example, Company A builds a project. It doesn't have sufficient credit to finance it. A separate Company B is set up which is owned by Company A. Company B does financing on the basis of a contract, such as a take or pay contract, with a group of companies which are going to buy the product of the plant. They will take and pay for products, or pay regardless of whether they get any products, a sufficient amount to service the debt. Company A keeps the debt off its balance sheet. Providing Company A will never rescue Company B, no matter what happens, it is not a liability to Company A. To the extent that Company A might rescue Company B, if it got into trouble, it is a contingent liability of Company A and Company A's credit would have to be weighed with that contingency in mind. However, the companies which sign the take or pay contracts are primarily responsible for the debt and should have their share of the debt of

Company B added to their long term debt. Certainly, the lenders to Company B in their analysis are looking for payment by the companies purchasing the product. The monkey has got to be on someone's back or no one would lend the money. That is the fact no matter how you slice it. But human nature being what it is, we like to avoid unpleasant facts if we can find an excuse to clear our conscience. And at times in finance some people's consciences have an almost infinite elasticity.

In spite of these critical comments, it is recognized that special types of financing are essential in certain situations for one of the reasons listed above. But they should be carefully analyzed in terms of their need to solve a problem, their cost and their advantages and disadvantages. They should not be justified on the superficial reason alone of getting debt off the balance sheet.

ABC or Carve-Out Financing

An old form of financing involving four parties is the so-called ABC transaction. It was used by oil producers and some other natural resource type of business to purchase assets. It may be structured in various ways depending on what is trying to be accomplished. A simple example might be as follows:

A owns oil producing properties or some other similar type of property such as a mine. As an example, we will assume that Company A has producing properties that are worth $1 million.

B wants the properties but doesn't want to pay for them until the oil is produced. A wants his money now. A sells the properties to B for $200,000 cash and in the conveyance with B receives a production payment in the amount of $800,000 to be paid out as the oil is produced together with interest on the unpaid balance.

Since A wants all his money now, he sells his $800,000 reserved production payment to C for cash. C borrows the money from the bank. The bank gets paid off by payments from C as the oil is produced. A has his money and is free and clear. B has an $800,000 obligation to pay C plus interest as oil is produced. Since C has the ownership, B avoids getting the obligation on its books.

The bank is protected by the strength of B's working interest in the properties and the fact that B has put up a $200,000 payment which he loses if he fails to make the payments. The amount that B will have to pay initially will depend on the amount the properties will support and how much the bank is willing to lend against the properties.

C may be a shell company which is a tax-free organization, such as a college endowment fund which will get a fee for acting as a conduit. The reason for the shell company is that production payment is an interest in real property which a bank is not permitted to buy.

The carved-out production payment may be used by a natural resource company for the purposes of raising capital as well as financing the sale of production. The financing takes a somewhat different form. Company A "carves out" a part of its natural resource and sells it to a tax-free shell. An institution makes a loan to the shell, which is used by the shell to pay for the "carved out" production. The lending institution looks exclusively to the proceeds of production to satisfy the payment. When the loan is repaid, the remaining production reverts to the natural resource company. The value of the "carve out" sufficiently exceeds the value of the loan so that the lending institution is protected. The natural resource company retains its working interest in the properties. If a natural resource is carved at a low figure on the company's books, the "carve out" financing will increase assets. On the liability side, the transaction is recorded as a deferred liability.

While this type of arrangement keeps the debt off Company A's balance sheet, there are good arguments why, for analysis purposes, it should be included with Company A's debt. To explain this statement, let's look at two companies, A and B, which start out both alike with a capital structure consisting 100%

of common equity. They both have an equal amount of undervalued natural resources on their books. Company A does straight debt financing so that its capital structure now includes 20% debt. Company B does a carve-out financing for the same amount. It appears as a deferred liability. If the natural resource of each company continues to be valuable, there is no difference between Company A and Company B for capital structure analytical purposes. Company B only has less liability if the natural resource turns out to be worth less than the debt. Then Company B can walk away and leave the holder of the debt holding the bag. However, there would be little likelihood of that because the holder of the debt would require adequate protection so that he would not get stuck.

This type of financing is particularly tricky as regards the tax and legal aspects and will require experts in these areas.

Leveraged Lease

In Chapter 4 we discussed the costs of a leveraged lease. Here we will point out the corporate setup.

In a simple lease there are two parties: the lessor, and the lessee who uses the property. In a leveraged lease, there are four parties.

- The lessee who uses the property.
- A shell company with a moderate amount of equity, which owns the property, leases it and is the medium for financing. The owner of the shell company has the equity.
- A trustee who has custody of the property and makes sure that it is administered properly for the benefit of the stockholders and debtholders of the shell company, and also collects the lease payments and distributes them to the stockholders and debtholders of the shell company.
- The lender of the senior capital.

The reason for the shell company is to put ownership of the property in the hands of investors who are in a higher tax bracket than the lessee and will receive a greater tax benefit from depreciation on the property. If the lessor shares some of their tax benefit with the lessee, the net financing cost is less for the lessee than if the property were owned directly and financed with debt.

The arrangement in a leveraged lease is shown in Exhibit 5-2.

Project Financing

In the utility industry, property in the process of construction is charged with interest during construction. For example, if a company builds a $100 million plant, there would be added to the plant the cost of financing the construction. Let's assume that the cost of financing is 10%; then each year there will be added to the plant cost 10% of the construction cost in that year. Let's assume that in the first year of construction $50 million of the plant was built, then $5 million in interest during construction would be added to the plant value.

In the year in which the construction is under way, the interest during construction that is added to the plant in the balance sheet is also added to the income after taxes in the income statement. This, in effect, reduces the company's total interest charges. Thus, earnings would be increased by the bookkeeping figure of $5 million in the first year.

Analysts have been critical of interest during construction, saying that it inflates earnings inappropriately. Project financing is one means that can be used to eliminate this effect.

Company A sets up a trust which has title to the project property.

Debt financing is done by the trust to take care of the cost of the project and also interest payments during the construction period. Company A agrees to buy the project at the end of the construction period. Thus, the interest charges for the project are added to the construction costs in the trust, but do not appear in the company's income statement.

Exhibit 5-2

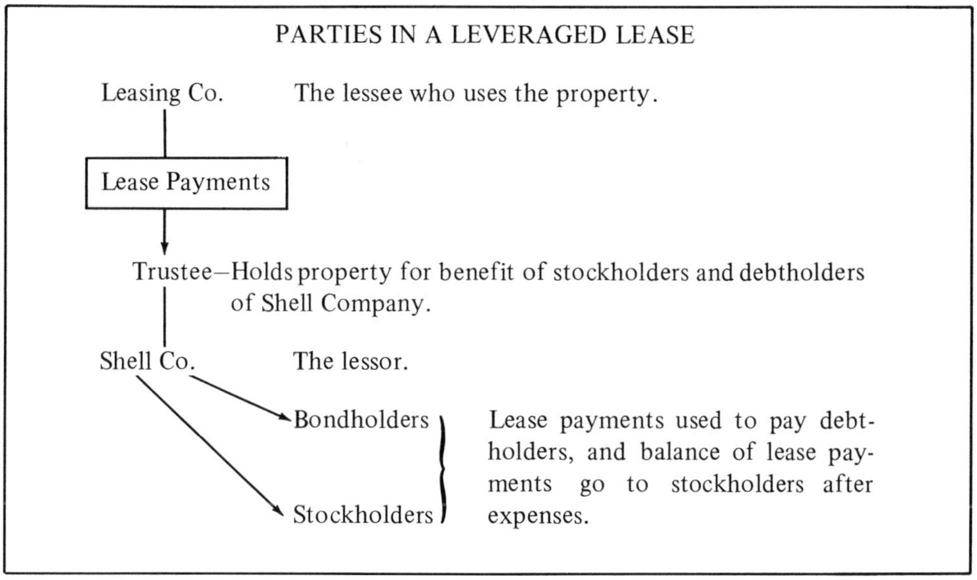

There may be some tax advantages. If Company A does not at present have any taxable income, the interest which piles up in the trust becomes part of the property value when it is taken over by the company. This is depreciable for tax purposes, and it also adds to the amount of investment tax credit because the tax base is larger.

Actually, an astute analyst should add the debt of the trust to Company A's debt because Company A guarantees it. And the interest charges paid by the trust should be added to the interest charges of Company A. In such an analysis, the picture would look worse in the income statement because there would be no deduction for interest during construction. A company which uses this type of project financing has to be betting partly on the fact that security analysts will not do a thorough job and add to Company A's capital structure the debt of the project company.

One thing more should be mentioned about this type of project financing. The company will be faced with a major refinancing problem when the project is completed. Its financing plan should include sufficient equity financing ahead of the completion of the project in order to be able to meet the debt maturity when the project is completed.

Nuclear Fuel Financing

Nuclear fuel for an electric utility requires a large capital outlay as compared to a coal pile or oil in storage tanks. When nuclear plants first came into operation, some companies were seeking ways to solve the fuel financing problem. The difference in treatment by the rating agencies of leases for nuclear fuel caused some companies to be interested in handling their nuclear fuel supply on a lease basis. One rating agency said they would treat the leases as another form of debt; another said they would treat nuclear fuel leases as an operating expense and not capitalize them.

An electric utility wants complete control of the nuclear fuel, so in order to set up a lease arrangement, a shell company is established, with nominal equity, which only has legal title to the fuel. For all other purposes, the utility handles the fuel as though it is its own.

We will call the shell company Nuclear Leasing Co. A bank, which is named as trustee for the company acts as a conduit for the funds.

The credit behind Nuclear Leasing Co. is the utility company. It would have a commitment to provide payments in two parts: one for repayment of principal as the fuel is burned up and the other for payment of interest. The reason for breaking down the payments in two parts is to provide flexibility. If the plant had to be shut down, the repayment of principal would be postponed. Both of these payments are covered by lease payments by the utility to the shell company, Nuclear Leasing, which in turn would pass the payments on to the lenders.

In order to get the lowest interest rates, financing was arranged with short term credits consisting of commercial paper and bank loan agreements, with Nuclear Leasing Co. being the obligor. One of the principal reasons for this type of financing was to take advantage of lower rates for shorter maturities.

Because of the complicated nature of the legal arrangements, it was necessary to have the commercial paper backed up by bank letters of credit. For this service the banks charged a fee, and the banks got a premium over the prime rate for their loan facilities.

One of the advantages of having the fuel owned by this separate entity was the ability to accumulate all related costs and start-up costs in the Nuclear Leasing Co. so that the utility company would not have to make any outlays until the plant started operating. Payment of interest charges during that period would be made out of principal.

An apparent advantage of this type of financing consisted in keeping this large amount of short term credit off the balance sheet of the utility company. This, however, is purely a subterfuge and any good analyst would assign the debt to the utility. The only possible tangible benefit was due to the fact that one of the rating agencies would treat the lease payments as operating expense. Since the utilities were having so much financing to do and also were having problems with their bond ratings, this was one other way to do debt financing.

A question can be raised as to the wisdom of doing so much financing on a short term basis. The part represented by the fuel which is burned up is ideal for short term financing, but there is a residual which requires permanent financing. In a credit crunch, financing might be difficult if short term funds dried up. Many utilities faced up to the problem and financed the residual part of the fuel with conventional long term financing.

Minority Interest

We have talked primarily about the corporate setup and financing with senior securities. Now we will discuss the use of common stock of subsidiaries. There may be two reasons for having common stock of subsidiaries outstanding:

To assist in evaluating the holding company common.
To assist in financing.

Minority Interest for Assisting Valuation of Holding Company

If a holding company has a number of subsidiaries, the unattractive ones may tend to dull the effect of the attractive ones for investors evaluating the common stock of the holding company. In order to overcome this problem, the holding company can sell a small minority interest in each of the subsidiaries. Then investors can determine a market value for the stocks of each subsidiary separately. After deducting any senior securities of the holding company, investors can arrive at a value for the holding company common. Thus, the full value of the attractive subsidiaries stands out. This sounds like a good idea, but it actually is not as good as it sounds for the following reasons:

1. Astute analysts will question whether a market value based on a small amount of stock in the form of minority interest represents a fair appraisal of market

value. And for this reason, they may disregard the market value. If the minority interest does not result in a floating supply of stock of at least 300,000 shares, an active market may not be created.

2. The weak subsidiaries may be a drain on the strong companies, if the strong ones are used to support the weak ones.
3. This approach assumes that analysts are not capable of analyzing the parts separately and coming to a conclusion as to the value of the holding company stock. If the company wishes to assist analysts in understanding the company, management should consider providing a consolidating balance sheet and income statement in addition to consolidated statements. Consolidating statements show each subsidiary separately and how they fit together.

   If a company has a sound investor relations program and gives out complete information both good and bad, informed investors should be able to appraise the holding company stock. Using a minority interest approach may give the impression that the management is playing games to promote the price of the holding company stock; this creates an unfavorable impression. Enhancement of value of either the parent or subsidiary's stock can be achieved without increasing minority interest. Stable earnings growth and good management will ultimately be recognized in the marketplace through a good investor relations program and financial statements with full disclosure.
4. A minority interest represents a prior drain of earnings out of the holding company system. If the subsidiary is attractive, and has good prospects, then a minority interest reduces the potential for the holding company stock. The market's appraisal of the parent may actually be impaired because of its reduced interest in an important, profitable subsidiary. This is illustrated below and in more detail in Exhibit 5-3.

   Holding Company Common
   - Holding company preferred —prior charge
   - Holding company debt —prior charge

   Subsidiary Minority Interest —prior drain
   - Subsidiary preferred —prior charge
   - Subsidiary debt —prior charge
5. If there is a positive influence on the parent's stock when the subsidiary's stock goes up, there should also be a negative effect when the subsidiary's stock goes down.
6. A minority interest may prove to be a hindrance to corporate changes such as:
   a) A merger of subsidiaries.
   b) Shifting assets from the holding company to subsidiaries, from one subsidiary to another, or sale of assets of subsidiaries.
   c) Sale of the entire subsidiary.
   d) Sale of the parent company.
   e) Dividend policy of the subsidiary to the parent company.
7. The larger the minority interest, the greater the possibility of minority interest law suits due to insider dealings and possible conflicts of interest between the parent and the subsidiary.
8. If in the future it becomes desirable to eliminate the minority interest, the holders have the company over a barrel, and it may be necessary to pay more than it is worth.

Companies that have lived with minority interest generally feel that it is more trouble than it is worth and would rather eliminate it.

Minority Interest for Financing

The advantages of minority interest for financing can be summarized as follows:

1. When the minority interest is sold, it provides funds for the parent company.
2. The minority interest may create supermoney; i.e., stock selling at a high multiple, which in turn may be used by the subsidiary or parent for acquisition pur-

Exhibit 5-3

HOLDING OR PARENT COMPANY
NON-CONSOLIDATED STATEMENT

Effect of Minority Interest

Holding Company

Current assets		$100	Current liabilities		$ 54
Investment in subsidiaries			Long term capital		
→ Company A	30		Debt	10	
→ Company B	24		Preferred	5	
		54	Common	85	
					100
Total		$154	Total		$154

Subsidiaries

Subsidiary Company A				
Assets				
Current assets			$ 40	
Plant, net			20	
Total			$ 60	
Liabilities				
Current liabilities			$ 20	
Long term capital				
	Debt	$10		→ Interest prior charge to earnings for holding co.
100%	Common	30		
	Total		40	
Total			$ 60	
Subsidiary Company B				
Assets				
Current assets			$ 40	
Plant, net			20	
Total			$ 60	
Liabilities				
Current liabilities			$ 20	
Long term capital				
	Debt	$10		→ Interest prior charge to earnings for holding co.
80%	Common	30		→ 20% minority ownership. Prior drain of earnings to holding company.
	Total		40	
Total			$ 60	

poses. The financing of an acquisition by a subsidiary through an exchange of stock cannot be considered as a "pooling of interests."

3. The creation of a minority interest offers flexibility in the following ways:

   a) The parent can issue incentive securities convertible into the shares of the subsidiary.

   b) The subsidiary can finance itself with common. This may enhance the growth potential of the subsidiary because it does not have to depend on corporate funds.

c) It may be possible to manage earnings per share by:

1) Reducing the parent's outstanding shares by swapping subsidiary's shares for them when the parent's stock is selling for a lower price-earnings ratio than the subsidiary.
2) Having the parent pay stock dividends in shares of subsidiaries rather than its own shares.

d) It should be possible to file a consolidated tax return if the minority interest does not exceed 20% of the voting stock. Per APB 23, the parent may be required to record deferred taxes on the undistributed earnings of a subsidiary which is not consolidated for tax purposes.

4. Depending upon the offering price of an issue by a subsidiary, the parent's investment in the subsidiary, and thereby its own equity, may be enhanced even though it owns a proportionately smaller share.

   Sale of subsidiary stock may build up the parent equity if a minority interest in a subsidiary is sold at a high price compared with the book value because of good earnings; the increase in price over the book value adds to the equity of the parent company.
5. A minority interest stresses decentralization and thereby serves to motivate management. The management of the subsidiary can relate its efforts to a market price for its shares. The use of stock options might also be made more effective. However, decentralization and management incentives can be realized without increasing a minority interest.
6. The minority interest may protect against a take-over of the parent.

Conclusions on Minority Interest

The public sale of a minority stock interest in a subsidiary for the primary purpose of improving the market price of the parent's common stock is not a realistic approach to obtaining a change in the market value of the parent. In effect, the public stockholder's appraisal of the parent's basic business will remain unchanged and may even be influenced negatively by the partial sale of a significant "earnings contributor."

In limited instances, a minority interest might be used effectively as a financing vehicle. These instances are as follows:

1. It might be possible to take advantage of a subsidiary's high multiple to finance an acquisition on more favorable terms than would otherwise be possible.
2. If the parent was unable to arrange needed financing, it could be beneficial to use the subsidiary to obtain the necessary capital.

So we conclude that it should be an unusual exception rather than the rule.

Conclusions on Corporate Organization for Financing

There are an almost unlimited number of ways that financing can be done outside of the principal corporation. However, there must be some credit strength on which to base the financing, and it must be pledged in one way or another. In order to justify special types of financing there must be some substantial reason, because they add to complications which generally adds to the cost of financing in the long run.

CHAPTER 6

Financial Planning

As background for financial planning you will have developed:

An average and maximum debt ratio.
A dividend policy.
A knowledge of types of securities.
A five-year financial forecast which shows the outlook for earnings and the capital requirements.

Three Reserves

We have already stressed the importance of establishing an average and maximum debt ratio so that the company's securities will have good quality and it will have borrowing reserve and financial insurance. Also keep in mind that there are only two other financial reserves for a corporation:

Short-term borrowing reserve.
Incentive security reserve.

It is financial stupidity to rely too heavily on short term borrowings under favorable conditions just to save some interest, and then when things turn down the company is unable to use short term borrowings to tide it over.

Also, using incentive securities such as convertibles and senior securities with warrants during a boom period results in a company using up a type of security which may be very helpful when earnings are poor.

Good financial planning should keep these three reserves open.

Plan Well Ahead—Forecasting

You may defend the Financial Vice President if a company's finances get in a jam, by saying, "He may affect profits or losses, but he doesn't make them." True, but he should handle his job so that a financial problem won't arise even if the company encounters difficulties. He should know in advance how he might maneuver. The only way he can accomplish this is to plan well ahead.

Anyone familiar with forecasts may feel that financial planning is a waste of time because earnings forecasts are so seldom realized. This is undoubtedly true. But good financial planning will handle this possibility or probability. That is the reason for having good quality securities, borrowing reserve, financial insurance, short-term borrowing capacity and incentive securities up your sleeve.

Perhaps more important than the earnings forecast is the forecast of requirements for outside funds. Financial planning requires that you have a forecast of your requirements for outside funds for a number of years ahead, preferably five, and revise it each year, dropping the previous year and adding another. The necessary flexibility in your financing program can be attained only if you have some idea of the magnitude of the requirements a number of years in advance.

It may seem elementary to stress this point, because officials of many companies take for granted making such a forecast; some feel that it is necessary to extend it for more than five years. However, there are others who protest that in their business it is impossible to do so for more than one year. No matter how difficult the task, put down some figures. Three years, and even two, are better than nothing, but unless you can stretch them for at least five, you haven't stepped out as far as you should.

You may need to make more than one forecast: a minimum, a maximum and the best estimate somewhere in between. Unexpected large variations cause the greatest strain on financing. The extent to which the nature of your company does make forecasting difficult for five years ahead will, in itself, be a reason for a conservative financial policy so that you will be able to meet unexpected situations.

Even in crude forecasting the very act of setting forth certain assumptions as to shipments, prices, costs, etc., over a five-year period, will provoke questions. In trying to answer these questions, you begin to think about problems which might not be brought to your attention otherwise. Moreover, each time a forecast is made, you will find ways of refining it, because, in some cases, you will have found answers or have narrowed your assumptions with greater confidence than previously.

It is important that all of the people who are involved in making estimates of sales, costs, capital requirements, etc., have a clear idea of the purpose of the budget and what its limitations may be. They should know what use will be made of it in order that their own contribution will make the budget a more effective device for planning.

This book in no way attempts to discuss the methods of budgeting; it takes up from the point after the budget has been made. However, we will say a word about working capital.

Working Capital

Working capital, which is the difference between current assets and current liabilities, for some companies may be a larger item than the plant itself. Working capital and current ratio (the ratio of current assets divided by current liabilities) may affect the quality of a company's long term securities. Some bond indentures and term loan agreements require that a company maintain a certain minimum working capital or current ratio as a control. The rating agencies at least look at the current position in determining bond ratings, and it is important in commercial paper rating. Some buyers of senior securities feel that current ratio is an indication of the soundness of a company's financial policies. Banks analyze the present and projected current position carefully in their credit analysis of a company. A company which tries to get along with too little working capital, and overuses its short-term credit facilities, may show a lack of understanding of a sound financial approach. And don't make the mistake of thinking that you can expand sales without expanding working capital.

Of course, the real problem is to arrive at the optimum working capital for your company; that is, the amount that will provide the proper balance between the minimum necessary to support the company's operations and the maximum for complete safety to creditors. In arriving at what the desirable ratio should be, figures of competitors and industry leaders are important since creditors will give some weight to your position as compared with others in your industry in analyzing your financial condition. If your figures vary substantially from the industry figures, you should have reasons to explain the difference.

Pattern of Demand for Capital

For our present purpose of financial planning, we are interested in a forecast which will show the need for outside requirements for financing. The budget should produce a top summary table which will look something like that shown in Exhibit 6-1.

A simple table, such as the one in the exhibit, will be easy for top management to review and discuss. Naturally, it will be documented by the detailed budget figures and other necessary background material.

The general magnitude and timing of the need for outside funds is all important in financial planning; it will show you what you may have to do to insure success in raising capital "come hell or high water."

Three things have to be tied together in financial planning:

The condition of the securities markets.
The pattern of demand for capital.
Earnings.

A forecast which shows most funds to be needed at the end of the forecast will call for one financial plan. If your stock is at a good price, you may want to build up your equity to assure that you can fall back on the use of debt if bad earnings are encountered.

On the other hand, if you have heavy demand for capital in the first part of your five-year plan and it falls off sharply in subsequent years, you may see your way clear to issue debt and repay it as the need for funds slackens.

Many types of companies only do some form of long term financing every five or ten years. For them, financial planning should be easy. Other types of companies call for heavy injections of capital. This is particularly true of a capital-intensive industry such as the electric utility business. In the seventies, many electric utilities had to sell an issue of bonds, preferred and common, each year. Their earnings outlook was uncertain and they had to rely heavily on rate increases to keep their earnings up. Because of the political implications, rate increases are fraught with uncertainty. Thus, in order to insure that such companies would be able to raise capital in later years, they had to sell common stock in the first few years, almost regardless of price. The real problem was whether the market would take the stock. It took guts to sell stock because the market was badly depressed. However, if utilities followed any other course, they would have been playing Russian Roulette. If they relied too heavily on debt and incentive types of securities, such as convertibles, in the beginning of their financing program, they would have had nothing to fall back on in later years if the common stock market dried up. It was bound to be a tight squeeze no matter how they did it, but if they took any other approach they might have gotten zapped.

A Company in Poor Financial Condition

A study of a company's forecast may show that because of its weak financial position or poor earnings outlook, it would be poor judgment to try to meet all of its needs for capital. In such a situation, a company has to tighten its belt and take the following steps:

1. Review the capital expenditure program carefully and only take on those capital expenditures which will provide an

Exhibit 6-1

FORECAST OF FINANCING REQUIREMENTS

	Actual Current Year	*Forecast by Years* 1st	2nd	3rd	4th	5th
Estimated Net Profit After Taxes						
Less: Dividends (Pfd. and Common)						
Income After Dividends						
Plus: Depreciation						
Plus: Other Items Providing Cash						
CASH GENERATED INTERNALLY	. . . .	. . . .	. . . .	. . . .	. . . .	. . . .
Capital Expenditures						
Additional Working Capital						
Plus: Other Items Requiring Cash						
CASH REQUIREMENTS	. . . .	. . . .	. . . .	. . . .	. . . .	. . . .
Less: CASH GENERATED INTERNALLY	. . . .	. . . .	. . . .	. . . .	. . . .	. . . .
FINANCING REQUIREMENTS (excess)	. . . .	. . . .	. . . .	. . . .	. . . .	. . . .
FINANCING REQUIREMENTS CUMULATIVE (excess).	. . . .	. . . .	. . . .	. . . .	. . . .	. . . .

Other items should be shown separately if they are large. Those providing cash might include proceeds from the sale of property, tax refunds, etc. Those requiring cash might include debt retirement, acquisitions, etc.

assured good return in the immediate future.

2. Review its existing divisions to determine whether there are any which are not earning their keep and should be sold.
3. Run a tight ship so that earnings will be realized to the fullest extent possible.
4. Work with banks and long term lenders to avoid having them pressure the company unnecessarily. Such pressure can be avoided by furnishing complete information before it is requested.
5. Consider various ways to raise capital in an emergency, such as sale and lease-back, subsidiary financing, receivable financing, etc. These types of financings might conflict with existing debt restrictions. Furthermore, they should be avoided if possible.
6. Take this period as an opportunity to upgrade and train the company's personnel.

This may prove to be a very valuable opportunity for a company to eliminate the fat and tighten up its muscles for a new start on a sounder basis. During this period of rehabilitation, a company should have in mind the capital structure goal it should try to achieve as improving operations permit.

Setting Up a Financing Program

If your company needs to raise only a small amount of money, or a large amount in only one out of five years, setting up a financing plan is easy. However, if fairly large amounts are required in each year for a number of years, the mechanics become similar to fitting a square peg in a round hole. It can be simplified, if done in rough form, in two steps.

We will explain these steps with an example. We will assume that the capital structure of our company at the beginning of the first year is a satisfactory goal for our company based on the considerations discussed in Chapter 2.

The first step is to determine the amount of each type of long term security which will have to be sold in each year of the five years to achieve the appropriate capital structure ratios in each year.

As a second step, we have to decide the amounts of each security to sell each year in order to keep the capital structure ratios from getting too far out of line in any one year, and offer securities in amounts neither too small nor too large.

An example is shown in Exhibit 6-2. Let's assume that the bottom line of Exhibit 6-1 shown previously, indicated financing requirements to be as in Exhibit 6-2, Part I. In figuring the capital structure ratios, we will have to allow for the fact that earned surplus will increase because of retained earnings. In Exhibit 6-1, shown previously, in the item "Income After Dividends," we have allowed for the cash that the company will generate from retained earnings. We will assume that retained earnings will amount to $4 million annually, or $20 million at the end of five years. This will have to be added to the common equity in figuring the ratios.

Shown in Part II is financing which will keep the ratios the same in each year. One plan might be as shown in Part III. Some financing had to be done in the first year. If the stock was selling at a good price, the sale of stock would strengthen the financial picture. If bank loans are used during the first part of year 1 and then common is sold, there would be sufficient funds to take care of year 2 after paying the bank loan. The company could use senior securities in year 3 and still have good ratios. Another issue of common would be needed in year 5 to meet the goals.

After you have set up such a rough plan, you will have to refine your figures, because the additional charges, etc. on the proposed securities will need to be included in a revised budget. Also, in order to provide interim cash, pending long term financing, you may have to use temporary bank loans.

And the final financial plan obviously has to be tested in terms of earnings forecast so as to determine the effect or earnings per share and coverage of fixed charges.

Use of Short Term Borrowings

Traditionally, short term borrowings are used for seasonal purposes such as inventory build-up. They are all cleaned up once a year. Providing a company is in a healthy position, the amount of funds used for this purpose depends entirely on the nature of the business and the need. There is no basic inhibition as far as amount is concerned. This type of borrowing may consist of bank loans or commercial paper.

To take advantage of lower short term rates, there are certain types of companies which use a band of short term borrowings to supply part of their long-term capital needs and continuously renew them when they mature. This is using a short term maturity for a long-term capital need. This is typical of finance companies. The nature of the finance business is such that in a credit crunch, they can shrink their assets and meet the payment of their short term obligations. Other types of companies, however, should use this type of financing with caution. If kept within limits, such as 5% of total long term capital, it has generally not proven to be a problem. However, such short term borrowings do cut into a company's short-term borrowing reserve which may be needed in an emergency. The overuse of short-term bank loans for long-term capital needs may be embarrassing in a credit crunch. It may force a company into the long term market under adverse conditions. Those in Wall Street who have been the greatest salesmen of short term funds for long term capital literally panic when things get bad. They turn their backs on you like you had the plague.

Exhibit 6-2

STEPS IN ESTABLISHING A FINANCING PROGRAM

(000,000's omitted)

PART I

REQUIREMENTS FOR OUTSIDE FUNDS

Year	1	2	3	4	5	Total
Amount	$10.0	$5.0	$20.0	$5.0	$10.0	$50.0

PART II

FINANCING REQUIRED EACH YEAR TO KEEP RATIOS EACH YEAR THE SAME AS THE GOAL

Year	Beginning		1		2		3		4		5		Total
Sales of Sec.													
Debt			$ 3		$ 2		$ 4		$ 2		$ 3		$14
Preferred			1		1		3		1		1		7
Common			6		2		13		2		6		29
Total			$ 10		$ 5		$ 20		$ 5		$ 10		$50
Cap. Struc.													
Debt	$ 40		43		45		49		51		54		
%		20%		20%		20%		20%		20%		20%	
Preferred	20		21		22		25		26		27		
%		10		10		10		10		10		10	
Common	140		146		148		161		163		169		
Ret. earn.			4		8		12		16		20		
Total	140		150		156		173		179		189		
%		70		70		70		70		70		70	
Total	$200	100%	$214	100%	$223	100%	$247	100%	$256		$270	100%	

PART III

FINANCING PROGRAM

Year	Beginning												
Sales of Sec.													
Debt			--		--		14		--		--		$14
Preferred			--		--		7		--		--		7
Common			14		--		--		--		15		29
			$ 14		--		$ 21		--		$ 15		$50
Cap. Struc.													
Debt	$ 40		$ 40		$ 40		$ 54		$ 54		$ 54		
%		20%		18%		18%		22%		21%		20%	
Preferred	20		20		20		27		27		27		
%		10		9		9		11		11		10	
Common	140		154		154		154		154		169		
Ret. earn.			4		8		12		16		20		
%		70		73		73		67		68		70	
	$200	100%	$218	100%	$222	100%	$247	100%	$251	100%	$270	100%	

Lenders of long term debt do not like to see a company play this kind of a game, and they will probably put a provision in a loan indenture requiring that a company clear up short term borrowings for a period of time each year such as a month. Long term lenders do this to prevent a company from choking with short term debt which will mature ahead of their loan. Payment might drain the company of resources or the long term bondholders may have to come in and rescue the company by paying off the bank loans to protect their position.

Using short term borrowings for long term purposes to take advantage of the fact that short term rates are generally lower than long term rates is what is known as playing the yield curve. Playing the yield curve is very tempting for eager financial officers who haven't been in the business long enough to have gotten burned. Of course, what a company can and should do depends upon its financial strength. A company with AAA bonds can break all the rules regarding the use of short term credit, and no one would give it a second thought. However, the weaker a company gets the more jaundiced will be the eyes that will scrutinize it.

Term Loans

In between the short term and the long term debt is the medium term such as term bank loans. The supply of this type of borrowing depends on conditions in the money market. Sometimes it is there and sometimes it disappears. Whether a company should use it will be affected by the rate, but more important it will depend on how it fits in with a company's financing plan. It doesn't make sense to use a term loan which will mature at the same time as some long term bonds, or when there is a large demand for capital. It may just compound the problem of raising capital.

Bank Loans Prior to Long Term Financing

The term, bridge financing, refers to short or intermediary financing which is paid off with some form of long term securities. A construction loan for a real estate operation is a typical example of bridge financing. This is a proper use of short term credit, providing it isn't used to gamble on a change in the long term security markets, and providing the company is in sufficiently strong financial position so that it can meet the short term maturity. Utilities do massive long term financings on a regular basis. They build up their short term borrowings and then repay them with a security offering. This prevents a company from having to do long term financing at the start of a construction program and hold funds temporarily idle. For this type of company, the amount of short term funds should be kept within limits. Short term loans up to 10% of total long term capital are manageable. As they approach 20% of total long term capital, they may become unmanageable, especially if the market for long term securities becomes sticky.

Bank loans should add to financial flexibility and not detract from it, as may occur if you stretch their use too far. Under ordinary circumstances, you should not plan to use bank borrowings for expansion purposes up to the maximum, either of length of time or amount, before refunding them with long term financing. The savings from the use of short-term bank loans in order to postpone permanent financing may seem quite large in terms of dollars for a year or two. However, such savings must be weighed in relation to the possible higher cost over a long period of time on long term securities.

The advisability of using short term bank loans and postponing the sale of long term securities until a construction program is completed, depends on all the surrounding circumstances at the time of the contemplated financing, including market conditions and a company's situation.

If conditions improve, an increase in security prices will naturally result. On the other hand, if conditions are favorable at the start of the construction program and adverse developments occur subsequently, there may be a decrease in the prices at which securities can be sold. Also, a change may occur in the type of terms of the securities that can be arranged. Severe deterioration in the market could prevent the sale of certain types of securities.

The following example, based on figures in Exhibit 6-3, will illustrate how any savings that might be realized through short term loans could be lost, if there were a relatively small drop in the market for long term securities.

Assume that a company wishes to raise $8 million for expansion purposes, that the construction will be done over a one-year period and that at the end of the year permanent securities will be sold to retire the short term loan. With a short-term bank loan interest rate of 7%, a 50% tax rate and with $2 million borrowed each quarter, the after-tax interest cost would be $175,000 as shown in Column IV of Exhibit 6-3, Part I.

We will test the possible savings by use of temporary bank loans, as contrasted with three possible means of raising $8 million through the sale of long term securities at the start of the year:

1. Bonds with 30-year maturity and a 7% interest rate, sold at a net price of 100 to the company.
2. Preferred stock with 7% dividend rate, sold at a net price of $100 per share to the company.
3. Common stock with a $1.20 dividend rate, sold at a net price to the company of $20 or 400,000 shares.

These figures are shown in Exhibit 6-3, Part II. Shown in Column V are the after-tax costs with these securities.

In Exhibit 6-3, Part III, the after-tax cost of the bank loan and long term securities are shown along with the interest that would be received from temporarily investing the idle funds from long term financing. And in Column V is the net extra cost of using long term securities at the start of the construction program.

In Exhibit 6-3, Part IV, the net after-tax extra cost of long term financing is shown per $100 or per share in Column I. In Column II the prices at which the securities were originally sold are adjusted for the extra cost, and in Columns III and IV, these figures are interpreted in terms of differences in yield. All of the above savings would be used up if long-term security prices fell the following amounts during the year that the permanent financing was postponed:

1. Bonds would have to fall $0.06 in price (from 100 to 99.94), or a change in yield of only 0.01% from 7.00% to 7.01%.
2. Preferred stocks would have to fall $3.56 in price (from $100 to $96.44), or a change in yield of 0.25% from 7.00% to 7.25%.
3. The net price the company received from common stock would only have to fall from $20.00 to $19.50, less than 2 1/2%, increasing the yield from 6.00% to 6.15%.

In order to appreciate the significance of these figures, they should be compared with the size of the actual market fluctuations of security prices and yields over a period of six months to a year. This will show that market fluctuations are far greater than these savings. Of course, the savings through the use of bank loans will vary, depending on the relationship of the bank rate, the rate on long term securities and the rate at which idle funds can be invested.

No allowance is made in these figures for the fact that the bank loan would require the additional cost of compensating balances.

The above remarks could be interpreted as suggesting that bank loans should be used primarily to assist in picking the very best market for the sale of long term securities. Subsequent remarks will indicate that this would be a wrong interpretation. The approach indicated above is merely for the purpose of placing the cost factor in the proper perspective. The essential point is to avoid inflexibility and not over-use bank loans.

The Value of Compensating Balances

Our banking system is based on the principle that, under ordinary circumstances, deposits should bear some relationship to

Exhibit 6-3

EXAMPLE OF CASH SAVINGS FROM USE OF SHORT-TERM BANK LOANS PRIOR TO LONG TERM FINANCING

For $8,000,000 Project Requiring $2,000,000 Quarterly at the Beginning of Each Quarter for One Year

PART I
SHORT TERM BORROWINGS AND INTEREST COST TO PROVIDE FUNDS FOR CONSTRUCTION

Column	I	II	III	IV
			Interest Charges Each Quarter	
Quarter	Bank Loans Outstanding	Interest Rate	Before Taxes	After 50% Tax Rate
1st	$2,000,000	7% for 3 mos.	$ 35,000	$ 17,500
2nd	4,000,000	" " " "	70,000	35,000
3rd	6,000,000	" " " "	105,000	52,500
4th	8,000,000	" " " "	140,000	70,000
Total				$175,000

PART II
THREE ALTERNATIVE METHODS OF FINANCING SALE OF SECURITIES AT BEGINNING OF YEAR

Column	I	II	III	IV	V
				Interest and Dividend Cost	
Type of Security	Rate	Price	Amount of Financing at Beginning of Yr.	Before Taxes	After 50% Tax Rate
Bonds–30 yrs.	7%	$100	$8,000,000	$560,000	$280,000
Preferred	7%	100	"	560,000	560,000
Common (4,000,000 shrs.)	$1.20 Dividend	20	"		480,000

PART III
CASH SAVINGS FROM USE OF BANK LOAN

Column	I	II	III	IV
Type of Security	Bank Loan Cost After Taxes	Long-Term Security Cost	Income from Investment of Idle Funds from Long Term Financing at 3% After 50% Tax Rate	Net Extra Cost of Long Term Securities
Bonds	$175,000	$280,000	$100,000	$ 5,000
Preferred	"	560,000	"	285,000
Common	"	480,000	"	205,000

PART IV
SAVINGS BY USE OF BANK LOAN IN TERMS OF
YIELD DIFFERENCE FOR SECURITIES

Column	I	II	III	IV
Type of Security	Net Extra Cost of Long Term Securities per $100 or per Share	Price Adjusted for Savings	Yield at Price Adj. for Savings	Difference in Yield
Bond	$0.06	$99.94	7.01%	0.01%
Preferred	3.56	96.44	7.25	0.25
Common	0.50	19.50	6.15	0.15

loans, commitments or lines of credit. When banks are short of funds, they naturally have to allocate their funds to those customers which have maintained good deposits. The officers of some companies don't seem to understand and appreciate this idea. They would prefer to pay a higher interest rate and forget the necessity of keeping balances. Without trying to argue the point, it is a fact that our banking system works on the basis of compensating deposit balances, and in order for a company to be able to call on short term funds in an emergency, it must have a good deposit relationship.

A company would be quite remiss in its finance planning if it did not recognize this necessity. It should keep its banks in a frame of mind so that they will be most willing to make loans to the company in an emergency under tight money conditions. For this reason, it is unwise for a company to spread its banking business to so many banks that it is unable to keep satisfactory balances in any of them. It will naturally wish to favor local banks, and should do so. However, if local banks do not have adequate loan capacity to take care of a company's needs, that company should spread its cash balances to its larger bank or banks outside its territory so that it will be able to obtain sufficient credit.

During tight money conditions, some banks may be hesitant to lend their full legal limit to any one customer because of their desire to spread available funds around to satisfy all customers. Therefore, as a rough rule of thumb, a company might consider having sufficient banks so that if each loaned 60% of its legal limit, they would in total be able to provide the company's maximum requirements. This, of course, depends on the relationship which a company maintains with its banks.

Test Plan in Terms of Good, Average and Poor Earnings

We have already said you have to test the effect of your financing plan on earnings. Because of the difficulty of forecasting earnings, you should make some estimate as to what you consider good, average and poor earnings for your company and test the final financing program under each of these conditions. Include earnings coverage figures for senior securities, and the earnings per share for the common, as well as the dividend payout ratio.

A similar type of test should be made with the cash budget, including any sinking funds on proposed new securities and coverage of total debt service from cash flow. This will help you visualize whether your program will stand up under adversity and whether it has the necessary flexibility. If poor earnings indicate the likelihood that certain sinking fund conditions may not be met, the whole program should be reviewed as to the magnitude of the capital expenditures.

With adverse earnings, you may need to resort to debt financing and postpone the scheduled sale of common or preferred. You should see how the use of debt would affect the financial strength of your company and how you would again restore the borrowing reserve. For example, see what would happen if you were forced into debt financing for a period of three years.

Study Future Maturity and Sinking Funds

Any sinking fund or maturity within the period of the budget will show up in the budget itself; however, sinking fund payments and maturities after five years will have to be reviewed in addition. They may have a bearing on how the program is arranged within the five years. You should observe the burden that these may entail. Sinking funds on existing debt may affect the design of sinking funds on new securities.

In setting the maturity of new debt issues, it is advisable to space maturities so that excessively large amounts do not fall due in a short period of time. If you have a large maturity after five years and your company is in a weak financial position, you may find it necessary to include as part of your five-year plan some program for reduction of that debt ahead of maturity.

Evaluation of these problems, subsequent to the budget period, will have to be on the basis of judgment. You should ask yourself how later maturities and terms of senior obligations, etc., would be handled if they were present today, under trying conditions. Would they be likely to present difficulties? Your financing program should be planned to anticipate such eventualities.

Common Financing

The ratio of common equity to total capital structure should be kept adequate and improved gradually if out of line. But in planning common stock financing, care should be taken, as far as possible, not to depress the market price. A 1 for 10 is considered an average-size offering. While offerings should not be too large relative to the outstanding shares, nevertheless too many small offerings strung out over a period of time increase financing costs and may also have a continuing depressing effect on the market.

The size and spacing of common stock offerings is a matter of judging the correct balance between the condition of the common stock market and the company's earnings outlook. A favorable market may suggest a step up in the size of the offering. The same applies when the earnings outlook is good, because the dilution in earnings per share will be lessened by the improvement. In fact, if your financing program will permit, you may be able to time your common offering when earnings per share are expected to bulge, in order to offset the dilution. Your aim should be to have a gradual, steady increase in your earnings per share.

As was pointed out in Chapter 3 on Dividend Policy, common stock financing will have an effect on dividend payout ratio, and on earned surplus per share.

Timing of Financing

When the time arrives to sell a security, the general market condition for securities will have to be taken into account. The condition of the market may affect the type of security your company will offer, it may require special terms in a security in order to attract buyers and it will govern the price. More specifically you will have to decide whether you should sell the security now or wait until later on. This will be dependent to some extent upon the urgency with which your company needs cash, but it may also be affected by the condition of the securities markets. Answer this question at an early date, because you don't want to go to the bother and expense of setting the machinery of finance in motion if the answer is to wait. If you do go ahead and the market changes, you will have to review the situation again just before the offering date.

There are certain rules which are worth keeping in mind in your efforts to make this decision. Obviously, you should avoid selling a security in a distressed securities market, but when capital is needed and the securities market is reasonably favorable, it is unwise to try to be too smart and outguess the market. By outguessing the market is meant trying to select a specific time, during a 12-month period, for example, when the market will be most receptive. The best of economists cannot forecast interest rates and the stock market with any degree of certainty. Underwriters learn their limitations in forecasting by the losses they incur if they fail to accept their limitations. And company officials should not plan their new money financing on the assumption that they can do more than try to avoid adverse markets. So the best rule might be: when you need capital, get it, if the securities markets are receptive.

Refunding of outstanding issues may require more emphasis on trying to guess the outlook for the market. This will be pointed out when the subject is discussed in Chapter 8.

If you have both common stock and bonds to sell within a relatively short period, it is generally best to sell the common first. This adds to the equity ratio and improves the debt picture. Furthermore, it saves the easiest security to sell to the last, in case an adverse stock market is encountered. Prevailing market conditions for the two types of securities will, of course, affect this decision.

When you decide to go ahead with your financing, you will have to pick the day for the sale in order to establish a time schedule. If you are a regulated company and offer securities competitively, you will be interested in the best day of the week for the bidding day. The choice is largely the result of the preference of the underwriters. They are not unanimous, but some prefer Tuesday and Wednesday. The underwriters can take a last-minute look at the market on Monday to see if anything happening over the weekend had any effect on the market. They can have their preliminary pricing meeting the day before the bidding without having a weekend intervene. Actually, Monday does not have serious drawbacks, but Tuesdays or Wednesdays are preferred. Friday is considered a bad day because underwriters do not like to take the risk of carrying the issue over the weekend. Thursday is not bad, but has some disadvantage because it is close to the weekend. Watch out for local holidays in areas where a large potential demand for your securities may exist.

A calendar of forthcoming issues should be consulted in order to avoid congestion and conflicts. Congestion will ensue whenever an excessive number of a similar type of issue is offered during a short period of time, such as a month or quarter. If there is a flood of issues, the buyers may use up funds immediately available for investment; the underwriters may accumulate a large inventory of unsold issues—which will detract from their eagerness to take on more. During periods of adverse change, buyers will be reluctant to purchase at a price which may prove too high tomorrow or next week.

Conflicts will occur whenever more than one similar type of issue is being offered on the same day at the same time. The problem of conflicts occurs mostly in competitive bidding. If there are conflicts, the buyers are in a more advantageous position since they can pick and choose between issues being simultaneously offered. Furthermore, the underwriters may be less anxious to stick their necks out if they have the opportunity to handle more than one issue at a time. In calculating their risk, underwriters bidding on more than one issue have to assume that they will get all of them.

If it is impossible to pick a day on which no other similar issue is to be offered, at least an hour should be chosen when there is no other issue. A bidding for senior securities should not be before 10:30, because underwriters must have time for their final price meeting before the bidding. It should be before 2:00 p.m. so that the price, etc., can be filed with the Securities and Exchange Commission to permit selling to start as soon as possible. You will be able to find someone in a large financial institution who keeps informed of forthcoming issues and will be glad to advise you.

Pricing of common stock usually takes place after the close of the market so that the price on the last sale may be used as a guide.

If senior securities are being sold which will be purchased by institutional investors, the summer vacations represent no real disadvantage. Institutional investors cannot let money lie idle merely because someone is on vacation. A few special types of institutional buyers may have larger accumulations of cash at certain times during the year, and at other times may be out of the market. If an issue must rely on such special buyers as the primary market, the sale may be timed when they are most flush. This is a rather unusual situation. For common stocks which are sold to many small investors, there might be reason to avoid the vacation period.

Team Play with the Experts

The Financial Vice President should call the shots and run the show in financing—not an outside lawyer, underwriting firm or advisor. However, he cannot be expected to know all the answers and he should not hesitate to rely on experts. There are four principal experts in the sale of a security—the lawyer, the underwriting firm if one is used, the tax expert and the accountant. The Financial Vice President may be knowledgeable in one or two of these fields, but it would be unlikely that he would be qualified to give the final word in all of them. He should run the operation on a team basis in order to assure best results.

There are two lawyers, the company's own house lawyer and outside counsel.

Security work is a very specialized field. The pattern changes and new and valuable legal provisions on securities, etc., are constantly being developed. The lawyers located in the large financial centers may not be any smarter than lawyers in small communities, but the fact is that because they are constantly working on financing, they keep up on and hear about new ideas in their field. These may be worth much to a company. When you choose outside counsel, you will do well to weigh the importance of having a top financial lawyer on your team. Bond indentures are seldom a matter of routine. It should be your hope to get a lawyer who can make financial law really live and who is on his toes for new ideas which will make your financing easy to live with.

In establishing a financial program, it may be important to have the lawyers consider its effect on the legality of the securities for some types of institutional purchasers. As an example of legal provisions, there are briefly summarized in Exhibit 6-4 some of the provisions for securities to be legal for investment for savings banks in New York.

It may not be possible to vary an entire program to fit into the pattern of the requirements of such purchasers, but in certain instances, a small change may be made so as to conform to the legal provisions. If a company's securities have previously been legal for certain purchasers, it is even more important to have this in mind, so that they will not be disturbed by a change in the legality.

In Chapter 4, it was pointed out that the accounting and tax effect of financing must be studied carefully. Some of the tests to determine the legality of investments for some institutions are defined in terms of certain accounts. Bookkeeping changes have resulted in the legal status of securities of a company being lost, when the effect of accounting changes has been disregarded.

The Financial Vice President and his counsel should prepare a schedule in detail of each step to be taken, with assignment of responsibilities for each participant. Above all, get the team working together at the start of the financing. This will keep down expenses and prevent steps being taken which the experts

Exhibit 6-4

EXAMPLES OF REQUIREMENTS FOR SECURITIES TO BE LEGAL FOR INVESTMENT BY SAVINGS BANKS IN NEW YORK

New York State Banking Law (Section 235)
(All Corporations Must Be Incorporated in the U.S.)

Mortgage Bonds—Electric and Gas Companies (Subdivision 13)

1. Either capital stock (including preferred and common), premium and surplus, must be at least 2/3 of debt secured by a mortgage; or capital stock, premium and surplus, plus unsecured debt (not maturing within 5 years and not in excess of 50% of such capital stock) shall be equal to 3/4 of the debt secured by a mortgage.
2. Mortgage indebtedness should not exceed 2/3 of net plant.
3. Reported net earnings before income taxes should have averaged in the past fiscal 5 years, 2 times the average annual interest charges on funded debt applicable to period.
4. Net earnings before income taxes in either of the past 2 years should at least equal 2 times pro-forma annual interest charges on funded debt outstanding at time of investment.

Preferred Stocks—All Industries (Subdivision 26,a.)

1. Net earnings after income taxes should average over the past 5 years at least 1 1/2 times annual pro-forma fixed charges, rents and preferred dividend requirements as of the date of investment.
2. Net earnings after income taxes in either of the past 2 years should at least be 1 1/2 times annual interest charges, rents and preferred dividends for that year.

Common Stocks—All Industries (Subdivision 26,c.)

1. They must be registered on a national or regional exchange.
2. They must have paid cash dividends on the common stock consecutively for the past 10 years.
3. They must have earned in the aggregate dividends paid over the last 10 years.
4. Preferred stock, if any, must be a legal investment for savings banks.

cannot later rectify, or which can be changed only at substantial cost to the company.

Example of a Financing Plan

Of course, it is always easy to use hindsight. However, for illustrative purposes, we will finish this chapter by looking at the mess an actual company got into and suggest how it might have been avoided. It used far too much debt and convertibles when it had the opportunity to sell common stock.

This is a typical manufacturing company. What actually happened is shown in Exhibit 6-5, Part I. Also included is an estimate of the average and maximum debt ratios that the company should have had to maintain an A rating.

As a consequence of using too much debt in the form of straight debt and convertibles, its senior debt was rated BBB and its convertibles BB. When bad earnings were encountered, the company had to cut its dividend. The company's stock turned out to be a highly volatile stock.

It is impossible to reconstruct the picture exactly to suggest what should have been done, because we don't know what the market price of the common would have been with different financing and with different earnings for the common stock caused by the financing. However, in Exhibit 6-5, Part II, an attempt is made to show what might have been the picture with a sound financial policy. Common stock financing at the average market price is substituted for the debenture financing in year 6 which would require a total common offering of about 1 for 10. In year 7, common financing is substituted for convertible financing which would have required an issue of about 1 for 10.

Undoubtedly, with the added common and revised earnings, the stock would not have sold so high, and therefore some more stock would have to have been sold in order to obtain the same amount of proceeds.

The earnings and dividends per share as occurred and giving effect to suggested financing are as follows:

	From Exhibit 6-5, Part I as Occurred		From Exhibit 6-5, Part II After Revised Financing	
	Earnings per Share	Dividends per Share	Earnings per Share	Dividends per Share
10 (most recent year)	$ .77	$ --	$ .76	$ .60
9	.71	.60	.73	.60
8	2.37	.60	2.16	.60
7	2.13	.60	1.89	.60
6	2.90	.40	2.96	.40
5	2.56	.30	2.56	.30
4	1.96	--	1.96	--
3	1.47	--	1.47	--
2	1.39	--	1.39	--
1	1.47	--	1.47	--

As can be seen, the earnings would not have been seriously lower with the greater amount of common stock and the company could have maintained its common dividend. In other words, the company would have had a better dividend record, the company's securities would have been of much better quality and the company would have been in a strong financial position. The market price of the common might not have risen so high but it certainly would not have fallen so low.

Exhibit 6-5

PART 1

INDUSTRIAL COMPANY – ACTUAL FINANCING

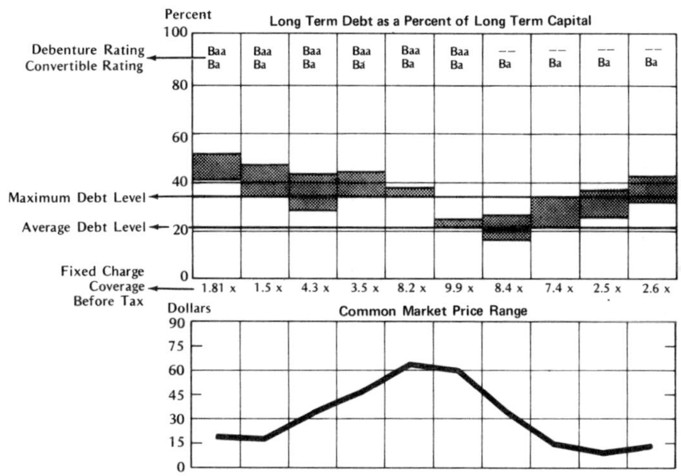

Financing and Common per Share Data

Financing: 000,000 Omitted										
Debentures		35		20	20					
Conv. Debentures			15	41						
Common					24					
Earnings per Share $	0.77	0.71	2.37	2.13	2.90	2.56	1.96	1.47	1.39	1.47
Dividends per Share $	–	0.60	0.60	0.60	0.40	0.30	–	–	–	–
Payout %	–	85	25	28	14	12	–	–	–	–
Average Hi-Low Market Price $	18	17	34	46	63	60	35	14	10	14
P/E Ratio X	23	24	14	22	22	23	18	10	7	10
Yield %		3.5	1.8	1.3	0.6	0.5	–	–	–	–
Book Value $	25	25	26	24	22	26	25	25	24	23
Market Value/ Book Value %	72	67	131	192	286	231	140	56	42	61
Return on Common %	3	3	9	9	13	10	8	6	6	6
Year	10	9	8	7	6	5	4	3	2	1
(Most Recent Yr.)										

Exhibit 6-5 (Cont'd.)

PART II

INDUSTRIAL COMPANY – WITH FINANCING REVISED

Long Term Debt as a Percent of Long Term Capital

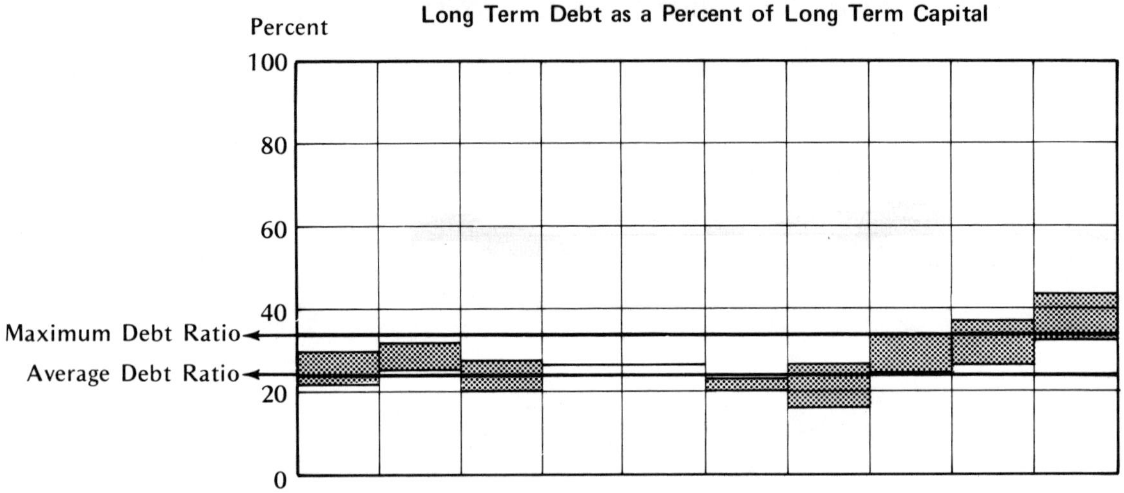

Financing and Common per Share Data

Financing 000,000 Omitted										
Debentures		35		20						
Conv. Debentures			15							
Common				41	44					
Earnings per Share $	.76	.73	2.16	1.89	2.96	2.56	1.96	1.47	1.39	1.47
Dividends per Share $	.60	.60	.60	.60	.40	.30	–	–	–	–
Payout %	79	82	28	32	14	12	–	–	–	–
Average Hi-Low Market Price $										
P/E Ratio X										
Yield %										
Book Value $										
Market Value/ Book Value %										
Return on Common %	3	3	7	7	13	14	12	10	9	11
Year (Most Recent Yr.)	10	9	8	7	6	5	4	3	2	1

CHAPTER 7

Sources of Capital – Long and Short

Sources of capital is a big subject. We will not attempt to cover the entire subject, but will just give you a bird's-eye view.

Need for Outside Funds

The extent to which companies may need to seek outside funds and the type of funds needed depends on the make-up of their long term capital, their capital intensity and their growth rate.

Retained earnings will take care of building up a company's equity position so it will not need to sell any new common stock, if it grows at a rate which corresponds to the growth rate of retained earnings. For example, a company can grow at a 6% rate, if it earns 12% on its book value and pays out 50% of its earnings in dividends so that common equity will grow at a 6% rate. Then it would only need to go outside for 6% new senior securities each year.

Exhibit 7-1 shows the extent to which corporations have been able to rely on internal and external funds. The contrast between all corporations and utilities which are very capital intensive is striking. The reliance on outside funds by utilities was double that for all corporations, and utilities had to rely seven times as heavily on equity financing as all corporations.

Meeting the Desires of the Suppliers

The desires of owners of capital vary all the way from wanting complete security with small income to being willing to take high risks with the potential of a substantial gain. Some suppliers have complete freedom of choice; whereas, institutional investors, such as insurance companies, are regulated as to the type of investment they can make. The desires of the suppliers of funds may differ in many respects:

1. Extent of risk.
2. Type and size of company.
3. Type of security and protective provisions—bond, convertible, common, etc.
4. Current income or market appreciation.
5. Maturity.

Exhibit 7-1

SOURCE OF FUNDS

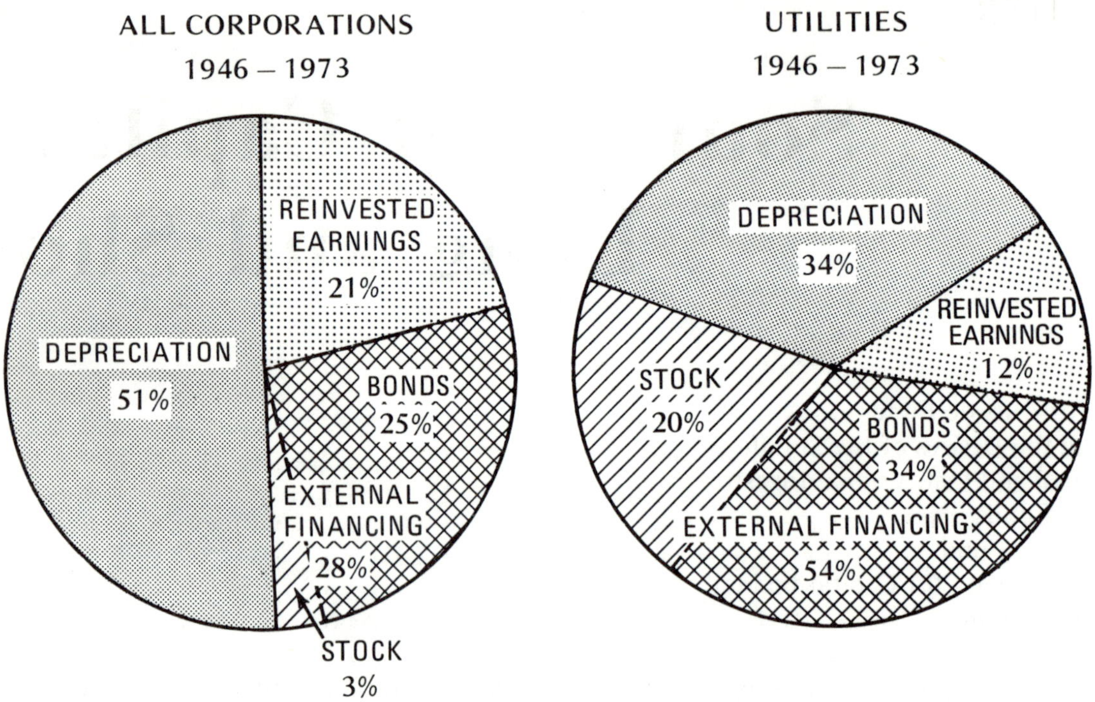

6. Marketability.
7. Tax situation.
8. Legal requirements.

Where investors choose to place their money may vary with business and security conditions and available alternative investments.

The financial officer of most companies cannot expect to be an expert on sources of capital. But since the supply of funds is such an important part of finance, he should have a general knowledge of the subject.

A clue as to the type of investors who are interested in your company can be obtained by analyzing your existing security holders. For your common and preferred stock, you can consult your stockholder list. Some of your stock may be held in nominee names by banks. You cannot find out who are the real owners, but by talking with the banks you may get an idea of the type of investors they represent. If your bonds are registered, you can readily find out who owns them. If they are not registered, you may be able to obtain some information from compilations of holdings of certain institutional investors. Some sources of information on security holdings are shown in Exhibit 7-2.

Individual and Institutional Investors

Investors can be broken down into two broad groups: individuals and institutions. Of course, all investments are owned either directly or indirectly by individuals because individuals own the institutions. But the broad classification of suppliers of funds between individuals and institutions is significant because the character of the investment policies are so different.

In analyzing the source of funds, we are interested in two things, the total source of funds and the source of funds for types of securities: senior securities and common stock.

Exhibit 7-2

SOURCES OF INFORMATION ON SECURITY HOLDINGS OF INSTITUTIONS

A.M. Best Company, Oldwick, New Jersey 08858. *Best's Market Guide,* Volume I, *Insurance Company Holdings of Common and Preferred Stocks.* Issued annually, $195. Volume II, *Insurance Company Holdings of Corporate Bonds.* Issued annually, $265.

Henry Ansbacher Long prepares quarterly reports on changes in investments of investment companies in *Barron's National Financial Weekly,* Barron's Publications, 22 Cortland Street, New York City 10007.

A book published each year by Wiesenberger Services, Inc., 1 New York Plaza, New York City 10004. Provides portfolios of principal investment companies. Price $65.

Vickers Associates, Inc., 226 New York Avenue, Huntington, N.Y. 11743 issues various guides to portfolio holdings:

Investment Company Portfolios gives the holdings of all the investment companies in the United States, Canada and offshore. Issued quarterly and common stocks are updated monthly. Vickers' Favorite 50, issued quarterly, is a part of this service, which ranks by dollar value the 50 stocks most popular with investment companies. Annual subscription to the Guide is $375 plus postage.

A special service for corporations shows the holdings and monthly changes by investment companies of a corporation's stock. Fee for this depends upon the number of investment companies holding the stock, but the minimum charge is $100 per year.

Guide to holdings of investment companies by management groups issued quarterly. Price $22.
Guide to Insurance Company Portfolios of Common Stocks covers 1,000 U.S. and Canadian companies. Price $210 per year. There is a similar service for corporate bonds. Price $245 per year.
Guide to College and Endowment Portfolios of Common Stocks. Price $150 per year.

Senior securities are largely owned by institutions.

Exhibit 7-3 shows how the holdings of stocks by institutions have been increasing and were 36% in 1973.

A breakdown of the holdings of common stocks in 1973 is shown in Exhibit 7-4.

The individual investors are those who chart their own course or rely partially or completely on assistance from a broker, a dealer, a written advisory service or an investment counsel firm. They may invest directly in a private company or purchase publicly traded securities.

As a result of a survey of individual shareholders, the New York Stock Exchange came up with the following information:

One out of four adults, or 30,850,000 individuals in America are share owners (50% women) in 10,000 publicly owned corporations. These companies have 36 billion shares outstanding, more than half of which are listed on the New York Stock Exchange.[1] The average share owner has a median household income of $13,500. Adult share owners are almost equally divided among those who attended college and those who did not. A study made a number of years ago[2] by the New York Stock Exchange showed that most stockholders acquired stock through brokers and dealers. A breakdown of the figures can be seen at the top of the following page.

A study[3] completed in 1974, showed that in 1971, 1% of U.S. families with the largest income owned 51% of stock owned by all

[1]New York Stock Exchange, 1974 Fact Book. Published by New York Stock Exchange.

[2]Share Ownership in America: 1959. Published by the New York Stock Exchange.

[3]Survey of Current Business, November 1974. Volume 54, Number 11. Stock Ownership in the United States: Characteristics and Trends.

	Number of Shareholders	Percentage of Total
Bought Through Broker and Dealer	6,080,000	49%
Through Company Worked for	2,592,000	21
Bought Through Bank	1,585,000	13
Gift or Inheritance	1,560,000	13
Other	381,000	3
Don't Remember	86,000	1
Sub-Total	12,284,000	100%
Not Classified by How First Acquired Stock	206,000	
	12,490,000	

Exhibit 7-3

INSTITUTIONAL HOLDINGS AS PERCENT OF ALL STOCKS (1)

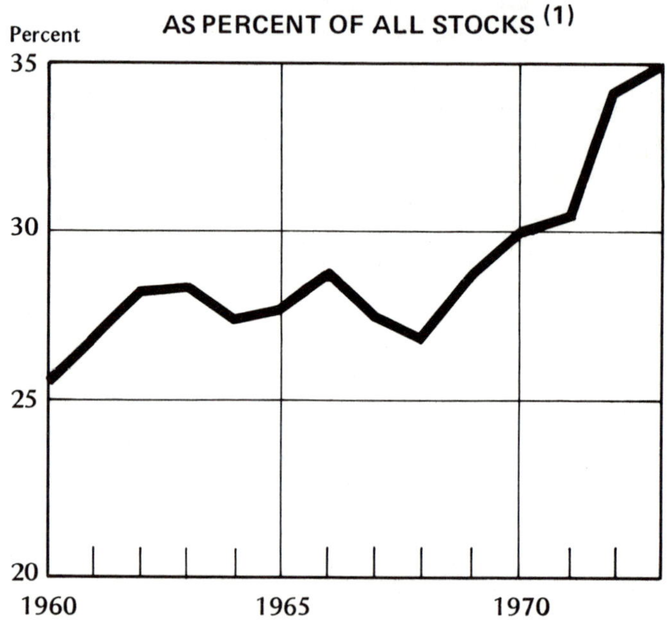

(1) Securities and Exchange Commission Statistical Bulletin, Volume 33, Number 26, August 1974.

families; and 10% of U.S. families with the largest income owned 74% of stock owned by all families. Of $780 billion of stock owned by individuals in 1971, 59% was in listed stocks.

Flow of Funds

Economists are continuously making estimates of the demand and supply of funds in order to determine the availability of funds for capital needs, and the effect on interest rates. The flow will vary with business conditions and conditions in the securities markets. In Exhibit 7-5 is shown a typical computation for a particular year.

While certain types of investors are restricted as to how they can invest their money, there is some fluidity of capital so

Exhibit 7-4

HOLDERS OF EQUITY

1973

Includes Common and Preferred Stocks, but Preferred Stocks Are a Small Part
Billions of Dollars

		Amount			*Percent*	
Personal Trust Funds		$ 95.5			28%	
Private Non-Insured Pension Funds		89.0			26	
Investment Companies						
Open-end	43.3			12		
Other	6.6			2		
Total		49.9			14	
Foundations		24.5			7	
Life Insurance Companies		25.9			8	
Property and Liability Insurance Companies		19.6			6	
State and Local Retirement Funds		17.8			5	
Educational Endowments		8.8			3	
Common Trust Funds		6.3			2	
Mutual Savings Banks		4.0			1	
Sub-Total			341.3			100%
Less: Institutional Holdings of Investment Shares			6.7			
Total Institutional Investors			334.6			36%
Foreign Investors			35.5			4
Domestic Individuals			550.6			60
Total Stock Outstanding			920.7			100%

Source: SEC Statistical Bulletin, August 1974, Volume 33, No. 26.

that funds available for investment will flow to the most attractive media. For this reason, in evaluating who might buy securities and what they might pay, you should have in mind the other broad types of investment that might be available. Your securities compete with other companies in your industry for investors' attention, but also directly and indirectly with other industries and other types of investments.

These figures on the supply side are on a net basis. That is, they are equal to the net increase in holdings by the various investors of the types of assets indicated under uses of funds. The gross flow of funds, which would include funds made available for reinvestment through the repayment of existing loans (amortization payments on mortgages are a prime example) would be equal to about twice the figures shown in the table. Savings and loan associations are a major factor in the supply situation, but not for corporate securities because they invest primarily in mortgages. Investment companies are included in the general category "Individuals and others."

On the demand side, the items do not provide for sinking fund and repayment.

Note the importance of mortgages. Life insurance companies and other types of investors which can buy mortgages may find them a

Exhibit 7-5

SOURCES AND USES OF FUNDS IN THE UNITED STATES
MONEY AND CAPITAL MARKETS*

(In billion of dollars)

Sources of funds	*1970*	*1971*	*1972*	*1973e*	*1974e*
Life insurance companies	$ 9.1	$ 11.7	$ 12.8	$ 14.7	$ 15.7
Non-insured pension funds	7.1	7.2	6.6	7.0	7.3
State and local funds	5.1	4.5	9.2	11.0	9.7
Savings and loan associations	11.6	29.4	36.5	30.0	32.0
Mutual savings banks	4.0	10.0	10.3	5.4	8.0
Commercial banks	31.8	49.8	72.4	69.3	74.0
Federal Reserve Banks	5.0	8.9	0.3	7.8	7.0
U.S. investment accounts	7.7	8.7	10.7	11.7	13.8
Federal loan agencies	8.0	5.2	5.4	11.7	10.0
Mutual funds	1.7	0.4	-1.8	-1.4	-0.5
Fire and casualty companies	4.8	6.5	5.8	6.2	7.3
Non-financial corporations	-0.1	10.2	13.6	18.0	10.2
Foreigners	11.0	27.1	10.5	6.0	†
Individuals and others	5.5	-11.5	16.5	23.2	1.8
Total sources	$112.3	$168.2	$208.7	$220.6	$196.2
Use of funds					
Corporate bonds	$ 22.8	$ 23.7	$ 19.1	$ 13.3	$ 19.0
Corporate stocks	6.8	13.5	13.0	8.2	9.0
State and local gov't. issues	11.4	17.0	12.3	8.8	11.0
Federal government issues	20.9	35.0	25.2	17.4	24.0
Federal agency issues	8.4	4.5	9.8	22.7	15.5
Mortgages: Residential	19.2	36.8	51.2	50.8	44.5
Non-residential	7.2	12.1	17.7	22.5	22.0
Business credit	6.7	8.4	28.5	51.6	37.5
Consumer credit	6.0	11.2	19.2	22.0	11.5
All other	3.0	6.0	12.6	3.3	2.2
Total uses	$112.3	$168.2	$208.7	$220.6	$196.2

*1973 Economic and Investment Report. A Report to the Membership of the American Life Insurance Association by Kenneth M. Wright, Vice-President and Chief Economist, American Life Insurance Association, Washington, D.C., Dec., 1973.

†$50 million or less. e–estimated.

The uses of funds measure the net changes in outstanding loans and securities; the sources of funds measure the net changes in ownership. Because of rounding, components may not add to totals shown.

more attractive media than corporates, particularly when interest rates are low as during a recession.

Forecasts of supply and demand figures are used as one clue to the future level of interest rates. However, it is necessary to be careful in interpreting the figures. It is the slight difference between supply and demand which can have an important effect on interest rates, and it is difficult to make accurate forecasts of supply and demand. Such figures can only be correctly interpreted for forecasting purposes if there is a thorough understanding of each item included, and a realization that interest rates are affected by other forces as well. These include Federal Reserve policy, the U.S. Government's financial needs, short-term credit demand and, last but not least, the psychological reactions of those who deal in the financial markets.

Short Term Funds

The availability of funds for different maturities ranges from funds available on demand to long term, and there is intermediate money in between.

The banks, of course, are the principal suppliers of short term funds. Total loans by the banking system amounted to $433 billion in 1973.[4]

Banks, of course, are not the only suppliers of short term funds. There are the finance companies, and even industrial companies, who may put money in the short term market if they have excess funds. Funds from abroad available for short maturities are becoming increasingly important.

The availability of funds from banks for intermediate maturities such as five or ten years depends on the general demand for funds. When banks are tight they tend to restrict loans to short term. When they get overloaded with cash, they reach out for the intermediary maturities. And the reverse situation may apply with regard to the institutions which ordinarily want long maturities. When they have excess funds available, they may reach back for shorter maturities.

Can the Demand for Capital Be Met?

At times, when there is a heavy demand for funds, a crunch may develop and then business becomes fearful that funds will not be available to carry on the capital growth of our country. When such a crunch occurs, it may be partly due to the Federal Reserve System putting on the brakes to prevent a runaway boom and inflation.

When businessmen look into the future, and see a great demand for capital, they worry whether there will be enough available capital. They seem to forget what history has shown. In the past, the savings of our nation have remarkably well-matched the demand for funds. They also forget that the amount of capital our nation can use depends on the available labor force and the time period to complete capital consuming projects. This country has financed world wars and regional wars, it has provided great giveaways to foreign nations and it still grew internally at a substantial pace.

Our banking system with the Federal Reserve has a flexible monetary system, and while we will have had crunches, the evidence from the past suggests that capital will be available to meet the demand in the long run for well-managed companies, providing our security markets do not become chaotic so that capital goes into hiding as it did in 1974.

Furthermore, our rate of savings is considerably lower than some other countries. For example,[5] in the period 1969-1971, savings in the U.S. represented 7.4% of gross national product; whereas, in West Germany it was 16.7% and in Japan 26.3%. So if there is a need and the incentive is right, there is an opportunity to increase the supply of capital with greater savings.

Venture Capital

This book is for the established corporate. But there is a step that has to be taken before a company becomes established—someone has to get the embryo going. We will say a few words about companies which are just getting under way. The capital they require is known

[4] Federal Deposit Insurance Corporation Annual Report, 1973. Figures are for all U.S. Commercial banks in the United States at June 30, 1973.

[5] 1972 Year Book of National Account Statistics, United Nations.

as venture capital. Webster's dictionary defines venture capital very well:

> "Funds invested or available for investment at considerable risk of loss in potentially highly profitable enterprises."

The risk is great and the investor is not going to take a gamble unless there is a possibility of making a large profit.

There are various types of enterprises which seek venture capital. They range all the way from a plan to an established operation which is in dire need of risk capital. If they are well established and in a very glamorous field, they may have access to the public market for capital. But this source of capital for this type of company has all the disadvantages of going public covered in another section of this book. Therefore, unless a company can become a viable publicly owned company it will be better off raising capital privately.

The sources of private capital for this type of operation include:

- Wealthy individuals or groups of individuals who have formed private venture capital companies.
- Limited number of venture capital firms publicly owned. SBIC's licensed by the U.S. Government which are independent or owned by another company.
- Venture capital companies owned by banks, insurance companies, industrial companies, investment bankers, etc.

There are three basic guides to sources of venture capital as shown in Exhibit 7-6.

The interest and skills of the various sources of venture capital vary widely. Some are able to understand technically oriented companies, others are able to handle companies which need a fusion of new management in certain areas. So it is necessary to match the type of venture with the right type of investor.

It takes considerable time finding someone who may be interested in taking a chance. And before a search is made, it is essential that a brochure be prepared describing the product, the amount of money needed, how it is going to be used, the future plans and profit potential.

The person seeking the venture capital has got to be prepared to give up a large part of his own potential gain to the capital provider. The record of venture capital companies has not been outstanding, and the people in the business know that they have got to have the potential to make a killing. It seems unreasonable that anyone would expect to multiply his investment from five to ten times in a few years, but this is what the venture capitalist may be thinking of. How much potential gain he will want will depend on the risk of the venture.

The type of security which the venture capitalist will require will vary considerably. Naturally, the capital provider will think in terms of a debt to protect his investment, and also a part of the equity or warrants in order to provide potential appreciation.

One of the things that will have to be presented in the brochure describing the company will be a forecast of financial statements for five years. After the capital provider feels that the estimates make sense based on a thorough study of the venture, he will make an estimate as to what the company might be worth at the end of five years. Then he can work backwards and determine what part of the ownership he will need in order to make the amount of profit necessary to interest him. Also he will have an important interest in how he might get rewarded at the end of a certain number of years. Can the company be set up so that it can be sold publicly or sold to another company at the estimated price.

To build a successful operation from nothing or very little takes a lot of guts, hard work, skill, judgment, optimism and a willingness not to be discouraged by even your friends. For an outsider to make an investment in such a project takes a sharp, cool, calculating brain willing to do a very careful job of analysis—and then have a lot of luck

Exhibit 7-6

SOURCES OF INFORMATION ABOUT SUPPLIERS OF VENTURE CAPITAL

Venture Capital ($29.95)—Published by Technimetrics, Inc., 919 Third Avenue, New York, N.Y. 10022. This book provides the investment criteria of over 400 venture capitalists. In addition, venture capitalists are broken down by the industries in which they have an investment preference.

Guide to Venture Capital Sources ($32.50)—Published by Capital Publishing Corporation, 310 South LaSalle Street, Chicago, Illinois 60603. This book provides the investment criteria of over 600 venture capitalists. It also contains a comprehensive bibliography of publications on venture capital.

Membership Directory/NASBIC (Free)—Published by the National Association of Small Business Investment Companies, 512 Washington Building, Washington, D.C. 20005. This directory provides the investment criteria of about 250 SBIC's.

thrown in. Most venture capital projects fall by the wayside, but those which succeed are the ones which build America and get the carrot.

CHAPTER 8

Selling Senior Securities

At this point, we will assume that it has been decided that our company needs to raise capital by the sale of some form of senior securities—bonds, debentures, notes or preferred stock. We will also assume that the tentative terms for the new securities have already been outlined.

This chapter tells how to handle the three major questions with which you will be concerned:

The Method of Sale
The Offering Price
The Amount of the Financing Costs

We will start off with a statement about the goal that is to be achieved. Next, we will cover what is meant by the price of a senior security and the two main items that make up financing costs. As further preliminary information, we will define briefly the methods that may be used in selling senior securities and show the extent of their use by corporations.

With the above as background, we will get into a more comprehensive look at the methods of financing. We will give you two complete examples of offering securities. They will take you behind the scenes so that you will know what the parties actually do, step by step.

You will need to know how to establish the price of a new security offering in order to be able to negotiate with underwriters or ultimate purchasers.

Any financing involves a knowledge of financing costs and the magnitude of the factors which may affect them.

The chapter concludes with two subjects which are closely related to senior security financing: refunding and exchange offers.

Since convertibles, either bonds or preferred, contain some elements of common stock, selling them is covered in the next chapter on selling common stock.

There have been some senior securities sold to existing security holders. This practice is so limited that it is not given special attention. However, the material in this and the next chapter will help you handle such a situation.

The Goal in Selling Senior Securities

What are we going to try to accomplish? The ultimate aim in selling a senior security is to obtain the most satisfactory price and terms at the least selling cost commensurate with the sales job to be done. The selling costs refer to all costs involved in the financing. In other words, the goal is to hire money at the least selling cost and at the best price and terms.

By satisfactory price is generally meant the highest price. When a company offers stock or a convertible issue to its own common stockholders, the meaning of the most satisfactory price will include making the offer attractive so that the owners will be happy. Even when common stock is sold directly to the public, rather than to its own stockholders, there is a school of thought that it should be priced so that the buyers will get a good buy. The advocates of this school contend that satisfied security buyers make it easier to sell future issues. They say that buyers who get burned aren't so eager the next time the company comes to the market. However, this problem pertains primarily to common stocks, and we will discuss its validity in the next chapter. Senior securities, such as bonds, are sold mostly to the sophisticated or informed buyers who know their way around and buy only if the price is right. Therefore, our original statement about our goal does mean obtaining the highest price for senior securities.

To illustrate, suppose a bond is offered for 100 and then shortly after the sale, it is traded in the market at 98, even though there has been no change in security markets. Naturally a buyer wouldn't be happy even if he bought it with his eyes open. However, suppose the price went up to 102, then the shoe is on the other foot. The company might have reason to complain that the offering price was too low and it "got took." Certainly, if good grade senior securities are sold to sophisticated buyers in normal market conditions, it doesn't look well for a company when the price jumps to more than a small premium of less than 1 point after the sale is completed.

The price of a security may be affected by the terms. Under certain circumstances, it may be worthwhile to accept a lower price or a higher yield in order to avoid too restrictive terms. A company, by concentrating on the price alone, may feel that it is doing a great job of saving 1/8 of 1% in the rate on a senior security; whereas, in reality it may accept terms which will prove to be far more costly, in one way or another, at some time in the future. The terms are usually difficult to analyze, and some take effect so far in the future that they get brushed aside. As was stressed in the chapter on "Types of Securities," the terms should be looked upon as part of the price and evaluated as to what they may be worth in terms of yield.

After the statement "the least selling cost," "commensurate with the sales job to be done" was added. In the sale of certain securities, much sales effort may be necessary, and in order to obtain the best price and terms, paying a higher selling cost may produce a better overall result. Furthermore, in certain instances, it may be advantageous to have the underwriters perform some functions connected with the sale other than just underwriting. Thus, "the least selling cost" should imply a cost commensurate with the most satisfactory performance toward achievement of the objectives for a particular offering. However, it is mostly in common stock financing and not in the sale of senior securities that the underwriters may have some special task to perform. Therefore, since we are now offering senior securities, which are largely sold to sophisticated institutional purchasers, we can still limit the goal as it was originally stated: to obtain the best price or rate at the least selling cost.

When we look at the price, from the company's point of view, we are talking about the price to the public less the underwriters compensation. This is the net proceeds the company receives.

What Are Price and Cost?

If you know what is meant by price of a bond, cost of financing, the difference between proceeds to company and net proceeds to company, etc., you can skip what comes under this heading. But if there is any question in your mind, it will be worthwhile for you to read it. You will need to have a precise understanding of these terms.

The first complete example which we shall use in explaining how to sell securities will be an offering by an actual company, which we will call Electric Company. The offering amounted to $50 million principal amount of mortgage bonds with an interest coupon of 7 1/8% and a 30-year maturity. We will use this offering now to define terms. Shown in Exhibit 8-1 are the figures from that sale in both percentage of principal amount and total amount.

The price of a bond is expressed as a percent of principal amount. For example, if a $1,000 bond is sold to investors for $1,000, the price is 100%. If the same $1,000 bond were sold for $900, the price would be 90%. Sometimes, the term par value is used in referring to a bond; this is incorrect. Par value is a term which applies to stocks, either preferred or common.

Price to public is the price at which the underwriters sell the bonds to purchasers or investors. It is sometimes referred to as the list price or original offering price.

Underwriters' compensation is the gross amount the underwriters obtained for their efforts. This is also referred to as fee, commission or spread. In a prospectus, it is called underwriting discounts and commissions. The terms "spread" and "discount" are in conformity with the idea that the underwriters, acting as principals, buy an issue, take title and sell it at an increased price.

The term "commission" is more nearly associated with a broker who acts as agent.

Exhibit 8-1

PRICE TO PUBLIC, FINANCING COSTS, PROCEEDS TO THE COMPANY AND NET PROCEEDS TO THE COMPANY

7 1/8% Bonds Maturity—30 Years

Line	Percentage of Principal Amount	Total Amount
1. Price to public	102.6550%	$51,327,500
2. Underwriters' Compensation	0.6151	307,550
3. Proceeds to company	102.0399	$51,019,950
4. Expenses	0.8654	432,700
5. Net proceeds to company	101.1745	$50,587,250
Financing costs—A total of lines 2 and 4.		
Underwriters' compensation	0.6151	$ 307,550
Expenses	0.8654	432,700
Financing costs	1.4805	$ 740,250
Financing costs—Line 1 less line 5		
Price to public	102.6550	$51,327,500
Less: Net proceeds to company	101.1745	50,587,250
Financing costs	1.4805	$ 740,250

We will generally use the terms "spread" or "compensation" for the amount the underwriters receive when they act in their capacity as underwriters. As will be discussed subsequently, the amount covers the underwriters' risk, the managing underwriters' fee, commissions for the underwriters' salesmen, discounts allowed to participating dealers, legal expenses, etc.

When an investment banker acts as an agent in a private sale, we will use the term "fee" for his compensation.

Proceeds to company is the amount the underwriters pay the company for the bonds. It is the price they bid for an issue when it is offered by competitive bidding. Then it is referred to as the "bid price" or "price to the company."

Expenses are the total cash outlays the company incurred in connection with the financing. These are the outside expenses for printing the registration statement, auditors' fees, fees to outside experts, etc. They do not include the wages and salaries of the company's own staff who worked on the financing.

Net proceeds to company is the amount of funds the company received from the financing after all outside costs were deducted including the underwriters' compensation and financing expenses.

Cost of financing, or financing costs, a term not shown above, is used to express the total cash costs for selling securities. It is a total of the two items "underwriters' compensation" and "expenses," or it is the difference between price to the public and net proceeds to the company. It is the cash cost to get the money to the company from the investors. The Securities and Exchange Commission uses the term "cost of flotation," but it means the same thing. The idea of "cash costs" is stressed, because as will be seen later on, there are some other items of non-cash nature which may have to be evaluated in a security offering.

Yield to Maturity

We haven't yet described the real "price" of the bond. It is expressed as a yield to maturity. There are two terms which apply to yield: yield to maturity and current yield.

Let's start our explanation with a simple example. When you buy a bond, whether you buy it at a premium over 100%, at 100% or at a discount below 100%, you still get 100% at maturity. In yield to maturity, the premium over 100% or discount below 100% is written off over the life of the bond. Thus, yield is a function of both price and coupon. It is the effective rate of interest to maturity as distinguished from the coupon rate stated on the face of the bond.

A simple explanation is as follows: A bond selling at 102, carrying a 7% coupon, with two years to maturity, would have a 6% yield; that is, the 7% interest less 1% per year for two years due to the write-off of the 2% premium. On the other hand, a bond selling at 98, carrying a 7% coupon, with two years to maturity, would have an 8% yield; that is, the 7% interest plus 1% per year for two years due to the write-up of the 2% discount. These figures are summarized in Exhibit 8-2. We have spread the premium or discount on an approximate basis; bond tables spread the premium or discount on a compound interest basis.

Now let's explain yield to maturity with the figures we used to illustrate bond pricing. When an investor bought one of the bonds, he paid a price of 102.655%. He would receive interest at the rate of 7 1/8% per year, and in 30 years he would be repaid 100% of the principal amount. If he holds the bond to maturity, he will gain, for each 100% principal amount, $7.125 in interest per year, but he will lose $2.655; that is, the premium price he paid over the 100% of principal amount he gets at maturity. So, the effective yield is a combination of the interest he gains each year and the premium he loses, which must be written off over the 30-year maturity of the bonds. The result is the yield to maturity. This can be calculated by means of a complicated compound interest formula, but there is no need for that; it has all been done for you in tables compiled in Bond Value Tables. Some Bond Value Tables give yields for each 0.01% of yield, others for each 0.05% and 0.10%. An excerpt, to fit our example, from a book with prices for each 0.10% in yield, is shown in Exhibit 8-3.

The left-hand column gives us the yield to maturity which we are after. We find the yield for our bond by first looking for the price of 102.66 in the column headed 30 years, which is for bonds with that maturity. We then look for the yield opposite that price in the left-hand column; this gives us the 6.91% by interpolation.

The problem of interpolation is eliminated today because some calculating machines are equipped to find yield to maturity to as many decimal places as you could wish.

The items which are shown in Exhibit 8-1 for our bond offering can be expressed in terms of yield to maturity, as shown in Exhibit 8-4. The figures for principal amount are rounded to the third decimal place, which is as far out as they need be carried in order to calculate an approximate yield.

These are a lot of figures on one point if you are not familiar with the subject; so if you want a review, here it is: The underwriters figure that they could sell the bonds to the public at 102.655 to yield 6.91%. They decided that their compensation should be 0.615, so they bid approximately 102.040, which was the proceeds the company received. The yield at the bid price is 6.96%. The company's expenses were 0.865, resulting in a net proceeds to the company of 101.175, making a cost of money to the company of 7.03%. The financing costs were 1.481, which was a total of the underwriters' compensation of 0.615, equivalent to 0.05% in terms of yield, and expenses of 0.865 equivalent to 0.07% in terms of yield. The financing expenses were high for this type of an issue because of a state mortgage tax.

Exhibit 8-2

YIELD TO MATURITY ILLUSTRATED

Year	Bond Price	Price at Maturity	Write-Off of Premium	Interest Coupon	Gain to Investor or Yield to Maturity
0	102				
1			-1%	+7%	6%
2		100	-1%	+7%	6%

Year	Bond Price	Price at Maturity	Write-Up of Discount	Interest Coupon	Gain to Investor or Yield to Maturity
0	98				
1			+1%	+7%	8%
2		100	+1%	+7%	8%

Exhibit 8-3

BOND VALUE TABLE ILLUSTRATION

7 1/8% Interest Coupon

Maturity

Yield	*29 Years*	*30 Years*	*31 Years*
6.60%	106.74	106.82	106.89
6.70	105.41	105.46	105.52
6.80	104.09	104.14	104.18
6.90	102.80	102.83	102.86
7.00	101.54	101.56	101.57
7.10	100.31	100.31	100.31
7.20	99.09	99.08	99.07

Note: If no price is in the column that corresponds to the price of our bonds, it is necessary to interpolate between the nearest two prices. Similarly, if the maturity does not exactly correspond, it is necessary to interpolate. Interpolation is accomplished by ratio and proportions. Interpolation is satisfactory for most purposes, but it is not entirely accurate, since the differences between the figures in the Bond Value Tables are not on a straight line basis.

Exhibit 8-4

BOND PRICES AND FINANCING COSTS EXPRESSED IN TERMS OF YIELD TO MATURITY

7 1/8% BOND–30-YEAR MATURITY

Line		Percentage of Principal Amount	Yield to Maturity
1	Price to public	102.655%	6.91%
2	Underwriters' compensation	0.615	0.05
3	Proceeds to company	102.040	6.96
4	Expenses	0.865	0.07
5	Net proceeds to company	101.175	7.03

We mentioned at the beginning of our discussion on yield, that there were two yields: yield to maturity and current yield. Current yield merely relates the coupon to the price. For example, a bond with a 7% coupon selling at 70 would have a 10% current yield. Current yields are seldom referred to in bonds because they have a maturity. The term is more likely to be used for preferred stocks or common stocks which have no maturity.

Basis Point

A term which you will continually hear in reference to yields is "basis point." It is sometimes erroneously referred to as bases point. Anyway, it is very simple: It is 1/100 of 1% yield, or, in other words, 0.01% yield. For example, 5 basis points would be 0.05% yield.

One very rough rule of thumb to quickly translate price into yield is that 5 basis points are equivalent to about 1% in the price of a bond. This rough rule should be used with caution. It varies with the interest rate on the bonds, the price and particularly with the maturity. It does not apply at all to bonds with short maturities. An idea of how it varies with maturity and interest rate can be gathered from the figures given in Exhibit 8-5, taken from Bond Value Tables. For a bond with a 4% interest coupon, 5 basis points are equivalent to 1.00 in price for a 40-year maturity. For other maturities and interest coupons, the rule of thumb may not be very close, as can be seen from the table. For example, for a bond with an 8% interest coupon, 5 basis points are equivalent to 0.60 in price for a 40-year maturity.

Average Maturity

If a bond has a serial maturity, the yield to maturity will be calculated for each serial maturity. If the serial maturities are different in amount, a weighted average yield can be calculated.

If a bond has a sinking fund, and the bonds are callable by lot, the investor would probably calculate the yield to final maturity. The investor would have no way of knowing if his bonds might be called for sinking fund. In other words, he might look at yield assuming that his bonds would be the last to be called. If all bonds were reduced equally by sinking fund, the investor would be interested in yield to average maturity. In any event, the company would be interested in yield to average maturity. Yield to average maturity is calculated on the basis of weighted average maturity. As a simple example, let's assume that a company has $10 million principal amount of bonds outstanding with $4 million paid off in one year and the remaining $6 million paid off in two years. The weighted average maturity would be calculated as shown in Exhibit 8-6.

Since this chapter also deals with preferred stocks, we should point out that the terms used above for bonds generally apply in the same way to preferreds. However, prices and

Exhibit 8-5

BASIS POINTS ILLUSTRATION

Yield to Maturity Equivalent to Difference in Bond Price for Various Maturities

4% Interest Coupon

	Yield	Bond Price 10 Yrs.	20 Yrs.	30 Yrs.	40 Yrs.	50 Yrs.
	3.95%	100.41	100.69	100.87	101.00	101.09
	4.00	100.00	100.00	100.00	100.00	100.00
5 Basis Points	0.05%	0.41	0.69	0.87	1.00	1.09

8% Interest Coupon

	Yield	10 Yrs.	20 Yrs.	30 Yrs.	40 Yrs.	50 Yrs.
	7.95%	100.34	100.54	100.57	100.60	100.62
	8.00	100.00	100.00	100.00	100.00	100.00
5 Basis Points	0.05%	0.34	0.54	0.57	0.60	0.62

other items are expressed in dollars per share, and since a preferred stock usually has no maturity, the yield is obtained merely by dividing the price into the dividend rate. This is what is called a current yield, as contrasted with a yield to maturity on a bond. If a preferred stock has a sinking fund, then elements similar to those of a bond with a sinking fund are present as far as yield is concerned. The yield would have to take into account the weighted average length of life of the issue.

So, while we can and do talk of the price of a bond and preferred stock, in itself it is meaningless, unless for a bond it is related to the interest rate and maturity, and for a preferred stock it is related to the dividend to obtain the current yield. The price and yield move in opposite directions: a high price means a low yield, and a low price, a high yield.

Methods of Sale

The methods of sale of senior securities can be classified under three headings:

1. Competitive public offering.
2. Negotiated public offering.
3. Private sale.

A few brief words about these methods: The first two involve public offerings. A public offering requires registration under the Securities act, with certain exceptions. Prospective purchasers must be provided a prospectus which has been cleared with the Securities and Exchange Commission. The underwriters purchase the securities as principals and then sell them to investors.

In a competitive sale, the price is determined by competitive bidding; the underwriters bid for the issue and the award is made to the highest bidder. There have been instances in which the underwriter has been eliminated by investors entering bids either directly or through agents in competitive offerings. These are very rare exceptions and can be disregarded for purposes of this book.

In a negotiated sale, an underwriting group negotiates with the company as to the price at which it buys the issue from the company.

In a private sale, the securities are sold directly to investors without any underwriting, although an underwriter may help the company arrange the private placement by

Exhibit 8-6

WEIGHTED-AVERAGE MATURITY CALCULATION

Column	I Principal Amount	II Maturity in Years	III Column I x Column II
	\$ 4,000,000	1	\$ 4,000,000
	6,000,000	2	12,000,000
Total	\$10,000,000		\$16,000,000

$$\text{Weighted average maturity} = \frac{\$16{,}000{,}000}{\$10{,}000{,}000} = 1.6 \text{ years}$$

OR

$$\frac{\$\ 4{,}000{,}000}{\$10{,}000{,}000} \times 1 + \frac{\$\ 6{,}000{,}000}{\$10{,}000{,}000} \times 2 = 1.6 \text{ years}$$

acting as an agent. Private sale eliminates the necessity of registering with the Securities and Exchange Commission, but in order to be exempt under the Securities Act a private sale must meet certain tests.

In some offerings, it may be possible to use any one of the three methods; so you may have to make a choice. If, for example, an issue could be sold competitively, it could also be sold by means of a negotiated public offering, provided no regulation required competitive bidding. Depending on the type and number of buyers involved, it could probably be sold at private sale. Such a situation may present a nice problem to determine which is best for the issuing company. Before we discuss each method more fully, let's take a look at the extent to which each is used for corporate financing.

Extent of Use of Methods of Sale

The type of industry has an important bearing on the method adopted. This is about the picture.

Debt securities in the railroad and utility fields are predominantly sold competitively. This has been a result largely of regulatory action with which these industries must comply. This regulatory action was due to abuses in finance. In 1926, the Interstate Commerce Commission ruled that, with certain exceptions, railroads must sell equipment trust certificates at competitive bidding. And as a result of a study in 1943, the Commission established that competitive bidding should be used for practically all railroad debt financing.

In the utility field, the companies which are subject to regulation of the Securities and Exchange Commission under the Public Utility Holding Company Act of 1935 must sell all types of their securities competitively as provided by Rule U-50, with few exceptions.[1] Many companies not under the jurisdiction of the Act, but subject to the Federal Power Commission or State Commission regulation, may be required to sell their securities competitively. Massachusetts was the pioneer in passing such a statute in 1870 for certain securities.

Some utilities, not forced to do so by state or Federal statute or ruling, use competitive bidding by choice. In the utility field, when competitive bidding is not used, the method is either negotiated public sale or private sale. In the industrial field, competitive bidding is practically unknown for any type of security. A greater number of debt securities of industrial companies are offered privately than by negotiated public sale.

For preferred stocks the picture in general is the same. Competitive bidding is limited to the fields where companies are regulated.

The material which follows gives more specific information. Exhibit 8-7, Part I shows that in the total financing for all types of securities, public offerings—that is, both competitive and negotiated combined—predominated. They represented 72% of the total in 1973, with the balance of 28% by private sale. However, private sale was more important for debt issues than indicated by Exhibit 8-7, Part I because it includes preferred and common stocks. Practically all commons are sold publicly. Since this chapter deals in senior securities, and since debt represents most of the senior security financing, let's now look at how the three methods were used in debt financing. The extent of use of each method will vary from year to year, as indicated in Exhibit 8-7, Part II. As previously stated, the picture varies with the type of industry, with competitive public offering predominating in the railroad and utility field and being almost unknown in the industrial.

Regarding the private sale of securities, the greatest number of issues are in the $5 million and under category, but by dollar amount the larger issues account for the greatest total dollar amount.

Now we will turn to the question of how each of the methods works. We will start with

[1]In October 1974, the SEC temporarily suspended competitive bidding for common stocks until March, 1975, because of the extremely adverse market for utility stocks.

Exhibit 8-7

PART I

PUBLIC VS. PRIVATE SALE FOR ALL TYPES OF SECURITIES*

(In Millions of Dollars)

Year	Amount: Private Placements	Amount: Public Offerings	Total
1973	9,127	22,935	32,062
1972	10,215	28,498	38,713
1971	7,256	35,645	42,901
1970	5,185	33,762	38,947
1969	6,025	20,719	26,744
1968	6,963	15,001	21,964
1967	7,163	17,633	24,796
1966	7,702	10,370	18,072
1965	8,549	7,446	15,995
1964	7,404	6,454	13,858

*Source: Securities and Exchange Commission Statistical Bulletin, September 1974 Volume 33, Number 27.

PART II

FINANCING METHODS FOR DEBT SECURITIES

	% of Total Debt Financing† 1972	1973	1969-1973
Competitive Public Offering	23%	26%	69.0% (Competitive and Negotiated combined)
Negotiated Public Offering	41	30	
Private Sale	36	44	31.0
	100%	100%	100.0%

†Estimated from figures of *Investment Dealers' Digest*.

competitive bidding, because this method requires the greatest number of steps and detail. It will provide good background material for an explanation of the other methods.

Competitive Public Offering

As we said in the introduction to this chapter, we will give you two complete examples, step by step, of methods of financing. We will start here with our first one on competitive bidding. You will obtain a first-hand picture of much of the general machinery and mechanics of selling any type of issue through underwriters.

Steps in Competitive Bidding—A Complete Example

To use as our example, we have chosen an offering of $50 million principal amount of bonds of an actual company we will call ELECTRIC COMPANY.

As a first step, the company must pick a tentative date for the bidding which does not conflict with other issues.

In getting ready for a security offering, the company must prepare a time schedule with its counsel, giving in detail the things to be done from the conception of the financing until its completion. This is necessary to assure a smooth operation of the financing, avoid delays, reduce overtime and keep down costs, particularly printing costs. A schedule will include most of the items shown below under the part played by the company.

Each step taken by the company and underwriter are so identified. The manager of our underwriting group is Underwriter-M, a leading investment banking firm. The procedure followed by Underwriter-M is basically similar to that of other firms. While Underwriter-M is doing the things described in each step marked "underwriter," the managers of other underwriting groups who expect to bid for the issue are taking similar steps.

A time schedule prepared by a company would include dates. However, in our explanation, in order to show the time interval throughout, the number in the left-hand column next to each step is the number of days before the bidding day. In other words, the left-hand column is a "countdown," as for a missile launching, to the "zero" day, the "blast-off," when the company either sells its bonds by accepting a bid, provided, of course, that some bids are received, or rejects them all. The number of days taken by each subsequent step after the bidding day to complete the financing, will be designated by a plus sign.

The first thing a person not following new issues would note regarding the offering would be an advertisement by the company in a leading financial newspaper, requesting bids a few days hence. *The Wall Street Journal* is often used for this purpose. The heading for the advertisement for our bond offering follows:

ELECTRIC COMPANY

Public Invitation for Bids for the Purchase of
$50,000,000 First and Refunding Mortgage Bonds,
% Series 0, due June 1 (30 years maturity).
Coupon rate to be specified in the bids.
ELECTRIC COMPANY
hereby invites bids, subject to the terms
and conditions herein stated.

The advertisement included the following additional information:

1. Where the papers, etc., describing the bidding requirements may be examined.
2. Where prospective bidders may meet with company officials to obtain answers to questions which may arise when they analyze the company and this financing. This is called the Information Meeting or the Due Diligence Meeting.
3. The time and place to hand in the bids.

This advertisement gives us a good basis for starting off the discussion of competitive bidding. However, it is largely a formality which is looked at by people in the financial community primarily for the three facts mentioned above.

The underwriting houses who expect to bid obtain information about the offering prior to the advertisement either directly from the company or by word of mouth in the street. Actually, before the advertisement has appeared, the wheels of finance have been turning for some time in preparation for the offering.

Before we start on our schedule of steps, some explanation is necessary to show what to expect.

The initial step taken by the prospective underwriters of an issue is the formation of bidding accounts; that is, groups of underwriting firms which act together in making a single bid. This is handled in each firm by the Syndicate Department. Unless the size of the issue is small—that is, below about $5 million—it is probable that any firm which wishes to submit a bid will want to do so in association with other underwriters. This is for the purpose of spreading the risk and to avoid tying up capital in a few issues. The formation of an account is undertaken promptly when it is first known that the financing is in the offing. Information as to the financing plans of a particular company comes from a number of sources, and underwriting firms are ever alert to acquire this knowledge. Some of the sources of information on forthcoming financings are: direct contacts with officials of the company, some of whom may be seeking advice as to financial plans; an article in the newspapers; information appearing on the news ticker; a meeting of the New York Society of Security Analysts at which some officer of the company discloses its financing plans; the prospectus relating to other types of financing of the issuer; company's annual report; one or more of the services giving financial information; reports that competitors are forming bidding accounts; etc.

A firm which desires to form and manage a bidding account must compete with others which have the same objective. Thus, it behooves a prospective manager to extend invitations to the firms his own firm wishes to have associated with it as promptly as possible upon receipt of knowledge of the new issue. Also, a firm which wishes to join an account to be managed by another promptly should seek a place in a bidding account of its choosing.

In each account, there is a manager, who is referred to as Manager, Head or Representative. The others are called account members. For our group Underwriter-M is the Manager. It is generally the larger firms, with adequate personnel and the financial capacity to assume relatively large underwriting commitments, which form and act as managers of corporate bidding accounts. Their position of leadership is based on experience and ability in setting up important underwritings and upon their history of success in this field.

Let us suppose that an underwriting firm hears of a prospective bond issue and decides to form a bidding account. Naturally, each managing firm wishes to form as strong an account as is feasible. In selecting the firms to be invited into the account, the manager gives consideration to such factors as underwriting capital, ability to distribute securities of the type in question, market judgment and willingness to assume underwriting risks. If a managing firm had previously managed an account which had bid on a prior issue of the company in question, it naturally would endeavor to form a new bidding account including firms which were associated with it on the prior issue. If the current issue is of an amount comparable to that of the previous one, the problem is then relatively simple. However, if the amount to be sold differs materially from the amount of the previous issue, it may be necessary to reduce or increase the size of the account. On a few occasions, where the size of the new issue of a particular company represents a substantial increase over a preceding issue, there may be mergers of certain bidding accounts whereby the managers may act jointly or one bidding account may be absorbed into one or more other accounts.

The number of separate accounts that may be formed to bid for a particular issue will depend primarily on the size and the quality of the issue in question. The resources of all underwriting houses do not permit formation of more than two or three groups for very large issues. The current condition of the market may influence the number of bidders. For bond issues which have ranged in size from $125 million to $250 million, there have been two large competing groups, and three groups have competed for issues as large as $80 million. In contrast, smaller issues may attract a number of bids.

Now we will begin our "countdown." We will start from the time when the news was first announced that the company was thinking of doing the financing. If you wish to breeze through the steps quickly, you can do so easily by just glancing at the headings opposite each step. The material under the headings describes what happens in more detail. Somewhat more emphasis is given to the part played by the underwriter in order to give you a complete picture of what goes on behind the doors of such an organization.

There are two particular days for which you should read all the material carefully. They are the day before the bidding and the day of the bidding. They include a description of the meetings of the members of the account and how the bid is arrived at. You must understand this part in order to have an understanding of competitive bidding. It will show you how the contact of the underwriters with potential buyers makes it possible for the underwriters to achieve a good estimate as to the price they should bid.

It should be pointed out that this example is particularly interesting because it shows that some flexibility in time schedule exists in competitive bidding. As will be explained, the offering was postponed after it was started. Thus, the total time that elapsed is not typical. Our schedule below shows 179 days from the start to the time of the bidding. Of course, some of the time consumed is due to the fact that, being a public utility, the firm had to obtain approval of the state regulatory body. This has no direct bearing on the time required to process a competitive public offering from the point of view of the Securities Act.

A more typical time schedule, without delays, was that for the offering by the same company which was authorized by the Board on April 26. Approval was obtained from the Public Service Commission on May 24. The Registration Statement was filed with the Securities and Exchange Commission on May

6 and became effective May 25. Bids were opened June 14. The schedule included, thus, a total of 48 days from the Board authorization to the bidding date, compared with our example below of 126 days from the day of the Board authorization.

Remember that the numbers at the left of each heading are the number of days before the "zero" day on which bids are received.

179 Underwriter—First news of issue—formation of account started.

In December, as a result of a report from a securities dealer, the Buying Department telephoned one of the officials of ELECTRIC COMPANY about a story regarding the construction program the following year. This official mentioned that there was a newspaper article about plant expansion and that the Company might need to sell about $60 million of bonds, but that there was nothing imminent. As far as he could then see, there would be no bond financing until the following fall. However, as a result of this conversation, Underwriter-M formed a nucleus of an account consisting of 24 firms, each of which had starting participations of $700,000 and over in the last previous deal, consisting of $60 million of bonds, for which they bid unsuccessfully a few months previously.

145 Underwriter—News of Company's change in plans.

The Buying Department again checked in January with an official of the company, who advised that while the management had been originally thinking of selling $50 million to $60 million of bonds in the fall, plans might be changed. His guess was that the Company might decide to sell bonds in April or May.

126 Company—Directors authorize issue.

The Company had a regular meeting of its Board of Directors at the end of January to authorize the issue and the filing of a petition to the State Public Service Commission and filing of a Registration Statement with the Securities and Exchange Commission.

126 Underwriter—Formation of underwriting account completed.

Underwriter-M, along with the other managers, was advised after the Company's Directors' meeting that it would sell $50 million of bonds in about three months; that is, around April. The company sent the managers of the bidding group a tentative time schedule. Underwriter-M completed its account by going to the other members who had bid with them on the last preceding account for $60 million. There were 118 members located throughout the country in that group.

113 Company—Review of bond market.

The Company reviewed the bond market situation to determine whether it was an appropriate time to go ahead with such an offering. It estimated the approximate interest rate and price it might receive, and whether the terms or amount might have to be altered in order to make the issue attractive to purchasers.

The Company discussed the matter of terms and general bond market conditions with some leading investment banking firms. It was advised to go ahead with the offering without making any special change in the terms of the indenture in order to attract purchasers.

Some investment banking firms are willing to give advice free of charge to companies contemplating competitive bidding. This provides an opportunity for a company to check its own independent studies on various aspects of the financing. It may be well to consult more than one firm because there may be a difference of opinion. However, it is unnecessary to contact more than two or three in order to get a good picture of the situation. As a point of interest, one question frequently asked by prospective issuers, when the bond market is tight, is the number of years which the bond will have to be made non-refundable in order to make the issue sell, and the price differential for different years of non-refundability. Other questions which might be asked investment bankers regarding a forthcoming bond issue are: the status of the current bond market, the most acceptable maturity and how much effect the maturity would have on market receptivity, what constitutes acceptable optional redemption provisions, the amount of sinking fund to be provided and what special restrictions, if any, might have to be included in the indenture under existing market conditions.

In such discussion with underwriters, the company may obtain some broad ideas as to the interest coupon and price which might be expected to be received. The estimate will only be an approximation, because no underwriting group wants to take a chance that the bid they are thinking about will leak out to any other group.

113 Company–Filing with Utility Commission.

The Company which is subject to regulation by the State Public Service Commission, filed a petition with the Commission requesting authority to sell the bonds.

99 Company–Hearing before Utility Commission.

Hearings were held before a member of the State Public Service Commission to review the Company's petition.

98 Company–Filing with the Securities and Exchange Commission.

Since this was a public offering, the Company had to file its Registration Statement with the Securities and Exchange Commission.

91 Underwriter–Manager sends first material to account members.

As Manager of their underwriting group, Underwriter-M sent to the members of the account copies of the following, which were obtained from the Company:

a. Prospective Bidders' Questionnaire–This must be filled in by each of the underwriters in the account and returned to the Company through the Manager. It covers questions referring to possible affiliation of the underwriters with the Company or trustee, which would disqualify them from being underwriters under the provisions of the Trust Indenture Act of 1939, or the Public Utility Holding Company Act of 1935.
b. A so-called blue sheet, on which each underwriter in the account fills in his exact firm name, address, etc., to be used in any circulars, advertisements or prospectuses issued in connection with the financing, and also a list of states in which the underwriter is registered as a security dealer. The latter part is for the purpose of indicating the states in which it may be necessary to get the issue cleared for sale by the state securities commission. This is known as Blue Sky procedure and is handled by the lawyers for the underwriters. In competitive bidding, one counsel is selected, early in the procedure, by the company to act for the underwriters. This is necessary because some things have to be done by the counsel for the underwriters prior to the time when the winning underwriter is known. The winning underwriter pays this counsel.
c. Preliminary prospectus, plainly marked that it has not yet been approved by the SEC.
d. So-called bidding papers comprising:

    Public invitation for Bids.

Statement of Terms and Conditions for Bids.

Form on which the Bid will be handed in to the Company.

Form of Purchase Contract between the underwriters and the Company.

88 Company–Order received from Commission.

The Public Service Commission issued an order granting the Company permission to sell the bonds.

57 Company–Amendment to Registration Statement filed, changing bidding date.

The Company filed an amendment to the Registration Statement, with the Securities and Exchange Commission changing the bidding date from 15 days hence to 57 days hence because of unusual congestion in the bond market.

56 Underwriter–Members informed of change in bidding date; revised papers sent.

The Manager informed the account members by letter that the company had changed its proposed bidding date, and sent members copies of amendment to Registration Statement, preliminary prospectus and other forms that needed to be updated.

37 Company–The Registration Statement as amended became effective.

The registration statement automatically becomes effective 20 days after filing with the Securities and Exchange Commission, unless a delaying amendment is filed, which is generally the case. Since ELECTRIC COMPANY had filed sometime previously and postponed financing, the registration statement was already effective.

After the winning bid is known on the day of the bidding, a post-effective amendment to the statement, including the price, interest rate, redemption prices and winning underwriting group, must be filed before the sale can take place. This automatically becomes effective immediately on filing.

22 Underwriter–Manager offered participations to smaller account members.

The Manager sent letters to the smaller individual account members offering them specific participations in the account. Generally these were accepted without complaint.

13 Underwriter–Manager sent further material to group members.

The Manager sent a letter to each account member advising all of them that no new bidding papers would be issued since no changes were contemplated in those last forwarded. Members were sent the following:

a. Blue Sky survey of counsel for the underwriters, which showed the states in which the bonds had been cleared for sale.
b. Survey of counsel as to legality of bonds for investment by certain institutions. This may be quite important in some issues. It is sometimes difficult to figure whether an issue is legal for investment by certain types of institutions in some states, and if this has not been definitely established before the offering, some potential purchasers will be eliminated.
c. Two copies of final prospectus. It is necessary for each underwriter to arrange with the Manager to have on hand a sufficient supply of prospectuses so that a copy can be sent to each potential purchaser who is offered the issue and does not already have a copy.
d. Drafts of opinions of counsel for the Company and of counsel for the successful bidders, concerning various legal matters.

12 Underwriter–More papers sent to members.

The Agreement among Purchasers–that is, the agreement among the members of the account in the underwriting group–and a list of account members in the group indicating the participation of each, were sent to the members.

11 Company–The formal advertisement appeared in papers, calling for bids 11 days hence.

This is the advertisement which was used to start off this description of competitive bidding. As we said then, the wheels of finance had been turning for some time before the advertisement appeared.

6 Company–Due Diligence Meeting.

The Company held a Due Diligence Meeting at 10:00 a.m. at a meeting room in the bank which was trustee for the bonds. This form of meeting is explained in Chapter 12, "Investor Relations." The meeting was attended by representatives of the underwriting groups, and by security analysts from various financial organizations which had an interest in the Company's securities. A representative of Underwriter-M and those of some of the other account members were present. The Company's representatives included senior officers of the Company, counsel for the Company, counsel for the prospective underwriters and accountants. The Company's President spoke about the company's operations. The Financial Vice President spoke briefly on the new issue and reviewed the prospectus; then questions were answered by company officials.

6 Underwriter–Data to assist in price appraisal, etc., sent to account members.

The Manager sent to account members a so-called form of Agenda showing high spots of Bidding Terms; time schedule of meetings of their underwriting group to discuss the issue; estimated expenses, such as legal fees to be borne by the underwriters; legality for investment in various states; redemption features; bond ratings; other groups of underwriters competing for the issue; amount of bonds to be retained by members of the group for their own retail sales. This material generally includes a statistical comparison of the company with a few other companies of similar size and rating which recently offered bonds.

There was also included a form of market tabulation comparing prices and yields for various series of ELECTRIC COMPANY bonds and certain other outstanding bonds of comparable rating.

5 Company–Deadline for bidding groups to qualify to bid.

This was the last day on which underwriters could file the questionnaire which would qualify them to bid on the issue. The Company now knew that there would be three bidding groups unless they subsequently withdrew.

1 Underwriter–Potential Demand survey of buyer interest, and preliminary meeting of Manager and account members to discuss price.

Prior to any discussion about what price to bid, the Sales Department of the Manager has made a canvass by phone of the principal buyers likely to be interested in purchasing the issue. This canvass is an effort to pry out of the potential buyers the amount of bonds they might be interested in buying if the price is right. Many buyers are not willing to tip their hands; thus it requires a nice bit of diplomacy in order to get as much information as possible. Through long experience in interpreting this information, the underwriters assess, insofar as possible, the extent of the immediate interest in the issue. This estimate aids in forming an opinion about price. The results of this potential demand survey or canvass of buyer interest is known as the "book."

An office meeting was held in the New York office of the Manager and was attended by the head of the firm and representatives of the firm's Sales, Trading,

Buying and Syndicate Departments. At this meeting there was a discussion of the current condition of the bond market, after which the Sales Department reported its finding from the canvass of interest of prospective buyers. Following this, each individual in attendance gave his views as to the market worth of the bonds.

A Preliminary Price Meeting of representatives of the account members is generally held the business day preceding the day of bidding. It was held in the office of the Manager, just after the Manager concluded the meeting of his own staff described above. It was attended by 33 members of the account. The purpose was to discuss the condition of the bond market, the significant features of the issuing company and the particular bonds. The Manager made a report on his survey of the interest in the issue, with specific mention of any large institutions which may have indicated an interest. Most individual account members make their own surveys of sales interest, although not as extensively as the Manager, and if they have any information differing from or in addition to the Manager's report, they have an opportunity to express themselves at this time. The "book" or potential demand survey by the Manager indicated an interest in the Eastern part of the country amounting from \$8,100,000 to \$10,450,000, and in the West from \$4,050,000 to \$6,500,000, exclusive of one large state fund upon which no specific report was available but which was believed to be a potential customer for at least \$2 million. This was a relatively thin demand. At times, the showing of potential demand will exceed the issue.

The concluding feature of the Preliminary Price Meeting is the expression of views of the various firms represented as to the yield basis on which the bonds should be offered to the public.

These ranged from 6.83% to 6.95%. In the interest of secrecy, the Manager did not express any views at this meeting.

Before we get to the point of finally determining the bid price, it may prevent some confusion in your mind if we review briefly what the underwriters in the account are trying to determine under the leadership of the Manager.

ELECTRIC COMPANY has called for bids for bonds with 30-year maturity. The underwriters are to name the interest coupon. The bidding terms called for an interest coupon in multiples of 1/8 of 1%. This is a usual provision. It assures that the coupon rate will fit Bond Value Tables figured in such multiples so that yields can be figured readily. One of the terms of the bidding is that the price paid to the Company—that is, the bid price—shall be between 100% and 102 3/4%. Utility companies subject to regulation of the Securities and Exchange Commission are generally required to receive 100% or better for their bonds, but there are exceptions. Some states have similar limitations. When not so required, there is no objection to a bid below 100%. In fact, some purchasers feel that a price slightly below 100% is more attractive because it gives more room to the call price. However, from the company's point of view it may, in effect, increase the call premium.

The underwriters have to decide what interest coupon they will use and what the bid price should be with that coupon, within the specified price range of 100% to 102 3/4%.

The process of reasoning starts with a determination of the yield to maturity at which it appears the bonds can be sold to the public. Based on the interest coupon and maturity, the yield is translated into a price to the public. This price, as well as the yield which corresponds to this price, is referred to as the list price. The next step is for the underwriters to figure how much compensation they should charge for underwriting the issue. As previously explained, this is also called the spread. By subtracting the underwriters' compensation from the list price, a price is reached which is the underwriters' bid for the bonds. Thus, the bid price requires two determinations: the list price and the underwriters' compensation. Since most of the account members were thinking of a list price which would produce a yield to the public in the range of 6.83% to 6.95%, then the interest coupon would have to be 7% or 7 1/8% to fit within the specified price range to the company and allow room for the underwriters' compensation to be tacked on to the price to reach the price to the public. This can be seen from the figures given below.

	7% Coupon	7 1/8% Coupon
To Public—Yield 6.83%	102.157	~~103.743~~
Assumed Underwriters' Compensation	0.700	~~0.700~~
To Bid	101.457	~~103.043~~
To Public—Yield 6.95%	~~100.627~~	102.194
Assumed Underwriters' Compensation	~~0.700~~	0.700
To Bid	~~99.927~~	101.494

These figures show the prices of two interest coupons for yields of 6.83% and 6.95% for a 30-year bond. Also shown is what the bid price would be, assuming an underwriters' compensation of 0.700. The crossed-out numbers are outside of the specified bidding prices. If more than one interest coupon will fit, the lowest one is finally used.

It should be emphasized that the discussion at the Price Meeting will involve both the list price and the size of the underwriters' compensation. There may be differences of opinion on both. Some underwriters tend to be willing to push for a higher list price, if there is a large enough compensation to take care of possible miscalculations; others feel that they are taking less risk by having a smaller compensation, with the list price so attractive as to produce a quick sale.

Now we will get back to our story.

"Zero"Day—Underwriter—Final Price Meeting.

Another office meeting was held in the New York Office of the Manager just prior to the Final Price Meeting, for the purpose of further discussion of potential demand, the bid and offering price and what maximum commitment or participation the Manager was willing to take. At that time the Manager's participation was $2,300,000 in bonds.

At this meeting it was agreed that the Manager would recommend, at the Final Price Meeting of the account, a bid price of 101.95 for a 7 1/8% interest coupon. This was based on a public offering price of 102.655, producing a yield to maturity of 6.91% and an underwriters' compensation of 0.705. It was further agreed that at this level the Manager would be willing to increase his commitment if necessary, from $2,300,000 to $10 million in order to absorb the slack; that is, participations of those firms who indicate they will withdraw from the account if the bid is too high for their liking.

The Final Price Meeting is generally scheduled by the Manager for as short a time before the hour for receipt of bids as will permit adequate discussion for determining the bid and allow for the completion of the paper work necessary in order to hand in the bid. One reason for scheduling this meeting for as late as feasible is that to do so affords members all possible time to secure the latest information on market conditions and sales interest. Another reason is to preserve the security of the bid. If the meeting breaks up too early, some of those present may talk, and information on the account's price may spread around the street like wildfire and get to the competing bidding groups.

Because some underwriting groups, particularly on an issue of large amount, consist of many members, it is not always practicable to allow each and every member to participate in the discussions at the Final Price Meeting. In such cases, the determination of the final bid and offering price is vested in a so-called Price Committee, which consists of firms having participations down to a certain minimum amount as pre-established by the Manager—which in this issue was $600,000. The Price Committee consisted of 24 members.

Members not on the Price Committee may attend the Final Price Meeting if they wish. Such members do not partake in the discussions, but each of them present is given the opportunity to declare whether or not he wishes to withdraw from the account or change the amount of his participation if he does not like the price decided upon by the Price Committee.

If an account member finds it inconvenient or impossible to attend the Final Price Meeting, such member may exercise the prerogative of filing with the Manager a price limit. This must be done by a certain designated hour in advance of the Final Price Meeting and indicates the maximum price which the account member is willing to bid for the bonds; at any higher bid such member no longer has a commitment to participate in the bid. The Manager had previously received price limits from 18 account members with aggregate participations of $4 million, none of whom had headquarters in New York. Two of these limits specified prices for 7% interest coupon, and the remaining 16, representing participations totalling $3,650,000, specified prices ranging between 100.0743 to 102.005 for a 7 1/8% interest coupon.

At the Final Price Meeting the Manager reviews the potential buyer interest in the issue and then gives his recommendations to the Price Committee. Each member of the committee is polled to determine the extent to which the committee members are willing to make the bid suggested. Usually some are willing and some are not, and perhaps certain of those who want to make the bid also will desire to absorb some of the slack.

It is found not feasible to achieve a bid at the level first recommended by the Manager, attempts are made at different prices until agreement on a bid is obtained. While the Manager makes the recommendation to the Price Committee, in some instances other members of the Price Committee may hold generally higher views than those expressed initially by the Manager; thus a bid higher than the Manager recommended may be achieved.

On the first canvass of the Price Committee, it was apparent that there would be no trouble arriving at the bid recommended by the Manager; namely, 101.95 for a 7 1/8% interest coupon and an offering price of 102.655 to produce a yield of 6.91%. The members were then canvassed to see how many would go through a 6.91% basis for a list price; that is, offer the bonds at a lower yield. Nine members were willing; whereas, 15 members of the Price Committee, with participations aggregating $14,850,000, were unwilling. After further discussion it was finally decided that the list price would be 102.655, which would give a yield of 6.91% for an interest coupon of 7 1/8%, but that the underwriters' compensation should be reduced so that the bid to the company would be higher. The final bid price to the Company agreed to was 102.0399, making the underwriters' compensation 0.6151.

The extra digits at the end of a bid may perplex some people. As explained above, basically, the way a bid is arrived at is that the account members decide on a proposed list price and deduct therefrom an underwriting compensation sufficient to cover the risks, expenses, and work involved for the particular issue. Any extra digits beyond this, such as two or more nines, are usually the results of someone's whim, but sometimes lead to startling results. Once an issue of $50 million bonds was won by the margin of $0.0001 per $100 bonds. In other words, the margin was $50 on a $50 million issue. Such things are sheer luck.

At the level of 102.0399, three members of the Price Committee dropped, eight non-Committee members in the meeting dropped, and two reduced participations, and 16 members not at the meeting dropped because of price limits they had filed. Five small members of the account had dropped before the final meeting. At the end of the meeting and at the agreed-to bid price, slack aggregated $8,750,000. This was absorbed by 22 members including the Manager, whose final participation was $7,950,000. There were finally 97 members in the account with participations ranging from that of the Manager down to the smallest of $100,000.

After determining the bid and the proposed price at which the bonds will be offered to the public, the Price Committee also decides the discounts to be allowed to dealers and the percentage of each underwriter's participation he will retain for his own retail sales. The latter two points will be explained subsequently.

At the conclusion of the Final Price Meeting, the Manager must quickly complete the necessary paper work in connection with executing the bid form and see that the bid is submitted correctly, in proper form, at the place and time designated for the opening of the bids.

There have been mistakes in bids which were submitted due to the stress and strain of the last-minute rush to get the bids in. There was a case of one underwriting group which, through clerical error by the person handing in the bid, put in the interest coupon rate 1/8% too low. The error was obvious and the company permitted the bid to be withdrawn. Other instances of mistakes have included handing in the price at which the bonds were to be offered to the public rather than the price to the company. This results in a serious problem for that underwriting group if they win the issue, as would be more than likely.

Some underwriters follow the practice of having one or more representatives of their Buying Department at the place of sale to receive by telephone the bid and the final changes in the membership of the account. The final bid forms were completed by representatives of the Buying Department of the Manager, who had been given use of desk space of the office of the Company. This work included changes in the list of account members in the group and the amount of their participations resulting from the final Price Meeting, as well as the insertion of the bid price and coupon rate. A "good faith" check must accompany the bid.

Promptly at the bid hour, just after the bids had been handed in, the Manager's Syndicate Department exchanged bids with the managers of the competing groups, so that the underwriting groups knew who won at the same time as the company opened the bids. This is a customary procedure, but it is quite surprising to company officials who don't know about it and discover that the underwriters knew who won at the same time as bids were being opened. This is done, of course, only after it would be too late for any group to change its bid.

"Zero" Day (Cont'd)—Company—Bids opened.

The company opened bids at 11:00 a.m. The bids, all specifying a 7 1/8% coupon, were:

Underwriter-M	102.0399%
Second place group	101.9099%
Third place group	101.7199%

The difference between the price submitted by the winning group and other bidders will depend on the type of issue and condition of the market. If the issue is high grade, about which there is little question, and the market is firm and steady, the difference between the bids of the groups tends to be infinitesimal compared with the magnitude of the undertaking. There have been a few instances of tie bids. One occurred when two groups each bid 101.7199% for an issue of $30 million of bonds bearing the same coupon. In this case, the tie groups were given a period of three hours in which to improve their bids if they so elected. One group raised its bid to 101.75% and the other to 101.86%, thereby winning the issue.

It tends to show how accurately well-known, high grade issues can be priced by competitive bidding. If the difference is great, it may hurt the sale by the winning group because it may be taken as a signal by potential buyers that the issue is over-priced. The difference in bids for ELECTRIC COMPANY is considered moderate in view of the circumstances.

The Company's Board of Directors was in session and it immediately approved the winning bid. The Company awarded the issue to Underwriter-M and associates, and a purchase contract was signed by the officials of the Company and Underwriter-M which bound each underwriter severally.

The Company and its counsel, working with Underwriter-M's Buying Department as well as with counsel for the Underwriters, collaborated on filing with the Securities and Exchange Commission the final amendment to the Registration Statement setting forth the price, interest rate, redemption prices and winning underwriting group. This is the so-called "post-effective amendment." The final prospectus was thus completed. As is customary, information about the offering terms, underwriters, etc., had been set up in type in advance in respect to each of the bidding accounts to the extent that it was feasible to do so. As previously stated, the post-effective amendment automatically becomes effective on filing.

The necessary approval of the price by the State Public Service Commission was obtained.

"Zero" Day (Cont'd)–Underwriting–Sales machinery gets set.

A final check was made by Underwriter-M's Buying Department on the status of the issue under various Blue Sky Laws. Night letter telegrams were sent:

1. To members, announcing that the issue had been released for public offering the next day, with information regarding delivery and requests for fully registered bonds;
2. To certain selected dealers, allotting them specific amounts of bonds at the list price less the dealers' selling concession of 1/4 of 1%–these dealers had previously made requests to the Syndicate Department for bonds;
3. To members who wanted additional bonds over and above the 80% of their participation which all members, including the Manager, had for retail sales.

The Manager retains a certain amount of each member's bonds in the so-called "pot," the rest of each member's participation being available for his own retail sales. The amount retained may vary in each issue. For small issues there may be no "pot." The manager kept 20% of this issue in the "pot," leaving 80% for retail sales.

This percentage was agreed to at the Final Price Meeting. "Pot" bonds are for three purposes: (a) Sales to certain large institutions at full list price for the account of all the underwriters. These sales are handled by the Manager out of the "pot" in order to afford a means for such investors to obtain large blocks of bonds to satisfy their requirements and to obviate the necessity of their having to get in touch with many members of the underwriting group to acquire sizeable blocks. (b) Sales to selected dealers at the dealer concession. In some instances, the Manager may release members of the group to make sales to selected dealers. Frequently, underwriters in the group that lose the bid will fill some orders from investors who are close to them, by taking down bonds from the winning group at the dealer concession. In so doing, they act in the capacity of a dealer. (c) In addition, with the consent of the manager, individual members may withdraw bonds from the "pot" which they contributed to the "pot" and which remain unsold.

+1 Underwriter—Sales begin.

The post-effective amendment was effective and firm sales began. Generally, it is possible to get the Registration Statement effective late in the day of the bid. In any event, firm offers to sell cannot be made without a prospectus; so they are generally held up until the day after the bidding. Actually, on the day before, as soon as the company accepts the bid, phones start ringing in the offices of the members of the successful group. If buyers are interested in the issue, they wish to record their interest so that they will be sure to obtain bonds when the Registration Statement becomes effective and a prospectus is available. This is what is termed circling bonds for interested buyers. If buyers are eager, it is possible that they may rush in and speak for all the bonds the day before the sale. It is illegal actually to sell bonds prior to the time when the Registration Statement becomes effective and without a prospectus. Such illegal practice is called "gun jumping."

Of the $10 million of bonds retained by the Manager in the "pot," there remained unsold at the close of business $5,294,000, and it was estimated that 25% of the entire issue was sold.

The advertisement of the issue in the newspapers, as placed by the underwriters, is shown in Exhibit 8-8. It included the name of the issue, the price and the names of the 23 underwriters with the largest participations. The advertisment may include more information, but it generally does not. This is the so-called "tombstone" advertisement, because it is usually so formal. If an offering is a quick sale, the issue may be largely spoken for by the time the advertisement appears. The statement in the ad to the effect that it is not an offer to sell and that the offering can only be made by prospectus is legal verbiage necessitated by the Securities Act. This advertisement is primarily a formality. It is of most interest to the lead underwriting houses in the group to show to the financial district and industry the important position that their firms are taking in underwritings. Most underwriters are very touchy about the position of their names on this totem pole. They feel that it is quite important as a matter of pride that they appear as near the head of the list as possible. The advertisement does have some significance as far as the agreement between the underwriters and company is concerned, because some of the clauses permitting the underwriter to withdraw are cut off by the formal offering.

+2 Underwriter—Sales effort continues.

There remained $3,503,000 bonds unsold in the "pot."

+3 Underwriter—Sales effort continues.

All of the remaining bonds in the "pot" were taken, of which $2,662,000 were taken by one account member.

+8 Company—Closing.

There was a closing held at 10:00 a.m., at which time Underwriter-M handed the Company a check for the total bid price for the bonds, plus accrued interest from the day the bonds were dated, less the amount of the good faith check. Some managing

Exhibit 8-8

ADVERTISEMENT OF SALE OF BONDS BY UNDERWRITERS

This announcement is not an offer to sell or a solicitation of an offer to buy these securities. The offering is made only by the Prospectus.

$50,000,000

ELECTRIC COMPANY

First and Refunding Mortgage Bonds, 7 1/8% Series 0,
due June 1 (maturity 30 years).

Price 102.655% and accrued interest.

The Prospectus may be obtained in any State in which this announcement is circulated from only such of the undersigned and other dealers as may lawfully offer these securities in such State.

Underwriter-M

The other underwriters names follow.

underwriters give the company their check for the full amount and collect from the account members. Others have the account members deliver their checks to the company directly, or through the Manager, for their share of the bonds.

The Trustee, on instructions from the Company, delivered the Bonds to the Manager, who in turn distributed them to the members of the group and selected dealers for final delivery to the ultimate purchasers.

+21 Underwriter—Agreement among purchasers extended.

It was estimated that the deal was about 60% sold. The agreement among account members was extended through the close of business for 20 more days.

+41 Underwriter—Syndicate dissolved.

The agreement among the account members was allowed to expire by limitation at the close of business. After these restrictions are removed, the price is free. The opening quotation on the next day was 100 - 100 ½. Three weeks later it was quoted 101 - 101 ¼.

This offering would be considered as a slow sale by the financial community.

When the underwriters bid on an issue, they try to bid the highest price possible so that they will win, set the price to the public to produce a satisfactory underwriters' compensation and yet sell the issue with reasonable promptness. It is their hope that the issue will be sold on the day that it is offered. Such a sale for a high-grade bond issue is referred to as selling fast, or, in street terminology, as being "out the window." If an issue is mostly sold within a week or ten days, this is considered satisfactory by the underwriters, depending on market conditions. However, if it takes the full period of the agreement among underwriters, usually between 20 and 30 days, then the issue is considered to be selling slowly. If a substantial amount of the issue is still left in underwriters' hands when the syndicate is terminated, then the sale is considered as a very slow one, and far from what the underwriters contemplated when they purchased the issue. The size of the underwriters' compensation is inadequate to take care of the risk of a change in the level of interest rates if they have to hold much of the issue as long as 20 days. The entire underwriting compensation for this issue of

0.615 only represents about 0.05% in terms of yield for the bonds. Thus, a very small increase in interest rates would make sale of the issue very difficult and the price would have to be reduced accordingly at the expiration of the agreement. Sometimes the agreement is extended for another 20-day period, as was done in the case of ELECTRIC COMPANY. Whether this is done will depend on the market situation at the time.

If there is any quantity of bonds left after the syndicate is broken then the market price will almost certainly drop. Members of the group can then sell or hang on as they wish. Some members sell, or as the term is ued in the street, they "cut and run." In many instances, experience has shown that if underwriters don't take their losses and sell, they may regret their decision to hold and continue hoping that the market will improve.

This finishes our step-by-step story of competitive bidding and the explanation that went with it. It should provide assistance to you in deciding on the knotty question of when to use competitive bidding, our next point.

Advantages and Disadvantages of Competitive Bidding

We will try to evaluate the pros and cons so that you can compare competitive bidding with the other forms of financing—negotiated public offering and private sale. Some of the answers are matters of fact and some are matters of opinion, because not all the advantages and disadvantages can be expressed in figures. There are experts in the field of finance who tend to favor one method or another. Naturally, underwriters begrudgingly say anything favorable about competitive bidding even where it is obviously advantageous.

First, here is a broad statement about the use of competitive bidding, which we will qualify when we get into more detail: the simple rule of thumb is that competitive bidding generally is most applicable to securities which are well-known to the potential investors and which require no special sales effort on the part of the underwriters to convince investors of their value. When underwriters bid for an issue, there is not the same incentive as exists in a negotiated public offering to do a sales job before the bidding date, because no bidder knows whether he will be the successful one. Now for a more detailed analysis.

Advantages:

1. An impartial assessment is made of the value of a security in the existing competitive market. The company does not have to negotiate the price or underwriters' compensation. The price the company obtains is established automatically by competitive bidding. The underwriters' compensation is also established automatically as far as the company is concerned. The underwriters set it themselves according to their overall appraisal of what they think should be the price to the public and how much they need to compensate them for their effort. The company may not be able to estimate the price to the public and the underwriters' compensation very closely, because the company is not close to the market. Thus, the company is relieved of having to rely heavily on the underwriters' judgment as is necessary in a negotiated public offering.
2. The underwriters will seek to pay the company the highest price commensurate with their estimate of their ability to sell the issue.

   For high-grade types of securities, which are well known to purchasers, under normal market conditions, the company may obtain a higher price for an issue through competitive bidding than in other methods of sale. In a rising market, the underwriters may even reach for an issue slightly above the indicated market demand, on the basis that the upward movement of the market may "bail them out." This practice, however, is usually not too long-lived because when the underwriters reach too high during a bull market, someone eventually gets burned and there is a corrective reaction.

3. The company is more free to set the terms of the issue which best meet its needs and then let the market pay the best price on the basis of those terms. This may be quite an advantage in some circumstances, when market conditions place the buyers in a strong bargaining position and they are more able to press their demands in a negotiated public offering and particularly in a private sale.

Disadvantages:

1. It is sometimes contended that competitive bidding requires a fairly rigid time schedule, and is not very flexible once it is started. However, a company can postpone the offering with little trouble. It can speed it up only within the limitations of all the formalities which must be completed. A negotiated public offering may be just about as rigid, because all the process of security regulation has to be gone through. The only thing eliminated is the bidding part.

   One feature which can add to the flexibility of a competitive bidding is to have the terms of the bidding set up so that bids can be called for on 72 hours' notice, rather than naming a specific hour at the start. However, when the financing calendar is congested with a large number of issues, this approach may not be feasible.

   If before the bidding day the company decides to postpone the financing or call it off, it should do so a few days in advance so that the underwriters will not go to the trouble of holding their pricing meeting.

   If on the final bid day the company rejects all bids because they are not satisfactory, it may receive some criticism from Wall Street. The underwriters may feel that they did all the work necessary to enter a bid and then were not given the chance to buy the security. This criticism is in no way justified. Anyone familiar with the procedure should know that a company is completely within its rights in rejecting all bids. The only criticism to which the company lays itself open is that of its financial judgment in appraising the bid price and then rejecting it. If later on the company doesn't do as well, it may look bad. However, this is something the company should be willing to face if it thinks it made a sound judgment on the basis of all surrounding facts at the time. There are relatively few examples of competitive bids having been rejected.

2. There may be some added expense as compared with a negotiated public offering, but it is negligible for large issues. Both types of public offerings require more expense than a private sale. Of course, the company may not receive all the benefit of the savings in a private sale; it may be offset to some extent by a lower price being offered by investors.

   Either method of public offering for small issues is substantially more expensive than a private sale. Thus, the expense element of a public offering is a real disadvantage for small issues.

3. Some underwriters will strongly argue that if there is a bad market situation, with underwriters' shelves overloaded with securities, the underwriters may be reluctant to bid aggressively. In such a situation, a better price may be obtained by a negotiated public offering or private sale.

   This is where there is a real clash of opinion. Those who favor competitive bidding will say that it isn't so; that in a competitive bid, the underwriters will make a thorough canvass of the market and bid for all the market justifies. Those who favor a negotiated public offering say that there are inherent risks in competitive bidding that prevent it from producing the best price in some poor markets.

   It is interesting to note that even in

past money crunches, except for 1974, competitive bidding worked successfully for good quality bonds.

4. It may not be suitable to issues which require much sales effort. This is primarily where those who favor negotiated public offerings should rest their case. They will explain that, with a negotiated public offering, they can put on a campaign with dealers and institutional buyers throughout the country within the limits of the Securities Act. Those who favor competitive bidding will not disagree, but they do point out that the amount of work that can be done with potential buyers is definitely limited by the Securities Act. Furthermore, in a competitive public offering, a company can arrange to put forth information itself if it wishes to do so. And underwriters in a competitive bid do some missionary work in stimulating buyers' interest. It is for you to decide for your particular issue the extent of the benefit that might be gained by any extra sales campaign through a negotiated rather than a competitive public offering.

In 1974 the underwriting business was in a shambles because of a major depression in Wall Street. Some houses had gone out of business and others had their capital depleted by losses. Interest rates were at an all-time high and the buyers of securities were very apprehensive. Some companies which offered securities competitively did not get any bids and were forced to switch to a negotiated offering. In other words, competitive bidding did fail in certain situations, especially where companies were having some financial difficulties. However, it is interesting to note that even under these circumstances, $150 million AA bonds of a telephone company were sold very successfully at competitive bidding.

Because of the debacle in Wall Street and high interest rates, the Securities and Exchange Commission permitted companies under their jurisdiction to sell common stock on a negotiated basis, and also senior securities if the company could show that no bids would be received. Because the buyers were in the driver's seat, they dictated very severe terms for senior issues which were offered on a negotiated basis.

You should understand that underwriters despise competitive bidding and they will go to extremes to talk a company out of it. If you were an underwriter, wouldn't you prefer to have an underwriting in your hot little hand rather than having to bid for it? Precisely!

Competitive bidding has been an excellent discipline in our securities markets. And a good rule of thumb to use, for a company which is subject to regulation such as a utility, is to use competitive bidding unless it can be shown conclusively that there would be a measurable savings in price, based on net proceeds to the company, and terms.

Negotiated Public Offering

If you have read the steps in a competitive public offering, you will have a good background for public offerings in general. Many of the details of a negotiated offering are similar, and there is no need to go through each step. The brief summary of a negotiated public offering which follows is for the purpose of bringing out its characteristics in order to assist you in your appraisal of when to use it and how to proceed.

How a Company Decides on Which Underwriter to Use

The choice of an underwriter by a company may be a result of previous dealings with an underwriter, recommendation of someone in another company or solicitation by an underwriter. There are a variety of types of underwriting firms, and the company should seek one which can best handle the type and size of offering contemplated.

If a company has a desirable security to sell, it will do well to visit three underwriting firms before it makes a decision as to which one to use. Such an approach is perfectly satisfactory but should be handled properly. It would be unwise and unnecessary to visit more than about three. The company should explain to each one visited that two other underwriters are being considered.

The company should provide the underwriters with complete information. What information will be necessary depends on the nature of the company and the extent to which detailed financial information is publicly available. A package of material might include the latest annual and quarterly report, a prospectus if one was issued within recent years, historical financial statements and a description of the nature of the business. It might be helpful to provide this information in a specially prepared brochure. It should include five-year forecast income and cash flow statements with an item showing the need for outside funds. Companies may be hesitant to give underwriters such inside information. However, underwriters should be hung if they failed to treat it as confidential, and any responsible underwriter ought to be able to be trusted in this regard. You should explain that after they have had time to review the material and decide on a recommendation that you will visit them again to hear their story. Prior to visiting the underwriters, the company should formulate its own financial plan, but it should not give its plan to the underwriters. The company should be seeking a completely independent view. When the company revisits the underwriters, it should expect to hear the underwriters' suggestions as to a proposed method of financing and alternate methods, with advantages and disadvantages of each. The company may wish to change its plan based on the recommendation of the investment bankers.

One company had an interesting experience with underwriters when they used this approach to pick an underwriter. They visited too many underwriters and got confused with the conflicting suggestions. In order to solve the problem, they invited all of them to meet with the management at the company's office at the same time to present their views. It was at a time when the stock market was at a peak. It was interesting to observe the various views and some of the superficial thinking that went into their reasoning. Three underwriters recommended straight debt, two convertibles and two common. The company's debt ratio was already on the high side and its stock was at a high price. It was a rather obvious situation for the sale of common, and subsequent events showed that the sale of debt or convertibles would have been a serious mistake.

When you meet with underwriters to seek their suggestions, there will naturally be some discussion of the price at which the security might be sold and the compensation that the underwriters would charge. However, the company should not base its decision on which one to use solely on price and compensation. It should form its opinion on an overall appraisal. Any price mentioned this far in advance of the offering date would only be a tentative price and might be subject to change due to circumstances which would occur before the offering date.

However, the company should track the action of the market from this point on with a comparable securities index so that when the time comes to actually set the price, the company will have an idea of how the price compares with the original suggested price of the underwriters in light of subsequent market changes.

At this time the company should pick one of the underwriters to handle the deal. The reason this should be done at this time is that, from here on, the company and underwriter will have to work closely together and it would be highly impractical to carry on any further contact with the other underwriters.

An underwriting firm will stress that, in negotiated public offerings, there is an advantage of sticking with one firm for all of a company's financing. This perhaps applies to the greatest extent when the company's business is of a very special nature. The underwriter develops a thorough knowledge of the company's business and can better advise the company on financial policy. However, a company should not by any means feel tied to an underwriting firm. It should expect to get the very best service and it should be alert to any indication that this is not being received. The company should not hesitate to make known any dissatisfaction, and, if it is not satisfactorily explained or corrected, the company should seek out another investment firm. There is no basic difference in the purchasing of the services of an underwriter from the purchasing of many other specialized services. Competition must exist in the underwriting business as in the rest of our economy.

Of course, if a company is not well known, reputable underwriters will also have a decision to make as to whether they wish to handle the issue. Securities are their merchandise and they do not wish to have their names connected with companies which do not have good management and a satisfactory outlook. If the company is a new venture, the underwriters may wish to hire some experts to study the company, at its expense, so that the underwriters can better decide whether they are interested.

Once the underwriter has been chosen and a financing program developed, the underwriter may wish to visit the company's plants and obtain more information. Then a financing schedule must be worked out between the underwriter and the company. This will include a decision as to who will be on the team doing the work and what each one will do.

Formation of the Underwriting Group

The company may first be asked what other underwriters it might wish to have as members in the group because of some past relationship, or because they are located in the company's territory. The manager will then decide on the other members of the group on the basis of various considerations, including their abilities to handle the particular issue. A final list will be submitted to the company.

The dealers who are to be included in the selling group will be added as they indicate an interest in the issue. These are the selected dealers. If a company wishes local distribution of its securities, it will wish to have local dealers favored. A certain amount of the issue can be set aside for them. Those favoring a negotiated public offering contend that this choice of underwriters and dealers by the company gives an advantage over a competitive public offering. However, this advantage is not necessarily entirely lacking in a competitive public offering. It is possible to arrange for certain local underwriters and dealers to be worked into the picture in one way or another.

Preparation of the Registration Statement and the Prospectus

This will be done by the managing underwriter and the company, along with lawyers and accountants, and other experts if necessary. Insofar as possible, the prospectus should present the facts in an interesting manner, since it is the basic sales document. It will have to be checked thoroughly by a lawyer and even rewritten in parts to make certain that it discloses all relevant information. It then has to be filed with the Securities and Exchange Commission.

Just before the Registration Statement is filed, the company should discuss with the underwriters the matter of price and compensation under the then-existing market conditions. Once the Registration Statement is filed, it is too late to change underwriters. This step is necessary so that everybody understands what to expect. If the market does change before the underwriters purchase the bonds from the company, the underwriters should so alert the company to avoid any subsequent misunderstanding. Of course, since the underwriters do not commit themselves at this point, price and compensation are of necessity matters of opinion.

Educational Program

For a large issue, the selected dealers should be thoroughly briefed by a series of meetings throughout the country, within the limits of the Securities Act. As previously discussed, this is one of the advantages suggested as favoring a negotiated public offering over a competitive. The underwriters have an incentive to see that the dealers are informed more than would exist in a competitive offering. Also, after the Registration Statement is filed, luncheons and meetings may be held with large potential investors in order to acquaint them better with the forthcoming issue. However, the means employed must be strictly within the bounds of the Securities Act.

Pricing and Spread

The underwriters are not committed for the security until the purchase contract is signed. Just before the signing, there will be a final meeting between the company and the underwriters in order to set the price to the public and the underwriters' compensation. In order to be able to negotiate, the company should have available a record of the price of all recent offerings of similar issues showing the spreads. Upon signing, the underwriters agree to buy the entire issue from the company regardless of market reception, except for the "out" clauses in the contract. This is discussed in Chapter 10.

A negotiated underwriting today has in some instances really become similar to a best efforts type of deal. The underwriters try to get the entire issue spoken for by investors before they agree to purchase the security from the company. There is, of course, some risk that potential buyers will back down when the issue becomes available. An underwriter may take on some of the issue without having it sold. However, don't labor under the impression that an underwriting firm buys the issue from you and waits until then to get purchasers lined up.

Advantages and Disadvantages of Negotiated Public Offering

The advantages and disadvantages of a negotiated public offering as compared to a competitive offering have been fairly well discussed already. To repeat, the principal advantage is the opportunity for the underwriters to conduct effective information meetings. This becomes more important for securities which are little known by potential purchasers. Further, underwriters may contend there is less of a hazard to them in a negotiated public offering, particularly when markets are adverse, and that they can get a better price from investors.

The principal disadvantage as compared to competitive bidding is that in competitive bidding the opportunity is given to every underwriting firm to make the best bid. Whether this is an advantage of competitive public offering will depend on the nature of the security; that is, whether it is sufficiently well known to potential investors so that the underwriters will make bids commensurate with the real worth of the issue.

A negotiated public offering, of course, leaves the company with the problem of having to negotiate the price and the compensation. In competitive bidding, the difference in bids by various underwriting groups for a particular issue is clear evidence that underwriters have different ideas as to the price at which the issue can be sold. If you are working with one underwriter, on a negotiated basis, how would you know whether you chose the underwriter who would give the best price?

To show how underwriters may differ in their idea of spread, we will use as an example a competitive common offering made in 1974 when Wall Street and security markets were in a mess. It was a utility rights offering.

The company had set the subscription price about 9% under the market. The company asked for bids on spread. There were three bids, \$2.05, \$1.24 and \$0.80. The \$2.05

figure represented 17% of the subscription price, an altogether ridiculous figure. The company rejected the bids and offered the stock to its shareholders without an underwriting. It got a 65% subscription and was very pleased with the results.

A negotiated public offering assumes that a company will have sufficient knowledge to handle the negotiation, and that it can rely on the soundness of the underwriter's judgment. An underwriter, of course, wants to stay in business, and you are his client. It should be in his interest to give you a fair deal so that there will be a continuing relationship. However, a company should be well armed with all relative data on recent offerings, etc. in order to negotiate the price and spread. It should not be a patsy and just put its life in the underwriter's hands.

The underwriter's compensation on negotiated offerings may be more than for competitive offerings.

Private sale will be discussed next. Then it will be compared with both types of public offerings.

Private Sale

Private sale is also referred to as private placement, direct placement and private deal. In this book, the term "private sale" will be used.

We have previously mentioned briefly what is meant by a private sale, but it will now be necessary to explain more fully what it constitutes. As we have already seen, under the Securities Act of 1933, a public offering of corporate securities, with certain exceptions, must be registered with the Securities and Exchange Commission, and each written offer to sell must be accompanied by a prospectus. Private sale is exempt from such procedure.

One of the characteristics of a private sale is that a company's securities are sold by the company in a non-public offering to sophisticated investors. Title to the securities passes directly to the investors from the company. There is no intermediate purchase and taking of title by an underwriter.

There may be someone assisting the company, who probably will be an investment banker but need not be. If there is a third party, ordinarily he will act as agent of the company, and, in this book, no matter who performs this function, he will be referred to as the agent. His pay will be called "agent's fee." He will not take title to the securities.

Requisites for Private Sale

The exemption of private sale from the Act applies, provided there are three features present:

1. The number of potential investors to which the security is offered are limited in number.
2. The purchasers are informed investors who are in a position to obtain the information as to the merits of the security without the protection of the provisions of the Securities Act.
3. The purchasers buy the securities with the original intention of holding them as an investment rather than for resale.

When the Securities Act first came into existence, test number 1 above was considered quite important. A conventional rule in the street was to limit the number of potential purchasers to which the security was to be offered to between 12 to 25. As time went on the number was gradually expanded. There have been a few instances in which as many as 100 purchasers have been solicited in a private sale for high grade bonds. If the number were indiscriminately increased, the spirit behind the exemption would be violated.

Today, the most important test seems to be the second, the type of purchasers. The Securities Act was primarily designed to protect unsophisticated investors against inadequate and misleading information; hence, the prospectus with all the penalties against such practices. The large institutional investors such as insurance companies, trustees of pension plans, investment companies, etc., with their trained staffs of analysts, can protect themselves better than the minimum requirements of the Securities Act. Therefore, offerings limited in scope to that type of investor can, justifiably, be exempt.

The third test—original intent of the purchasers to hold the security as an investment—is for the purpose of preventing circumvention of the Securities Act by means of a private sale to a few large, sophisticated purchasers, who then turn around and resell the securities, without registering with the Securities and Exchange Commission and without a prospectus, to a broad list of purchasers who should be protected by the Act. This test must be met. Obviously, if there is an intent to resell, the exemption does not apply, because the purchasers in effect become underwriters, buying for the purpose of resale. This does not mean, however, that the investors who buy securities at a private sale can't resell them. They can do so, and without registering them with the Securities and Exchange Commission, provided in the first instance they bought the securities with the original intent to hold them as an investment.

There is no fixed time limit as to how long they must be held. The fact that the original purchaser must buy with intent to hold as an investment, requires a thorough analysis of the security by the purchaser and a willingness to assume all risk involved in the security, rather than just the risk of price involved in quick resale to someone else. A company selling securities at private sale may require a letter or statement from the purchasers affirming their intent to acquire for investment. This is for the purpose of protecting the company. On the other hand, the purchasers may require that the company agree to use its best efforts to register the securities in case they should decide later to sell them. This protects the purchasers against the expense of registering if the SEC later requires it. For convertible issues and warrants which were originally sold privately, the resulting stock may have to be so registered.

The third test obviously eliminates an investment banker from acting as an underwriter, as defined in the Act, in a private sale, because an underwriter by definition does not purchase for investment but for redistribution. An underwriter can only act as an agent in private sale.

The private sale of senior securities does not raise much of a problem, but there can also be a private sale of common stock to insiders. And there may be a private sale in an acquisition. In those situations the question becomes much more sticky. In 1974, the Securities and Exchange Commission issued a Rule 146 covering private sales in general. Some of the points it covered are:

1. Sophistication and access.

   The potential purchasers must be knowledgeable in finance and be able to get adequate information on which to make a judgment.
2. Restriction on resale.
3. Size of offering units.

   Large units look more like a private sale because they tend to be sold to large investors.
4. Manner of offering.

   A face-to-face offering would point more to private sale than less-direct contact.
5. The relationship of the offerees would have an effect. For example, executive officers of a company are a related group.
6. The number of purchasers.

   The rule includes 35 as the number of purchasers, but excluded from this number is any purchaser who acquires an amount greater than $150,000 for cash. In determining the number, the clients of one investment advisor would each be treated as a single person.

   Since most purchasers of senior securities buy in amounts greater than $150,000, there is no real number limitation for such securities.

We can summarize the above discussion in a definition: a direct sale is an offering of securities by a company, with or without the assistance of an agent, to informed investors not indiscriminately unlimited in numbers, who have original intent to purchase for investment purposes and not for resale. The problem is a simple one for good-grade senior securities. The problem of applying Rule 146 arises with common stock issues.

Agent's Use

In either a competitive or negotiated public offering of senior securities, you will use an underwriter, but in a private sale you have a choice as to whether to handle the sale yourself or use an agent. Therefore, before we get to our example of private sale, we will give you the pros and cons to weigh in answering the question: Should you use an agent?

The agent need not necessarily be an investment banker. Some consulting firms and banks assist with private sales. However, an investment banker has an advantage because his regular dealing in securities keeps him in close contact with prices of securities, potential purchasers and terms in recent offerings.

The advantages of using an agent, assuming that he is an investment banker or that he is equally qualified to act as an agent, are as follows:

1. He should know the potential purchasers who will be most interested in the issue. If a company has only a limited knowledge of the potential purchasers, it may miss the best possible market.
2. He is thoroughly familiar with the current market for securities and can assist the company in deciding on the price it should receive, and the terms necessary to attract purchasers.
3. He can assist in negotiating with the purchasers both as to price and terms. The agent, being in between the two, is in a better position to bargain than the company dealing directly. The company should not delegate this job entirely to an agent, however, because the agent may have a tendency to favor terms which will facilitate closing the deal quickly in order to minimize his time and effort. In fact, a company should be certain that the agent gives no indication that he is trying to favor the buyers in order to compensate them for past tough deals or to keep their goodwill for future deals.
4. He can advise the company on financial policy, as to type and amount of security to sell.
5. He can help prepare the company's story to present to purchasers with the company's assistance, so that it will include all necessary information in the proper form. There may be some advantage to the agent doing the job, because the agent can appraise the situation more favorably than the company itself without appearing self-serving.
6. He can do a "no-name canvass" to determine potentially interested purchasers. This is discussed subsequently.

The buyers of securities generally have no objection to having an agent introduce the issue or be a party to the negotiations. The only disadvantage of using a competent agent is the cost. While it is relatively small for a large, high grade bond or preferred stock issue, it increases for small issues and ones which are more speculative and harder to sell. Figures on cost are given subsequently.

Agents tend to be used more for larger issues than small. Size of issue is a factor because of the higher relative cost for small issues. Whether a company uses an agent will depend on the experience of the company's financial officer, the character and size of the security being offered and the conditions of the security market.

Steps in Private Sale–
A Complete Example

Since the procedure in private sale is quite different from either type of public offering, we will outline the steps which are taken as we did for the competitive public offering. This will help you see how private sale works and assist you in deciding whether it is best suited to your financing.

Instead of using dates when each step is taken, we will use the same method of countdown by days up to the time the company has obtained an agreement as to price and terms, the day of the moral commitment by both parties. That date will correspond to the day in competitive public offering when the company receives bids, or in a negotiated public offering when the underwriters sign the agreement to purchase. Thus, the figures in the left-hand column opposite each step are the number of days prior to the day when the company knows it will get the money and the price. The number of days taken by each subsequent step necessary to button up the financing will be designated by a plus sign.

Our example is an industrial company which has decided to sell $5 million of debentures to retire short-term bank loans. The material is disguised, but it is based on an actual offering. We are assuming that the type of financing is such as to justify private sale as the best method.

The company's Financial Vice President has not done any long-term financing in recent years and is not familiar with the best potential purchasers or security markets. Therefore, he has decided to use an underwriting firm as an agent to assist him.

24 Company–Choice of agent–preliminary conference with underwriter.

The Company sold some common stock through an underwriter ten years ago and was satisfied with the performance of that firm; so the Financial Vice President decided to use it as their agent. If the Company had not already had an investment banking firm in mind, it could choose one in the manner explained under a negotiated public offering by visiting two or three firms. But it should make its choice before proceeding further with sale of the issue.

The Financial Vice President visited the investment banking firm to have a preliminary discussion. He outlined his financial requirements, explained why he had decided on debentures, went over his financial statements and discussed the feasibility of private sale. The investment banker suggested that because the Company was not very well known–it was only moderate in size, and it was in a highly competitive field–the debentures would barely have the equivalent of *A* grade credit rating, even though they would represent a moderate percentage of total capitalization.

The investment banker was asked his fee to act as agent, and his reply was one-half to three-quarters of 1% of the principal amount. He would think the matter over and let the company know a definite figure at their next meeting.

The investment banker outlined the type of report for the Company to prepare for review at their next meeting. In the meantime, the investment banker would make a "no-name canvass" for a potential purchaser.

23 Agent–"No-name canvass."

In a private sale, a security should not be shopped around among potential purchasers. If all of the issue could be taken by one purchaser, then the company should decide on the most likely candidate and work with that purchaser until the deal is consummated or until it becomes evident that the parties cannot reach an agreement. Then another purchaser may be sought out. If more than one purchaser is required in order to absorb the issue, he will readily agree that others may be contacted. In certain special instances the original one contacted may be willing to bring in others. Or the Company or its agent may do the job. Who will do this should be made clear at the start.

Informed investors will show no interest in a security offered at private sale if the company attempts to offer it to other purchasers at the same time when there is no need to do so in order to absorb the issue. News travels fast in the financial community, and such a wrong approach will cool off a deal. It will make the security shopworn. Once that news gets around, potential purchasers will shy away.

There are various reasons why shopping around does not work in private sale. Consider the attitude of the institutional investors. Many securities sold through private sale are of a type that requires much study. A purchaser does not like to go to a lot of trouble and then find out that he may not have an opportunity to buy the issue.

But perhaps more important is the fact that no purchaser wants a price which he may suggest used as a means to trade with other potential purchasers. And if a company shopped around, that is just what would happen. One purchaser would name a tentative price; then the company would merely go to another and say, "I have already been bid such a price; will you make a better bid?"

Finally, the following thought naturally runs through the heads of potential purchasers, if it gets rumored around that the issue has been shopped: "There must be something the matter with the security, for no one seems to want it. Why should we bother with it?"

In certain instances, regulatory authorities have insisted in a private sale that "best efforts" be made to assure some competition for an issue. Then the company must offer the security in a limited way to more than one purchaser. It may ask several in succession, provided each knows what is going on, or it might ask each purchaser to submit a price at a certain date. A security must be of a standard quality without any special features for even this limited type of shopping to work. The extent of shopping in such a situation will be dependent upon the regulatory authorities' wishes. The company should, of course, resist being pushed in this direction, and if it is forced to shop, it should explain to any purchaser contacted all the facts of the situation. It will get a cool reception from some potential purchasers.

Of course, if a company handles a private sale itself, it may inquire of an institutional investor whether he is interested in considering purchase, but the company is more limited in this respect than an agent. A form of shopping to find out potentially interested purchasers, the so-called "no-name canvass" mentioned above, only can be done through an agent or third party.

The agent can talk with investors without mentioning the company's name, but just describe approximately the amount of securities to be issued and the type of industry in which the company operates. Potential purchasers can be asked whether they might be interested in this type of investment.

Since this form of shopping involves no effort on the part of purchasers and no discussion of price, it is not frowned upon. Its only purpose is to seek out the best market. However, once it is decided to offer the security to a purchaser and the data are turned over to that purchaser for investigation, all shopping should cease.

For our Company, the agent was so familiar with the type of purchasers that would be most interested that, after only three phone calls, it was decided that a particular insurance company would be the best candidate.

20 Agent and insurance company—Preliminary discussion.

The agent telephoned the insurance company explaining the name of the Company, the amount of financing, that the money would be needed immediately to repay bank loans, that a report would be available shortly and also asking what terms the insurance company might be thinking of. The insurance company requested a few days to think the matter over.

20 Company—Preparation of report.

During the week after the preliminary meeting with the underwriter, the Financial Vice President and his staff prepared a report to be used in the sale as suggested by the agent. The agent, rather than the company, may prepare the report. This will depend on the individual situation.

The report included complete information necessary to evaluate the security: a description of the Company's business, some figures on the industry, where the Company fitted into the industry, complete audited financial figures for ten years and pro forma figures for the current year giving effect to the financing.

The Company's financing needs were spelled out with a where-got, where-gone statement, or cash budget, and a statement of how the new money would be used. The report included five-year forecast statements and information as to future financial requirements for the next five years, so that the purchaser could tell whether the financing would be adequate. A brief summary was included of the principal terms of the debenture which the Company desired.

A good report is well worthwhile. It may affect the purchasers' interest; it will speed the decision by the prospective purchasers; it may well affect the price and terms. While preparing the report, the Company discussed some of the points on the phone with the agent. When the report was finished, a copy was sent to the agent, who then visited the Company to go over the properties and get the report in final form. At this time, the agent said that his fee would be one-half of 1% of the proceeds of the offering, which would mean $25,000. The agent showed the Company the fees it had charged on other debt issues recently and that one-half of 1% was in fact its minimum fee. The reason for the low fee was because it appeared that the financing could be arranged without too much difficulty, and because the Company was preparing the report. The Company considered this quite reasonable. The Financial Vice President was acquainted with financial officers of two other industrial companies which recently arranged somewhat similar financings through private sale. One was larger and better known; the fee was one-half of 1%. The other was smaller and the fee was 1%. The one-half of 1% for this issue also checks as being low in comparison with published average figures for similar-sized offerings for industrial companies. The $25,000 is the minimum for which it is worthwhile for a large underwriting firm to act.

16 Insurance company–Preliminary analysis.

After the insurance company's staff made a brief analysis of material available to them from published sources, the insurance company called the agent back to say that they might be interested in $5 million principal amount, 7 1/8%, 15-year debenture with an annual sinking fund of $250,000 resulting in an average term of 9.8 years, with a ten-year non-refundable provision.

The agent relayed this information to the Company, and suggested that the terms were satisfactory as a basis of preliminary negotiation. The Company wanted a special call provision and a lighter sinking fund provision for the first few years. The agent suggested that these points be outlined in the report.

13 Company and agent–Price discussion.

Because shopping around doesn't work, a company must know well the price it should receive. As stated above, this is one of the advantages of using an agent if a company is not thoroughly familiar with security markets.

The Company had gathered information on indexes of yields on outstanding issues of *A* grade industrial bonds and recent new issues of such grade bonds offered through negotiated public offering, in order to become acquainted with yields on bonds. The agent prepared a similar table as well as a list of recent private sales. In a conference between agent and the Company, it was decided that a 7 1/8% interest rate and a price of 100 was generally satisfactory. It appeared slightly on the generous side under then existing market conditions, but since the Company wished to press its demands for reduced sinking fund provisions and a special call feature, it was felt that the rate should be accepted.

11 Company, agent and insurance company—General conference.

A conference was held at the insurance company, with the following present:

Company Financial Vice President
Company Comptroller
Company Counsel
Agent
Insurance Company Vice President in charge of Industrial Investments
Insurance Company Analyst
Insurance Company Counsel

The report was handed to the insurance company, and the agent explained that the Company wanted reduced sinking fund payments during the next few years because of substantial capital improvements. The Company also wanted the right to retire the debt at 100% for three years if it did so through sale of common. It was considering the sale of common for such a purpose, provided earnings improved and market conditions permitted.

The insurance company representatives had a list of questions. The Company showed where the answers were contained in the report, answered them verbally or agreed to furnish data as soon as they returned to their office. The insurance company requested time to review the report and the Company's special requests on sinking fund and call feature.

9 Insurance company—Counterproposal.

The insurance company called the agent and said that they were satisfied, but they proposed that the sinking fund be reduced during the first three or four years, with the average life no longer than 11 years, and that the debt be redeemable at 101 for the first three years if it is retired through the sale of common stock. The insurance company, in looking over the Company's financial needs, felt that it should have $500,000 more working capital, and suggested that the amount of bonds be increased to $5,500,000.

6 Company, agent and insurance company conference—Final conference on principal terms.

All members of the three parties met again to iron out final terms. After much discussion covering all phases of the financing, including indenture provisions, etc., the following was agreed on regarding the principal points which had been in controversy:

a. Increasing the amount to $5,500,000;
b. Sinking fund which would produce an average maturity of 11.1 years;
c. Special call feature of 101 for four years if debt is refunded through common equity financing.

5 Insurance company—Outline of terms, sometimes called letter of interest, purchase suggestion or memorandum of terms.

The insurance company prepared an outline of the proposed financing and submitted it to the agent. It included interest rate, sinking fund payments, schedule of call prices, outline of restrictive covenants relating to dividends and creation of additional indebtedness, lease rental obligations and restrictions on loans to subsidiaries and subsidiary indebtedness. The purpose of this memorandum is to reduce the terms of the agreement to writing. It is not an agreement to buy.

It is quite important that prior to this point the Company consider with its management team all possible effects the financing might have on the operations of the company. If a company discovers some difficulties after the Financial Vice President has agreed to the memorandum of terms, and the loan committee of the insurance company approves the deal, the insurance company will be embarrassed to seek further approval from its loan committee. The memorandum of terms is subject to satisfactory legal documents being prepared, and the condition that nothing is found out about the Company on further investigation by the insurance company, which is contrary to previous representations.

3 Company–Acceptance–moral commitment.

The final terms were accepted by the Company with minor changes. Thus, the Company became morally committed.

At this stage of the negotiation, the insurance company expects the Company to go ahead with the deal if its Finance Committee approves. In other words, now is the last time for the Company to withdraw if it has reason to object to the price or the terms. It has happened occasionally that working out all of the complete terms subsequent to the moral commitment has taken considerable time and that insoluble disagreement has arisen.

The Company informed the insurance company of the bank that would act as trustee. Where there is only one purchaser, the insurance company may be willing to eliminate the trustee.

"Zero" Day–Insurance Company–Finance Committee approval, moral commitment.

Before the insurance company representative can morally commit his company, the financing must be passed on by the Finance Committee. The Finance Committee of the insurance company met and approved the deal, and the agent was so informed. Thus, at this time both parties are morally committed to the terms expressed in the letter of interest.

The price is set as of this date just as it is set in competitive bidding on the day a bid is accepted, or in a negotiated offering on the day the underwriters agree to buy the bonds. If interest rates decrease before the final papers are signed, the Company cannot expect to have a change made; nor will the insurance company seek any change if interest rates go up. Billions of dollars of financing have been arranged on this basis, and there have been practically no cases in which either party has welched.

Thus, it was 24 days from the start of negotiations to the time that the Company knew it would get the money and the general terms.

As we previously stated, our competitive bidding example was not typical as far as time is concerned; under ordinary circumstances, a competitive bid can be completed, even for a utility, in about two or three months. The comparison is still not fair, because a utility offering takes additional time due to special regulatory procedure. Although no set rule can be given because of the many variables in each offering, private sale does represent a quicker method of obtaining a commitment on price. In a private sale, much additional time may elapse before the Company gets its money, because there are still many things left to be done after both parties are morally committed. Part of the delay which ensues may be due to the lack of need to hurry, since the price has been set.

+1 Insurance company–Preparation of purchase agreement and indenture.

A revised outline of the terms was forwarded to the insurance company counsel for preparation of legal documents.

Outside counsel for the insurance company started preparing the Debenture Purchase Agreement, and Indenture, both of which will be submitted to the insurance company's counsel for review. The Company will pay these fees.

When completed they were released to the Company and trustee for review by their outside counsel. The Company also pays these counsel fees.

Sometimes the legal work has been completed in a week, but generally it takes a month or longer.

+1 *Insurance company—Representatives visit company.*

Two representatives from the insurance company visited the Company's plant to examine the conditions of the building and equipment, familiarize themselves with the products and production methods, meet members of the management and gather statistical data and other information.

They prepared a brief memorandum stating that no unfavorable conditions were found. Subsequently an extensive report was prepared saying that the debentures represented a satisfactory investment.

If there is some uncertainty regarding the credit of the Company, the visit to the plant will take place prior to the signing of the memorandum of terms. Under the circumstances existing in this situation, the memorandum of terms was subject to no unfavorable circumstances being found on examination of the Company's property.

+31 *Company, insurance company and trustee—Conference to iron out details.*

Representatives and legal counsels of the company, the insurance company and the trustee met to discuss the legal documents and iron out any problems. Subsequently, this required numerous phone calls and one further conference.

+109 *Company and insurance company—Sign Debenture Purchase Agreement.*

The Debenture Purchase Agreement, or Letter of Agreement, comes some time after the moral commitment of both parties. It may appear an unnecessary document at this late date. As far as the moral commitment is concerned, it *is* unnecessary; however, it contains certain additional information and provisions, such as:

Conditions which must be fulfilled before the closing, including required legal documents and legal opinions stating validity of corporate existence and the proposed new issue, and the existence of good title to properties.

A statement of existing liens, litigation, taxes, large contracts and conditions of properties.

Agreements to furnish financial statements regularly, and to permit the purchaser to inspect properties, etc.

+110 *Company, insurance company and trustee—Closing.*

A meeting was held at the offices of the insurance company with representatives of the insurance company, the Company and the trustee present, at which time the insurance company delivered a check for $5,500,000 and accrued interest. The trustee, in turn, delivered the bonds to the insurance company—which were dated on the first of the month.

Generally, interest starts to accrue from the date on which the company gets the money. A bond may be dated on any working day of the month, but generally new issues are dated on the 1st.

If it is going to be a long time from the time of the commitment to the final closing, there may be a commitment fee to the closing date when interest will start to accrue.

If you are seeking information about the time that a private sale is consummated, the interest date may be an approximate clue, or if there is a commitment fee, the date from which the commitment fee started running.

These are the basic steps which occur in a private sale of securities. They will vary with different purchasers and different circumstances surrounding the security; however, the general pattern will be similar and the basic principles the same.

Advantages of Private Sale

The advantages of private sale, from the point of view of the company considering its use, are as given below:

1. *Speed and flexibility.* The Securities Act, necessitating a registration statement,

prospectus, etc., for public sale of securities, requires much preliminary work and time scheduling. In a public offering, there is a 20-day waiting period, unless shortened by the commission, between the date of filing of the registration statement and the effective date, at which time the securities may be publicly offered. A private sale can be arranged more quickly because all of this is eliminated. Large institutional buyers of securities will stick to their word once they have agreed to such matters as interest rate. Drawing up the final papers can be done subsequently.

There have been cases, for companies well-known to the purchasers, where a commitment has been obtained in a week. Such speed is the exception rather than the rule. It could not be expected for a new and complicated type of situation, but it illustrates this advantage. As previously pointed out, from the day of the commitment on price to the day when the company gets its money may be longer in a private sale than in a public offering, because of the details to be completed after the moral commitment.

The timing is more flexible in a private sale. Once the process of registration for a public offering gets underway, a company may hesitate to postpone the offering, because certain of the material will have to be redone in order to bring it up to date when the offering is renewed. The extent to which the material will have to be redone will depend on the length of the postponement. A private sale can more easily be postponed or abandoned. Thus, if for some unusual reason a company needs money in a hurry, or may have some uncertainty about its money requirements, a private sale has this advantage.

Also, if the market for securities is uncertain, then the speed and flexibility of a private sale may appear advantageous. However, this latter point assumes that it is possible to make some judgment as to future movement of the securities markets, which is a hazardous guessing game. In other words, if you used private sale in order to speed up the financing because you thought the market was going to get worse, you would, in effect, be trying to forecast future market movements.

2. *Financing costs savings.* There is no underwriters' spread as such. If an investment banker is used as an agent to assist the company in arranging the sale, the fee is smaller than the payment to an underwriter if the issue were underwritten and publicly offered.

Financing expenses are lower than with a public offering because there is neither the expense of a prospectus nor of other costs of a public offering.

With all public offerings of debt, there is a trustee whose purpose is to see that the company complies with the terms of indenture. This means the bondholders' position is protected without their having to watch the details themselves. In some private sales, a note may be used as the debt instrument and the trustee dispensed with. There may be other expenses eliminated, such as listing fees.

The dollar savings in financing costs become more important for small issues. Exhibit 8-9, Part I brings out the general difference in magnitude compared to public offerings, by size of issue for total financing costs—underwriters' compensation and expenses combined.

These figures on financing costs should be used with caution, because as will be seen when the matter is discussed more fully, they may vary with market conditions and all the circumstances surrounding a particular issue. If you are concerned with this point for a particular offering, you will wish to obtain comparable data under existing market conditions. However, the figures do illustrate that for issues under $10 million, the savings in financing cost, as a percent of proceeds, start to be of real significance.

It is of interest also to view the savings in terms of difference in yield to maturity. For this purpose, we have assumed that we are dealing with a bond with a 7 1/8% interest coupon and a 30-year maturity, and that both in a private sale and a public offering the ultimate purchasers paid a price of 100%. Then the yield based on the net proceeds to the company, after deducting the financing costs as shown in Part I, can be compared in Exhibit 8-9, Part II. Thus, the yield difference might be more than 0.50% for a small issue, but might amount to less than 0.05% for $50 million. As will be pointed out later, a company should not by any means expect to realize all of these savings. These are what might be termed apparent savings. Purchasers are well aware of them, and expect to participate by receiving a higher yield. For larger issues, which could be sold satisfactorily publicly, it would be questionable whether any net savings would be realized. However, the picture is different for smaller issues. Financing costs are an important factor accounting for the greater use of private sale for small issues, as was previously pointed out.

3. *Future readjustment of terms.* Due to unforeseen developments, a company may in the future have to seek waiver of covenants, or a change in debt repayment schedules, etc. If a company's debt is publicly held and it is unable to obtain necessary consents, it may have to call all of the outstanding debt and issue new bonds.

In a private sale, it may be easier to

Exhibit 8-9

GENERAL MAGNITUDE OR DIFFERENCE IN FINANCING COSTS FOR DEBT SECURITIES SOLD PRIVATELY AND PUBLICLY

PART I

FINANCING COSTS–UNDERWRITERS COMPENSATION OR FEE AND FINANCING EXPENSES

	Private Sale		Public Sale	
Size of Issue	Amount	Percent of Proceeds	Amount	Percent of Proceeds
$ 1,000,000	$ 17,500	1 3/4%	$ 80,000	8%
10,000,000	75,000	3/4%	150,000	1 1/2%
50,000,000	250,000	1/2%	500,000	1%

PART II

DIFFERENCE IN FINANCING COSTS TRANSLATED INTO YIELD FOR 7 1/8% BOND MATURING IN 30 YEARS. SOLD AT PRICE TO PUBLIC 100.

	Private Sale		Public Sale		
Size of Issue	Net Proceeds to Company	Yield at Net Proceeds to Company	Net Proceeds to Company	Yield at Net Proceeds to Company	Difference in Yield
$ 1,000,000	98.25	7.27%	92.00	7.82%	0.55%
10,000,000	99.25	7.19	98.50	7.25	0.06
50,000,000	99.50	7.17	99.00	7.20	0.03

make a change, because there may be only one or at least only a small number of purchasers, who are all known to the company. The holders may be willing to make an adjustment. Of course, they may ask for some form of compensation, such as an increase in the interest rate if the change adversely alters their credit position.

This advantage may be quite important for a company which is not standard in nature and for which it is difficult to foretell the company's future requirements at the time of financing. If a company runs into financial difficulty, and is unable to meet its commitments, bankruptcy or receivership would result with a publicly held debt issue. In a private sale, it may be possible to work out a readjustment.

If a company contemplates that changes may be required, it should keep the number of purchasers of the bonds to a minimum so that it will be easier to get agreement to changes. It might even be worthwhile to accept a higher yield in order to keep the number of purchasers small.

This advantage disappears if the original purchasers redistribute the issue to a broader group of investors. And it does not apply to a similar extent if the company has previously offered another series of the same security or other debt publicly so that there are already a large number of holders.

4. *A complicated financing can be explained to experts.* Private sale makes it possible to explain in detail a complicated financing to a small group of expert purchasers. In a public offering, purchasers cannot be approached without a "red herring" prospectus, and then the material covered should be restricted to that included in the prospectus.

This is an important advantage for certain types of complicated offerings. In fact, it may be the governing reason in such a situation. A new, untried, intricate deal may have to be financed at the start by a small group of experienced investors. Even if the issue were sold publicly, the buyers would undoubtedly be limited to the same ones contacted in a private sale. Nothing would be gained by a public offering.

5. *Special features.* It may be possible to work out some special feature more readily than in a public offering. The delayed takedown represents such an example. In a delayed takedown, the purchasers agree to take the full amount of the issue. However, the company can postpone receipt of some of its money if it does not need it all immediately. In this way, the company temporarily avoids the full interest payments. On that part of the issue on which there is a delayed takedown, the company will pay a commitment fee, which is far less than the charges on the security itself. For example, the commitment fee might be at the rate of one-half of 1% per annum. There have been instances of short delayed takedowns in public offerings, but not to the extent of their use in private sale. The security markets and surrounding circumstances will determine whether delayed takedown might better be handled by the company borrowing temporarily from banks for its first money requirements, and then doing its permanent financing to repay the bank loans and provide the balance of the needed money.

In a tight money period when investors do not have funds, the company may agree to postpone taking down the funds. In such a situation, the delayed takedown is for the benefit of the purchaser and no commitment fee should be charged.

Another type of feature which has been included in some private sales is an option on the amount of the security, with or without a delayed takedown. For example, if a company is uncertain as to the ultimate cost of a project or how much earnings may be generated for construction purposes, it may wish to have an option to increase the amount. Of course, there will be a fee for this option.

Not only may special features be worked into a private sale, but, in fact, new techniques of financing may be developed.

6. *Maintain trade secrets.* If a company has a trade secret which it does not wish to reveal publicly, and the secret would have an effect on the price of its securities, it can feel free to disclose the information, on a confidential basis, in a private sale.
7. *Development of personal lender-borrower relationship.* A small company, which needs funds fairly often and can rely on one institutional lender, may be able to develop a mutual understanding with such a lender so that it has a ready source of funds.

Disadvantages of Private Sale

1. *Limited in scope.* In view of the legal restrictions on private sale, it is applicable only to securities which can be sold to well-informed investors. If a large number of investors have to be solicited and some of them are not experts in finance, private sale is out.
2. *Price may be lower.* The price at which the issue is sold will generally have to be lower than could be obtained with a public offering.

   In the first place, the purchasers are well aware of the savings in financing costs in a private sale *vs.* public sale, and they expect to share some of the savings. They feel that private sale is possible only because of them.

   Furthermore, the investors have only three basic reasons to be interested in a private sale:

   a. To get a better price or rate;
   b. To get better terms such as are in an indenture;
   c. To obtain a substantial amount of the issue as an outlet for their investable funds.

   Only when investments are scarce does point *c* exclusively represent the purchasers' main interest in a private sale. Otherwise, the purchasers would expect some additional compensation in one form or another. A possible exception to this generalization may exist in a period of chaotic security markets, when underwriters are hesitant to act with any enthusiasm because of the risks of the situation. Then private sale may produce a better price. The debatable nature of this point was discussed under competitive bidding.
3. *More restrictive terms.* The purchasers are in a relatively strong bargaining position in regard to restrictive provisions. When the securities market is in their favor, they can name certain provisions as prerequisites to a private sale. For example, in tight money markets when institutional investors are able to place all of their money at relatively attractive rates, they will require a non-refundable feature as an absolute necessity. However, in a public offering, it may be possible to avoid this feature, depending on market conditions. This may require a higher interest rate, at times from one-eighth to three-eighths of 1%. No increase in rate will budge the purchasers in a private sale to give up the non-refundable feature if they are not pressed for an outlet for their funds.

   As was previously pointed out, an effort on the part of buyers to get such restrictive features as non-refundability should not be condemned. They are not being arbitrary or dictatorial. It is their job to get it if they can. It is part of the price the company may have to pay to get money. A company should merely weigh such additional restrictions in deciding whether or not it might be better to go the public route in order to avoid them. Needless to say, a company must thoroughly understand all the possible future ramifications of restrictive provisions in order to protect its own position. If it fails in such understanding, it cannot blame someone else. Some purchasers may try to abuse their position and try to "hog-tie" a company. This is a rare exception. Well-informed purchasers are genuinely interested in giving a company freedom of financial action so that it can operate successfully. Their primary concern must be to protect their investment.

4. *No market for sinking fund purchases.* There is no market available in which to repurchase the security for sinking fund or other purposes. When a security is sold at private sale, the terms at which a company can reacquire it are spelled out in the indenture. For sinking fund purposes, the price is generally keyed to the price at which it is purchased.

   If a company sells bonds publicly when interest rates are low, and then the general level of interest rates increases, the market price of bonds will fall correspondingly. For example, a bond with a 7% interest rate and 30-year maturity would have the following prices at various yields, as shown in bond yield tables:

Yield	*Price*
7.00%	100.00%
7.50	94.07
8.00	88.69
8.50	83.81

   From these figures, it can be seen that if such a reversal in interest rates occurs, a company can achieve a substantial savings, provided there is an existing market for its securities and it is able to reacquire bonds for sinking fund or other purposes.

   When interest rates increase substantially, under special circumstances, the purchasers at private sales may be willing to resell their bonds to the company at a reduced price. However, the company must be in a good bargaining position. This situation might occur where there are a relatively large number of holders and a company has an optional sinking fund, or already has filled its fixed sinking fund requirements and wishes to anticipate future sinking funds. In other words, where the company has a choice as to whether to purchase or not, then the purchasers at private sale may be willing to accept a lower price than provided in the indenture. This is not a usual occurrence, and the price the company would have to pay undoubtedly would be higher than if there had been a public market. Where the company has a fixed amount to provide for sinking fund purposes and there are only one or two holders, it is in a poor bargaining position. In some instances, if a public sale is confined to a limited number of holders, the same situation would occur.

   In a private sale, the call for sinking fund may contain a provision that purchases for sinking fund will be on a pro rata basis among investors. If one or more investors subsequently sell their bonds publicly, the provisions still apply to the portion of the bonds held by the original investors. This type of restriction largely eliminates the possibility of purchase below the call price for sinking fund purposes while the bonds are held by the original investors. If there is no such provision, the company may find it worthwhile to try to acquire some cheap sinking fund bonds. Such a procedure is not generally frowned upon by the purchasers at private sale.

   The inability to repurchase bonds for sinking fund purposes represents a very substantial objection to private sale. It should be weighed very carefully when senior securities are sold during a period of low interest rates. Companies which have sold publicly large debt issues with heavy sinking funds in times of low interest rates, have saved millions of dollars in repurchase of their bonds in the market to satisfy the sinking fund when interest rates have increased. The extent to which it is possible for the company to retire bonds through purchase in the market, after a public offering, will depend on how well the bonds are scattered among a large number of investors, and on the extent of market activity.

5. *No rating.* The rating agencies feel that there is no purpose in rating an issue sold privately. Ratings are for the purpose of guiding the less informed purchasers as

to the general credit standing. The purchasers in a private sale have adequate statistical staffs to arrive at their own rating.

Under some circumstances this may prove to be an advantage. If a company has no ratings on its bonds already outstanding and has to issue an excessive amount of debt due to special circumstances, it may wish to avoid any rating until it has an opportunity to correct its financial picture. However, if the original purchasers do eventually resell an issue to the public, it may then be rated.

If a company already has other series of the same security which were offered publicly, this point does not apply, because the outstanding issues would be rated and the rating would be the same for all series. Nor does it apply if the company has other types of debt publicly held and rated, from which the ratings for various types of debt can easily be imputed. The rating agencies are not so lax as to disregard the private sale of additional debt if there are bonds publicly held which are rated.

You can't use private sale to hide an increase in debt from the rating agencies or from any astute investors, and you should not wish to do so.

If for some reason a rating is required for a private sale, the rating agencies will rate the security.

Summary of Advantages and Disadvantages of Private Sale

Such an array of advantages and disadvantages may make it difficult to determine when a private sale should be used. These pros and cons should be evaluated in each situation. However, it may be well to summarize them briefly.

There are certain types of issues which, by their very nature—new, complicated ventures with risks difficult to appraise—can be handled only through a private sale. They would have to be offered to a small number of well-informed investors. Nothing would be gained by having a public offering. In a public offering, the same buyers would have to be contacted and there would be the added expenses.

Private sale may permit the development of untried techniques in financing.

Aside from these points, the principal advantages are: speed and flexibility of arrangement, the possibility of changing provisions by contacting a few holders in the future and the saving in financing costs. The saving becomes a real advantage for a small issue and accounts for its greater use by small companies.

The principal disadvantages are that the purchasers may be in a position to obtain a better rate and terms, particularly the latter, and that there is no market in which to repurchase securities for sinking fund or other purposes. This may be a substantial disadvantage if a company has sold senior securities when interest rates were low and it has heavy sinking fund payments to meet in a period of higher rates.

Summary Comparison of Financing Methods

Exhibit 8-10 may help you quickly review the advantages and disadvantages of the three methods of sale of senior securities. This may help you sort out your thinking so that you can pick out the points which are most applicable to your financing and then review them more carefully.

Pricing of New Senior Securities

When a company offers securities, it must have some idea of the price or rate it may expect to receive. This will be one of the determinants of whether to do the financing. Furthermore, if the company offers the securities at competitive bidding, such information will be necessary in deciding whether to accept a bid. In a negotiated offering, it will be a deciding factor as to whether to accept the underwriters' proposition. In a private placement, the matter of rate is equally as important as in a negotiated offer-

Exhibit 8-10

SUMMARY COMPARISON OF FINANCING METHODS

ADVANTAGES

Public Offering		Private Sale
Competitive	*Negotiated*	
Avoids problem of negotiating price and spread.		Company not limited by Securities Act:
Company can establish desired terms without direct pressure from investors or underwriters.	Company can establish desired terms without direct pressure from investors, but may experience pressure from underwriters to make issue easy to sell.	a. can use forecast figures. b. can explain difficult situation. c. can try new financing approach. d. can keep trade secrets. Fast.
Generally, company receives best net proceeds and terms.		Develop lender-borrower relationship.
Wide distribution.	Wide distribution.	Readjustment of terms is facilitated.
Subsequently, company can buy bonds in market.	Subsequently, company can buy bonds in market.	If company does not want to advertise its credit rating, it may be able to avoid a bond rating when all its debt is privately held.
	Sales promotion can be applied within limits of Securities Act.	
		Financing costs are reduced. This is particularly important for small issues.
		Well-adapted to small issues which would not be suitable for public offering and complicated types of financing.

DISADVANTAGES

Public Offering		Private Sale
Competitive	*Negotiated*	
Securities must be registered.	Securities must be registered.	Probably higher net cost to company and worse terms.
Cannot be used for small issues.	Generally not worthwhile for small issues.	Can only approach limited number of investors.
Relatively rigid time schedule.	Rigid time schedule, but not quite as rigid as competitive.	Cannot buy bonds back in open market.
No pre-offering sales promotion by underwriters.		
Only used for regulated companies like utilities.		
	Company is at a disadvantage with underwriters in negotiating price and spread.	

ing, particularly if the company handles the financing itself. If it uses an agent to do the negotiating, it will still have to have a good idea of the rate, so that it will know what to accept.

As explained at the start of the chapter, for bonds the rate means the yield to maturity. This can be translated into a price for the bonds by referring to bond yield tables on the basis of the number of years to maturity and interest coupon. For preferred stock, the rate means current yield, which can be translated into price on the basis of a dividend rate.

In solving the problem, the company should first seek to determine the rate at which the security can be sold to the public. Then, in a public offering, the underwriters' compensation will have to be estimated in order to get from the price to the public, to the proceeds to the company. In the material which follows, we will be concerned exclusively with the rate at which the securities can be sold to investors. The next sections cover the underwriters' compensation and expenses.

How is the rate that investors will pay for a new issue of long-term debt or preferred stock determined?

A reply that the rate is a matter of supply and demand, like any other price, is not much help, but the idea is basic in trying to solve the riddle. Therefore, from necessity, we will have to take time to discuss the elements that affect price before we give you an actual example of pricing a security.

On the demand for funds side, there are these factors:

1. The security being offered:

   (a) *Its quality.* This may be exemplified by the credit ratings, which take into account all of the factors affecting the inherent risk. Obviously, the greater the risk, the higher the rate. Privately placed bonds are not rated, but the same principle applies. The same idea also applies to the quality and risk for other senior securities, such as preferred stocks.

   (b) *The size of the issue.* Very large issues may require a somewhat higher rate, meaning lower price, because of the added supply. Very small issues, in the neighborhood of $3 million or less, will undoubtedly require a higher rate, because the purchasers will have to do as much work in analysis of the situation and will have less investment over which to spread their cost analysis.

   (c) *Size of company.* Not only does size of the issue affect the rate but the size of the company may also have an additional effect. A small, unknown company will require a higher rate than a larger, well-known company for the same size issue. A small company is less well-known to investors, and there is thus not as much of a potential market for its securities.

   (d) *The general character of the industry.* Certain types of industries are more difficult to analyze and have less appeal to investors for many different reasons. They will command higher rates. On the other hand, there are some issues which are known as museum pieces. They are the *creme de la creme* and in limited supply; they command premium prices. Therefore, the rate is affected by the type of industry and company.

   (e) *The terms of the offering.* Such factors as maturity, call price, sinking fund, restrictive provisions, etc. may affect the rate.

2. Other media available for investment:

   This includes sources of investment of both a similar and a dissimilar nature, but which represent a possible substitute source for investment, and thus compete either directly or indirectly for the purchasers' available funds. This may include both outstanding issues and new media for investment. Similar new issues being offered at about the same time represent the most direct competition, as do unsold issues in the hands of underwriters. A large offering of U.S. Government bonds may affect the whole market.

On the supply of funds side, there are these factors:

1. The overall supply of funds:

   There are many different types of funds seeking investment in the broad field of capital, some short term, some restricted by certain legal requirements, some seeking tax exemption, some seeking income, others appreciation, etc. There are, thus, many different rates in the money market. There is not complete fluidity of capital from one field to another, but there is sufficient fluidity so that a movement in the rate in one field may have an effect on the supply of funds to another.

2. Availability of funds for the type of issue:

   The amount of funds that are in investors' hands available for possible purchase of the type of security being offered.

3. Potential purchasers' interest in the issue:

   The extent to which potential purchasers for the new issue may already have enough of the company's securities. As already mentioned, if a well-known company brings out a new issue of which none is now outstanding, it may command a slight premium. On the other hand, if a company already has outstanding a large amount of securities similar to the proposed new issue, potential investors may already hold so much that they will be less eager to purchase more.

4. Freedom of underwriters' capital:

   By this is meant the extent to which underwriters' capital is tied up with issues which they purchased and have been unable to sell. In other words, how much unsold securities are on underwriters' shelves. If the proposed new issue is being offered competitively, this may be quite important. It is less important in a negotiated offering, but it still cannot be disregarded.

5. Action of the Federal Reserve System and other general influences in the money market:

   Through its open market policy, a change in the rediscount rate or a change in the commercial bank reserve requirements, it can influence the level of interest rates through the effect of its actions on supply. There may be other important general influences on the money market, such as U.S. Government fiscal policy.

Now let's determine the yield to maturity at the price to the public for an actual issue. Let's refer to ELECTRIC COMPANY, our competitive bidding example, and assume that we are the management of the company on Monday, June 2, making a rough approximation of what might be obtained the next day when the bids are opened. Our job is to arrive at an estimate of the rate from current prices of other securities as nearly similar in nature as possible. We must make allowance for any lack of similarity and for prices which are not current. If we are able to find comparable securities, we ought to be able to arrive at a fairly good guess, if the market stays level.

We should look at both outstanding issues and new offerings. However, since we are concerned with the price for a new offering, we will primarily have to rely on other similar new offerings. They have to be priced lower, meaning a higher yield, than similar outstanding seasoned issues in order to attract buyers to absorb the supply. The price for an outstanding issue is determined by a relatively thin market representing purchases and sales of a small amount of the security. Furthermore, the published quotations for such issues are often nominal and do not necessarily give a good clue as to the market. They should be observed with this in mind.

The extent of the difference in yield between new offerings and similar outstanding issues will depend on market conditions.

When interest rates are low and buyers have a large supply of funds to invest, the difference becomes narrow. As interest rates increase, the difference widens out.

While outstanding issues may not necessarily give us a good clue, they should be observed, keeping in mind that the price for a new issue will have to be lower and the yield higher. We will first look at other outstanding issues of ELECTRIC COMPANY. It had a number of mortgage bond issues with which the new issue would be on an identical basis. The K and L series have maturities and interest coupons nearest to those for the new issue. Market quotations for these issues, preceding the bidding, were as shown in Exhibit 8-11, Part I.

From these figures it would appear that a reasonable yield to maturity might be slightly less than 6.85%, judging from the bid prices that were being offered by investors for the outstanding issues.

The reason for including the call prices is to make certain that the market quotations were not above the call prices so that they might be affected by the possibility of call. Obviously, the prices of these bonds are sufficiently below the call price that there would be no effect.

The interest coupon rate may affect the price. A bond with a very high coupon tends to sell at a slightly higher yield than a low coupon bond with the price at a discount below par. The reason for this is that the price of a low coupon bond generally has more room to the call price. By "room" is meant possibilities of appreciation before the price is checked by the call price. As noted in the above prices, the highest interest coupon shows a slightly higher yield.

Quotations for the bonds of ELECTRIC COMPANY may be affected by the forthcoming issue of new bonds. Therefore, we should look at prices of other comparable electric company bonds. The mortgage bonds of ELECTRIC COMPANY are rated AA by Fitch, Aa by Moody's and AA by Standard. As a sample, the quotations for two other bonds of electric companies rated Double A and unaffected by current call are shown in Exhibit 8-11, Part II.

Electric Co. A's bonds would suggest a yield slightly better than 6.91%. Electric Co. B's bonds would indicate a lower yield, but this was due partly to the non-refundable feature.

Then, using hindsight, why did the interest coupon turn out to be 7 1/8%, the price to the public 102.655% and the yield 6.91%? The principal answer is the fact that, as already explained, outstanding issues generally sell at a lower yield than the price at which similar new issues can be sold.

The spread between outstanding and new issues is illustrated in Exhibit 8-12, showing an index of yields on outstanding Aa issues and like-rated new issues of electric companies. The spread may vary widely depending on conditions in the bond market.

Now let's take a look at three new offerings just prior to June 3, our bidding date in Exhibit 8-11, Part III.

Electric Co. C's bonds came out early in the month. The rates were higher at 6.96%, but the price rose so that the quotation on the now outstanding issues gives a yield around 6.87%. The two more recent new issues of Electric Co. D and E indicate a yield of 6.91%. There were no quotations on these bonds because they were still in syndicate. Thus, under existing circumstances, the officials of ELECTRIC COMPANY could have estimated just prior to the bidding that the rate to the public would have been about 6.91%, as was actually the case.

When rates hold level, it is possible, if comparable issues are available, to determine quite closely what a company might receive for a new issue of senior securities. However, this foresight is dependent on being able to obtain an adequate sample of similar new issues and on the existence of a stable market. When the market is changing rapidly, this approach will be inaccurate to the extent of the change that takes place in the market right up to the bidding hour. This may be

Exhibit 8-11

DATA FOR PRICING A NEW BOND OFFERING

PART I

YIELDS ON OUTSTANDING BONDS OF THE SAME COMPANY

Thursday, May 29

	Bid		Asked		Current
	Price	Yield	Price	Yield	Call Price
Series K 6 1/2s, due 27 yrs.	96 1/2	6.785%	97 1/2	6.695%	105.62
Series L 6 3/4s, due 28 yrs.	99	6.83	--	--	105.88

PART II

YIELDS ON OUTSTANDING BONDS OF OTHER COMPANIES OF A SIMILAR QUALITY

Thursday, May 29

	Ratings*			Price		Price		Current
	F	M	S	Bid	Yield	Asked	Yield	Call Price
Electric Co. A 7s due 30 yrs.	AA	Aa	AA	101.1/8	6.91%	100.5/8	6.875%	107.000
Electric Co. B 6 7/8s due 20 yrs.	AA	Aa	AA	101.	6.78	101.1/4	6.76	106.457**

*F–Fitch, M–Moody's, S–Standard and Poor's.
**Non-refundable first 5 years.

PART III

YIELDS ON NEW ISSUES OF BONDS OF SIMILAR QUALITY

		Ratings†				Offering Price to Public		Quotation June 2		Call
	Date	F	M	S	Amount	Price	Yield	Price	Yield	Feature
								Bid	Ask	
Electric Co. C 7s due 30 yrs.	5/13	AA	Aa	AA	$16 Mil	100.50	6.96	101.1/2	101.3/4	107.50
Electric Co. D 1st 7 1/8 due 30 yrs.	5/20	AA	Aa	AA	$20 Mil	102.655	6.91	6.88% (in syndicate)	6.86%	109.79
Electric Co. E 1st 7 1/8 due 30 yrs.	5/21	AA	Aa	AA	$25 Mil	102.655	6.91	(in syndicate)		109.79

†F–Fitch, M–Moody's, S–Standard and Poor's.

Exhibit 8-12

SPREAD BETWEEN YIELD ON OUTSTANDING* AND NEWLY ISSUED** Aa CORPORATE BONDS

	1974			1973			1972		
	Out-standing	New Issues	Differ-ence	Out-standing	New Issues	Differ-ence	Out-standing	New Issues	Differ-ence
January	7.97%	8.32%	0.35%	7.37%	7.61%	0.24%	7.52%	7.36%	(0.16%)
February	7.97	8.21	0.24	7.47	7.67	0.20	7.52	7.57	0.05
March	8.08	8.60	0.54	7.49	7.75	0.26	7.53	7.53	0.00
April	8.28	9.04	0.76	7.49	7.70	0.21	7.57	7.77	0.20
May	8.42	9.39	0.96	7.49	7.69	0.20	7.56	7.61	0.05
June	8.55	9.59	1.04	7.55	7.73	0.18	7.51	7.63	0.14
July	8.76	10.18	1.38	7.64	7.97	0.33	7.50	7.72	0.22
August	9.05	10.30	1.25	7.84	8.45	0.61	7.43	7.59	0.16
September	9.35	10.44	1.09	7.86	8.10	0.24	7.41	7.72	0.31
October				7.84	7.97	0.19	7.45	7.66	0.21
November				7.90	7.95	0.05	7.39	7.47	0.08
December				7.92	8.09	0.17	7.36	7.50	0.14
Average			0.85%			0.24%			0.12%

**Moody's Public Utility Manual 1974*, Moody's Investors Service, Inc.

**Treasury Bulletin, October, 1974, United States Treasury Department, office of the Secretary. Treasury Series based on reoffering yields of new corporate bonds with 5 years' call protection and rated Aa by Moody's Investors Service. Prior to 1973, this series reflected bonds without call protection. The value of 5 years' call protection in that period ranged from 10 to 25 basis points.

surprisingly large when a market becomes chaotic. A company, however, can go no further. The underwriters, of course, rely not only on such information, but upon their up-to-the-minute appraisal of the interest of potential buyers, on their knowledge of new security offerings pressing on the market and the extent to which unsold issues are on underwriters' shelves. In a rapidly changing market, it is only underwriters, who are close to the market and to potential purchasers for the new issue, who can make an accurate appraisal.

Our ELECTRIC COMPANY example illustrates the principles involved in determining the yield to maturity and offering price to the public for a new bond issue. The same principles apply for preferred stocks. However, ELECTRIC COMPANY represented a comparatively simple problem. The bonds are high grade and of a very standard nature. There were both new and outstanding closely comparable issues. As a guide to comparability, we were able to rely quite heavily on the three rating agencies.

For lower grade issues, and for issues of companies which are not well-known and less standard in nature, frequently found in industrial issues, the matter of finding comparable issues is a more difficult one. Then it may be necessary to rely on issues which are not in fact comparable, and to make an allowance for the differences on the basis of judgment. This requires a more detailed statistical comparison or table, sometimes called a stack-up, showing the principal data and ratios used in security analysis in evaluating such securities. It will include factors surrounding the issue, such as the amount of the issue, rating if available, sinking fund provision, call feature, etc., and the principal balance sheet and income statement ratios. They will be the standard ones of capitalization and coverage, and, in addition, any special ratios which are applicable to the type of company involved. The figures in the stack-up will not reveal the answers directly, because security prices cannot be determined on the basis of mathematics alone. The job requires judgment gained from practical experience in investment analysis. Thus, the Financial Vice President of a company might not be able to come to a very accurate conclusion. However, he must tussle with the problem and arrive at some rough estimate. The level of his ability and the extent of his knowledge in this field will determine the extent to which he will have to lean on the underwriter's judgment. If a company handles a private sale without an underwriter acting as an agent, it may wish to pay a financial expert for a study to show the approximate price the company should obtain. Some underwriting firms may be willing to make such a study for a fee. There are a few consulting firms which are qualified to make an approximation, but to the extent to which they are not right on top of the market, they may not come too close.

A special problem arises in using new issues sold through private sale as a guide to determine the price of a forthcoming issue. Most announcements of private sales give the principal amount, the interest coupon or the preferred dividend rate, but fail to give the proceeds paid to the company. Another problem which may be equally important is the matter of the date the agreement for the private sale was made. When an issue is sold privately, the public announcement is generally made one, two and perhaps even more than three months after the price was actually established. The pubic announcement almost never says when the deal was consummated. In order for the price to be meaningful, it must be viewed in relation to the market as it existed at the time that the price was set. If there has been a significant change in the general market, such private sales will be of little value unless the correct date can be obtained. As previously suggested, the day the bonds are dated, or the date that the commitment fee starts running, if there is one, may give an approximation to the day the price was set.

Financing Costs for All Types of Offerings

We will now discuss the financing costs for senior securities, which include:

- Underwriters' compensation for public offerings,
- Agent's fee for private sale,
- Expenses for public offerings,
- Expenses for private sale.

Underwriters' Compensation for Public Offerings

First, a word about the make-up of the underwriters' compensation. The manager of an underwriting group has the principal burden of work for handling the issue. For this he receives a fixed percentage of the total commission. For a high-grade bond issue sold at competitive bidding, it may be about 5% of the total amount of the gross compensation. It runs higher for negotiated offerings and may be about 15%. It comes out of the compensation of each member of the group on a proportionate basis.

Selected dealers can obtain bonds to sell to their customers from the "pot" or from any one of the underwriters in the group at a concession. For example, if the offering price to the public is 102, the dealer concession may be one-quarter of 1%. Thus, an underwriter would sell bonds at 101 3/4 to a selected dealer who, in turn, would sell them to an investor at 102, making the one-quarter of 1% for his effort. The allowance to selected dealers comes out of the underwriters' compensation. Its size will depend upon how much the underwriters feel they will need the sales effort of the selected dealers. The allowance has to be enough to induce dealers to spend their time selling the issue rather than trying to make money as a dealer in already outstanding issues, or from some other new issue. For a high grade bond, it may be one-quarter of 1%, but may be one-third of 1%. For a high-grade preferred stock it may be one-half of 1%. It may be increased for issues not readily salable, and when market conditions are adverse. Then the underwriters will have to increase their compensation accordingly. As a practical matter, most high grade bonds are sold directly to investors by underwriters, with selected dealers taking a small part. This is partly due to the fact that most underwriting groups are large and the bonds are well spread among account members.

A transaction which takes place entirely outside of the underwriting group is the reallowance which a selected dealer may make to any dealer who is a member of the National Association of Securities Dealers. This reallowance may also be made by members of the underwriting group to members of the NASD. Let's assume one-eighth of 1% for such an allowance. Then, in our example above, the selected dealer who bought the bonds from the underwriter for 101 3/4, instead of selling them to an investor, could sell them to a member of the National Association of Securities Dealers at 101 7/8. The latter, in turn, would resell them at 102 to an investor.

The size of the Selected Dealer Concession has to take into account the size of the reallowance which selected dealers can make to members of the National Association of Securities Dealers.

There are the outside costs which must be borne by all members of the underwriting group, such as the legal fees for the lawyers who represent the underwriters. In competitive bidding, since it is not known which underwriter will win the issue, the company selects a law firm to represent the winning underwriter. Even prior to the bidding this firm has some functions to perform. Since this legal fee is paid by the winning bidder, a question is always asked at a Due Diligence Meeting—How much will be the fees for the lawyers representing the underwriters?

For an unusual type of offering, the underwriting firm may hire some other outside experts, such as engineers, in their investigation of the company in order to help them decide whether to do the financing.

The underwriters will generally have to pay interest on bank loans, used to carry the issue until it is sold. However, if the deal sells quickly, the settlement may be arrived at promptly. There may be miscellaneous expenses.

After the above items are deducted (except for the reallowance by selected dealers to members of the NASD) from the underwriters' compensation, the amount which remains is to cover the underwriters' own firm's expenses, underwriting risk, sales effort and a profit on their own capital. Well-known issues may require little work and expense of the underwriters' own staff. On the other hand, a complicated type of financing by an unknown company may need much analysis, investigation and thought. To summarize the above remarks, we will refer to the figures for our old friend the ELECTRIC COMPANY which offered $50 million of bonds competitively. They are shown in Exhibit 8-13.

The balance represented by line 5 must be sufficient, among other things, to cover the underwriting risk. Let's now review this risk to see what it encompasses and how it may vary.

The risk consists in being unable to dispose of the issue at the offering price. Underwriters expect to price an issue which they purchase at competitive bidding so that it can be sold within a few days. If this cannot be done,

Exhibit 8-13

UNDERWRITERS' COMPENSATION BREAKDOWN FOR
$50,000,000 COMPETITIVE BOND OFFERING

Line/Column		I	II	III	IV
			Per $100 Principal Amount	Total	% of Total
1	Management Fee for Heading Group (5% of total underwriters' spread)	$0.0307		$ 15,577.50	5%
2	Estimated Direct Expenses	0.1070		53,500.00	17
3	Total Expenses		$0.1377	$ 68,877.50	
4	Allowance to Selected Dealers–1/4 of 1%		0.25		41
5	Underwriters' Profit		0.2274		37
6	Total Underwriters' Spread		$0.6151	$307,550.00	100%
7	Reallowance by Selected Dealers on Their Sales to Members of NASD–1/8 of 1%. (This comes out of the Selected Dealer Allowance.)		$0.125		

Line Above

2 Estimated Direct Expenses
Includes counsel fees ($12,500) and disbursements, advertising, taxes ($25,000) and miscellaneous expenses.

4 Allowance to Selected Dealers–1/4 of 1%.
The amount of bonds sold by selected dealers varies. To the extent that bonds are sold by the underwriters themselves, they keep this amount. However, the 1/4 of 1% may be looked at as compensation for their own firm's sales efforts.

5 Underwriters' Profit
The so-called "profit" must cover underwriters' own firm expenses, interest on bank loans to carry the issue, risk and profit on underwriters' own capital.

7 Reallowance by Selected Dealers on their Sales to Members of the NASD–1/8 of 1%. This reallowance may also be made by members of the underwriting group to members of the NASD.

then after the underwriting agreement is terminated, usually within about three weeks more or less, bonds may trade in the market at a reduced price and the syndicate members may have to reduce the price in order to attract buyers to purchase the unsold portion.

Even though an unusual demand develops when the issue is first offered, the price cannot be increased over the offering price unless an amendment to the registration statement is filed and a sticker is added to the prospectus.

The Securities and Exchange Commission frowns on the idea unless the syndicate is first dissolved. That doesn't happen; when an offering price is set, the underwriters are expected to sell the entire issue at that price if they are able to do so. And it would be circumventing the Act if an underwriter withheld securities with the intention of reoffering them at a higher price after the underwriting agreement is dissolved. Thus, as far as the risk element is concerned, it is a one-way street, and the underwriters must include in the compensation an amount sufficient to cover that risk.

There are three elements of risk:

1. The risk of something happening either directly or indirectly to the company which will affect the security before it is sold. This risk is inherent in any security offering, but it is usually borne by the issuing company. The underwriters' contract has an "out" clause which permits them to withdraw from the issue if the company experiences a material adverse change.
2. The risk of misjudging the demand for the new issue.
3. The risk of an adverse change in the general market. This element is the most serious, and the one over which the underwriters have no control.

The degree of risk of an adverse market action is affected by the elements which comprise the risk of the security and which determine the acceptable yield for the debt or preferred stock. As the quality of the security decreases and the yield increases, the underwriters' compensation tends to increase.

The level and condition of the market as it shows investors' willingness to purchase also affects the risk. Obviously, when purchasers are eager for new issues, the underwriters take less risk of getting stuck than they do in a dull market when there is apathy on the part of the purchasers.

Thus, we can summarize the principal factors that will affect the spread for senior securities in a public offering as a percent of proceeds as follows:

1. The size of the issue.
2. The quality of the issue.
3. The condition of the security market.
4. The method of sale; that is, whether it is negotiated or competitive.
5. The type of senior security.

When you get ready to do some financing, you will wish to analyze other recent comparable offerings to determine what are the going charges. If yours is a negotiated offering, you might also wish to assemble data for comparable competitive offerings.

Shown in Exhibit 8-14 is a general indication of how size of issue might affect underwriters' compensation. As an issue gets small, the cost of a public offering becomes relatively high. Competitive offerings may show a smaller spread. The table only covers bonds. Preferred stocks might show spreads twice as great. Also shown in the exhibit is an indication of the financing expenses for a negotiated debt financing, as well as the items which make up the total expense.

Shown in Exhibit 8-15 is a general indication of the agent's fee and expenses as a percent of proceeds for debt issue of different sizes. The agent's fee is substantially lower than the underwriters' compensation and expenses are also somewhat lower. Also shown are the expense items which might be encountered in a private sale. Which ones are applicable would depend on the circumstances surrounding the placement. For a preferred stock, the agent's fee in a private sale would be somewhat more than for a debt security.

Refunding

If you have senior securities outstanding which have a high interest or dividend rate compared with existing markets and they can be called for redemption, you should be weighing whether or not to refund them. Two questions will be involved.

What will be the savings?

Should you proceed to refund now or wait for a better market?

An example follows: Our Company had outstanding a $10 million principal amount of mortgage bonds which had an interest coupon of 8% and a 24-year remaining maturity. The

Exhibit 8-14

UNDERWRITERS' COMPENSATION AND EXPENSES FOR NEGOTIATED PUBLIC OFFERINGS OF DEBT SECURITIES AS PERCENT OF PROCEEDS

Size of Issue	*Underwriters' Compensation*	*Expenses*	*Financing Costs*
$50,000,000	0.80	0.20%	1.00%
10,000,000	1.00	0.50	1.50
1,000,000	6.00	2.00	8.00

Expense items:

SEC fees
Listing fees
Federal revenue stamps
State taxes and fees
Trustees' fees, etc.
For preferred stock this would be replaced by Transfer agent's fee, etc.
Printing and engraving
Legal
Accounting
Engineering, etc.
Miscellaneous
Total

Exhibit 8-15

AGENT'S FEE AND EXPENSES FOR PRIVATE SALE OF DEBT SECURITIES AS PERCENT OF PROCEEDS

Size of Issue	*Agent's Fee*	*Expenses*	*Financing Costs*
$50,000,000	0.50%	0.25%	0.75%
10,000,000	0.75	0.30	1.05

Expense items:

Federal revenue stamps
State taxes and fees
Trustee's fees, etc.
Printing and engraving
Legal
Accounting
Engineering, etc.
Miscellaneous

bonds are rated *Double A*. The regular call price is now 104 3/4, callable on 30 days' notice, then decreasing 1/4 point each year thereafter until the price reaches 100.

Interest rates have decreased. The Company made a study of current rates and asked underwriters what rate the company might expect if it sold new bonds to refund the existing bonds. The conclusion was that new bonds could be sold to the public with a 7% interest coupon and a 25-year maturity at about 100. Underwriters' compensation and expenses would amount to about 1.50, so that the net proceeds to the company would be 98.50. Thus, the cost to the company to raise new money to accomplish this refunding would be 7.13%, as shown by referring to Bond Value Tables.

Now then, we have to decide what to compare the 7.13% cost of our new money with in order to determine the savings in terms of yield. In effect, what we are doing is selling new bonds and reinvesting the proceeds in our old bonds at their call price. Thus, we are interested in the rate to call the outstanding bonds. They have an 8% interest coupon, a 24-year remaining maturity and a call price of 104 3/4. The yield at the call price is 7.57%, as shown by referring to Bond Value Tables. On the basis of yield, we would realize a saving of 0.44%, which is a result of subtracting the cost rate for the new bonds of 7.13% from the cost to call the oustanding bonds of 7.57%. This is a gross saving and must be adjusted for the tax effect to get the net savings.

Another approach to the problem of determining the savings is to charge the call premium on the bonds to be refunded to the cost of doing the new financing. This process is shown below.

1. New bonds—7% coupon, maturity 25 yrs., to be sold @	100.00%
2. Less compensation and expenses	1.50
3. Net proceeds	98.50%
4. Less premium to call old bonds	4.75
5. Net to company after calling old bonds	93.75%
6. Cost of old bonds: 8% coupon—price 100%	8.00%
7. Cost of new money: 7% coupon, maturity 25 yrs. Price 93.75 (line 5 above)	7.56
8. Saving before taxes	0.44

This method may produce a slightly greater apparent savings because the call premium is written off at the lower interest rate, over a longer period of time.

We have answered our first question on an approximate basis—What will be the savings? Now, we must decide our second question, whether to refund now or wait? This represents a nice problem of judgment. We must attack the problem in this manner: Accept the fact that we cannot forecast interest rates. If the savings are significant, then go ahead and realize the savings by doing the refunding. For our company, the savings are significant. But if the savings were less, how do we decide whether they were sufficiently large to go ahead? This is a matter of weighing the extent of the savings in relation to the level of interest rates.

There is a very rough rule of thumb as follows: The yield to maturity for the new issue, at the net proceeds the company would receive from the underwriters, should be about one-half of 1% less than the yield at the call price for the outstanding issue, in order to make refunding worthwhile. Note that in this rule, the price on the new issue would be after deducting the underwriters' compensation from the public offering price, but before deducting the expenses of the offering.

However, this rule should be tempered by considering the level of interest rates and their outlook. You would not wish to do a refunding, and then have to repeat it all over again within a relatively short period of time, with duplication of financing costs, if interest rates drop further. If interest rates are at a low level, the refunding operation might be advisable with a smaller difference in yield. The prospects of further potential savings decrease as the level of interest rates declines.

At least, there must be sufficient savings, as measured by a difference in yield, in order to take care of possible adverse security market changes in the period that is required to complete the sale of the new issue and the call of the old one. You would not wish to go to all the effort and expense of financing and then find that a small change in the market wiped out the calculated savings. In this connection, you should consider the possible fluctuations in security prices similar to your issue in the time interval required to sell the new issue and call the old bonds.

From the above comments, it can be seen that it is first necessary to make a mathematical estimate of the savings to be realized, but that the final decision must be a matter of judgment. The mathematics in itself will not give the answer whether or not to proceed.

The above approach will give you a good start on making your decision. However, you may wish to make a more accurate analysis before coming to a final conclusion. The calculations thus far have been based on yield rather than total dollar savings. The reason for this is to express the savings in such a way that it will be easy to apply judgment in terms of bond yields. A company should also make an analysis on a dollar basis, as the size of the issue will govern the dollar savings involved, and it should make a careful analysis of each of the items affecting taxes and also the time effect of each item. The call premium on the outstanding bonds is immediately deductible for tax purposes, and the financing costs, with exceptions, on the new issue are deductible over the life of the new issue.

It should be noted that inasmuch as the call premium is immediately deductible for tax purposes, the net expenditures by the company to pay for the call premium are only half of the stated premium with a 50% tax rate. Therefore, the saving derived by applying a tax rate to the savings in terms of yield is understated. In the example used, the net savings after taxes would be increased over the above figure of 0.22%.

A further item which must be considered in a detailed analysis is the duplication of interest payments which may have to be paid on both the new and old bond issue until the call is completed. Of course, some income may be obtained from a temporary investment of the proceeds of the new issue.

And there can be considerable argument in making a careful discounted cash flow analysis as to whether to use the common cost rate, the overall cost-of-capital or the bond rate for the capital required for the call price. The overall cost-of-capital rate is most logical, but for practical purposes the bond rate is satisfactory.

The example we used was a relatively simple one. Some of the complications which arise are:

1. If debt has a sinking fund or serial maturity, you will have to determine the average maturity to use in calculating the yield.
2. If the call price drops in the future, the yield may have to be figured at each call price, to see if there is a sufficient drop to justify waiting to do the refunding at the lower call.
3. The maturity of the outstanding issue as compared to the new issue may be important. In our example, the outstanding issue had a 24-year remaining maturity and the new bonds 25 years, so that this little difference in maturity was not significant. As the spread in maturity gets larger, there may be some advantage to the longer maturity. For example, if a bond is due, say, in five years, the call price is low and the market favorable, then the company might decide to refund at relatively little savings. There might be the advantage of anticipating the maturity at a favorable rate. The maturity problem and how it affects the final decision is again a matter of judgment.

The principles of refunding a preferred stock with another preferred are the same, except that the maturity factor is generally missing. The yield is a current yield and the tax adjustments are obviously different.

Exchange Offers

Exchange of securities is not really a new offering, but it is largely treated as such under the Securities Act. Exchanges can involve senior securities as well as common stock, and any combination of the types of securities. They can apply to just one security or may involve an entire capital structure in a reorganization, a recapitalization or a merger. An exchange has one feature similar to a new offering in that it involves establishing a value on the old securities and the new securities to be received in exchange. In order to induce the existing security holders to accept the exchange, it will be necessary to offer a premium in the new securities either in the form of better protective provisions, price or income, or a combination.

Exchange offers require some different mechanics than a new offering and may at times seem vastly complicated. Actually, there are two basic steps:

1. A new security or securities must be devised which may be offered in exchange and which will fit the company's financial requirements. This calls for basic principles of finance. It may be necessary to depart from an ideal capital structure to effect the exchange. The extent to which this should be done will be determined by the urgency with which the old security must be eliminated and the extent of the improvement that might be accomplished as a result of the transaction.
2. A price and the features of the new securities must be decided upon which will be sufficiently attractive to induce holders to make the exchange and will not be unduly costly to the company. This involves appraising values of securities and their returns–which includes determining the investors' appraisal of the potential values in the old and new securities. If the old securities have real possibilities of appreciation, the holders may be reluctant to make the exchange unless the offer fully compensates for this potential in one way or another.

Exchange of Preferred for Debentures–The Mechanics

Here is an actual example, which, in effect, was an exchange in connection with a merger when interest rates were at a relatively low level. An industrial company had outstanding 1,340,641 shares of $20 par value 7% preferred stock (dividends per share $1.40) which was non-callable.

Prior to the announcement of the offer, the preferred stock sold for 32 1/2 and the approximate price range is shown in Exhibit 8-16, Part I.

The company offered for each 14 shares of preferred, $500 principal amount of 25-year 4 1/2%-subordinated debentures, which is equivalent to $35.71 principal amount for each share. Any fractional balance of less than $500 was paid in cash at the rate of $35.71 per share.

The holder of 14 shares of preferred had a dividend income of $19.60. On $500 principal amount of debentures, he would receive $22.50 in interest. This would be equivalent to $1.61 in interest for each share of preferred.

When trading started in the debentures the price was slightly above 100%, which resulted in a little over the equivalent of $35.71 principal amount for each share of preferred.

The holder of a share of preferred received a more senior security and an increase in market value and income as shown in the table at the bottom of the next page.

This would appear to be a rather generous offer. Of the preferred stockholders, 86.9% voted for the plan, 2.3% against and the balance didn't vote. Less than 1% of the

Exhibit 8-16

EXCHANGE OF 7% PREFERRED STOCK
FOR 4 1/2 SUBORDINATED DEBENTURES

PART I

PRICE RANGE OF PREFERRED PRIOR TO
ANNOUNCEMENT OF EXCHANGE

	Prior 10 Years		Prior 5 Months	
	Price	Yield	Price	Yield
High	$37	3.8%	$33 3/8	4.2%
Average of Highs	35 1/4	3.9	32 1/4	4.3
Low	26	5.4	30	4.7
Average of Lows	30 1/2	4.6	30 1/2	4.6

PART II

ILLUSTRATION OF MARKET PRICE ACTION OF 7% PREFERRED

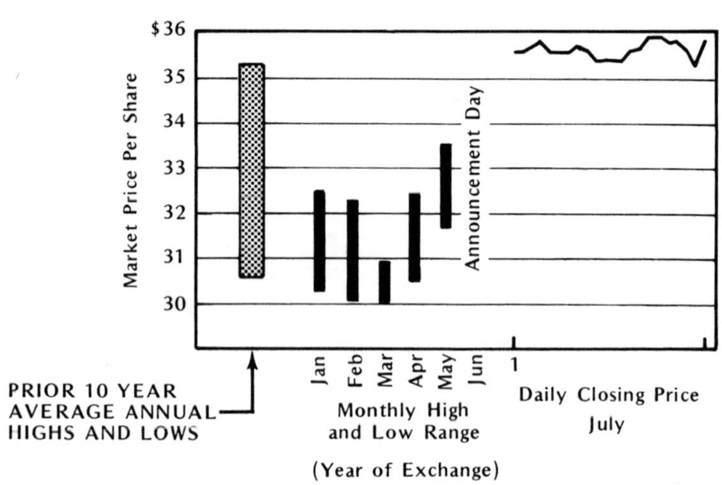

	Preferred	New Debentures Equivalent to 1 Share of Preferred	% Increase
Market Value	$32 1/2 (prior to announcement)	$35.71	10%
Income	$1.40	$ 1.61	15%

stockholders were paid off in cash pursuant to their rights of an appraisal.

Exhibit 8-16, Part II gives the price action of the preferred stock before and after the announcement of the offer. When trading starts in the new securities on a when-issued basis, the old and new tend to reach a parity due to arbitrage. This is illustrated on the chart. The arbitrageurs will sell the new security short and purchase the old. They will cover their short position by delivery of the new securities that they eventually receive in exchange for the old ones. The closeness to parity will depend on the extent of the assurance that the exchange will be consummated.

The size of the premium which must be given in the new securities is a matter of judgment and depends on the interest which the company has in making a successful exchange, existing market conditions, nature of the holders who own the old securities and their interest in retaining the old securities, and tax features which may affect the company and the holders.

A company may, and most likely will, elicit the aid of an investment banker at least for advice. Certain types of exchange offers may, in fact, be underwritten. For example, if a company has a high dividend preferred stock outstanding which is callable, it may under special circumstances wish to give the existing preferred stockholders an opportunity to purchase a new lower dividend rate preferred. An underwriting of the exchange will involve the underwriters agreeing to purchase any new preferred not exchanged so that the money will be available to call the old preferred.

If your exchange is a complicated one, you may be involved with additional experts in many fields, including accountants, lawyers, tax experts and even engineers where appraisal of assets and manufacturing processes are important. Thus, exchanges present an intriguing problem which involves pricing securities, evaluating market conditions and knowing the interest of existing holders.

Exchange of One Convertible Debenture for Another—Cost Elements

In the previous example, we explained the mechanics of an exchange offer. In this example, we will be concerned with the cost elements. Does the company come out ahead or behind?

Generally, an exchange involves a cost to the company because an inducement must be offered to the security holders in order to get them to make the exchange. Therefore, there must be some sound reason for a company to make an exchange in order to compensate for the extra cost. Because unlike securities may be exchanged, the extra cost may be camouflaged. This will be illustrated with the following example.

The outstanding security was a convertible debenture as follows:

4% coupon (19-year maturity)	
Principal amount	$100,000,000
Conversion price	$80
Market price of common	$20
Market price of convertible debenture	48 1/2
Yield to maturity of convertible debenture	10.18%
Total market value of convertible debenture	$ 48,500,000

Suggested exchange for a new convertible debenture is as follows:

7 1/2% coupon (19-year maturity)	
Principal amount	$ 60,625,000
Conversion price	$30
Market price of convertible debenture	$100
Principal amount of new convertible debentures for each $100 principal amount of old convertible debenture	$60.625
Premium received by old convertible debenture holder ($60.625 ÷ 48 1/2)	25%

The advantages of the exchange were suggested to be as follows:

1. Reduction in the company's outstanding debt because the principal amount of the new debentures would be much less than the principal amount of the old debentures:

4% convertible debentures	$100,000,000
7 1/2 " "	60,625,000
Decrease in principal amount of debt outstanding.	$ 39,375,000

2. Retirement of the old 4% convertible debentures at $60.625 results in a non-recurring extraordinary earnings gain of $39,375,000. This would be subject to the corporate tax. It was suggested that a tax rate of 24% only need be applied since that was the company's effective tax rate.

The disadvantages were suggested to be as follows:

1. An increase in annual interest charges.

Interest on old 4% debentures	$4,000,000
Interest on new 7 1/2 debentures	4,547,000
Increase in interest charges	$ 547,000

2. Increase in shares upon conversion.

Shares if old 4% debentures were converted	1,197,000
Shares if new 7 1/2 debentures were converted	2,020,833

The total market price of the outstanding 4% convertible debentures was $48,500,000 and the market value of the new 7 1/2% convertible debentures was $60,625,000, so the company paid a substantial premium or cost to make this exchange of 25% or $12,125,000. But let's examine the picture more closely.

First, we will comment on the above-suggested advantages.

1. The reduction in outstanding principal appears impressive but the real effect has to be tested in terms of how much it will affect the debt ratio in the capital structure, and this will depend on the size of the issue compared to the total amount of the company's long term debt.
2. The extraordinary earnings gain should be calculated with the incremental tax rate of 48% and not 24%, the company's average effective tax rate. Furthermore, it is doubtful whether an informed investor would give much weight to this bookkeeping temporary increase in earnings per share.[2]
3. The increase in interest charges will reduce coverage of interest charges, and this may be more important in affecting the quality of the company's debt than the reduction in principal.
4. The increase in dilution is not measured by the difference in the common shares resulting from the conversion of each convertible because the old convertible had no prospects of being converted. The current market price of $20 is so far away from the $80 conversion price as to have no prospects of conversion for practical purposes. However, the new 7 1/2% convertibles with a $30 conversion price could convert if the stock rose from its present price of $20 to over the conversion price. Therefore, the company was adding a potential dilution of 2,020,833 shares.

Therefore, to summarize the results as above outlined, they are:

1. A reduction in principal.	$39,375,000
2. A non-recurring extraordinary earnings gain after 48% tax.	$20,475,000
3. An annual increase in interest charges pre-tax.	$ 547,000
4. Potential earnings per share dilution from the new 7 1/2% convertible due to increase in shares.	2,020,833
5. Possible increase in common if new 7 1/2% convertibles convert.	$60,625,000

[2]The Financial Accounting Standards Board issued a proposal in February 1975 to require companies to treat any gain or loss on "extinguishment" of debt as an extraordinary item in their income statements.

6. A tax on the extraordinary earnings gain.

This comparison is hard to analyze from a cost point of view because the two securities are entirely different. The old 4% convertibles are really a debt security since they have lost the potential of conversion. The new 7 1/2% convertibles are true convertibles, so the company gives in exchange a call on its common stock at $30 per share. The interest cost picture is camouflaged because the new 7 1/2% convertibles carry a low interest rate because of their conversion feature.

The cost effect of such an exchange can be brought out more clearly if the old 4% debentures are exchanged for new debentures without a conversion feature. Then we will be comparing like with like, since the old 4% debentures are really a debt security at this point.

The 4% debentures due in 19 years, selling at $48 1/2, yield 10.18% to maturity. As a first step in our explanation, we will look at the picture by exchanging the old 4% debentures for new debentures with a 10.18% coupon selling at $100. We will not offer any premium but make the exchange on the basis of $48 1/2 principal amount of 10.18% debentures for $100 principal amount of old 4% debentures. This would result in the following:

1. Decrease in principal amount outstanding.	
4% debentures	$100,000,000
10.18% debentures	48,500,000
Decrease in principal	$ 51,500,000
2. Pre-tax, non-recurring extraordinary earnings gain.	$ 51,500,000
3. Increase in interest charges.	
Interest on old 4% debentures	$ 4,000,000
Interest on new 10.18% debentures	4,937,300
Increase in annual interest charges	937,300
Increase in total interest charges for 19 years maturity.	17,808,700

Now the increase in annual interest charges are substantial, or a 25% increase. The conversion feature kept the interest charges low in our previous figures.

Let's carry the picture a step further and include the 25% premium or $12,125,000, which would be necessary to get investors to make the exchange. Then we would have to offer $60.625 principal amount of new 10.18% debentures for each $100 principal amount of old 4% debentures selling at $48 1/2. This would result in the following:

1. Decrease in principal amount outstanding.	
4% debentures	$100,000,000
10.18% debentures	60,625,000
Decrease in principal	$ 39,375,000
2. Pre-tax, non-recurring extraordinary earnings gain.	$ 39,375,000
3. Increase in interest charges.	
Interest on old 4% debentures	$ 4,000,000
Interest on new 10.18% debentures	6,171,625
Increase in annual interest charges	$ 2,171,625
Increase in total interest charges for 19 years to maturity.	$ 41,260,875
4. A tax on the extraordinary earnings gain.	

This results in a major increase in interest charges.

Up to this point we have only explained the situation. In order to analyze costs correctly, we have to allow for the complete tax effects and also the time value of money. The interest payments are spread out over a period of years and the larger principal payment doesn't come due until maturity. The figures for our exchange of convertible debenture 4's for straight 10.18% debentures with a 25% premium are laid out in Exhibit 8-17, Part I and Part II.

It shows that for each 48 1/2 market price of the 4% bonds there is an after-tax cost giving effect to discounting at 10.18% of $22. To simplify the calculations, we have charged the tax on the extraordinary gain at the beginning. The company has the option of deducting it from the property which was built with the proceeds from the bonds. This would result in lower depreciation charges so that the effect would be to write off the tax over the remaining life of the property. This would result in reducing the effect of this tax because of the time value of money.

In our original example, in which the exchange was done with new convertibles the interest rate was lower, but this was due to the convertible feature which is a cost from the company's point of view.

Exhibit 8-17

EXCHANGE OF SUBORDINATED DEBENTURE
10.18% DUE IN 19 YEARS FOR SUBORDINATED CONVERTIBLE
DEBENTURE 4's DUE IN 19 YEARS. 25% PREMIUM

PART I

CASH DIFFERENCE

Column		I	II	Difference
	Interest coupon	4%	10.18%	Col. II less I
	Security	Sub. Conv. Debt.	Sub. Debt	
	Maturity	19 years	19 years	
	Conversion price	\$ 80		
	Market price	\$ 48½	100	
	Exchange offer–principal amount	100	60.625	
	Principal amount outstanding	100%	60.625%	
	Tax on extraordinary gain at 48% paid by Co.		\$ 18.90	
Years	Interest			
1		\$ 4.00	\$ 6.17*	
2		"	"	
3		"	"	
4		"	"	
5		"	"	
6		"	"	
7		"	"	
8		"	"	
9		"	"	
10		"	"	
11		"	"	
12		"	"	
13		"	"	
14		"	"	
15		"	"	
16		"	"	
17		"	"	
18		"	"	
19		"	"	
	Total Interest	\$ 76.00	\$117.23	
	What investor gets at end of 19 years			
	Interest	\$ 76.00	\$117.23	\$ 41.230
	Principal	100.00	60.625	(39.375)
	Total	\$176.00	\$177.855	\$ 1.855)

*Interest rate 10.18% times principal \$60.625 equals annual interest charge \$6.17.

PART II

DISCOUNTED CASH FLOW ANALYSIS OF PART I FROM COMPANY'S POINT OF VIEW DISCOUNTED AT 10.18%

Column		I	II	III	IV	V	VI
			4% Sub. Conv. Debentures		10.18% Subordinated Debentures		
			After-Tax Interest	Cash Flow Discounted	After-Tax Interest	Cash Flow Discounted	Difference Column V Less Column III
Year							
0	Tax on extra-ordinary gain	$18.90*				$18.90	
1			$ 2.08	$ 1.888	$ 3.21	$ 2.913	
2			"	1.713	"	2.644	
3			"	1.555	"	2.400	
4			"	1.411	"	2.178	
5			"	1.281	"	1.977	
6			"	1.163	"	1.794	
7			"	1.055	"	1.629	
8			"	.958	"	1.478	
9			"	.869	"	1.342	
10			"	.789	"	1.218	
11			"	.716	"	1.105	
12			"	.650	"	1.003	
13			"	.590	"	.910	
14			"	.535	"	.826	
15			"	.486	"	.750	
16			"	.441	"	.681	
17			"	.400	"	.618	
18			"	.363	"	.561	
19			"	.330	"	.509	
		Principal	$100.00	15.85	$60.625	$ 9.61	
		Total		$33.04		$55.04	$22.00

*Income tax rate 48%.

Since there is a cost, there has to be some real reason for making the exchange rather than just the bookkeeping results of a reduction in principal amount. If the company has too much debt, the new convertibles might represent a way to increase the common equity when conversion takes place. If this is the aim, then the conversion price should be close enough to the market price to assure conversion. Perhaps the company should have given consideration to an exchange for common stock so that the debt would immediately be eliminated. The answers to these questions, of course, depend on all the circumstances surrounding the company's financial picture and outlook. But you must assume that an exchange generally involves an additional cost.

CHAPTER 9

Selling Common Stock

This chapter presupposes that you are familiar with the general ideas about offering securities as described in the chapter on "Selling Senior Securities." Selling common stock is more complicated; consequently, this chapter is not easy. However, if you like finance you will find it interesting.

What We Will Cover

We will be primarily concerned with public offerings of common stock which have to be registered under the Securities Act of 1933. Private placements which are exempt from the Act are spelled out in Rule 146 under the Securities Act of 1933. We outlined briefly how the rule applies to senior securities in the previous chapter. The new rule follows much of the past thinking about the need of the offeree to be sophisticated, etc., but it defines much more closely the limitations surrounding a private sale. It limits the number of purchasers to 35, but excludes from the count purchasers who make an investment of over $150,000. It includes the idea that an unsophisticated purchaser can hire a sophisticated representative. Each private placement of common stocks represents a special situation and must be analyzed by itself in terms of Rule 146 to make certain that it will be exempt. The Rule also has implications in mergers, etc. of closely held companies. Exemption in such a situation may save considerable expense and effort.

One of the reasons for the complicated nature of offering common stock publicly is that there are two methods which are quite different: direct sale to the public and sale through rights to existing stockholders.

Direct sale is easy and we will cover it first. We will then spend considerable time in explaining the rights method. Only after an understanding of the two methods can we attempt to answer the tough question as to whether you should use a direct or rights offering. We will also cover various other subjects which are related to offering common stocks as well as investment letter stock.

Most of our explanation of direct sale will pertain to financing by companies which already have some stock publicly held and for which there is a market quotation. However, before we finish the subject, we will say a word about the situation in which, previous to the new issue, there was no publicly held stock.

We will not go into all the steps required in the sale of common stock, such as the proxy statement, filing of the registration statement, writing the prospectus, etc. Many of the ideas on the mechanics of financing that were discussed in the chapter on selling senior securities apply to common stocks.

Goal in Offering Common Stock

Our goal in offering common stock is somewhat different from that for senior securities, since we are dealing with the security which stands for ownership. We wish to raise the largest amount of money per share of common stock at the least cost, combined with the greatest benefit to the existing owners. You should be concerned with what is good for the stockholders and not what is good for the company as distinguished from the stockholders. The reason for emphasizing this point will become apparent when we get to the comparison of direct and rights offerings.

And your decisions have to be made on the basis of what is good for existing stockholders. When you sell new stock, the new stockholders are not members of the family until after they buy the stock.

Generally, management thinks that their stock is underpriced and that when they sell new stock they are giving it away. There may be times in a bull market when a few managements feel that their stock is over-priced. They may fear that if they sell over-priced stock, there will be a bad reaction on the part of the new investors when it falls. If this does occur, there is bound to be a bad reaction, but the management does have to accept the market's appraisal. If the Company has done a complete and honest investor relations job, the over-pricing is not the fault of the management. Furthermore, it may be noted that managements are notoriously wrong in their evaluation of the price of their company's stock.

Is Your Stock Reasonably Priced?

When you get ready to sell new stock, it is a puzzle to try to decide whether your stock is at a reasonable price. In the short run, the stock market is irrational and there is no way to account for its action. However, there are some things you can look at to tell whether the price of your stock is at a reasonable level:

1. *What return should an investor get?* In the first place, an investor buying the stock should get a reasonable return on his investment. What do you think is a reasonable return for the investor from both dividend yield and percent market appreciation? Should it be 10%, 11%, 12% or more based on experience such as in 1974? Pick a figure and then relate it to the long range return you think your company can earn on book value. An investor cannot get more than the company earns. For example, if you think an investor should get a 12% return and your company will earn 12% on book value on the average over a long period of time, then the stock is worth

book value and about eight times earnings. Only if your company can earn a higher rate of return should the price-earnings ratio be higher.

An approach to stock value based on a return to investors is discussed in the last chapter of the book.

2. *The earnings level.* With the above comments in mind, what is the current return on common book value in relation to the long range average? Is it low and likely to go up or is it at a peak?
3. *The price-earnings ratio.* What is the price-earnings ratio in relation to your historical average and to other comparable stocks?

   A company earning 20% on common book value and selling at ten times earnings will have the same market price related to book value as a stock earning 10% on book value and selling at 20 times earnings.
4. *The dividend yield.* If dividend yield is a significant factor as far as price is concerned, what is the yield compared to the past and related to other similar stocks with similar payout ratios?
5. *Market price related to book value.* What is the relationship of the market price to book value compared to the past and other similar stocks? This is a function of the rate earned on the book value and the price-earnings ratio.
6. *The outlook for earnings.* What is a reasonable appraisal of the outlook for the company? Perhaps put less weight on this factor because of management's general optimism regarding the outlook for their company.

With these figures before you, stand back and take a look at the broad picture to see if you can get some idea of whether your stock is reasonably priced, keeping in mind that, in the long run, investors should get a fair return. Ask yourself—would you rush out and buy the stock at the current price? You cannot pick the peak of the market to sell stock. You can only tell whether your stock is selling at a reasonable price level. You should attempt to do stock financing in good markets if your plan calls for common and not try to postpone it in the hopes of higher earnings and a higher price-earnings ratio. Reaching for the moon when common is needed has resulted in many companies being forced to sell common at low prices when the market took a nose dive.

Size of Common Stock Offering

How much common stock to offer will depend on the company's need for outside funds and what has to be done in order to maintain a sound financial position. However, there are some rules of thumb with regard to the size of an offering in terms of the effect on earnings per share. As we pointed out in Chapter 6, a 1-for-10 offering, or one new share for each ten shares outstanding, is considered an average-sized offering. It will mean an immediate decrease in earnings per share of 9.09%. A 1 for 20, which will result in a 4.76% decrease in earnings per share, is a light offering. A 1 for 5 is a heavy offering; it will result in a 16.7% decrease in earnings per share. We do not suggest what is right to do in a particular case because it will depend on all the factors surrounding the situation. We are merely suggesting how it may be thought of in the marketplace.

NEGOTIATED DIRECT OFFERING

In a direct sale, the underwriters purchase the stock either on a negotiated basis or at competitive bidding, and then resell it to investors at the offering price. We will first cover negotiated direct offerings.

Setting the Price

We will start our discussion of a negotiated direct offering just prior to the announcement of the offering. Undoubtedly, you will be talking with underwriters prior to the announcement of the offering. They may give you some preliminary ideas on pricing the issue and how much they will charge. They may over-state their case in order to prevent you from going to some other underwriter. Furthermore, such comments may not mean much if the whole market changes by the time the stock is offered. In order for you to follow how subsequent changes in the general market may affect their preliminary comments, you should keep an index of stock prices as nearly similar to your issue as possible.

The market price of a stock will tend to decline relative to other similar stocks from the day of the announcement of the financing to the day of the offering. This is known as pre-offering pressure. It may take effect prior to the formal announcement if the financial community has anticipated that the common offering will take place.

Pre-offering pressure results from buyers withholding their orders for the following reasons:

1. They may feel that the added supply will result in a lower price and they can buy it cheaper.
2. The added number of shares may cause some dilution in earnings per share.
3. They can get stock at the offering price without paying a brokerage commission.

The extent of the pressure will depend on all the circumstances surrounding the company, the offering and the prevailing market for securities.

The signing of the agreement with the underwriters and setting the offering price will take place in the afternoon after the close of the market on the day prior to the offering. At that time, there are two questions to be resolved:

1. The offering price to the public.
2. The amount the company will pay the underwriters, also referred to as underwriters' compensation, or the spread.

The offering price less the spread gives the price the underwriters will pay the company.

Where should the price be set relative to the closing market price? For example, if the closing market price is $100 per share, should the offering price be $100 1/4, $99 or some other figure? It depends on many factors, such as:

1. *The pre-offering market action.*
   How has the market price for the stock reacted after the announcement of the financing in relation to the general market; in other words, what is the extent of the pre-offering pressure? If it has been great, the market price may have over-reacted. This will tend to justify a high offering price in relation to the closing market price. On the other hand, if the stock has held up better than would be expected, there may be reason for placing the offering price lower.
2. *The issue.*
   All the circumstances surrounding the issue such as the size of the offering and the offering ratio.
3. *The market for the stock.*
   The nature of the existing market for the company's stock, including whether it is closely held or widely distributed, whether the potential interest comes from individuals or institutions, whether it is listed or over-the-counter.
4. *The quality of the stock and its outlook.*
   Everything which affects the quality and outlook for the company and its stock, and its relative attractiveness compared with other types of stock.
5. *Investor interest in the issue.*
   The potential interest of investors in the new offering, as indicated by the market canvass by the underwriters prior to the offering. The underwriters, through their contacts with purchasers, will feel out the attitude of buyers carefully before the price is set.
6. *The condition of the securities market.*
   The general condition of the securities market, including its relative level, and the general interest of investors toward the purchase of new issues. This is a very important factor in setting the price.

During a bull market with strong demand for stocks, the price can be set high.

With a strong demand for a stock, the offering price may be at a small premium of 1/4 or 1/2 point over the market price. Purchasers of the new issue get stock at the offering price without paying a brokerage commission, which would be necessary if.they bought the stock in the market. Without favorable circumstances, it would be expected that the offering price would be set at a slight discount of 1/4 or 1/2 point below the market. The discount will range higher as the factors become less favorable. It may have to be substantial for a small, little-known, speculative type of stock.

It is generally considered beneficial to all concerned if a common stock is priced so that it can be sold within a reasonable length of time. If after the offering it immediately sinks in price, then the unsophisticated investors who bought it may feel some dissatisfaction and may not be as interested when the company offers more stock. Sophisticated buyers know what price they want to pay and don't need to be mollycoddled. These remarks assume a level securities market; investors cannot expect to be protected against a change in price due to a break in the general market.

Underwriters make a big pitch about the importance of pricing an issue so that it will go to a slight premium after the sale in order to make investors happy. Of course, such a procedure makes it much easier for the underwriters and reduces their risk. However, to be realistic, the period directly after the offering is over rather quickly, and whether investors are happy will depend on whether the stock goes up over the long run. Only the company's performance and the general movement of stocks will determine this action.

Certainly pricing a stock so that the deal will be successful does not mean setting it so low that it is obviously a bargain. The company must try to get as much net proceeds per share as possible, within the qualifications suggested above of making the deal a success; the company owes this to existing stockholders. If, after the offering, the stock jumps to a substantial premium, without any change in the general level of the market, then it may indicate that the price was too low and that the company has been taken by the underwriters. By then it is too late, as far as the company is concerned; the cat is already out of the bag.

Once the offering price has been set and filed with the Securities and Exchange Commission, that is the price at which the underwriters must sell the issue as long as the agreement among the underwriters in the group is in effect. This may be for about two weeks; it may be extended for another short period if the underwriters in the group think they can sell the issue at the offering price, given more time. As pointed out in the chapter on Selling Senior Securities, it is illegal under the Securities Act of 1933 to sell the stock above the offering price. If the issue is a failure when the agreement among underwriters terminates, the members may then sell the remaining securities at whatever lower price than the subscription price they can obtain. It would be quite unethical, and illegal according to the Securities Act of 1933, for them to withhold securities of a successful deal in order to benefit by a price rise after the underwriting agreement is terminated.

Review of Pricing an Issue and Financing Expenses

If you wish to review the discussion of pricing a direct offering, you can refer to Exhibit 9-1, which shows the facts in a diagram. The exhibit includes the term total underpricing. Total underpricing refers to the net amount the company receives related to the market price before there is any pre-offering pressure. Total underpricing includes the pre-offering pressure, the amount by which the price is set below the market, the underwriters' compensation and the expenses of the

Exhibit 9-1

UNDERPRICING FOR A DIRECT OFFERING OF COMMON STOCK

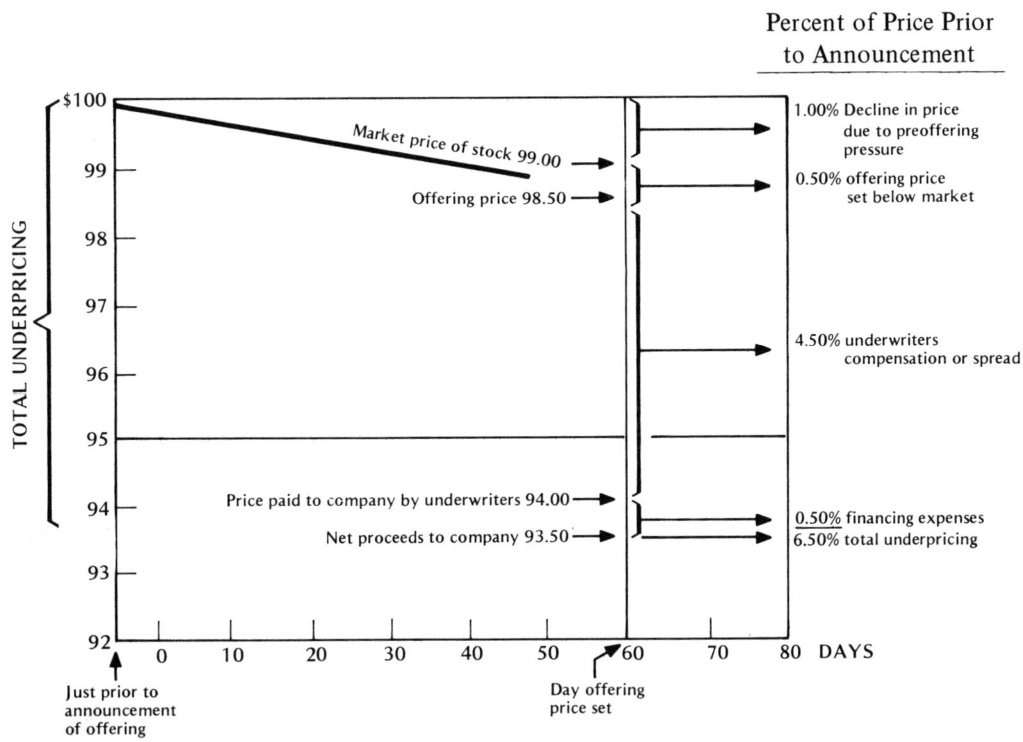

		Percentage of Price Prior to Announcement
Market price of stock just before announcement	$100.00	
Decline in price due to pre-offering pressure	1.00	1.00%
Market price on day offering price set	99.00	
Amount by which offering price is set under market	0.50	0.50
Offering price	98.50	
Underwriters' compensation or spread	4.50	4.50
Price paid to company by underwriters	94.00	
Corporate expenses	0.50	0.50
Net proceeds to company	93.50	6.50

offering. Expenses include: SEC fees, listing fees, Federal revenue stamps, state taxes and fees, transfer agents' fees, printing and engraving, legal, accounting, engineering and miscellaneous expenses.

The underwriters' spread expressed as a percent depends to some extent on the price of the stock. The selling concession has to be somewhat more than the brokerage commission a security salesman could make on a listed stock. And as the share price decreases the brokerage commission becomes a larger percentage. Therefore, for a low-priced stock, the total underwriters' spread may be a higher percentage than for a similar higher-priced stock.

Financing Costs

How much should you agree to pay the underwriters for a direct offering? They may perform two services:

1. Buying the security from you and taking the risk of disposing of it. This is their principal service.
2. Assistance and advice in preparing the financing for market. The value of this service will depend on how complicated your deal is.

The risk the underwriters assume depends upon all the factors discussed above which affect the pricing of the issue. If there is very strong demand, they may see where the stock can all be sold almost as soon as it is bought; then their risk is small. In fact, the underwriters will probably have the issue already sold before the underwriting agreement is signed. To actually sell the issue prior to filing the price with the Securities and Exchange Commission is illegal. However, prior to the offering, the underwriters will obtain ideas as to the amount the buyers might take and how they might react to a price. If the buyers are interested, they will tell the underwriters to "circle" a certain number of shares for them. This means that when the issue is priced and offered, the buyers expect to buy that number of shares. This is not a contract or agreement because that would be illegal; either party can back out. But the custom is that neither party withdraws. As a practical matter, in many negotiated deals, the underwriters have the issue "sold" before they buy the securities from the company.

If the issue is a difficult one to sell, and the underwriters expect to hold at least a part of it pending a vigorous sales effort, their risk mounts up.

As we pointed out in the chapter on Selling Senior Securities, the gross compensation paid the underwriters has to cover four items. For a high-grade stock, a breakdown of the underwriters' compensation might be as follows: allowance for selling cost 60% which covers dealer concession; management fee for head underwriter 20% and allowance to cover the underwriting function 20%, which includes expenses of 5%.

A typical prospectus for a direct offering will include data as shown in Exhibit 9-2. The stock was offered at $24.25. The underwriters' spread was 3.09% of the offering price. This offering was in a period when the

Exhibit 9-2

CERTAIN DATA INCLUDED IN PROSPECTUS FOR DIRECT OFFERING

	Price to Public	Underwriting Discounts and Commissions	Proceeds to Company*
Per Share	$24.25	$.75	$23.50
Total	$17,581,250	$543,750	$17,037,500

*Before deducting expenses estimated at $82,870.

The Underwriters have advised the Company that they propose to offer the additional shares of Common Stock to the public initially at the public offering price set forth on the cover page hereof, and to certain dealers at such price less a concession of not in excess of 40¢ per share. The Underwriters and such dealers may allow a discount, not in excess of 25¢ per share on sales to other dealers.

stock market was favorable and the spread was relatively low. The estimated expenses of the offering which the company had to pay were 0.47%.

You may wonder what is meant by the statement about dealer discount which was 40¢ per share or 53% of the underwriters' compensation. We explained this for sale of debt securities but will review it again. What it says is that the underwriters can allow, out of their spread of 75¢ per share, a discount to selected dealers up to 40¢ per share. The underwriters and selected dealers can allow up to 25¢ to other non-selected dealers.

The selected dealers are the ones who have been specifically chosen by the underwriting group to help market the issue. They will include the principal dealers who will be expected to be interested in working on the issue. These selected dealers do not have an underwriting commitment. However, if they sell some stock at the offering price of $24.25, they can obtain the stock from the underwriters at 40¢ less than the offering price, or at $23.85. They can then sell it at $24.25; thus they make 40¢ per share.

Any dealer, other than selected dealers, can sell the stock for $24.25 and obtain it from the underwriters or selected dealers at a 25¢ discount or $24. Thus they would make 25¢ per share. It is never expected that the dealers, other than the selected dealers, will play much of a part in the marketing effort; their discount merely permits them to accommodate their customers.

The allowance to the selling group—that is, to selected dealers—must be sufficient to induce dealers to take an active interest in pushing the issue. The size of the allowance will depend on the extent of the sales effort needed. It may be related to the commission for a trade on the New York Stock Exchange, but be larger in order to provide incentive to sell the new issue. It may vary up to two times a Stock Exchange commission under some circumstances. It should be noted that only a small part of an issue may be sold by dealers; it is only on those shares that the allowance to dealers is paid. However, the underwriters will need some compensation for the sales effort of their own firm. Underwriters may use the need for a large discount to selected dealers as an argument for a large underwriting spread.

The New York Stock Exchange Commission for 100 shares for a stock selling for $24.25 might be approximately 44¢ per share today. At the time the stock in the exhibit was offered, the New York Stock Exchange Commission was lower.

The amount required to cover the underwriting risk may be small for a high grade issue in a favorable market. The underwriters' compensation will increase for a more speculative type of stock in a poor market.

The underwriters' compensation may be quite dependent on where the offering price is set, as that will have a lot to do with the attractiveness of the offering to potential buyers and how quickly the issue can be sold. The company should recognize that where the price is set determines the amount it gets. For example, if the market price is $100 and the offering price is set at 100 1/2, with an underwriters' spread of $4 the company gets a net of 96 1/2. On the other hand, if the price is set at 99 1/2 with an underwriters' spread of $4, the company gets a net of 95 1/2.

Financing costs depend on all the circumstances at the time of the offering, including general market conditions and the nature of the offering.

Exhibit 9-3 gives financing costs for common stocks over a ten-year period. Note how the underwriters' spread varies from year to year.

Size of issue has a major effect on financing costs and Exhibit 9-4 shows the effect of size. Note how the costs become relatively large for small issues. This is due to two factors: the smaller issues tend to be of less well-known companies, for which there is more risk, and underwriters' expenses do not decrease proportionately with size. When you get ready to finance, you will want to compile up-to-date information for comparable issues.

New Untried Offerings of Common

For small and untried companies, underwriters may take part of their compensation through allocation of some of the common stock at a discount below the public offering price. The amount of this discount must be considered as part of financing cost. It may turn out to be very sizeable. Generally, the underwriters hold their stock for more than six months in order to turn their profit into a long-term capital gain for tax purposes.

Two examples of offerings in which the underwriters walked off with a large share of the company follow:

1) The underwriter paid $50 for 50,000 shares or .1¢ per share. The public paid $2 a share.
2) The insiders picked up 50% of the company for $16,000. The public got the other half for an investment of more than $1 million.

It is not easy to raise money for small, new ventures and the underwriters deserve adequate compensation. However, such a company should weigh carefully whether the cost

Exhibit 9-3

FINANCING COSTS FOR ALL COMMON STOCKS*

As Percent of Gross Amount of Issue

Year	Underwriters' Compensation	Expenses	Total
1973	5.08%	.91%	5.99%
1972	4.83	.64	5.47
1971	5.59	1.10	6.69
1970	5.56	.91	6.47
1969	4.93	1.04	5.97
1968	6.05	1.36	7.41
1967	5.93	1.13	7.05
1966	5.29	.87	6.15
1965	4.51	.58	5.09
1964	4.00	.67	4.67
Average	4.15	.80	4.95

*Securities Industry Association, 20 Broad Street, New York, New York, Special Study.

Exhibit 9-4

FINANCING COSTS FOR ALL COMMON STOCKS*
EFFECT OF SIZE OF ISSUE

Average Figures 1964-1973

As Percent of Gross Amount of Issue

Size of Issue (000's Omitted)	Underwriters' Compensation	Expenses	Total
$ 0– 499	11.07%	8.74%	19.81%
500– 999	10.18	6.52	16.70
1,000– 1,999	8.80	4.41	13.21
2,000– 4,999	7.63	2.24	9.87
5,000– 9,999	6.19	1.45	7.64
10,000–19,999	5.18	.87	6.05
20,000–49,999	4.41	.52	4.93
50,000–over	3.96	.25	4.21

*Securities Industry Association, 20 Broadway, New York, N.Y. Special Study.

to raise capital can be justified by the prospects for the company. The cost of financing for small companies may be astronomical; a new venture would have to be "really" successful in order to achieve a profit goal sufficient to compensate for such financing costs.

Generally, financing of this type takes place at the peak of a bull market when investors are eager to buy almost anything. Then, even junk can be sold relatively easily.

In your negotiation with underwriters, how can you know where the offering price should be set and the amount to pay them? You can't do too much because you do not have the direct contact with the buyers which gives the potential interest in the issue. That is why you should be sure when choosing your underwriters that you evaluate their ability and integrity carefully. However, the difficulty of your being able to do a refined job does not suggest that you should not be conversant with all available information so that you can negotiate intelligently. This will call for a study of all reasonably comparable issues which have been offered within the past few months prior to your offering as well as what has happened to the general market during this period. But you should realize that you are at a disadvantage because the underwriters hold all the cards.

Best Efforts Financing

Sometimes small issues which may be hard to sell are handled by small underwriting houses on a best efforts basis. They will sell "all or nothing"—in effect, on consignment. It entails no underwriting risk. The underwriter does not put up any cash, as he would if the stock were on a "firm commitment." A company which is so weak that it has to resort to this type of financing probably has its back to the wall.

Formula Offering

The price of an offering may be established on a so-called formula basis in relation to the market on the day the stock is offered. For example, the company and the underwriters will agree on the underwriting spread, either in terms of a percent or dollar amount, and that the offering price shall be within a certain range of the market price on the day the stock is offered. This information is filed with the Securities and Exchange Commission and is included in the prospectus. This method has the advantage of getting the registration effective before the final price is established. It permits the underwriters to start selling as soon as the underwriting agreement is signed. Otherwise, they have to wait until the price and underwriting compensation is filed with the Securities and Exchange Commission. It has the disadvantage of not being able to set the offering price and underwriters' spread on the day immediately prior to the offering based on the most recent market information.

Stabilization

Stabilization may be used in some types of financing. Its purpose is to maintain the price of a security at a certain level. In order for this to occur, a bid is placed in the market on the floor of the Exchange to purchase any of the security coming on the market at a specific price. As long as the bid price is continued, the market price cannot fall below that level.

Price maintenance can be done only in a limited way. The price of a stock is determined by the supply and demand. If the supply becomes great, it will be necessary to purchase that supply in order to maintain the price. And if securities are being offered, the net effect is to reduce the amount offered by the amount purchased for stabilization purposes. Therefore, stabilization can be used only to prevent a small supply of stock from causing a price decline due to a temporary imbalance in the market. To this extent, stabilization may be helpful.

A simple example of how it is used is as follows: An underwriting firm in a negotiated financing of a direct offering of common stock signs the underwriting agreement with the company and agrees to pay to the company $95 per share.

The underwriters' plan is to offer the stock at a price of $100, so that their spread is $5. At the time of the signing of the underwriting agreement, the market price of the stock is $100 1/4. Once the underwriting agreement is signed, the underwriters may put in a stabilizing bid at a price of $100. Thus, the public offering price agreed upon with the company is protected against a decline as long as only a small amount of stock is thrown on the market by the public. If the general market for stocks sinks and the underwriters are hit with a large amount of stock, they may have to "pull" their stabilization bid; otherwise, they would be defeating their own purpose. They would be buying stock on balance rather than selling the stock they had underwritten. When the market sinks, they have a turkey on their hands as far as the underwriting is concerned. But they would only be aggravating the situation by trying to stem the tide through stabilization.

Stabilization is largely limited to companies listed on an exchange where purchase and sales are funneled through one point.

A utility company which offers its stock directly on a competitive basis might like to stabilize the price just before the bids are opened. However, the bidding underwriters may object to such a procedure if the company produced an artificial market price on which underwriters had to base their bid. A company might wish to include the right to stabilize in its prospectus for the issue, but it should recognize the problem which it might produce.

If a rights offering is underwritten, the underwriter will handle any stabilization which might be done just prior to the time that the subscription price is set. If a rights offering is not underwritten the company might like to have the right to stabilize in the prospectus, but it would probably not have sufficient knowledge to use it. Stabilization cannot be used in a rights offering once the subscription period starts.

Stabilization requires an intimate knowledge of security markets and must be handled by experts. It must be spelled out in the prospectus. The company will probably wish to employ an underwriting firm, familiar with security markets, to handle the operation. In order to prevent manipulation of security prices, the Securities and Exchange Commission carefully limits the procedure followed in stabilization. A stabilization bid must be reported to the Securities and Exchange Commission. If a stock is listed, the bid goes on the quotation tape and is so designated.

Why should the Financial Vice President know about stabilization? For two reasons: so that he will realize that it may play a part in assisting the market action of his company's stock during an offering, and secondly, that if it is applied, except to assist the market in a limited way, a serious financial fiasco may result in a sinking market.

Over-Allotment

In a negotiated direct offering of common stock, the underwriter will probably over-allot the issue. By that is meant that a small amount of extra shares will be sold in addition to that specified in the underwriting agreement. For example, if 1 million shares are underwritten, the underwriter might sell up to 1,050,000 shares or 5% more than the shares underwritten. The purpose is to put the underwriter in a short position when the offering is complete so that he can go into the market to obtain the shares to cover the over-allotment. By so doing he helps to give the market a boost, so that the stock will go to a slight premium and make an attractive picture for the investors.

Another reason for over-allotment is the fact that a few investors who agreed to purchase the stock may not take up their stock and a few investors may even sell the stock as soon as they get it. Over-allotment provides a way to absorb this stock.

Green Shoe

An underwriter can get caught by over-alloting if the market moves up sharply after the offering so that a premium has to be paid in order to purchase shares to meet the over-allotment. To overcome this problem, the Green Shoe approach may be used. The company agrees to sell the underwriter up to 10% more stock at the offering price in order to cover over-allotment. This puts the underwriter in a safe position. If the market declines after the offering, the underwriter can step in and buy stock in order to support the market. If, however, the market moves up after the offering, the underwriter is protected by the company furnishing the stock at the offering price to cover over-allotment. It is called Green Shoe, because it was first used in an offering by that company.

Over-allotment is perfectly legal and it is subject to the regulations of the Securities and Exchange Commission.

Offering When no Previous Stock Outstanding

When a company has no stock publicly held and there is no market quotation available, there is no price which can be used as a guide to judge the offering price. Such a situation will occur if a company has been privately owned or is a new venture. Then it will be necessary to make some estimate of how much the stock might be worth as compared with similar types of stocks for which there are available market quotations. This estimate will take the form of a statistical comparison with principal ratios. The pricing of the issue in relation to comparable issues will be affected by how well the company is known to investors and the interest that can be developed with potential investors. If the company is a large, well-known company, there may be a strong potential demand and it can be fully priced; otherwise, there may have to be a significant discount. An offering of stock in a new, speculative venture might have to be offered at a substantial discount to make it attractive in relation to potential uncertain earnings. There is no market for such a type of stock except in a bull market.

In a bull market with investors crawling all over each other to get new stocks, pricing presents a special type of problem. It may be possible to price the issue for more than it is worth. Then the question arises whether the issue should be fully priced, with the prospects that it will subsequently fall in price and the stockholders will be very unhappy. There is relatively little a company can do about such a situation when fools want to be parted from their money. However, a company should be aware that it will mean some trouble in the future, and it should proceed with some conscience.

COMPETITIVE DIRECT OFFERING

Competitive bidding is used by companies which are regulated, such as utility companies. Underwriters despise competitive bidding just as we all dislike competition for ourselves but not for the other fellow when we are on the buyer's side.

Underwriters may contend that companies only use competitive bidding for common stocks which are forced to do so by regulation. This is not altogether true because some utility companies use it by choice. Exhibit 9-5 shows how principally electric utility stocks were offered in 1971, 1972 and 1973. These were years in which there was a large volume of such financing and very uncertain market conditions, supposedly a time when competitive bidding would not work. In 1973, the number of issues offered competitively was 28% of the total and 34% by amount. In 1974, when Wall Street was in a state of shock, when utilities were having major problems and investors were in hiding, competitive bidding had to be largely abandoned. Regulatory authorities recognized the situation and permitted negotiations providing a company would visit a number of underwriters to seek the best deal.

Exhibit 9-5

PRINCIPALLY ELECTRIC UTILITY COMMON STOCK
FINANCING BY METHOD OF SALE
ISSUES OVER $10 MILLION IN SIZE

PART I

NUMBER OF ISSUES

	Negotiated		Competitive		Total	
Year	Number	%	Number	%	Number	%
1973	36	72	14	28	50	100%
1972	35	78	10	22	45	100
1971	31	71	13	30	44	100

PART II

AMOUNT
(000,000 Omitted)

	Negotiated		Competitive		Total	
Year	Amount	%	Amount	%	Amount	%
1973	$1,600	66	$832	34	$2,432	100%
1972	1,474	73	542	27	2,016	100
1971	1,335	69	597	31	1,932	100

There may be circumstances under which negotiated offering of a utility common stock may produce better results such as:

1. A company with serious problems which require much analysis on the part of the underwriters and a special marketing job.
2. An issue which is too small to make it worthwhile for underwriters to bother to bid on a competitive sale—an issue of under $5 million.
3. An issue which is too large to make it possible for two groups of underwriters to be formed so that there will be competition.
4. Very adverse and uncertain security markets.

However, as we have noted, competitive bidding has worked successfully for common stocks of utility companies. As one example, note the comparison of a competitive vs. a negotiated financing for two utilities as shown in Exhibit 9-6. Here we only present a few statistics because it is such a clear-cut case that competitive bidding was better.

In Exhibit 9-7 is a story about how members of a syndicate got into a hassle in deciding on what they should bid. One of the lead members felt the pricc to the public was too high and pulled out. Suppose the company had negotiated with that firm rather than with the one that was more aggressive?

It would be quite incorrect to say that these limited examples prove that a utility company should offer common stock competitively; they are presented merely to focus attention on the point. A utility in making a decision should consider all the surrounding circumstances as we have suggested, such as the nature of the company, the size of the offering, market conditions, etc.

It should also make a study of all comparable competitive and negotiated offerings in

Exhibit 9-6

COMPARISON OF COMMON STOCK OFFERING

Competitive vs. Negotiated

	(Competitive) Company C (Bonds Rated Aa)	(Negotiated) Company N (Bonds Rated Aa)
Day Price Set	2/13/73	2/8/73
Number Shares Offered	750,000	1,500,000
Outstanding Prior to Sale	6,600,000	15,487,408
Approximate Dilution	11%	10%
Price-Earnings Ratio	11	9 1/2
Price to Public	$31.875	$20.00
Underwriters' Discount	$ 0.689	$ 0.75
Net Proceeds to Company	$31.186	$19.25
Closing Price on Day Price Set	$32.35	$20.375
Price to Public Under Market	1.14%	1.75%
Underwriters' Cost as % of Offering Price	2.16%	3.75%
Net Proceeds to Company Under Market	3.30%	5.50%

Market Action Prior to Offering:

	Dow Jones Index	Market Price	Market Price
2/6	113.46		$21.625
2/7	113.27		21.000
2/8	113.15		20.375
2/9	113.34	$31.75	
2/12	114.04	32.50	
2/13	113.75	32.35	

the last year to see what the results have been in terms of the net proceeds the company received after deducting the underwriters' spread as a percent of the closing market price just prior to the offering. The problem in such a study is to obtain a sample of companies which are comparable. Therefore, you should include in a statistical comparison the principal factors which may have affected the offering, such as: size of offering, offering ratio, price-earnings ratio, yield, quality of company's securities as shown by bond ratings, the percent of revenues derived from electricity and gas, common equity as a percent of total capital, etc.

The condition of the market at the time of each offering may have a lot to do with net proceeds a company received. Therefore, the samples should be matched as nearly as possible as to the times of offerings. Since it will be virtually impossible to get comparable negotiated and competitive issues at the same time, care should be taken to study the possible effect of different offering times. A background as to what happened in the market during the period is essential in order to be able to interpret the figures correctly.

There is one other major disturbing factor in such a comparison; that is, how the stocks acted marketwise prior to the time of the offering. If an issue moved down just before the offering, the price might represent a more attractive buy to potential investors and an easier issue for underwriters to sell than an

Exhibit 9-7

COMPETITIVE BIDDING STORY FOR A UTILITY

February 28, 1973

By a *Wall Street Journal* Staff Reporter*

NEW YORK—The Corporation's 1.2 million common share public offering reached investors at $44.75 apiece despite an unsuccessful attempt by some syndicate members to trim that price, dealers said.

The offering, made after the market closed yesterday, divided the 11-manager group, causing four members, including the chief underwriter, to desert. Infighting aside, the offering was reported over-subscribed by "Underwriter X," which assumed control of the books from "Underwriter Y."

"There was substantial institutional interest in the stock, but we differed over whether those institutions would be willing to pay a premium over the last sale, particularly in this weak market," an "Underwriter Y" spokesman said.

An "Underwriter X" official asserted: "The balance of the group felt there was a justifiable business risk in underwriting it."

The Corporation's common closed unchanged at $44.50 apiece on a volume of 4,800 shares in New York Stock Exchange trading. The stock market closed lower for the fifth consecutive day, with the Dow Jones industrial average ending 947.92, down 5.87 points from the previous session.

"Underwriter X" said most of the pre-sale orders for 1.1 million shares weren't canceled as a result of the 25-cent premium above the stock's closing price, and those who balked "were replaced." The offering price was "near the bottom of the stock's 1972-73 trading range of $53 to $39.50, which made it attractive to investors," the spokesman said. Buyers included insurance companies, pension funds, banks and investment advisers, he added.

The .... company awarded the stock to the "Underwriter X" group on a bid of $44.189 a share, a mere 6 cents more than a rival bidding group. Had the rival bidding group won, the price to the public also would have been $44.75.

issue which had moved up. There is opportunity for pressure being brought to bear on a direct offering of common just prior to setting the price, particularly for competitive bidding.

In a competitive bid, the bidding takes place in the afternoon after the close of the market. Suppose an institution which owns some stock is interested in buying a large amount more. Just before the close of the market, the institution hits the market with enough shares to knock the market price off a point or more. The underwriters will be influenced by the last sale in determining their bid prices. The institution will then be in a position to buy a large amount of the stock from the underwriters at some savings. This is dirty pool and manipulation. It is illegal for a prospective underwriter to participate in such action, either directly or indirectly. However, it is legal for a prospective purchaser to do so. Such action should be made illegal by preventing an investor who sells stock two weeks before an offering from buying any stock until two months after the offering.

Theoretically, if a stock is listed, the specialist should prevent a stock from going off as a result of such action. A company offering stock should be in touch with its specialist and explain that it will expect a clear explanation for any unusual market action just prior to the offering.

A company offering stock on a direct basis may wish to ask the Securities and Exchange Commission to provide surveillance of the market prior to the offering date in order to scare off this type of action.

In the over-the-counter market where trading is widely dispersed, there may be more adverse unaccounted for market action when new stock is about to make its appearance.

Trying to decide whether to sell a common issue negotiated or competitive is a difficult question for the management of a utility company. Competitive bidding has the distinct advantage of absolving the management of the difficult task of justifying to regulatory authorities the price it received. A good approach for a company to take is to use competitive bidding unless it can be shown beyond any reasonable doubt that there would be a savings with a negotiated offering.

OFFERING THROUGH RIGHTS

You undoubtedly know what is meant by offering stock through rights to existing stockholders, but here is a little review.

As an example, we will take a company with 1 million shares of common. The management decides to sell 100,000 new shares through rights to existing stockholders; the ratio is one new share for ten held. The stockholders are given the right to subscribe to the new stock in proportion to their existing holdings at a price below the market price. This valuable right must be exercised in a certain number of days.

This is a public offering and must be registered with the Securities and Exchange Commission. The procedure in such financing is to send to each stockholder an announcement of the offering, a prospectus describing the company and terms of the offering and a warrant to subscribe.

Each stockholder receives one warrant stating the number of rights to which he is entitled; that is, one right for each share of stock he owns. In our example, if a stockholder owned 100 shares, his warrant would show 100 rights. Since the offering of new stock is on the basis of one new share for each ten shares held, then the 100 rights would permit a stockholder to subscribe to ten new shares. In other words, there is one right for each share of stock outstanding before the new offering.

The warrant states the subscription price and the day on which the warrant expires.

Division of New Shares into Three Groups

The new shares will fall into one of the three categories as a result of stockholders' actions:

1. *Shares subscribed by original stockholders.*

   Some stockholders subscribe by signing the warrants and sending them to a subscription agent with a check for the subscription price for the number of shares to which they are entitled.

2. *Shares subscribed by purchasers of rights.*

   Some stockholders sell their rights through a broker and deliver the warrant so that the purchaser can subscribe.

3. *The tag end shares unsubscribed due to lapsed rights.*

   Some stockholders fail to do anything and let their rights lapse for various reasons: stockholders may die during the rights period, others may be away from home and not receive their mail and still others may forget. The extent of lapsed rights will depend somewhat on the nature of the stockholder list. For example, a company which has been through financial difficulties and reorganization will probably have more stockholders who disregard their rights than a relatively new company which has been prosperous. These unsubscribed shares are referred to as "tag end."

There is not much information available on the amount of shares represented by categories 1 and 2 above. In compiling results of rights offerings, companies generally do not distinguish between subscriptions by the original stockholders and those who purchase rights and then subscribe. There may be considerable variation in the amount of shares in categories 1 and 2 for different offerings. For purposes of this chapter, we will assume that the rights continue to have value during the subscription period and use the following figures for the three categories:

1. Shares subscribed by original holders–50%
2. Shares subscribed by purchasers of rights–47%
3. Tag end shares unsubscribed due to lapsed rights–3%

Of course, if the market price falls below the subscription price, there is no incentive for anyone to subscribe and the number of lapsed rights would be large.

Confusion may arise between the number of stockholders and the number of shares represented by these three categories. We are interested in the number of shares and not the number of stockholders. In discussing a rights offering, be careful that someone doesn't mislead you by using the number of stockholders rather than the number of shares.

If the issue is underwritten, the tag end or unsubscribed shares go to the underwriter to sell. If there is no underwriter, then the company may do nothing with the tag end and reduce the offering by that amount, or it may arrange to sell them to an underwriter after the subscription period is over. Tag end shares can also be taken care of through over-subscription, discussed subsequently. In some instances, companies have arranged to offer the unsubscribed shares to employees either at the market price or the subscription price.

The Subscription Period

One of the important elements in a rights offering is the number of days between the day the company sets the subscription price and the end of the subscription period. It is this period which the company must study in setting the subscription price, and which affects the risks to be allowed for; the shorter the period, the less risk of something happening which might depress the market price of the stock below the subscription price.

For stocks listed on the New York Stock Exchange, the Exchange has something to say about the procedure in a rights offering, particularly as to the length of the subscription period. The Exchange wants to be certain that there is enough time to permit stockholders to act. The length of the period will depend on the number of stockholders, their location and the extent of the facilities which the company provides for assisting stockholders to subscribe. Under some circumstances, the New York Stock Exchange will permit a period of 16 days from the day the warrants are mailed to the stockholders to the end of the subscription period. The subscription price has to be set before the warrants can be printed and mailed out. For very large offerings, where stockholders are scattered throughout the world, a period as long as 55 days has been used.

The sequence of important dates is shown in diagram form in Exhibit 9-8. We have used a slightly longer interval than presently allowed by the New York Stock Exchange.

A study of rights offering has to begin just before the announcement of the proposed new common stock financing, because the market price of the existing stock will generally be affected by the announcement. As our take-off point, we will use one or two days prior to announcement of the offering; our "countdown" starts here. The day the subscription price is set is our "launching day."

The subscription price has to be set in order for the value of the rights to be established. When the subscription price is filed with the Securities and Exchange commission, the registration statement becomes effective. Trading in the rights will start on a "when issued" basis as soon as the registration statement is effective. The term "when issued" means just what it implies: the rights have not yet been sent out to stockholders.

Exhibit 9-8

SEQUENCE OF EVENTS FOR RIGHTS OFFERING

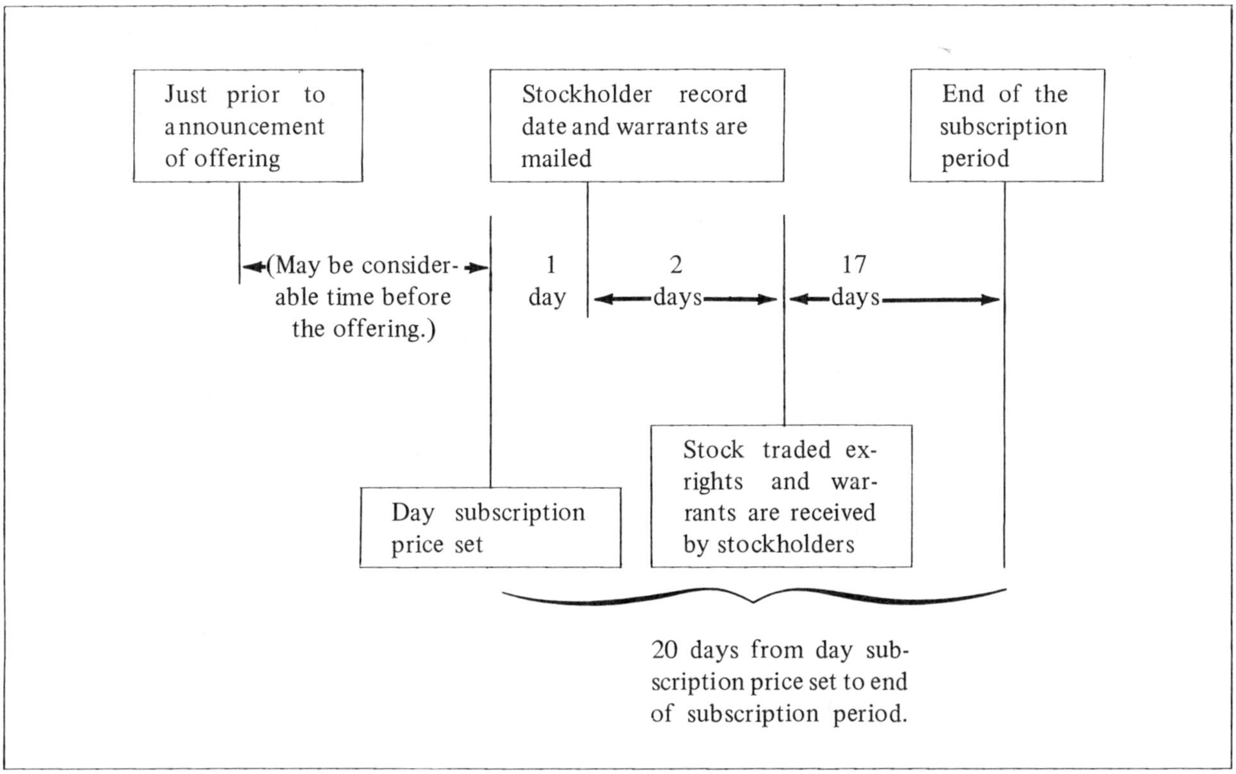

The stockholder record date establishes the stockholder list for mailing warrants. This may also be the day the registration statement becomes effective. The New York Stock Exchange fixes the day for listed stocks on which trading is ex-rights; that is, when the stock no longer has the rights attached, usually the second day after the record date. If a stockholder sells his stock after the record date but before the stock is traded ex-rights, then when he receives the rights, he will have to forward them to the purchaser of the stock.

Questions to Be Answered in a Rights Offering

There are three major questions you will need to answer:

1. How far should the subscription price be set below the market price?
2. Should the issue be underwritten?
3. If underwritten, how much should you pay the underwriter?

Since a large amount of explanation must follow, it might be of assistance if we give you a brief answer to the first question at this point.

There is a wide range within which a company may decide to set the subscription price below the market price on the day the subscription price is set, from a few percentage points up to 25% and more. In this book, we will call this figure, which is expressed as a percent or dollar amount, the discount.

Four Categories of Discount

The amount of discount can be put in four different categories. The figures we will use assume a generally favorable stock market.

1) *A small discount.*

An offering generally falls into this category if the subscription price is set 6% or less below the market for a moderate-sized issue of a stable type of stock. For a larger, less stable type of stock, the percentage would be higher.

This would be an unsound policy for many reasons. The rights would have very little value and the stockholders would become annoyed. There would be a substantial risk that the market price of the stock would fall below the subscription price and there would be no subscriptions. The underwriters would charge a high spread because the risk would be high.

2) *Sufficient discount to make the rights have a reasonable value and reduce to a nominal amount the risk that the stock will go below the subscription price.*

For a stable stock like a moderate-sized utility—7%, 8% or 9%. For a more volatile stock like an industrial—12% to 15%. With this discount you would probably want to have an underwriter to assure that you would get your money unless you were willing to take the small chance of failure.

3) *Sufficient discount to assure a successful offering so that no appreciable risk of failure would occur.*

This would require a few percentage points more than in category 2. Depending on the size of the issue, the nature of the stock, etc., the range in discount for this category would be between about 10% for a stable stock of a moderate-sized company to perhaps as much as 20% for a larger issue and for a less stable stock. The underwriter would be eliminated.

4) *A large discount.*

This would represent 25% or more. This is more discount than is needed. The amount of shares would have to be increased substantially in order to raise the same amount of money. The immediate dilution in earnings per share would be more than necessary. Such large discount includes the elements of a stock dividend.

We will be working with categories 2 and 3.

Now we will gradually explain how you may estimate the amount of discount to use for your offering. Due to the complicated nature of the subject, we will attack it in two steps: first, with a qualitative explanation, and then a quantitative one. Thus, we will first show what happens, and then we will get down to actual figures.

Qualitative Explanation of Rights Offering

We begin poised just prior to the announcement. In order to bring the picture down out of the clouds, we will use some figures but they should only be viewed as props at this time.

Let us assume that the market price of the outstanding stock is $100 per share. After the new offering is announced there is a tendency for the price to decrease somewhat, relative to the movement of the general securities market, from the time of the announcement to the day the subscription price is set. This is due to the action of potential purchasers withholding their orders to buy in anticipation of lower prices when the effect of the added supply actually takes place. This is called pre-offering pressure. We will assume that while the general market for securities remains level, the market price of the stock declines to $99 on the day the subscription price is set due to the pre-offering pressure.

From the day the price is set, there are 20 days before the end of the subscription period. The management faces the difficult task of establishing the subscription price. We will assume that it decides on $92, which is $7 under the market price of $99 on the day the subscription price is set. The management decides to have the issue underwritten, and after negotiating with underwriters, a compensation of $1 per share is agreed upon. Financing expenses for printing the prospectus, for legal fees and so forth are estimated to be $1 per share.

Therefore, the picture, on a per share basis, is as shown in Exhibit 9-9.

Value of One Right

We must depart from our general theme long enough to explain how the value of a right is determined. If you are familiar with the formula, you can skip this section. A right's value was discussed under arbitrage, but we will review it here as it applies to our example.

An owner of the rights gets a bargain. A person who owns ten shares gets ten rights and can subscribe for one share of stock for \$92, which is worth more in the market. When the subscription is first announced and before the warrants have been mailed to the stockholders so that the stock is with rights, each share of stock has one right still "attached" to it. The market price of the stock then includes the value of one right and will be greater than after the ex-rights date by the value of the right. Therefore, in order to obtain the value of a right before the stock goes ex-rights, we have to include an allowance for the one right. To do this a "+1" is added to the offering ratio in the denominator of the rights formula, as follows:

$$\text{Price of Right Before Ex-Rights} = \frac{\text{Market Price of Stock with Right, Less the Subscription Price}}{\text{Offering Ratio} + 1}$$

$$= \frac{\$99 - \$92}{10 + 1}$$

$$= \frac{\$7}{11}$$

$$= \$0.636$$

After the stock has gone ex-rights, the market price per share will decrease from \$99 by the value of one right, \$0.636, to \$98.364. Now the formula with the stock ex-rights, would be as follows:

$$\text{Price of Right After Ex-Rights} = \frac{\text{Market Price of Stock Ex-Rights, Less the Subscription Price}}{\text{Offering Ratio}}$$

$$= \frac{\$98.364 - \$92}{10}$$

$$= \$0.636$$

Note that the only difference in the two formulas is the "+1" added to the offering ratio in the denominator before the stock goes ex-rights and the market price of the stock includes the right.

You may hear the expression "the Parity Table" when discussing a rights offering. This is merely a table showing the mathematical value of the rights, based on the formula, for various prices of the stock. From the table you can quickly obtain the equivalent rights value for various stock prices. A simple table, using our example, would be as shown in Exhibit 9-10.

To see how the formula works, consider that a person, who was not an original stock-

Exhibit 9-9

UNDERPRICING FOR UNDERWRITTEN RIGHTS OFFERING

Market Price of Stock Just Before Announcement of Offering	\$100.00		Total Underpricing
Decline in Price Due to Pre-Offering Pressure	1.00		
Market Price on Day Subscription Price Set	\$ 99.00	The Discount	
Subscription Price	92.00		
Underwriters' Compensation	1.00		
Financing Expenses	1.00		
Net Proceeds to Company	\$ 90.00		

Exhibit 9-10

EXAMPLE OF RIGHTS PARITY TABLE
FOR A 1-FOR-10 OFFERING WITH
THE SUBSCRIPTION PRICE $92

Market Price of Stock Ex-Rights	Equivalent Rights Value
$100.00	$0.800
99.00	0.700
98.36	0.636
98.00	0.600
97.00	0.500
96.00	0.400
95.00	0.300
94.00	0.200
93.00	0.100
92.00	0.000

holder, buys ten rights in the market in order to subscribe. At a cost of $0.636 per right, the total cost of ten rights would be $6.36. He would use these rights to subscribe to one share of stock at $92 per share, so that his total cost would be $6.36 plus $92, or $98.36, which is the market price of the stock ex-rights. Thus, he would come out the same whether he bought the stock in the market or indirectly through purchase of rights, and then subscribed. As discussed under the subject of arbitrage, there generally is a spread between the rights price and the stock price because of expenses involved in purchases of rights, transfer taxes and so on.

An owner of rights who wanted the common stock might subscribe even though the stock price fell slightly below $92, the subscription price, because using the rights would make it possible for him to avoid paying the brokerage commission to buy the stock. A buyer of rights, who wanted to subscribe for the common would have to consider the brokerage fees and expenses of buying the rights and subscribing versus the brokerage commission and expenses of buying the common directly.

Factors Affecting the Subscription Price and Net Proceeds to Company

Now let's go back and see what factors have to be weighed in setting the subscription price They are not all necessarily additive. We will put the pieces together after we discuss each one. The problem is estimating the possible risk of the market price of the stock declining to or below the subscription price during the offering period so that the rights would be worthless. For example, if the stock declined below $92 per share, the rights would have no value, and no stockholder in his right mind would subscribe, since he could purchase the existing stock in the market at less than $92. As we have explained, even if the market price of the stock is slightly below $92, it might pay a holder of rights to subscribe rather than buy stock in the open market, because in the purchase of stock there would be a brokerage fee. This is a minor qualification. If the stock stayed below $92 for the entire subscription period, then, at the end, the underwriters would have to pay the company the $92 per share, less the underwriters' compensation of $1 per share, or a net of $91. They would own the stock. The extent of their loss would depend on the price at which they could sell the stock within a relatively short time. Ordinarily, they would not wish to hold it very long and gamble on the market.

Starting from just before the announcement of the offering, the factors which may cause a decline in the market price of the stock may be grouped under the headings given below. The capital letters next to each are for identification purposes in a chart which follows.

P–Pre-Offering Pressure

We have already noted the decline in price due to pre-offering pressure from $100 per share to $99 per share from the day the company announced the offering to the day on which the company set the subscription.

The extent of this decline will be affected by the same factors to be discussed under subscription period pressure.

R—Rights Value

Purely as a matter of mathematics, the stock will drop in price the value of one right on the day the stock goes ex-rights. In our example, a right was worth $0.636 so now the ex-rights price of the stock is $98.364 per share.

When you offer stock through rights, there are many stockholders who will wish to sell their rights. They are directly interested in the market value of their rights. If you set the subscription price so close to the market that the rights are worth only a few cents, stockholders will find that the brokerage charges and transfer taxes to sell the rights may be more than the value of the rights. This is bound to cause annoyance. Therefore, the subscription price should be established sufficiently below the market to make the rights have some value.

A bare minimum rights value for a very stable stock in a favorable market might be about 2/3 of 1% of the value of the stock.

For a stock selling at $100, this would mean a rights value of $0.67. The subscription price would have to be set under the market price 6.7% for such a rights value with a 1-for-10 offering. The figures would be as follows:

$$\text{Price of Right After Ex-Rights} = \frac{\text{Market Price of Stock Ex-Rights, Less the Subscription Price}}{\text{Offering Ratio}}$$

$$= \$100 - \$93.33$$

$$= \frac{\$6.67}{10}$$

$$= \$0.67$$

For a stock selling at $25 per share, and with a 1-for-10 offering, the same figures would be as follows:

Rights value 2/3 of 1% of market price of $25 ex-rights	=	17¢
Subscription price set below market price ex-rights to make rights worth 17¢	=	$1.67
Subscription price below market price ex-rights as a percent of market price	=	6.7%

If a person owned 100 shares of a stock selling at $25, the 100 rights at 17¢ per right would be worth $17. For a stock listed on the New York Stock Exchange, the brokerage charge to sell the 100 rights would amount to approximately $1, so the net amount the stockholder received would be approximately $16.

The offering ratio will have an important effect on rights value. For example, a subscription price which would produce a rights value of 17¢ per right on a 1-for-10 offering for a $25 stock, would result in a rights value of only 8¢ per right for a 1-for-20 offering, and this would be too small. Actually, there is no set rule for a minimum rights value, but it should be sufficient to promote stockholder goodwill.

In figuring an appropriate allowance for rights value, you should allow for the fact that the stock may be depressed somewhat due to subscription period pressure and that the estimated rights value should be after this allowance. Pressure always causes a downward tendency in price, and not, as in the case of market break, either upward or downward.

S—Subscription Period Pressure

When the stockholders do not wish to subscribe and sell their rights, the market value of the rights tends to decline, but the price of the stock is kept in parity with the rights value due to action by the arbitrageurs. This is the way the added supply of the stock acting through the rights has a depressing effect on the market price of the stock during the subscription period. The extent of the decline will depend on:

1. All the circumstances surrounding the new offering, including the size of offering, the offering ratio and such offering features as over-subscription, dealer

compensation, etc. These latter points will be explained at the end of the chapter. The larger the issue, other things being equal, the greater will be the pressure.

2. Everything which affects the quality and outlook for the company and its stock.

   A high quality stock with favorable outlook will tend to resist pressure more than a poor quality stock with an unfavorable outlook. A stock with a high yield tends to resist a market decline.
3. The nature of the existing market for the company's common stock, including whether it is closely held, the type of holders, whether it is listed or not listed. A broad active interest will tend to reduce the effect of pressure.
4. The general condition of the securities market, including its relative level, and the general interest of investors toward the purchase of new issues.

   The condition of the securities market is one of the most important factors affecting pressure. An active market tends to reduce pressure, and, in fact, in some "boiling" bull markets no pressure may appear whatsoever.
5. Special advantages which may exist for holders of the rights as compared to the purchase of the oustanding stock. This pertains primarily to the matter of margin requirements as established by the Board of Governors of the Federal Reserve System. There have been times when persons who subscribe could borrow from banks on margin up to 75% of the subscription price for a certain period of time; whereas, they could only borrow 10% of the market price if they purchased the outstanding stock. The reason for the more liberal treatment accorded in a rights offering is to assist stockholders in their effort to maintain their position in the company. Banks' willingness to lend, of course, may also have a bearing on the situation.
6. The tendency for the stock to decline due to the investors' appraisal of the immediate dilution effect on earnings per share caused by the added number of shares. The offering ratio has an important effect on this element. The maximum dilution would be on the assumption that the new capital earned nothing and that the earnings per share were reduced proportionately by the new shares. If the new capital were to be used for a project which would definitely increase the earnings per share, then there might be a tendency for the stock to increase in price; this, however, would be unlikely. The actual extent of dilution will depend on how quickly and to what extent investors expect earnings to materialize on the new capital.

Therefore, lumped together under this heading, "S–Subscription Period Pressure," are the effect of the added supply and the temporary dilution effect on earnings due to the greater number of shares.

The company is most interested in the pressure towards the end of the subscription period, which we will consider as being the last five days of the subscription period. The reason for the emphasis on the last five days is that most subscriptions are made during that period and the success or failure of an offering will depend largely on what happens then to the market for the stock. Most subscriptions are made in the last few days because, a stockholder would be foolish to exercise his rights if the market price of the stock fell below the subscription price. It makes sense for stockholders to wait until the end of the subscription period to subscribe in order to see what will happen to the market price. Actually, it is primarily the professionals–that is, the brokers and dealers–who wait until the last few days. They have an added reason to wait until the end. They may use bank loans to finance their subscriptions, and they will not wish to pay interest any longer than necessary. The small stockholders can't be bothered with such close calculations.

From the point of view of the risk factor, we will take the last five days as the most important part of the subscription period. Of course, it should be realized that if the market price of the stock does go below the subscription price in the first part of the subscription period, it will undoubtedly reduce the number of shares subscribed.

A–Adverse Developments for Company

The next factor is the possibility that the company may encounter some adverse development from the time the subscription price is set to the end of the subscription period. For example, if an oil company struck a dry well in one of its best areas during the offering period, the price of the stock might be depressed. As another example, suppose one of the important products of a drug company, such as a vaccine, was found to be defective.

The likelihood of an adverse development occurring during an offering is relatively slim, because a company would not plan an offering if there were a likelihood of such a problem. We will note this potential hazard, but we will make no specific allowance for it because the possibility of it occurring is too remote.

Some favorable development may occur for the company during the subscription period and cause the stock to advance in price. If it does go up, so much the better, but in deciding where to set the subscription price, our efforts are directed at determining the danger of a decline, rather than the possibility of an upward as well as a downward movement.

M–Market Break

This pertains to the action of the general market for common stocks, which may be level, up or down. Since stock prices represent relative values, individual stocks tend to move up and down with the general market unless there is some special development which would cause them to move counter thereto. In other words, if all stocks go down, they will have a depressing effect on our stock, and if they go up, there will be a buoying effect.

In evaluating the risk of having an unsuccessful offering, market break is one of the most important elements to allow for.

What we are interested in determining is the possibility of a general market break occurring in a 20-day period and the extent of that possibility. Remember, we are most interested in the last five days of the subscription period, because that is when most subscriptions take place. This can be determined from an analysis of the action of the market price of a company's stock during many 20-day periods over a number of years.

U–Underwriters' Compensation

E–Financing Expenses

After the subscription price is set, there are further deductions to get the net amount per share that the company will receive. Underwriters' compensation, if any, and financing expenses must be deducted from the subscription price in order to get the net proceeds per share.

Total Underpricing

The expression, total underpricing, which is perhaps not very descriptive, has grown up to represent the total of all the additive items discussed above. It must be allowed for in determining the cost rate for common equity in the chapter on Cost-of-Capital. It is not to be confused with the discount; that is, the amount by which the subscription price is set below the market on the day the subscription price is set. Total underpricing includes three additional items: pre-offering pressure, underwriters' compensation (if any) and financing expenses.

A Review of Qualitative Explanation

The elements we have discussed are:

P –Pre-Offering Pressure
R–Rights Value
S –Subscription Period Pressure
A–Adverse Developments
M–Market Break
U–Underwriters' Compensation
E –Expenses

We have said that all these items are not necessarily additive. This statement applies to R–Rights Value and M–Market Break. The general market for stocks may go up or down, and R–Rights Value may be enough to absorb the possibility of a market break if one occurs.

Exhibit 9-11

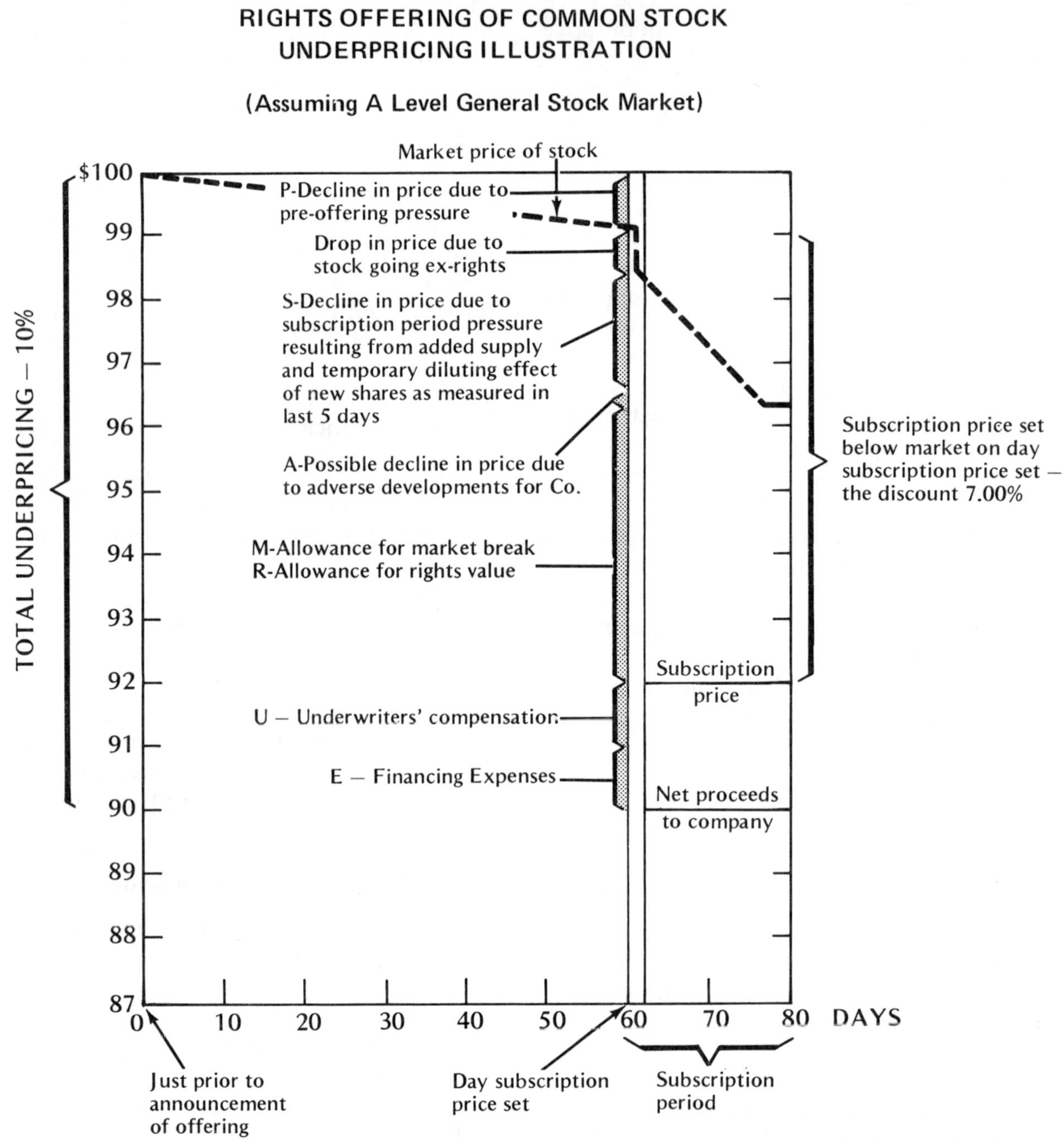

For a picture of what we have been discussing, look at Exhibit 9-11. It is based on the figures which were used for illustrative purposes in Exhibit 9-9. It presupposes that the general stock market is level during the offering.

Actual Market Action in Rights Offering, Not a Regular Pattern

If a rights offering always followed the pattern of the explanation given above, the professional security traders would make a fortune. It would be like shooting fish in a barrel. They would merely go short stock at the beginning of an offering and make money by covering their short position when the stock had gone off due to pressure. The professionals would like to do just that, but the pattern is almost never "normal." Furthermore, the professionals by their own actions may change the pattern of pressure. Occasionally, they make some bad judgments, known only to themselves, and the consequent market effect is hard for the outsider to understand. Therefore, don't expect a consistent pattern. There are many other reasons which will confuse the actual results, as we will see shortly.

You may say: "And now you tell me that there are even more complications to come." Well, if you had been told before, you wouldn't have read this far. Our task is not as hopeless as it may sound. This is merely a warning to keep you from expecting precision. We can make estimates within some reasonable degree, and we are, in fact, forced to do so in order to determine answers to our three major questions: Where to set the subscription price, whether to use an underwriter and, if one is used, how much to pay him. So let's continue, being ready to use a good pinch of judgment on the way.

Separation of Pressure

The principal operation we must perform is separating out the effects of pressure. Pressure may be defined as the decrease in the market price of a stock caused by the new issue, as compared with how the price would have acted if there had been no new offering. In order to determine pressure, it is necessary to separate out other influences on the price of the stock.

As previously stated, the market price of a stock will have a tendency to go up or down as a result of a change in the general level of other stocks. We can eliminate the effect of the change in the general level of the stock market by the use of an index of comparable types of stocks. In making this elimination, we must start our study just before the announcement of the offering because pre-offering pressure may begin to take effect as soon as the announcement is made.

Starting Date

As a rule of thumb, we take one or two days before the formal announcement when it is not more than about two or three months before the offering itself. When the announcement is more than about three months prior, this rule of thumb may not be used, because then the time interval is so long that something may happen to the company, such as a new earnings report, which may affect the price of the stock much more than pre-offering pressure and which cannot be isolated. In such a situation, we use an arbitrary starting date two months before the offering. If the formal announcement is closer than two months, we still use our two-month arbitrary starting point, on the assumption that undoubtedly the news has already leaked out some time ago. Some experts criticize the use of such an artificial date. Their criticism is a valid one because we may miss some pressure. However, we feel that if we go back too far many factors other than pressure may influence the price.

Illustration

To illustrate the separation of pressure from the effect of a change in the general level of other stocks, we will take an actual offering of about \$329 million of common stock by a large company. The offering ratio was 1 for 20 and the subscription period was 26 days from February 9 to March 7. The subscription price was \$75 per share. Shown in Exhibit 9-12 are the market price of the stock, including the value of one right during the subscription period, and the Dow-Jones Industrial Stock Average. Both are represented by index numbers with 100 at the starting point just prior to the formal announcement of the offering. The Dow-Jones Average is used to measure the upward

Exhibit 9-12

PRESSURE IN A RIGHTS OFFERING OF COMMON STOCK

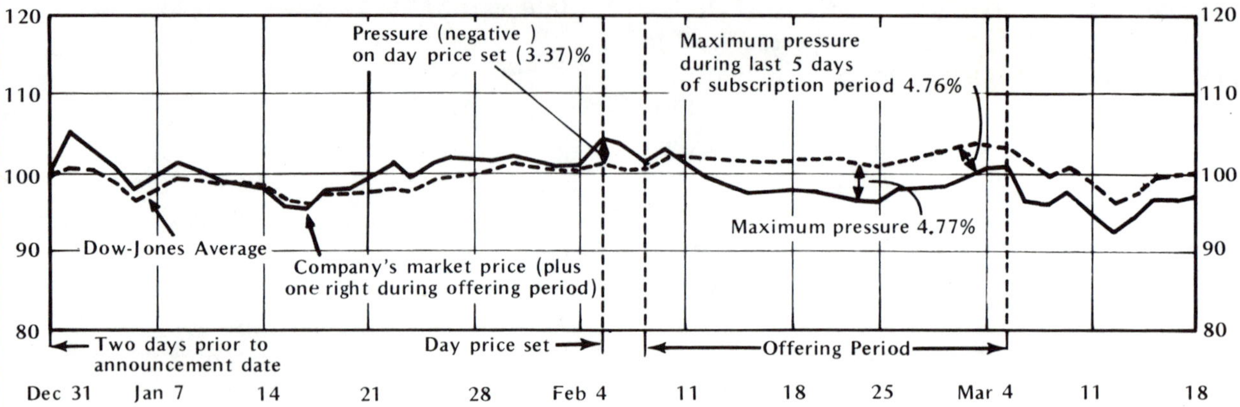

Pressure from 2 days prior to announcement of offering:		
On day subscription price set	(3.37%)	Parentheses signify negative pressure.
Maximum pressure during subscription period	4.77%	
Maximum pressure during last 5 days of subscription period	4.76%	
Pressure from day subscription price set:		Derived by subtracting the pressure on the day the subscription price is set from the maximum pressure as measured from 2 days prior to the announcement of the offering. Since the pressure at the time the price was set was negative, it was added.
Maximum pressure during subscription period	8.14%	
Maximum pressure during last 5 days of subscription period	8.13%	

and downward movement of the general market. If it goes down, that is the market break we have to worry about. Pressure is measured as the difference between the Dow-Jones Index and the index for the company's stock. The results are given in the exhibit.

The figure we are most interested in for setting the subscription price is the maximum pressure in the last five days of the subscription period from the day the price was set. It was 8.13%.

Reasons for Possible Errors in Pressure

There are various reasons why our pressure figures may not be very accurate in either direction.

1. Our starting date probably understates pressure. It is seldom that we have a clear-cut date. Comments may be made by a company about new financing long before the press release with the details about the issue. Furthermore, the well-informed analysts may, as a result of knowing the company's financial needs, make their own estimates of the effect of a forthcoming issue. Therefore, generally all pre-offering pressure cannot be determined by starting from the formal

announcement of the financing. But we must start somewhere.

2. Our tool, the Dow-Jones Average, may not be very good for the purpose. It may be influenced in an up or downward movement by many factors other than just the general supply and demand for stocks. For example, the Average includes metal stocks, and a change in metal prices might make those stocks move counter to the rest of the market. However, unless we were to construct a special average, which would be quite laborious and of doubtful additional value, the Dow-Jones Industrial Average is the best available for our immediate purpose. If we were studying another type of stock such as a utility, we would select an index with stocks of companies as nearly like our company as possible. Be sure to interpret the results in light of the possible error due to the tool used.
3. Aside from the effect of the general market movement of stocks and the pressure of a new offering, the market price of a stock may be influenced by adverse or favorable developments affecting the earnings of the company either directly or indirectly. For example, suppose some good or bad news about the company came out after the announcement of the financing; then the stock would react and this would cover up or exaggerate pressure figures, depending on whether the news was favorable or unfavorable. All we can do in this respect is to note any such news which would tend to throw off the results of our analysis of pressure.
4. During the short run, the price of a stock may hop up or down due to temporary imbalance in the supply and demand for the stock. This may make some peculiar day-to-day price fluctuations. For example, as previously mentioned, the arbitrageurs in a rights offering are continuously trying to guess the future market movement of a stock. If they guess wrong and have to cover their position, they may cause a temporary swing which will be hard for an outsider to understand.
5. One possible offset to pressure may result if at the time of the offering there is a large demand for the stock by speculators who like to buy on margin. Generally, the margin requirements for a stock purchased through rights is much more liberal than the margin requirements for a direct purchase of stock.

We referred to the negative pressure in our example on the day the subscription price was set without explaining what is meant by it. Theoretically, and in fact quite practically, there is little reason for negative pressure, because pressure is the result of added supply, and, according to the law of supply and demand, with an added supply the price should go down. Then why the apparent negative pressure? Perhaps you have already caught on. It may be caused by any one of the five factors mentioned above.

Therefore, in our study of pressure we must not expect precision, and in any particular offering there may be other influences which throw off our results. The figures must be interpreted with this in mind, and this is where that good pinch of judgment is required.

With all these qualifications, you may feel like throwing up your hands and saying a few unprintable words. Do so, but then accept the fact that pressure is an important item in a stock offering. Its effect can be observed, and while its pattern is erratic and unpredictable and at times unexplainable, we can get some idea of its general magnitude and we must allow for it in a rights offering. With these cautioning words, let's turn to some quantitative figures.

Quantitative Explanation of Rights Offering

P–Pre-Offering Pressure;

S–Subscription Period Pressure

In Exhibit 9-13 are figures for pre-offering pressure and subscription period pressure for actual offerings by four large industrial companies and 22 electric utility companies. The offerings were made during favorable

Exhibit 9-13

PRE-OFFERING AND SUBSCRIPTION PERIOD PRESSURE
IN COMMON STOCK RIGHTS OFFERINGS

Column	I	II	III	IV	V
				P	S
	Amount of Offering (000's omitted)	Offering Ratio	Discount, % Subscription Price Set Under Market Price on Day Price Set	Pre-Offering Pressure on Day Subscription Price Set. From 2 Days Prior to Announcement	Maximum Subscription Period Pressure during Last 5 Days of Subscription Period. From Day Subscription Price Set
4 Industrials					
Average	$226,000	1 for 16	18.9%	2.6%	5.9%
Range					
Maximum	329,000	1 for 5	25.8	6.8	8.1
Minimum	87,000	1 for 30	14.2	(3.4)(*)	3.2
22 Electric Utilities					
Average	14,000	1 for 10	8.1	1.4%	2.3%
Range					
Maximum	42,000	1 for 7	15.3	10.2	8.2
Minimum	1,000	1 for 20	4.5	(11.8)(*)	(3.9)(*)

(*)Represents negative pressure.

stock market conditions and were generally successful with high subscription percentages. When you look at them, keep in mind the previous comments on possible errors that may occur in measuring pressure.

These observations may be made:

1. The ranges in pressures are not necessarily for the same company for both pre-offering and subscription period pressure; therefore, they are not additive. As already explained, there may be factors other than pressure to account for the large maximums and minimums.
2. The offerings by the four industrial companies are very large. The large size tends to increase pressure. On the other hand, these companies are well-known to a broad group of investors and there is wide demand for their stocks. There would be a tendency for greater pressure for less well-known companies. Thus, their large size was offset to some extent by the character of the companies.
3. The electric utilities, which represent moderate-sized offerings and are more stable types of stocks than industrials, showed less pressure on the average. Note the wide range in pressure.

   Sixteen of the utility issues were underwritten and six not underwritten.

Can we come to any conclusion regarding pressure figures which you can use for your offering? We might think in terms of the average figures shown above, having in mind the wide range that may occur and that the pressure pattern depends on all the circumstances surrounding an issue that we discussed previously. Before a company offers stock through rights, it may wish to study new offerings of a comparable nature by other companies and, of course, any previous offerings by the company itself.

M–Market Break

In deciding on how far to set the subscription price below the market, the next factor to evaluate is market break. We will use the Dow-Jones Industrial Average as our guide for the performance of an industrial stock in a market break, although, of course, each individual stock will react differently. The figures are shown in Exhibit 9-14. It covers two years, 1972 and 1973, from the first day of each 20-day period to the lowest point reached in the final five days.

In order to make a thorough study of market break, a number of years should be included which covers a complete cycle so that there is not a bias of a trend downward or upward. The year 1972 was probably more representative. In that year there were about as many periods in which there was no decline as there were declines. It showed that 5% would cover market break completely. In 1973 the market was on a downtrend. In both of the years, an allowance of 6% for market break would cover about 90% of the declines.

A company should make such a study of its own stock to see how it reacts to market breaks. In the study, allowance must be made for the fact that much of a stock's movements may be due to favorable or adverse developments for the company. We are not now interested in such movements. It is impossible to isolate them but they must be weighed in interpreting the results of a market break study of a single stock.

Setting the Subscription Price

With these ideas of how a stock might react during an offering, you can get down to the problem of setting the subscription price. On the day that we face this problem, we already will have observed how much the stock has reacted due to pre-offering pressure. In setting a subscription price, a company should take the following steps:

1. Estimate how much the stock may go off from the day the price is set to the last five days of the subscription period, due to subscription period pressure with a level general securities market.
2. Calculate how much lower the subscription price will have to be set in order to give an adequate rights value. We can determine R–Rights Value on the basis that the market will remain level. There is an equal chance that it will go up or down, and on the average stockholders will receive a satisfactory rights value.
3. Estimate the extent to which the stock may decrease due to market break in the last five days of the subscription period.
4. If three is greater than two, then an underwriter will be required and it will be necessary to estimate how much will have to be paid to the underwriter.
5. If three is less than two an underwriter can be eliminated.
6. Finally, estimate the expenses of the offering in order to get the net amount the company will receive for the new offering.

Each stock will have to be evaluated by itself. In the previous discussion on pressure, rights value and market break, you have some figures on which to begin your thinking and some suggestions as to how you might study your own stock and other comparable issues in order to form a background for your decision.

Use of Underwriter

When you establish the discount–that is, the amount by which you will set the subscription price below the market–you will have decided the extent of the risk of the market going below the subscription price. Next you will have to decide whether you are willing to take whatever risk exists, or

Exhibit 9-14

MARKET BREAK POSSIBILITIES DURING 20-DAY PERIOD FROM FIRST DAY OF EACH PERIOD TO GREATEST BREAK AS SHOWN BY DOW-JONES INDUSTRIAL AVERAGE DURING LAST 5 DAYS

				% of cases	
	1972	1973	TOTAL	NON-CUM.	CUM.
NO DECLINE	120	63	183	37.9%	37.9%
LESS THAN 1%	40	13	53	11.0	48.9
" " 2	38	15	53	11.0	59.9
" " 3	27	20	47	9.7	69.6
" " 4	18	22	40	8.3	77.9
" " 5	7	27	34	7.1	85.0
" " 6		23	23	4.8	89.8
" " 7		18	18	3.7	93.5
" " 8		5	5	1.0	94.5
" " 9		7	7	1.5	96.0
" " 10		3	3	.6	96.6
" " 11		2	2	.4	97.0
" " 12		1	1	.2	97.2
" " 13		4	4	.8	98.0
" " 14		4	4	.8	98.8
" " 15		3	3	.6	99.4
" " 16		2	2	.4	99.8
" " 17		1	1	.2	100.0
" " 18					
" " 19					
" " 20					
TOTAL	250	233	483	100.0	100.0

whether you will use an underwriter as insurance and to assist in the offering.

Generally, in the industrial field, an underwriter is used. In the utility field sometimes an underwriter is dispensed with. For example, of the seven electric utility issues of rights offerings of common stock, in 1973, six were underwritten and one was not.

If you decide to use an underwriter, it will be on a negotiated basis for an industrial company. Regulated companies have a choice between negotiated or competitive unless they are required to use competitive by regulations. In the electric utility field, in 1973, of the six issues offered by rights which were underwritten, four were done on a negotiated basis and two competitively. If all a utility company wants from an underwriting is the insurance part of that function and the company is a well-known standard type of stock, competitive bidding will perform satisfactorily under most market conditions. However, if some further assistance is needed in managing the offering, the negotiated method will be used.

When you come to negotiating with underwriters, you will have to decide how much to pay them and in what form. You will be like a "babe in the woods" if you haven't done much financing or haven't made a thorough study as we have suggested. Do the underwriters make the same type of studies? No. They arrive at their decision as to how much they should be paid by looking at the overall effect of the numerous items mentioned, having had firsthand experience with many issues under varied circumstances. You will have to rely heavily on your underwriters' advice; they know much more about markets than you. However, this does not mean that you should turn the job of setting their compensation over to them "carte blanche" any more than you would do with any other expert, nor should they expect you to do so.

The principal consideration in determining the amount to pay underwriters, as far as the risk factor is concerned, is the extent of the danger of the market price of the stock declining below the subscription price. This will depend on all factors surrounding the offering and on how far the subscription price is set under the market. Other things being equal, the risk decreases as the discount of the subscription price below the market price increases. Remember that there are three factors which may cause a decline after the subscription price is set: subscription period pressure, market break and possible adverse developments for the company.

If you read your underwriting agreement carefully, you should realize that the underwriters do not assume responsibility for all risks. Underwriting agreements may have an "out" if there is a material change in the company's condition or the market turns so badly that the issue cannot be sold. However, as a practical matter, it is only under rare circumstances that an underwriter pulls out.

Some general figures on underwriters' compensation and also expenses for rights offering are shown in Exhibit 9-15. They are primarily of interest to give some idea of the effect of size of offering and type of industry. The underwriting spread will vary depending on the market conditions. Therefore, in obtaining an estimate for a proposed offering, you will wish to consider recent offerings of a comparable nature. Unfortunately, these figures are not very helpful, because they don't show the amount by which the subscription price was set below the market price.

Two-Fee vs. Single Fee Deal

In a rights offering there are two types of underwriting compensation: a two fee and single fee.

In a two-fee deal, the underwriter is paid one base fee per share for all shares, and an additional fee per share on those shares which are unsubscribed and are purchased and sold by the underwriter. If the unsubscribed shares represent about 3%, a company would thus pay one fee on 97% of the offering, and a somewhat larger combined fee on 3%. If the issue turns out to be unsuccessful and a large amount is unsubscribed, then there is a corresponding increase in the cost.

The base fee is to compensate the underwriter for the risk he assumes, his expenses and the fee for the underwriting firm which acts as manager. The additional fee on the unsubscribed portion is to take care of the job of selling that portion of the issue. It must be large enough to provide a sufficient incentive to selected dealers to sell the issue.

In a single fee deal, the underwriter is paid a fixed amount per share for all shares offered. It rolls into one fee the risk involved in the underwriting and the additional cost to sell the unsubscribed shares.

A company should figure out what the overall average fee would be for a two-fee deal, with the two fees combined for various percentages of stock subscribed, in order to be able to compare it with a single fee deal. In making a comparison, the company will have to weigh the extent to which shares may be unsubscribed.

The advantage of a two-fee deal is that it adjusts ex post facto the commissions to be paid according to actual results. An advantage of a single fee deal is that the company knows at the start the maximum that the underwriting will cost, no matter how much is subscribed. While some underwriting firms prefer the single fee arrangement, some do not.

Exhibit 9-15

FINANCING COSTS
COMMON STOCK OFFERINGS THROUGH RIGHTS
1971 and 1972*

All Industry
Classified by Size of Issue
(Costs as Percentage of Proceeds)

Size of Issue ($ Millions)	No. of Issues	Total Cost	Underwriters' Compensation	Other Expenses
Under .5	2	21.18	8.94	12.24
.5– .99	7	12.25	7.43	4.82
1.0– 1.99	6	6.27	4.51	1.76
2.0– 4.99	4	6.62	4.24	2.38
5.0– 9.99	6	4.01	2.83	1.18
10.0– 19.99	10	4.00	3.14	.86
20.0– 49.99	5	3.41	2.77	.64
50.0– 99.99	––			
100.0–499.99	1	2.36	1.90	.46
500.0–over	––			
Total	41			

*Source: Cost of Flotation of Corporate Securities (Date), Securities and Exchange Commission, Washington 25, D.C.

Tag End Split

One additional feature, which may be contained in either type of agreement, is the split on the unsubscribed shares. The underwriter gets the shares which are unsubscribed and sells them at the best possible price. This produces an additional amount of money above the subscription price; who receives this additional amount will depend on the underwriting agreement. In the utility field, it may be split 50-50 with the company or on some other basis. The basis of the split may depend on the amount unsubscribed. For example, in an industrial offering, the company may receive the entire amount if the unsubscribed is 3% or less, the theory being that such a percentage represents the amount of rights which fail to be exercised if the issue is a complete success. However, if the percentage of unsubscribed is greater, it may be due to adverse market developments which increase the underwriter's risk. Then the profit on the unsubscribed may be split with the company on some formula basis, with the underwriter receiving a greater proportion as the amount of unsubscribed increases.

It is suggested by some underwriters that the amount which the company receives from the tag end split is a profit for the company from the sale of any unsubscribed shares at a price in excess of the subscription price, and that it should represent a reduction in the overall cost of underwriting. Any amount which the company receives from the tag end split should be treated as additional net proceeds. Consider the situation in which a company does not have its stock underwritten and sells the unsubscribed shares in the open market. The additional amount received would be added to the proceeds from the issue; there would be no other way to account for it. Any amount the underwriter receives from the tag end split should be considered as part of his compensation. In the first place, everything belongs to the company and anything the underwriter receives is derived from the company. Certainly, when studying underwriting costs, the part the underwriter receives from the tag end split must be included with the underwriters' compensation in order for various forms of underwriting agreements to be comparable.

Layoffs–Payments at the Second Fee Rate

Starting around 1947, there was an innovation in the operation of a rights offering, fostered to a large extent by the late Eugene Barry of the underwriting firm of Shields and Company. It is known as the layoff, Barry or Shields plan. The term itself, *layoff,* refers to the act of selling stock.

The original purpose of the plan was to permit underwriters to reduce their risk and lower underwriting costs, by providing an orderly distribution of stock purchased by the underwriters on the exercise of rights bought in the market. When this provision is included in the underwriting agreement, it may permit offering shares to stockholders at a slightly higher subscription price and for a lower underwriting compensation than could be obtained from underwriters without such a provision.

As an example of a two-fee deal, the wording might be as follows on the front of the prospectus: "The Company has agreed to pay the underwriters 75¢ a share in respect of all the shares offered hereby, plus an additional $1 a share in respect of each share of capital stock acquired by them through the exercise of rights purchased by them . . ."

The rights held by stockholders who exercise them never come on the market; the underwriter's risk is reduced to that extent. If, before the stockholders get around to subscribing, the market price falls below the subscription price, then they would not subscribe. There is nothing that the underwriters can do about it. The unsubscribed shares would belong to the underwriters at the end of the subscription period.

The rights that are sold come on the market. While the rights have value someone will buy them, and as long as they continue to have value throughout the subscription period, the purchasers will subscribe. If, subsequent to their purchase, the market price of the stock falls below the subscription price, then subscriptions will not take place. Thus, the underwriters would have to take up this stock. Under the layoff plan, the underwriters can protect themselves against this occurring. In essence, it works this way: underwriters purchase rights during the offering period; they exercise the rights and sell the stock directly to investors, not through the stock exchange, so as to avoid depressing the Stock Exchange market. They cannot get stuck with this stock at the end of the subscription period if, following the layoff, the market price falls below the subscription price.

When the layoff plan was devised, it had to be cleared with the Securities and Exchange Commission, in order not to violate the regulations regarding market price manipulation of a stock. The Investment Bankers Association issued a memorandum setting forth the principles that govern the conduct of underwriters during the rights period. Layoffs have to be carried out in a carefully prescribed manner. It requires a detailed knowledge of trading regulations. You do not need to know them but merely that they exist.

The extent of decrease in risk of the underwriters depends upon the amount of stock laid off. It is only that particular stock which the underwriters have assurance will not have to be taken up at the end of the subscription period if the market price should fall below the subscription price.

There is another reason advanced for layoffs; they help provide an orderly market for the rights during the subscription period. When there is a flood of rights coming into the market, the underwriters buy them, thus supporting their price, and sell the stock. If underwriters feel that this is necessary in a single fee deal, they may require compensation large enough to cover it. The underwriters will explain that a generous selling commission will lead to orders in excess of the shares to be supplied. But remember that when they sell the stock some pressure may be put on the market, which may cause a decrease in the stock price and be reflected back to the rights through parity. You can't go too far in this operation without defeating your purpose. Furthermore, you must be familiar with arbitrage to complete your understanding of market operations during a rights offering. When there is a sag in the rights price, the arbitrageurs will be providing support to the market in a manner similar to the layoff operation. Arbitrage is explained in Chapter 10.

Why should the Financial Vice President worry about layoffs? He ought to know what is back of the market action of the stock and rights; more important, the company may pay for layoffs. The underwriting agreement may include a fee to be paid for stock taken up by the underwriters through purchase and exercise of rights; that is, through layoffs. In the two-fee deal, the underwriters usually get the same fee on layoffs as the additional fee for unsubscribed stock. Therefore, layoffs may substantially increase the cost of the underwriting to the company.

Of course, if the risk to the underwriters is reduced by layoffs, then there is an advantage to the company, as a smaller risk may reduce the overall underwriting cost. However, a company should make certain that this is the reason for layoffs. If the subscription price is set well below the market price so that there is relatively little risk of the rights becoming worthless, then there would be no occasion for a large amount of layoffs in order for the underwriters to protect themselves, and a small amount of layoffs reduces the underwriters' risk to that extent.

Underwriters will contend that they only lay off stock to help the offering. The company has no way of knowing whether the layoffs were essential and whether the second fee they got stuck paying could be avoided. Unless you want some real surprises in your total underwriting cost, you better have a clear understanding with your underwriter that you don't want any stock laid off unless it is absolutely necessary. And you ought to follow what happens as the offering progresses. It has been suggested that an underwriter might want to lay off stock to give its salesmen, who have been steamed up about an issue, some stock even if the layoff isn't necessary. In studying your agreement with underwriters, the way the second fee works is important to understand. For example, the second fee may not apply if layoffs are less than 10% of the issue, but if layoffs are 11%, you pay the fee on the whole 11%, not just the additional 1%. The second fee may increase as the amount of stock which is unsubscribed or laid off increases. Know what to expect for your total underwriting cost for various amounts of unsubscribed and laid off stock.

Some underwriters prefer a single fee deal so that there will not be the temptation to lay off stock and so that the company will not feel that it may have been taken.

As a matter of interest, it may be noted that the largest offering ever of common stock, over $1 billion by American Telephone and Telegraph Company in 1964, was done through rights with no underwriting, and the market action during the subscription period was remarkably good. Of course, it is a relatively stable type of stock, and the discount was substantial. The right to lay off becomes more important to underwriters when the subscription price is set close to the market. Then they might need to make substantial layoffs in order to reduce their risk.

In certain situations, a form of layoff may be used to assist in the distribution of stock of certain larger holders who are known in advance of the offering not to be interested in exercising their rights because of the large additional investment, or in order to avoid further concentration of investment. This type of layoff will be planned in advance to take care of those specific rights.

Over-Subscription

The tag end shares in a rights offering can be eliminated by means of an over-subscription privilege included with the regular subscription. When the holders of the rights subscribe, they can be given the right to request allotment of the tag end shares at the subscription price. After the subscription period is over, the shares which become available are allotted, generally in full shares, pro rata, among those who put in an over-subscription, on the basis of their original number of rights.

In favor of the over-subscription are these arguments:

- The unsubscribed shares are eliminated. This may become more important if an offering is not underwritten, because it will assure that all the shares will be sold, and that the company will not have the unsubscribed shares to sell after the subscription is over.
- The stockholders are given the opportunity of obtaining some additional stock at the subscription price.
- It gives some added value to the rights, and to this extent, tends to help the price of rights. The arbitrageurs like it because it affords them a small extra play in the rights. If the issue is touch and go, it may give it a little boost.

An example of how over-subscription might affect the rights value is as follows:

Assume:

Shares outstanding	1,000,000
Shares offered	100,000
Offering ratio	1 for 10
95% of shares subscribed, leaving 5% for tag end	5,000
Stockholders, owning 1/2 of the stock, apply for over-subscription	

There will be available 5,000 shares to allow pro rata to original holders of 500,000 rights.

Assume:

Market price of stock per share, ex-rights	$32.00
Subscription price	$30.00
Rights value without allowing for value of over-subscription	$0.20

A holder of 100 rights who over-subscribed would get ten new shares through direct subscription and one share through over-subscription. He would thus have 11 shares worth $352 at the market price, for which he would pay $330, the subscription price. This would make his 100 original rights worth $22, or 22¢ per right. The over-subscription privilege added 2¢ per right for those who availed themselves of the privilege.

Against over-subscription are these arguments or complaints:

- If the issue is underwritten, most underwriters don't like it. They lose any possibility of a split on the tag end or unsubscribed shares. Furthermore, they feel strongly that it makes the issue more unmanageable as regards layoffs.
- Those who oppose over-subscription contend that the average stockholder doesn't really understand it and therefore doesn't take advantage of it. The professionals, such as the arbitrageurs, are the ones who benefit. Of course, if they like it, that tends to create additional interest in the rights.
- The company gives up the opportunity of any tag end split on the unsubscribed shares.
- One thing is certain, over-subscription will not save an unsuccessful offering. If the market price falls below the subscription price, over-subscription will not make it any more worthwhile to subscribe.

  If you decide to place the subscription price close to the market so that the underwriters will have a substantial risk, you may find it better to bow to their objections to over-subscription. With a greater spread between the market price and the subscription price, you may wish to weigh its use more carefully, particularly if the issue is not underwritten, because then the company would not have to take care of the tag end. These are the questions you should be thinking about in making your decision about over-subscription: Do you want to eliminate the unsubscribed shares and give a little kicker to your rights value with over-subscription? Or would it be better to do without it and get some profit on the unsubscribed shares? Actually, over-subscription is not a major financial issue, but more of a fine point. It will show your financial finesse if you know how it works and all the pros and cons as to whether it should be used in your offering.

One company used a variation of over-subscription. It offered 3 million shares to its stockholders on the basis of one new share for each 15 shares held. It also permitted each stockholder to subscribe to 100 new additional shares under a supplemental subscription privilege regardless of the number of shares held. This supplemental privilege might amount to 2 million shares. The company reserved the privilege of providing these shares at the subscription price or buying them in the open market.

Dealer Compensation

In a rights offering, the greater the amount of stock subscribed by the original stockholders the less will be the rights coming on the market; the pressure will be reduced accordingly.

The small, unsophisticated stockholder may not know what to do or how to handle a subscription. He may turn for advice to his security dealer. Giving such advice takes up the time of the dealer, and if he should recommend that the stockholder subscribe, the dealer will undoubtedly have the warrant processed through his firm with the ensuing paper work and expense, similar to what would be done if a security were purchased. The dealer receives no compensation for this work, since there is no established way to charge the stockholder. Many security dealers are very vocal on this point. They feel that it is an imposition, caused by the company which issues the stock. In view of this fact, human nature being as it is, there may be a tendency for a dealer to recommend to a stockholder that, instead of subscribing, the rights be sold and another security purchased. In this way, the dealer would make money on both the sale of the rights and the purchase of the other stock. But this will mean more rights coming on the market and more pressure. Many security dealers have contended that the company offering the security should pay a fee to dealers for the work involved in helping stockholders subscribe. Some companies do. This is what is known as dealer compensation. A dealer who helps a stockholder subscribe has his name stamped on the warrant, and the company pays a fee on the basis of the number of shares subscribed. Payment of the fee tends to increase the amount of subscriptions and thus reduces the pressure.

If dealers purchase rights themselves in order to subscribe, dealer compensation may be paid on those rights. An additional incentive is thereby provided for dealers to trade in rights, which tends to improve the market. However, the Securities and Exchange Commission frowns on this practice and special approval must be obtained. If a firm accepts dealer compensation, it cannot actively trade in the offering. Some large firms would rather trade and are not interested in the compensation.

The fee is around 1% of the price of the stock. For a stock selling at $30 per share, the fee would be 30¢ per share for each share for which a dealer assists in the subscription. A limitation is imposed on the maximum payment on any one transaction, which may range from $150 to $250. If about one-third of the entire issue passes through dealers' hands, the overall cost will be less than one-half of 1% of the total issue. The fee per share should bear some relation to the New York Stock Exchange brokerage commission, because it represents the type of work a dealer would have to do in selling a stock to a customer. The fee can be somewhat less because the stockholder initiates the action giving rise to the compensation, and it is not initiated by the dealer. Since the cost is so small, not much of a decrease in pressure is necessary in order to pay for the cost.[1]

If an issue is not underwritten, the company may handle payment of dealer compensation itself. However, some companies have employed an underwriting firm to act as a dealer-manager and supervise the operation. If an issue is underwritten, then the company can arrange with its underwriter also to act as dealer-manager.

Some companies which have used dealer compensation swear by it. They point out that it not only compensates dealers who are approached by stockholders, but acts as an incentive to dealers to help little stockholders. Thus, subscriptions by original stockholders are increased, and the supply of rights coming on the market, which tends to lower their price, is reduced. If dealers know that a company will pay dealer compensation when there is a rights offering, they may be more interested in recommending the stock to their customers at other times.

Some company officials are strongly opposed to dealer compensation. They state that it is completely unethical for a dealer to be swayed in his recommendation of investment policy merely because he gets a fee for assisting with subscriptions. He should give his best advice to his customer regardless; it is a service which dealers should provide their customers. If anyone should pay the dealer, it should be the stockholder who uses the dealer's services. Furthermore, a company should set up adequate machinery to assist stockholders to subscribe, and if that is done, dealer compensation is a duplication of costs.

American Telephone and Telegraph has in the past opposed dealer compensation; however, they used dealer compensation in their gigantic financing of debentures and warrants in 1970, of $1,569,000,000.

Underwriting houses generally oppose dealer compensation. They would rather have a straight underwriting. Some have expressed a fear that if dealer compensation came into general use, companies would pay a smaller underwriting fee, or not use an underwriter at all. This argument does not seem well-founded. Whether or not an underwriter is used will depend on whether the subscription price is set sufficiently below the market price to eliminate the risk of failure of an offering. Dealer compensation will have some beneficial effect on an issue but not enough in itself to eliminate the use of an underwriter. It may improve the rights value somewhat and benefit the stockholders, or a company may wish to take advantage of the slightly better rights value and set the subscription price slightly higher in order to recoup the cost of dealer compensation. While dealer compensation may reduce the risk of a decline in rights value and to that extent shade the amount paid to underwriters, they should not fear that it will have any major adverse effect on their business. In any event, be prepared to have most underwriters say that it is a waste of money.

Even though some dealers feel that it is unfair not to pay dealer compensation, many such firms are also engaged in the underwriting business. Consequently, the ones who

---

[1] In a comparison of 12 offerings having dealer compensation with 12 approximately similar offerings without dealer compensation, the average pressure for the former was slightly lower than the size of the dealer compensation as a percentage of the market price per share. For those issues with compensation, the fee was paid on only about one-third of the number of shares, so that the cost related to the entire issue was relatively small. Since pressure is difficult to measure, reliance should not be placed on these figures as to the exact effect of dealer compensation, but they do show that it tends to be beneficial and pays for itself. See "A Technique of Offering Common Stock Through Rights" by John F. Childs, *Public Utilities Fortnightly Magazine,* November 11, 1954.

are strictly dealers have not been able to get all dealers to join together in a united front in their favor. Furthermore, some dealers have gotten so wrought up on the subject that they haven't helped sell the idea. Some have even hurt their own cause. Apparently a few have threatened to boycott offerings and recommend sale of all rights, unless dealer compensation were paid. It has been said that dealers have approached large institutions, requesting that the institutions process their rights through the dealers so that they can collect the dealer compensation. This, of course, is unsound, because institutions do not need assistance and can send their rights in directly. In certain instances, it has been reported that some dealers have requested institutions to break up a subscription into smaller pieces so that they could get the maximum allowed compensation on each part. That is wrong! The fee should only be sought by dealers who help stockholders needing assistance. It is on the basis of this benefit alone that they should seek its acceptance. In order to avoid unnecessary payments, a company may wish to include, in the material sent out with warrants, a clear and simple notice in large red type warning stockholders not to have dealers' names stamped on warrants unless their assistance is actually needed. It is the company's, and therefore the stockholders' money, which is being spent, and it should not be wasted.

The technique of handling dealer compensation is not altogether simple. If it is handled incorrectly, some money will be wasted. A company which decides to use dealer compensation should not try to do a rush job. It should contact other companies which have used dealer compensation, and take advantage of the techniques they learned through actual operation. That will pay off, and, in fact, it is quite necessary. Rush jobs will be bound to produce poor results.

Dealer compensation has not been widely used, but some companies have found it worthwhile and stick to it each time they offer common stock. You may wish to investigate whether it is worthwhile for your company, particularly if you do not have your issue underwritten.

Delayed Payment

There are some special features to assist in an offering of common stock. As one illustration, there is the delayed payment plan. It was used in one of the large common stock offerings by American Telephone & Telegraph Co. The subscription price of that issue was $100 per share. Upon subscription, the stockholders were given the option of paying the full subscription price, or only $50. If stockholders opted for delayed payment, the company held on to the stock and then sent it out a few months later when the balance was due. The stockholder got interest on his down payment.

The reason for this feature was the tremendous size of the issue and the drain which it placed on funds available for purchase of common stock. The delayed payment provided time for additional funds to be generated in investors' hands. About 4% of the subscriptions were made on this installment plan.

Underwriters' Compensation

After the subscription period is over, the underwriters' compensation can be figured out from the sticker which is subsequently added to the prospectus. Exhibit 9-16 shows an actual offering.

Part I shows how the shares were sold. The difference between the shares of D (648,025) and the shares of E (635,766) is 12,259, which are the excess shares to which the underwriters subscribed but did not lay off. These shares are added to B, the tag end (53,596), to get F (65,855), the shares the underwriters sold after the end of the subscription period.

On the shares of B—that is, the tag end or the unsubscribed (53,596)—the company

Exhibit 9-16

UNDERWRITERS' COMPENSATION FOR A RIGHTS OFFERING

PART I

SHARES SOLD

	Number of Shares	Percentage of Total
A. "Subscribed through rights by original stockholders or purchasers of rights other than underwriters and through purchase of rights by underwriters"	6,495,528	99.2%
B. "Unsubscribed shares"—tag end	53,596	0.8
C. Total "shares offered by company"	6,549,124	100.0%
D. "Underwriters subscribed for," through purchase of rights for purpose of layoffs	648,025	
E. "Underwriters sold during the subscription period" for layoffs	635,766	
F. "Shares offered by underwriters after the subscription period at $49.75"—shares subscribed for by underwriters not laid off plus unsubscribed shares	65,855 (D − E + B)	

PART II

UNDERWRITERS' COMPENSATION

Shares		Fee Rate	Total
6,549,124	(Base rate on all shares)	$0.75	$4,911,843
648,025	(For stock purchased for layoffs)	1.00	648,025
53,596	(Unsubscribed)	1.00	53,596
	Total Underwriters' Compensation		$5,613,464

received the difference between the $49.75 market price and the subscription price of $44, or a total of $305,808.06, after deducting transfer taxes. The underwriting agreement provided that all proceeds (after all expenses, including transfer taxes, but excluding concessions to dealers) on unsubscribed shares should go to the company, if the unsubscribed shares were 3% or less. If the unsubscribed were between 3% and 10% of the total offered, the company was to split with the underwriters, on a 50-50 basis, the profit on sale of the unsubscribed. If the unsubscribed were 10% or more, all profit would go to the underwriters.

The underwriters' compensation for the issue is included in Exhibit 9-16, Part II.

In Exhibit 9-17 are some average figures for underwriters' compensation and expenses for certain rights offerings, which were issued under generally favorable market conditions. The average figures for underwriter's compen-

Exhibit 9-17

UNDERWRITERS' COMPENSATION FOR CERTAIN RIGHTS OFFERINGS

Type of Company	Underwriters' Compensation as a Percent of Market Price on Day Price Set	Expenses of Offering as a Percent of Market Price on Day Price Set
4 Industrials		
Average	1.7%	0.4%
Range		
Maximum:	2.4	0.5
Minimum:	0.9	0.3
16 Electric Utilities		
Average	0.9%	1.1%
Range		
Maximum:	4.3	2.3
Minimum:	0.1	0.5

sation are somewhat lower than the comprehensive figures in the previous Exhibit 9-16.

In determining a reasonable underwriting compensation for your offering, you should study all issues reasonably comparable with yours offered in recent years, keeping in mind particularly the percent discount by which the subscription price was set below the market. You will have to weigh all factors of each issue which affected the risk.

DIRECT vs. RIGHTS

With the above background about the two methods of offering common stock, we can now consider which method you should choose—direct or rights.

Here are typical superficial reasons advanced by some underwriters and company officials against a rights offering:

- The rights get depressed during an offering; the small stockholders sell and take a beating. The professional traders take advantage of the situation, buy and make a killing.
- A company gets less net proceeds in a rights offering and has to sell more shares to get the same amount of money. Thus, there is greater dilution in earnings per share.

These points have to be considered, but, as stated, they are quite misleading.

Comparison—Direct vs. Rights

We must make such a comparison from the point of view of the greatest benefit to the stockholders since they own the company. This is fundamental. We cannot make the comparison from the point of view of the effect on the company alone. The importance of this distinction will become apparent as we proceed.

With regard to rights, these points are often left out:

1. The stockholders receive some benefit from the rights. While the company may receive less cash per share through a rights offering, it is the stockholders who own the company, and the benefit they receive from the value of the rights has to be taken into account.
2. In calculating the benefit to the stockholders, the extent of their benefit will depend on the action the stockholders

take. On this basis, the shares offered can be divided into three groups.

a. *Shares subscribed by original stockholders.*

These stockholders get the full benefit of the rights value.

b. *Shares represented by stockholders who sell their rights.*

They benefit, but less than the first group, to the extent of the decreased rights value, due to the pressure on the rights when they sell.

c. *Shares represented by stockholders who let their rights lapse by failing to subscribe or sell.*

They receive no benefit, but this group is generally small.

To lump all stockholders together and assume that they are affected alike is quite erroneous. In our analysis, we will take into account the difference in these groups.

Before we make a detailed comparison, we point out that, in a direct offering, the underwriters' compensation is a large cost. In a rights offering, it is relatively small if the subscription price is set at a reasonable amount below the market price. Some of the risk is absorbed through the rights value, which goes to the stockholders rather than the underwriters.

If you were an underwriter, which method would you prefer? Would you rather have a direct deal with a large commission and have the offering over in short order, or would you rather make a small commission and wait 20 days during the subscription period, to find out how the market may react and to get paid? Obviously, underwriters are prejudiced in favor of direct offerings.

We will use Exhibit 9-18 as an aid to our explanation. In the exhibit, there is shown how a comparison can be made between a direct and a rights offering. It is based on certain assumptions in order to simplify the picture and is primarily for illustrative purposes. These are the assumptions:

1. The stock is a relatively stable type.
2. The figures for underwriters' compensation and financing expenses are as previously shown in the exhibits used to illustrate a direct and a rights offering.
3. The shares in the rights offering represented by the three groups of stockholders are:

shares subscribed by original stockholders	50%
shares represented by stockholders who sell their rights	47%
shares represented by stockholders who let their rights lapse	3%
Total:	100%

The results of the comparison will, of course, depend to a great extent on these percentages.

Exhibit 9-18 provides a form for a company to use in deciding whether to go direct or rights. Figures can be substituted which fit its situation. Let's go through the exhibit to explain it in detail.

Part I makes the comparison on the basis of the net proceeds the company receives for both a direct and rights offering from the time prior to the effect of the new offering. From the market price prior to the effect of the new issue is deducted:

Pre-offering pressure.
The discount or amount by which the offering price is set under the market on the day the price is set.
Underwriters' spread.
Financing expenses.

This results in a net proceeds for the company as follows:

Direct	Rights
$92.00	$80.30

Thus, the company receives $11.70 less per share with a rights offering.

Part II calculates the benefit to stockholders in a rights offering from the fact that the stockholders get new stock at a discount. It takes into account the fact that the effect on the stockholders depends on what they do with their rights. On this basis, it divides the

Exhibit 9-18

DIRECT vs. RIGHTS OFFERING OF COMMON STOCK COMPARISON
1-FOR-10 OFFERING FOR LARGE INDUSTRIAL COMPANY

PART I
Net Proceeds Received by Company

Line	Column		I Direct		II Rights
1	Market price per share of common prior to announcement of offering		$100.00		$100.00
2	Pre-offering pressure up to time price is set		2.00		2.00
3	Market price of common at time price is set		98.00		98.00
4	Amount by which price is set under the market		0.50		14.70*
5	Offering price		97.50		
6	Subscription price				83.30
7	Underwriter's commission	$5.00		$2.00	
8	Expenses	0.50		1.00	
9	Total		$ 5.50		$ 3.00
10	Net proceeds received by company		92.00		80.30

*Subscription price set 15% below the market price of $98 on the day the price is set.

PART II
Value of Rights to Stockholders

Original stockholders who subscribe–50% of the shares: They hold on to the stock and receive the full value of the discount, $14.70 (Part I, Line 4), and the pre-offering pressure, $2.00 (Part I, Line 2), since the market will recover to $100 after the sale is completed. They represent 50% of the shares. The benefit is $16.70 x 50%	=	$ 8.35
Rights sold–47% of the shares: The stockholders who sell their rights get the value of the discount, $14.70 (Part I, Line 4), less the amount by which the rights value is driven down by subscription period pressure. Assume that the pressure is about 4% or equivalent to $4.00 of the market price prior to announcement of the offering. This group of stockholders gets ($14.70 less $4.00) times 47%, the amount of shares affected	=	$ 5.03
Rights lapsed–3% of the shares: This 3% of the shares receives nothing	=	$ 0.00
Total value of rights to stockholders	=	$ 13.38

PART III

Benefit to Company and Stockholders Combined

Add the benefit the stockholders receive from the rights to the net proceeds to the company in order to obtain the correct net effect.

	Direct	Rights
Net proceeds to company—see Part I, Line 10	\$ 92.00	\$ 80.30
Rights benefit to stockholders, Part II		13.38
Combined effect on company and stockholders	\$ 92.00	\$ 93.68

Thus, evaluated from the point of view of the stockholders, these assumed figures show a rights offering to be preferable.

new shares into three groups and calculates the benefit to each group in order to get the total benefit.

The original stockholders who subscribe get the full benefit of the right to subscribe at the subscription price. After the offering, the stock should recover to the price prior to the announcement of the offering.

The stockholders who sell their rights benefit to the extent of rights value. Compared to the market price of the stock prior to announcement of the offering, they are affected by the pre-offering and subscription period pressure. Their gain is equivalent to the market price of the stock at the time the price is set, less the subscription period pressure.

Those stockholders who let their rights lapse get nothing.

In Part II, our final figures are the total benefit the stockholders receive from the rights.

In Part III, we add the total benefit to all stockholders, as calculated in Part II, to the net proceeds received by the Company in a rights offering, in order to get a correct comparison with a direct offering.

In Exhibit 9-18, we left out four factors to keep the exhibit simple. They are not sufficient to throw off the results. They are as follows:

1. The rights that are lost—i.e., neither subscribed nor sold—are a total loss to the individual stockholders but not necessarily a total loss to the company. If the offering is not underwritten, the company can sell these shares at the market price and thus get the full amount. If the offering is underwritten, the underwriting agreement may provide for division between the company and the underwriters of the difference between the subscription price and the market price at which these shares are sold. Thus, the company gains some of the benefit lost by the stockholders. This amount is generally small because the number of rights involved is small.
2. When stockholders sell rights, their benefit is reduced by the brokerage charges in connection with the sale.[2]
3. It was assumed that the pre-offering pressure for a direct offering and a rights offering were both 1%. Since all the stock in a direct offering comes on the market, whereas that amount subscribed by original holders in a rights offering never comes on the market, it might be expected that it would be greater for a direct offering because of the greater supply. Because of the problems

[2] As an example, if a right had a market value of 30¢, and a stockholder owning 100 shares sold 100 rights, he would receive \$30 less brokerage commissions of about \$1.80, which is 6% of the rights value. If we apply this to the full 7% for the amount the subscription price is set below market on the day the price is set, it would mean a reduction of .42% from our Benefit to Stockholders, but it only applies to 47% of the stock so that the net effect is only .20%, a negligible overall amount.

involved in measuring pre-offering pressure, this refinement may be worth keeping in mind without specifically allowing for it in the figures.

4. For exact calculations, the subscription period pressure should be the weighted average of the pressures existing at the time various amounts of rights are sold.

Complete Comparison—Direct vs. Rights

With the above discussion as a background, let's go over the points you will have to weigh in making a decision as to which method you should use.

1. *Dilution of earnings per share.*

   As we have pointed out, opponents of rights offerings say that the lower net proceeds resulting from a rights offering is a real disadvantage, because it results in greater dilution of earnings per share. They over-emphasize it.

   Let's assume, that the net proceeds are 10% less in a rights than a direct offering. How would this affect earnings per share if the company sold enough additional stock in a rights offering in order to obtain the same net proceeds? We will assume that, with a direct offering, the company will sell one new share for each ten shares outstanding, or a 1 for 10. The calculations are shown in Exhibit 9-19.

   The exhibit shows that the diluting effect per share is about 1%, whereas there was about 10% less net proceeds per share with a rights offering. Why so little diluting effect? The answer is easy. Earnings per share are figured on the basis of total number of shares and the diluting effect is thus decreased. It is only the new shares which affect the full dilution, and they are 10% of the outstanding shares.

   In other words, if a company offers stock on a 1-for-10 ratio, which is 10% more stock, and there is 10% less net proceeds per share for the new shares with a rights offering, then this will produce only 1% dilution in per share earnings on total shares outstanding after the financing. It would take ten such offerings of stock, or a 100% increase in the total shares, before the diluting effect on earnings per share would be as much as 10%.

   Furthermore, the stockholders get some benefit from rights. Only if a company is determined to get the greatest net proceeds per share, without regard to the benefit of rights to stockholders, will it probably prefer the direct sale method, because as pointed out above, in a rights offering it is generally not wise to set the subscription price so high that the rights have little value.

2. *Legal aspects.*

   Some state laws require companies incorporated therein to offer common stocks and securities convertible into common stock by means of preemptive rights to existing stockholders. The charters of some companies have provisions requiring the use of preemptive rights. Some regulatory authorities have shown a preference for companies under their jurisdiction to use the rights method.

   The primary basis for this obligatory requirement was the original reason for rights—to prevent the management of a company from selling additional stock without each stockholder having an opportunity to maintain his existing position. This was for the purpose of preventing two types of abuses by management: sale of stock to a select group at a cheap price so that the select group would receive a monetary benefit, or sale of stock to a select group acquiring control so that it could subsequently benefit.

   For large companies with a broad group of stockholders, this original reason for rights is not very important today. It is unlikely that insiders would try any such shenanigans to benefit a select group. Financing by this type of company is so much in the public eye that the management could not easily conceal such wrongdoing, even if they wished to do so. Furthermore, the matter of control is relatively unimportant because the

Exhibit 9-19

DILUTION OF EARNINGS PER SHARE WITH DIRECT OFFERING COMPARED WITH RIGHTS OFFERING

Assuming: 1-for-10 offering
net proceeds per share in rights offering 10% less than direct.

Before financing	
Earnings available for common	$10,000,000
Shares outstanding	2,000,000
Earnings per share	$5.00
Direct offering	
Offering ratio	1 for 10
Shares offered	200,000
Net proceeds per share	$50.00
Total net proceeds	$10,000,000
Rights offering	
Offering ratio	1 for 9
Shares offered	222,000
Net proceeds per share	$45.00
Total new proceeds	$10,000,000
Assuming: No additional earnings on new capital	
Earnings per share, after direct offering (2,200,000 shares)	$4.55
Earnings per share after rights offering (2,222,000 shares)	$4.50
% Decrease with rights	-1%
Assuming: Additional earnings from 10% return on new capital	
Earnings per share, after direct offering (2,200,000 shares)	$4.96
Earnings per share, after rights offering (2,222,000 shares)	$4.91
% Decrease with rights	-1%

ownership of a large, publicly owned company is in most instances so widely spread that no one stockholder has any effective control.

For smaller corporations, which are less in the public eye and where stockholders do have a substantial interest which they wish to maintain, a requirement for preemptive rights may provide some protection to existing stockholders. Generally today, the principal factors in deciding on direct offering *vs.* rights do not center around the question of protection against management's abuses.

3. *When stock is below book value—use rights?*

   It is sometimes contended that rights should be used if a new offering has to be sold below book value.

   For example, if the book value per share is $50 and the market price of the stock is $48, new stock would have to be sold below book value. This would result in dilution of the existing stockholders' equity. If there was a new offering of stock on a 1-for-10 basis to produce net proceeds per share of $45, the book value per share after the offering would be $49.55. This does not seem to be a compelling reason to use rights.

If an analysis of the net benefit to the company and stockholders, based on the method of calculation in Exhibit 9-18, showed that a direct offering would produce the best results, this analysis should carry more weight than the mere fact that the stock was selling below book value.

4. *High offering ratio—relatively small issue.*

The rights value is dependent on the discount and the offering ratio.

When a relatively small amount of stock is offered, the offering ratio is high and the rights value will be relatively small. For example, if a stock selling at $30 has a subscription price of $27, the rights value, when rights are detached, would be 30¢ with a 1-for-10 offering. If half the amount of stock were offered so that the offering ratio was 1 for 20, the rights value would be 15¢.

Thus, for relatively small issues of stock, a company might prefer a direct offering in order to avoid a low rights value.

5. *Benefit to stockholders.*

In a rights offering the stockholders get the benefit of the option to purchase at a reduced price, as discussed above. This advantage should be properly analyzed as in the exhibit. If the benefit to the stockholders is deducted from the cost to the company to get the combined effect, the picture becomes quite different than it appears when the emphasis is placed on point 2 above net proceeds per share alone.

6. *Stockholders' preference.*

Some stockholders are outspoken in favor of rights. They like the added benefit. It has the advantage of being taxed as a capital gain. Other stockholders just don't like them. For example, institutions, which handle the investments of a large number of individuals, must do a lot of paper work and correspondence with their clients when there are rights offerings.

The following passage from a survey of 891 large and small individual stockholders in large- and medium-sized companies is perhaps of some interest:

> Rights to subscribe to new stock at prices below the market were overwhelmingly approved by all classes of individual stockholders. Small stockholders, whose tendency to allow rights to expire unused has worried many managers, are more emphatic in their approval than other classes. And comparison with the 1951 survey indicates that rights are even more popular than seven years ago.[3]

Many companies have been able to obtain a favorable vote from stockholders to change their charter, giving management the choice as to whether stock should be offered through rights or direct. This should not necessarily be interpreted as a vote against rights. A stockholder might feel that it was wise to give management flexibility in this regard, and yet still prefer rights if there was no compelling reason for management to do otherwise. If such a change is made in a charter, it may be provided that stock offered without rights must be offered publicly in order to prevent an inside deal.

A company might do well to make a survey based on a scientific sample of its stockholders in order to determine their wishes on the subject. The results should be calculated on the basis of number of shares and not of the number of stockholders.

7. *Effect on market price.*

Since there is a benefit to stockholders in a rights offering, it would be reasonable to expect that the market price of a

---

[3]Survey made under the auspices of the Bureau of Business and Economic Research of the University of California. As reported in the article, "What Do Stockholders Like?" by John Clendenin; Volume I, Number 1, Fall 1958, *California Management Review.*

company's stock, other than when new stock is being offered, would reflect this benefit to some extent. While the benefit might be difficult to measure in most cases, because so many other factors affect the price of a stock, nevertheless it cannot be completely overlooked. This would apply particularly if a company followed a consistent policy of offering stock through rights.

8. *Assist in raising capital.*

   Sometimes, it may be necessary to use a rights offering in order to raise the amount of money required in a common stock offering. For example, when an issue is very large, a rights offering might be helpful by inducing stockholders to dig down into their pockets and put up the money; whereas, they might not bother if there was a direct offering. Thus, an added source of new capital is tapped which might not be reached through a direct offering.

   At certain times, margin requirements for shares purchased through rights are substantially less than for direct purchases. This may provide an added market appeal for rights and assist in raising capital. For example, borrowings by stockholders in order to subscribe might add to the amount of money available to take up the issue. For large issues this may be a significant factor.

   On the other hand, if a company has offered stock on a rights basis often, it might find that a decreasing number of stockholders would subscribe, because they did not have the funds or already had enough of the stock. In such a situation, a direct offering might be advisable in order to bring in a new group of stockholders. A company should be sure of its ground before using this as a reason. Keeping a record of the number of original stockholders who subscribe will assist in making this decision.

   If a large amount of a company's stock is held by a small number of investors, who are known not to want additional stock, then a direct offering might fit the picture better. If a rights offering were used, an arrangement would have to be made for underwriters to handle the rights which would be received by this group of stockholders.

9. *Cultivation of dealers in a rights offering.*

   If a stock is listed on a stock exchange, dealers tend to lose interest. Payment of dealer compensation in a rights offering represents a way to keep dealers interested in a listed stock.

Summary–Direct Offering vs. Rights

Where does this all lead us?

The original purpose for rights–to prevent management abuses, by sale of stock to insiders–may still be worthwhile in smaller companies not in the public limelight. However, the large companies couldn't hide such a maneuver even if the desire to do so were present. Therefore, in deciding on which method is preferable, we must look to what is best for the company; that includes the stockholders, since they own the company.

Direct sale may produce the greatest net proceeds per share, but the argument that it thus prevents the serious dilution caused by a rights offering is not sound. The added dilution of rights offering is not serious. Furthermore, mere emphasis on the greatest amount of net proceeds per share clearly disregards allowance for the benefit to stockholders of a rights offering. If rights are appreciated by stockholders, they may have a favorable long range effect on the price of the company's stock. Make proper allowance for this benefit and keep your stockholders in mind as the real owners of your company. You should heed your stockholders' wishes, but be sure you have a comprehensive sample based on the number of shares.

There are, of course, situations in which direct sale may be preferable, but it would appear that you would do well to have good reasons for not using rights before you decide otherwise.

So, if you are forced to use the rights method of offering stock by state law where your company is incorporated, don't feel too badly. If there is no such requirement, a company's charter which permits the use of either method may be preferable, because it provides greater flexibility. However, given the choice, it would appear that when weighed from the point of view of the combined benefit to the company and stockholders, the balance generally favors the rights method.

PRIVATE SALE OF COMMON–INVESTMENT LETTER STOCK

A seldom used method of raising common stock money is by means of investment letter stock. This method is generally used in a bull stock market when there are eager stock buyers. It has been used by a few companies which have a dire need for common in a hurry. Such companies will undoubtedly have sold all the debt possible, they have an interesting project which requires a large amount of capital so they must sell common. Their stock is selling at a good price, probably more than it is worth, but the market is soft. The public market might not take much stock. So the company sells stock privately to certain sophisticated investors. Or it may be used by a company which has poor earnings but bright prospects. Forecast information can be given the investors.

No registration is needed, because it conforms to the definition of a private sale since the buyers are knowledgeable and can protect themselves. In order to conform to a private sale, it must comply with Rule 146 of the Securities and Exchange Commission which was mentioned at the start of this chapter. The purchasers of the stock must have the intent to buy it for investment purposes and not for resale. The company will require the purchasers to sign a letter stating that they purchased the stock with intent to hold it as an investment and not for resale. This restriction, of course, puts the buyer of the common at a disadvantage, since the stock cannot readily be sold. The length of time the purchaser has to hold the stock in order to show that he bought it as an investment is now defined by the SEC under Rule 144. Because of the restriction on resale, the purchasers will expect to get the stock at a substantial discount from the market. This may range up to 20%. Thus, this method of raising common money is very expensive. Existing stockholders might feel that their company was being given away. An advantage is the speed with which the transaction can be handled since no registration statement is required.

PRICING OF A CONVERTIBLE FOR A NEW OFFERING

A convertible debenture or convertible preferred can be offered either directly or through rights. The same general ideas apply as to which method is better, as applied to an offering of common. If it is a rights offering, then after the terms and price of the convertible have been established, the subscription price is set in a similar way as for a common offering. In Chapter 4, we explained how to price a convertible.

GOING PUBLIC

A privately owned company has three ownership choices:

Stay private
Sell out
Go public

The principal reasons for going public are:

1. To permit the owners to sell some of their investment for estate reasons.
2. To provide an opportunity for the company to raise common equity capital from outside sources.
3. To provide a publicly traded stock which could be used for acquisition purposes.
4. To make it more practical to offer incentive securities such as convertibles and warrants, or stock options for key company personnel.

This is a vital decision. The stakes are high and the wrong move may ultimately spell disaster.

If a privately owned company is expanding rapidly it will probably borrow to the hilt, and then if it does not generate enough common equity through retained earnings to permit further borrowing it will have reached the end of its rope. If at that time its earnings are down, it can't go public and it will be at a disadvantage to sell out. Many owners love what they have built so much that they just can't face up to the problem, particularly when the company is doing well. These questions have to be answered:

How long can it stay private?
Can it go public?
Would it be better to sell out?

Simple rules of thumb used by some underwriters for a company to go public include:

Minimum Net Income After Full Taxes	$1,000,000
Minimum Size of Common Issue	$3,000,000
Minimum Number of Shares Offered	300,000
Minimum Price per Share, Approximately	$10

However, these figures alone are not the answer. All the circumstances surrounding a company have to be considered. Is it in an attractive industry? Is it soundly financed? Has it had a good earnings record over a period of years? Is there any depth of management? Has the company a bright future with prospects of major growth?

There are, of course, disadvantages:

1. The management will now be responsible to its outside stockholders. If management takes this as seriously as it should, it may mean a new way of life. Outside directors should be put on the board.
2. Certain types of actions require approval by the stockholders.
3. It will have to make public information about its operations.
4. There are additional administrative problems and expenses. There are additional liabilities for directors and officers.
5. Once a company goes public it may be more difficult to sell it to another company because of the outside stockholders.
6. If a company's stock becomes a dog, it will be unable to raise equity capital and the stock remaining with the original holders can't be sold.
7. A dividend policy has to be established which will assist the market price of the stock. This may be opposed to the desires of the original owners who still have a large investment in the company.
8. It may complicate estate situations, because for estate evaluation purposes the market price will have to be used; whereas, with a privately owned company an appraised value is used.
9. Salaries and expense accounts of the senior officers should be in line with comparable public companies. There is less freedom than for a privately owned company.

Even if a company seems to fit the criteria which would permit it to go public, the answer is not that simple. The important question is how will it survive once it goes public. It is sad to watch companies which have been taken public by investment bankers in a bull market hang by their thumbs and twirl in the breeze once the boom is over. Their stocks sell at low price-earnings ratios and below book values. That is a disastrous position and one that can't be reversed. Remember, there is no written obligation by the investment banker to maintain a market after the offering.

A company may show a real growth in earnings per share because its return on common book value is increasing say from 6% to 7% to 8% to 9%. The resulting earnings per share growth may make it an attractive dish for an investment banker to offer. However, in order for a company to be a viable public entity it must continue to represent an attractive common stock investment. A company should be able to maintain a good return on book value of its common of about 12% *on an average,* with a sound capital structure, even after the bloom is off, and even here there is no assurance about market price. With markets as they existed in 1974, this rate of return would be inadequate.

So a company should not just assume that going public is an easy way out. And it cannot be done overnight. A private company that may, and we repeat the word "may," have to consider going public or selling out in the future should plan for that possibility even though it may be able to avoid it. It should get its finances in shape so that its historical balance sheet and income statement will present a good picture to the public. Also it should review its legal "posture" with counsel experienced in Securities and Exchange Commission work. And the best procedure to follow is to take action when the company is in a strong financial position and not wait until the last minute when estate problems or capital needs have reached a climax.

If a company gets to the point of going public it will need to work with three people in whom it has faith: a lawyer who has had broad experience in securities work, an underwriter who will want to do a good long range job and an accounting firm with stature. Good Luck!

Going Private

Some small companies which have gone public, and which do not have a viable market for their stock, may consider reversing the process if the owners can see their way clear in the future to operate without outside equity, and if funds can be obtained to make the transition without putting the company in a bad financial bind. However, this is a delicate step to take. It involves the possibility of future law suits by outsiders who give up their stock at a low price in relation to what they purchased it for, and subsequently discover that insiders had great plans to make the company very profitable. This operation must be handled with complete disclosure in fairness to stockholders and in order to avoid future law suits.

CHAPTER 10

The Financial Community–Who Does What

Wall Street and all the machinery of finance seem like an unlimited maze of people and firms doing many complicated and mysterious things.

However, as you get to know who does what, much of the mystery disappears. You see that many of the organizations find their counterpart in other types of business where the middleman trades in a commodity; in finance the commodity just happens to be securities and money. The same forces work as in other businesses: the law of supply and demand, the incentive to make a dollar and regulation through competition and government.

There are, of course, some organizations connected with the money market which are special in their nature; the Federal Reserve System is one. It can assist in adding to or subtracting from the supply of money as one of its functions. But even for such organizations, the principles governing their operations are not too difficult to understand.

Besides giving information about the financial community in order to reduce the mystery, there are some practical reasons for this chapter. It will help you better understand the type of firms that deal in your company's securities, affect their prices and perform many other functions. You will be rubbing elbows and transacting business with them in raising capital and keeping investors informed.

To simplify the picture, we will sort them out into six groups with their principal components.

1. The users of funds
   - Individuals
   - Corporations
   - Government bodies—federal, states cities and authorities
2. The providers of funds
   - Individuals
   - Institutions
3. The middlemen
   - Underwriter or investment banker—raise new capital.
   - Broker and dealer—buy outstanding securities from one investor and sell them to another.
4. Service organizations
   - Stock exchanges—New York, American and local exchanges with their specialists.
   - Corporate Trust Departments of banks and private service organizations.
     - The machinery of finance acting as transfer agents, registrars, trustees for bond issues, etc.
   - Central depositories of securities.
   - The Federal Reserve System—regulating the money supply.
     - Federal Reserve Bank of New York acts as agent in selling U.S. government bonds.
   - Rating agencies.
5. Security analysts—wherever securities are evaluated
6. The Policemen
   - The Securities and Exchange Commission operating under five Federal Acts.
   - The State securities departments operating under so-called Blue Sky Laws.
   - The banking authorities having regulatory authority over banks.

We will not have to cover all these groups because some are described in other parts of the book. The corporate users of funds is the subject of the entire book. The second group, the providers of funds, is covered in Chapter 7, Sources of Capital—Long and Short. In the fourth group, the stock exchanges are covered in Chapter 11, Markets for Outstanding Securities. And in the sixth group, banking authorities, are covered in Chapter 13 on bank financing.

Underwriter or Investment Banker

When you sell securities, you may sell them directly to the ultimate purchasers, but more than likely you will deal with an underwriter. Thus, an underwriter generally will take part in the process of distribution to the ultimate investors in one way or another.

The underwriter is a middleman. He is a merchandiser of securities. In his normal function he does not wish to continue to be the owner of the securities for any length of time. Securities are merely his stock in trade, which he moves into the hands of investors with the greatest possible speed. He makes his money by turnover and not by holding. In most cases, his capital is not large enough to use for both underwriting and investment purposes.

An underwriting firm may also be called an investment banking firm. This latter term is more appropriate when referring to such a firm's overall business, which may include financial services related to underwriting. In the past, practically all investment banking firms were privately owned. Today, there are many with stock outstanding with the public, so if you want to study their operations you can look at their annual reports.

Investment banking firms handle billions of dollars of issues each year with relatively little capital. This is accomplished because securities in the hands of underwriters are largely financed by short-term bank loans. The banks call these loans brokers' loans, whether they are to brokers, dealers or underwriters. On high grade bonds, the banks may lend nearly the full price. The commercial bankers would not make such loans unless they expected the securities would be sold quickly and the loans repaid. An underwriting firm must have capital equivalent to a certain percentage of its commitments at any one time. The percentage is different for bonds and stocks. However, an underwriter hopes to buy and sell an issue in a short period of time so that it has a high capital turnover. For this reason an underwriting firm can do billions of dollars of business during a year with millions of dollars of capital.

There are many different types of underwriting firms, some large, which take large positions in a new security issue, and some small, which participate on a scale commensurate with their capital. Size of a firm may be measured by the amount of capital, size of issue which they can handle, volume of securities which they underwrite in a year, number of employees and number of branches.

Some are wholesalers of new issues almost exclusively; they have one main office in New York and perhaps one other outside. When a wholesale type of underwriting firm buys an issue, it will sell to large institutional purchasers. If the security is a type which has to be sold to a large group of investors scattered throughout the country, such a firm will rely heavily on dealers throughout the country to assist in selling. There are other firms which have many branches throughout the country and do much of the distribution to individual investors through their own branches. There are still other firms which might be considered as in between, with a limited number of branches in key cities. Some firms have foreign branches.

A few firms tend to do more business in senior securities. Some are known as specialists in certain types of industries, such as oil companies, department stores, etc. Some do more competitive deals; whereas, others may be heavier in negotiated offerings or private placements.

Some firms are strictly in the underwriting business; whereas, others are in many other types of security businesses, functioning as broker, dealer, arbitrageur, trader in U.S. Governments and Municipals, investment counsel service, etc. Some of the firms also handle trading in commodities.

Large investment banking firms are departmentalized, and when you deal with one you will find it easier if you have an idea what the different departments do. They are as follows:

- Buying or Underwriting Department—This department handles all the operations of buying the securities from the issuing company, including developing new business for the underwriting firm, developing financial plans, framing terms of security issues and assisting companies in setting up financing in a negotiated deal, such as writing the prospectus, etc.
- Syndicate Department—Arrangements are made in this department with other underwriting firms that may participate in the underwriting of a new issue, and relations are handled with dealer firms that may assist in the sale of the issue.
- Sales Department—This is self-explanatory. Once a new issue is set up and underwritten, the sales department handles the selling of the firm's own commitment in the issue.
- Trading Department—This department is staffed with men sitting at banks of phones, which are connected with other firms and some institutional investors throughout the country. Don't try to tell a securities trader a new joke; chances are he has heard it long ago, no matter in what part of the country it originated. Teletype machines are handy for further instantaneous communication. This department looks like a madhouse to someone who isn't accustomed to it. There is much shouting of bid and asked prices and other lingo of the trade, flashing of telephone lights and large boards

on the wall with up-to-the-minute quotations. The trading department is not a necessary adjunct of the underwriting business, but many firms have such departments because they perform functions in the securities business other than underwriting. They mostly buy and sell issues already outstanding.

- Statistical Department—This department is staffed with security analysts who write reports and make various types of studies about companies, industries and securities. It is also known as the investment analysis department, the research department and the security analysis department.

There are other departments necessary to keep a large organization going, such as accounting, security handling, etc. They are referred to as the back office. You will have no contact with them as far as offering securities is concerned.

An investment banking firm provides three related services for a company selling securities:

1. Buying the securities from the company at a specific price and on a certain date. Thus, the company gets its money. In this capacity, the firm is acting as an underwriter and has the risk and the job of selling securities to investors.
2. Acting as agent for the company if the securities are sold at private sale.
3. Acting as a financial advisor either as a separate function or while handling a new offering.

An investment banking firm should have three things to offer you: people with know-how, capital and reputation. When you choose your underwriter, these are the points you will wish to have in mind:

1. The size—The size of the firm to choose will depend on the size of the offering. Most large underwriting houses don't like to handle issues under $4 million. A small company may find that its securities could better be handled by a small underwriting firm geared to such financing. This may involve the use of a local firm familiar with the situation and local investors who would be the most interested purchasers.
2. The type of firm—whether it is a wholesaler with a good dealer setup, or a retailer with many branches, and whether it does business in bonds or stocks.
3. Knowledge of the personnel—Long experience in handling many deals is a prerequisite to build up adequate knowledge in this specialized business. If your business is of an unusual nature, the more experience the firm has in your industry the better. Watch out for the young smarties who have not been seasoned with some bad as well as good years.
4. Integrity—This should probably be put first. Unless you are an expert in finance and right up-to-the-minute on financial markets, you will have to rely heavily on your underwriter's advice. You can only be sure that you will be fairly treated if the underwriter has the highest possible integrity. Does he try to snow you? Does he try to push you so that he can get a commission in the bag?
5. Capital—The firm must have sufficient capital to handle your financing.
6. Sufficient staff—You will not wish to be given summary treatment by a firm which has a large volume of business and inadequate personnel.

Some underwriters claim that they alone can handle large common stock offerings because they have a great many branches which can sell the issue to the individual investors. However, underwriters with a small number of branches will contend that they can do just as well by forming a syndicate with local securities dealers; thus they can get as good or better sales power because they can select the best dealer in each community who will give an issue the best sponsorship. Some of the very large houses of this variety handle some of the largest common deals.

Underwriters seldom handle a large public offering alone. In order to spread the risk, the underwriter who originated the deal will invite other underwriters to form a syndicate. The originating underwriter will act as manager of the offering and will get a fee out of the spread for acting in this capacity. Each of the underwriters in the syndicate will have securities to sell, the amount of which will depend on the underwriter's capital, his sales ability and how much the managing underwriter wants him to have.

In order to help sell an issue, the managing underwriter may arrange with a group of dealers to participate in the offering. The dealers do not act as underwriters but only as salesmen. The managing underwriter handles relations with dealers and provides them with securities to sell.

For some large issues, two large underwriting firms may work jointly in managing an underwriting. In most situations, the large underwriting firms can handle an issue alone. Unless necessary, there may be some disadvantage of a joint manager. There have been instances where joint managers got fighting over the issue and the financing suffered accordingly. One underwriter who was asked what he thought about having joint managers put it this way: "When I am not the manager, I try to become the manager and at least a co-manager. However, when I am the managing underwriter I don't want or need a co-manager." That is an honest statement.

There are two publications which list investment bankers each year. They are:

Finance Magazine, the Magazine of Money, in its July issue, gives the principal firms with their capital, number of offices, volume of equity and debt issues managed and participated, number of offices and key personnel.[1]

The Investment Dealer's Digest issues a "Corporate Financing Directory" twice a year, which gives the volume of corporate financing done by each firm.[2]

In choosing an underwriter, you will first wish to pick out about three who will be interested in handling your financing and generally fit your requirements as to size of issue, type of security and type of company. You should then visit each one and explain the financing you contemplate. Tell them to study the situation and that you will visit them subsequently to hear what they have to offer. You should explain that you are talking to two other underwriters and will make a choice after you have heard what each has to offer. You should make your decision on the basis of what they tell you about their previous experience, how they operate and what they can do with your issue. The people you are dealing with should be an important factor in your decision.

On your first visit, you should not put too much weight on the price at which an underwriter tells you he can sell your security, because conditions may change before the issue is ready for sale and you sign the underwriting agreement. In order to suck you in, some underwriters may over-state what they think they can get for your security. In order to guard against this problem, you should use an index of securities similar to your security from the time an underwriter suggests a price in order to track subsequent changes in market conditions. This will help you tell whether the market has changed or the underwriter is changing his idea on price. For example, if your company is an industrial and you are selling an A grade bond issue, you should track the yield on similar bonds with an index of A grade industrial bonds.

Remember in listening to the financial advice of underwriters that they have an ax to grind. They want to sell an issue and make a fee as soon as possible. A bird in the hand is one that another underwriter won't get. They will

[1]Finance Publishing Corp., P.O. Box G, Lenox Hill Station, New York, N.Y. 10021. $10 per copy.

[2]*The Investment Dealer's Digest,* 150 Broadway, New York, N.Y. 10038. $10 per copy.

be thinking about the type of issue which will sell readily. This may be in conflict with what would be best for your company in the long run. Also remember their likes and dislikes because of the benefit to them, such as:

A direct offering of common stock makes more money for the underwriter than a rights offering, and a direct offering is easier to handle.

A private sale eliminates risk to the underwriter which exists in a public offering.

Underwriters hate competitive offerings.

They prefer a debt issue over a common offering because of the greater ease of sale. Convertibles may even be easier for them to sell.

If you are satisfied with the job your investment banker is doing, you should stick with him. But if you are dissatisfied in any way, do not hesitate to try another one. Don't listen to the "malarky" that you should stay with one investment banker because he knows your company; that alone should be no reason whatsoever to prevent you from moving. You are hiring a service and you should seek the best possible service.

One thing any underwriter should have, if he is worth his salt, is a good "feel" of the market. He should know the instantaneous thoughts of the buyers in regard to price. An underwriter can be immeasurably helpful in this regard. Furthermore, an underwriter should be aware of the terms which investors are currently seeking. An underwriter will tell you that there are security patterns which are continuously evolving. In order to sell your security most advantageously, you should know the proper dress to put your security in, to make it appealing to investors. This is a sound approach provided due consideration is given by the company to the fact that the dress should wear well and not hurt the company's subsequent appeal when some of the security provisions come into effect in future years. Remember you are behind the eight ball in dealing with the underwriter on price and terms because you are not close to the market. You may have to be shrewd to make certain your company gets well-treated.

Practically everyone in a large underwriting syndicate would like the price to be low in order that it can be sold quickly. Certainly, the salesmen are of this mind. The other underwriting members of the group would like to see the price low so they can sell the issue quickly and not put their capital at risk. The only ones who have an interest in working for you are the members of the buying department of the managing underwriter; they should wish to please you so that they will get your repeat business.

If you have a new offering of securities underwritten, you will sign an agreement with the underwriter on the day he buys the securities. Such an agreement says that he will pay you the money a few days hence on the closing day. If you read most agreements, you will note that they may include certain clauses which permit an underwriter to get out of the contract if the issue could not be sold at practically any price. Such clauses cover the company experiencing a material adverse development affecting its financial strength, a major law suit, a war or other national catastrophe, etc. These out clauses may jolt you when you first read them. They make it look as though you do not really have the underwriter on the hook. However, underwriters have to depend on their reputation in order to get business, and if they did not lean over backwards in interpreting these out clauses, their name would be mud. As a practical matter, reliable underwriters would not use them except under extreme circumstances. Therefore, you don't have too much to worry about. This does not mean that you shouldn't be sure that you have a good underwriting agreement; you might be unlucky and then your contract with the underwriters would be important. Furthermore, the agreements which underwriting firms are willing to sign may vary regarding the out clauses. Some firms pride themselves in being willing to sign a tight agreement. You should read the out clauses so that, at least, you will know whether you are getting the protection you thought you were paying for. One thing to note is that the agreement with underwriters who act together in offering a single issue is several and not joint.

In the chapters on selling securities, we analyzed the risks involved in offering a security and pointed out which risks the underwriters assume if the issue is underwritten. We also discussed the charges for their services and how to negotiate with underwriters.

Broker and Dealer

One firm may act in both capacities, at one time as a broker and at another as a dealer, and, in fact, it may also do business as an underwriter. A firm may be loosely referred to as a broker, a dealer or an underwriter, and do all three types of business. On the other hand, one firm may specialize in a single one of these functions.

The distinction between a broker and dealer is as follows:

> A *broker* is an agent. The legal definition of an agent, in simple terms, is one who acts under the instructions of a principal to buy or sell a security; an agent never takes title. The broker is a middleman. He receives a commission.
>
> A *dealer* acts as a principal and generally has title to a security before he sells it to you, and he takes title if he buys it from you. His compensation is measured by the spread between the price at which he buys and sells. This spread is in lieu of the commission which the broker receives.

The men in brokerage houses and dealer organizations who sell securities to investors are known as registered representatives.

The broker has no securities or merchandise on his "shelves" to sell you. When he receives an order, he contacts someone who owns the security through the facilities of a stock exchange and buys for you, not for himself. This is accomplished by the broker going to the proper "post" on the floor of the exchange through his representative there and engaging in bidding in that market as your agent. The dealer, on the other hand, usually has merchandise on his "shelves" which he owns and which he sells to you. If he has none he will buy some, take title and then sell them to you at an increased price.

When you bought some stock for your personal account, you probably did not notice whether the firm acted as broker or dealer. If you looked on the slip of paper you received confirming the transaction, you would note that the brokerage transaction showed a figure for a commission and included a statement:

> "As agent we have BOUGHT for your account and risk."

The dealer transaction without showing a commission would include a statement:

> "As principal we confirm SALE to you."

It gives the price you paid the dealer, but not what the dealer paid or how much he made.

Securities which are listed on an exchange must be handled on a brokerage basis by firms which are members of the exchange. Securities which are not listed are mostly handled on a dealer basis. There are exceptions. It is possible to purchase or sell an unlisted security on a commission or agency basis. Firms which are not members of an exchange may handle listed securities on a dealer basis.

The National Association of Securities Dealers

The dealers have a national organization known as the National Association of Securities Dealers, Inc. This organization has 3,212 member firms, from the big to the little dealer. This compares with 510 organizations which are members of the New York Stock Exchange. Most of the New York Stock Exchange firms are also members of the NASD and trade in over-the-counter securities. If your stock is traded over-the-counter, you ought to keep the dealers in mind as part of your investor relations program. You should know what makes them click and how to keep them interested in your securities.

The Securities and Exchange Commission has regulatory authority over all markets, but the National Association of Securities Dealers, Inc. is a self-regulatory body.

Arbitrageurs

Many experienced Financial Vice Presidents have hardly heard of the word arbitrage as it applies to securities. An arbitrageur is not strictly a middleman, because he is not acting for a corporation or an investor; he is acting for his own account. However, in carrying on his business he will be buying and selling securities from investors.

Arbitrage is a specialized field of finance. In certain transactions it is quite important. If you offer securities through rights, you will need to understand it in order to know one of the forces acting on the market price during the offering. Arbitrage may also come into play in conversion of convertible issues and in other fields, such as exchange offers.

Definition: Briefly, it is the simultaneous purchase and sale of equivalents. In other words, it is the purchase and sale of exchangeable securities for the purpose of profiting upon price differentials in the market between the equivalents.

Let's take an example in the field of rights offerings to stockholders. The sale of common stock through rights, the value of a right, etc., are all described in detail in Chapter 9, Selling Common Stock. However, so that you won't have to review that chapter before proceeding with arbitrage, we will say a few words about the value of rights at this stage.

A company has stock outstanding with the public. It announces that it will offer one new share of stock to its existing stockholders for each ten shares held. Stockholders are given 17 days to subscribe. Assume that the market price of the stock after the rights have been issued—that is, after the ex-rights date—is $100. The subscription price is $90.

Each existing share prior to the ex-rights date includes the right to purchase one-tenth of a new share at the subscription price. The existing stockholders are issued warrants, which are pieces of paper stating the number of rights to which a stockholder is entitled as well as other information regarding the offering. Those who do not wish to subscribe can sell their rights in the market.

An owner of the rights gets a bargain. A person who has ten shares receives a warrant showing that he is entitled to ten rights. When he gets the warrant he can buy one share of stock worth $100 for $90, or at a $10 discount. The ten rights are worth $10, each right being worth $1.

Now back to arbitrage—the simultaneous purchase and sale of equivalents:

Purchase ten rights for $1 per right, or a total of $10.

Simultaneously, sell one share of stock for $100.

We are short one share of stock; that is, we sold a share which we didn't own, so we use our ten rights to subscribe at a price of $90 per share. Thus, we purchased ten rights at $10 and subscribed for one share at $90, making a total of $100. We deliver this share to the person to whom we had sold one share for $100. This would not be a worthwhile arbitrage because we came out all even. It merely serves as a simple illustration.

Arbitrage in rights can just as well take place in the reverse of the above transactions.

Sell ten rights for $1 each, or a total of $10.

Simultaneously, purchase one share of stock for $100 per share.

We have gone short the rights, since we didn't have any to start with, but we own one share of stock.

In general, there is no market risk in these two arbitrages, because there is an equivalent offsetting transaction in the market in each of them at the same time. If the market goes up or down, there will be a gain in one and an equal loss in the other as long as parity exists. There are two qualifications which need to be made to this statement. In the first place, if the market price falls below the subscription price and the rights become worthless, the arbitrage no longer holds, because one of the equivalents is eliminated. The second situation occurs when the arbitrage consists in going short rights, buying common and then covering through delivery of the stock. If, because of margin rules, more money can be borrowed to purchase stock obtained through the exercise of rights than for the purpose of purchasing stock directly, the party to whom the rights were sold short may be unwilling to accept stock.

In carrying out an arbitrage, the rules of the Securities and Exchange Commission must be obeyed, as well as those of a stock exchange if the security is listed. There are some mechanics which are necessary to make these arbitrages possible. When an arbitrageur goes short stock, he may have to borrow stock temporarily in order to deliver on time. In our second example, he would have to borrow rights, and subsequently might have to reverse his position to cover. You don't need to know how these mechanics work, since they are routine matters in the financial community.

In our simple examples above, as previously stated, we just broke even. No arbitrageur could work on that basis. He would not make any money, and in fact he would lose money. In addition to the paper work in his own organization, there are expenses to be covered; and, of course, he must make a profit. There must be a sufficient spread between the rights value and the stock price to make arbitrage worthwhile.

Let's assume that a person wanted to carry out an arbitrage of 100 shares for a stock listed on the New York Stock Exchange as in our first example. He might have four or five principal expenses: brokerage fees, transfer taxes, Securities and Exchange Commission fee, interest on loans if the transaction is done on margin, and perhaps some charge for borrowing stock The first three expenses would be as shown in Exhibit 10-1 for a transaction taking place in New York.

In order just to cover these expenses, the rights would have to be bought for 91¢ per right and the stock sold for $100.80 per share. Arbitrage cannot ordinarily be done by individuals, because the spread isn't sufficient to cover such expenses and also allow a profit. The professionals in brokerage firms do not have to pay the brokerage fees, and they can handle the transaction on a narrower spread and still make money. It is a penny business in large volume.

In calculating the spread in an arbitrage, careful attention must be paid not only to the expenses and when the stock goes ex-rights, but also to the dividend date and accruals, etc.

A word here about the justification of arbitrage. Is it a skin game in which the professionals make money and do no good? Not at all. Visualize what happens in a rights offering. Those stockholders who don't wish to subscribe sell their rights, and with the increase in the supply of rights, the price of rights would be driven down. There would not necessarily be any corresponding action in the stock. As a consequence, the stock would stay up in price as the rights fell. The two would not remain in approximate parity which means the same equivalent value. Here is where the arbitrageurs come in. As the spread gets great enough between the rights value and the stock, enabling the arbitrageurs to make money, they will sell the stock short and buy the rights. Thus, buying comes into the market for the rights—which holds their price up. The selling of the stock short puts pressure on the stock price and tends to adjust it downward so that the rights and stock approach parity. Therefore, the arbitrageurs do perform a worthwhile function. In fact, they are so quick to take advantage of any spread between the rights and the stock that it is seldom that any spread exists. Therefore, there is relatively little true arbitrage in rights offerings of common stocks.

Exhibit 10-1

EXPENSES IN AN ARBITRAGE

Expenses to Purchase Rights:		
For 1,000 Rights @ $1 per right		
Brokerage Fee	$92.40	Per Right $0.09
Expenses to Sell Stock:		
For 100 Shares @ $100 per share		
Brokerage Fee	$75.00	
Taxes: N.Y. State	5.00	
S.E.C. Fee	.20	
	$80.20	Per Share $0.80

Remember that true arbitrage means a simultaneous transaction.

Much of the arbitrage in rights offerings is so-called "delayed" arbitrage. It is based on an expected price differential developing between the two equivalents over a period of time, due to variations in supply and demand factors. For example, you buy rights today at what you think are depressed prices, and then hope to sell the stock later on at a higher price in order to complete the arbitrage. "Delayed" arbitrage, unlike true arbitrage which is simultaneous, involves market risk during the interim while the transaction is being completed. This type of so-called arbitrage also performs an economic function in tending to level out the price movements during the subscription period. The arbitrageurs provide buying power when prices look low and provide a supply when prices look high. This has to be based on their best judgment, and, of course, there are many times when they are wrong; then they may push markets out of line in their efforts to correct their error. But they have to be right more often than they are wrong or else they would be out of business.

As previously mentioned, there is arbitrage in convertible issues, and in some situations it hastens the conversion. For example, if a bond is convertible into stock, and the stock sells at a premium over the equivalent conversion value for the bond, an arbitrageur may sell stock short, buy the convertible bond, make the conversion and deliver the stock.

There are numerous other arbitrages in finance, such as in refundings, mergers and reorganizations where one security is exchanged for another. In most of these situations, trading takes place in "when issued" securities. Where there is uncertainty as to whether the exchange will ultimately be accomplished, there may be a lack of parity between the market value of the two equivalent securities due to the risk of possible failure of the exchange. The arbitrageurs estimate this risk and make the spread between the two equivalents sufficient to cover it.

If you are involved in any financial situation in which arbitrage may occur, you will have to investigate how the arbitrageurs will be operating in order to understand the market action for your securities.

While many firms on Wall Street do some arbitrage business, it is a specialized field; the bulk of it is done by a few large firms which are members of the New York Stock Exchange. Arbitrage is, of course, only a part of their business.

Corporate Trust Operations

There are any number of services which have to be performed with securities. Some can be performed by the issuing company;

some have to be performed by another party. These are mostly handled by corporate trust departments of large money center banks. Some of the services are performed by service organizations.

A bond indenture covers many provisions which must be met by the company. It would be a laborious task for each bondholder to make sure that the company was living up to the covenants. For this reason a trust department of a bank is named as trustee to act on behalf of all the bondholders. The trustee has to issue regular reports to the bondholders. The Trust Indenture Act requires that the trustee meet certain criteria so that it is equipped to perform its duties and is financially responsible.

The trustee will probably also pay the interest to the bondholder for the company and keep the records of bondholders for a registered bond.

For stock, there are two functions to be performed: transfer agent and registrar. When someone sells shares of stock, he will send in the old certificates to the transfer agent to be cancelled. The agent will then issue new stock certificates to the buyer. A record of the holders of the stock is an outgrowth of the transfer service which calls for posting and maintaining an up-to-date list of the stockholders. The transfer service is performed mostly by the corporate trust departments of large money center banks, but may be handled by service organizations or the company itself.

Another service performed for a stock is "registrar." This provides an independent check of the total shares outstanding so that there will not be an over-issue by the transfer agent. In the past, it was a requirement that the registrar be separate and independent of the transfer agent. It is now permissible for one agent to act in both capacities, provided that certain criteria are met. If a company acts as its own transfer agent, it will need an independent registrar.

Dividends can be paid by the company, but in many instances the transfer agent also acts as the dividend disbursing agent. The agent who maintains the security records will also act as a disbursing agent for such material as quarterly reports, annual reports, proxy material and any other corporate mailings to security holders.

With the advent of dividend reinvestment, this is another service which may be performed by a corporate trust department or a service organization which pays a company's dividends.

There are many other services they perform such as assisting in:

Spin-offs
Subscriptions
Tenders and exchanges
Stock splits
Annual Meetings
Redemptions
Escrow agent for two or more parties who have entered into a contingency agreement.
Holding property in trust under agreement for special types of financing.
Depository for protective agreements under foreclosure, recapitalizations, reorganizations, tenders, etc.

Thus, the corporate trust departments and similar organizations serve the securities industry by handling the mass of paper work, acting as watchdog over property and making sure that companies live up to their contractual agreements with investors.

Depository Trust Company

The management of a company generally is little concerned with the paper work in Wall Street. However, in the wild 1960's, management became painfully aware that the paper mess was causing many stockholders concern because they couldn't get delivery of stock they had purchased and their dividends were not being received. The subsequent drop in trading volume cured many problems, but Wall Street has taken major steps to improve the situation

When a person sells a security through a brokerage house to another person who buys it from another brokerage house, the security must be processed through the transfer agent, which kills the old certificates and issues new ones in the buyers' names. Many investors leave their securities in custody of their brokers. With the ebb and flow of securities between Wall Street houses, there is much unnecessary movement of securities and paper work.

A major step to reduce the paper work and handle it better was the formation of what is today known as the Depository Trust Company. While it was originally owned by the New York Stock Exchange, it now encompasses all segments involved in processing and holding securities: brokers, dealers, banks, insurance companies, mutual funds and others. It is now chartered as a New York State Trust Company and is a member of the Federal Reserve System. It is in the process of being sold by the New York Stock Exchange to the many institutions which use its services.

It is the largest non-government depository in the country. By mid-1974, it had on deposit 2 billion shares of stock in more than 5,000 issues and over 500,000 corporate bonds in 1,210 issues.

The Depository keeps the records, and the securities are held in its vaults and a number of custodian banks in New York City.

The participating financial firms can transfer ownership of securities by book-entry, thus greatly reducing the cost and improving security processing operations. The full range of services include:

Deposits of securities.
Custody of securities.
Withdrawals by transfer or in the name of the Depository's nominee.
Collection of dividends which are then passed on to the beneficial owner by the participating firms.
The Pledge Bank Program permits participating banks to accept pledges from brokers by book-entry as a basis for a loan. Total loans on this basis generally amount to $3 billion at any one time.
The Regional Depository Facilities Program permits a broker-dealer to turn securities around the same day they are received even though the point of receipt is in some distant city.
The Institutional Delivery system permits broker confirmations to be relayed electronically to institutions around the country.
The Remote Terminal System permits a participant to inquire directly into the depository files to determine its cash settlement position and position in any issue.

Elaborate safeguards and a comprehensive insurance package have been developed to protect its participants' assets.

The Depository is in the process of further expanding the institutions and securities covered.

Federal Reserve System

A Financial Vice President can't expect to be an expert on the daily operations of the Federal Reserve System. It requires the work of an economist following it regularly in order to interpret its actions and resulting effects on business, price levels and interest rates. However, you should have sufficient knowledge to follow an economist's explanation. If you have not had courses in money and banking, you will not completely understand how the Federal Reserve does certain things described below, but this discussion should give you a general idea of how the results are obtained.

There are 12 Federal Reserve Banks located throughout the country. Commercial banks, representing about 85% of total bank deposits, are members of their local reserve banks. They contribute the capital of their local Reserve Bank, and own it. But it is rather a nominal ownership since the return on their stock is limited to 6%, any excess going to the Federal government after a specified appropriation to surplus. Supervision of the system is in the hands of the seven-man Board of Governors in Washington, appointed by the President of the United States. The seven-man Board appoints the president and three of the nine directors of each local reserve bank.

By direction of Congress, which established it, the Federal Reserve System operates for the welfare of our economy. Were you to study its methods of gathering information about our economy through its local Federal Reserve Banks and other media, you would realize that, insofar as humanly possible, it has a very close feel of the pulse of our economy.

One of the primary functions of the Federal Reserve System, as it may affect our economy, is its influence over the money supply. As you know, there are two kinds of money: cash and checks. The commercial banking system adds to the money supply by creating bank deposits when the banks add to their assets by making loans, or buying investments like government bonds. However, a commercial bank must have a certain percentage of its deposits represented by deposits or so-called reserves, in the Federal Reserve System. It is this tie which gives the Federal Reserve System its influence over the deposits of the commercial banking system and the money supply. This influence can be exercised in four ways:

1. The Federal Reserve has power within certain limits to vary the percentage of deposits which commercial banks must keep on deposit with the Federal Reserve as reserves.
2. If the commercial banks have too little deposits or reserves, with the Federal Reserve they can get additional reserves by temporarily borrowing from the Federal Reserve System. The Federal Reserve can vary the rate it charges on those borrowings and can restrain or encourage such borrowings.
3. Reserves which the commercial banks have on deposit with the Federal Reserve can be increased or decreased through the Fed's open market policy. If the Federal Reserve sells government securities to commercial banks, reserves are reduced as the banks pay for the bonds. If it buys government bonds from commercial banks, reserves are increased. The local New York Reserve Bank carries out such money market transactions.
4. When the Fed is not able to hold down the supply money by one or more of the above operations it may finally resort to control of the amount of loans that banks can make.

When there is a recession, the Federal Reserve tends to loosen the reins, make money easy and cheap to borrow. On the other hand, when business is booming and there is a threat of inflation, the Federal Reserve tries to keep the reins tight, and through holding back on reserves, it can make money more difficult and costly to borrow.

There seems to be a general misconception about the ability of the commercial banks to borrow from the Federal Reserve. Commercial banks cannot freely use the Federal Reserve as a source of funds. The Federal Reserve frowns on a commercial bank being indebted to it except for a short period of time. It will use pressure to see that such indebtedness does not occur. Commercial banks have to adjust their business in order to prevent themselves from getting in that spot.

You may wonder how the control over the commercial bank reserves affects the interest on long-term corporate securities. The rate of interest results from a chain of reactions in the money supply. The general idea is as follows. If the Federal Reserve takes action to add to the supply of money and reduce interest rates, the first affected will be the commercial banks. They will have more funds available. In seeking to keep invested, they will buy short term governments, and this added demand for the bonds will reduce their rate. This, in turn, will make the higher rate on longer governments more attractive, and banks and other investors will then purchase the longer ones. As a further step, investors who have been buying long term governments because of their previous attractive interest yield will be forced to seek other more interesting investments as the yield on governments decreases. They will turn to corporate bonds; and so the chain goes on. When interest rates are tightened, the chain reaction works in reverse. Actually, the market in long term securities may not await the chain reaction; it may anticipate the expected result.

As far as the subject of this book is concerned, the Financial Vice President will be primarily concerned with the way the Federal Reserve System may affect interest rates, and hence the rate at which long term debt can be sold. Interest rates also may have an effect on yields on high-grade preferred stocks. And the effect of the action of the Federal Reserve on interest rates and on business may carry through to the common stock market. As pointed out in other parts of the book, financing plans should not be based on an assumption that interest rates and stock market can be forecast with any degree of accuracy. But the problem cannot entirely be ignored, so you will wish to be able to follow experts when they talk about the action by the Fed.

Officials of the Federal Reserve System would be the first to deny that they can control the economy through their actions. All they can do is assist and encourage our economy in the right direction through their positive or negative effect on the availability of bank funds, and thus on interest rates established by the overall demand and supply of funds for investment.

When we get into a recession, the Fed can't make businessmen borrow and increase production and employment if they don't want to. When we get into an inflationary boom, the Fed can't stop businessmen from borrowing if they want to keep on increasing production in spite of the high cost of borrowing. And unfortunately, politicians, quite illogically, start yelling at the Fed for creating high interest rates which supposedly benefit the bankers and hurt the small borrower. So by its efforts to vary the supply and demand of money, its power over our economy is limited.

There is no need to include more on this subject. If you wish to pursue it further, the Federal Reserve will furnish you with excellent reading material. Write to the Federal Reserve Bank of New York, 33 Liberty Street, New York City, for "A Day at the Fed" and "The Federal Reserve System—Purposes and Functions," Board of Governors of the Federal Reserve System. And if you are interested in following the money market operations of the Federal Reserve, your best bet is to have your name added to the mailing list for the "Monthly Review of the Federal Reserve Bank of New York."

Rating Agencies

There are three organizations in New York City which assign quality ratings to securities, as was explained in Chapter 2:

Fitch Investors Service, Inc., 12 Barclay, N.Y.C. 10007

Moody's Investors Service Inc., 99 Church Street, N.Y.C. 10007

Standard and Poor's Corporation, 345 Hudson Street, N.Y.C. 10014

They are the three so-called "legal" rating agencies. The reason this term is attached to them, is that their bond ratings have been referred to in laws which govern the legality or eligibility of investments for certain institutions.

Ratings were originally thought of in terms of debt securities, because all three agencies assign comparable ratings to that type of security. While bond ratings are most important, they have extended their coverage and rate other securities. If you are selling preferred stock, the rating will have an effect on the price. The securities they rate are as follows:

Fitch
- Bonds.
- Preferred stocks upon request.

Moody's

Bonds and preferred stocks, upon request.

They rate bonds of bank holding companies but no banks.

They rate bonds of finance companies, but not real estate investment trusts.

Standard

Bonds and preferred stocks.

They rank common stocks but on a different basis.

They rate bonds of bank holding companies but not banks. They rate real estate investment trusts, with a five-year operating record.

Originally they did not charge for ratings, but now all three services charge. The charges vary; as an example, Moody's has a minimum of $1,000 and a maximum of $10,000.

Ratings reflect in part the financial policy followed by management. They give a good indication of a company's ability to borrow and the approximate cost of debt money. When a company sells a bond, management, the underwriters and the potential buyers of the securities are all vitally interested in the rating assigned to it. Indirectly, debt ratings are a clue to the quality of equity securities. They are a valuable tool in various phases of finance, as pointed out in Chapter 2.

The executives of some companies have made "uncomplimentary" remarks about the agencies, out of their hearing of course, when the securities of their companies did not receive the ratings to which they deemed them to be entitled. This is to be expected because everybody loves his own baby. A few people in high finance have pooh-poohed ratings. Be that as it may, ratings are well accepted in financial circles.

The rating symbols used by the agencies for bonds, preferred and rankings for common stocks, from high to low quality, are shown in Exhibit 10-2.

As explained in Chapter 2 for purposes of this book, you can forget bond ratings of B and lower for debt issues, because they are too speculative.

Exhibit 10-2

SECURITY RATING AND RANKING SYMBOLS USED BY THE RATING AGENCIES

Bonds

Fitch	Moody's	Standard
AAA	Aaa	AAA
AA	Aa	AA
A	A	A
BBB	Baa	BBB
BB	Ba	BB
B	B	B
CCC	Caa	CCC
CC	Ca	CC
C	C	C
DDD		DDD
DD		DD
D		D

Preferred Stocks

Fitch	Moody's	Standard
(Same symbols used for preferred stocks)	"aaa"	AAA
	"aa"	AA
	"a"	A
	"baa"	BBB
	"ba"	BB
	"b"	B
	"caa"	C

Common Stocks

Fitch	Moody's	Standard (Rankings)
(Not Rated)	(Not Rated)	A+
		A
		A–
		B+
		B
		B–

Issues of new and untried companies usually are not rated because there is no record on which to base a rating. A company usually must have an operating record for at least three years in order to be rated, but this does not always hold for Standard; it depends on the character of the company. Corporate debt issues are generally not rated by Fitch if they are under $500,000, by Moody's if under $600,000, as a class and by Standard if under $2 million. There are a few types of companies having large enough issues and a sufficiently long record which are not rated for special reasons.

The agencies work completely independently and are jealous of their own ratings. However, the debt ratings are comparable in the same category. Rather than use the symbols of one agency, the terminology in the street may be:

Triple A
Double A
Single A
Triple B
Double B
Single B

How did the ratings of these agencies get to have such significance? Their use grew slowly at first and then rapidly after the bankruptcies in 1930. Years ago, these organizations were in the business of furnishing published information and advice to investors on securities. In order to assist their clients, they devised the symbols to designate the investment quality of securities; that is, the extent of assurance of payment of principal and interest. Then, as laws were established with regard to the quality requirements for investments of certain institutions, the lawmakers latched on to these ratings to assist in defining the investments to which the institutions should be restricted. At one time most commercial banks were restricted in the purchase of bonds to those rated Triple B or better by two or more of the agencies. Bond amortization requirements of some life insurance companies are linked with ratings; a bond which is rated in the first four classifications may be fully amortized; others may have to be carried at market.

Now the agencies have a responsibility which they never expected.

How Ratings Are Made

Ratings in each agency are the considered opinion of a rating committee. They are based on a careful analysis of all factual information amassed by the agencies and on their experience. They study all the statistics, ratios, history of the company and the industry; talk with management, and even competitors, and then arrive at a rating on the basis of judgment.

The rating agencies attempt, insofar as possible, to make ratings comparable not only among companies of the same industry but among industries.

Management may be puzzled at times when a statistical comparison shows two companies to be very similar and yet to have different ratings. The shadings between a high Single A and a low Double A may be very thin, but it is the analysts' experience and judgment rather than pure statistics which will put the issue in its particular class. As stated above, each of the agencies determines the rating it will put on a security entirely independently of the other agencies. Yet, if a comparison is made of the ratings of these three services, it will reveal how closely they agree.

If you want to know how ratings are made, don't ask someone in one of the agencies, "What formula do you use?" Even if they don't show it, their reaction will be slightly jaundiced. The first thing that they will tell you is that there is *no* formula. You can quiz them until they and you are blue in the face as to what ratios, etc., make a Triple A, Double A, etc., and you will get nowhere. This is not to say that capital structure ratios, earnings coverage and certain other ratios are not vital in arriving at an answer. The agencies have selected numerous statistical tests to serve as points of comparison between one issue and another. But the weight given to each one may vary with the circumstances, and for this reason the agencies themselves may not specify what the ratios should be. There are various factors involved which cannot be reduced to figures. For certain types of companies, where there is relative uniformity of operations and risk, there may be some recognizable correlation between ratings and such a ratio as debt to total capital structure, but it is up to you to make some comparative analysis to find it out.

Junior debt will generally be graded at least one notch lower than senior debt, even though there is only a smaller amount of junior debt and even though it matures before the senior debt. Maturity does not affect Moody's or Standard's ratings. If there is a large amount of junior debt, it may be rated more than one notch lower. Junior debt may reduce the rating on the senior debt if it so adds to the total debt burden of the company as to adversely affect the company's financial strength.

The market price of securities does not have any effect on ratings. The agencies may note any substantial change in the market price of a company's securities and it may suggest to them to look into the matter of ratings, but it is not taken into account in assigning the rating. In other words, the reverse is the case: ratings affect the market, rather than the market affecting the rating.

The ratings are continuously under review by all the agencies. When there is new debt financing, close attention is paid to the effect on the capital structure, and at such times a special review is made. However, ratings are not changed unless there is a definite, non-transitory change in factors affecting the rating. This is because the ratings are established for lasting quality. The theory is that if the ratings are soundly arrived at, then they should be rather constant, unless there is a marked permanent change in the company's position. The analysts have carefully reviewed a company's financial policy and character before assigning the rating. They do not find it necessary to modify the rating whenever a few figures get out of line. Some investors buy securities by their ratings and would be confused if there were rapid changes. The agencies recognize their responsibility to investors and try to decide upon a rating with the long range view in mind.

The slowness of change in ratings is one of the things that results in annoyance on the part of company executives. When their company's position improves, they expect the agencies to immediately upgrade the rating. This is seldom done. The agencies wish to make certain that the change is a permanent one, and time alone proves this to the agencies.

Companies fail to realize that the slowness of upward change in ratings works to a company's advantage when a company's credit temporarily deteriorates either because of poor operating results or the temporary addition of an excessive amount of debt. The agencies will listen to a company's story in such a situation and consider whether it is temporary in nature.

If one of the agencies is about to lower a rating it will almost always contact the company and ask if there is any explanation for adverse developments which justifies a continuation of the existing rating. On the other hand, this policy is not always followed. This highlights the importance of a company keeping in close contact with the agencies and continually providing them with all the facts.

Do not try to pressure the agencies or over-sell them on ratings. They have had too much contact with companies to be fooled. They have just as much interest in assigning a proper rating as you have in receiving the correct one. You should only want the rating which truly represents the credit standing of your company. Since the ratings are used as an indication of risk involved, it is only fair to your security holders that the rating be accurate. A rating too high would be just as bad as one too low from this point of view.

Don't overlook any one of the three rating agencies. If the rating on the debt of your company by one of the agencies is lower than by the other two, there is what is called a split rating. This tends to pull the overall quality down. A composite rating is a term often used in financial circles when such a situation exists. The composite rating is the rating of the two alike ratings. For example, if the ratings are AA, AA and A, the composite rating would be Double A. Should either of the Double A ratings be lowered, then the composite rating drops to a Single A.

Publications and Investment Advisory Services of Agencies

The agencies make their money primarily from the great mass of written material which they provide to investors.

Actually, the basic function of these organizations is to gather and present complete data on all fields of investments. Their printed services are among the most comprehensive sources of information available of their kind. They are the encyclopedia for people interested in investments. The factual publications include manuals, corporation records, current supplementary services and bond and stock quotation guides. They publish current guides to investors. These guides are weekly releases giving opinions on individual issues of stocks and bonds and also on general market conditions. Thus, the material ranges from pure statistics and description about various types of investments and industries to specific recommendations on securities and securities markets.

The services are widely used in the financial districts for determining investment policy, for appraising security prices of both seasoned and new offerings and for gaining much other financial information. The agencies' importance can be illustrated by enumerating the audience reached by their services. The publications mentioned above are consulted by every type of investor—institutional and individual, informed and uninformed. Among the subscribers are: banks, insurance companies, investment houses, pension trusts, industrial corporations, brokers, managers of investments—in short, everyone dealing with any phase of finance.

As a supplement to their publications, the agencies are continuously answering telephone and written requests for up-to-the-minute information and advice about specific securities.

In order to keep informed, you should know how they operate, what information they want about your company and how they want it. That is what we will now discuss.

Contacting the Agencies

The method of contacting each agency is somewhat different. It also depends on the type and size of company, but some generalizations can be made.

Your aim should be to give the agencies all the facts about your company, whether good or bad. They will treat any information as confidential if you ask them to do so. Some companies that operate in a complicated type of business have found it worthwhile to prepare elaborate statistical booklets on their operations for the special use of the agencies.

In sending in regular written material, you can address it to the library of each organization. The library will route it to the person or persons who will be concerned with your company. Then it will be added to their extensive files on company information. But be sure that the information is pertinent, and will have some bearing on the outlook for your securities. If something unusual happens, be sure to keep them informed.

After material about your company is prepared for inclusion in their manuals and corporation records, they will send you a copy to check and for suggestions. You should treat this as a real opportunity. You should go over it promptly; they have a publishing deadline to meet. If you do not do so, they will use the material as is and there may be something you could have corrected, added to or changed which would better present the facts. Of course, you must accept that they will be the ones to decide whether to include any material you suggest.

Make personal calls on them according to the nature of your company and as they indicate a desire to see you. If you are located outside of New York, you might consider writing a letter when you come to New York, saying where you will be staying and can be contacted if desired. Or you might enclose a return postcard on which they can indicate if they wish you to call while you are in New York. If you feel it necessary to see them, arrange an appointment by phone. Don't pester them with too many calls, but don't ignore them. Remember that they are as busy as you are, and recognize this in your contact with them. If you have major securities rated, you should attempt to see them at least once a year. Attention to details will help in your relationship with the agencies. For example, give them as much notice as possible. If you invite them to luncheon, they may not wish to take two hours. In order to save time, you might find that arranging for a place to eat close to their office would be appreciated.

In these personal calls, you should keep your ear open for prejudices or concerns which they may have about your company. You will gradually have to overcome them by continually presenting the facts. It might be well for you to follow what they say about your company in their opinion services.

Each agency operates differently, and there is some difference in the same agency among industries. At Standard, the group following the common stocks are separate from the bond experts, although they both sit on the rating committee. You should see both if you have both securities publicly held. In other words, find out how each service works and who to contact.

Standard is the only one with a field staff stationed throughout the country and spends much time visiting companies.

If you offer securities at competitive bidding, send the agencies prospectuses and other material as soon as they are available. You should pay them a visit before the sale date, after they have had an opportunity to digest the material and before they hold their committee meetings to assign a rating. In order to determine the correct day for your visit, be sure to make an appointment by phone well in advance. If you offer securities on a negotiated basis, the underwriting firm will arrange these meetings, but it is up to you to get thoroughly prepared. Underwriters, in some cases, have been very lax in advising companies how to get prepared. Never permit an underwriter to represent you before the rating agencies without you being present. If an underwriter suggests that they visit the agencies alone, you might look for another underwriter. These meetings are so vital that you should know what goes on and direct how it is handled. Suppose an underwriter had handled an agency poorly, it may reflect on your company.

Commercial Paper Ratings

All three agencies rate commercial paper for certain types of companies for which they charge a fee. Moody's has a separate department which rates commercial paper. They use the following symbols:

Fitch	Moody's	Standard
F–1	Prime 1	A–1
F–2	" 2	2
F–3	" 3	3
F–4	Not rated	B
		C
		D

In order to be readily marketable in all types of markets, it will have to be in the top quality. Category 2 may be hard to market in a crunch, and category 3 may be unmarketable in a crunch.

The rating of a company's long term debt will have an effect on the commercial paper rating. However, in analyzing a company's credit for commercial paper rating purposes, each of the agencies puts much more emphasis on short range credit strength, including cash flow and access to other short-term debt sources. They watch more closely a company's short-term financial strength than they do with a bond rating. And they may change commercial paper ratings more frequently.

The relationship between the bond and commercial paper ratings of Moody's and

Standard for a group of industrial and utility companies was as follows:

Bond Rating	Commercial Paper Rating					
	Moody's			Standard		
	P–1	P–2	P–3	A–1	A–2	A–3
Triple A	6			6		
Double A	7			11	1	
Single A	4	4		3	10	
Triple B		4			1	

Certain types of companies may be able to sell commercial paper under certain conditions without back-up bank lines of credit, but generally such lines are required.

Summary of Rating Agencies

If you have not had any experience in contacting the agencies, perhaps a brief summary might help to orient your thinking. If yours is a large, publicly owned company with no senior securities, or with senior securities held privately, you will want to pay close attention to the agencies primarily because of the material they publish about your company, and the recommendations they will be making. If your company, in addition, has senior securities publicly held, you will have some additional contacts to cover.

If commercial paper is important to your company, you will want to pay close attention to these ratings.

As the size of your company decreases, so will the attention that these agencies give to your company and the attention that you will have to give to them. But no matter how small, as long as you have securities publicly held and the agencies include information about your company in their manuals and other publications, you will wish to be sure that they are given all necessary information.

In Exhibit 10-3 is an outline of material you might prepare for the agencies. The financial ratios will vary to some extent with the type of industry. Each agency calculates some financial ratios differently. In the material you prepare for the agencies, you should calculate the ratios according to their method. In Exhibit 10-4 are the ratios used by Standard and Poor's for industrial companies and how they are calculated. In Exhibit 10-5 are some ratios used by Moody's for various types of securities of industrial companies with some explanation as to what is included in the items.

The Financial Analysts Federation

In Chapter 12, on Investor Relations, we will spend a lot of time on security analysts because they are the backbone of an investor relations program. Here we will just describe the analyst societies and how analysts may perform their functions.

The Societies

There are 47 local analyst societies tied together in a national organization known as The Financial Analysts Federation. Four of the local societies are in Canada. There are 14,135 individual members with varying interests in different types of securities. In order to be a Chartered Financial Analyst, it is necessary to take comprehensive examinations. The analysts hold an annual convention in the spring at which some companies make it a point to be represented, so that the analyst can be contacted. The analysts welcome participation.

The largest society and one which meets the most often is the New York Society of Security Analysts.[3] It has about 5,000 members interested in various types of security analysis. It meets every weekday at luncheon, at which time the president or principal financial officer of some company presents his story. Attendance will vary from about 100 to 400, depending on the type of company. The Society also holds occasional dinner meetings at its headquarters for its members and guests. At these meetings, some of the

[3]Address: New York Society of Security Analysts, 15 William Street, New York, N.Y. 10005. Meetings are held at 15 William Street. The Financial Analysts Federation, 219 East 49th Street, New York, N.Y.

Exhibit 10-3

OUTLINE OF REPORT FOR RATING AGENCIES

I. Description of offering including sinking fund and redemption provisions for senior securities. An exhibit including an outline of indenture provisions.

II. Use of proceeds.

III. Existing and pro-forma capital structure giving effect to financing with percentages for each type of security.

IV. Brief history and description of its present business. Properties: size, location, condition. Major developments in the past five years.

V. Organization chart with explanation.

VI. Directors with affiliation and management with age and responsibilities. Describe how your management team functions.

VII. Detailed description of product groups with relative importance of each, competition, your market share and your advantages and disadvantages. Show trends and tell where the industry is headed and where you are headed in the industry and how you expect to get there.

VIII. Principal customers, selling methods, importance of a few large customers. New products. Research and development policies. Patents.

IX. Be sure to explain your problems or litigation and how you plan to handle them.

X. Financial policies including goals for capital structure ratios, dividend payout policy, use of short term borrowings and, if many subsidiaries, how cash flow is managed.

XI. Describe budgeting and planning methods.

XII. Financial review.

1. Each agency calculates some financial ratios differently. You should use the method the agency uses for which you are providing the data.
2. Five- or ten-year historical financial statements (income statement, balance sheet and source and application of funds statement) in complete detail with financial ratios as calculated by the agency for which the material is prepared.
3. Forecast financial statements as above for five years. However, these should be handled with great care. They are confidential information and should be clearly marked accordingly. Forecasts that don't come out may cause loss of credibility. You should explain what is behind your forecasts and list your assumptions carefully. Be sure not to be too over-optimistic. When you visit the agencies subsequently, you should be sure to explain any reasons why the actual figures turned out differently from the forecasts.
4. Consider whether a special explanation is needed for any items in your financial statements: inventories, depreciation, natural resources such as timber lands, etc.
5. Include a discussion of your future financing with reasons.
6. Schedules on
   a. Sinking fund and debt repayment schedules
   b. Guarantees
   c. Complete detail on lease payments
   d. Banking arrangements.
7. Five-year analysis of principal divisions for sales and income.
8. If there have been any major acquisitions or mergers, show effect on sales and profits.
9. If a number of subsidiaries, show statements on a consolidated basis, and also consolidating financial statements for the latest year, so as to show how the system is made up.

Exhibit 10-4

FINANCIAL RATIOS USED FOR RATING SENIOR SECURITIES OF INDUSTRIAL COMPANIES BY STANDARD AND POOR'S

Ratio	Definition
Acid test	$\frac{\text{Cash items (including marketable securities)} + \text{receivables (current only)}}{\text{Current liabilities}}$
Current ratio	$\frac{\text{Current assets}}{\text{Current liabilities}}$
$\frac{\text{Short term debt}}{\text{Current liabilities}}$	$\frac{\text{Notes payable (less than one year)} + \text{current maturities of long term debt}}{\text{All liabilities due in one year}}$
$\frac{\text{Cash flow}}{\text{Current liabilities}}$	$\frac{\text{Net income} + \text{depreciation}}{\text{All liabilities due in one year}}$
$\frac{\text{Cash flow}}{\text{Long term debt}}$	$\frac{\text{Net income} + \text{depreciation}}{\text{All debt with maturities exceeding one year}}$
$\frac{\text{Working capital}}{\text{Long term debt}}$	$\frac{\text{Current assets} - \text{current liabilities}}{\text{All debt with maturities exceeding one year}}$
$\frac{\text{Long term debt}}{\text{Net plant}}$	$\frac{\text{All debt with maturities exceeding one year}}{\text{Gross plant} - \text{depreciation}}$
$\frac{\text{Net tangible assets}}{\text{Long term debt}}$	$\frac{\text{Net plant} + \text{working capital} + \text{all tangible assets} - \text{all deferred charges and reserves on liabilities side}}{\text{All debt with maturities exceeding one year}}$
$\frac{\text{Total liabilities}}{\text{Stockholders' equity}}$	$\frac{\text{All liabilities}}{\text{Preferred stock} + \text{capital stock} + \text{capital surplus} + \text{retained earnings}}$
$\frac{\text{Net worth}}{\text{Capitalization}}$	$\frac{\text{Stockholders' equity}}{\text{Stockholders' equity} + \text{long term debt}}$
Fixed charge coverage: After income tax coverage	$\frac{\text{Interest charges} + \text{*adjusted net income}}{\text{Interest charges}}$
Including rentals (total rentals)	$\frac{\text{Interest charges} + \text{rentals} + \text{adj. net income*}}{\text{Interest charges} + \text{rentals}}$
Before income tax coverage	$\frac{\text{Interest charges} + \text{*adjusted net income} + \text{income taxes}}{\text{Interest charges}}$
Operating ratio	$\frac{\text{Operating expenses before income taxes, depreciation and interest}}{\text{Net sales}}$
Return on invested capital	$\frac{\text{Pre-tax income} + \text{gross interest expense}}{\text{Total assets}}$

*Adjusted for minority interest and non-recurring items.

Exhibit 10-5

FINANCIAL RATIOS USED BY MOODY'S INVESTORS FOR VARIOUS TYPES OF SECURITIES OF INDUSTRIAL COMPANIES

TIMES CHARGES EARNED

This is shown where the company has bonds, notes or other instruments of indebtedness outstanding. It is a figure which reveals the relationship between the amount of fixed charges and the earnings which are available therefor. "Charges," where it is possible to do so, are the aggregate of all interest payments, debt discount and items of like character. The figure is computed before deduction of Federal or other income taxes where such taxes are separately shown; also after deduction of these taxes in most instances. In all cases, the figures are computed after deducting minority interest.

EARNED PER SHARE

Earned per preferred share is based on the number of shares outstanding at the close of each year.

Earned per common share is generally shown as reported by the company in its annual report. Where shares outstanding have increased during the year, earnings per common share is usually based on the average number of shares outstanding during the year (in some cases including common equivalent shares). Earned per share based on common on a fully diluted basis, is shown when reported by company.

On some of the larger companies, Moody's has also computed the earnings per common share based on number of shares outstanding at end of year after allowance for the required dividends (whether or not such dividends were paid) on stock issues with a priority right as to dividends. Accumulations of unpaid dividends or payment of dividends with respect to accumulations in excess of the amount of annual requirements are ignored in the compiling of this figure.

"Preferred Dividends Times Earned" is shown to provide an indication of dividend coverage which eliminates the necessity of adjusting the per share earnings to the annual per share dividend requirements. This is particularly useful in those cases where preferred stocks are of less than $100 par value or no par, indicating, as it does, the extent of dividend coverage more clearly than "Earned per Share."

NET TANGIBLE ASSETS AVAILABLE PER EACH $1,000 OF LONG TERM DEBT

These are theoretical calculations usable only to designate the aggregate dollar value of tangible assets as shown by the company's books less all current liabilities and reserves and directly applied to the indebtedness and stock capitalization. In arriving at "Net Tangible Assets per $1,000 of Long Term Debt," all the capital stock and surplus (stockholders' equity), less intangible assets, as shown on the company's books plus the aggregate of long term debt (excluding current maturities) is divided by the amount of long term indebtedness outstanding.

NET TANGIBLE ASSETS PER SHARE

"Net Tangible Assets per Share" of preferred and common is similarly computed except that long term debt is deducted from the sum of tangible assets and in the case of the common stocks all senior stock issues are deducted. The calculation is simply a reflection of tangible book values applicable to the securities outstanding.

NET CURRENT ASSETS—WORKING CAPITAL

Represents excess of total current assets over total current liabilities.

INTANGIBLE ASSETS

Such assets include "excess cost of acquisition" (excess of cost over equity in net assets of subsidiaries at dates of acquisition) or goodwill, patents, subscription lists, trademarks, etc.

SIGNIFICANCE OF FINANCIAL AND OPERATING RATIOS

We show a percentage analysis of operations representing a breakdown of income account figures on a percentage basis by years for a seven-year period and affording a convenient comparison of income accounts of companies in the same line of business, and for tracing the distribution of revenues from sales

Exhibit 10-5 (Cont'd)

to net profits. By use of these percentages, changes in costs such as labor and materials, the relation of taxes to volume of sales, etc., become more understandable. Also, it is more readily apparent whether expansion of sales has occurred at the expense of profits.

The financial and operating ratios are of a practical nature for the purpose of making the facts and figures shown of greater informative value.

Ratios used are as follows:

(1) Current assets to current liabilities—indicates the relation of cash or items which theoretically are readily convertible into cash to the current claims of creditors.

(2) Percent cash and securities to current assets—a measurement of the cash items to the total of items which are in theory readily convertible into cash.

(3) Percent inventory to current assets—shows the amount of quick assets tied up in raw and finished materials.

(4) Percent net current assets to net worth (stockholders equity)—shows the percentage of the equity capital represented by net quick items.

(5) Percent property depreciated—indicates the extent to which the fixed assets have been written down by annual depreciation charges.

(6) Percent annual depreciation, etc., to gross property—indicative of the rate of annual charges to the balance sheet values of fixed assets.

Capitalization:

(7) Percent long term debt—

(8) Percent preferred stock—

(9) Percent common stock and surplus—

These three ratios simply break down the long term debt and stockholders' equity in relation to the whole and quickly indicate whether or not there is leverage for the common stock and whether or not the capital structure possesses reasonable balance.

(10) Sales—by inventory—shows rapidity of turnover; i.e., how often raw materials and finished goods are converted into sales during the year.

(11) Percent sales to net property—this is a measure of productivity of depreciated property account.

(12) Percent sales to total assets—a measure of the usefulness of assets in relation to the gross volume of transactions.

(13) Percent net income to total assets—this is a measure of the profits related to the aggregate of money invested in the business.

(14) Percent net income to net worth (stockholders' equity)—this is used to indicate the relation of profits to the equity capital.

---

leading corporations may be asked to cover special topics.

The operations of the other societies vary considerably as to type of membership and frequency of meetings.

There is an annual "Directory of Members" each year, which can be purchased for $40 per copy through the office of The Financial Analysts Federation or any of the local societies. It classifies the members according to the industry in which they are interested.

Security Analysis[4]

An understanding or feel of security analysis—that is, how it is performed—is a necessary background for finance. Security analysis is the method by which the price of your "commodity" is established, and you will wish to know how that is done. If you get into finance very deeply, you will be making price estimates yourself, or at least studying price estimates made by someone else. If you cultivate the analysts by keeping them informed about the operations of your company, you will do a better job by appreciating how they try to perform their job. What follows is a simplified statement of how a security analyst works.

The purpose of security analysis, or financial analysis, as it is also called, is: to determine the characteristics and quality of a security in order to determine suitability as an investment for various types of investors, and whether it should be bought, held or sold at a particular price.

There may be other supplementary reasons for security analysis. The rating agencies

[4]If you are interested in security analysis, some of the books on the subject are: *Security Analysis* by B. Graham, Dodd, Cottle and Tatham, published by McGraw-Hill Book Company, Inc., New York, 4th edition, 1962, price $13.50. *Investment Analysis and Portfolio Management* by Cohen, Zinbarg and Zeikel, revised edition, 1973, Dow Jones-Irwin, Homewood, Illinois, price $13.95. *The Financial Analysts Handbook,* two volumes, 1974, Dow Jones-Irwin, Homewood, Illinois, price $50.

study a security in order to evaluate the risk and place a rating on it. Underwriters study a security in order to determine whether it is the type that they should underwrite, and the price which they should pay as intermediaries in the distribution of securities.

The forces which will change the value of a security must make themselves felt through the balance sheet and income statement of a company. These are the two usual starting places.

First of all, what security is the analyst studying–a senior security or common stock? Let's assume that our company has three types of securities outstanding–bonds, preferred stock and common stock.

After glancing at each security to see its type, the next consideration is of how much of the capital structure each represents; that gives the analysts an immediate idea as to whether there is a heavy or light burden of senior securities.

Other things being equal, the percentages which each security represents of long term capital give a picture of the protection afforded the debt by the size of the preferred and common equity and, correspondingly, the risk added to the common equity by obligations having a senior position. But all other things are practically never equal. As explained in Chapter 2, a relatively stable, well-situated electric company may have as much as 50% debt to total capital structure and be rated Double A, while most large industrial companies with that much debt would receive a very low rating on their bonds.

So from here on the security analyst has to start to work. The analyst will study the balance sheet to discover what the assets consist of, whether they are properly stated, whether there are sufficient reserves, whether there are any items of dubious worth on the asset side of the balance sheet, whether assets are leased or owned, etc. He will need to know the principal terms of each security.

But assets generally aren't worth much unless they can earn; so the analyst is primarily interested in the prospects for earnings.

For bonds, the analyst is ultimately interested in the number of times that earnings available for interest payments cover those payments. Many analysts prefer a pre-tax coverage; others use the after-tax figure. For preferred stock, the test is the number of times earnings, after taxes available for interest, cover both interest and preferred dividends. For common stocks, the ultimate aim is the earnings per share.

Now the analyst's heavy work really begins. He will look for non-recurring items in the income statement and make allowances for them. He will have to try to find out the amount of earnings that will continue to be available to service the company's securities and their stability. He will want to consider every factor which might increase or decrease these results–possibilities of increasing or decreasing sales and expenses. In order to do this, he will need to understand the industry and its prospects, the nature of the company and how it stands in the industry.

The approach in bond analysis is somewhat different from analysis of the common stock. In bond analysis, the analyst is interested in determining that both assets and earnings are sufficient so that interest and principal payments will be assured, but, more important, that the quality of the security will be maintained so that the bonds can be sold in the future at satisfactory prices in the market. The same applies to preferred stock analysis.

For common stocks, the analyst must perform a more difficult task. He must determine the prospects for the earnings per share, because it is primarily those prospects which affect the value of a common stock. Future dividends will come from those earnings, and the amount of earnings plowed back in the business will build up the investment. Common stock analysis is much more difficult, because the analyst is dealing with the last security out on the limb, and it is the future residual left over to the common which will determine its value. Bond analysis is more of a defensive type of analysis–its purpose is to determine whether there are sufficient assets and earnings behind the bonds to assure protection, and it can be done with a much greater degree of accuracy.

Does all this sound easy? Perhaps it does, but it isn't. The management of a company, knowing all about its operations, may find it most difficult to properly evaluate the risks in the business and the outlook; yet the security analyst, on the outside, must do just that.

Security analysis is far from being a science. The analyst will start off with a scientific approach, by making a thorough study of all factors affecting a company, and in his analysis he will subject a company's balance sheet and income statement to any number of ratios in order to bring out various relationships. However, in the end, the final result is a matter of judgment.

Since security analysis is not an exact science by any stretch of the imagination, there is no set pattern of analysis followed by all analysts. Many analysts use different types of ratios. As an example, which has already been mentioned, some will figure interest coverage before Federal Income Taxes; whereas, others will figure it afterward. However, whatever ratios they use, they will always have in mind how they were calculated when weighing their significance; so there is compensation for their different approaches. Furthermore, an analyst will be consistent in his application of ratios from one company to another.

The price of a security is generally looked at first in relation to prices of other securities. What is its relative value to other securities, with due allowance for any difference between the securities? Is it over, under, or reasonably priced? In other words, is it attractive as compared to other securities? As an aid in determining relative values, analysts often make a statistical stack-up or comparison of one security with a number of other securities. Such a comparison will include the principal ratios, which show important relationships in balance sheet and income statement figures, as well as some operating statistics. If a company official should study such a "stack-up" or make one himself, he might wonder why the prices of the securities did not conform closely to relative values as shown by the ratios. The answer is as already stated: the ratios are only to aid in interpreting the picture which each company presents. For example, one important element in analyzing a security, not yet mentioned, is the quality of management, particularly for common stocks. An appraisal of management cannot be put into figures.

You, as an executive of your company, may question how security analysts can place a value on your company's securities when they don't have more than what may appear to you to be a superficial knowledge of your company and the industry. This observation on your part may be correct. But remember, there is something they do have if they are good analysts, and that is a broad knowledge of many companies and relative values of securities, gained through long experience. The more the analysts know about your company, the better, but without the broad knowledge they would not be able to weigh the relative values. Some of the questions they ask you may seem foolish and may well be foolish. They may even be groping for the right question to ask. You may not see fit to answer all their questions for a very good reason.

Company officials at times are prone to criticize security analysts, and say that equally good results could be obtained by flipping a coin.

As a matter of fact, the common stock analysts in general did fail badly in the 1960's. One reason some of them got taken to the cleaners, or rather their customers got taken to the cleaners, was because they tended to follow each other like sheep, and they concentrated on forecast earnings in the coming years rather than looking at return on investment and fundamental values.

There are good, mediocre and bad security analysts. Be as critical as you wish about security analysis; nevertheless, it is only through security analysis that at least an approach can be achieved towards the proper evaluation of a security. It is better than the way many investors buy and sell stocks, without any effort at analysis whatsoever, but merely on the basis of general optimism or pessimism or some "inside" tip.

Furthermore, whether you like it or not, someone is going to perform that function as long as we have a system of private capital. Your contact with security analysts will be facilitated if you appreciate what they are trying to do, the difficulty of their task and its importance to your company and our economy.

The Policemen

Securities and Exchange Commission

The unethical and unsound financial practices which occurred in the late 1920's became glaringly evident during the great depression in the early 1930's. As a result, Congress decided that it was in the general public interest that the investor be protected. The Securities Act of 1933 was passed and subsequently the Securities and Exchange Commission was set up to administer it.

After the Act was first passed, the howls in Wall Street could be heard far and wide: "We can't do business under the Act, the penalties are too great." "There will be no more underwriting of securities." "The Government is crucifying Wall Street and blocking the flow of capital."

After a while some brave souls started to function under the Act, and then others followed. Now most people in Wall Street will say that the idea of the Act is sound. There must be some regulation since the average individual investor is not sufficiently knowledgeable to protect himself against the unscrupulous financial operator. Naturally, with all the money involved in finance, there are unscrupulous men in the industry. They are best able to operate during a bull stock market when the small investors, hoping for quick profits, buy on tips. The Securities and Exchange Commission has a tough job on its hands to ferret out the rascals and prosecute them. Handling of other people's money should be done on the basis of the highest trust and with expert knowledge; these attributes combined, in their highest sense, are not easy to come by.

You cannot sell securities today without knowing about the Securities Act of 1933. It covers the distribution of securities. Since it is a Federal law, it pertains to securities sold through the mails or in interstate commerce. Certain securities are exempt from registration though not from the fraud provisions. One broad group of exempt corporate securities are those of the railroads. The companies issuing these securities are regulated by the Interstate Commerce Commission; so when the Act was passed, it was felt unnecessary to include them.

Banks, thus far, have been exempt from the Act because they are regulated by the bank regulatory authorities. Bank holding companies are subject to the Act.

A basic purpose of the Act is to make certain that a company, when selling a new issue, gives full and fair disclosure of all the facts necessary for a potential purchase to make a proper evaluation. The Act is for the purpose of preventing the issuance of misleading information or the withholding of material information in connection with the distribution of securities.

Unless a security or a transaction is exempt, a company must file a registration statement with the Securities and Exchange Commission prior to the public offering. Offers to sell a new security must be accompanied by a prospectus which includes most of the information filed in the registration statement. Although there are registration forms and prospectuses for many types of issues and offerings, there are two types commonly used by industrial, commercial and utility companies. The form S-9, which is a simplified form, can be used for bonds of companies meeting certain standards; the longer form, S-1, has more general application.

The Act provides that a registration statement becomes effective upon the expiration of a 20-day period unless extended by the filing of a delaying amendment. But most registration statements become effective by administrative action of the Commission. Acceleration of the 20-day period from the time of original filing is unusual, but more readily applies to the time applicable to amendments. As soon as the registration statement becomes effective, sales of the security can begin.

A company must be careful about what information it gives out while financing is in process, or it might be suspected of trying to sell its securities without using a prospectus. Also, it is important for a company to consider how an offering affects its general program to keep its existing investors fully informed during the period.

The Act starts to apply when a company expects to offer securities. When this occurs is a matter of judgment in many instances. From this starting date, until the registration statement is filed, dissemination of information for purposes of financing is limited to that provided by the company to the underwriters. There is no restriction at any time as to the type of information for this purpose.

When the registration statement is filed and until it is effective, there will be available a preliminary or so-called "red herring" prospectus.[5] At this point, the underwriters may distribute this prospectus to investors and dealers, but no other written sales material may be provided by the company or underwriters. Offers to purchase the securities may be made by dealers and investors during this period, but such offers cannot be accepted by the underwriters until the statement has become effective. The underwriters cannot sign up selected dealers, but they can find out which ones will be interested in handling the issue and make all arrangements for signing them up as soon as the registration statement becomes effective.

When the registration statement becomes effective with all amendments, all offers to sell must be accompanied by a final so-called offering prospectus. Now, other written material supplementary to the prospectus may be used with the prospectus, but from the point of view of the company, it would be preferable that the prospectus include all pertinent information, and the prospectus should be written as the basic sales document.

The Act continues to apply as respects the material that can be given out by the company, until all the issue is sold by underwriters and dealers. There is a statement sometimes made to the effect that the period continues until 40 days after the day on which the issue was offered publicly if all of the security has been sold in a shorter period. However, the section in the Act in which the 40 days is mentioned applies to dealers and underwriters, and not to the company.

Although the statute does not attempt to govern the nature of negotiations between issuers and underwriters on the subjects which may be discussed in such negotiations, the information used in the public sale of a security must be limited to facts. Anything of a "puffing" nature is obviously not permitted. The Securities and Exchange Commission formerly took the approach that forecast earnings are not matters which can properly be included in a registration statement and prospectus. The commission has changed its attitude on this subject, but a company might be well advised to proceed cautiously in making forecasts. If a company should give out information to potential purchasers during an offering, which is not included in the prospectus, the offering may be stopped

[5] There is another form known as a summary prospectus which may be used for certain purposes. It applies to both the preliminary and final forms.

There is a type of prospectus, which comes into play in a competitive bidding, known as the bidding prospectus. It is the same as a final prospectus and is used for bidding purposes, but does not include the price, call prices, etc., which can only be filled in after the bidding has taken place. It is final in all respects, except for these items.

and the company penalized. If an underwriter commits such an error, it too might be penalized, or, in the alternative, might have to withdraw from the underwriting group.

The above comments are important to a company in evaluating the extent to which a so-called "sales campaign" can be developed in a negotiated public offering during the period prior to the effective date. In this connection, it may be noted that the protective provisions of the Act are intended to operate for the benefit of the dealers as well as the investors.

In carrying out its regular investor relations program, a question may arise as to what type of information a company can give out during an offering of securities. Things of a routine nature, such as quarterly and annual reports which have been issued regularly without regard to financing, are, under ordinary circumstances, permissible. Of course, care must be taken not to include information which might suggest that it is in fact part of the program to sell the securities.

As a practical matter, a company need not worry about the penalties under the Act, even though they are severe, if, in good conscience, it does its best to carry out the principles of the Act. The philosophy behind the Act is essential for the protection of the providers of capital, and thus of our economy. For the most part, the Securities and Exchange Commission has done a realistic job in administering the Act.

A company must rely on counsel familiar with the Act in complying with its provisions, or in determining whether a transaction is exempt. Too technical a lawyer can make the Act appear unnecessarily burdensome.

Many of the costs incurred in the public sale of a security, other than the underwriting discount, taxes and engraving, are a result of the Act. The printing business has benefited materially.

Other important Federal legislation, which was passed at about the same time as the Securities Act, was the Securities Exchange Act of 1934, the Trust Indenture Act of 1939, the Investment Company Act and the Public Utility Holding Company Act.

The Securities and Exchange Act covers trading in securities and governs such matters as exchange operations, margin requirements, full disclosure for listed securities, buying and selling by insiders and the procedure that must be followed in a short sale in order to prevent bear raids, broker-dealer relationship with customers, proxies, etc.

The Trust Indenture Act supplements the Securities Act of 1933 and establishes certain provisions which must be included in indentures for large, publicly offered debt issues. This aspect was referred to in a previous chapter on types of securities.

State Blue Sky Departments

Most states have some laws regulating the sale of securities. When a new issue is offered, the term "Blue Sky" is often used. It refers to making the necessary filings in the states where the security will be sold in order to comply with the state laws. The term "Blue Sky" to denote state security laws arose many years before the Securities Act, when the states were struggling with the prevention of the sale of fraudulent securities. The statement was made, in the discussion of the subject in a state legislature, that security dealers would try to sell you the blue sky. So state laws were passed to prevent frauds, and that term became attached to such state laws. Large high-grade issues can be processed rather easily through the state securities commissions, but a complicated type of issue may take time. It is essential that it be completed in time for the sale; otherwise, the securities cannot be offered in the state. The states have exclusive jurisdiction over the intrastate security sales which do not use the mails or means of interstate commerce. Processing of applications for compliance with Blue Sky Laws is the job of the lawyers for the underwriters.

CHAPTER 11

Markets for Outstanding Securities

When you are publicly owned, you should be concerned with the market for your securities. By this we do not mean that you should be a tape worm, watching the quotes on the tape, and scheming how to get the price of your stock up. We have continuously stressed throughout the book that you should not want your stock to be over-priced any more than you should want it to be underpriced. There is a reasonable price which will provide investors a fair return depending on the return you are able to earn on your capital.

It is essential to the formation of capital in our free enterprise system that there be sound markets for outstanding securities. Investors who provide new capital to industry by purchasing new issues of securities will have as one of their principal considerations whether subsequently there will be a good market so that they can dispose of their investment at a reasonable price.

It is doubtful that very many people who make up the marketplace appreciate the importance of good security markets to the functioning of our free enterprise system. In fact, it is unfortunate that many of them are so selfish and short-sighted that they view security markets solely from their own point of view as a place to make a killing regardless of who gets hurt. Otherwise, the stupidity and greed in the marketplace would not stand out in such stark ugliness when a slump occurs after years of a boom, such as ended in the 1960's.

A good market for your securities should include:

1. The best price for your stock commensurate with the nature of your company which will provide a fair return to investors.
2. A stable market which does not fluctuate widely. A market in which an inves-

tor can buy or sell a reasonable number of shares without unnecessarily disturbing the market price.
3. Reasonable cost for your security holders to buy and sell.
4. A market that is not manipulated, but is strictly the result of supply and demand.
5. A market that will assist in the sale of new stock.

A good market will depend on the facts surrounding the stock, such as:

1. The nature of the company's business and its size.
2. The quality of the stock; that is, whether it is speculative or high quality.
3. The company's earnings performance and dividend policy.
4. The number of shares outstanding and in the hands of the public.
5. The extent to which the stock has been seasoned or outstanding for a reasonable length of time.
6. The information the company provides about its operations.
7. The type of investors who make up the market.
8. The market in which the stock is traded.

In this chapter, we are concerned with how the different markets operate, which one will suit your company the best, how your stock will act in the market and how you might monitor the market you choose in order to be sure that your stock is fairly treated.

In our discussion of markets, we will first explain the two types of markets which have traditionally existed. We will then touch on the foment which is taking place in the markets today. Traditionally, the two types of markets were:

- The market for unlisted or over-the-counter securities. This market is "over-the-counter" as contrasted with the "floor" of an exchange.

- The market for listed securities which are handled on the "floor" of one or more of the exchanges.

The Market for Over-the-Counter Securities

The Retail Market

In the financial newspapers, and some of the large metropolitan newspapers, you will find an over-the-counter section. These quotations are furnished to the newspapers by the National Association of Securities Dealers. Over-the-counter trading is done on a negotiated basis. You will note that there are no sales prices, but bid and asked quotations. These are the prices at which a dealer will buy securities: the bid prices; and the prices at which he will sell securities—the asked prices. The dealer makes his money by the difference between the price at which he buys and sells. He acts as principal and owns the stock as contrasted with a broker who acts as an agent. A dealer may maintain an inventory of securities and sell to you out of his inventory. Or, if he has no inventory, he will purchase the securities in the market in his own name and sell them to you at a mark-up.

At one time the quotes in the newspapers for over-the-counter market reflected the retail prices. However, today the quotes are representative quotations and close to the wholesale quotes. In other words, it would be expected that it would cost the small investor more than these figures indicate.

It is beneficial for an unlisted company to have its stock included in the over-the-counter columns of the newspapers because it gets the company's name before investors. Furthermore, having the quotations readily available is a service to investors. The securities quoted are limited to those which are quoted on NASDAQ. In order to qualify a company must have two members of the NASD make a market in the securities, and you will need their cooperation. If a company thinks it should be included, it should apply to the President of the National Association of Securities Dealers in Washington, D.C.

The Wholesale Market

Some dealer firms are wholesalers. They trade only with other dealers and large institutions—just like wholesale merchants, as contrasted with retail stores. The many small retail security dealers throughout the country may get their merchandise from the wholesale dealers. Some dealers are both wholesalers and retailers. In the wholesale market the spread between the bid and asked is smaller, because, among other reasons, the number of shares traded in a transaction is generally larger and there is vigorous competition.

The wholesale market is referred to as the inside market. For many years, there has been a written quotation system for the wholesale dealer fraternity. It is known as the "Pink Sheets."

The "Pink Sheets" are a product of a unique firm, The National Quotation Bureau, Inc., 116 Nassau Street, New York City 10038. It has been an essential cog in the over-the-counter security market, where a beehive of activity exists in the afternoon on each business day after the close of the market.

Here is what the Bureau does. Each dealer who is interested in making a wholesale market in certain securities will fill out IBM cards for each security, showing the name of his firm and the price at which he would be willing to buy or sell. Every day around noon a messenger from 116 Nassau Street starts picking up these slips. They are rapidly sorted by name of the security. By computer this information is compiled on the so-called "Pink Sheets." It lists all the principal over-the-counter securities with the dealers' names and their quotations. The "Pink Sheets" are rushed to the airport for airmail delivery out-of-town. They are delivered by hand in New York early the next morning.

This service of the National Quotation Bureau is restricted to the dealers who are registered with the Securities and Exchange Commission and meet other requirements of the Bureau. The dealers pay the Bureau on a contract basis to list their quotations.

While outsiders do not have direct access to the "Pink Sheets," a company may, for a small fee, obtain the wholesale quotations for its securities. Elaborate files have been maintained by the Bureau. The authenticity of these quotes has been recognized by courts. So if your company's stock is traded over-the-counter and you want the wholesale market price on a certain day, or ranges over the years, here is where you can get it. Furthermore, if you want to know who trades in your stock, ask a dealer to take a look at the "Pink Sheets."

There is more to the service than just the "Pink Sheets." The Bureau also provides quotations for bonds and other securities.

Even today, the "Pink Sheets" are still a basic tool used by securities dealers operating in the over-the-counter market. They cover 8,000 to 10,000 stocks.

However, now there is an instantaneous quotation service available to dealers for over-the-counter stocks called NASDAQ, which we previously referred to. It is operated by the National Association of Security Dealers and provides quotes for about 2,750 over-the-counter stocks. A computer screen gives instantaneous quotes on these selected stocks and shows the dealers who are making the market.

How Markets Are Made in Over-the-Counter Securities

Dealers keep close contact with one another by direct wires or by the regular telephone system. They are continuously checking quotations with each other, either in carrying out a transaction, or in order to keep abreast of the market.

Making markets in securities requires skill. It must be done on an ethical basis, but an astute dealer must sense what the other fellow has in mind and reveal his own hand only when necessary; otherwise, his ability to trade is lost, and he would be merely acting as an order clerk, paying the other fellow's price. A dealer, making up his mind whether to be a buyer or a seller, will weigh such factors as: his existing or potential orders one way or the other; the condition of securities markets and all factors affecting the market of the particular security.

There is a limit to what is considered a reasonable mark-up or mark-down for an unlisted security. The National Association of Securities Dealers sets the policy and polices the dealers. A maximum figure for a reasonably active stock is 5%. For example, a mark-up between the price at which a retail dealer buys a security from a wholesale dealer and the price for which he sells it to a customer should not be more than 5%. This figure is subject to many variations depending on the circumstances.

As we have pointed out, the dealers also play an important role in the distribution of new securities issues. They do part of the selling job and form what is known as the selling group.

A dealer may handle a transaction for a customer by acting as an agent and charge the same as a stock exchange commission. But this is not the general rule throughout the over-the-counter market.

The Stock Exchange Market

Now let's turn to the stock exchanges and see how prices for outstanding securities are arrived at there. The other element that makes up an exchange besides the securities is the members who own the seats. A seat is merely the term for a membership. The seat can be sold and there is a market for seats when any are available. In order to be permitted to buy a seat, you must have a certain amount of capital and be investigated for integrity, to mention one criterion.

The market for listed securities is made on the floor of the exchange. Only members are permitted to trade in securities on the floor. Members may operate as individuals or be affiliated with member organizations. Operating on the floor of an exchange are representatives of brokerage houses carrying out the orders for their brokerage houses, members who trade for their own account, odd-lot traders who handle the small orders and the specialists.

The responsibility for making markets in listed securities rests with those members who have been accepted as specialists, which is their sole function. They are assigned stocks by the stock exchange according to their ability to handle the trading task. When you are first listed you can request that your stock be assigned to a certain specialist, but the exchange will have the final say.

The purpose of the exchange is to provide a market place for the purchase and sale of securities. The exchange stresses that it provides an orderly market. By orderly market we mean two things—reasonably narrow spread between bid and asked prices, and, insofar as possible, a smoothing out of erratic price fluctuations due to temporary imbalance of the demand and supply.

It is the job of the floor specialist to carry out the purpose of the exchange. In order to do so, he may have to participate in the market by increasing his own holdings and providing a demand if there is a temporary flood of sell orders without corresponding buy orders—and vice versa; that is, if there is a temporary flood of buy orders with no sales, he will sell or go short stock and provide a supply. In this respect, his function is like that of a dealer trading in unlisted securities who buys and sells for his own account.

He makes part of his income from the difference between the prices at which he buys and the prices at which he sells, depending on the condition of the market. He, of course, is in business to make money, and he can only assist in smoothing out the fluctuations in the purchases and sales of securities. If there is a continuous flood of sales, he cannot keep buying and holding up the price. He will have to keep lowering his bid price based on his estimate of the flood of selling as compared with purchases. If the situation becomes too chaotic in a particular stock, the exchange can suspend trading for a short period of time until it is possible to assess the situation and determine at what level the stock should reopen.

As a second function, the specialist acts as an agent for brokers seeking to buy or sell. For this service he is paid a commission. The commission the specialist earns, when he acts as agent for a broker, is paid by the broker and not by the broker's customers. In his capacity as agent, the floor specialist keeps a "book" on the number of shares and the prices at which there are offers to buy and sell the securities which have been assigned to him. Many orders are entered at the market, which means that the buyer or seller will accept the price prevailing at the time. An example of a book of a specialist on the New York Stock Exchange is shown in Exhibit 11-1.

Exhibit 11-1

EXAMPLE OF SPECIALIST'S BOOK ON THE EXCHANGE

THE PRICES AT WHICH HE HAS ORDERS TO BUY AND SELL A CERTAIN SECURITY FOR VARIOUS BROKERS

50	1 Loper 2 Gaw 1 Green	50	
1/8		1/8	
1/4	2 Evans ~~1 Brown~~ C	1/4	
3/8		3/8	
1/2	~~1 Kind GDE~~ ~~1 Sail FGH~~	1/2	
5/8		5/8	1 Ball 1 Lean
3/4		3/4	1 Moon 1 Pike
7/8		7/8	

The numbers opposite the prices are the number of shares in units of 100 with the names of the buying and selling broker. The orders to buy at 50 1/2 have been executed by the specialist for the two buying brokers. The initials after the names indicate the selling brokers. The order to buy 100 at 50 1/4 has been canceled.

The orders must be executed by the floor specialist in accordance with well-defined rules of the exchange in order to protect the position of each buyer and seller against any possible favoritism.

Transactions on the floor of the exchange may occur by a third method. A broker may sell directly to another broker without the specialist participating in any way. However, when this is done, it must be done in the presence of the specialist, so that he knows what is going on in the stocks in which he specializes.

Thus, all transactions by members of an exchange in a listed stock are concentrated at one focal point; that is, the specialist.

The specialist is in a position to make money and make it easily if he was not also required to carry out his economic function of maintaining a close market in which there is only a narrow gap between the price being bid for a stock and the price at which it is offered. He may make money on part of his business, but he must be ready and able to lose on part. The exchanges watch the operations of the specialist and should not tolerate poor performance, since the exchanges seek to provide a fair and orderly market place.

The market on the floor of the stock exchange has been referred to as an auction market. This is not an exact description since all people in an auction are supposed to be on an equal footing; whereas, the specialist holds all the cards.

If an investor, Smith, wants to sell a listed security through a firm which is a member of an exchange, here is the way it works: Smith calls his broker and instructs him to sell 100 shares at the market, which is bid 20, asked 20 1/8. To execute the order the broker calls the firm's partner on the floor of the exchange, who goes over to the post where the stock is traded. From here on let's assume that the transaction is handled by the specialist in his role of providing a fair and orderly market. There are no buyers immediately available for the stock; so the specialist buys Smith's 100 shares at $20 per share. Smith gives his broker the 100 shares he wanted to sell and receives $2,000, less brokerage fees of approximately $42. He will also have to pay some transfer taxes, which are paid by the seller, not by the purchaser.

Before 1974, brokerage commissions were established by the Stock Exchange with the approval of the Securities and Exchange Commission. However, at the insistence of the Securities and Exchange Commission, fixed commissions were phased out. This was completed in May, 1975. Now rates are not to be fixed but are to be established by each firm. An approximation of commissions for 50- and 100-share trades is given in Exhibit 11-2.

To continue our story about selling and buying on the Exchange, let's assume that with no change in the market price and no new sellers entering the market, Jones wants to buy 100 shares. To execute the order he calls his broker, who contacts the firm's floor member. The floor member goes over to the specialist who sells the 100 shares he bought from Smith to Jones at $20.125 per share, or a total of $2,012.50. Jones pays his broker fees of approximately $42.

Exhibit 11-2

APPROXIMATE BROKERAGE COMMISSION FOR THE NEW YORK STOCK EXCHANGE
NOVEMBER 1974

	50 Shares			100 Shares		
		Commission			Commission	
Price of Stock per Share	Total Value of Stock	Per Share	% of Value	Total Value of Stock	Per Share	% of Value
$ 10	$ 500	$ .33	3.3%	$ 1,000	$ .30	3.0%
15	750	.43	2.9	1,500	.35	2.3
20	1,000	.50	2.5	2,000	.42	2.1
25	1,250	.57	2.3	2,500	.49	2.0
50	2,500	.94	1.9	5,000	.72*	1.4
75	3,750	1.18	1.6	7,500	.75*	1.0
100	5,000	1.43*	1.4	10,000	.75*	.8
125	6,250	1.50*	1.2	12,500	.75*	.6
150	7,500	1.50*	1.0	15,000	.75*	.5

In figuring total cost to buy an odd-lot when the round-lot is figured in 100-share units, add $1/8 per share to the round-lot market price. In selling an odd-lot, subtract $1/8 per share from the round-lot market price to obtain proceeds before commissions.

Commissions for odd- and even-lot transaction under $2,000 are not set by the Securities and Exchange Commission but are as mutually agreed. The figures supplied are intended to be representative commissions.

All commissions for total amounts above $2,000 were computed by using the Securities and Exchange Commission minimum commissions schedules effective Sept. 25, 1973. Actual brokerage transactions are typically 5% higher than the minimum commissions.

*The minimum commission on any order for 100 shares or any odd-lot order shall not exceed $71.50 on orders not in excess of $5,000 and $74.75 on orders involving an amount in excess of $5,000.

The specialist gets the $0.125 per share difference between the price at which he bought the stock and that at which he sold it, or a total of $12.50. This spread may be larger but we will use this figure for illustrative purposes. Thus, one broker made $42 and the other $42. The specialist made $12.50, less transfer taxes which must be paid by the specialist, since this is a separate transaction from the original sale by Smith. These figures are summarized in Exhibit 11-3, Part I. Also, Part II shows how the over-the-counter market works. No figures are filled in because they vary depending on the nature of the stock. For an inactive stock, the total spread between the customer selling and the customer buying will be substantially larger than for a stock exchange transaction, because stocks on the stock exchange are larger and more active. The "dealer wholesale" may be likened to the position of the specialist on the stock exchange. And wholesale dealers may claim that they can trade on about the same basis as the specialist for equally active stocks. The difference between the bids and askeds by the first and second retail dealers is akin to the brokerage commissions to the customers selling and buying on the stock exchange. And some dealers do charge stock exchange commissions for active stocks rather than take mark-ups and mark-downs.

It looks as though the specialist member got something for doing very little work. As it appears in this transaction, he did, but remember that the specialist did assume the risk of an adverse development in the market when he bought and held on to Smith's stock until Jones came along and bought it.

Exhibit 11-3

SPREADS AND COMMISSIONS FOR OVER-THE-COUNTER AND LISTED STOCKS
(Excluding Transfer Taxes, not shown)

PART I

LISTED MARKET

	$19.16	Net Price to Customer Selling	↑
Brokerage Commission	0.84	(2.1%)	
Sale Price by Smith	$20.00		
Specialists Spread	0.125	(0.6)	4.8% Spread
Purchase Price by Jones	$20.125		
Brokerage Commission	0.84	(2.1%)	
	$20.965	Gross Price to Customer Buying	↓

PART II

OVER-THE-COUNTER MARKET

1st Dealer Retail–Bid	$20	. . . . Price to Customer Selling	↑
Asked	$	. . . . % (Limited by N.A.S.D. to Maximum of 5%)	% Spread
Dealer Wholesale–Bid	$*	. . . . % (Limited by N.A.S.D. to Maximum of 5%)	
Asked	$		
2nd Retail Dealer–Bid	$**	. . . . Price to Customer Buying	↓
Asked	$		

*Dealer Wholesale Bid the same as 1st Dealer Retail Asked.
**2nd Retail Dealer Bid the same as Dealer Wholesale Asked.

There are two principal national exchanges located in New York, and what might be termed four major regional exchanges. There are altogether a total of 11 registered exchanges which trade in securities in the United States. They are shown in Exhibit 11-4 in order of importance as measured by percent of total dollar market volume of securities traded in July, 1973. Of the total dollar market volume traded on all exchanges, about 95% were accounted for by stocks.

The New York Stock Exchange lists about 2,200 stocks of which 1,600 are common stocks. The American deals in securities of 1,251 corporations. The largest local exchange, the Midwest, provides a market for over 729 securities, practically all of which are stocks. Of these, 38 are listed only on that exchange.

Exhibit 11-4

TRADING VOLUME ON PRINCIPAL U.S. EXCHANGES

July, 1973

	% of Total Market Value* Traded
New York Stock Exchange	84.8%
Midwest (Chicago)	4.4
American (New York City)	3.8
Pacific Coast (San Francisco)	3.6
Philadelphia-Baltimore (Philadelphia)	1.9
Boston	1.4
Other (Cincinnati, Intermountain, National, Spokane, Detroit)	0.1
	100.0%

*Data from Securities and Exchange Commission, Statistical Bulletin, Washington, D.C.

Listing vs. Non-Listing

We can attack the problem of listing by first trying to decide whether your stock should be listed on the largest national exchange, the New York Stock Exchange or over-the-counter.

Before a company can list on the New York Stock Exchange it must meet certain requirements. They are summarized in Exhibit 11-5. There are considerations other than these set rules, such as the degree of national interest in the company, its standing in its field, etc.

If you meet the listing requirements, you will then wish to review the advantages and disadvantages in listing, keeping in mind that the principal thing you are trying to achieve is the best market for your stock. As far as price alone is concerned, we reiterate that there are three elements: a narrow spread between bid and asked, an orderly market so that there are not erratic or wide fluctuations and the best price level commensurate with the nature of your company.

Important, as regards whether listing or over-the-counter will provide the best price level for your stock, is a correct evaluation of the interest that may be generated in the two markets on the part of investors and those who trade in securities; that is, brokers and dealers. This necessitates an understanding of securities markets, which we discussed previously. We will now discuss the advantages and disadvantages of listing before pulling the entire subject together.

Advantages

1. There are certain types of investors who in some instances limit their investments to stocks listed on the largest exchange. Some state laws governing the investment of common stock for certain institutions require that they be listed on some exchange. Thus, listing may open up a new market for a company's securities.
2. There are more newspapers throughout the country which report a complete list of market prices of stocks on the New York Stock Exchange, than report quotations for over-the-counter securities. This is an advantage to the individual owner of the securities.

Exhibit 11-5

LISTING REQUIREMENTS FOR THE NEW YORK AND AMERICAN STOCK EXCHANGES. AND REQUIREMENTS FOR OVER-THE-COUNTER STOCKS TO HAVE SAME MARGIN FOR LOANS AS LISTED STOCKS.

	NYSE	ASE	OTC Margin Stocks
Numbers of holders	––	1,200	1,500 (Not including officers, directors and holders of more than 10%.)
Round-lot holders	2,000	800	
Number of shares publicly held	1,000,000	400,000	500,000
Market value of public portion	$16,000,000	$3,000,000	$10,000,000
Earnings before taxes			
Latest year	$ 2,500,000	$ 750,000 ($400,000 after taxes)	––
Preceding 2 years	$ 2,000,000	––	––
Net tangible assets	$16,000,000	$4,000,000	––
Total equity	––	––	$ 5,000,000
Minimum stock price	––	$5.00	$10.00
Other			5 market makers. Regulation under the Securities Act. Daily quotes. Six months of trading.

3. A company's common stock is automatically exempt in most states from "Blue Sky" laws if it is listed. This permits new issues of the stock and also senior securities of a company to be sold in those states. This can be handled in another manner at some expense, but the automatic qualification results in savings in time and money.
4. When a listed company desires to acquire a closely held or family owned company, the Exchange Market may have an appeal to the owners of the company to be acquired.
5. When new stock is offered, the stock exchange provides a better opportunity to prevent adverse market developments. For example, when a new issue is offered, the underwriters may put in a stabilizing bid on the floor of the exchange. This is impossible in the over-the-counter market because it is so widely scattered. Likewise, there is more danger that the price of a stock will get knocked down in the over-the-counter market prior to an offering.
6. Listing makes it easier to raise capital abroad. This might apply particularly to the sale of convertibles, which would have a more attractive convertible privilege if the stock is listed.
7. Banks may be more willing to lend on listed stocks. Banks and brokers are subject to laws regulating margin requirements. Collateral loans by banks, dealers and brokers are on about the same footing for listed stocks as for unlisted ones which are of a size to be on the over-the-counter margin stock list. This size criterion for an over-the-counter stock to be on the margin stock list falls in between the New York and American Exchange listing tests and is shown in Exhibit 11-5. For over-the-

counter stocks not on the margin stock list, there is a difference compared to listed stocks. Banks can loan any amount they wish, but dealers cannot make any loans on such stocks.

Disadvantages

1. Dealer interest is lost when a stock is listed. If dealers are members of an exchange, they cannot make a market on a negotiated basis; they must handle transactions as brokers and accept the regular exchange commission. If they aren't members of an exchange, their interest may be lost because they are not the primary market and cannot readily deal with members of the exchange. In the past, a major reason for loss of dealer interest was the fact that dealers could make a larger spread in over-the-counter stocks as compared with commissions on the stock exchange. With the narrowing of spreads in the over-the-counter market, this is not as important a reason today.
2. There are some additional requirements: non-voting stock can't be listed; a company must agree to solicit proxies; shareholder approval must be obtained when additional shares are listed for certain purposes and mergers of a certain size must be voted on by stockholders. Controlling persons and recipients of stock in certain kinds of mergers are restricted in immediate sales of stock to 1% of the stock outstanding for both listed and over-the-counter stocks, but the restriction is more stringent for listed stocks.
3. There is some cost,[1] but it appears reasonable in the light of publicity obtained and the advantage to stockholders of a fair and orderly market.

In finally deciding on whether to list or not, you will wish to weigh the nature of the two different markets for your security and what the exchange provides, as outlined above.

A large company with a broad market for its securities will generally gain more by listing. The over-the-counter market functions as a seasoning ground for new companies, some of which should eventually be listed. On the other hand, a company which is not suited to being listed and which will not gain additional stockholder interest by doing so, may hurt the market for its stock by listing. The price of your stock may sag if there is not an offsetting gain in stockholder interest when the stock is listed. If the stock is suitable to being listed, such gain in stockholder interest will occur.

In carrying out our plan to determine whether or not to list, and where, we will next consider the other principal national exchange, the American. You cannot list on both national exchanges, and there would be no advantage in doing so, because most of the firms which are members of the New York Stock Exchange are members of the American. Much of the same basic reasoning applies in weighing listing on the American as on the New York Stock Exchange.

First, with regard to the American, size requirements are smaller as was shown in Exhibit 11-5. Thus, many companies which would not be eligible for the New York Stock Exchange may qualify for listing on the American. Secondly, the cost of listings is lower on the American.

If you look at the American's booklet on the advantages of listing, you will find practically the same ones given above for the New York Stock Exchange about the advantages of a supervised market, etc.

Basically, the American is the foremost exchange for new enterprises—a national exchange on which the securities of smaller and newer corporations are eligible for listing. However, it also has many old and well-established companies. For example, as of the end of 1973, about one-quarter of the common stocks traded on the American paid cash dividends for five consecutive years or more.

[1]For New York Stock Exchange

	Initial Fee, per Share*	Continuing Annual Fee, per Share ($10,000 Minimum)
First 2 million shares	1¢	1/10¢
3rd and 4th million shares	1/2¢	1/20¢
5th million to 300 million shares	1/4¢	1/20¢
In excess of 300 million shares	1/8¢	1/20¢

*For original listings of common stock there is a further one-time charge of $25,000.

One point made by the American is that greater overall attention may be given to a smaller company. There is a natural rivalry between the two exchanges, and the New York Stock Exchange contends that it does not slight any company.

In making a final decision as to whether to list on the American, you will wish to go over the advantages and disadvantages as discussed under the New York Stock Exchange, with the differences, as noted above, for the American.

Regional Exchanges

If you decide to list on either the New York or American Exchange, you will next have to decide whether to list on one or more of the regional exchanges. You will wish to consider only those exchanges which are located where there is an active market in your stock.

The first question of importance about listing on a regional exchange for a stock which is already listed on a national revolves around whether a regional exchange will produce more interest on the part of investors and brokers without decreasing the volume on the national exchange so as to affect the market adversely. The market on the local exchanges will follow that on either of the national exchanges. A stock must be actively traded for a specialist to keep a narrow spread between bid and asked price. You would only hurt your market if listing on a local exchange pulls too much trading from New York. This is what is known as diluting your market. The specialist and other experts on the national exchange on which you are listed can help you on this point. Provided it will not hurt your market, then there might be an added advantage in listing on the local exchanges where there is an active interest in the stock. It may add to the local interest. Brokers who are members of the local exchange, but not of the New York Exchange on which the stock may be listed, have to pay a commission to members of the New York Exchange when they purchase or sell the stock through that route. If it is listed on their local exchange, they can handle it themselves and get the full commission.

There is a New York State transfer tax on all sales of stock on either of the New York exchanges which amounts to 5¢ per share for a stock selling at $20 per share or more. It is less for lower-priced stocks. This can be avoided for people located outside New York by going through a local exchange, if a company has a transfer agent outside of New York. However, if in putting through the transaction on another exchange you miss the market by as much as 1/8 of a point, any advantage of avoiding the tax is more than lost.

Exhibit 11-6 shows the ten companies listed on the New York Stock Exchange with the greatest number of stockholders, and the regional exchanges on which they are also traded.

If you are not listed on either the New York or American, you will have a different decision to make with regard to listing on one or more of the regional exchanges. Then the effect of the loss of dealer interest again arises. You will need to know the number and importance of the dealers in the area and their interest in your stock, and the number and importance of the brokers who are members of the exchange. For example, as previously mentioned, the Midwest has 38 issues which are listed exclusively on that exchange. Thus, listing on an exchange outside of New York City may be considered by some companies either on a permanent basis or as a transition from the over-the-counter market to a national exchange.

You may run into the fact that some stocks are traded on exchanges on an unlisted basis and wonder what it means. Before passage of the Securities Exchange Act of 1934, some stocks were traded on certain exchanges on that basis. Those stocks were traded as all other stocks, but the companies avoided having to comply with any of the exchange's requirements. Their status was frozen with

Exhibit 11-6

TEN COMPANIES WITH THE GREATEST NUMBER OF STOCKHOLDERS ON THE NEW YORK STOCK EXCHANGE WHICH ARE ALSO TRADED ON LOCAL AND FOREIGN EXCHANGES

Company	Midwest	Pacific Coast	Phil. Bost. Wash.	Boston	Other* U.S.	Other* Foreign
American Telephone & Tel.	X	X	X	X	C,D	P
General Motors	X	X	X	X	C,D	B,D,F,L,M,T,P
Exxon Corp.	X	X		X	C	B
Int'l Business Machines	X	X	X	X	C,D	A,B,Ba,F,G,L,La,M,T,P,Z
General Electric	X	X	X	X	D	
General Tel. & Electronics	X	X	X	X	C,D	A,Ba,L,La,G,To,Z
Ford Motor	X	X	X	X	D	M,T and others
Gulf Oil	X	X	X	X	C,D	
Texaco, Inc.	X	X	X	X	C,D	L,T.
Consolidated Edison	X	X	X	X	D	A

*Letters indicate the other exchanges on which stocks are listed as follows:

A–Amsterdam, B–Brussels, Ba–Basil, D–Dusseldorf, F–Frankfort, G–Geneva, L–London, La–Lausanne, M–Montreal, P–Paris, T–Toronto, To–Tokyo, Z–Zurich

the passage of the Act. Now an exchange can apply to the Securities and Exchange Commission to have a stock traded on an unlisted basis if it is registered on another exchange, or if the company is giving such information as if it were registered; and if the stock has aroused a wide public interest and is widely distributed, leading to an active market in the locality of the exchange. A company cannot initiate or block such a move without real cause.

A correct decision on the proper market for your stock will mean dollars and cents to your stockholders in their purchases and sales and a better price level for your stock. You have an obligation to your stockholders to give it your careful consideration.

In making a decision on whether or not to list and where, you should compare your stock with others of a similar nature and size which are listed and unlisted, as regards brokerage commissions, spread between bid and asked, erratic price movements and price level. If such information can be obtained, it would be well to study the new types of stockholders which may have been added as a result of a similar type of company being listed. You may wish to consult with the management of listed companies like your own to determine what happened to them when they listed. The exchanges issue brief booklets giving their story. They have experts you can consult on an informal and confidential basis. You should review your situation with them as a first step in deciding what decision to make. You should talk with some of the larger dealer firms which are not members of the stock exchange in order to get their picture of the advantages of the unlisted market for your stock. This is not a difficult question if you understand security markets.

Whatever the market for your stock, you should follow it to ascertain that a proper market is being continuously maintained. As your company grows, you should review the picture to see if any different action is required. Once you are listed, this does not mean that you can abandon the market for your securities—you should follow it carefully. You should get to know your specialist and see him regularly. If you do not believe your specialist is doing a good job, you should talk to the Exchange. And if you do not get satisfaction, you should request that your specialist be changed. However, this is not very easy to do because the specialist carries a lot of weight with the Exchange.

Markets for Senior Securities

Our discussion of markets has pertained to common stocks. Most of the trading in bonds takes place over-the-counter. Of the value of all securities traded on all exchanges, only about 5% was accounted for by bonds.[2] The institutional investors are served satisfactorily by the over-the-counter market, except that there may be a few who only buy listed bonds. Some debt issues are listed. About 360 companies have their debt issues listed on the New York Stock Exchange, and that exchange accounted for practically all of the listed trading in bonds. The listing fee is small. A possible advantage is the published record of prices as a result of listing. The ticker carries bond prices. Bond prices are reported separately in the newspapers from stocks, but only a few newspapers carry these quotations. If higher interest rates encourage individual investors to go into the bond market, there may be more reason for listing.

More preferred stocks are listed because there is some interest in them by individual investors. However, the market is thin. If a company's preferred stock does have a public interest, then there may be some advantage to listing. Preferred stock prices are reported along with those for common stocks. There is one school of thought to the effect that quotations on a preferred stock will be better if it is listed, and that this will assist in getting better prices on future offerings of preferred stocks. The question of listing a preferred may be important in some instances, but it isn't such an important question as is listing of common.

Some institutional buyers of senior securities are limited to listed securities. The underwriters and lawyers will tell you whether this is important in order to help sell a new issue.

Perhaps more consideration should be given to listing senior securities which are convertible into common stock on the same exchange as that on which the common stock is traded in order to provide a comparable quotation for the two issues. This may be of some benefit to your security holders when it appears advantageous to convert. More individual investors are interested in convertibles than senior securities without the convertible privilege.

Changes in the Marketplace

We have described the traditional view of the market for securities. This knowledge is necessary to understanding the securities markets and following the current changes. However, securities markets are in a state of flux because of changes in economics, regulation and electronic systems.

What is known as the third market sprang up because dealers who are not members of an exchange found that for large orders, they could handle a transaction at less cost to the customer than a broker could on the exchange. The investors in this type of transaction are the institutions such as trust accounts of banks, mutual funds, corporate pension funds, etc. And dealers who are not members of the Exchange can service their customers with Stock Exchange stocks by going to a third market maker. Trading of this type exists in up to 400 stocks of the larger companies listed on the New York Stock Exchange. This was due to four factors:

1. Brokerage commissions were previously fixed rather than negotiated as they are today. Block traders claimed that they

---

[2] Data from Securities and Exchange Commission, Washington, D.C.

could handle a transaction at about one-quarter the cost of the New York Stock Exchange Commission.

2. According to the houses doing the business, the specialists' capital was inadequate so they could not step in and take on large blocks of stock.
3. The substantial growth in institutionalization of the investment business which resulted in increased size of trades.
4. The great communication ability with electronic systems which can make market information readily available.

This off-the-exchange trading has been a thorn in the side of the exchanges. The New York Stock Exchange will claim that they have a system to handle such transactions after the close of the exchange.

Block trading of shares of stock by a few of the large member houses is also a part of the third market which grew up in the booming 1960's. A block trade is considered to involve 10,000 shares or more. An institution which wants to sell a large block may feel that it would hurt the market if it gradually sold the stock on an exchange, so it offers the block to a large house which specializes in such transactions and which will make a bid for the stock. Depending on the market, the bid may be below the bid on the stock exchange, but the seller may feel that if he sold it gradually on the exchange he would drive the price down. The block trader will find one or more buyers who will absorb the entire block. The block trader may get a stock exchange commission from the buyer and the seller. If the entire issue cannot be placed, the block trading house may position some of the stock, hoping to be able to find a buyer in the near future. Members of an exchange must put all transactions through the exchange. Block trading houses are members of the New York Stock Exchange and also regional exchanges. Block trades by member firms are put through a regional exchange which is more liberal in allowing such transactions than the New York Stock Exchange.

With the collapse of the market in the early 1970's, some people on Wall Street feel that the block trading market will stay at its dampened pace. Others feel that it will come to life with a bull market. Block trading represented about 20% of the total volume on the New York Stock Exchange in January, 1973 and fell to about 15% a year later.

As we have previously pointed out, there are computer screens available such as NASDAQ which readily gives up-to-the-minute quotes for the over-the-counter market securities. Some institutional investors subscribe to computer screens on which they can show their interest in buying and selling a certain number of shares without going through any intermediary.

Such developments may change the marketplace for securities, and even more far-reaching ideas are in the process. Some of the major developments which are in process or under consideration are:

1. Ownership of exchange seats by institutions so they can cut down their trading costs. It is permitted by some local exchanges, but not the New York or American Exchange. This is opposed by most of the brokerage community.
2. Negotiated rates. This change took place May 1, 1975.
3. A central securities market which will include a consolidated ticker tape giving the last sale price on all securities regardless of where traded. And as a second step, a composite quote system which will show up-to-date bid and asked prices so that a buyer or seller can obtain the best market.
4. A national clearing process in order to eliminate much of the unnecessary physical movement of certificates.

Putting any of these current developments in a book is rather futile because the scene is changing so fast. However, if you understand the workings of the traditional markets and know the reasons why changes are occurring—regulation trying to improve the markets and the economics of the large institutional investors—you will be able to understand the up-to-date picture.

Foreign Markets for Securities

Your interest in foreign markets for securities should rest primarily on the extent to which they may represent a source of capital. The availability of funds changes so rapidly in foreign countries that you will have to rely on the advice of an investment or commercial banker unless you are so large and have such an extensive foreign operation that your own financial people can follow the situation. And the problems involved will depend on whether you want to use the funds abroad or in this country.

If your stock has some foreign ownership, you will wish to provide the best market for the stock, so that it will be of most use in raising capital. At times, convertibles have been a major source of capital in the European market to provide funds for expansion in that area. Listing on a foreign stock exchange may increase the interest in a convertible. Some other reasons suggested for listing are:

1. It will make it easier to sell new stock abroad. Certain institutional investors are restricted in their purchase to stocks which are listed on certain exchanges.
2. It may assist in foreign acquisitions and mergers.
3. It provides publicity for a company.

The principal exchanges in Japan and Europe are shown in Exhibit 11-7.

In deciding on whether you should list, you might wish to determine what other similar companies have done. You can find where companies are listed by referring to Standard and Poor's or Moody's Manuals.

Of those that are listed abroad, you might inquire as to the results.

Exhibit 11-7

STOCK EXCHANGES IN EUROPE AND JAPAN WITH NUMBER OF U.S. CORPORATIONS LISTED

	Number of U.S. Companies Listed	Initial Introduction	Approximate Cost
Tokyo		One of major Japanese banks with offices in N.Y.	$100,000
Zurich		One of major Swiss banks with offices in N.Y.	Approximately $20,000 including bank fee.
Geneva and Brazil		When approved for Zurich, listing on these 2 exchanges is automatic.	
London		By British banks and broker.	$12,000 (any stock listed in a major foreign exchange can be traded in London).
Paris	40	By French bank and American bank with branch in France.	Up to $50,000
Frankfort (There are 8 others in West Germany)	20		Up to $50,000
Amsterdam	300	By Dutch bank	Up to $10,000
Brussels	40	By Belgian bank	Up to $6,000

The most active exchange in Europe is the Amsterdam Exchange. Principal dealers in securities throughout Europe have access to that market. The expense of listing on that exchange is relatively small and it does add to interest in a company's stock in the European market.

There are certain requirements for listing on foreign exchanges. The requirements vary with the exchanges, but if you are large enough to make it worthwhile to list, you will undoubtedly meet the requirements. The process of listing for most of the exchanges is initiated through a well-known financial organization such as a commercial or investment bank.

Transfers of securities take place in the foreign markets in various ways: with actual shares, by bookkeeping entry with shares held in a depository or by depository receipts.

If your stock is actively traded abroad, it will take some time of your top management to keep foreign investors informed. And the act of listing does require top management participation. There are some requirements for reporting such as furnishing annual reports translated into foreign languages.

CHAPTER 12

Investor Relations

This chapter explains the purpose of an investor relations program and how and to whom a company should disseminate information about itself; that is, any information which will affect the value of its securities. This subject is now well-known by the term investor relations.

The Purpose

Years ago, there was a feeling in industry that managements were, in effect, the owners or perhaps trustees of the stockholders' property. There was no reason to give out information about a company's operations. Management was the group which made the decisions. Why, then, was it necessary to bother to keep anyone else informed? This feeling may have resulted from the fact that in the early stages of our industrial growth, companies were small and owned by a family or a few people. In most cases, management and owners were one and the same. This situation no longer exists for the companies large enough to have a broad list of stockholders.

Industry today should recognize that it is the stockholders who own the company and that managements are working for the stockholders. Managements which persist in the old theory that "we are the company" are out of step with the times. They fail to recognize their true responsibility. They hurt their companies and render a disservice to our system of private capital.

Management has an obligation to keep its stockholders informed. A person buys a security at a certain price. The price he is willing to pay is determined by an appraisal of information by the investor himself or his advisor. When he wishes to sell that security, his decision will be made on a similar basis, as will the decisions of subsequent buyers and sellers. The price should reflect as far as possible the risks and potentials present in the stock. It should be obvious that those who make such appraisals and determine the market price must be given adequate information at all times.

Furthermore, prices of securities tend to direct the flow of capital. It is not healthy for our economic system to have security prices out of line with the economic risk of the enterprise. It is not healthy for the individual company, in raising new capital, to have a market evaluation which does not fairly reflect the realities of the business. This applies when security prices are too high as well as when they are too low.

In carrying out a program of keeping investors informed, it is essential that management conceive the correct purpose. Otherwise, the goal will not be achieved and managements may become discouraged because of some surprising and irreconcilable reactions from investors. It may be expressed briefly in the following principle:

> THE PURPOSE OF AN INVESTOR RELATIONS PROGRAM SHOULD BE TO COMMUNICATE EFFECTIVELY AND PROMPTLY ALL INFORMATION HAVING AN EFFECT ON A COMPANY'S SECURITIES, WHETHER GOOD OR BAD, SO THAT THOSE WHO EVALUATE SECURITIES WILL HAVE COMPLETE INFORMATION ON WHICH TO BASE THEIR JUDGMENT.

There are going to be times when there will be unfavorable information to give out. For example, earnings may be off, or a major accident may have occurred. Publicizing this information may make a company's securities decrease in price. There is nothing wrong in such an occurrence.

If there are some unfavorable developments about a company which require a reappraisal of its securities in the market, it is foolish for management to assume that it can avoid such action by hiding the facts. The day of reckoning will come. It is far better for the reappraisal to be made by investors when the events happen. An honest, clear-cut picture of the facts will usually help avoid too erratic a reaction in the prices.

Advantages

To be more specific, here are the advantages of an investor relations program:

1. Generally, it will tend to assure a more reasonable price level for a company's securities. It will help reduce short or violent swings in the market. Lack of information may cause unreasonable fears and induce investors to sell the stock. But with a good information program this may be prevented.
2. It will facilitate raising capital. It will increase the number of investors interested in the company, thus broadening the market for capital. This is directly beneficial to the company and thus its stockholders.
3. It will help prevent unnecessary proxy fights. Onc of the important tests of good management, as far as investors are concerned, is its investor relations program. Stockholders will naturally be prejudiced against a company that has failed in this responsibility. If a satisfactory program has been maintained, and a company runs into trouble, then the stockholders will be more inclined to support the management, because they believe in it.
4. It will aid in obtaining approval of necessary changes in the charter and terms in outstanding securities from security holders. Why should the management of a company expect security holders to go along with requested changes if it has chosen to ignore them until making such a request?
5. It will minimize the risk of violating the misuse of insider information.

Disadvantages

There are really no disadvantages to a well-thought-out investor relations program. However, there are certain obstacles which probably will be encountered, such as:

1. There are some unreasonable security holders and financial analysts. No matter what you do they may say you are doing a poor job. They may ask and almost demand information which should not be given out.
2. Some information you give out at times will be misinterpreted. Those who receive it may view it differently than you, who know the entire situation. Occasionally, this cannot be avoided; don't let it discourage you.
3. It will involve some expense and time of the company's officers.

Management's Attitude Most Important

The attitude of management towards an investor relations program is all-important. If the attitude is wrong, there is no possibility that the program will be successful. In fact, if the management's attitude is wrong, the company would be better off having no program.

The one all-important word is credibility. If investors lose faith in the information a company gives out, all is lost because they will either ignore the company or downgrade the value of the earnings. And once credibility is lost, it is a rather hopeless task to rccrcatc.

The quickest way to lose credibility is to come up with surprises. Wall Street abhores surprises! A company must be willing to discuss subjects which are adverse in order to rule out surprises.

Certain types of people are just not constituted to do a good investor relations job. Investor relations has absolutely nothing to do with public relations. And with no apologies whatsoever, most PR people are just not the type for the job. Another type is the president of a company who is sales oriented.

Any time such a president appears before a group it represents an opportunity to give a sales pitch of one kind or another. If the president of a company is this type, he should talk about the company's products and let the financial vice president cover the financial matters. Another type is the nit-picking lawyer, who spends his time thinking of reasons not to give out information in fear of the Securities and Exchange Commission. Presidents of some companies fall in this category. The Securities and Exchange Commission, in policing this area, is not out to get anyone. If a person uses good common sense he can feel safe.

One more word about credibility. A company's results have to appear in the financials as time rolls on. There is no quicker way to lose credibility than to play accounting games. When investors don't believe your figures, you have sunk to a low level. Some companies are known for jazzing up their earnings with accounting gimmicks; others are known for "managing" their earnings in one way or another. Some companies are always arguing with their accountants and the Securities and Exchange Commission. If a company really wants to tell the truth, it isn't just that hard and the names of the companies whose figures can't be trusted get around fairly fast.

Here is a comment by an analyst about a credibility gap developed by a company which should make you think twice before getting your company in the same position:

> They put on a big campaign earlier in the year, meeting with analysts and painting a really optimistic picture. A lot of guys moved into the stock because of it. And, then, after the stock is down 40%, they issue a press release. I say they had an obligation to let the street know sooner.
>
> There isn't any doubt but that a sizeable credibility gap has developed between management and the financial community. It has now become difficult to have any high degree of confidence in its revised earnings estimate. And it will undoubtedly take the company a long time to recapture the confidence of the investment community.

Comments by management often give away the fact that they have a wrong attitude:

> "Certain information might be misinterpreted; therefore, we feel that it would be wrong to give it out."
>
> "Our situation is very complicated at present. Therefore, we feel that the best course is to postpone discussions with investors until matters straighten out."
>
> "We have got to put more time in on investor relations because the price of our stock is down."

A good approach to take is that you will say the same thing whether earnings are going up or down. Some companies become quite vocal when the picture looks rosy, but they become clams when the earnings turn down.

Management should not follow the price of its stock primarily for the elation of seeing it go up. It should be followed in relation to the general securities market, and also in relation to securities of other companies in the same type of business. If the price is out of line, it may give a clue that investors are appraising the company incorrectly. If so, management will want to find out why. Is the investor relations program being handled correctly? If the stock is relatively over-priced, is it because overly optimistic information has been given out or is it because other companies are not doing a good investor relations job?

Unfortunately, we have to accept the fact that some managements are manipulators. They do everything possible to push up the price of the stock for personal reasons. They unload their stock when they can get a high price regardless of what happens to the stock subsequently. And, thereafter they live high on the hog with money which was, in effect, stolen. A boom period permits this type to flourish and the 1960's developed its share of this miserable type. Talking about a sound investor relations program for that type of management is a total waste of breath.

Program

In order to do an effective investor relations job, a company should map out a program at least two years ahead. It should be reviewed at the end of each year and extended for another year, with changes made on the basis of the last year's experience.

Why a program and why for two years? Some investors will be analyzing your stock at all times. A program assures a regular continuous flow of sufficient information, and the use of all necessary media to reach investors. It provides proper spacing of meetings, etc. and prevents duplication of effort. The program should be completely planned for one year in advance and be well thought out for the succeeding year. Some media may be used only every two years; thus, at least a skeleton outline is required for the second year, to see how the entire picture will be developed.

A program must be tailor-made to fit the needs of the individual company. There isn't just one correct plan for all companies. The two major factors which will affect the elaborateness of the program are:

1. The size of the company and the number and location of its investors. Obviously, a small company could not and need not have as expensive a program, but it should have an equally thorough program.
2. The nature of the company. A company which is in a very changeable type of business will need to put forth more effort than a company in a stable business.

Is this a laborious task? At first, it seems endless. After one or two years' experience has been gained, it settles down to reasonable proportions. It will take a little time on the part of the president and somewhat more time from the top financial officer. The amount of staff required will depend on the size of the company and its list of investors. Companies which have set up a complete program for investor relations have not found it over-burdensome in relation to the benefits. There is no need to jump into an extensive program all at once. A company can feel its way and build gradually.

Some large companies have found it worthwhile to have a specialist assigned to the proper handling of this task. Such an approach has an advantage, in that it relieves the top officers of much of the work involved and assures a more consistent companywide approach. This person, in turn, must be completely familiar with all the figures of the company and must be able to present a balanced and comprehensive picture. However, this person should not block the analyst's access to the financial vice president and president. He should screen the people he believes have need to see top officials.

As part of the program, there should be a complete understanding of who does what and the principles which will be followed.

It is preferable that contacts with analysts be limited to a few people so that the information released will be uniform. And there should be a clear understanding of who these persons will be and what part they would play. For a large company, analysts may wish to visit with non-financial executives; these visits should be monitored by the person in charge of investor relations.

The person in charge of investor relations should write out the policies he feels should be followed in giving out information. And this should be agreed to by the persons who will be involved in the program. This will result in a structured and disciplined program which will provide consistent information for all persons interested in a company's stock.

Outside Advisors

Should a company perform this function itself? There are sound reasons why it should.

1. It is more effective, because investors like to know that they are dealing directly with company officials; that they are getting information directly from the "horse's mouth." Furthermore,

part of the problem of analyzing a security involves evaluating management. Investors want to become acquainted with management so that they can appraise it.

2. It gives your company officials contact with the financial community. If you assign an up-and-coming assistant to handling the details, it provides an opportunity for training him in finance.

Should outside advisors be used, and, if so, in what way? Perhaps it is worthwhile at the start and for smaller companies that cannot afford a staff which devotes its entire time to investor relations. However, for larger companies, it is relatively inexpensive to perform the service themselves. Furthermore, management should take a personal interest in this function.

If an outside firm is used, it should be on a consulting basis only. Written material should be sent out from the company under its own name. Mail in the envelope of a financial public relations firm may cause an unfavorable reaction on the part of some analysts.

Questions from the investors should be answered by company officials. Consider the reaction of investors if a company official tells an inquirer that the financial public relations firm will handle it.

Suppose your company's program is run by an outside expert who speaks for your company, and at the same time he is also speaking for 20 other companies. Suppose that he has given out over-optimistic information about one of the companies and that the information turns out to be faulty. How will that reflect on your company? The stigma of being associated with that financial public relations firm may be felt by all its other clients.

Consulting firms claim that because they are expert in the field, they can do a better job than management. The consultants say that they know just what is needed and whom to contact. They can do it inexpensively because they can spread the cost over a number of companies. Perhaps they can, but they should not place themselves between you and the investors. They can give you ideas on techniques and assist in planning your program, but management should carry it out.

And, also, beware of what they mean by "better job." Do they mean pushing the price of your stock up? If so, that may work in a bull market. And it may be helpful just before you sell stock, but it won't fit your needs during a bear market or when you run into trouble. It can spell failure over the long run because it will hurt credibility.

If you decide to use an outside advisor, make sure he doesn't have any of the PR characteristics, and that he does not take a short term, glamorous approach of bulling your stock. The main purpose is to see that more and more investors have a better knowledge of your company. That cannot be accomplished unless the management at least keeps in the act.

Distinction Between Types of Investors

Should you treat security holders, such as bond holders and preferred stockholders, differently than you treat common stockholders? Basically no, because it is advantageous to a company and to its stockholders to keep all security holders well-informed. Just review the advantages listed above of an investor relations program. Most of them are applicable to all security holders.

Nevertheless, in setting up a program, it is essential to distinguish between two types of investors, no matter what kind of security they own—the uninformed and the informed. They are quite distinct, and the approach to each is entirely different.

The uninformed investors are the great mass of investors who are unskilled in analysis of securities.

The informed are those who make a profession of security analysis, and also those who have acquired a sufficient knowledge of securities to make a studied decision as to whether to buy or sell. In order to make sound decisions, two attributes are necessary:

1. A thorough understanding of income statements, balance sheets, types of secu-

rities, financial policy and a myriad of factors that may affect the profits of a company, including, importantly, management and research.
2. Training in analyzing securities, so that an opinion can be made as to the relative value of one security as compared to another.

Uninformed Investors

Let us first consider the uninformed group. There are three schools of thought regarding the uninformed:

1. One believes that they are so hopelessly lacking in knowledge of finance that it is impossible to get across any meaningful story to them. The president of one company, who made extensive tours of the country holding regional stockholders' meetings, tells vividly of how he became totally disillusioned as to the ability of the small stockholders to absorb financial matters. He quotes one woman as saying after a regional meeting: "Mr President, I didn't understand what you were talking about, but I just know there must be something wrong if you came all the way from New York to Chicago to talk to us. Can't you tell me if I should sell my stock in your company?" After numerous other similar experiences, he concluded, "Don't waste your time on the uninformed."
2. The second school of thought is that the uninformed investors should be given as much as seems reasonable for them to absorb. They are not specialists and do not have the time or training to analyze securities carefully. So do not burden them with volumes of statistics. But don't neglect them.
3. The most optimistically minded contend that our capitalistic system cannot survive unless the great mass of the people are helped to understand how our economy works. For example, they urge that emphasis be placed on appealing annual reports and that they should be used extensively as educational media. The optimists say that every means possible should be used to get stockholders to understand our system of private capital.

One of the most practical studies on the uninformed investor was made many years ago by The Controllership Foundation, Inc. It was entitled, What Information People Want About Policies and Financial Conditions of Corporations. The late Dr. Julian Woodward, Research Executive, Elmo Roper & Associates, played a major part in that survey. He personally interviewed many stockholders.

His conclusions were that most stockholders just do not have sufficient knowledge about finance to understand income statements, balance sheets, complicated annual reports, etc.; that, in most instances, they bought securities on the advice of a professional—a security analyst, a broker, a banker or an investment advisor.

It seems that the second school of thought, or the middle course, makes the most sense. Those who take the first approach may be overly pessimistic. Those who take the last seem to be working towards a rather long term goal as to what their audience someday should be like. Certainly no one should be criticized for this kind of worthwhile effort to get the public better informed about our system of private capital. There is no question that it is woefully needed. If it can be achieved by efforts with the small stockholder, so much the better. This is somewhat outside our immediate problem of informing stockholders specifically about the company.

Getting back to our theme, it was Dr. Woodward's contention that the average stockholder wants to know just three things about a company:

1. Dividends per share;
2. Earnings per share;
3. A general statement about the strength of his or her investment.

The place to cover this information is in the President's Letter in the annual report. In some annual reports, the President's Letter is written in very small, hard-to-read type, smaller than the type in the rest of the report.

Why? Is it done to fit the material into a page? If so, it is no excuse. Too small type is annoying and discourages reader interest.

If some space is to be devoted to the uninformed stockholder, it is essential to make certain that the audience is reached. Visualize a small stockholder who owns ten different stocks and receives ten elaborate, complicated annual reports. Do you expect him to read all of them? If he reads part of each, he will be doing well. The first thing that should be done in order to get him to read even part is to make the report very readable. This also applies as far as the informed investors are concerned. It is interesting to test annual reports for readability. Try the Rudolf Flesch test, included in *The Art of Readable Writing.*[1] You will be surprised to find that many annual reports, even those directed specifically at the uninformed, fall into the hard-to-read category. A glamorous report with nice pictures and charts in themselves won't make stockholders actually read it. Charts should be used as an integral part of the story in order to increase readership and understanding.

The various annual report "awards" have helped stimulate companies to do a better job. However, some managements have been carried away by the idea of winning an award. They seem to feel that this means they have accomplished their goal. But too much emphasis along these lines may prevent a company from keeping its eye on the ultimate audience to which the report should be directed. Write the report for the correct audience; if an award results, well and good.

This discussion is not meant to imply that the annual report is written for the uninformed investor. It should be directed to all types of investors and particularly the analysts. A more thorough discussion of the annual report will be given later.

We have drifted somewhat off the subject of supplying information to uninformed investors by pursuing a discussion about the annual report. There are various other media you may wish to use in order to cultivate the uninformed investor. Don't take these as recommendations, but merely some possibilities you may want to look into:

1. A post-meeting report on the annual meeting;
2. Letters of welcome to new stockholders;
3. Letters to stockholders when they sell the stock;
4. Letters in response to complaints;
5. Letters of thanks for sending in proxies;
6. Dividend stuffers;
7. A small sample of your products if your business is such that you can do it—say, a company in the food business;
8. A small booklet on understanding your company;
9. Regional stockholders' meetings.

You shouldn't go in for all of these! You would snow your stockholders under. Consider which ones might be best for your management to build good stockholder relations. Number 4 is essential. Letters from stockholders should be answered quickly, courteously and adequately to give a good answer. As stockholders they have a right to question. Even an unreasonable request deserves an immediate answer.

Remember the three essential factors to stress for the uninformed investor—dividends, earnings and the general condition of the company. Don't talk over the stockholders' heads, but don't "talk down" to them either.

American Telephone and Telegraph Company, with about 2.9 million stockholders, has been running a program for many years to reach as many stockholders as possible through personal contact. Selected management personnel in their subsidiaries throughout the country are trained on the type of information stockholders might wish to know. Visits are made as a part of the day-to-day jobs of these telephone people. This can't help but assist in a better appreciation on the part of their stockholders of the company's objectives.

[1]Revised 1974, published by Harper and Row Publishers, Inc., 10 East 53rd Street, New York City 10022. Price $7.95.

The type of cultivation required for the uninformed stockholder is more a part of the general problem of public relations. It is most important for you to distinguish between the types of investors. What might seem completely right to the uninformed might appear foolish to the informed; what might be interesting and informative to the informed, might be incomprehensible to the uninformed.

Some of the large annual stockholders meetings have become a circus. Certain stockholders try to make a show of themselves. This has made management cynical about such meetings and rightly so. It is questionable how much is really accomplished. However, it is an integral part of the democratic process, and it, at least, shows management's willingness to come into the open and give an account of its stewardship. It is this aspect alone which justifies the annual stockholders meeting. To further the idea from a public relations point of view, a post-meeting report on the annual meeting sent to all stockholders is worth considering.

As previously noted, the writer believes in a middle course towards the uninformed. Don't by any means ignore them. However, they cannot be expected to use complex information to arrive at a definite conclusion regarding a security. We will not dwell longer on the uninformed, because the most important audience to cultivate is the informed investor. However, before leaving this group, a word of caution should be added. A college professor, who was a finance teacher, was heard to complain that there should be no distinction between the uninformed and the informed. He objected strenuously to not receiving all information about companies in which he had investments. He had a right to object. Furthermore, there may be some small investors, not professional analysts, who do their own analysis work in deciding what securities to buy. They want all information, and they should receive it. Keep this in mind when setting up a program. All information should be made available to anyone who wants it. For some companies, such as railroads, utilities and certain types of industrials, where much additional statistical information is publicly available, this can be handled quite readily by including a statement in the back of the annual report. This statement would explain that the company sends out this kind of additional information and would be glad to include any security holder who might wish to receive it. However, don't be alarmed. Companies which have asked the great mass of stockholders whether they wish the additional information have received only a few requests. The note included in the annual report to the effect that information will be sent acts as a precaution to prevent someone from having a justifiable complaint.

Informed Investors

The informed investors are the primary ones who determine the market price for your securities. They have the ability and training to evaluate securities. Furthermore, the uninformed largely rely on the informed group for advice as to what action they should take. By giving complete information to the informed group so that they can make sound decisions, you are directly benefiting the uninformed investors.

Security Analysts

More specifically, to whom do we refer by the term *informed investors?* Primarily to the security analysts who are regularly engaged in the study of all the factors which have an effect on individual securities. They are the individuals who make recommendations on the quality of securities and on whether to buy, hold or sell them. In Chapter 10 we described the Financial Analysts Federation and discussed how analysts perform their function. Here we will discuss how to contact them and keep them informed.

Security analysts are found in practically all types of organizations which are directly engaged in investing money or in recommending to others how they should invest—in investment companies, investment counsel firms, investment banking firms, personal trust departments of banks, mutual funds, pension funds, open- and closed-end funds, insurance companies, savings banks, brokerage houses, rating agencies, etc. They are the ones who make up the department in these organizations which is referred to as the research department, the statistical department or the analytical department.

The security analyst may not always be the one who will make the final decision whether to buy or sell, or have the contact with the customer. For example, in an investment company, that decision may be made by a committee. In a brokerage house, a registered representative, or so-called customer's man, may talk with the client and suggest what action to take. However, it is most important in setting up an investor relations program to realize that behind the scenes it is the security analyst who pores over the information about your company. It is he who makes the original recommendations on the action to be taken. He is the one to whom a company should send its information. A failure to realize this point will cause a company to direct its efforts to the wrong people. For example, one company comes to mind which gave a luncheon in Boston for the purpose of telling the story of its operations. It invited the top officials of various types of financial organizations. They turned out, apparently, because they did not want to say no to such an important company. The company was quite elated because of the high caliber of those who attended. However, relatively little good resulted from the meeting. The officials took no notes, nor did they tell their own security analysts any of the facts given out at the meeting. The security analysts were heard to grumble, and rightly so. In their eyes, the company actually hurt itself by showing that it did not know who did the work on its securities.

This is not to suggest that in many organizations security analysts have not attained top positions. There are many who are partners or vice presidents. However, be sure that you direct your efforts to them and not to some officer just on the basis of his title. For example, letters are sometimes sent to presidents of banks inviting them to a luncheon at which a company wishes to tell the story of its operations. Perhaps the company does not know whom to invite. If so, the letter may be directed to the president, but it should read, "We would like to have as our guest the person in your organization who is interested in analyzing the securities of our company."

You may wish to do some top executive cultivation in the financial community as a part of your investor relations program, so that the name of your company will become better known in top financial circles. This, too, is part of your investor relations program, but you should not confuse it with the problem of getting information across to those who use the information.

Another example of the importance of knowing where to direct your efforts occurs in the case of the commercial bank. There are persons in the commercial bank who are interested in your company from the point of view of the regular commercial banking business—loans, deposits, corporate trust, etc. There are others in a bank who analyze your securities as a medium for investment in the accounts managed by the personal trust department. The commercial banker does not and should not pass on the information he receives to the security analyst in his bank. They are in different departments, very much separated, and they should be.

Visualize the reaction of an investor who employs the personal trust department of a bank to give impartial advice on investing his funds. Suppose that person found out that the bank bought securities of certain companies in the personal trust accounts in order to influence those companies to do commercial banking business with it. There might be good grounds for a law suit in such a case. The commercial banking and trust department must be absolutely and completely separate. Some companies have made the mistake of opening deposit accounts with commercial banks because those banks held a large amount of their securities in personal trust accounts and pension funds. This may have been due, in some instances, to the fact that representatives of commercial banking departments have hinted that because the personal trust department holds a large amount of securities, it would be well to do commercial banking business with the bank. Anyone who makes such an intimation should be told that the recipient is not quite that naive.

Keeping the commercial bankers who lend you money informed is quite necessary, but it is a separate operation. It might serve a purpose to include them in meetings with security analysts and send them the same information; however, their different interest in your company should be recognized. Reaching them will not substitute for covering the security analysts in the same organization, and you are not restricted in the type of forecast material you give commercial bankers. They are insiders and should not trade in your stock.

Some investment bankers, in order to get underwriting business, have insinuated that they should be given business because they have so much stock under their control in nominee names. This is so wrong that you might even consider taking up the matter with the Securities and Exchange Commission. In any event, such tactics should be enough to convince you not to use them as investment bankers.

Getting back to the security analysts, there are all degrees of experience and specialization to be found among the analysts. In experience, they range from beginners to those who have spent many years in the field. A company is naturally most interested in reaching the knowledgeable analyst, no matter what his age. Since an investor relations program must be a long term project, the inexperienced analysts should also be included, because the earlier they get to know about your company, the better.

There is a wide variation in specialization among analysts. Some firms handling a large volume of investments may have a sizeable analytical staff, divided into different industry groups, with one or more analysts working on just one group—such as utilities, rails, oils, chemicals, etc. On the other hand, small investment firms may have only a few or even just one man doing analysis work on interesting situations as they arise. In fact, in small brokerage houses, the partners who do the brokerage work also may be doing analytical work. They should be included, if they are interested in your company, just as much as the specialist.

With all this about "Who is who?" among the analysts group, you may conclude that cultivating the analysts is a hopeless task and that it is very difficult to seek out the ones who are actually interested in your company. Not at all; it is relatively easy. The number of analysts to be kept informed for a large company is only a small fraction of the number of its stockholders. And the analysts can be located with reasonable effort.

There are two schools of thought regarding which analysts to cultivate. Some companies use the selective approach. They limit their cultivation to the senior analysts who are the leaders and opinion makers. Companies that take this approach claim that it is a waste of time to cultivate a broad group including the junior analyst. They say the juniors follow the leaders. There is a danger in carrying this too far because a company may give the impression of playing favorites, and this will damage their image. You need to keep equally informed all analysts who are interested in your company. As time goes on the juniors will step into the senior positions and the groundwork will then pay off.

Building a List

The total membership in the analysts' societies includes all types of analysts interested in utilities, industrials, municipal bonds, etc. The membership requirements of the societies are not uniform and there are many included in the list who are really not security analysts. There are some who work for industrial companies, service organizations and so forth. The Directory is coded as to the type of industry in which the analysts are primarily interested. This coding is not altogether complete and should not be fully relied on. Not all analysts are members of the societies; therefore the Directory does not give a complete list.

How, specifically, can you build a list of analysts who are interested in your company?

First on your list should be the institutional holders and large owners of your securities. Study your stock and bond records for this information. You can find out readily who should be on the list in each such organization by a simple letter. The letter should state that you wish to know who is interested in analyzing the securities of your company, and to whom written material should be directed. Sometimes large organizations prefer that you send material to their library.

There are three organizations in New York which should be next on the list of every company with securities publicly held. They are the rating agencies—Fitch Investor's Service, Moody's Investors Service, and Standard and Poor's Corporation. These organizations are such an important part of the financial community that they are described separately in Chapter 10. It is necessary to understand thoroughly what they do, what they want to know about your company, how to furnish information to them and how to handle your relationship with them. These matters are covered in that chapter. Suffice it to repeat here that their ratings of publicly held securities have an important bearing on the quality and price appraisal by most investors; and their many publications, which are used almost universally by analysts, may be as important in furnishing information about your company as the material you send out directly.

It was stated above that a majority of analysts throughout the country are members of their local financial analysts' society, and that these societies are members of the Financial Analysts Federation. A good method to use to determine who is interested in your company is as follows: After you have given a speech about your company before one of the societies, send out a return postcard to the entire membership of the Federation. Ask those who wish a copy of the talk and who wish to be placed on the mailing list to return the attached postcard. This can be handled easily by using the up-to-date address plates maintained by the mailing house facilities (Ace Press and Letter Company, Inc., 9 Murray Street, New York City 10007) of the Federation and the New York Society. The mailing house will send out the card for you. The cost will include the mailing and printing cost and a moderate fee paid to the Federation for the use of the list. The number of return cards you will receive will depend on the nature of your company. A large company might receive a 20% return. Don't use the Directory for this purpose; it is not corrected for current changes.

To build a list of non-members is not quite as easy. You may ask an underwriting house that is familiar with your company to suggest a list of names of persons who might be interested. Write directly to these persons and ask if they wish to be included. You may wish to refer to directories of certain types of large institutional investors as a source of names.

You now have a list started, and you should use every opportunity to build it. For example, when you appear at a meeting of an analysts' society, be sure to have cards available which the audience can fill out. If new names appear, write those persons a letter asking if they wish to be added. The same applies when you have a Due Diligence Meeting prior to the sale of your securities, or other similar types of meetings.

For some industries, there are splinter groups of analysts who meet on an informal basis to discuss problems of that industry. At some of their meetings they have industry representation. If your company is in such an industry, you should know about these meetings and who attends as they represent the core of specialists in that field.

There are other types of people who should be prominent on your financial list. If you are listed on a stock exchange, there is the specialist assigned to your stock on the trading floor. Get to know him personally.

As you develop a list, you will encounter some special situations which exist for some types of investors. For example, one organization may manage the investments for more than one investment company. You will only need to cover one analyst for all the investment companies in the group. The same idea applies to the fire and casualty insurance companies; there may be a number of different companies in one group. These special situations will become apparent as you become more familiar with the financial community.

In New York City, members of the financial community can obtain annual reports, quarterly reports and other material such as 10-K's and proxy statements from The New York Clearance Systems, Inc. This organization maintains copies of financial material of 14,000 companies which are sent out on request. The companies pay a service charge to the New York Clearance Systems, Inc. to provide this service to the street. Annual and quarterly reports are sent out free upon request. There is a charge for other material such as a 10-K. They also have an office in San Francisco.

The Security Dealers

If your securities are traded over-the-counter, a worthwhile group to know about is the security dealers who make a market in your issues throughout the country. As we suggested in Chapter 10, you can find out from some dealer the list of firms that are included in the quotation sheets published by the National Quotation Bureau, Inc., 116 Nassau Street, New York City. The importance and position of the dealers should be thoroughly understood. You will wish to consider sending written material to them, the effect of loss of dealer interest when a stock is listed, etc. Payment of soliciting dealers' fees is covered in Chapter 9. Be sure to include them in your investor relations program, particularly if your stock is over-the-counter.

Senior Security Holders

Holders of your senior securities should be on your list to regularly contact as part of your investor relations program. However, the information you give out can be quite different. They are insiders and can be treated as such. You can give them forecast financial plans. Commercial bankers, whom we have already referred to, are in this group. However, in your contact with this group, you should make it clear that the information is for their interest in your loans or investments in your senior securities only, and *in no way should be used for decisions regarding your common stock.*

Reviewing Your Mailing List

Having now started a list, you should comb it to make certain that you do not have duplications, with too many people from one organization, etc. As an example, one company sent complete sets of material to four members of a small investment advisory firm who were members of the New York Society of Security Analysts, Inc. At various times each had signed cards given by the company saying that they would like their names added to the mailing list. Neither knew the others had signed. This was a waste for all concerned. An annual review of the mailing list should be used to iron out such duplication, to take care of changes of address and title and so on. The annual review letter should include:

1. A statement that the company is pleased to have the person on their mailing list; that it hopes all desired information is being received and that, if further information is needed, the person is invited to write or telephone, or call in person. Be sure to indicate which executives should be contacted by the analysts.
2. A list of those who are being sent the information in the same firm. Ask whether all the names should be continued or any added.

3. A request to make any changes in titles or spelling, etc.
4. A return, stamped postcard to cover the information above.

When the annual review is done, you may be surprised at how many changes of addresses occur. When the stock market is booming analysts are successful and many move from one job to another in order to get an increase in salary. When the stock market falls, firms in the financial community tighten their belts and analysts have to seek new jobs. If you do not review your mailing list once a year, it may get badly out of wack. This job should be turned over to an assistant who finally cleans it up after a mailing, with phone calls to take care of the batch of cards that are not returned. You don't want to create ill-will by taking an important analyst off your mailing list.

Some companies apparently do not feel that it is necessary to develop a mailing list. They follow the policy of sending their annual report to all members of the analysts' societies. The number of annual reports that get thrown in the waste basket each year in the financial community is phenomenal. That is a waste of stockholders' money. A company should know which analysts are interested. One of the largest manufacturing companies discovered that most analysts get their annual report as a result of the general mailing to stockholders, and arranged their mailing to analysts to prevent duplication.

Now what do we do for the analysts in order to give them all the facts?

How to Tell What Analysts Want

Don't sit back in your office and try to imagine what the analysts want and how they want it. There may be great mystery as to what the uninformed investor wants, and you may never know the exact answer. Surveys on the uninformed investor seem to differ widely. However, with the informed group you don't have to guess. You can hit the bull's-eye just by asking. You should have close contact with a few top analysts representing different types of organizations. They can act as your listening posts and tell you what information they want. Don't use just one analyst, because each analyst has special methods of approach, and special likes and dislikes. You will not reach the needs of most analysts if you rely on one as a guide. Five analysts ought to give you a good cross-section, and their ideas should be representative of the analysts as a whole. Be sure that you explain your objective carefully and make certain that they understand that you are seeking criticism and suggestions; otherwise, they may take the easy way out by flattering you rather than being critical. This isn't something to be brushed aside lightly, or you will get poor results. It is surprising how far off base companies sometimes get with regard to the things they think analysts want to know or are worried about. And when companies fail to cover material which analysts consider necessary, it creates a bad impression.

Not let's go over the different media that are available to a company. As pointed out, how much and what is used will depend on the type of company, its size and other special characteristics. It is well to divide the media into two types—personal contact and written material.

Personal Contacts

Financial analysts' society luncheons—Companies probably achieve the most personal contact with security analysts through appearance at the regular luncheon meetings of the New York Society of Security Analysts. The notice for the meetings goes to all the 5,000 membership but attendance ranges from 75 to 400. Of the total membership, many specialize in certain types of securities and do not have an interest in securities outside of their field. Generally, small or closely held companies do not appear on the program, because there is not enough interest.

The Program Committee of the New York Society is divided into subcommittees which cover industrials, railroads and utilities; and is further subdivided by industry specialization. These subcommittees arrange the program about six months ahead. In most instances, companies are invited to appear. However, if the management of a company feels that it would like to be included and has not received an invitation, it should contact the Committee and inquire whether arrangements can be made. The company should feel no compunction whatsoever about asking. The program includes the top companies in the country and fills up so fast that a company should ask for a spot at the beginning of the year in order to be included. An appearance before the New York Society of Security Analysts every two or three years would be about the best a company could expect because of the large number of candidates. If the Committee should decide that there would not be sufficient interest at the time, the company should not feel hurt. It merely will have to use other media to get its story across.

Some investor relations experts of large companies feel that meetings of the New York Society of Security Analysts are a waste of time. They say that such meetings include mostly juniors and generalists who are not the leaders. These experts prefer to cultivate the leading analysts. It may be a mistake to forego the opportunity to appear before the New York Society even though some of the criticisms are justified. It does represent a way for a company to get before an open forum with its investor relations program. And it opens up the opportunity to use the Federation's mailing list to send a card asking if any analysts throughout the company would like a copy of the speech as we have explained above.

The other societies are much smaller than the New York Society, and their membership is somewhat different in character. Their meetings are less frequent. If a company wishes to appear at their meetings, it should make it a point to find out how they operate.

Luncheons given by a company—At the analysts' societies' luncheons, the companies are the guests. A company may decide to give a luncheon on its own for the security analysts rather than appear at one of the societies' meetings for the following reasons:

1. It wants a select list of analysts.
2. It may wish to include non-members; there are numerous analysts who are not members.
3. The societies' programs may already be filled.
4. It may wish to alternate between the society's and its own luncheon for variety.
5. It may not be large enough to be included on the program.

There are a number of ways to handle these luncheons. The company can give a large luncheon for as many as 200, or a series of smaller ones. The latter give the company officials a better opportunity to get to know the individual analysts personally, but they are more time-consuming.

One of the problems which arises in connection with giving a luncheon for analysts is the invitation list. If a company doesn't have its own list, it will have to try to get suggestions from an investment banking firm or commercial bank which is familiar with the analysts who might wish to attend. A company may also want to send invitations to all the members of the local society. If this is done, caution should be used not to include anything in the invitation intimating that the luncheon is under the auspices of the society. If invitations are sent to such a large number as the membership of the New York Society, it will obviously be necessary to have return cards so that the company will know how many to expect. Additional planning is necessary to keep things under control.

It is possible that more acceptances may be received than can be accommodated. In order to be able to handle such a possibility, the letter of invitation should state that if the number of acceptances exceeds the capacity of the luncheon room, then selection will be made on some defined equitable basis, such as one person to a firm, first acceptances considered first, etc. Those who cannot be accommodated should be sent a letter of explanation, and an alternative should be given to them so that they can hear the same story. It should be remembered that analysts dislike very much being excluded from a luncheon if they have sent in a reply card that they will attend and have a real interest in the company's securities. Don't be too exclusive in your invitations, but don't be so apprehensive of offending someone that you hesitate to hold a private luncheon.

Receptions—After you have presented your story at an analysts' society or given a large luncheon, you may wish to hold a reception on the afternoon of the same day. At a large luncheon you have an opportunity to tell your story and answer some questions; however, you cannot speak to all analysts personally, and a reception affords this opportunity.

There are some details which should be followed in order for a reception to be effective. They may seem obvious, but enough companies miss them to make them worth mentioning. In New York, it should be held from about 4:15 to 6:00 p.m. This gives those who wish to catch a 5:15 train an opportunity to drop in, and also allows time for those who can't leave the office until 5:00. It should be held in a place convenient to the financial center. At least four officers of a company should be present so that if 100 or more analysts attend, there will be adequate coverage and the analysts won't spend the time talking with each other. One company representative could be assigned the job of making certain that the officers circulate so that all analysts will be covered. Some analysts may monopolize an officer. The officers should have name tags including their titles as it is embarrassing to talk to an official without knowing his position. You may wish to have name tags for the guests as well so that your officers will know with whom they are talking.

Invitations should be sent out saying who will be present from the company, with a return card so that the company will know how many expect to attend. It is not sufficient to issue an invitation at the luncheon held on the same day. By that time many of the analysts may already have accepted other engagements.

If a company has already told its story at a regular luncheon meeting of an analysts' society, it is unnecessary to repeat the story again at a reception in the afternoon. There may be an exception when there were some who could not be accommodated at a luncheon. Then the company may repeat the story before the reception. The invitation to the reception should make this item of the agenda clear, so that those who have already heard it will not have to sit through it again.

If a company does not hold a luncheon, it may hold a general meeting in the afternoon and tell its story the same way as it would at a luncheon. Timing is important. It should not be too early, or else there will be poor attendance. It should start at 4:00 p.m. This method has an advantage in that a larger number can be accommodated than could be included at a luncheon, and there is no need to have as close account of those who will attend. The principal disadvantage is that people may wander in late and miss part of the talk, which would not happen at a luncheon.

With regard to invitations to an afternoon meeting, they should be handled similarly as those to a luncheon, but because of the greater number that can be accommodated, the invitations can be sent on a much broader scale. In addition, invitations might be issued to the security dealers, already mentioned. A company might even include an advertisement in financial papers announcing the meeting. If it is done on such a broad scale, those answering the advertisement should be requested to write or telephone the company giving the reason for their interest. Then tickets should be issued to those who request to attend. This will help reduce freeloaders. In any of these large meetings there are bound to be a certain percentage of freeloaders; a company must accept that as inevitable.

Due Diligence Meetings—When a utility company offers securities at competitive bidding, the general practice is to hold an open meeting in the financial community in which most prospective bidders will be located, generally New York City, Chicago or Boston. It is advisable to hold it at a place convenient to the financial community. Most often, if a company does not have an office in New York, the place is a conference room in one of the commercial banks with which the company does business. It is conducted by the executives of the issuing company, but also will include lawyers, accountants and perhaps technical experts.

The announcement of the meeting is made in the advertisement for bids. Some companies, in addition, send a letter to the analysts on their list, telling them of the meeting. Whether or not the letter is sent, many of those who attend will be analysts.

This meeting is referred to by the term *Due Diligence Meeting* or *information meeting.* It is not a legal requirement of the Securities Act. It grew up as a matter of practice. Its purpose is to give prospective bidders an opportunity to meet with company officials and make sure that they have used "due diligence" in obtaining all information affecting the securities which will be sold to the public. Underwriters are subject to certain penalties under the Securities Act if they fail to use due diligence in investigating the securities. A thorough analysis of a company generally should include a visit with the management to clarify any questions which may arise about the company.

This meeting may be held in the morning or afternoon. In setting the time, it is important not to have it conflict with Due Diligence meetings which may be held by other companies offering securities. A conflict may reduce the audience for one of the companies.

It should be held at least five days before the bidding date, so that there will be sufficient time to use the information in arriving at the price to bid. Some companies have made the mistake of holding the meeting one or two days before the bidding. By that time the bidders have already completed their analytical work. The meeting includes a coverage of the prospectus and time for questions. The company officials should take the opportunity to tell the same story as it would at a meeting with analysts.

The practice evolved for companies to use this meeting as an opportunity to cultivate the financial community. In other words, they included the Due Diligence Meeting as part of their investor relations program. Thus, in order to win good will, the company officials made more out of the Due Diligence Meeting than a mere formality. This proved advisable, since many people who attended the open meeting were not necessarily interested in the particular security being offered, such as a bond, but were there to get information about the company which would help in analysis of all the company's securities.

If a company has told its story at an open meeting with analysts in the same financial community within a reasonable time or expects to have such a meeting in the not too distant future, then presenting a complete story at the Due Diligence Meeting may result in duplication. Duplication of effort through Due Diligence Meetings and analysts meetings should be eliminated through proper programing.

Some companies feel that it is preferable to treat the Due Diligence Meeting as strictly a routine matter and not try to make it a part of their investor relations program. They limit the meeting to a review of the prospectus and a question period. Their argument is that the people who attend are relatively limited and not necessarily those who would be covered as part of an investor relations program. This may be a poor procedure and may build ill will in the financial community. Those who attend generally expect something more than just a routine review of the prospectus. What a company should do will depend on what else it does in keeping investors informed. The company must weigh the possible adverse reaction on the part of some people who attend if it is strictly a routine matter.

A possible substitution for a Due Diligence Meeting is to advertise that company officials will be available at a designated place on a certain day for a period, say, between 10:00 a.m. and 4:00 p.m., during which time the officials of the company will answer questions. Interested persons may call for an appointment or just come and wait their turn. This method has certain advantages and disadvantages. The company knows the individuals with whom it is talking, and it assures that any unauthorized statements will not appear in the press. This method has the disadvantage of preventing an open discussion of the company's situation. Some of the questions one person asks may turn out to be of interest to the others who would attend an open meeting. This type of Due Diligence Meeting started to be used a number of years ago by some companies after the Securities and Exchange Commission investigated certain companies for information given out about new offerings which got into the press, but was not included in the prospectus.

A company will have to use caution about the type of information it gives out around the time of a sale of a security, to any investor or prospective investor. The Securities Act of 1933 limits such information. In your personal contacts with investors during this period, you will have to explain why you are under wraps and are limited in what you can say. This explanation will have to be handled tactfully because it is not appreciated by some analysts. The value of a meeting with security analysts around the time of a sale of a security has been largely limited by this factor. This provision of the Act does not apply to giving information to potential underwriting firms, provided they do not turn around and pass it on to dealers and investors.

If a company's securities are offered publicly through a negotiated financing rather than competitively, the principal underwriter will undoubtedly wish company officials to discuss its operations with members of the underwriting group. This is a closed meeting and is run by the head underwriter. Attendance is limited. For this reason, it may play a less important part in an investor relations program.

Dinners—Dinners are not very effective in New York City because of the problems of getting people to attend, due to the commuting problem. Dinners may best be used for a small, special group. There are exceptions; the New York Society of Security Analysts has arranged some very successful dinner meetings with large companies. And outside of New York City, dinner meetings may be more successful.

General considerations regarding meetings—How often should some form of large meeting be held in an important financial community? This depends on the nature of the company and the problems of the analysts in keeping informed. If its operations are subject to change, if they are complicated in nature and require a lot of explanation, then as often as once a year may be necessary. For a stable company, every two years may be sufficient. The frequency of meetings should also depend on other factors than stability. How large is your company? How well are your management policies known throughout the country? Is yours an easily understood type of operation?

Variety may be injected into the program by using different types of meetings. However, coverage is most important, and don't attempt to achieve variety if it results in any loss of coverage.

It is worthwhile to stress again that a company should be meticulous not to have its meeting conflict with a meeting held by a similar type of company, so that analysts who may wish to attend both will have to make a choice. Both meetings suffer as a result of these conflicts. The program for the analysts' societies can be readily determined by checking with a committee member. Dates of other Due Diligence meetings, luncheons, etc., can be obtained by asking a leading underwriting house to check for possible conflicts. There are some times when meetings can't be held successfully, such as when a local analysts' society is having its annual outing or the local members are attending the national convention. Check with well-informed analysts to avoid such conflicts.

Special types of meetings—There may be new ways to present your company's story. A major oil company got the idea that junior analysts in the New York area might be interested in a course in the analysis of oil companies' securities. They set up such a program, with the top men in various phases of their company's operations as speakers. It turned out to be such a success that senior analysts clamored to be included and the company had to repeat it many times. It was also held in four cities outside New York. While the course was directed on the subject of the oil business in general, it won many friends for the company and provided a better understanding of its operations on the part of investors. Some other large companies with operations which were hard to analyze adopted the idea.

Trips and plant visits—Visits to a company's properties may prove to be an excellent medium to use in order to give analysts a thorough knowledge of a company's operation. Such trips should not include too many guests, otherwise there is not sufficient opportunity for individual attention. About 25 guests is a good number, depending, of course, on the nature of the trip. This necessitates having a series of trips in order to cover a large number of analysts. However, such tours can be spread over a long period of time so as not to put a burden on the company's staff. There may be situations in which trips can be arranged for four or five analysts, depending on what is sought to be accomplished. In a few instances, trips for large numbers have been most successful, but don't try to do a mass job just for the sake of coverage.

Top personnel should be available for a substantial part of the trip, so that analysts can get a view of the management and have their questions fully answered. The financial man should be on hand at practically all times. On one particular trip the analysts were handled by salesmen. They did a good job in explaining the product, but were totally lost on all financial questions. The analysts received a very unfavorable impression of the company. Another reminder: Don't wear out the analysts so that they can't absorb what you show them. On the other hand, don't make it a junket. You will lose their respect. It should be a working session, so that when it is over, the analysts will feel that they have made a worthwhile addition to their knowledge.

A trip has the advantage of so thoroughly acquainting analysts that they will tell other analysts about your company's operations. Thus, the benefit is not limited to just those who go on the trip. Furthermore, once they have been on a trip, there is no reason to include them on another. They have a lasting knowledge of your company. Other types of cultivation, such as luncheons, do not have as lasting an effect and must be repeated regularly.

Personal calls and individual contacts—Certain organizations and large investors may deserve personal calls, particularly the rating agencies; they may be high on the list for most companies. Also holders of your senior securities if they are limited in number should be called on regularly.

How far you can go with personal contacts depends on your location in relation to the large financial centers. Some companies make it a practice of keeping a list of large investors, such as insurance companies, investment companies, large individual holders, etc., segregated by cities. Then, when one of their senior officers is in one of the cities, he calls on them.

When the financial officer of the company is in a large financial center and finds that he has free time, he might invite five or ten analysts to join him at an informal luncheon. This can result in a two-way benefit. The financial officer can check with these analysts on their feeling towards the company and its program to keep them informed.

Your personal contacts with the well-informed analysts represents one of the best ways of keeping a complete story about your company before the financial opinion makers. How far you can go in this regard depends on the circumstances surrounding your company.

Presentations by a company—All types of formal presentations before a group of analysts—at luncheons, Due Diligence Meetings, etc.—are basically similar, and there are certain rules which should be followed.

It is not so important whether one man does the speaking or a team approach is used, so long as the speakers are senior officers who can speak with authority for the company. If one man speaks, it generally should be the President or the Financial Vice President. Due Diligence Meetings which are held in connection with an offering of securities at competitive bidding should not be conducted by an outside lawyer. It gives the impression that outside counsel really runs the company. In special situations, there may be a place for men in production, research, etc., to explain an important part of a company's operations.

A careful observation of timing is essential. Nothing will defeat the effectiveness of a meeting more than too long a talk. A good rule of thumb to follow for a regular meeting with analysts is a 30-minute talk and 30 minutes for questions. A pause between the talk and question period gives those a chance to leave who may have to return to their offices. Even if more than one person talks, no more than 40 minutes should be taken for the formal presentation. At a luncheon, remember to finish everything by 2 o'clock. People have to get back to their offices. If there seem to be too many questions, then close the meeting at 2:00 and suggest that anyone who has more questions may stay after the close.

What to cover will of course depend on each company. However, don't waste time on history. Analysts are familiar with the background material on your company. They are interested primarily in those factors which will affect the future. What are the problems the company has to face, and the favorable developments? They will be most interested in items which will eventually affect the balance sheet and income statements.

Expansion requirements and methods of financing are most important—particularly, cover factors about which the analysts may have unjustified prejudices or may not understand. If something is said about earnings per share and dividend policy, it should be saved for last. We will subsequently comment on how to handle forecasts of earnings and dividends.

One of the important factors analysts are weighing when they hear the management of a company present its story is the quality of the management itself. It will be judged on the manner in which it presents its story as well as what is included. Analysts realize that the company is dependent on the quality of its management if it is to prosper.

If a company has appeared recently before the same group of analysts, it may wish to vary the type of material presented. However, be careful not to develop such a novel approach that the analysts will receive the impression that the company just doesn't have a firm understanding of what makes securities sound. A standard type of approach, even with the risk of being repetitive, is the safest and will produce the best results.

Talking from notes is preferred to reading a speech. Enthusiasm in a talk before analysts is naturally to be desired. However, it should be based on facts. Occasionally, the president of a company will go too far in terms of unrealistic "dreams." This definitely creates an unfavorable impression unless the "dreams" are clearly labeled as such.

There are various aids that may be used in presenting a story. What is used will have to depend on the preferences of the person who gives the speech. Beware of the use of wall charts or slides. They may seem attractive to the management, but a chart is no good unless all the audience can see all of it, including the bottom line. The bottom line is one of the two scales and if it cannot be read, the chart loses its significance. Have you ever sat in a room with more than three or four rows of seats and visualized how high a wall chart must be in order for the person in the back row to see the bottom line?

If you do use charts, have someone inspect the meeting room ahead of time and design the charts and the stand so that everyone can see them.

One way to solve the problem of using charts is to print them in a small booklet which can be handed out to the audience and referred to by the speaker. This has three advantages: it can be easily seen, the audience can make notes on the charts as the speaker talks and it can be filed for reference purposes. It has one disadvantage: the audience may thumb through it during the talk and not give full attention to the speaker. The advantages seem to far outweigh the disadvantages, as compared to wall charts or slides.

Films showing a company's plant or operations may be effective if they are brief shots and do not take too much time. A full length film may take away from the time allotted for the talk. The full-length film might be fitted in by showing it during the lunch hour prior to the talk, or a film might be used at a reception just prior to the social part. If so, it should be announced in the invitation. Do not use the film, whether it be long or short, unless it really adds to the presentation and can be properly fitted in.

Even if a speaker does not read his speech, it is well to have copies available to distribute after the meeting. This guards against misunderstanding what the speaker has said. We have already explained how a card can be sent to the entire membership of the Financial Analysts Federation asking if they wish a copy.

If a company is scheduled to appear at an analysts' society in another city in the near future, it should wait until after that appearance to broadcast copies. Otherwise, the story will already have been read by these analysts. Copies of the speech should also be sent to all those already on the company's mailing list.

If a company does not have copies of the speech to hand out at the end of the meeting, it may wish to have copies of a few pages of the material covering subjects which are difficult to explain, such as earnings adjustments, etc. This may help prevent misinterpretation of statements.

An effort at one time was made to keep meetings of the New York Society of Security Analysts "off the record." However, there were so many slips and annoyances as a result that all speakers are told that anything they say may be quoted. Even if the press is not present, the far-flung wire system of some of the large brokerage houses is so great that a quotation transmitted over those wire systems may get to many financial people just as readily as a quotation in the press. Therefore, in large meetings a company would be unwise to assume that it can be "off the record." And the question may be raised as to whether it should be off the record. Sometimes the press does attend, and it is well to have a press release available. This should be handed out with copies of the talk. If no copy of the talk is made but a press release is available, there should be sufficient copies for all those present.

Standing exhibits around the room may be effective and add a sparkle to the meeting. This all depends on whether they tie in with the factors affecting the company's securities.

Some companies provide a door prize of one of the company's products. If this is to be done, the product should definitely be tied in with the company in some way. It should, under no circumstances, be used merely to win goodwill, or be so elaborate as to give an impression of trying to influence the analysts. It will only backfire. Unless a company is careful, this is a practice which should be frowned upon.

We have referred to New York City as the principal financial center. It is that. However, there are many other important financial communities, and in a complete investor relations program other cities should be included, if investors in those communities are interested in the company's securities. If a company does not have a national following, the financial center nearest its office may be more important than New York City.

Written Material

Annual reports—First on the list of written material, of course, is the annual report. Some companies design their annual report primarily for the security analysts and use it as the principal written medium to get across their story to them. There are very few annual reports which are written without being partly directed at the security analysts.

Writing annual reports is not an easy task. By the time all the "brass" has approved it, the unfortunate person in charge of the report is about ready to jump out a window. The real audience has been lost sight of, the lawyers have cut out much interesting material and fears have been expressed by someone in top management about practically every word.

One reason why some annual reports seem to fail is that they are not directed to a clearly defined audience. The report finally becomes a story by the management, which makes very good reading for them and the directors, but for no one else. This failure may result from the fact that the person in charge of the report is not truly aware of the audience to whom the report should be directed. If he has selected an audience, he should make it known to those who contribute to and have the final say on the report.

Obviously, many groups have to be kept in mind in writing a report. Material should not be included which will harm employee or union relations, because some of the reports are bound to get into their hands. Nothing should be included which will adversely affect customer relations, or public relations. Nevertheless, if an effort is made to write an annual report for use by directors, uninformed stockholders, informed stockholders, the employees, consumers, etc., the report is bound to fail.

In some companies, the public relations expert is allowed to usurp the job of writing the annual report away from the Financial Vice President. Unless he is an expert in finance, he may be so carried away with general public relations ideas as to miss the audience to which the report should be intended. Of course, the public relations expert should be consulted to make certain that the report does not include anything at cross-purposes with a public relations program, and, at its best, he should work as part of the team. The important point is that whoever works on the report should have as his goal the problem of achieving communication of the financial story, and not just of producing a report that looks well.

With regard to annual reports, analysts differ as to what they desire in general design. Some want no pictures and charts, whereas some want a lot. It seems best to reach a balance. Include pictures or charts so that they add to the story. Mere glamorization for its own sake is not impressive to the analysts. Charts should be so designed that the analysts can read off the figures if they wish to use them in a story. For example, bar charts are very effective when the figures are also shown within the bars. But be sure to make the report easy to read and interesting, because a company is competing for an analyst's time. During the report season, the financial community literally rains annual reports.

Size of the report would seem to be unimportant, but this is not so. Analysts prefer the regular letter size of 8½ by 11, approximately. It is much easier to file than one of odd size.

In designing your annual report, don't try too hard for variety each year and thus hurt the effectiveness of the report. The form of the report may seem monotonous to you, but not to the audience which receives it once a year. A similar format makes it easier for analysts to absorb.

There is only one theme—What Happened Financially and Why. Each annual report should be complete in itself. If you have covered a subject in a previous annual report, but it is still a necessary part of this year's report, you must repeat it again.

A good example of a company's efforts to tell what happened to earnings during the year and why, is a table regularly included in a company's annual report, regardless of whether earnings go up or down, as follows:

Primary earnings a share—Current year	$0.00
—Previous year	0.00
Change—Current year over previous year	$0.00
Analysis of Major Causal Factors	
Sales-related factors:	
Change in sales volume and product mix	$0.00
Lower selling prices	0.00
Total sales-related factors	0.00
Cost-related factors:	
Lower raw material prices	0.00
Higher manufacturing costs	(0.00)
Higher non-manufacturing costs	(0.00)
Lower start-up costs	0.00
Total cost-related factors	(0.00)
Other factors:	
Lower interest expense	0.00
Higher income credits—Net	0.00
Lower tax rate	0.00
Other	(0.00)
Total other factors	0.00
Change—Current year over previous year	$0.00

A good report should be complete, it should be easy to read and it should have analytical qualities. Once you have achieved a good format keep it the same and improve on it, don't try to change it.

A good way to aid in designing an annual report so that it will fit the needs of the audience, is to ask five of your analyst friends to go over carefully last year's annual report, and then meet with them at a luncheon at which you sit back and listen to them go over the report, page by page, saying what they like, what they don't like and what is missing. Specifically tell them that you want them to be critical, and when they are critical don't defend your position. Take notes and go back to your office and mull over how their thoughts can help you do a better job next year.

The Securities and Exchange Commission's regulations regarding material companies are required to include in annual reports is a push in the right direction. However, it is a sad commentary on management that it has to be told what to report to the people the management is supposed to be working for—the stockholders. It just shows how far the arrogance of some top managements have gone, to the point of thinking that the company is their baby to satisfy their own personal greed rather than to be run on a basis of high standards for all concerned.

In Exhibit 12-1 at the end of the chapter is an outline of ideas and material you might wish to use as a check list when you get to write your annual report.

Statistical book—Some companies, especially those in regulated industries which have to file considerable amounts of statistical information with public agencies, use a combination of the annual report and a statistical book for security analysts. It may be difficult for some of these companies to satisfy analysts completely with an annual report. There may be so much extra statistical information of interest to them, that it cannot all be presented in the annual report. However, don't compile a statistical report unless there is some worthwhile information which can be of real use.

What a company includes in the annual report will depend to some extent on whether or not it plans to issue a statistical booklet for the analysts. A relatively uncomplex annual report, containing the essential information which would go out to all the stockholders and a detailed statistical book for the analysts, would appear to be the ideal combination. The analysts, however, do not like to have a company cut down the annual report to a bare skeleton, even if the statistical booklet is issued. If a statistical book is issued simultaneously with an annual report and reference is made to the statistical book in the report, then the annual report can be reduced in size and the excluded material put in the statistical book.

The purpose of a statistical book is more than just a supplement to the annual report. It may be used to gather together a large quantity of information for the analysts which originally appeared in many different sources. It may be used by some companies to present explanatory information about operations and finances which cannot be included in the annual report. For example, in the operations of a company in the food products business, the hedging of wheat plays an important part and has an effect on the income statement and balance sheet. It is somewhat complicated, but most important to a thorough understanding of the company's finances. A section on this subject in a statistical book was very effectively employed to educate the analysts.

Analysts vary in their preferences for design of a good statistical book. A combination of good charts, tables and explanatory material seem to fit the needs of the majority. Pictures generally need not be included unless they contribute to the analysts' understanding in some special way—perhaps, in areas of new technology; for example, pictures of the company's products or its various plants may help.

A statistical book with tables alone just does not do the job it is supposed to accomplish. An explanation of the important factors affecting the company's operation is necessary. Elaborate footnotes are well worthwhile, but be sure to have them in large print. If they are used, then make them readable.

It is an important decision whether or not to issue a statistical booklet concurrently with the annual report and, in effect, make it a supplement for the analysts. There is another choice, and that is to issue the statistical booklet every two years or as the occasion seems to necessitate it. Do not decide to issue a statistical book until you have arrived at a definite decision on this point. It will influence what you will include in it.

In a statistical booklet, the question often arises of whether a company should figure out the financial ratios, or leave them for the analysts to calculate. Some of the ratios, which are of a standard nature and figured the same by all analysts, such as earnings per share on total shares outstanding, should be included. There are many ratios which analysts have their own pet way of calculating. If you choose to figure those ratios, there should be included a detailed footnote stating how you did them, so that the analysts can see if it is in agreement with their own method.

In your development of a statistical book, you would do well to discuss it with about five analysts so that you will be sure of the data and ratios to include and how to present them.

10-K reports—Some companies send 10-K reports to analysts. This should not be a substitute for a complete annual report. One way to handle the distribution of the 10-K is to make a statement in the back of the annual report that the report will be furnished on request. Companies that have followed this policy find that there are relatively few requests for the report.

Quarterly reports—Annual reports become obsolete a few months after they are issued. Earnings and balance sheet items change and new developments arise regarding the company's operations. Interim reports are the ideal way to keep the investors up-to-date.

Quarterly seems to be the best time interval for issuing such interim reports. Analysts are quite outspoken about their need of such reports.

Some types of companies have brought the quarterly report to perfection. They include an explanatory statement as to what has happened since the last report, three-months and 12-months comparative statements and a balance sheet. At least, include as much information as possible. If you can't furnish what analysts want in a quarterly report, then accept it as one of your problems to explain why. Don't think you can fool them; they are too close to too many companies, and know too much about financial statements.

Other written material—There are many other written media, such as prospectuses, general press releases, company house organs, court or government agency decisions, special reports, etc. All written material should be weighted as to the part it will play in keeping the analysts currently informed about all the company's operations. For example, a prospectus issued in connection with a new security offering should not be viewed as a legal requirement, but as an opportunity for a company to tell a real story, unless investors are already well informed through a recent annual report and statistical book.

Above all, don't burden analysts with written material which is not pertinent. They are deluged with reading material. The importance of laying out a program comes in right here. Planning will make it possible to see just what is required to do an effective investor relations job.

Don't overlook material published by others about your company, such as that by the three agencies, Fitch, Moody's and Standard and Poor's. The importance of the manuals for annual figures, etc. is covered in Chapter 10. In their regular current services they carry interim reports and other pertinent data.

Analytical material and opinions about a company are also furnished to investors in reports or studies made by security analysts in various types of financial firms. Often companies are asked to review these reports before they are sent out. A company should welcome this review as a real opportunity, since the reports may be given wide distribution. This can also prevent publication of material which may be erroneous. However, in reviewing the reports, make it clear that you are passing on the facts and not the opinions of the analyst who may cover forecast earnings.

The Financial Press

The financial press represents an excellent medium through which to disseminate information to investors. The approach is somewhat different from that used with the analysts. Very probably, a company will have someone handling press relations, and if there is such an expert, the financial officer may best work through him. The following comments are made with this in mind.

You cannot tell the press what, when and how to publish information. Editors publish what they wish, when they have space. But if you ignore them or fail to do your part with the press, you may not receive as much coverage as you would like, and some stories may be published which will not do justice to your operations. Treating the press fairly and keeping it informed produce the best results. A company representative should get to know the financial editors and their staffs personally, and get to know what, when and how they want material about his company.

The type of material will depend on the nature of your company. The test is whether it has a broad interest to the people who read the financial pages—or, occasionally, an interest even to the public at large. Earnings reports are a regular item. They should be comparative. Annual reports should be sent in with a press release. Changes in management get some play. Other items might include expansion programs, financing, new ideas on the science of management and advanced planning, new technology, etc. A speech made at an analysts' society is well worth sending in with a press release.

In sending in material to the large metropolitan newspapers, one copy should be sent to the financial editor. You should know who specializes in your type of company and also send him a copy. On each copy, mark the names of others on the same newspaper to whom you have also sent copies. When you are going to make a speech, send in a copy so that it arrives at the newspaper one day ahead of time. The time and day for release should be conspicuously marked on the release. For Sunday papers, the material should be in the hands of the press at least by Thursday evening. Except by pure mistake, the release date will be carefully respected. Some company officials are so afraid that a speech will appear in the press before it is given that they won't send in a copy until afterwards. If this is done, the papers can't print it until a day or so later and then it has lost its news value. When you do send in a speech or other material, indicate where you can be readily reached in case there are any questions, and how the newspaper can verify that the speech was delivered.

In building your personal relationship with the press, you should see that its members are invited to major meetings, such as stockholder meetings. When something important happens which the financial press considers newsworthy, one of the top men in your company should be available and willing to talk. The press should know who your spokesmen are and where they can be reached. If a large, unusual piece of financing has been announced and the press calls and cannot find anyone who will discuss the matter, the ill will resulting may not be overcome for a long time. Furthermore, the reporters will have to write a story based on inadequate information. It may hurt your company.

Whether or not your story will be printed will depend on its newsworthiness and also on the space available in the paper. It will also depend on how it has been handled and on the timing. Even if you have done a perfect job of presenting it to the press, there is terrific competition for the limited space available. Each paper has a limited number of pages in which to cram an almost limitless amount of possible copy. The editor has to use his best judgment under pressure and in a great hurry.

In addition to the newspapers, the wire services are very important—the Associated Press, United Press International, Dow-Jones and Company Ticker Reports, and Reuters. They should be at the top of your list. Magazines should not be overlooked. Getting attention by magazines is a much longer process and must be treated on an individual basis. In most instances, they prepare a long study rather than use spot news.

The press does not particularly care whether you handle your own press relations, or use an agent. If someone in your company has the time and can learn the proper way to handle it, you may get better coverage. There is always the personal relationship that can be developed, and, also, agents have to spread their efforts over a large number of companies.

Financial Advertising

Financial advertising may have a limited place in a company's program. The message should fit your particular need in communication with investors. If you are trying to reach the financial analysts, find out the few media they read in your field and design an advertisement which will catch their eye. They are unimpressed by run-of-the-mill material about dividend notices, etc. Don't waste your money on an advertisement unless you can give it sufficient attention, and even then it may be an ineffective way to reach the analysts.

Problems Encountered

Investor relations is not always a smooth road. Some problems are sure to develop. For example, a company cannot proceed very long without having to decide what to do about giving out forecast earnings.

Forecast Earnings

It should be amply clear, that a company cannot give forecast earnings and dividends to some investors and not all, because they would be giving a preference. If a company decides to give out such forecasts it must make them public.

When the Securities and Exchange Commission first became deeply interested in this subject, some people in the Commission pushed hard in favor of requiring companies to give out forecasts. The purpose was to put everybody on an equal basis and eliminate any preference to a few insiders. This sounds like a simple solution, but it isn't that easy.

Anyone familiar with earnings forecasts by companies is aware of the fact that they may be far off the mark. To this extent investors would be misled. Also, this would open up the door for unscrupulous management to make false forecasts in order to manipulate their stock. If the forecast is correct, management will get no credit for giving it out. If it is wrong management will lose creditability. In the long run, this would hurt the company's stockholders. Therefore, the most sensible approach is to be very clear with financial analysts that it is the company policy not to give out forecast earnings and dividends per share. Companies that have taken a strong stand on this point seem to have sounder investor relations in the long run.

A further question, however, arises as to what you should do if an analyst makes an erroneous earnings per share forecast? Should you do nothing or should you try to get it changed? No matter how carefully you proceed in trying to get the analyst back on track, you may reveal what you believe is a correct forecast. When you go that far, you have given out forecast earnings.

Let's take a case of an analyst who has forecast earnings per share for your company of $4. You believe earnings will be only $3. You tell him his forecast seems out of line. After some discussion, he corrects his forecast to $3.10 per share. Then you don't say anything. It is obvious that his forecast must agree reasonably well with your company's forecast. Then, for all practical purposes, you are on the spot of having given him your forecast and you should make it public, with all the problems which ensue from that.

Some companies claim that they can help an analyst correct an erroneous forecast without giving out the company's forecast. You would have to be very clever to do that juggling act.

Companies tussle with this problem because they worry about their stockholders being misled if an erroneous forecast by an analyst is not corrected. But who did the misleading, the analyst or the company? And how far does a company go in policing the market. Suppose an analyst has the same forecast earnings as the company and the analyst is pushing the stock even though it is selling at a very high price-earnings ratio and as a consequence the stock subsequently collapses. This kind of incorrect recommendation may have just as much adverse effect on the investors as a wrong earnings per share forecast. A reduction in price-earnings ratio from 20 to ten times has the same adverse effect on the market price as a 50% reduction in earnings per share.

There is no agreement in industry on how to handle the erroneous earnings forecasts by analysts. However, the cleanest approach would seem to be to tell analysts that management will help them with facts, but they will not comment on any forecast or opinion by an analyst.

This problem might be alleviated to some extent if the Securities and Exchange Commission required that an analyst state in any written report that the earnings per share forecast was the analyst's estimate and in no way reflected the opinion of company's management.

A company should be constantly on guard to avoid giving out inside information. It is illegal, but even more important it is unfair to its stockholders. This requires that directors and management who are privy to such information guard it with great care.

What we have just said does not mean that a company should hesitate to give out information which will help the analysts form their own judgment. There is a vast difference. In many cases, even the analyst who most persistently seeks an earnings forecast can be satisfied if you will discuss with him, realistically and in some detail, the factors which may affect earnings in the coming year, so that he will be able to make a reasonable forecast for himself. It is only that ultimate figure of forecast earnings and dividends which may get a company into serious difficulty.

Handling Emergencies

When an emergency arises which will have an important effect on your company, be prepared to handle it. The minute the news leaks out, it will have an effect on your securities. Investors, either directly or indirectly, will be calling analysts immediately, asking whether to buy or sell. It is not up to you to decide what they should do, but the analysts should be given all the information you have, so that they can form their own opinions. In such an emergency, the Financial Vice President should be prepared to handle phone calls personally in order to prevent conflicting stories being given out. If a press release is prepared, it should be mailed to analysts. The event should be explained in detail in the next interim statement to security holders.

The importance of proper handling of emergencies would be fully realized if a Financial Vice President could be in a large financial community when such an event occurs. The phones start to ring. Investors call their brokers and investment advisors as soon as they hear the news. Partners of firms call their analysts on the interoffice phone. The analysts call around among themselves and also call the company. Everybody is trying to estimate the effect and trying to decide whether to buy or sell and at what price. If a company "clams up" at such a time, real ill will develops and everyone becomes overly suspicious.

That has happened, and produces the worst possible results. Of course, in some cases, there may not be a complete answer readily available. Then the company may find it desirable to postpone giving out any answer until the full story is available; for half an answer may not represent the company fairly. In such a case, as soon as the full story can be told, it should be communicated as broadly as possible.

Declining Earnings

What does a company do when its earnings are on the decline or it is facing a number of problems? Does it then ignore the financial community? Absolutely not. And this is where a soundly conceived investor relations program comes into play. If a company handles its investor relations on the basis of a regular, well-planned program, it will never have to face the problem of doing a job when things are bright and then crawling into its shell when things look bad. A regular program will not be as glamorous as making an appearance only when the company has an optimistic report or there is some unusual development to explain. Nevertheless, it is the only way that proper results can be achieved over the long run. It helps avoid the very unfavorable impression and ill will which result from withdrawal during adverse circumstances. That is why so much stress was placed in the first part of this chapter on managements' understanding the true purpose of an investor relations program.

Dissatisfied Analysts

No matter how perfectly a company handles an investor relations program, a few analysts will be dissatisfied. There are unreasonable analysts, just as there are unreasonable people in every group. Don't antagonize them: they will probably talk against your company in the financial community, building ill will for you. Do the best you can, diplomatically, and you will be successful in your program. If you do a good job with the high grade analysts, and especially with those analysts who most regularly follow your company and thus become experts in it, you will find that your image will be such in the financial community that those who make unreasonable comments will not affect your reputation.

The unreasonable analysts include those who want inside information for themselves exclusively. If an analyst has written a fine story about a company and that company has helped the analyst with some figures, there is no need for management to feel it should immediately broadcast the information to all analysts. An analyst who ferrets out information has a right to it. However, the company should be willing to treat all analysts the same and give information and assistance freely to all. Don't play favorites. Of course, it should be recognized, in this connection, that even if all analysts are satisfied with the company's investor relations' program, there still will be some who, with justifiable reasons, will wish to sell your stock. This should be recognized as a natural process of investment.

A few analysts seem to feel that a company should withhold information which it may have given out to a small group, until that group has had time to take advantage of it and buy securities before the information is distributed generally. In fact, analysts have been heard to complain because some companies have issued press releases after meetings with analysts. No analyst has a right to object to such a policy and the company would be most foolish to yield to such pressure. Everything should be open and aboveboard.

Sometimes rumors start around Wall Street to the effect that the analyst in an investment banking firm may get some information about future earnings and dividends because one of the partners of the firm is a director of the company—totally inexcusable. It is one of the disadvantages of having directors of investment banking and other types of financial firms on a board and should be guarded against meticulously.

Restrictions During a Securities Offering

As previously mentioned, some special considerations arise when a company is going to sell new securities, since it will have to comply with the Securities Act of 1933. A company should check with its lawyers to make certain that there is no legal conflict if a meeting is scheduled with analysts, or if written material is issued at that time. Some lawyers will over-emphasize caution to a point that a company may eliminate all of the investor relations program for a period before and after the offering. This is unnecessary. No company which has been doing a conscientious job of keeping investors informed will be accused of violating the provisions of the Act. However, because the problem exists, the new financing schedule should be included among the items to consider in designing an investor relations program.

Conclusion

We conclude with a very few words. Much stress has been laid on detail in this chapter on investor relations. It is important; by lack of careful attention, an investor relations program can be damaged. Analysts are a critical bunch, and they compare how different companies perform. Slips become only too obvious. As a final word, we repeat that the most important idea to keep in mind is credibility.

Exhibit 12-1

OUTLINE OF IDEAS FOR ANNUAL REPORT

Theme:	WHAT HAPPENED FINANCIALLY AND WHY Don't have a special theme each year—there is only one theme.
Balance:	Space given to each subject should depend on its importance to the financial picture.
Completeness:	It must present all the facts, both favorable and unfavorable, about a company's operations during the year and immediately contemplated, which may have a significant effect on the value of its securities. This requires that material included in past annual reports must be repeated if it is necessary to make a complete report. Regardless of the other qualities of a report, the omission of any fact will seriously damage its value. Face up to adversities by explaining them and what management is doing about them. Don't hide meaningful material in the 10K.
Analytical Quality:	The material must be presented in such a way that it can be used readily in evaluating the securities. As a simple example, a wage increase must include the annual amount and also the date it became effective.
Readability:	The material must be presented in an interesting way and it must be easy to read. Test the readability by a readability test such as that devised by Rudolf Flesch, included in "The Art of Readable Writing."*
Balance:	Space given to each subject should depend on its importance to the financial picture.
Headings and Type:	To aid readability have ample descriptive headings. Large type throughout the report. At least 10-point optima large face type with 2 point leading.
Size:	8 1/2 x 11. Odd sizes are hard to file. Two-column pages. No half pages. Fold-outs if necessary.
Charts and Pictures:	Only those that add to the financial story. Charts should include figures so that analysts can read off the numbers. Bar charts are very effective when figures are shown within the bars. Maps if needed to show location of plants, etc.
Cover:	Name of Company Year and month of fiscal year Picture of design—which ties in with a major part of the company's operations
What Your Company Does:	This might be included on the inside cover.

*See footnote 1.

Exhibit 12-1 (Cont'd.)

Format:	Index Highlights President's letter Body of report Comparative financials for two years Ten-year summary of financials and related data
Highlights:	Two years comparative with percent change. At least the following: Net sales Income before income taxes Federal income taxes Net income Earnings per share—primary —fully diluted Dividends per share Book value per share Working capital Capital expenditures Number of shares
President's Letter:	1 or 2 pages in large type. Earnings and dividends per share comparative. Why they changed. Very brief summary of important developments during the year.
Body of the Report:	Break down into divisions or groups which would be meaningful to analysts. Use copious headings.
Financial Statements:	Consolidated, consolidating and parent company financials where needed to tell complete story as well as statements of important subsidiaries which are not consolidated. Source and application of funds statements.
Ten-Year Financial Summary:	Operating data Net sales Cost of sales Gross profit Payroll, including benefits Depreciation Interest on long term debt Income before taxes Federal income tax Net income Net income as percent of sales Capital expenditures Production—barrels or tonnage per day, etc. Order backlog Number of employees Balance sheet data Current assets Current liabilities Net plant and equipment

Exhibit 12-1(Cont'd.)

Capitalization: In dollars and with percent for each item
- Long term debt
- Preferred stock
- Common equity
- Total

Common stock data
- Earnings per share—primary
  —fully diluted
- Cash dividends per share
- Dividend payout percentage
- Book value per share
- Return on common equity
- Shares outstanding
- Number of stockholders
- Annual high-low price of stock
- (See check list at end of Exhibit for possible additional data to include in these tables.)

Leases: Where significant there should be complete data at least in footnotes. Payments—total and minimum. Average maturity. Additional information might include type of property leased, number of leases and renewal options.

Security List: After financials, a complete list of individual security issues outstanding.

Miscellaneous: Address of company, with phone number, date and place of annual meeting.

Corporate trust agents for stocks—transfer agent, registrar, dividend disbursing agent.

Stock Exchange ticker symbol.

Principal officers with descriptive titles.

Directors—with outside affiliations.

Reference to statistical book—If company prepares a separate statistical book, a clear reference to it should be made in the annual report.

Footnotes—In large type with simple explanations. Not just to comply with legal requirements and confuse.

Reference Material: Review the annual reports considered best by analysts for all types of companies and for your industry.

Check List of Data: The type of data included in an annual report or a statistical book will depend on the nature of the company. A broad list of items for an industrial company are included below.

1. Sales:
   a. In dollars and physical units (tonnage, barrels, yards, pounds, etc.).
   b. The major product groups in dollars, physical units or both.
   c. In dollar volume by major consuming markets.

Exhibit 12-1 (Cont'd.)

This kind of information permits comparison of an individual company's progress against the industry's background, figures for which are usually available. It also will reveal what markets are served by the company—and normally a great deal of industry data is made constantly available through trade papers, trade associations, financial newspapers and publications, government bureaus, etc.

2. The following major expense items should be detailed:
   a. Wages
   b. Material costs
   c. Selling, general and administrative expense
   d. Depreciation, depletion and amortization
   e. Cost of goods sold
   f. Profit from operations, excluding non-operating income
   g. Non-recurring items
   h. Federal income taxes
3. Other important information desired by security analysts is:
   a. Number and location of plants and total capacity in physical units. A good map is very worthwhile.
   b. Number of employees—either at the year's end or the average for the year.
4. Sufficient detail with respect to the extent of integration, control of raw material supply sources, etc.
5. Percentage of total dollar sales volume representing defense shipments.
6. Unfilled order backlogs vs. year-earlier totals.
7. Government business and its importance.
8. Details on foreign business covering sales, earnings, dividends and undistributed profits. Tax status of earnings. Location of foreign sources of business by countries and the above breakdowns by countries. It does not matter from the analysts' viewpoint whether you consolidate your foreign operations or not, as long as you give all the pertinent information.
9. Annual amounts spent for research, together with other details of research activities; staff; discussion of new products; percentage of most recent year's sales volume representing new products developed by the company over the past, say, ten-15 years.
10. Major raw materials used in the business and sources of supply.
11. Methods of distribution employed.

Exhibit 12-1 (Cont'd.)

12. Explanation of hidden assets; i.e., such as timberlands undervalued on the books, or investments in affiliates or subsidiaries carried at values well below prevailing appraisal or sale values.
13. Capital outlays for the most recent year, and contemplated for at least the next year. Discussion of expansion plans and programs; also, methods for financing them and financial philosophy.
14. Comments on dividend philosophy or policy, in relation to indicated capital needs.
15. Significance of any patents and their expiration dates.
16. For extractive industries, estimates by competent persons of net proven reserves; also, production, new discoveries and similar data.
17. Employee relations: Training programs, unions, union contracts, profit sharing plans.
18. Acquisitions: Purpose, effect on sales and earnings, price paid and method of purchase, accounting treatment.
19. Pollution problems and solutions.

CHAPTER 13

Financing for a Bank

Viewing a Bank's Capital

A commercial bank primarily takes in deposits and uses the money to make loans. In looking at the long term capital of a bank, you might think that the principal consideration would be the relationship of long term debt and common equity. Many people in finance do look at it that way. We cannot disregard this relationship, but in our analysis of capital structure for all types of companies, we stated that any short term debt which is rolled over and provides funds on a continuous basis should be included with long term capital. We approach a bank in the same way. Deposits vary, but the great mass of deposits remain on the bank's books year after year; we consider them part of long term capital.

Our analysis first requires that we divide the total capital into two parts.

1. Senior obligations—including deposits and other forms of indebtedness in an equal position with deposits.
2. Capital base—securities junior to deposits, including subordinated debt and equity.

Capital base is necessary to protect depositors, and bank regulatory authorities keep a close watch on it. Thus, the ability of a bank to expand is limited by its ability to get capital base from retained earnings, the sale of common and subordinated debt.

The approximate relationship of these two categories in our banking system is shown in Exhibit 13-1.

Since all banks on an average have about \$93 of deposits and unsubordinated debt for each \$7 of capital base, in the form of either subordinated debt or equity, the banking system can expand deposits by \$93 for each \$7 of capital base or on about a 13-to-1 ratio. Thus, securities in capital base perform a dual function. They provide money to invest in loans, etc., but, more important, every \$1 of capital base provides the ability to increase deposits about \$13 for the banking system. Consequently, we stated that any security in capital base should be viewed primarily for its effect on a bank's ability to expand.

In deciding on how much capital a bank needs, there are two principal considerations:

1. The requirements of regulatory authorities.

   Some banks watch regulators looking over their shoulders and wait until the regulators push them to get more capital. This is short-sighted and shows lack of financial planning. When the regulators get tough, it may turn out to be a poor time for the bank to sell securities; the bank's stock may be low or there may be a crunch in the bond market.

2. The quality of its securities.

   What the regulators require in terms of capital in order to just protect the depositors may not be enough to provide a good quality for a bank's common stock.

   In financial planning, a bank should achieve a good quality for its long term debt and common stock for the same type of reasons we suggested in the chapter on Capital Structure for all types of companies. It should keep its financing options open so that it will be able to finance at its own choosing on satisfactory terms. It should avoid being pushed into financing on an emergency basis. In this way its stockholders will benefit most over the long run.

Exhibit 13-1

DEPOSITS AND CAPITAL BASE
ALL INSURED COMMERCIAL BANKS IN THE U.S.*
(000,000's omitted)

	I	II	III	IV
Year	Deposits, etc.**	Capital Base	Total Deposits, Etc. and Capital Base	Capital Base as a Percent of Total Deposits, Etc. and Capital Base
1973	\$744,538	\$57,839	\$802,376	7.2%
1972	659,291	52,367	711,658	7.4
---	---	---	---	---
1964	308,821	27,438	336,259	8.2
1963	278,224	25,322	303,456	8.3

*Federal Deposit Insurance Corporation Annual Reports. Domestic commercial bank statistics.

**Includes time and demand deposits, Federal funds purchased, other liabilities for borrowed money, mortgage indebtedness and acceptances outstanding.

Thus, a bank should evaluate capital base securities in terms of satisfying regulatory authorities, but more important to maintain good quality for its securities and financial flexibility with borrowing reserve.

Subordinated Debt

Subordinated debt came into prominence in the 1960's. It added flexibility to bank financing in that a debt security became available which would satisfy regulatory authorities. Bank management grabbed on to this form of security as a God-given opportunity to satisfy regulators without having to sell common.

The capital base has been gradually getting smaller in relation to deposits, and the common stock related to total capital has been sinking even further. Finally, in the early 1970's, regulatory authorities began to focus more on the need for common equity. The banks screamed bloody murder and offered ridiculous arguments why regulation should keep hands off. This, of course, is typical of what other industries have done in the past when they have been short-sighted and gotten on the wrong track with unsound financial planning.

Subordinated debt does add protection to depositors, but it is still a debt obligation. Interest is a fixed charge and must be met regardless of earnings, and the maturity must ultimately be provided for. Furthermore, it cannot be used to absorb losses, if the bank is a going concern.

Balance Sheet for All Banks

We can look at the balance sheet for all U.S. banks and use a few simple ratios to bring out the broad relationships of the figures. The balance sheet for all U.S. banks is shown in Exhibit 13-2.

One item on the right-hand side of the balance sheet about which you may have a question is "reserve on loans and securities." A bank may use one of two methods for loan loss charges:

1. Actual for the year.
2. A historical average of past five years.

One of these methods is used as a charge to operating expenses during the year and is credited to loan loss reserve. Actual losses are taken out of the reserve.

In capital structure determination, we include reserves which are in excess of those permitted as tax deductions. In general, the Internal Revenue Service prevents banks from building up loan loss reserves to more than 1.8% of eligible loans.[1] However, if a bank has previously built up an excess reserve for tax purposes, the Internal Revenue Service will permit the reserve to be restored to the extent that it is depleted.

Ratios applied to the balance sheet should bring out the extent to which the bank is keeping its assets in non-risk vs. risk assets. This will affect the amount of capital a bank needs.

The simple ratios most generally used relate various assets to deposits, since deposits make up most of the liabilities. The first three ratios (see bottom of page 441) are based on this approach. The fourth ratio brings in capital base. The figures are for all insured commercial banks as shown in Exhibit 13-2. There are numerous other such ratios but these give some picture of the balance sheet.

Financial Planning for a Bank

It is necessary to take the three basic steps in financial planning for a bank as we do with other corporations:

1. Develop a five-year forecast. Forecasting for a bank should not be a major task in most instances because it can be built around one or more of the principal balance sheet items.

   For example, a bank should have a good idea of how deposits will grow and may build its forecast around deposits. The growth in deposits will be the primary determinant for capital needs. The return on beginning common equity

[1] Eligible loans refer to total loans less government guaranteed loans, unearned discount, federal funds sold, dealer reserves or holdbacks, loans to U.S. branches of foreign banks, cash collateral. The 1.8% reduces to 1.2% in 1976.

Exhibit 13-2

BALANCE SHEET
ALL INSURED COMMERCIAL BANKS IN THE U.S.*
1973

(000,000,000's omitted)

Assets				*Liabilities*			
Cash and equivalent			$117	Deposits—Demand	$309		
Securities				—Time	373		
U.S. Govt.	$83			Total			$682
Municipals	91			Federal funds purchased, etc.		63†	
Other**	15			Other		22	
Total		189		Total			85
Federal Funds sold		34		Reserve on loans and securities			8
Loans and discounts		460					
Other earnings assets***		6		Capital accounts			
Earnings assets			689	Notes and debentures		4 (7%)	
Bank premises			13	Equity		54 (93%)	
Other			14	Total			58
Total			$833	Total			$833

*Federal Deposit Insurance Corporation Annual Report. Domestic commercial bank statistics.

**Includes other securities $6, and trading account securities $9.

***Includes real estate owned other than bank premises $1, investments in subsidiaries non-consolidated $1 and customers' liabilities on acceptances $4.

†Includes:	
Federal funds purchased	$51
Other liabilities for borrowed money	7
Mortgage indebtedness	1
Acceptances outstanding	4
Total	$63

I. Loans/Deposits $= \frac{\$460}{\$682} = 67\%$

Loans in general represent risk assets which cannot be liquidated in a hurry. Thus, this ratio shows how much of the deposits are tied up in part of the banks' non-liquid risk assets.

II. Cash and U.S. Govt. Securities/Deposits $= \frac{\$200}{\$682} = 29\%$

This shows the liquidity position. But it is a very rough measure. If the securities have long maturities, they are not really liquid.

III. Risk Assets/Deposits $= \frac{\$633}{\$682} = 93\%$

Risk assets are represented by non-liquid assets. They are total assets less cash and U.S. Governments.

IV. Capital Base/Risk Assets $= \frac{\$\ 58}{\$633} = 9\%$

This shows how much capital base is available in relation to assets which have risk.

book value and the percent of earnings paid out in dividends will determine the growth in common equity capital from retained earnings. A comparison of the growth rate in deposits with the growth rate in common equity will determine whether outside capital will be needed. For example, if deposits are expected to grow at 5% a year, and the bank earns 12 1/2% on beginning book value with a 60% dividend payout ratio, the common equity will grow at 5% from plowback of earnings. Thus, the deposit growth rate will be balanced by capital growth. The growth rate in earnings from plowback was explained in Chapter 3.

2. Establish a dividend policy. It will vary depending on the bank's earning ability and the nature of its stockholders.
3. Determine a capital structure policy which will provide good quality of securities. This is our present interest.

Capital Structure for a Bank

The items which we will use in the two categories in our analysis of long term capital for a bank are as follows:

Total Capital

- Senior obligations, including deposits
  - Deposits—demand
    - —time, including certificates of deposits
  - Federal Funds purchased in excess of Federal Funds sold
  - Other liabilities for borrowed money
  - Mortgage indebtedness
  - Leases capitalized
  - Acceptances

Capital Base

- Subordinated debt—notes and debentures, straight and convertible.
  - Subordinated notes with a short maturity must have reserves in the Federal Reserve Bank just the same as time deposits. If the maturity of a note is under seven years it might not be considered as capital, and sinking funds on subordinated debt must be approved by the Federal Deposit Insurance Corp.
- Preferred stock—straight and convertible.
- Common equity.
- Loan loss reserves to the extent that they exceed the amount allowed for income tax purposes.

With regard to a bank's capital, we are interested in three things:

1. The average and minimum percent that the capital base represents of the total capital.
2. An average and maximum division of capital base between debt and equity and excess loan loss reserves. If preferreds are significant, they should be shown separately.
3. The average and minimum percent that the equity and excess loan loss reserves represent of total capital.

Bond Ratings for Banks

In our determination of capital structure for all types of companies, we sought to provide good quality securities; we used bond ratings to designate quality of debt.

Fitch Publishing Company was the first to rate bank debt. Then Moody's Investors Service[2] started rating bank holding company debt in 1974. Standard and Poor's entered the field in 1974. These organizations also rate commercial paper of bank holding companies.

In general, the rating agencies have done a good job in rating securities, but banking is a strange field for bond ratings. It is our opinion that some of the ratings may be too high in view of the minimum equity which banks have today. Therefore, we have not used ratings to signify quality in our approach to capital structure although we will use the same general approach.

Capital Structure Figures for All Banks

A bank can have a relatively small capital base and equity, because of the nature of its assets. Part of a bank's assets are in cash and

[2]Moody's Investors Service will only rate bonds of holding companies with equity over $40 million and will only consider rating a bond AAA if equity is over $150 million.

short-term high grade bonds. Most of the other part of a bank's assets consists of loans which to a large extent are short term and relatively high grade. In other words, its assets are liquid and much of them riskless.

The average capital structure figures for all banks, as shown in Exhibit 13-2, are as follows:

Capital base as a percent of total capital[3]	7.2%
Subordinated debt as a percent of capital base	7.1%
Common equity as a percent of total capital	6.7%

Bank Compared to a Finance Company

We can make a comparison between the amount of common equity required for a bank and a finance company.

A bank and a finance company are basically in the same business of making loans. A bank, however, only keeps about 55% of its assets in loans; whereas, a finance company has about 85% of its assets in loans. This is shown in Exhibit 13-3. It gives figures for all insured commercial banks in the U.S. and two representative finance companies with senior debt rated A by Standard and Poor's. On the basis of these figures, a bank should have 55/85 of the amount of common of a financing company. This is based on the following assumptions:

1. That the loans of both types of companies have equal risk.
2. That other assets of a bank and a finance company have the same risk.
3. That earnings of each are equal.

Actually, the other assets of a bank do have some risk. They are substantial in amount compared to the other assets of a finance company.

The finance companies have 14% of total assets in common equity, and 55/85 would represent 9%. On this basis and under the above assumptions, banks would require common equity of slightly more than 9% of long term capital, as we have defined it, in order to provide equal protection to that provided by the equity of an A grade finance company.

This type of reasoning doesn't solve the problem regarding the amount of common equity for a bank, but it may help to put the figures in perspective. We might raise the question of whether banks would lend money to finance companies if they had let their common equity position drift off as badly as that of the banks.

Guidelines for Bank Capital

We will consider financial policy for large banks and suggest ratios as shown in Exhibit 13-4. These figures assume that the bank's balance sheet is made up approximately as that for the composite figures for all banks and has adequate earnings.

With these standards, a conflict arises between the use of subordinated debt and the maintenance of an adequate common equity. For example, if capital base is 8% of total capital, and subordinated debt represented 15% of capital base, common equity would be reduced to 6.8% as follows:

Senior obligations, including deposits		$ 92
Capital base		
Subordinated debt	$1.20 (15%)	
Common equity	6.80 (85%)	
Total		$ 8
Total capital		$100

Thus, the 6.8% ratio of common equity to total capital is slightly below our 7% average standard consistent with good credit, which we recommend in Exhibit 13-4.

If subordinated debt is 30% of capital base, the common equity would be reduced to 5.6% as follows:

Senior obligations, including deposits		$ 92
Capital base		
Subordinated debt	$2.40 (30%)	

[3] Total capital is defined as time and demand deposits, Federal Funds purchased in excess of Federal Funds sold, other liabilities for borrowed money, mortgage indebtedness, leases capitalized and acceptances outstanding plus capital base.

Exhibit 13-3

COMPARISON OF COMMON EQUITY STRENGTH OF COMMERCIAL BANKS WITH FINANCE COMPANIES

December 31, 1973

All Insured Commercial Banks in U.S.*		Average of Two Finance Companies with Senior Debt Rated A by Standard and Poor's**	
Assets			*Assets*
Cash and equivalent	14%	2%	Cash
Investment and trading account securities	23	9	Marketable securities
Loans and discounts	55	85	Receivables, net
Other assets–Bank premises and other assets including Federal funds sold	8	4	Other assets
	100%	100%	
Liabilities			*Liabilities*
Long term capital			Long term capital
Deposits	82%	29%	Notes due in 1 year, etc.
		37	Senior long term debt
Subordinated debt	0.5	9	Subordinated long term debt
Common	6.5	14	Common
Reserves	1.0		
Other liabilities–Miscellaneous liabilities, including Federal funds purchased	10	11	Other liabilities–savings account deposits and other payables and accruals
Total	100%	100%	Total
Loans or receivables as a percent of total assets	55%	85%	Loans or receivables as a percent of total assets
Common equity as a percent of total liabilities	6.5%	14%	Common equity as a percent of total liabilities

*Federal Deposit Insurance Corp. Annual Report. Domestic commercial bank statistics.
**Commercial Credit Company December 31, 1973, and Dial Financial Corp. December 31, 1973.

Common equity	5.60 (70%)	
Total		$ 8
Total capital		$100

Then, common equity would be close to the figure we consider to be too low as a percent of total capital. What is the solution? There is no complete answer. In order to have borrowing reserve, subordinated debt should probably not average over 15% of capital base for a large bank. When it is necessary to use borrowing reserve and go higher, it should be realized that the common equity position is being violated, and plans should be under way to sell more common.

Some banks have used subordinated debt primarily as a source of funds. We have explained why we believe this to be a wrong approach. Furthermore, it may present a problem of borrowing long and investing short. Whether such a source of funds proves to be worthwhile will depend on whether interest rates on the investment for which the funds are used remains above the rate on the subordinated debt. In other words, using long-term subordinated debt as a source of funds is

Exhibit 13-4

CAPITAL STRUCTURE RATIOS FOR LARGE BANK

	Average	Minimum with Good Credit	Not Recommended
Capital Base as a Percent of Total Capital	8%	7%	5%

	Average	Maximum with Good Credit	Maximum Available Not Recommended
Capital Base			
Subordinated Debt	15%	30%	35%
Common Equity	85	70	65
Total	100%	100%	100%

	Average	Minimum with Good Credit	Not Recommended
Common Equity as a Percent of Total Capital	7%	6.5%	5%

a gamble on future interest rates. This depends on the rate and maturity of the subordinated debt and the possibility of call, compared with the various rates and maturities of investments with which they can be matched.

Capital for a Specific Bank

It is hoped that these broad figures presented above will help to provide some general perspective. However, each bank has special characteristics which will have an effect on how much capital is required.

The size of a bank is very important as far as risk is concerned and the amount of capital base required. Very small banks with $1 million of total assets and under may require a capital base as a percent of total capital of 13%. As size increases, the percentage drops rapidly to about 8% for banks with $10 million of assets and over.

Small banks do not have access to the open market for subordinated debt market. They may be able to sell notes locally to their customers or medium term notes to their correspondent bank. Most institutional investors would not purchase securities of banks under $5 million in total assets, and a significant market is not available for banks much under $25 million. Moderate-sized banks should plan to meet their capital needs with equity and borrow only if the market for their stock is poor. Large banks can provide capital with subordinated debt.

The amount of capital base for a particular bank will depend on all relevant factors such as:

The quality of its management.

This should show up in the bank's balance sheet, income statement and operating procedures.

The character of its assets as regards liquidity and quality.

The amount of cash.

The type, maturity and quality of its investments.

- The amount of assets represented by loans and their maturity, quality and diversification.
- The amount invested in building and fixtures.
- The extent of foreign operations and their nature—whether they are financing foreign trade or represent loans and other assets in foreign countries which have a high risk factor.
- The type of other assets.
- The extent to which assets may be over- or understated.

The character of its liabilities.

- The nature of its deposits as to whether they are volatile and subject to unexpected withdrawal which would force the bank to liquidate assets at a loss.
- The extent to which deposits may be inflated by excessive float which would also inflate cash.
- The other types of instruments it uses as a source of funds.
- The dividend policy as it may affect the buildup of capital through retained earnings.
- The nature of its other businesses, such as its trust activities.
- The size of the banks—a small bank will tend to have more risk than a large one.
- The future prospects for the bank as it may affect the above factors.

The amount and variability of its earnings.

Earnings Protection for Bonds

The ratio generally used for earnings protection for bonds is the number of times interest charges are covered.

If all interest charges are used in the ratio for a bank, the coverage figure is relatively low and so insensitive to changes in debt in the capital base that it is not a very helpful figure. For example, the pre-tax coverage of all interest charges[4] as shown in the income statement for all banks, which is shown subsequently in Exhibit 13-9, is 1.36 times. All banks had 7.1% of capital base in subordinated debt. If the subordinated debt were approximately doubled with an 8% interest rate, the coverage would only change to 1.34 times.

It has been suggested that interest on time deposits be treated as an operating expense and the coverage be figured on the basis of income after such interest charges. The applicable interest charges would then be primarily interest on the subordinated debt in the capital base. This would be even more misleading because it would be so leveraged with the prior charges.

Actually, earnings coverage for debt of a bank is not as meaningful as for other types of businesses. The assets of a bank are so liquid that they have value based on their intrinsic worth. If a bank has adequate equity, the debt of a bank should be well protected. However, having made this concession regarding the less significance of interest coverage for bank debt, we will reverse ourselves and say that as with any type of company, adequate earnings are an absolute essential for a bank to be a strong operating entity. This is true because like any other corporation a bank must be able to raise equity money to protect the debt and permit it to expand. Only if earnings are adequate for the common will a bank be in such a position. Therefore, we suggest that the way to test the earnings of a bank is in terms of return on common equity. And for this figure to be meaningful, the amount of common equity must be adequate for there to be a sound common.

If a bank's common equity is adequate, the calculation is a simple one. Merely divide the book value of the common equity by the income after taxes and before net securities gains or losses. The figure for all banks based on the balance sheet figures in Exhibit 13-2 and the income statement in Exhibit 13-9 which appears subsequently was as follows:

$$\frac{\text{Income after taxes before net security gains and losses}}{\text{Common equity}} = \frac{\$\,6.6}{\$53.7} = 12.3\%$$

[4] This is calculated by adding interest on deposits of $19.84 to expenses of Federal funds purchased, and other interest charges of $4.66 to income before taxes and security gains and losses of $8.71, making a total of $33.21, and dividing by $19.84 plus $4.66.

The common equity was 6.7% of total capital.

If the common equity is inadequate and the bank is over-leveraged, it is necessary to make adjustments in order to get a meaningful return. Accordingly, decrease the debt and increase the common equity a like amount so as to make the common equity sound. Then add to the earnings available for the common the interest applicable to the debt that has been eliminated, and subtract the increase in taxes which will result from the lower interest charges. Divide the new adjusted sound common equity by the adjusted earnings.

A few figures may help:

Total senior capital—deposits and other debt	$ 95.00
Common (5%)	5.00
Total capital	$100.00
Earnings available for common	$ 0.50

Assume that the common for this bank should be 7% of total capital in order to be good quality. Then the total capital would be as follows:

Total senior capital—deposits and other debt	$ 93.00
Common (7%)	7.00
Total capital	$100.00

We have shifted $2 of debt to common. We will assume that the interest rate on this debt is 8%, so the interest charges would be 16¢. Shifting the interest charges to common would increase taxes by 8¢ with a 50% tax rate, so the net additional to earnings would be 8¢ (16¢ interest less 8¢ increase in taxes). Therefore the earnings of 50¢ would be adjusted upward to 58¢. This would produce a return of 8.3% on the sound common of $7. If an 11% return is considered a minimum historical return to meet the cost of common, the earnings rate would be 25% below a minimum figure. This low rate of earnings would make the sale of common very difficult if investors expected that the rate would not improve. In the markets of 1973 and 1974, even 11% would not permit common financing on a reasonable basis.

Bank Regulatory Approach to Capital Adequacy

In determining the financial policy for your bank, you should understand the methods used by your regulatory authorities to determine capital adequacy. We have suggested that for sound financial policy you will wish to have a stronger capital than the minimum required by regulatory authorities. And you will be more concerned with the common equity portion of capital. However, an understanding of the approaches used by regulators may help you come to a sound conclusion.

Regulation is interested in the amount of capital of a bank because of the importance of the bank being able to meet customers' demands. This involves the matter of losses due to bad loans and investments and liquidity. Liquidity provides protection against losses that could develop if demands were made on the bank for funds and it were forced to liquidate assets at a loss in an adverse market. Demands on a bank can come from withdrawals by depositors or requests for loans by borrowers, but the demands of depositors is far more important because a bank can turn down loans if things get tight.

Practically all banks are chartered as either national or state banks. Most banks are members of the Federal Reserve System and practically all banks are insured by the Federal Deposit Insurance Corporation. Regulation can be summarized as follows:

- *National Banks.* Primarily by the Comptroller of the Currency. The Federal Reserve and FDIC have authority but generally don't use it.
- *State Banks—Members of Federal Reserve.* Federal Reserve Districts and state banking authorities in cooperation.
- *State Banks—Non-Members of the Federal Reserve, but insured.* FDIC and state authorities in cooperation.
- *Holding Companies—Federal Reserve Board.* They may examine subsidiaries. If they are state banks, then state authority also.

Securities sold by banks are not subject to the Securities Act, but securities sold by a bank holding company are subject to the Act.

Each of the regulatory agencies has its own system to determine bank capital adequacy.

The Comptroller of the Currency uses the liquidity test shown in Exhibit 13-5. As a first test of capital adequacy the comptroller uses net loans to adjusted capital ratio as follows:

Net loans. Total loans excluding:

- Commercial paper purchased
- Brokers' loans
- Municipal loans
- Loans guaranteed or insured by the government

Adjusted capital

- Capital notes
- Equity
- Loan loss reserve after deducting 50% of assets classified as doubtful and 100% of assets classified as loss.

This ratio should not exceed 7.5x. We cannot obtain the figures for adjusted capital and net loans for all insured commercial banks in the U.S., but, we can arrive at an approximation by referring to Exhibit 13-2. Total capital base and reserves amounted to $66 billion. Total loans and discounts were $460 billion. Based on these figures, the ratio would be 7.0x.

It should be noted that the comptroller's analysis does use various ratios such as the one above, but much reliance is placed on the quality of assets and ability of management.

Quality of assets is measured by relating the aggregate volume of assets classified as substandard, doubtful or loss to gross capital base, including the total reserve for loan losses. Each bank is assigned one of four categories.

Exhibit 13-5

ITEMS USED TO CALCULATE THE RATIO
NET LIQUID ASSETS/NET DEPOSITS AND UNSUBORDINATED
SHORT TERM LIABILITIES*

Net liquid assets		
1. Cash and due from banks.		xxxx
2. Unpledged U.S. Govts. at market.		xxxx
3. Other unpledged securities with 2-year maturities or less at market.		xxxx
4. Federal funds sold; U.S. securities and other securities with up to 2 years maturities purchased under agreements to resell.		xxxx
5. Gross liquid assets.		xxxx
6. Less: Reserve requirement excluding vault cash.		xxx
7. Net liquid assets.		xxxx
Net deposits and unsubordinated short term liabilities		
1. Total deposits and unsubordinated short term liabilities.	xxxx	
2. Less: Liabilities secured by U.S. Govt. securities and other securities.	xxx	xxxx
3. Interest collected not earned.		xxx
4. Net deposits and unsubordinated short term liabilities.		xxxx

*Comptroller of the Currency, Treasury Department. Revised 12/69.

Rating	Classified Assets/Gross Capital	Comptroller's Action
A	Less than 20%	
B	More than 20%, less than 40%	Letter from Regional Administrator
C	More than 40%, less than 80%	Problem bank. Meeting with Board of Directors to insure that correction will be instituted
D	More than 80%	Real trouble

In addition, the following are taken into consideration:

a. Quality of management
b. History of earnings and retention
c. Quality and character of ownership
d. Burden of meeting occupancy expenses
e. Potential volatility of deposit structure
f. Quality of operating procedures
g. Ability to meet present and future financial needs of the bank's trade area considering competition

Based on a combination of all factors cited, the Comptroller groups banks in four categories.

Group 1—Banks sound in every respect.
Group 2—Banks with one or more unfavorable factors such as moderate capital inadequacy.
Group 3—Banks with excessive volume of asset problems in relation to capital, serious management problems, extremely adverse economic conditions in the area.
Group 4—Banks with extremely serious asset problems in relation to capital, with a D rating and gross inadequacy of management.

The Federal Reserve System which includes both Board and Banks, uses several ratios, comparisons and formulae. It also relies on judgment in determining the appropriate level of capital for any bank, including considerations as to earnings, asset quality, geographical location, diversification of assets and liabilities and management. The Federal Reserve Board method is not used as often as those of the Districts, but it is comprehensive and gives a detailed approach based on an analysis of capital required for different types of assets, and liquidity required for various liabilities. An example of the form used by the Federal Reserve Board is shown in Exhibit 13-6.

Some Comments on Capital Requirements

We will now make some general observations about risks which affect the amount of common equity.

The basic risks on the asset side consist of the quality of loans and investments and their length of maturity. There is no way an outsider can tell about the quality of loans except possibly from the historical record of loan losses. But loan policy can change very quickly with new management. Bond ratings can give a clue as to quality of bond investments. Bonds rated AAA or AA would have relatively little risk.

The length of maturity of bond investments can add substantially to risk. For example, a 1% and 2% increase in interest rate for a 5% bond originally selling at 100 will result in the percentage losses as shown in Exhibit 13-7. (See page 456.) The amount of decline depends on the maturity and the change in interest rates. For example, for a bond with a 25-year maturity, an increase in interest rates to 7% would result in a 23% decrease in the price.

A major risk for a large bank is the amount of foreign business. As we will indicate in the chapter on cost-of-capital there is a substantial increase in risk in almost any foreign investment. This, of course, will vary widely with the nature of the asset and the country in which it is located.

The Federal Reserve Board Form shows capital requirement for trust business equal to 200% of revenues for this business. This would seem to be somewhat on the high side. It is not likely that trust departments could make an adequate return on capital if this amount was required. A figure of 100% might be more in line with reality.

Float, which consists of checks not yet cleared, is present in all banks, and in com-

Exhibit 13-6

FEDERAL RESERVE BOARD

FORM FOR ANALYZING BANK CAPITAL

LIQUIDITY CALCULATION

	Amount Outstanding	Percent	Calculation
Demand deposits, IPC		35	
Savings deposits		25	
Time deposits, IPC, under $100,000		30	
Time deposits, IPC, $100,000 & over		80	
Deposits of banks		80	
Other deposits		80	
TOTAL DEPOSITS			
Borrowings		100	
Other liabilities (a)		100	
Special factors: ______		100	
TOTAL LIQUIDITY CALCULATION (b)			

MEMORANDA

(a) "Other liabilities" and "Loans: Consumer installments" are shown net of:

Dealers reserves . . . . ______

Income collected but not earned . . . . ______

(b) "LIQUIDITY AVAILABLE FROM ASSETS" is to be aggregated only until it equals "TOTAL LIQUIDITY CALCULATION."

(c) "Cash assets" are shown net of:

Required reserves . . . . ______

(d) "TOTAL ASSETS" are shown net of assets classified as:

Doubtful . . . . ______

Loss . . . . ______

	AMOUNT OUTSTANDING	CAPITAL CALCULATION CREDIT RISK		CAPITAL CALCULATION MARKET RISK		LIQUIDITY AVAILABLE FROM ASSETS (b)	
		Percent	Amount	Percent	Amount	Amount	Aggregate
(1) PRIMARY RESERVE							
Cash assets (c)		0	0	0	0		
Federal funds sold		0	0	0	0		
(1) TOTAL			0		0		
(2) SECONDARY RESERVE							
Commercial paper and bankers acceptances		1		1			
Securities maturing under 1 year:							
U.S. Treasury		0	0	*			
Government agencies		0	0	*			
State, county and municipal		0	0	*			
Other Group 1		0	0	1			
(2) TOTAL							

(3) MINIMUM RISK ASSETS							
Securities maturing 1-5 years:							
U.S. Treasury		0	0	*			
Government agencies		0	0	*			
State, county and municipal		2		*			
Other Group 1		2		8			
(3) TOTAL							
(4) INTERMEDIATE ASSETS							
Securities maturing 5-10 years:							
U.S. Treasury		0	0	*			
Government agencies		0	0	*			
State, county and municipal		3		*			
Other Group 1		3		15			
Loans specially secured or guaranteed		3		15			
(4) TOTAL							
(5) PORTFOLIO ASSETS							
Securities maturing over 10 years:							
U.S. Treasury		0	0	*			
Government agencies		0	0	*			
State, county and municipal		5		*			
Other Group 1		5		25			
Loans: Real estate		5		25			
Consumer installment (a)		5		25			
All other		5		25			
(5) TOTAL							
(6) FIXED, CLASSIFIED AND OTHER ASSETS							
Bank premises		50					
Furniture and fixtures; other real estate		100					
Group 2 securities		50					
Groups 3 and 4 securities		100					
Assets classified substandard		20					
Accruals and other assets		0	0				
(6) TOTAL							
(7) TOTAL CAPITAL CALCULATED FOR MARKET RISK							
(8) TOTAL CAPITAL CALCULATED FOR CREDIT RISK				→			

*See continued Exhibit for SECURITIES COMPUTATIONS which take account of quality, yield and narrower maturity ranges.

Exhibit 13-6 (Cont'd.)

(9) **TOTAL ASSETS (d)** ________ 2 ________

(10) **TRUST DEPARTMENT GROSS EARNINGS** ________ 200 ________

(11) **SPECIAL FACTORS:** ________ ________

(12) **TOTAL CAPITAL CALCULATION** (sum of lines 7 through 11) ________

(13) **ADJUSTED CAPITAL STRUCTURE**† **AND CAPITAL STRUCTURE INDEX** (Adjusted capital structure divided by line (12)) . . . . $ ________ ________

(14) **ADJUSTED EQUITY CAPITAL**†† **AND EQUITY CAPITAL INDEX** (Adjusted equity capital divided by line (12)) . . . . $ ________ ________

CAPITAL RATIOS

Adjusted capital structure as a percent of:
total assets ________%; total assets minus primary reserves, U.S. Treasury and Agency securities ________%; total deposits ________%.

Adjusted equity capital as a percent of:
total assets ________%; total assets minus primary reserves, U.S. Treasury and Agency securities ________%; total deposits ________%.

†Adjusted capital structure–Total capital accounts plus reserves on securities and loans minus assets classified loss and 50 percent of assets classified doubtful.

††Adjusted Equity Capital–Adjusted capital structure minus debt capital.

NOTES REGARDING FORM FOR ANALYZING BANK CAPITAL

A thorough appraisal of the capital needs of a particular bank must take due account of all relevant factors affecting the bank. These include the characteristics of its assets, its liabilities, its trust or other corporate responsibilities and its management—as well as the history and prospects of the bank, its customers and its community. The complexity of the problem requires a considerable exercise of judgment. The groupings and percentages suggested in the Form for Analyzing Bank Capital can necessarily be no more than aids to the exercise of judgment.

The requirements indicated by the various items on the form are essentially "norms" and can provide no more than an initial presumption as to the actual capital required by a particular bank. These "norms" are entitled to considerable weight, but various upward or downward adjustments in requirements may be appropriate for a particular bank if special or unusual circumstances are in fact present in the specific situation. Such adjustments may be entered under "Special factors" indicated on the Analysis Form.

The requirements suggested in the Analysis Form assume that the bank has adequate safeguards and insurance coverage against fire, defalcation, burglary, etc. Lack of such safeguards or coverage would place upon the bank's capital risks which it should not be called upon to bear.

SECURITIES COMPUTATIONS which take account of quality, yield and narrower maturity ranges. For determining market risk, take the following steps:

1. Distribute the bank's holdings of U.S. treasury, U.S. Agency and State and Political Subdivisions in the following matrices:

		U.S. Treasury			U.S. Government Agencies and Corporations			States and Political Subdivisions		
Years Over	Through	Avg. Cpn. Rate*	Par	Book	Avg. Cpn. Rate*	Par	Book	Avg. Cpn. Rate*	Par	Book
	1		$	$		$	$		$	$
1	2									
2	5									
5	10									
10	20									
20										
Totals			$	$		$	$		$	$

*Average coupon rate. The preferred method is to obtain by computing actual annual coupon income generated by securities in a given cell and dividing such annual coupon income by the par value of the cell. In the alternative, the average coupon rate may be imputed as described below.

Years		U.S. Treasury		U.S. Government Agencies and Corporations		States and Political Subdivisions		HIGH YIELDS		
Over	Through	Avg. Cur. Mkt. Yld.**	Market**	Avg. Cur. Mkt. Yld.**	Market**	Avg. Cur. Mkt. Yld.**	Market**	U.S. Treasury	U.S. Government Agencies and Corporations	States and Political Subdivisions
	1		$		$		$	7.75	8.21	5.02
1	2							7.78	8.23	5.11
2	5							7.82	8.29	5.32
5	10							7.64	8.39	5.65
10	20							7.30	7.98	6.08
20								7.07	8.12	6.43
Total market value			$		$		$			

(Not necessary to complete if average coupon rate is known.) Average current market yield (approximate yield base for market value shown) may be obtained from actual knowledge of yields used to obtain above market value or by selecting a single investment issue for each cell that is representative of that particular cell; e.g., for state and political subdivisions with maturities of from 10-20 years, select a medium grade issue maturing in 15 years or as close to 15 years as is available. Divide the market value of the issue by par value and locate the resultant value in the **Comprehensive Bond Value Tables under the coupon rate of the issue selected and trace across to maturity yield. Enter maturity yield under "Avg. Cur. Yld." above. If information concerning the individual securities comprising each cell is unavailable, enter market yields obtained from a general review of rates prevailing at or near the time of pricing.

2. Price the securities in each cell to yield at the high yield rate set forth in the high yield matrix. Note: Price as though each cell was a single issue using average coupon rate and total par value. Assume maturities for each cell as follows: 1–(1 year); 1-2 (1½ years); 2-5 (2½ years); 5-10 (7½ years); 10-20 (15 years); 20 (25 years [except assume 20 years for U.S. Agencies]). Note: If bank has a concentration of lower quality municipal securities, add about 50 basis points to high yield for "States and political subdivisions."

3. Determine the amount of maximum probable market depreciation in each cell by subtracting the market value obtained from step 1 above from the book value of securities. Enter actual figure for maximum potential market loss in the appropriate market risk column, combining where necessary in order to conform to distribution as appears on the front of the Form. If computations show potential market appreciation, enter zero for market risk.

Method for Imputing Coupon

Par value ÷ Market value = Assumed price.

Locate assumed price in the Comprehensive Bond Valuation Tables assuming a coupon equal to average current yield. Trace the price to the yield to maturity column in the tables. **The yield to maturity is the imputed average coupon rate of that particular cell.** (Note: Owing to the restraints of the table size the yield may have to be interpolated; a more precise method for obtaining the yield may be achieved by utilizing the mathematical equation for determining such yields.)

Note: If the above data are unavailable, as an alternative but less desirable method, the following percentage charges may be used:

All securities maturing under 1 year, 1 percent; 1-5 years, 8 percent; 5-10 years, 15 percent; over 10 years, 25 percent.

Exhibit 13-7

EFFECT OF MATURITY ON DECREASE IN PRICE OF A BOND DUE TO AN INCREASE IN INTEREST RATES

5% Bond Originally Selling at 100 to Yield 5%

	Increase in Yield to Maturity to 6%		Increase in Yield to Maturity to 7%	
Maturity of Bond	Price	Percent Decrease	Price	Percent Decrease
1	99	1%	98	2%
5	96	4	92	8
10	93	7	86	14
15	90	10	82	18
20	88	12	79	21
25	87	13	77	23

paring ratios of one bank with another, no adjustment should be made for float. However, some banks which do a lot of clearing for other banks have an excessive float so that the ratio of capital base and equity to total capital is distorted. In such a situation, the excessive float may be deducted in calculating the capital ratios. Of course, capital base related to risk assets is not affected by float so that ratio excludes the problem.

Federal Funds Sold should not be netted against Federal Funds Purchased. On the left-hand side of the balance sheet, the Federal funds category is considered a risk asset for the application of the capital base to risk asset standard. Federal funds sold are not riskless in the sense that cash or U.S. Government investments are, but could be considered next in line in the risk spectrum. An abnormally large percent of total assets employed in this category would necessitate some adjustment in the risk asset standard. On the liability side, Federal funds purchased represent a source of funds and should be recognized as such. However, there are situations which may call for special treatment if a bank does a Federal funds trading business with other banks. Then the Federal funds picture would be distorted, and for bank capital adequacy tests, it might be preferable to net out the Federal funds which were represented by the trading account.

Acceptance Liabilities represents the use of the banks' credit as a backup for the credit of one of the bank's customers. It is not a source of funds in the strict sense, but it requires capital and should be included in the total capital picture in determining capital adequacy. The corresponding entry on the asset side is customers' acceptance liability. It should be considered as part of risk assets in considering capital adequacy.

Acceptances not on the balance sheet which represent unused guarantees should be put on the balance sheet for analytical purposes in capital determination; otherwise, a potential risk requiring capital would be overlooked.

Of particular interest in the Federal Reserve Board Form shown in Exhibit 13-6, is the attention that is paid to the adequacy of common equity. Ratios for common equity are calculated under CAPITAL RATIOS in the exhibit.

Bank Building Treatment

There is wide divergence as to how bank buildings are treated by regulatory authorities. Some authorities require 100% capital base for bank buildings. This doesn't seem reasonable. Certainly, a building is not a liquid asset and should be given no credit from the point of view of liquidity. However, probably most bank buildings today are undervalued. From an asset analysis point of view, it would seem reasonable to require common equity to represent 35% of a building. As noted in the Federal Reserve Board form, capital base is required up to 50%. Some regulatory authorities treat buildings which are leased on the basis of the burden of lease payments as compared with other comparable banks. Leases of home office buildings from non-affiliated companies may be capitalized by some Federal Reserve Districts, but this is a gray area. The same attitude may be taken by the Federal Reserve Board for subsidiaries of holding companies. If the holding company owns the building and it is financed with debt and leased to a subsidiary bank, the total indebtedness against the building is added to the subsidiary's investment in bank premises. State policy varies with each state.

It would be more consistent if leased premises were required to be capitalized and put back on the balance sheet by all regulatory authorities.

The Liability Side and Liquidity

Turning to the liability side, elaborate tests have been developed with regard to volatility of deposits to determine the liquidity necessary to meet demands for deposit withdrawals. Seasonal increases in deposits should be completely covered with liquid assets. And any large deposits such as time deposits which are known to be subject to unpredictable withdrawals should be covered by equally liquid and high grade investments. Of course, if the volatile part of the deposits are not covered by liquid assets, more capital is needed to protect against forced losses when assets have to be liquidated. However, as far as capital adequacy is concerned, it is questionable whether this kind of analysis serves much purpose.

With regard to bank regulation in general, a constructive move would be for the regulatory authorities to get together and at least use one statistical form for testing capital adequacy. There seems to be little reason why this can't be done.

Other Types of Securities

Preferred stock has only a limited place in bank capital. Because a bank has such a low common equity, the addition of a senior security ahead of the common, in addition to subordinated debt, would push the common too far out on a limb. Convertible preferred may be useful in a bank acquisition program. It permits tailoring the dividend to the dividend on the common stock of the acquired bank without changing the dividend of the acquiring bank.

The general principles which apply to the use of incentive securities such as convertibles and senior securities with warrants, also apply to a bank. They should be saved for a time when the bank's stock is down and it needs common but can't get it directly. Since convertible debentures may turn into common, they would generally be preferable to debentures with warrants.

Bank Holding Company Financing

A bank holding company system has a number of different financing problems, such as:

- It is subject to the Securities Act and security offerings must be registered.
- A holding company and its subsidiaries come under regulation of the Federal Reserve Board.
- A holding company can sell commercial paper without back-up lines.

However, these special situations do not change the fundamental principles that we have discussed for bank financing.

In a holding company system, it is the holding company which supplies the common equity to the system. For a viable system, the common stock of the holding company must have good quality. Therefore, the ratios for the system on a consolidated basis should conform to the principles we have previously outlined.

It is ridiculous to believe that a holding company can pile on debt, use the proceeds to buy common in the subsidiaries and still have a strong system. Such a policy may push the common of the holding company too far out on a limb. This is what the electric utility holding companies did in the 1929 era and with disastrous results. The Public Utility Holding Company Act had to be passed by Congress to clean up the mess.

If a holding company is in a number of different businesses, such as a leasing company and finance company, which require a larger amount of common, it is necessary to determine a proper common equity for each business. The common equity of the holding company should be the weighted average of the common equities of the banks, the leasing company and the finance company.

Consideration may be given to financing the bank building in the holding company and leasing it to its subsidiary. This will depend on all the surrounding circumstances, including whether the bank is a state or national bank, and the applicable regulation and tax laws. However, it does not change the need for adhering to sound capital structure ratios.

Whether senior security financing should be done in the holding company or subsidiaries depends on the nature of the subsidiaries. If the subsidiaries are all small, then senior security financing could probably best be done in the holding company. However, large, strong subsidiaries could probably best do senior security financing on their own.

A Bank That Got into Trouble

The capital of a bank that encountered problems because of bad asset and liability management and inadequate capital is shown in Exhibit 13-8. In the first year in the exhibit, the capital base was 6% and the common equity was 4% of total capital, including deposits, unsubordinated debt, subordinated debt and equity. In year 3, the capital base ratio fell to 4% and the common equity to 3%. An attempt was made to increase the equity with preferred in year 4. The prospectus covering the new issue of preferred (with warrants attached) states: "The growth in the bank's deposits and business in recent years, the continued increase in the demand for loans and other banking services and the importance of maintaining a proper ratio of capital funds to deposits has made it advisable to increase the Bank's capital funds." However, this increase only brought the capital base up to 6% and the equity up to 5%. In year 5, the capital base fell to 5% and the equity to 4%. By that time it was apparent that the bank was in trouble.

In turning down the bank's application for certain expansion steps in year 5, the Federal Reserve stated: "The general character of the ______________ management and the bank's financial history and conditions, including its liquidity and capital position, militate against approval of the present applications."

This bank did not get into trouble because of lack of capital alone, but primarily because of overall bad management. However, the example does illustrate that because of the small capital of the banking business, management must run a tight ship.

Earnings of a Bank and Return on Capital

Now we turn to the earnings picture.

The amount a bank must make in interest on loans to provide an adequate return on capital depends on: the expenses of handling the deposits, the interest it must pay on the various forms of indebtedness and the income it can earn on liquid investments.

Earnings per share are reported after loan loss expense and after taxes in two ways:

1. Income before security profit or losses, net of tax.
2. Net income after security profit or losses, net of tax.

Security profits or losses, net of taxes, means that security profits or losses are reported after adjusting for such taxes. For example, if there were security profits of $1 million and applicable taxes of $500,000, taxes as reported would include $500,000 and

Exhibit 13-8

CAPITAL OF A BANK THAT ENCOUNTERED TROUBLE
(000,000's Omitted)

Year	1		2		3	
Deposits and unsubordinated debt	$791	94%	$1,008	96%	$1,257	96%
Capital base						
Subordinated notes	15	2	15	1	15	1
Preferred						
Common	31	4	32	4	34	3
	$837	100%	$1,055	100%	$1,306	100%
Capital base						
Subordinated notes	$ 15	33%	$ 15	32%	$ 15	31%
Preferred						
Common	31	67	32	68	34	69
	$ 46	100%	$ 47	100%	$ 49	100%

Year	4			5		
Deposits and unsubordinated debt	$1,349	94%		$1,367	95%	
Capital base						
Subordinated notes	15	1		15	1	
Preferred	30	2	} 5	30	2	} 4
Common	39	3		24	2	
	$1,433	100%		$1,436	100%	
Capital base						
Subordinated notes	$ 15	18%		15	22%	
Preferred	30	36		30	43	
Common	39	46		24	35	
	$ 84	100%		$ 69	100%	

security profits net of taxes would be reported at $500,000.

Both of the above incomes are before extraordinary charges.

For our purpose in calculating return on capital, we use income before security profit or losses, net of tax.

The income statement for all U.S. banks is shown in Exhibit 13-9. The only financial ratio we will show here which applies to the income statement alone is dividend payout ratio.

$$\text{Dividend payout} = \frac{\text{Dividends}}{\text{Income Before Securities Gains or Losses}} = \frac{\$2.4}{\$6.6} = 37\%$$

The other ratios tie in with the income statement and the balance sheet because they pertain to return on investment.

The goal of a bank in the past should be to earn a minimum of 11% on the common equity with an adequate amount of common equity. With security markets as they were in

Exhibit 13-9

INCOME STATEMENT
ALL INSURED COMMERCIAL BANKS IN THE U.S.*
1973
(000,000,000's Omitted)

Line			
1	Operating Income		
2	Interest and fees on loans	$35.4	
3	Interest on investments, etc.	11.6	
4	Trust income	1.5	
5	Other income	4.5	
6	Total		$53.0
7	Operating Expenses		
8	Salaries, etc.	$10.1	
9	Interest on deposits	19.8	
10	Expenses of Federal funds purchased, and other interest changes	4.6	
11	Occupancy expense, net	1.8	
12	Furniture, equipment, depreciation, rental, etc.	1.2	
13	Provision for loan losses	1.3	
14	Other operating expenses	5.5	
15	Total		$44.0
16	Income Before Income Taxes and Security Gains and Losses		8.7
17	Income taxes		2.1
18	Income before securities gains and losses		6.6
19	Securities gains or losses, net		0.0
20	Net income before extraordinary items		6.6
21	Extraordinary charges or credits, net		0.0
22	Net income		6.6
23	Dividends		2.4

*Federal Deposit Insurance Corporation Annual Report. Domestic commercial bank statistics.

1973 and 1974, this would be highly inadequate to satisfy investors.

The return for all banks was as follows in 1973.

$$\text{Return on common equity} = \frac{\text{Income after taxes before securities gains and losses}}{\text{Common equity}} = \frac{\$6.6}{\$54} = 12.3\%$$

We can also calculate a return on two other bases—earning assets and total assets. These calculations are shown below.

$$\text{Return on earning assets} = \frac{\text{Income after taxes before securities gains and losses}}{\text{Earning assets}} = \frac{\$6.6}{\$674} = 1.0\%$$

$$\text{Return on total assets} = \frac{\text{Income after taxes before securities gains and losses}}{\text{Total assets}} = \frac{\$6.6}{\$833} = 0.8\%$$

These two ratios eliminate the problem of leverage which might occur using return on common, if there was an inadequate common equity.

There is a general tie-in between the three return figures. Earning assets may be about 80% of total assets. Therefore, an 0.8% return on total assets is about the same as a 1% return on earning assets. Since common equity is about 7% of total capital as we define it, and total capital is close to total assets, then an 0.8% return on total assets or a 1% return on earning assets results in a return around 11% on common equity. The way the three different bases, on which these figures are calculated, tie together is illustrated with the hypothetical figures given below:

Earning assets	$ 80
Other assets	20
Total assets	$100
Deposits and other items	$ 93
Equity	7
	$100

Now let's back up and see in very broad terms where the 1% return on earning assets for All Insured Commercial Banks in the U.S. came from.

The operating income for all banks represents 7.8% of earning assets. The cost to obtain funds in terms of interest paid represents 3.6% of earning assets. Operating expenses including taxes, but excluding interest paid, represents 3.2% on earning assets. As a result there remained 1% return on earning assets for net income before securities gains and losses. These figures can be summarized as follows:

Of course, these figures include the deposit and loan operation of a bank and also the trust departments operations. It would be preferable to have figures for these two distinct parts with an allocation of capital for each.

Dividend Policy

We covered dividend policy in detail in Chapter 3. We will now just make a few comments on how dividend policy might apply to a bank. Dividend policy for banks will vary widely because there is so much difference between banks and the type of stockholders which are naturally attracted to them.

The average payout for all banks is below 50%. Banks as a whole show a relatively low return on common of about 12%. It would appear that such a dividend policy is too low. A large bank with these figures might be better for its stockholders in the long run with a higher payout in the neighborhood of 65%.

Some moderate-sized banks outside of the money centers, where competition is less severe, are able to earn a relatively good return, even as high as 15% with a sound amount of common. For them it makes sense to keep the payout in the neighborhood of 35%.

Banks which have stocks locally held with a small stockholder list may be able to follow dividend policies successfully which are

	Percent of Earning Assets	Percent of Total Funds Provided by Obligations (Total Liabilities Less Reserves and Equity and Other Liabilities)	Percent of Total Assets	Percent of Common Equity
Operating income	7.8%			
Less: Cost of funds	3.6	3.3%		
Operating expenses, etc.	3.2			
Income after taxes before security gains and losses	1.0%		0.8%	12.3%

totally out of line with dividend policy in general, because of their special circumstances.

National banks and state member banks are required to obtain approval from regulatory authorities before paying dividends in excess of net income in a year.

PART TWO

Capital Management

Introduction

In order for management to run a company well, it must understand return on investment and how to employ it. As we have said, profits are not the ultimate goal of our free enterprise system—the ultimate goal is the production of goods and services. But profits are a key in management decision making and profits must be related to investment; consequently, the importance of return on investment.

Return on investment is used in three ways:

1. As a goal for your company as a whole.
2. As a tool for decision making in capital investments and acquisitions so that your company will achieve its goal.
3. As a measure of performance for various divisions of your company so that the managers will play their part on the team to meet the company's goal.

We will cover return on investment from these three points of view. We will show you why it is essential and how to put it to work. Our explanation will require a discussion of various related subjects:

1. How earnings per share grow.
2. The elusive subject cost-of-capital and how it is the basis for setting a profit goal.
3. The importance of taking account of the time value of money in calculating return on capital investments.
4. A reasonable price for your stock based on a fair return to investors.

These subjects will be covered in this part of the book in five chapters:

14—Earnings per Share Growth
15—Cost-of-Capital—Profit Goals
16—Capital Investment Analysis and Acquisition Pricing
17—Division Performance Standards
18—A Fair Return for Investors and a Reasonable Price for Your Stock—Completing the Cycle

CHAPTER 14

Earnings per Share Growth

Managements of publicly owned companies know that their shareholders will be watching earnings per share intently, so managements are sensitive to changes in earnings per share. And some managements use increasing current earnings per share as a primary tool for decision making.

As far as return on investment is concerned, earnings per share is the end result. But we will start here and work backwards because of the importance of earnings per share to stockholders and management.

Management should understand how earnings per share increase and how an increase in earnings per share is related to return on investment. Therefore, we will interpret changes in earnings per share in terms of return on book value of stockholders' investment.

We will finally show how earnings per share is a poor management guide for capital decision making. It can lead to serious mistakes because it does not relate profits to investment. You can follow many policies which will increase earnings per share in the short run but will produce poor and even disastrous results in the long run. This does not mean that management should not have a target for increasing earnings per share; they should have. But this target should be derived from their primary goal, return on investment; the two should tie together.

How Earnings per Share Grow

There are five ways earnings per share grow:

1. Plowback of earnings.
2. Increase in return.
3. Sale of common stock above book value.
4. High price-earnings ratio company acquires low price-earnings ratio company.
5. Repurchase of common stock.

1. Plowback of Earnings

We have already explained in Chapter 3 on dividend policy how plowback of earnings increases earnings per share. By way of review, the rate of increase depends on the amount of earnings retained, which is the balance left after dividend payments, and on the rate earned on the additional capital. The formula is as follows:

> Percent Earned on New Capital x Percent of Earnings Retained (100% Less Percent of Earnings Paid Out in Dividends) = Growth Rate in Earnings per Share

The simplest example we used was a company earning 10% on its beginning common book value and expecting to continue to earn the same rate. It paid out 50% of its earnings in dividends and retained the other 50%. Therefore, the growth rate in earnings per share would be as follows: 10% x 50% = 5%. And the book value per share and dividends per share will also increase at the same rate.

The return on common book value is based on beginning book value because it is used to calculate the growth rate in earnings per share from plowback. The retained earnings come out of earnings during the year and are added to beginning book value to get book value at year end. Consequently, the compounding effect of plowback takes place during the year, with beginning book value as the base.

A company must set a long-range target growth rate in earnings per share which is consistent with its dividend policy and return on capital goal. For example, if it has a dividend payout policy of 38% and has a goal to earn 13% on beginning common equity book value, its growth in earnings per share target would be 8% from plowback: 13% x 62% = 8%. Calculations for this type of company are shown in Exhibit 14-1, Part I. Such a company might anticipate that it would have some additional growth in earnings per share for other reasons.

A true long-range growth company should have a growth rate in earnings per share of more than 8%. Why do we pick 8% as the low side? It is a rather arbitrary choice, but if a company's price-earnings ratio is constant in the long run, the market price of a stock will increase at the same rate as the growth in earnings per share. If investors get an 8% return from market appreciation, the return they would want from dividend yield to provide a satisfactory total return would be smaller compared to the return from appreciation. For example, if investors wanted a 13% total return, and got 8% from market appreciation, they would only have to get 5% from dividend yield. If they wanted 14%, they would have to get 6% from yield. In other words, market appreciation from growth in earnings per share would produce the greatest part of their total return.

Growth rate in earnings per share from plowback is the only growth that can be sustained. All other ways earnings per share grow are transitory.

In Exhibit 14-1, Part II is an example of how earnings per share would grow for certain returns on common and dividend payouts. We have lowered the payout as the return increased, which is consistent with the idea that the higher the return the more a company can benefit stockholders by retaining earnings. Each of the payouts would result in the same dollar dividend payments. For example, if a company had a common book value per share of $25 and earned 10%, earnings per share would be $2.50. If it paid out 50%, the dividend would be $1.25. If the return was 15%, the earnings per share would be $3.75, and with a $1.25 dividend, the payout would be 33%. The dividend in both cases would represent the same 5% on common book value.

2. Increase in Return

If a company paid out all of its earnings in dividends, or in other words, had a 100% dividend payout policy, there would be no growth in earnings per share from plowback. However, earnings of such a company would

Exhibit 14-1

PART I

GROWTH IN EARNINGS PER SHARE FROM PLOWBACK

Return on Beginning Common Book Value 13%. Dividend Payout Ratio 38%.

Line		Year 1	Year 2	Year 3
1	Beginning common book value	$25.00	$27.01	$29.19
2	Return on beginning book value	13%	13%	13%
3	Earnings per share	$ 3.25	$ 3.51	$ 3.79
4	Less: dividend–38% paid out	1.24	1.33	1.44
5	Retained earnings	$ 2.01	$ 2.18	$ 2.35
6	Ending book value	$27.01	$29.19	$31.54
7	Growth in earnings per share	––	8.0%	8.0%
8	Market price (price-earnings ratio = 20)	$65.00	$70.20	$75.80

PART II

GROWTH IN EARNINGS PER SHARE FROM PLOWBACK FOR CERTAIN RETURNS ON BEGINNING COMMON BOOK VALUE AND DIVIDEND PAYOUT RATIOS

Column	I	II	III	IV
Line	Return on Beginning Book Value	Percent Earnings Paid Out in Dividends	Percent Earnings Retained	Growth Rate in Earnings per Share Column I × Column III
1	10%	50%	50%	5%
2	11	45	55	6
3	12	42	58	7
4	13	38	62	8
5	14	36	64	9
6	15	33	67	10

Factors affecting increase in earnings per share from plowback:

1. The rate of return on new capital.
2. The percent of earnings retained, which is 100% of the earnings less the percent of earnings paid out in dividends.

grow if the return on the common book value increased.

For example, if a company has a book value of $25 per share and earns 10% on the book value, it will earn $2.50 per share. With a 100% payout policy, the dividend would be $2.50. There would be no growth from plowback. If next year it earned 11% on book value, the earnings per share would be $2.75, which would be a 10% increase in earnings per share.

As a result of an increase in the return on common book value, a company may be able to show a substantial increase in earnings per share for a few years, particularly if it starts with a low rate of return. For example, if a company earns 6% on common book value and in the next five years it increases the rate to 7%, 8%, 9%, 10%, 11%, it will show a high growth rate in earnings per share.

The growth rate from increases in rate of return would be added to the growth rate from plowback to the extent that all earnings were not paid out in dividends.

The stock market may interpret a growth from an increase in rate of return as though the company was a true growth company. The market does not distinguish between the different ways earnings per share grow. However, growth from a change in rate of return is only transitory. There is some point at which the return on common book value must level off, depending on the nature of the company's business, and competition, etc. The true long-range growth rate depends on the typical rate of return that the company can maintain over the long run and the dividend payout policy.

In Exhibit 14-2, is an example of how earnings per share would grow from an increase in rate of return alone. In year 2 earnings per share increased due to the increase in rate of return but there is no increase in year 3 since the rate of return is the same as in year 2. We have paid out all earnings in dividends so that there was no increase in earnings per share from plowback.

In the exhibit we have assumed a constant price-earnings ratio so that the market price of the stock increases as the earnings increase. This assumes that the earnings in year 2 are of the same quality as in year 1, and that the increase in return on common has not been due to some factor which would increase the risk, such as leverage.

The return on common book value may increase for a number of reasons:

1. An increase in return on existing assets.
2. A reduction in charges on senior securities from refunding at a lower rate.
3. A reduction in the amount of senior securities, with the proceeds from the sale of assets earning less than the rate on senior securities.
4. A change in the capital mix with more leverage.
5. Added investments, which if financed with senior securities, earn more than the rate on senior securities. If financed

Exhibit 14-2

INCREASE IN EARNINGS PER SHARE
FROM INCREASE IN RETURN ON COMMON BOOK VALUE

Return on Beginning Common Book Value 13% in Year 1, increasing to 14% in Year 2 and remaining at 14% in Year 3.
All Earnings Paid Out in Dividends

Line		Year 1	Year 2	Year 3
1	Beginning common book value	$25.00	$25.00	$25.00
2	Return on beginning book value	13%	14%	14%
3	Earnings per share	$ 3.25	$ 3.50	$ 3.50
4	Less: dividend—100% paid out	3.25	3.50	3.50
5	Retained earnings	0.00	0.00	0.00
6	Increase in earnings per share	—	7.7%	0%
7	Market price (price-earnings ratio = 20)	$65.00	$70.00	$70.00

Factors affecting increase in earnings per share from increase in return on common book value:

1. The size of the increase in return.

with common, the assets must earn more than the existing rate on the common.

6. In the unusual situation in which senior securities are refunded with the sale of common, if the earnings-price ratio of the common is less than the after-tax rate of the debt.

This is not to suggest that such increase in return on common book value will necessarily justify the action to cause the increase, or that it is an appropriate way to look at an increase in rate of return.

3. Sale of Common Stock Above Book Value

To explain the effect of sale of stock above book value on earnings per share, let's take a very simple example. Let's assume that a company has one share of stock outstanding with a book value of $100. It is earning 10% on the book value or $10 per share. The company sells one new share at 20 times earnings or $200. Now the company's new book value is a total of $300 or $150 per share. It earns the same 10% on the new investment and earnings per share are $15, a 50% increase in earnings per share. These figures are shown in Exhibit 14-3, Part I. In this example, we have used an extreme case where there has been a 1-for-1 offering of new common stock, so that the shares outstanding have doubled. Ordinarily, a company offers much less stock, in the neighborhood of 1 for 10 or a 10% increase in shares outstanding. Consequently, the effect on increasing earnings per share would be much less.

Exhibit 14-3, Part II shows the effect of increasing earnings per share from a 1-for-10 offering, with stock sold at 2.6 times book value and 20 times earnings. The increase in earnings per share is 14.5%. If the stock were sold at 50% above book value on a 1-for-10 offering and a 13% return on beginning book value, the increase in earnings per share would be 4 1/2%. Again, we have kept the dividend payout at 100% so that there would be no increase in earnings per share from plowback.

In the examples, we have assumed that the capital was put to work immediately. Actually, there would be a temporary decrease in earnings due to the time required to put the capital to work.

The important points to keep in mind with regard to this way to increase earnings per share are:

1. It depends on the amount that the new stock is sold above book value.
2. The amount of stock offered.

If stock is sold below book value, and the return is the same, earnings per share would decrease. Continuous sale of stock below book value will have a serious deteriorating effect on earnings per share.

If you are interested in more detail on this method of increasing earnings per share you may wish to study Exhibit 14-4.

If instead of sale of common stock, the company sold bonds to raise the same amount of money, there would be a greater increase in earnings per share. But this further increase would be due to an increase in return on common book value from leverage. This was covered above under the second way that earnings per share increase—increase in return. If an excessive amount of debt is added, the quality of the earnings would be lower. Sale of common builds up the company's borrowing reserve, the quality of its stock and financial flexibility, so the resulting increase in earnings per share from sale of common vs. the sale of debt are not directly comparable.

4. High P/E Company Acquires Low P/E Company

If an acquiring company's price-earnings ratio is higher than the price-earnings ratio of a company acquired, then current earnings per share will increase. This is illustrated in Exhibit 14-5. The acquiring company is selling for ten times earnings. The company acquired is one-quarter the size of the buying company. Current earnings per share increased 8.5%. Note that this method may decrease return on common book value if the return on the acquired company is lower than the acquiring company.

If an acquisition is made with senior securities, current earnings would also increase

Exhibit 14-3

INCREASE IN EARNINGS PER SHARE FROM SALE OF COMMON STOCK ABOVE BOOK VALUE

PART I

1-for-1 Offering

Line		Before Sale of Common	After Sale of Common
1	Beginning common book value	$100	$100
2	One new share sold at 2 times book	––	200
3	Total book value	$100	$300
4	Common book value per share	$100	$150
5	Return on common book value	10%	10%
6	Earnings per share	$ 10	$ 15
7	Growth in earnings per share	––	50%

PART II

1-for-10 Offering

Sell 1/10 of a New Share for Each Share Outstanding at a Market Price of 2.6x Beginning Common Book Value in Year 2.

Line		Year 1	Year 2	Year 3
1	Beginning common book value	$25.00	$25.00	$31.50
2	1/10 of a new share sold at 2.6 times book value ($25 x 2.6 x 1/10)	––	6.50	––
3	Total book value	25.00	31.50	31.50
4	Shares outstanding	1	1.1	1.1
5	Book value per share	25.00	28.64	28.64
6	Return on common book value	13%	13%	13%
7	Earnings per share	3.25	3.72	3.72
8	Less: dividends–100% paid out	3.25	3.72	3.72
9	Retained earnings	0.00	0.00	0.00
10	Increase in earnings per share	––	14.5%	0%
11	Market price (price-earnings ratio = 20)	$65.00	$74.40	$74.40

Factors affecting increase in earnings per share from sale of stock above book value:

1. The extent to which stock is sold above book value.
2. The return on the new investment.
3. The amount of stock sold.

Exhibit 14-4

EFFECT OF SALE OF COMMON ON CURRENT EARNINGS PER SHARE ASSUMING CAPITAL IS IMMEDIATELY PUT TO WORK AT SAME RATE AS ON EXISTING COMMON COMPARED WITH EFFECT OF DEBT FINANCING

PART I

COMMON OFFERING 1 FOR 20–A 5% INCREASE IN NUMBER OF SHARES

Column	I	II	III	IV	V
Line	After-Tax Return on Common	Price-Earnings Ratio	Ratio of Market Price to Book Value	Increase in Current Earnings per Share from Sale of Stock	Increase in Earnings per Share if Financing Done with Debt at 8% Interest Rate (4% Net Rate After Taxes)*
1	8%	6.3	50%	– 3%	+2.5%
2	10	8	80	– 1	+3.0
3	10	10	100	+ 0	+3.0
4	11 1/2	11.8	178	+ 4	+3.3
5	12	12 1/2	250	+ 7	+3.3
6	15	20	300	+ 10	+3.7
7	20	40	800	+ 33	+4.0

PART II

COMMON OFFERING 1 FOR 10–A 10% INCREASE IN NUMBER OF SHARES

Line	After-Tax Return on Common	Price-Earnings Ratio	Ratio of Market Price to Book Value	Increase in Current Earnings per Share from Sale of Stock	Increase in Earnings per Share if Financing Done with Debt at 8% Interest Rate (4% Net Rate After Taxes)*
1	8%	6.3	50%	– 5%	+5.0%
2	10	8	80	– 2	+6.0
3	10	10	100	+ 0	+6.0
4	11 1/2	11.8	178	+ 7	+6.5
5	12	12 1/2	250	+ 14	+6.7
6	15	20	300	+ 18	+6.7
7	20	40	800	+ 64	+8.0

Formula

$$\left(\frac{100\% + \text{Number of Times Market Price Is of Book Value x \% Increase in Shares}}{100\% + \text{\% Increase in Shares}}\right) - 100\%$$

Example: Part I, Line 6

$$\left(\frac{100\% + 3 \text{ x } 5\%}{100\% + 5\%}\right) - 100\% = 10\%$$

The percent increase in earnings per share is equal to the percent increase in book value per share, providing the same rate is earned on the new capital as on the existing capital. This percentage increase in book value per share depends on the number of shares offered and the extent to which the stock is sold above book value.

*Return on capital raised by debt financing is assumed to produce the same rate as the return on capital raised by common.

Exhibit 14-5

INCREASE IN EARNINGS PER SHARE FROM HIGH PRICE-EARNINGS RATIO COMPANY ACQUIRING LOW PRICE-EARNINGS RATIO COMPANY

Acquisition of a Company 1/4 the Size at 1/2 the Price-Earnings Ratio
Return on Common Book Value of Company Acquired 10%

Line		Year 1	Year 2	Year 3
1	Beginning common book value	$25.00	$25.00	$31.25
2	New company	––	6.25	––
3	Combined book	––	31.25	31.25
4	Return on common beginning book value			
	Acquiring company	13%	13%	13%
	Acquired company		10	10
	Combined		12.4%	12.4%
5	Shares outstanding	1	1.1	1.1
6	Book value per share	$25.00	$28.41	$28.41
7	Earnings per share	3.25	3.52	3.52
8	Less: dividend–100% paid out	3.25	3.52	3.52
9	Retained earnings	0.00	0.00	0.00
10	Increase in earnings per share	––	8.3	0%
11	Market price (price-earnings ratio = 20)	$65.00	$70.40	$70.40

Factors affecting increase in earnings per share from high P/E company acquiring low P/E company:

1. Size of the acquisition.
2. The amount by which one P/E is above the other P/E.

provided the net after-tax cost of the senior securities is less than the earnings-price ratio of the acquired company. But again the effect of the leverage on the quality of earnings would have to be weighed. And since pooling is not allowed if the acquisition is with debt, the earnings would be affected by the intangibles to be written off.

5. *Repurchase of Common Stock*

If the return on the source of funds used to repurchase common stock is less than the earnings-price ratio, current earnings per share will be increased.

In Exhibit 14-6 is shown a simple example of a company which repurchases 10% of its stock. It used idle cash which is not earning anything. In such a situation if the company earns anything for its common stock, current earnings per share would increase.

If the company sold an asset in order to provide funds to repurchase stock, current earnings per share would increase if the after-tax return on the asset sold was less than the earnings-price ratio. This is shown in the figures on page 473.

If the company sold bonds to provide funds to repurchase stock, current earnings per share would increase if the after-tax cost of the interest was less than the earnings-price ratio of the stock.

The ways current earnings per share can be increased by repurchase of stock are not necessarily financial maneuvers that should be

Exhibit 14-6

INCREASE IN EARNINGS PER SHARE FROM REPURCHASE OF COMMON STOCK

1/10 of Share Repurchase

The common book value in year 1 is represented by assets consisting of $6.50 cash and $18.50 of earning assets. The $6.50 in cash is used to purchase 1/10 of a share of common stock at the end of year 1.

Line			Year 1	Year 2	Year 3
1	Beginning common book value represented by:				
		Cash	$ 6.50		
		Earning Assets	18.50		
		Total	$25.00	$18.50	$18.50
2	Return on beginning book value		13%		
2	Return on beginning book value		13%	17%	17%
3	Total earnings		$ 3.25	$ 3.25	$ 3.25
4	Number of shares		1	.9	.9
5	Earnings per share		$ 3.25	$ 3.61	$ 3.61
6	Less: dividends–100% paid out		3.25	3.61	3.61
7	Retained earnings		0.00	0.00	0.00
8	Increase in earnings per share		0	11.1%	0
9	Market price (price-earnings ratio = 20)		$65.00	$72.20	$72.20

Factors affecting increase in earnings per share from repurchase of stock:

1. The amount of stock repurchased.
2. The relationship of the earnings price percentage and the net after-tax return on the asset used to purchase the stock, or the net after-tax cost of the senior security used to provide funds to repurchase the stock.

Assets Sold	After-Tax Return on Assets Sold	Market Price of Stock	Earnings per Share	Earnings-Price Ratio	Net Gain in Earnings for Shares Remaining Outstanding
$100	$3 or 3%	$100	$4	4%	$1

done. The advantages and disadvantages of repurchase of stock was covered in Chapter 3.

Summary of Growth in Earnings per Share

In Exhibit 14-7 are summarized the five examples we used to show how earnings per share increased.

The important thing to note is that there is only one which provides a permanent increase–that is plowback. All the others are one-shot and temporary. This is not to say that such increases are necessarily wrong; they may or they may not be. However, the mere fact that current earnings per share increase is not adequate reason in itself for making these management decisions, and they are not a source of permanent growth rate in earnings per share.

Actual growth in earnings per share in any one year may be the result of one or more of the ways earnings per share grow. And they may take place in varying degree during the year, rather than at the beginning of the year as we have applied the figures. Therefore, it may be difficult to separate them. But in the long run, the reason for the growth rate should be discernible.

The above five reasons for increasing earnings per share can also be used to describe how current earnings per share decrease when the reverse of these actions occur.

Why Is Increasing Current Earnings per Share a Poor Guide?

We can show why earnings per share is a poor guide for management decision making with a few figures.

When any investment is made, no matter in what form or by whom, the investor expects to get a return. The size of that return must

Exhibit 14-7

SUMMARY OF TABLES ON GROWTH IN EARNINGS PER SHARE

		Year 1	Year 2	Year 3
Exhibit 14-1	Plowback	$3.25	$3.51	$3.79
	Percent change in earnings per share	––	8.0%	8.0%
	Return on beginning book value 13% Dividend payout ratio 38%.			
Exhibit 14-2	Increase in rate of return on common book value	3.25	3.50	3.50
	Percent change in earnings per share	––	7.7%	0%
	Return on beginning book value 13% in year 1, increasing to 14% in years 2 and 3.			
Exhibit 14-3	Sale of new stock above book value	3.25	3.72	3.72
	Percent change in earnings per share	––	14.5%	0%
	Sale of 1/10 of a new share for each share outstanding at 2.6 times beginning book value in year 2.			
Exhibit 14-5	Acquisition of company with common	3.25	3.52	3.52
	Percent change in earnings per share	––	8.3%	0%
	Acquisition of company 1/4 the size at 1/2 price-earnings ratio in year 2. Return on common book value of company acquired 10%.			
Exhibit 14-6	Repurchase of stock	3.25	3.61	3.61
	Percent change in earnings per share	––	11.1%	0%
	Repurchase of 1/10 of a share at 20 price-earnings ratio in year 2 with idle cash.			

depend upon the willingness of the investor to provide the funds and the degree of risk involved. In other words, there is some minimum rate which is necessary to be just sufficient to induce the investor to put up the funds. If this rate is not met, the earnings per share in the future will not be sufficient to maintain the price of the company's common stock.

As an example, we will take a company with 1 million shares outstanding. It is considering a $10 million capital investment. The company evaluates the risk in the $10 million project and considers that it should make a minimum return on investment of 10% after taxes to satisfy investors.

The company has $10 million invested in municipal bonds earning 4% tax free. This contributes 40¢ per share to the company's earnings. A forecast for the $10 million project shows that earnings after all expenses and taxes will be $700,000 annually or 7%. This would amount to 70¢ per share on the company's outstanding shares. Thus, relying on increasing current earnings per share, the company decides to sell the municipal bonds and go into the project because it will increase current earnings per share by 30¢. This results from a 70¢ increase in earnings per share from the project less a 40¢ loss in earnings per share from sale of municipal bonds. These figures are shown in Exhibit 14-8, Part I.

As another way to finance the project, the company could sell $10 million 8% bonds which would result in an after-tax interest cost with a 50% tax rate of 4%, or $400,000. The results would be the same—a 30¢ increase in earnings per share. These figures are shown in Exhibit 14-8, Part II.

Or the company might sell common stock at 25 times earnings or a 4% earnings-price ratio so that the project could be financed with common stock and increase earnings per share by 27¢. These figures are shown in Exhibit 14-8, Part III.

However, if we look at the rate of return on the project of 7% and compare it to the 10% return required to cover the management's estimate of the risk, we should turn the project down. A company should not invest in any project which did not give a return to cover more than the risk involved.

So we say at this point, that earnings per share cannot be used for decision making purposes in capital investments. If the point is not clear at this time, we hope at least it will be clearer after you have read the next chapter on Cost-of-Capital. In it we will explain that there is a minimum return which is acceptable to investors; it may vary from industry to industry and company to company depending on the risk involved. And if the minimum return acquired by investors is not earned on a capital investment, the increase in earnings per share will be insufficient to compensate investors adequately, regardless of the short run effect on current earnings per share. Ultimately, the market price of the stock represented by the investment will suffer.

Exhibit 14-8

INADEQUATE INCREASE IN CURRENT EARNINGS PER SHARE FROM INVESTMENT IN NEW PROJECT

Assumptions

Shares outstanding	1,000,000
Earnings per share for company prior to project	$ 4.00
Project	$10,000,000
Estimated earnings on project after taxes–7%	$ 700,000
Management assesses risk of project to require a minimum return after taxes	10%

PART I

CAPITAL INVESTMENT FINANCED WITH PROCEEDS FROM SALE OF ASSETS CONSISTING OF MUNICIPAL BONDS

Earnings per share from project	+70¢
Proceeds from sale of asset consisting of municipal bonds	$10,000,000
Income from municipal bonds	$ 400,000
Earnings per share from municipal bonds	–40¢
Net gain in earnings per share	+30¢

PART II

CAPITAL INVESTMENT FINANCED WITH PROCEEDS FROM SALE OF BONDS

Earnings per share from project	+70¢
Proceeds from sale of bonds	$10,000,000
Interest cost rate pre-tax 8% and 4% after 50% tax rate	$ 400,000
Interest cost after taxes per share	–40¢
Net gain in earnings per share	+30¢

PART III

CAPITAL INVESTMENT FINANCED WITH PROCEEDS FROM SALE OF COMMON STOCK

Market price of stock	$ 100
Shares offered	100,000
Proceeds from sale of common stock	$10,000,000
Price-earnings ratio	25
Earnings-price ratio	4%
Earnings after taxes required to prevent dilution	$ 400,000
Earnings resulting from project	$ 700,000
Net gain in earnings per share	+27¢

CHAPTER 15

Cost-of-Capital–Profit Goals

The Significance of Cost-of-Capital and Profit Goals

You must have some goal for the three purposes we suggested in the introduction to capital management:

1. Company goal.
2. Capital investments and acquisition decisions.
3. Division performance.

Various goals used by some managements are:

1. Return on sales.
2. Improve the operating ratio.
3. Earn more than the interest rate on debt.
4. Earn the interest rate on debt and dividends on common.
5. Company's historical return on capital.
6. What other companies in the industry earn.
7. Growth rate in earnings per share.
8 Payback of investment.

Are any of these adequate?

A profit goal should be compatible with the way our free enterprise system works; competition is supposed to drive prices down to cover all costs so that the consumers are protected. If we start from this premise, we must develop a goal that fits into what is meant by all costs.

Costs to produce goods and services include all operating expenses such as wages, materials and taxes.

What if management of a company in an unregulated industry decided to produce goods which could be sold at prices only sufficient to cover these elemental costs? It would not make sense. The consumers, with freedom of choice, would be saying that they did not want the goods enough for society to justify their production. There are other costs which must be met. Products must satisfy a need sufficiently so that the consumers will be willing to pay prices which will also cover the costs associated with capital.

One cost associated with capital is depreciation. If a $10 million building is used to produce goods, it will decline in value as time goes on due to depreciation. And the investor who puts up the money will want to get his original investment back as the asset depreciates. Depreciation provides a flow of funds to replace assets; it is a return *of* capital. If the goods produced in the building could be sold at prices which would be just enough to cover operating expenses and depreciation, the investor would end up, after the building wore out, with his $10 million. He would have received no return for the use of the capital.

Therefore, there is another element which must be met. It is return on capital to compensate the investor for the use of the money.

For a project to be economically successful, the resulting goods or services must be able to be sold at prices which will cover:

1. Operating expenses–wages, materials, taxes.
2. Depreciation–return *of* capital.
3. Additional earnings sufficient to provide an adequate return *on* capital.

A decision by management to make an investment must be based on whether sales will be sufficient to cover these three elements. And whether the third amount is adequate must be determined by relating earnings to the capital employed. None of the goals we mentioned which are used by some managements provide an answer based on a proper return on capital.

There is a competitive market for capital. And investors consider the returns that might be available on alternative investments. Thus, there is a certain return which investors require to induce them to put up capital; we call this cost-of-capital. The term cost-of-capital fits into the idea of the way our competitive system works; that is, that capital investments should only be made if all expenses are covered including cost-of-capital.

It is interesting to note that Donaldson Brown, a vice president of General Motors stated way back in 1924 in an article[1] entitled, "Pricing Policy in Relation to Financial Control":

> . . ."A sound pricing policy must be founded upon a clear conception of what might be implied in the phrase, economic return attainable upon capital required."
>
> . . ."Management's principal control over capital outlays involves rigorous attention given before authorization to the expected profit return after tax on capital to be employed."
>
> . . ."The fundamental consideration is the economic cost-of-capital to the individual business."

By cost-of-capital, we do not mean just an interest cost. A company obtains its capital through various types of long term securities, such as bonds, preferred stock, and common stock. There is a competitive market for all types of securities, just as there is a competitive market for goods and services. You must focus on the capital market because that is where capital has to be obtained.

Cost-of-capital includes two elements:

1. Pure interest–This is the amount necessary to induce people to save their money and invest rather than hold it idle or spend it without any risk.

---

[1] *Measurement and Administration,* Volume 7, No. 4, April, 1924.

2. An additional amount necessary to compensate investors for the risk of the investment. This is affected by the business itself and the amount and terms of the other securities in the particular capital structure.

Therefore, our problem is essentially one of determining the cost-of-capital by assessing the risk of an enterprise as it is judged in the competitive capital market.

Cost-of-capital is the starting point for a company's profit goal. As we will subsequently discuss, management should establish a profit goal above the cost-of-capital.

To develop a goal based on an adequate return on capital requires an answer to three questions:

1. What do we mean by capital and how should it be raised?
2. What rates should be applied to the various types of capital?
3. What is an adequate overall return on capital?

Application to a Privately Owned Company

In our discussion of cost-of-capital, we will be talking about rates for capital in the competitive capital market. A publicly owned company gets all its capital, not generated internally, in the capital market. A privately owned company depends on its limited number of owners to supply the common money, so it does not have to conform to the disciplines of the market place for this part of its capital. The owners of the company can make their own rules regarding the return on their capital. However, unless the owners want to run the company as a toy, it should earn the same as though it were publicly held; otherwise, the owners would be better off selling out and putting their money in the stock market. Thus, it only makes sense for the owners to conform to the same discipline as if the company were publicly held. And if the owners contemplate going public some time in the future, they should build a record which is acceptable for publicly owned companies.

Capital

To start, we will have to see what we mean by capital. To do so, we will refer to our simple balance sheet for an industrial company.

Balance Sheet

Assets		Liabilities		
Current assets	$100	Current Liabilities		$ 50
Plant, net	50	Long term capital		
		Debt	$25	
		Common	75	
				$100
Total	$150			$150

You have heard it said many times throughout the book that the savings of our nation flow into corporations through the sale of long term securities, on the right hand side of the balance sheet, and also from retained earnings which are recorded with common equity. The capital is used for plant, equipment and working capital on the asset side. Remember, we include in long term capital short term debt which is not cleaned up annually, and finance leases capitalized.

Current liabilities may include short-term seasonal bank loans, which do supply some capital. But capital provided through current liabilities, which require a payment of interest, is dependent on the seasonal nature of the business and is generally small. Any expenses connected therewith can be taken care of in operating expense. We will be concerned primarily with the principal source of capital—long term capital and the rates associated with it. The amount of long term capital will depend on the nature of the business, but, within limits, the way it is divided up is at the discretion of management.

Division of Long Term Capital

Our first step in determining cost-of-capital is to decide on the make-up of the long term capital. Theoretically, we could use any capital structure to determine cost-of-capital as long as we assigned to each type of security a rate which reflects the market's appraisal of risk for that security.

This can be done for senior securities. However, as a practical matter, a problem arises with regard to the rate for the common stock. The rate for the common stock must reflect the increased risk if a company is highly leveraged. It is hard enough to determine a rate for common stock for a soundly capitalized company; it is generally impractical to try to find evidence of a rate for a common stock which is excessively leveraged for its type of business. The rate should reflect the return required by investors in both good and bad times. A company which has too much leverage may fare well in a boom period, but it may suffer seriously if bad earnings are encountered. It is difficult to get representative data to show the effect of adverse conditions on rates for a highly leveraged company which can be used for common equity for cost-of-capital purposes.

Therefore, as a practical matter, we will have to use a long-term capital structure which will provide a sound rating on bonds and which will not have a financial risk due to excessive leverage. This would require that the debt be rated at least A grade. As we pointed out in our discussion of capital structure, it would be preferable to have a higher rating, but many companies are unable to do so.

If we use debt up to the point where a financial risk is not added, we will, on the basis of logic, be raising capital at the lowest cost. If a company has a more leveraged capital structure, we should determine the cost-of-capital based on a hypothetical capital structure which would provide good quality securities. On the other hand, if a company is underleveraged, a hypothetical capital structure can also be used which will include the appropriate amount of debt. There is a reasonable range within which a company's securities will be accorded good quality.

Sometimes the question is raised as to whether the capital structure ratios should be calculated with the market prices of the securities rather than book figures. Some financial analysts do calculate the ratios on this basis in addition to the book figures in determining the quality of securities. For purposes of cost-of-capital, book figures are the ones to use. The ratios based on market prices of securities will vary widely, depending on the level of security prices. Furthermore, the book figures more nearly represent the capital which a company has available on which to earn a profit and from which it must calculate the composite cost.

The extent to which book figures represent true present values of assets can be easily challenged. The book figures may be under- or over-stated. It would be nice if all balance sheets were stated on the basis of true present values, but that would be expecting the impossible. In determining the quality of a company's securities, analysts will give some weight to such values where they may be known. For cost-of-capital purposes, the extent to which book figures vary from true present values should be kept in mind in deciding on the significance of capital structure ratios. Probably this is the best that can be done.

Based on the book figures, a moderate-sized industrial company with sales around $300 million and satisfactory earnings might have debt to total long term capital of about 25% to provide an A rating. This is the same as the percentage we used in our example of a simple balance sheet at the start of this chapter. This is about the average debt ratio for all industrial companies. The long term capital would then be:

Debt	25%
Common	75
Total	100%

Assuming that our company has such a capital structure, our next step is to determine the rates to apply to the debt and common equity. But before making such a determination, we will have to discuss two subjects which we will need to use in calculating these rates; that is, financing costs and the appropriate time period.

Financing Costs

In determining the rates to apply to the securities in the capital structure, we have to allow for financing costs. A company only has the capital to use which it receives from the sale of securities after deducting financing costs from the price at which the securities were sold to the public.

For example, if a company sells an 8% bond with a 30-year maturity without a sinking fund at a price to the public of 100, the yield to maturity would be 8%. However, the company has to pay the underwriters for selling the bonds, and there are financing expenses connected with the bond sale such as legal, accounting, regulatory, etc. These have to be deducted from the price at which the bonds are sold to the public to get the net proceeds to the company. For a good quality bond, the effect of financing costs on yield to maturity might be as follows:

Price to public	100	Yield 8.00%
Underwriters' fee	1	
Price to company	99	
Financing expenses	1	
Net proceeds to company	98	Yield 8.18%

The rate that should be used for cost-of-capital purposes is the yield to maturity based on the net proceeds the company receives, which is 98 and results in a rate of 8.18%.

The size of the underwriters' fee and financing expenses depends on many factors such as quality of the issue, its size, the condition of the market, etc. The effect of these costs on yield depends on the size of the interest coupon and the length of maturity. A sinking fund would affect the maturity.

The same type of allowance for financing costs should be made for other types of senior securities and also common stock in order to obtain the rate based on the net proceeds.

Time Period for Rates—Embedded, Spot, Average or Future

There are four possible time periods to consider for calculating rates for senior securities and common stock.

1. *Embedded*—Embedded rates refer to the rates on a company's existing securities; that is, the company's historical rates. They are based on what the company received at the time the securities were sold. The sales of the securities may have taken place any number of years ago and bear no relationship to current rates.

   If a company has more than one issue of a similar type of security outstanding, the rate to apply to the combined amount would be the weighted average. As an example, for a company with two issues of bonds with equal security, the weighted average rate would be as follows:

Amount	Yield to Maturity Based on Net Proceeds Received at Time of Sale	Interest
\$20,000,000	5.70%	\$1,140,000
30,000,000	6.70%	2,010,000
\$50,000,000		\$3,150,000

$$\text{Weighted average embedded rate} = \frac{\$\ 3{,}150{,}000}{\$50{,}000{,}000} = 6.30\%$$

   If an issue of bonds were used to refund previously outstanding bonds, there are financing costs associated with the transaction which have to be included as part of the financing costs for the existing issue in order to get the embedded costs. These are the debt discount and expense on the previously outstanding bonds which has not been amortized, and the call premium to call the previously outstanding bonds. These amounts should be deducted from the net proceeds of the new issue in figuring the yield.

   A company cannot totally disregard the embedded costs of its senior securities. In the income statement, the interest on existing securities will be the actual expense. However, past financing, just like an old plant, is "over the dawn" as far as use for determining pricing policy in our competitive society. It may be merely some evidence in arriving at a proper rate.

   It would be futile to try to calculate the embedded cost of common stock for a company which has been in existence for many years. The embedded cost of common stock would include the historical record of each common stock issue which has been sold since the company's inception and all the earned surplus which has been piled up each year—a rather impractical task.

2. *Spot*—Spot or short term refers to rates based on a day, or an average for a month, a quarter or even a period of a few years. This would not be satisfactory because the cost-of-capital might go up and down as senior security prices changed in a short period of time. When a company makes a capital expenditure, it is concerned with a much longer time period.
3. *Average*—By average we do not mean "spot." We have already eliminated that possibility. By average we mean a period covering a sufficient number of recent years to give a figure which would represent the cost to raise capital under varying conditions of good and bad years, bull and bear markets—in other words, a business cycle. It would appear necessary to use at least five years in order to get away from "spot." A ten-year period might give more reasonably average results. Keep in mind that to the extent that the period does not include a complete cycle, it may be biased on the high or low side. What period to use depends on the circumstances and is a matter of judgment.
4. *Future*—How well a company is doing, based on return on existing capital, will be affected by the rates at which it has raised senior capital in the past. However, for deciding on capital expenditures, the costs which will be pertinent will be those that it will have to incur to raise the capital in the future. If rates have recently risen so that the financing will probably have to be done at high rates compared with any average past period, it is only sensible to take into account possible future rates. A problem arises here because it is difficult to forecast rates with any accuracy for even a short term ahead. However, the difficulty of the problem does not suggest that it should be disregarded.

Conclusion on Period for Rates

Now that we have described the time periods available, what do we use? We should eliminate embedded and spot so we are left with average and future. However, it should be noted that for regulated companies, commissions rely heavily on embedded rates.

Companies should only provide new supplies of goods if estimated future prices will be sufficient to cover all future operating costs and produce a fair return on capital. But we have to estimate the future by looking at the past.

If rates on securities were repeated from one cycle to the next, we could use an average of the past five or ten years. But this is not necessarily the way rates move; there may be a long upward or downward trend.

Since estimating the future is so difficult, what do we do? Judgment has to be applied to come up with a reasonable figure.

If rates have been moving in a cycle, a ten-year average might be appropriate. If they have been trending upward or downward for a number of years, a five-year average might be more appropriate. If it appears that a present high or low level of rates will continue for some time in the future, then some allowance should be given to a projection of existing levels.

As an example, we will refer to the interest rate on outstanding A grade bonds of industrial companies for the ten-year period 1964-1973. They were as follows:

1964	4.57%	1969	7.40%
1965	4.63	1970	8.57
1966	5.35	1971	8.03
1967	5.86	1972	7.66
1968	6.54	1973	7.84

Ten-year average 1964-1973—6.65%
Five-year average 1969-1973—7.90%

In view of the upward trend, it would appear that the most recent five years would be more representative of what a company might face. And it would not be unreasonable to expect that the present high level might continue for some time. Therefore, a final figure might be based on an average of the last five years with two more years added on at the same rate as in 1973. This would produce an average of 7.90%. In view of the fact the rates increased substantially in 1974, this figure would be on the low side.

In these figures we have not allowed for the fact that new issues generally have to be sold at a higher yield than outstanding bonds, and also an allowance has to be made for financing costs to get the net proceeds to the company. Making these adjustments, we might use a rate for illustrative purposes of 8¼%.

Admittedly, we are relying heavily on judgment, but that has to be an essential element in determining cost-of-capital.

Sources of Data for Rates on Senior Securities

Whatever source is used, the rates on senior securities must be compatible with the type of capital structure and nature of the company's business. In other words, the rate tied to each security should represent the risk associated with that security. Bond ratings are generally a helpful guide in matching up the quality of debt securities. Care should be exercised to make certain that the issues are comparable not only as to quality, but also for size, maturity, terms, etc.

There are three principal sources of data for rates for senior securities.

1. New issues.
2. Outstanding issues.
3. Indexes of rates for senior securities.

New Issues—New issues are an ideal source of data. In calculating the cost rates, the net proceeds received by the company after financing costs should be used.

The principal disadvantage of this type of data, is that there may not be an adequate sample of new issues so that a representative average over an appropriate period can be obtained.

Outstanding Issues—Market quotations over an appropriate period for comparable outstanding issues may be a good source for data for senior securities. However, it is necessary to make two adjustments: an adjustment on outstanding issues to get the rate on new issues, and an allowance for financing costs. So this source of data requires two steps: first to obtain the rate on the market prices, and then get the equivalent rate on net proceeds that would be received by the company for new issues. This may require an increase in yield from 0.10% to many times that amount depending on the market situation at the time.

Indexes of Rates for Senior Securities—There are numerous indexes of rates for different quality bonds and preferred stocks. They give a good, broad perspective—but representing an average, they may include low and high coupon bonds, varying maturities, etc. These indexes have to be adjusted in the same way as for outstanding issues in order to get a rate based on the net proceeds.

Common Cost Rate

Now we come to the most difficult question in cost-of-capital: Does common have a cost?

Your reaction may still be: "Who ever heard of common stock having a cost?"

We reply: "It does not have an accounting cost. However, common stockholders have to be satisfied and common stock does have a cost in the economic sense. The rate can be expressed as a percentage, just as the debt cost is expressed as a percentage interest rate."

Some people contend that it is a misnomer and confuses the picture to use the term "cost." They prefer to say that common has an "earnings requirement." Whatever terminology you prefer, you must arrive at a rate to apply to the common equity.

Importance of Future Earnings

For a debt security, such as a bond, it is the expectation of receiving interest payments in the future and repayment of the principal amount at maturity that attracts investors to pay a price for a bond. We emphasize that it is the prospect of future interest payments which induces investors to buy a bond. Past payments are over the dam.

What is it that attracts common stockholders to pay a price for common stock? In essence, stockholders receive two things: future dividends, and market appreciation–the difference between the price at which they buy the stock and the price at which they sell it. It is these two elements, both in the future, that induce investors to pay a price for common stock.

Where do both dividends and market appreciation come from? They both derive from future earnings per share. In total, it is the expectation of future earnings per share which induces investors to buy a stock and which determines the price they will pay.

It is the relationship of market price to the future earnings per share that is the guide to the common cost. We will try to build up gradually to the full meaning of this concept.

On the basis of what has been said, if a stock earns \$10 per share and sells at \$100 per share, the apparent cost rate for the common would be \$10 divided by \$100 or 10%. This is similar to the situation for a bond which sells at \$100 and pays \$5 interest. The cost rate would be 5%. Presumably, in this simple example, if the company continued to earn \$10 per share the stock would continue to sell at \$100. The company would be just earning the rate that investors required in the competitive capital market. Unfortunately, it is not quite this simple.

Suppose we have a bond which matures in two years and pays 4% interest the first year and 6% the second year. What would be the cost rate for the bond? Would it be 4%–the relationship of price to interest being paid immediately? Hardly. It would be the relationship of price to a combination of all future payments. A simple average of future payments would give us 5%. Similarly, if a stock earned \$8 next year and \$12 the year after, it might be some combination of the two figures which would affect the price of the stock.

The important point we are stressing is that the common cost is the relationship of market price to future earnings rather than to present earnings per share. Present earnings are past earnings once a stock is purchased; all gain to the stockholder comes from future earnings. Past and present earnings may be some guide to future earnings, but they are not what benefits the common stockholder and they are not what he buys. This idea is summarized in Exhibit 15-1, Part I.

Without going into minor refinements, it is the future earnings in Column III and not the present earnings in Column II which determine the market prices and thus the cost rates shown in Column IV.

We should note that in our explanation, we will use a 10% common cost rate for illustrative purposes, because it makes it easy for the reader to follow the figures. However, as we will explain, such a figure is much too low, particularly in current markets.

Investors' Expectations

There is another more subtle point with regard to the common cost. There are actually three earnings per share from which we have to choose in order to arrive at a definition of the common cost. This is illustrated by the simple figures shown in Exhibit 15-1, Part II.

For future earnings in Column II and III–that is, \$8 and \$10–we have used single figures to represent future earning power per share. Actually, future earnings will be a stream over a period of years rather than one single figure. However, using these figures for explanatory purposes, what is it that makes investors pay \$100 per share for the stock–the current \$5, or future \$8 or \$10?

The stock sells at 20 times the present earnings per share of \$5. The reciprocal, or earnings-price ratio, is 5%. The greatest misconception about the common cost is that it is this 5% figure. The \$5 reported present earnings per share is already history when a stock is purchased.

It is not the $8 per share estimated by the management which determines the market price of the stock because that estimate is known only to management; it is a secret. Managements generally do not give out such forecasts. Secrets cannot affect public market prices. It is the investors who buy and sell the stock who affect the market price.

The investors' expectation of $10 is what makes the market price. In Exhibit 15-1, Part II we have indicated that not only is it future earnings that determines stock prices, but also it is future earnings *expected by investors.* Thus, the cost rate for common has to be based on the price investors pay for a stock related to the earnings that they expect to receive in the future.

We qualify this rate in the exhibit by the word "approximate" because we have to allow for financing costs.

Eventually, if the company's estimate of $8 proves to be correct, investors will revise their expectations from $10 to $8. Since investors want a 10% return, the price of the stock will fall to $80 per share. The common cost will still be 10% before allowing for financing costs.

By now, you should be beginning to switch away from the concept of profit as shown in the last line of an income statement and appreciate the fact that a company is losing money for its stockholders if it does not earn the common cost. To make a profit it should earn more. We admit that these are categorical statements. The remainder of this chapter provides explanation.

As to the size of the common cost, we can make one very definite statement at this point. Regardless of the price-earnings ratio, the common cost must be substantially higher than debt cost or any other senior security cost because the common stock is in the most risky position in the capital structure. Senior securities are protected by the common stock and have their risk reduced thereby.

Before we go further with the common

Exhibit 15-1

COMMON COST ILLUSTRATED

PART I

COMMON COST DEPENDS ON FUTURE EARNINGS

Column	I	II	III	IV
Company	Market Price of Stock	Present Earnings per Share	Future Earnings per Share	Approximate Common Cost Rate
A	$100	$ 5	$10	10%
B	100	10	10	10
C	100	20	10	10

PART II

COMMON COST DEPENDS ON INVESTORS' EXPECTATIONS

Market Price of Stock	Present Earnings per Share	Estimated Earnings per Share by the Company	Expected Future Earnings per Share by Investors	Approximate Common Cost
$100	$5	$8	$10	10%

cost rate we will have to review briefly three subjects: the significance of the taxes investors pay, the relationship of book value and market price per share and financing costs for common.

Investors' Taxes

It is sometimes argued in rather vigorous fashion that taxes paid by investors should be taken into account in calculating the cost-of-capital for a company.

Taxes which investors pay may affect the supply and demand for various types of securities. However, the effect is registered in the market prices. The company must meet the market rates.

We will use the following example in order to clarify the idea that we do not have to allow for the taxes paid by investors.

Interest on municipal bonds is exempt from Federal income taxes. Consequently, the interest rate investors require and the rate municipalities have to pay is relatively low. If the tax law were changed so that investors had to pay a tax on the interest they received on municipal bonds, the interest rate that municipalities would have to pay on new financings would be increased through investors' reaction and corresponding change in demand.

Let's put this in terms of figures. We will assume that a municipality could sell a tax-exempt bond to yield 4% with the interest exempt from personal income taxes. Now assume that the tax laws are changed so that investors would have to pay income taxes on such interest. Then the interest rate that investors would be willing to accept would increase on the basis of supply and demand to reflect the rate they could get on similar quality corporate bonds subject to income taxes. Assume that this resulted in a 6% rate. The net income which investors obtained, after the tax law was changed, might be roughly the same as their return of 4% when the bonds were tax exempt. However, it would not follow that a municipality would only have to pay the net income that investors obtained after taxes; it would have to pay 4% if the bonds were tax exempt and it would have to pay 6% if the law were changed so investors had to pay taxes on the bond.

Likewise, a company has to determine the rates it has to pay investors without regard to the taxes the investors pay.

Is the Rate Determined on Market Price or Book Value?

Even after there is an understanding of common cost, some confusion seems to linger regarding the relationship of market price and book value as the base which is used for figuring the cost, and how the rate figured on one base ties together with the other.

The common cost rate must be based on market price. We wish to obtain the rate investors require in relation to the amount of money they will supply. But this statement does not always clear up the matter. The question still remains: "How can the rate be obtained from the market price and then be applied to book value?"

A simple example may help:

> A company's capital structure consists solely of one share of common stock with a book value of $100 per share. Assume that the book value represents a true present value of the company's assets. It earns 20% or $20 per share on the book value. The stock sells for $200. If we assume that investors do not anticipate any growth, the common cost is 10%, leaving out financing costs to simplify the picture.
>
> A company can earn only on the capital with which it has to work. It has $100 to work with, not the market price of $200. In order to meet its cost-of-capital it would only have to earn 10%. In fact it is doing much better, so the stock sells well above book value.
>
> The company needs to increase its capital for expansion purposes and sells one new share for $200. The book value will now be as shown on the next page.

	Book Value
Original Share	$100
New Share	200
Total	$300
Per Share	$150

If we assume that the company continues to earn 20% on the original $100 investment and just earns its 10% cost-of-capital on the new investment of $200, the earnings would be as follows:

	Book Value	Rate	Earnings
Original Share	$100	20%	$20
New Share	200	10	20
Total	$300		$40
Earnings per Share			$20

With no change in risk as appraised by investors, the stock will sell at 10 times earnings or $200 per share.

So we conclude that the common cost must be obtained from the market price and not the book value. The company must earn on assets.

Our example may raise a question in your mind as to what would happen if the original part of the business making 20% is gradually liquidated through depreciation. What happens is obvious. This lucrative investment will gradually be reduced to zero and the cash would flow back from depreciation. If the company invests this cash flow at the cost-of-capital rate, the stockholders will receive a return equivalent to the risk and the book investment recaptured through depreciation will be preserved. However, the market price of the stock would suffer seriously. Only if the return on that investment reaches 20% will the stockholders be as well off as before in the market price of their stock. But the company cannot be limited in its use of the cash by the 20% rate which was earned on a previous investment. Once the cash flows back, the next step, is a new and independent decision.

In this discussion, it might incorrectly appear that we are suggesting that the market price should be about equal to book value. We discuss further the relationship of market price to book value in Chapter 18.

One more subject before we get to a rate for common cost.

Financing Costs for Common

Allowance must be made for financing costs for common stock just as for senior securities. For example, if a new issue of common is sold at $100 per share and financing costs are $10, so that the company received net proceeds of $90, this later figure would be used as the basis for determining the common cost rate. It would be divided into the future earnings investors expected when they bought the stock. If the earning power expected by investors was $10 per share, the common cost would be 11.1% (expected earnings per share of $10 divided by net proceeds per share of $90).

There is another way to make this calculation for common stock. First calculate the common cost rate by using the market price and then adjust that rate to allow for the financing costs. This latter step is done by dividing the common cost rate, based on the market price of the outstanding stock, by the percent that the net proceeds represent of the market price of the outstanding stock. These calculations are shown in Exhibit 15-2.

Two questions can be raised regarding the financing costs to use for calculating the common cost:

1. Should the financing costs for a direct or rights offering be used? Generally, the net proceeds for a direct offering is greater than a rights offering because of the need to set the subscription price low enough to provide a rights value. There are various reasons for using the net proceeds approach for a rights offering in calculating the common cost rate:
   a) Some companies have to offer stock through rights because of charter or state laws.

Exhibit 15-2

ADJUSTMENT OF COMMON COST RATE BASED ON MARKET PRICE OF OUTSTANDING STOCK TO OBTAIN THE COST RATE BASED ON NET PROCEEDS COMPANY RECEIVES AFTER FINANCING COSTS

1. $\dfrac{\text{Expected future earning power per share by investors}}{\text{Market price of outstanding stock}} = \dfrac{\$\ 10}{\$100} = 10\%$

2. Net proceeds received by company after financing costs as a percent of the market price of outstanding stock.

   $\dfrac{\text{Net proceeds per share after financing costs}}{\text{Market price of outstanding stock}} = \dfrac{\$\ 90}{\$100} = 90\%$

3. Common cost rate based on net proceeds after financing costs.

   $\dfrac{\text{Rate based on market price of outstanding stock}}{\text{Net proceeds per share after financing costs as \% of market price of outstanding stock}} = \dfrac{10\%}{90\%} = 11.1\%$

b) Stockholders generally like rights.

c) If a company uses rights and the stockholders recognize the value of the rights by paying a higher price for the stock, the company will recoup the extra cost of the rights by a better market price at the time of the offering.

2. Should financing costs be applied to earned surplus?

One sometimes encounters complete misconceptions regarding the cost of earned surplus, even from supposedly financially sophisticated people. For example, a senior official in bank regulation talking about bank capital to a group of bankers said, "Earned surplus is your cheapest form of capital." Fortunately, the reaction of the group indicated that they were not impressed with the idea.

There is no distinction in the various parts of common equity as far as the common stockholders are concerned. It all represents part of their ownership. Surplus arising from retained earnings is equivalent to raising new common equity. In fact, as earnings are plowed back, a company regularly raises new common equity every day. If management made a distinction regarding the rate to be earned on earned surplus, stockholders would be well advised to have the company pay out all its earnings in dividends and then raise new equity money by sale of stock. If you question this statement, consider a private company with one stockholder. Will he accept a lower return on money he *leaves* in than on money he *puts* in? Stockholders of a publicly owned company should not be treated differently by management.

There is one possible difference between common stock sold to the public and earned surplus. A stock sale involves financing costs, including underwriter's compensation and financing expense; none of these is associated with retained earnings, which build up without financing costs. Therefore, it may be contended that a slightly lower rate should be applied to earned surplus to the extent of financing costs. There is a good argument against any difference: a company should earn enough on its common equity to be able to pay out all its earnings in dividends if it chooses to do so and still cover its cost-of-capital. In other words, dividend policy decisions should be made free from any pressure of capital requirements. As another argument, a company should not accept less profitable ventures than would be required to stand the test of the capital markets. This book treats all common equity the same.

The allowance for financing costs in order to get the net proceeds per share to the company for a moderate-sized rights offering for a stable stock might be in the neighborhood of 10%. The net proceeds per share, after allowing for financing costs, would be 90% of the market price. For a volatile stock or a very large issue, the allowance would have to be larger, perhaps in the neighborhood of 15%. On this basis, the net proceeds per share, after allowing for financing costs, would be 85% of the market price.

Definition of Common Cost

At this point, we will pause to give a definition to common cost and then go into further explanation in the hope of clearing up questions which may be plaguing you.

Common equity cost is the relationship of the market price investors are willing to pay for a stock, adjusted for financing costs, to the long-range future benefits that they expect to receive, or:

$$\frac{\text{Return Investors Expect to Receive from Future Dividends and Market Appreciation}}{\text{Market Price of Stock Investors Are Willing to Pay, Adjusted for Financing Costs}}$$

The figures which we have used to describe the common cost are shown in diagram form in Exhibit 15-3. For comparative purposes, the bond cost is also included.

The common cost represents what investors require on the average in the way of future earning power in order to justify their paying the market prices they pay, in view of their appraisal of the risk.

Throughout the book, we will use many examples involving common cost. They have to be based on investors' expectations. We may use a single figure for earnings per share to represent this concept. Actually, as already mentioned, investors' expectations consist of a stream of earnings rather than one figure, and, generally, the stream will be on the increase. Using a single figure, with no growth, is unrealistic, but it is satisfactory for explanatory purposes.

Six Different Views of Common Cost

Now we will suggest six different ways to look at a rate for common equity to give you a better feeling for the subject and the general magnitude. You should appreciate that none of them are cost of common since they do not represent investors' expectations to market price. Some are figured on book value and some on market price. For those on book value, we are trying by indirection to determine what investors might want on market price. All of the figures are historical and based on a period when interest rates were considerably lower so that they are not representative of the common rate today. However, they do give some interesting clues.

The Case of an All-Debt Capital Structure

Let's take an unusual view of the long term capital in our simplified balance sheet; that is, the \$25 of debt and \$75 of common equity. Our purpose will be to illustrate the idea that common equity does have a cost. For this purpose, let's reason in terms of debt securities. You will undoubtedly agree that debt has a cost.

If we assume an interest rate of 7% on the \$25 of debt, the picture would start out as shown below:

	Amount	Rate	Cost
Debt	\$25	7%	\$1.75
Common	75		

Forget about the tax savings that interest produces for the company; we are now talking only about the rates that investors require, and they do not pay the corporate tax. We will cover the effect of interest on the taxes the company pays subsequently.

Now let's change the composition of our capital structure and substitute a layer of \$25 of junior debt for $25 of common equity. Since the added debt would be junior and in a more risky position, it would require a higher rate. Let's use 8%.

For an industrial company, we already have added much more debt than would be wise from the viewpoint of sound financial policy. However, purely for illustrative purposes, let's go further and use a third layer of debt; with practically no common equity for protection, any interest rate we assign to it would be a pure guess. It is conceivable that the rate on

Exhibit 15-3

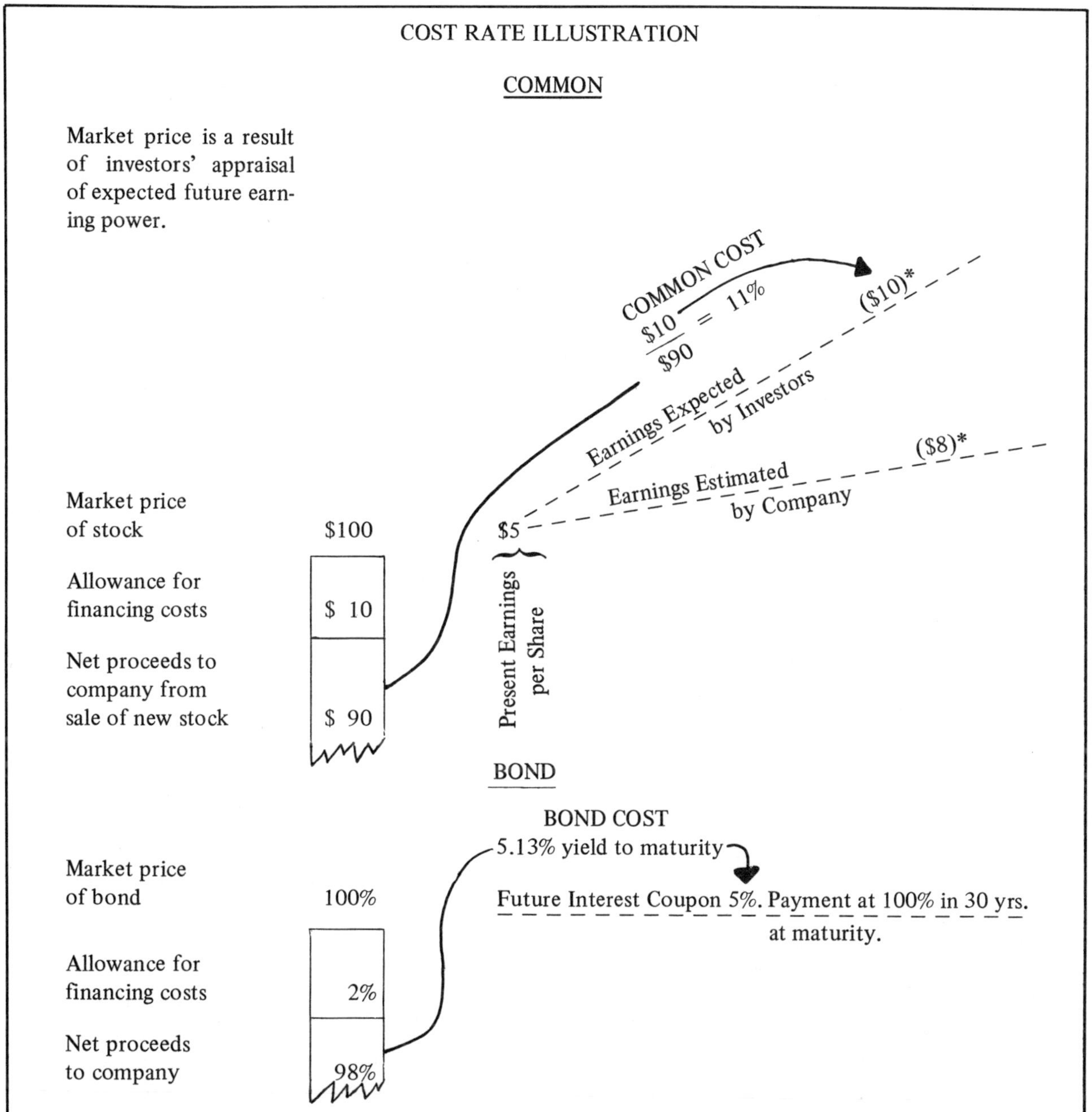

*The $10 and $8 figures are each supposed to represent in one figure the potential stream of future earnings per share.

this third layer of debt might be 15%. As a matter of fact, it might not be possible to sell the issue under any circumstances.

However, for illustrative purposes, with the two additional layers of debt, the picture would be as shown below:

	Amount, $	Rate, %	Cost, $
Debt	$ 25	7	1.75
Jr. Debt	25	8	2.00
Jr., Jr. Debt	49	15	7.35
Common	1		
	$100		11.10

Thus, leaving out the cost for the remaining $1 of common and using the debt costs as above, the overall cost for 99% of our capital is about 11%.

It is hoped that this approach makes it easier for you to understand that all capital has a cost whether it be debt or common equity. Merely substituting debt for common or common for debt shouldn't change the fact that all capital has a cost.

This illustration should also indicate that capital is not cheap, and that as securities become more junior the risk increases, so the rates should increase regardless of the type of security.

What Return Do You Think Investors Should Receive from an Investment in a Common Stock?

When talking to management groups, in order to get them to think about a common cost rate, it is interesting to ask them to give their answers to this proposition:

> You are in charge of the pension fund for your company. You have decided to hire a new outside money manager for the fund. You want all of the fund to be invested in good grade common stocks. In other words, it will not be a balanced fund with part bonds and part stocks–it will be all common stocks; not high fliers but good quality stocks. While interviewing prospective new money managers for your fund, they turn the tables on you and ask what you consider the minimum satisfactory performance for the fund in terms of dividends and market appreciation over a ten-year period; that is, the minimum average annual rate of return from dividends and market appreciation combined.

This question has been presented to various management groups over a period of years when interest rates were considerably lower. The replies very interestingly averaged in the neighborhood of 11%. Some individual answers ranged as low as 8%. That was obviously too low because that rate could be attained on good grade bonds. The answers ranged as high as 15%.

This approach suggests that, as a supplier of funds from your pension plan, you expect to get a satisfactory return from future earnings on the common stocks of companies in which your pension fund will be invested.

Now turn the picture around and look at it from the point of view of the companies in which your pension plan will have investments. You can't get a return as a *supplier of funds* unless the companies which are *users of the funds* earn that return. Therefore, from the point of view of the managements running companies in which your pension fund is invested, the 11% becomes the minimum earnings requirement rate after taxes on market value of the common stock.

What Industry Earns

Now let's look at the rate of common from another point of view.

If our free enterprise system works correctly, and competition drives prices down to the level at which all costs are covered, then it might follow that what industry earns represents the cost-of-capital. Here we are talking about all industry and not one particularly depressed or very profitable industry. According to Exhibit 15-4, Part I, the average return on year-end common equity for all manufacturing companies was 11.3% for the most recent ten-year period. On average beginning and year-end capital, the average figure would be closer to 12%.

It is interesting to note the median returns on common equity for the 500 largest companies included in the *Fortune* magazine survey for the past ten years as shown in Part II of the exhibit. The average of the medians is 11.1% on year-end common equity. On average beginning and year-end capital it would be closer to 12%.

Part III shows the return on common equity for companies included in the principal stock indexes. These returns show a higher figure of over 13%. Thus, the figures in Exhibit 15-4 suggest a rate of over 11% for common equity.

Exhibit 15-5 depicts the returns on average common book value for the 500 largest companies in the *Fortune* magazine survey in 1973 on a dispersion chart. Very interestingly the returns fall in a bell-shaped curve with the median at 12.4% and the best companies making 20% and over.

We may note that a company or industry may earn below cost of capital for an extended period. Once capital is sunk it cannot be retrieved. Furthermore, a company can use money from depreciation and retained earnings and put it in capital at too low a rate of return. It can borrow money and do the same thing. This represents serious loss to a company's stockholders and to our economy. However, management can persist in following wrong policies for a long period if the directors do not have enough guts to replace the management. If the returns for a sample of companies or certain industries are used for clues as to common cost, sensible selectivity must be used to come up with appropriate figures.

What Common Stockholders Have Received

As another approach let's look at what stockholders have received over a period of years. This does not represent a common cost rate unless we assume that investors received what they expected to get and what induced them to pay the prices they did for stocks. For this reason, this is a dangerous approach, because the stock market for many investors is like betting on the horses. Their exaggerated dreams make them pay too much for stocks; like the people who bet on horses, they disregard the long term odds. If investors' expectations are not realized, stocks take a plunge. In any event, a figure on this basis is shown in Exhibit 15-6. It shows that investments in all stocks on the New York Stock Exchange produced a return of 9.3% from 1926 to 1965. This is a rather interesting figure, but it is for such a long time span that it is not very helpful for our present purpose.

What Investors Think They May Earn—Expectations

In order to better comply with the definition of common cost rate, we should measure the market price of stocks in terms of what a representative group of investors expect to receive. To illustrate the idea of investors' expectations there are two quotations below giving some idea as to what investors might expect. They suggest a rate of 11 1/4% and 12%.

The Financial Research Center of the Department of Economics, Princeton University issued, on December 9, 1970, the results of a survey of financial institutions on stock prices:

> Stock prices are expected to gain about 7 3/4% per year over the next decade. Since dividend yields for stocks in general are now about 3 1/2%, investors are anticipating an overall return (including both dividends and capital gains) of about 11 1/4%. This compares with present yields to maturity of about 8% for high-grade long term corporate bonds and about 6 1/4% for long-term government bonds.

Of course, 1970 is outdated today.

In May 1973, Byron Klapper in the column, "Heard on the Street," in the *Wall Street Journal* made the following comment about electric utilities:

> Analysts note that the 7% dividend yield is only part of a total of about 12% that

Exhibit 15-4

RETURNS ON COMMON EQUITY FOR
BROAD COMPANY GROUPS

PART I

RETURN ON YEAR-END COMMON EQUITY,
ALL MANUFACTURING COMPANIES*

Year	%
1973	12.4
1972	10.3
1971	9.4
1970	9.2
1969	11.2
1968	11.7
1967	11.4
1966	13.1
1965	12.6
1964	11.4
Average % profit, 1964-1973	11.3%

*Includes all manufacturing corporations except newspapers. Source: Quarterly Financial Report for Manufacturing Corporations, Federal Trade Commission, Securities and Exchange Commission. Figures for preferred stock are included with common equity, but the amount of preferred is relatively small.

PART II

MEDIAN RETURN ON YEAR-END EQUITY,
500 LARGEST COMPANIES†

Year	%
1973	12.4
1972	10.3
1971	9.1
1970	9.5
1969	11.3
1968	11.7
1967	11.3
1966	12.7
1965	11.8
1964	10.5
Average % return, 1964-1973	11.1%

†Reprinted from *Fortune Directory* by permission, © 1970 Time Inc. Year-end equity is referred to as invested capital by *Fortune* magazine; it includes capital stock, surplus and retained earnings.

PART III

RETURNS ON AVERAGE COMMON EQUITY FOR PRINCIPAL STOCK INDEXES

	% Earned on Average Equity	
	1954-1973	1964-1973
Moody's 125 Industrials	13.0%	13.2%
503 Compustat Companies	12.8	12.8
S & P's 425 Industrials	13.8	14.1
50 Largest Mfg. Corps.	13.8	14.0
Average	13.4%	13.5%

Exhibit 15-5

RETURN ON YEAR-END EQUITY

500 Largest Companies 1973*

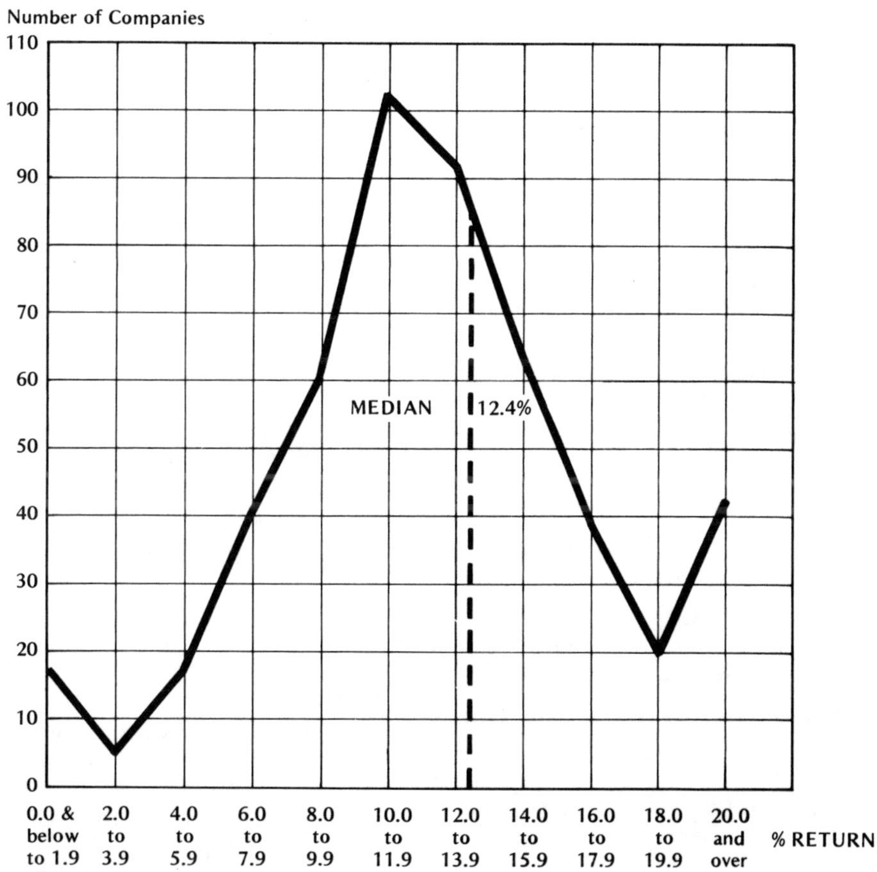

*Reprinted from FORTUNE by permission; ©1970 Time Inc. Year-end equity is referred to as invested capital by FORTUNE Magazine; it includes capital stock, surplus and retained earnings.

Exhibit 15-6

RETURN RECEIVED BY INVESTORS ON COMMON STOCKS FROM MARKET APPRECIATION AND DIVIDENDS

Return from Market Appreciation and Dividends with Dividend Reinvestment for All Stocks Listed on the New York Stock Exchange

University of Chicago, Center for Research on Security Prices

1926-1965–9.3%

investors should receive as dividends increase an average of 5% annually.

Regulated Utility Companies

A major controversy in a rate case for a utility company is the fair rate of return which the company should be allowed to earn on its total long term capital. The evidence in rate controversies before state and Federal regulatory authorities is voluminous. The companies present one view and representatives of the consumers present another view.

Company witnesses present data to show that a fair return on common equity may be 15% or higher. So-called opposition witnesses, may argue for a figure as low as 10%.

Since regulation is a substitute for competition, commissions should allow a return which would be appropriate if competition did exist. Commissions have allowed returns on common varying up to as high as 15% depending on the circumstances. For example, in 1974, the New York Public Service Commission allowed a 14% return on common equity and the Public Service Commission of Colorado allowed 15%. It is interesting to note that the Massachusetts Supreme Court ruled in a telephone case in 1971 that a minimum non-confiscatory return on equity was 11%.[2]

Summary of Views on Common Cost

The different views on common cost are summarized in Exhibit 15-7. On the basis of these figures 12% would appear to be on the conservative side. Adjusting that figure for financing costs by dividing by 90% would increase it to over 13%. However, these data include years in which interest rates and inflation were about half what they are today. In 1974 a figure of 13% for a well-capitalized company with its debt rated at least A would certainly be too low.

Returns on both short-and long-term senior securities in 1974 suggest that investors would be fools if they did not expect a much higher return on common than they did in the past. Investors would be better off putting their funds in bonds with far less risk. This is illustrated by the yields in 1974 on certain bonds compared with ten years ago as follows:

	1964	November 1974
Treasury bills–3 mo.	3.55%	7.60%
Taxable U.S. govt. bonds–Due 10 yrs. and longer	4.15	7.04
Moody's index of A grade industrial bonds	4.57	9.51

Measurement of Common Cost for a Particular Company

So far we have given you a broad perspective of the common cost. You should have sufficient feel of its magnitude to decide on an approximate figure for your company providing it has adequate size and a sound capital structure.

You may be wondering how you might calculate a common cost rate. We will now

[2]New England Telephone & Telegraph Co. vs. Department of Public Utilities 275 NF. 2nd 493 or 92 PUR 3rd 116.

Exhibit 15-7

SUMMARY OF VIEWS ON COMMON COST

Exhibit		Approximate Returns
15-4, Part I	Returns on year-end common equity for all manufacturing companies, adjusted for return on average common equity–1964-1973.	12%
Part II	Median return on year-end common equity *Fortune* 500, adjusted for return on average common equity–1964-1973.	12%
Part III	Average returns on average common equity for four principal stock indexes–1964-1973.	13%+
15-5,	Returns received by investors in common stocks from market appreciation and dividends for all stocks listed on the N.Y. Stock Exchange–1926-1965.	9%+
What investors think they may earn–expectations:		
	Survey of financial institutions by Financial Research Center of Dept. of Economics, Princeton University–December 9, 1970–Return from market appreciation and yield.	11%+
	Analysts' opinion of return from dividend yield and increase in dividends for electric utilities. Quote from *Wall Street Journal,* May, 1973.	12%
	Regulated utility companies–Ruling by Massachusetts Supreme Court as to minimum return on common figure for non-confiscation for telephone company–1971.	11%

discuss various methods, but we should prepare you for some discouragement because direct measurement presents a major problem. In making such a calculation, you must keep in mind that the definition of the common cost depends on the idea of *expected* earnings.

Companies for Which Investors Have Not Expected Growth in Earnings per Share

If investors expect that a company is static in earnings per share, then the average earnings in the past are expected to be repeated. Under these circumstances, since past earnings represent what investors expect in the future, an average of ratios of past earnings per share to the market price of the stock in the same year will give a common cost. In other words, we are talking about non-growth companies. The ratio for any single year might be unrepresentative because of swings in earnings from year to year, but if we use an average of such ratios over a period of years, adjusted for financing costs, we should be able to obtain a reasonable result.

This is the easiest situation in which to determine the common cost, but there are pitfalls which must be avoided:

The fact that a company's earnings have exhibited no growth does not in itself mean that investors believe there is no growth. For example, a company which has spent large sums on research and development may not yet have reaped the benefit of those expenditures. Past earnings may have been disappointing. Nevertheless, investors may have bought the stock in anticipation of future growth in earnings when the results of research and development will materialize. Under these circumstances, ratios of earnings per share to the market price in the same year would not produce a common cost.

Furthermore, since most companies only pay out a part of their earnings in dividends and build up the common stockholders' equity with retained earnings, investors logically can expect some growth in earnings per share. Therefore, whenever you use this approach for companies which apparently have no prospects of growth, you must keep in mind that the resulting common cost may be on the low side. The same idea applies to a company with earnings at an abnormally low level; investors can expect that earnings will return to a more normal level. Companies in which investors had no hopes of an increase in earnings in the future when they bought the stock would seem to be a rare situation.

If a company had no growth and investors expected it to have no growth, then all investors would get is dividend yield. In such a situation, in order for investors to be sure of the dividend being paid, investors would want adequate protection of the dividend by earnings. Such a common stock becomes more like a preferred stock. The company in deciding on how much it should earn to keep investors satisfied would have to think in terms of the earnings protection needed for the dividend. For example, suppose investors were satisfied with an 8% yield on a common stock which had a market price equal to book value, a 12% earnings rate on common book value would result in a 66 2/3% dividend payout ratio. This is a high payout for an industrial company. From a practical point of view, an investor would be better off buying a preferred stock which would provide better earnings protection for the dividend. This, in itself, suggests that investors practically never buy a common stock for yield alone without expecting some appreciation.

Market Price Related to Forecast Earnings per Share

Financial analysts make forecasts of earnings per share. Some of the financial services carry estimates of earnings per share at least a year ahead. For certain industries, analysts make forecasts a number of years ahead. Such forecasts may give a limited clue to common cost.

This idea may be applied to a study of the historical relationship of market price and earnings per share a certain number of years ahead, if we assume that what the company earned was, in fact, on the average what the analysts expected the company to earn.

For example, we might examine the historical relationship of past market price, adjusted for financing costs, to earnings per share five years ahead. We could do this over an extended period of time to obtain an average figure. We refer to this method as the "lead and lag" approach—that is, the lead in earnings vs. the lag in price. It should be used with extreme caution for these reasons:

1. The number of years which investors look ahead may vary.
2. When we relate past market prices adjusted to actually reported earnings a number of years ahead, we are assuming that the actual earnings are the same as those which investors expected, and which actually affected the prices at the time. This may or may not be the case.
3. The worst error that may be made in this approach is the assumption that investors expect no further growth past a specific year's earnings. Such a measure is thus too low to the extent that further growth may be expected. This idea is illustrated in Exhibit 15-8.

In spite of the many dangers inherent in using the ratio of market price, adjusted for financing costs to future earnings, there are some companies for which this approach may give a clue to the common cost. It may work for a company which has had depressed earnings for a considerable period, but for which the future looks encouraging. Analysts forecast a return of earnings to a more normal level. The current market price may be largely affected by analysts' expectations. A discussion with analysts may give a gauge as to the general level of their expectations.

Exhibit 15-8

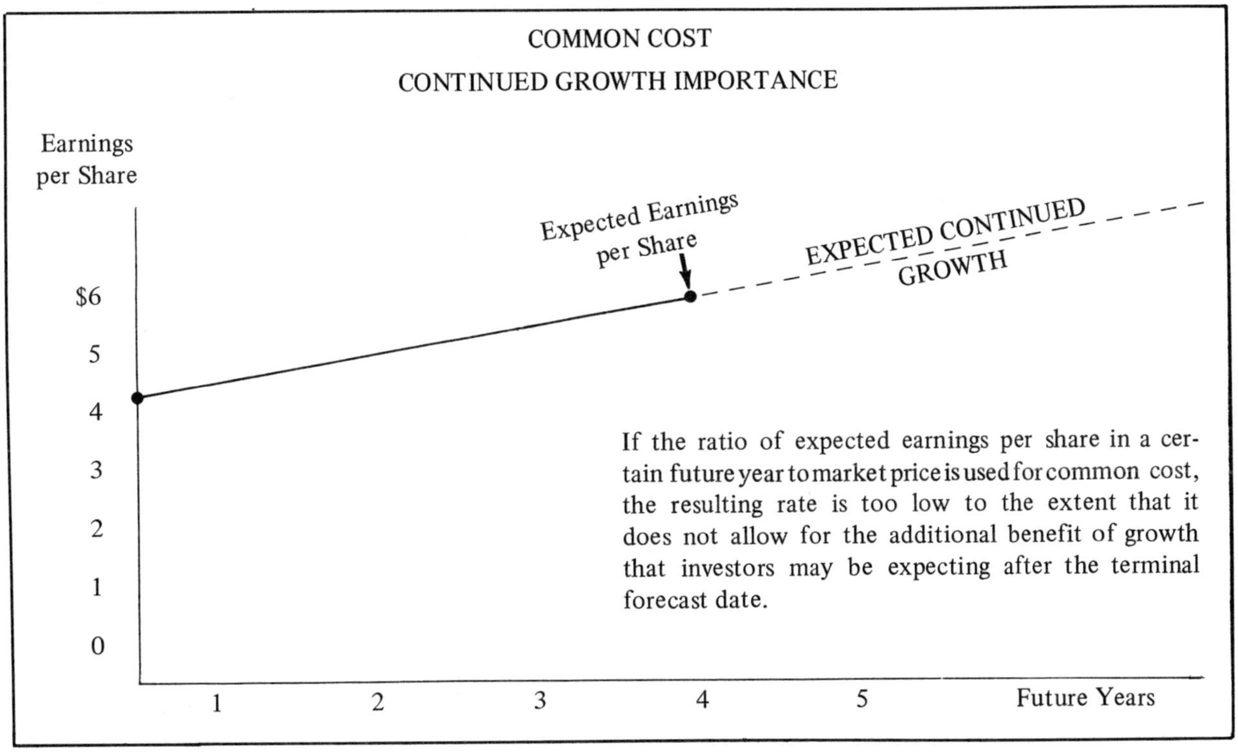

Growth Rate Approach

There are more sophisticated approaches to the valuation of common stocks in terms of prospective returns to investors. They generally involve an estimate of the combined return from future dividends and market appreciation, both of which are derived from earnings.

The simplest method assumes that an investor expects the stock can be sold at the same price-earnings ratio at which it is bought and that the dividend payout ratio will remain the same. An estimate is made of the growth rate investors expect in earnings per share. On the basis of these facts, the approximate return to the investor, no matter how long he holds the stock, is the total of the present dividend yield plus the growth rate in earnings per share. This is illustrated in Exhibit 15-9, Part I.

If you are not familiar with this method, you might wonder how it works out. This is shown in Exhibit 15-9, Part II. The return on the $100 invested on a Time Value Profitability Rate Basis is 10%. This is the same as we obtained above by adding the dividend yield of 4% at the start, to the compound growth rate of 6%. The Time Value of Money technique is explained in Chapter 16.

The 10% figure, representing the return to the investor, would have to be increased for common cost purposes to allow for financing costs.

The limitations of this approach must be appreciated. The number of years does not affect the results, but the idea assumes that the investor expects that the stock can be sold at the same price-earnings ratio at which it is bought, and that there will be a constant dividend payout ratio. This, of course, is a very broad assumption and one which materially affects the final result.

Exhibit 15-9

GROWTH RATE APPROACH TO COMMON COST FOR STOCK WITH CONSTANT PRICE-EARNINGS RATIO AND DIVIDEND PAYOUT RATIO

PART I

DIVIDEND YIELD PLUS EXPECTED GROWTH RATE IN EARNINGS PER SHARE

Constant price-earnings ratio	10
Present dividend yield	4%
Constant dividend payout ratio	40%
Expected growth rate in earnings per share	6%
Total expected return to investors:	
Present dividend yield	4%
Expected growth rate in earnings per share	6%
Total return	10%

PART II

RETURN ON COMMON STOCK FROM DIVIDENDS AND MARKET APPRECIATION

Column	I	II	III	IV	V	VI
Year	Earnings per Share	Dividend Payout Ratio	Dividends per Share	Price-Earnings Ratio	Market Price	Dividend Yield
Purchase	$10.00	40%	$4.00	10	$100.00	4.00%
1	10.60	"	4.24	"	106.00	"
2	11.24	"	4.49	"	112.40	"
3	11.91	"	4.76	"	119.10	"
4 Sale	12.62	"	5.05	"	126.20	"

Column	I	II	III	IV
		RETURN TO INVESTOR		
Year	Purchase Price	Dividends	Sale Price	Total Return
0	–$100			–$100.00
1		+$4.24		+ 4.24
2		+ 4.49		+ 4.49
3		+ 4.76		+ 4.76
4		+ 5.05	+$126.25	+ 131.30
Total				+$ 44.79
Time Value Profitability Rate				10.00%

A refinement of the yield-plus-growth-rate method is based on the same assumptions as above, but covers estimates of price-earnings ratios at the time of sale of the stock different from the price-earnings ratio at the time the stock was purchased. Elaborate tables[3] have been devised so that an investor can read off the estimated total return. However, this refined approach is of little value for cost-of-capital purposes because of the difficulty of finding out what terminal price-earnings ratio investors may have been expecting.

How do the methods based on growth rate help a company determine a common cost? They are just another tool that may be useful to arrive at an approximate return investors expect to receive. A company which has close contact with financial analysts may be able to obtain an idea of what they expect of growth in earnings per share.

Other Approaches to Growth Situations

There are various other approaches to the valuation of common stocks based on estimated future returns. One such approach proceeds on the assumption that the only stream of value which flows from a company to its stockholders over an indefinite period of time is the cash dividends. Viewed another way, the individual stockholders may change from time to time with sellers and buyers, but as a whole the entire mass of stockholders continues intact. The only benefit they receive as a whole from the company is cash dividends. This method attempts to place a value on a stock on the basis of the present worth of the expected flow of dividends for an almost indefinite period in the future. Actually, those who use this method make certain assumptions about the growth rate in dividends per share for a substantial number of years in the future, and further assume that the growth rate will gradually slow down over a subsequent period and finally level off.[4]

[3]One of the first major studies of this type was contained in a book published in 1931, *Stock Growth and Discount Tables,* by Samuel Eliot Guild, Financial Publishing Co., Boston, Massachusetts.

[4]One of the leading proponents of this school is Nicholas Molodovsky, Vice-President of White, Weld, and Co., Inc. See "Common Stock Valuation: Theory and Tables," by Nicholas Molodovsky, Catherine May, and Sherman Chattiner, *Financial Analysts Journal,* March-April 1965, Volume 21, Number 2.

This method may be of value to some highly skilled analysts in estimating whether certain common stocks may be over- or underpriced. However, it would seem to be of limited value to the financial executive of a company who is trying to obtain an interpretation of how much return investors expect to receive in the future to justify their purchase of a stock. From the practical point of view, the average investor thinks about what he may receive in terms of dividends and market appreciation.

Conclusion on Common Cost Rate

Six important points to keep in mind about common cost are:

1. There is such a thing as common cost.
2. It is not cheap.
3. It has to be higher than the rate on any senior securities.
4. If excess leverage is added to the capital structure, the common rate must increase substantially.
5. Serious errors may arise in determining the common cost if a person is not thoroughly familiar with the principles involved.
6. The best that can be done is to arrive at some reasonable figure for a company that is well capitalized with good quality securities.

In our summary on common cost, we suggested, for a soundly capitalized company, that a figure of 13% adjusted for financing costs may have been appropriate in the past, but it would be on the low side on the basis of present interest rates and the high level of inflation.

As far as the common cost rate for your company is concerned, you should have your ears attuned to any evidence of the return investors might require to induce them to buy your stock. You may find that you cannot get any such evidence and will have to fall back on an acceptable figure for a large, well-capitalized company. This will certainly be satisfactory for you to use in order to get a gauge of your overall cost-of-capital.

Exhibit 15-10 summarizes the definition of the common cost rate and some related ideas.

What Follows from an Understanding of Common Cost

If a company with long term capital consisting only of common stock sells stock and uses the proceeds in an expansion program so as to earn less than the common cost, and investors' appraisal of the risk remains the same, the stock will ultimately fall in market price, regardless of the short range action. The company will have misdirected capital so as not to provide a return commensurate with its cost.

By way of further explanation, let us think of this idea in terms of bonds. If a company sells bonds to investors, it will have to offer an interest rate which will satisfy investors' appraisal of the risk in the bond.

If the company sells a 30-year bond at \$100 with a 6% interest rate, the bond will continue to sell at \$100 (assuming stable interest rates in general) as long as the company continues to pay 6% and there is no change in investors' appraisal of the risk. Assuming, hypothetically, that the company could cut the interest rate at will and reduced it to 5%, the price of the bond would fall to about \$86, so that the yield at the new price would be 6%. Investors would have lost money.

The same idea applies to a common stock when a company fails to earn the common cost as measured in the competitive capital market by the relationship between market price and investors' expectations.

You may feel that investors' expectations are limitless and that a company could not hope to earn enough to satisfy them. If this troubles you, we have failed to make the point clear. If investors' expectations of earnings are high, then they will pay a correspondingly high price for the stock. To illustrate, suppose that investors would buy a 30-year bond at \$100 with a 4% interest rate on the basis of their

Exhibit 15-10

OUTLINE SUMMARY OF COMMON COST

Definition: Return a Company Is Required to Earn to Attract Investors to Provide Common Equity Capital

or

$$\frac{\text{Return Investors Expect to Receive from Future Dividends and Market Appreciation}}{\text{Market Price Investors Are Willing to Pay, Adjusted for Financing Costs}}$$

Both dividends and market appreciation come from earnings per share, so cost of common can also be measured in terms of investors' expectation of future stream of earnings.

Allowance must be made in the market price for financing costs to obtain the rate based on the net proceeds the company receives from financing.

The return investors require includes:

1. A return sufficient to compensate them for providing capital with no risk.
2. An allowance for risk.

Risk is affected by the nature of the business, the amount of senior securities ahead of the common and the credibility of the company's investor relations program. Since common is more risky than any senior security, the rate must be higher.

What common cost is not:

1. The current earnings-price ratio—unless investors expect future earnings to be the same as the current earnings.
2. What investors have received as a return in the past—unless what they received is what they expected to receive.

appraisal of the risk. For no good reason, let us suppose that the company decided to pay 6% interest. Then, in the competitive capital market, the company could sell the bond at a price of about $135. The price would go up in proportion to their expectations. The yield to maturity to investors would still be the 4% rate they required in terms of their risk appraisal.

Likewise, with common stocks, if investors' expectations of earnings are high, prices of stocks will be high. During a bull stock market, the common cost may not decrease. The increase in the prices of stocks may be due to investors' optimism and an increase in their expectations about earnings, and not the fact that they are willing to accept a lower return.

By now, you should have a feeling as to why merely increasing present earnings per share is not necessarily the right goal for management to use in deciding on expansion and acquisition policies. Present earnings do not focus on the rate of return that the capital must earn in order to satisfy the cost in the competitive capital market.

You may insist that, if a company's reported earnings per share increase, the price of the stock will increase. Therefore, you should concentrate on present earnings per share. You are right about the immediate market action. This is why we have to spend so much time on this point. Investors do have to place much reliance on trends in reported earnings to make their estimates of the future. However, regardless of past trends, if investors' expectations of earnings based on their appraisal of prospects for the company, are not realized in the future, then the price of the stock will ultimately be bound to suffer.

Common stockholders require a rate of return on their investment based on their appraisal of risk. If they do not get it, they will sell their stock down to a price where the earnings represent the rate they require. For example, if stockholders require a 10% return and they believe the company only has prospects of earning $5 on $100 of common book value, stockholders will only pay $50. The $100 of investment is now worth only $50 in the market. And every dollar that management plows back in the business will represent a 50¢ loss to the investors.

Let's take another view of why it is disastrous to go into projects which do not earn the cost-of-capital.

If you want to ask executives a fun question in order to tell whether they have good judgment in making capital investments, put this question to them:

> Company X, an average industrial company, has $10 million invested in municipal bonds selling at 100 with a 5% coupon to yield 5%. The $500,000 annual interest is an after-tax income. The company has an opportunity to sell the bonds and put the money into a $10 million typical industrial project which will show an after-tax return on the investment of 8% for the life of the project, or $800,000 annually. Company X has no other project which will require this amount of capital in the near future. Ask executives whether Company X should keep the municipal bonds or sell them and put the money in the industrial project?

This question has been tried on many management groups, and usually, there will be a majority who will vote in favor of selling the bonds and going into the project. It was tried on one particularly interesting group consisting of 20 young presidents of companies and their wives. To have some fun, their wives were asked to give their answers first. They voted 18 to 2 not to go. When the presidents voted, they voted 16 to 4 to go.

The correct answer is NO GO! In fact, the project will mean at least a $2 million loss of principal the minute the decision is made to go. That is how bad it is!

The wives were asked why they had voted 18 to 2 not to go. They explained that their husbands complained so much about all the problems they had running their companies that the municipal bonds looked like a better bet even though the income was lower. The wives, without realizing it, took risk into

Exhibit 15-11

ILLUSTRATION OF LOSS OF INVESTMENT BY GOING INTO PROJECTS BELOW THE COST-OF-CAPITAL

	Book Value	Level Earnings for Common	Return on Investment	Cost-of-Capital Return Required by Investors	Market Price
Step 1–Steel Company	$100	$10	10%	10%	$100
Step 2–Municipal Bonds	100	5	5	5	100
Step 3–Steel Company	100	8	8	10	80

account while their husbands ignored the difference in risk and concentrated too much on the increase in earnings per share.

We will use a slightly different example to explain why, at least, $2 million was lost in the project. The figures are shown in Exhibit 15-11.

In step 1, the Steel Company has $100 invested in plant, earning $10 or 10%. Investors want a 10% return so investors will place a market value on it of $100.

In step 2, the company decides to go out of the steel business and invest the $100 in municipal bonds earning 5%. Since the risk has decreased from 10% to 5%, investors would still place a market value on it of $100.

Finally, in step 3, the company decides to increase earnings per share so it goes back in the steel business. However, over-production has developed in the steel business so that it can only earn $8 or 8%. This increases earnings per share 60% from $5 in the municipal bonds. Temporarily, it would probably drive the stock market crazy. However, eventually when the market settled down and investors wanted a 10% return in the steel business, the market price would sink to $80.

Now the Steel Company is very depressed by the $80 market price, so it decides that it should get out of the steel business. It finds willing buyers, but they are sufficiently intelligent to know that they have to raise their capital in the competitive capital market, and therefore they will only pay $80 for the plant since the earnings of $8 must provide a 10% return. Thus, by taking step 3 at a return 20% below the return required by the market, which is cost-of-capital, $20 of their investment was lost regardless of the book figures.

Similarly, Company X lost at least 20% or $2 million of its principal when it sold the $10 million of municipal bonds and went into the industrial project with an 8% return. A hell of a poor decision! Anyone making capital investment decisions should know that 8% is a totally inadequate return for an average industrial project, and, of course, the return of 10% we used for illustrative purposes, is too low.

The company should have kept the money investment in municipal bonds in order to preserve the principal until a project materialized which would earn more than cost-of-capital, or it should have paid the $10 million back to its stockholders.

Convertible Rate

We should say a word about the rate to use for convertibles. For calculation of the return on long term capital on the books of a company, the components to use for convertible debentures and convertible preferred are interest and dividends respectively.

However, for cost-of-capital purposes, it has to be considered differently if the price of the common stock is close enough to the conversion price for there to be prospects of conversion in the future. A convertible consists of a debt instrument and a call on the common stock. For cost-of-capital purposes, it may be contended that the rate for a convertible should be a combination of the interest cost, and another rate to cover the part of the convertible which represents a call on the common. However, for practical purposes, the common cost rate should be used for convertibles; otherwise, there will not be sufficient earnings to cause conversion.

Overall or Composite Cost-of-Capital

The capital which you raise for your company is represented on the liability side of the balance sheet. Capital is used on the asset side. Tracing individual funds from the right side to the left for cost-of-capital purposes is seriously wrong.

Suppose you raise $10 million for a project by the sale of bonds with an 8% interest rate and a net cost of 4% after a 50% tax rate. You might contend that the capital cost associated with that project is a net 4%. Wrong, wrong, wrong! The only reason you were able to sell bonds was because your company had some common equity to protect the bonds.

Suppose instead of selling bonds you sold common and decided the net cost rate after taxes was 13%. Would you now say the capital cost rate for that project was three times as much? Wrong again! If you did raise the funds from the sale of common it would give your company the opportunity to subsequently sell bonds.

What we have been leading up to is that in project analysis you should use the composite cost-of-capital rate regardless of the way the particular project is financed.

If the project has the same risk as that for your company as a whole, you can use the composite cost rate for your company. If the project is different in nature and risk, then you will have to adjust the overall rate depending on the risk.

Let's now look at the composite cost for a company with the capital structure with which we started out. If we arbitrarily use an 8% rate for debt, and an historical rate of 13% for the common equity, the overall cost-of-capital, after taxes on a To Investor Rate Basis for a typical large industrial company would be about 11% as shown below.

	Amount	Rate	Total
Debt	25%	8%	2.00%
Common	75	13	9.75
Total	100%		11.75%

Profit Goal

The purpose of profits are to:

1. Reward investors.
2. Act as an incentive.
3. Provide a tool for decision making.

In evaluating a proposed capital project, the standard procedure is to make a forecast of sales, expenses and capital outlays, and then make a profitability calculation based on the forecast by allowing for the time value of money.

It is necessary to establish a profit goal as a cutoff rate of return on capital. This is the rate with which the project's profitability can be compared in order to determine whether there is sufficient return to justify the project.

We start out with cost-of-capital as the breakeven point. If a company established a profit goal equal to its cost-of-capital, it would show no true economic profit. If a company earned anything less than the cost-of-capital and we theorized that a company's capital was all in debt, the company would be in the red and become bankrupt.

The profit goal should be higher than the cost-of-capital for three reasons:

1. A company will wish to achieve a return above the cost of capital.
2. Some projects may have to be undertaken which provide no return, such as eating facilities for company employees and environmental investments. Some projects may have to be undertaken which do not completely cover cost-of-capital. These deficiencies below cost-of-capital must be made up by setting the profit goal on other projects above cost-of-capital.
3. Uncertainties in forecasting the results for a new project require an allowance

above cost-of-capital. There may be lags in start-up time, disappointing sales, unforeseen expenses, additional investment, etc. If a company only achieved the cost-of-capital on some projects and, because of unexpected difficulties, failed to earn the cost-of-capital on others, the average result would be below cost-of-capital.

4. In the case of regulated companies, there should be an allowance for attrition due to regulatory lag with increasing costs.

A distinction should be made between expansion and diversification. Diversification should generally require a higher standard because of unfamiliarity. Of course, we are talking not about immediate profits but about all future profits that are expected to accrue as a result of an investment.

It has been reported that some manufacturing companies have used an after-tax profit goal as high as 20%.[5]

It is interesting to note that the managements of companies which show good profits generally recognize the importance of setting high profit goals. On the other hand, some companies which show poor results argue that they cannot find projects which will provide high profits. They struggle with their consciences, and in the end usually lower their profit goals. This can only lead to perpetuation of poor performance with all the unfortunate consequences of misdirecting capital.

The amount by which a profit goal should be above cost-of-capital is a matter of judgment depending on various factors. The nature of the business is an important determinant. If the business is standardized and highly competitive and the type in which even good management has little opportunity to do better than its competitors, it couldn't set a profit goal far above the cost-of-capital, without pricing itself out of the market. If the overall cost-of-capital is 11%, such a company might establish 12% to 13% as its profit goal.

[5]"Variability of Private Investment in Plant and Equipment." Materials submitted to the Joint Economic Committee, Congress of the United States (87th Congress, 2nd Session); Part II, Some Elements Shaping Investment Decisions, p. 14.

On the other hand, a specialized type of business, which has an excellent product which consumers are eager to buy, would be foolish to establish the profit goal close to the cost-of-capital. Why should the company put money into research and development if it did not have an incentive to earn a real profit if consumers were eager to buy the products and benefited as a result of the research? Consumers in a free market place reflect the benefit they receive from the products by being willing to pay a full price rather than spending their money on something else. Such a company might decide as a matter of policy that it wanted to be in a class with the top profit earners, with an after-tax return on total capital of 15% or over; providing, of course, that through ingenuity it can do better than its competitors in satisfying consumer needs.

A company can set a profit goal by increasing the return it wants to earn on its common equity in calculating the overall composite rate; or it can add on an increment above the overall cost-of-capital. For example, the To Investor Rate on both bases would be as follows:

			Rate		Rate	
Debt	25%	x	8%	2.00%	8%	2.00%
Common	75	x	13	9.75	15.67	11.75
Total	100%			11.75%		
Allowance above cost to get profit goal				2.00		
Profit Goal				13.75%		13.75%

Thus, adding on 2.00% to the cost-of-capital is the same as setting the rate on the common at 15.67%.

An outline summary of cost-of-capital and profit goal is shown in Exhibit 15-12.

A company which has been very profitable in the past as a result of good products may ultimately run into the problem of generating so much capital from earnings that it can't find sufficient new ideas which will provide a high profit goal. It has two choices:

1. It can pay back the extra capital to its stockholders and only take on limited projects which require special research and maintain its profit goal at a high rate.

Exhibit 15-12

OUTLINE SUMMARY OF COST-OF-CAPITAL AND PROFIT GOAL

Capital Structure		Cost Rates		Total
Proportions of long term securities which will provide good quality securities. May include three basic types of securities:		Current (not "spot" or historical) over sufficient number of years, representing average market conditions for raising capital with some allowance for future rates.		
Long term debt	00.% times	0.00% (Yield from bond tables based on interest coupon and net proceeds per $100 bonds.)	=	0.00
Preferred stock	00. times	0.00% (Dividend rate divided by net proceeds per share.)		
Common stock and surplus	00. times	0.00% ("EXPECTED" earnings per share divided by net proceeds per share. Apply common rate to convertibles if there are prospects of conversion.)	=	0.00
	100			
COST-OF-CAPITAL				0.00%
Allowance above cost				
Profit Goal				0.00%

2. It can go into more mundane types of business with lower profit opportunities which would earn a smaller spread above cost-of-capital.

Either decision might be right, but the end result and nature of the company will be quite different.

If a company decided on the second choice and maintained a high profit on its existing business, but went into new business with a lower profit goal, the overall return on investment would gradually decrease. The market price for the stock would continue to increase but at a slower rate than it had in the past.

This becomes a major decision for some large companies. The larger they get the more money they develop to put into new projects, and the harder it becomes to develop unique ideas which will absorb large amounts of capital and produce high rates.

Tax Treatment–Before or After Taxes

Thus far, we have used the To Investor Rate. You have waited a long time for a discussion of the effect of tax deductibility of interest from the company's point of view. We are interested in three rates:

The To Investor Rate
The Pre-Tax Rate
After-Tax Equivalent Rate

They all tie together very neatly, but they are used for different purposes.

To Investor Rate

This rate is based on the rates required by investors. It does include adjustments for financing costs, but it disregards any consideration of the effect of corporate income taxes.

This rate is the one we have already discussed as the starting point for figuring cost-of-capital. It is directly comparable with the company's past experienced return. The company's experienced return is derived as shown on top of the next page.

To determine how well a company is doing, the company experienced rate is compared

Long Term Capital		Return	
Common equity	0.00	Earnings available for common stock after taxes before common dividends	0.00
Preferred	0.00	Preferred dividends	0.00
All types of long term debt	0.00	Full interest payments on long term debt	0.00
Total long term capital	0.00	Total return	0.00

$$\text{Company's experienced return on long term capital} = \frac{\text{Total Return}}{\text{Total Long Term Capital}}$$

with the To Investor Rate composite cost-of-capital rate or the composite cost-of-capital rate plus an allowance above cost-of-capital to get a profit goal.

This is the rate also used for regulatory purposes for the regulated companies such as electric, gas and telephone companies. The actual reduction in taxes due to interest charges is taken into account in figuring the amount of revenue increase needed.

Pre-Tax Rate

The nature of this rate is obvious; it gives the cost to the company before income taxes. Interest is applied at the full rate because it is before interest has any effect on tax savings. The common rate has to be increased sufficiently to allow for the amount of the income that will be absorbed by income taxes. The same treatment has to be given to the preferred stock rate and to the amount of allowance above cost-of-capital. This rate may be used for division performance standards.

After-Tax Equivalent Rate

An expansion project's profitability rate is generally calculated on a fully taxed basis with no reduction made for the tax savings if the company has interest charges on long term debt.

Therefore, to make the cost-of-capital comparable with the profitability rate calculated for a project, adjustment is made in the cost of debt for the related tax savings. The interest rate is reduced to the extent that the interest reduces taxes. The common cost is the same as that used for the To Investor Rate.

These three rates are illustrated in Exhibit 15-13, assuming a 50% tax rate on a cost-of-capital basis without allowing an added amount for a profit goal. It is worth spending some further time on these rates because they seem to confuse people.

Here is how they tie together. We will take the figures out of the Exhibit without any allowance above cost-of-capital for a profit goal and put them in a simple statement.

Income before interest and taxes	$21.50
Interest	2.00
Income after interest before taxes	19.50
Income taxes	9.75
Income for common	$ 9.75

To Investor Rate:

Interest	$ 2.00
Income for common	9.75
Total	$11.75

Dividing by $100 of long term capital gives an 11.75% To Investor Rate.

Pre-Tax Rate:

Income before interest and taxes	$21.50

Dividing by $100 of long term capital gives a 21.50% pre-tax rate.

After-Tax Equivalent Rate:

Interest reduces the amount of income on which taxes have to be paid. The $2 in interest saves $1 in income taxes so that the net cost of interest is $1. Thus:

Interest giving effect to tax savings	$ 1.00
Income for common	9.75
Total	$10.75

Exhibit 15-13

COST-OF-CAPITAL

TO INVESTOR RATE, PRE-TAX RATE, AFTER-TAX EQUIVALENT RATE

Column		I	II	III	IV	V
					50% Tax Rate	
Line	Long Term Capital	Amount	Rate	To-Investor Rate	Pre-Tax Rate	After-Tax Equivalent Rate
1	Debt	25%	8%	2.00%	2.00%	1.00%
2	Common Equity	75	13	9.75	19.50	9.75
3	Total	100%		11.75%	21.50%	10.75%

Dividing by $100 long term capital gives a 10.75% after-tax equivalent rate.

Let's also illustrate why the after-tax equivalent rate should be used for a project analysis, which will use $100 of capital.

The forecast earnings of the project are as follows:

Sales	$200.00
Expenses	178.50
Income after expenses	21.50
Interest	0.00
Income after interest before taxes	21.50
Taxes at 50%	10.75
Balance	10.75

These calculations do not make allowance for the fact that taxes would be reduced when the project is thrown in with the company's operations by the interest in the income statement. Now if we assume that the $100 project is financed with $25 of debt and $75 of common equity, and thrown into the income statement, the figures would be as follows:

Sales	$200.00
Expenses	178.50
Income after expenses	21.50
Interest	2.00
	19.50
Taxes	9.75
Income for common	9.75

So if the company decided to do the project on an after-tax equivalent rate basis of 10.75% and earned $10.75 on the project with no tax savings from interest, it would show a return of 11.75% ($2.00 interest plus $9.75 for common) on long term capital on a To Investor Rate Base when it was thrown into the income statement and got the benefit of the tax savings of interest.

Effect of Capital Structure Mix on Cost-of-Capital

One of the controversies about cost-of-capital revolves around the question of the effect of varying the debt ratio. There are three schools of thought.

Pure Theory–Capital Structure Has no Effect

Pure economic theory tells us that cost-of-capital is dependent on the risk of the enterprise and not on the way the capital structure pie is divided between debt and equity. Here we are talking about the To Investor Rate and not considering the effect of interest on tax savings.

This idea is based on the principle that as debt is increased, both the debt and the common equity become more risky and the rate on both must rise so that the two combined equal the same over-all cost.

For example, suppose one person owned all the company. Could he change the cost-of-capital by exchanging half of his stock for debt so that his investment would consist of 50% debt and 50% common? Obviously, it makes no difference to him how the pie is divided, the overall risk of the enterprise is the same.

Now, suppose the two different securities are owned by different investors. Would they take lower rates on each, or on either one, so that the overall cost would be lower than with common only? Not on the basis of pure theory. And in our thinking about cost-of-capital, we should not lose sight of the fact that basically it is the risk of the enterprise that determines the rate.

However, this is not a very practical approach in view of the nature of the securities markets, and it does not take into account that interest does create a tax savings.

Practical Approach—Proper Use of Senior Securities

We do have to allow for the fact that tax savings reduce the net cost of debt because interest reduces taxes. Furthermore, the markets for debt and common are not entirely overlapping. Debt may be used up to a certain point without significantly increasing the debt and common cost so that there will be a decrease in the overall cost. Within a limited range of debt, so that the quality of the debt and common are maintained as high grade, there will be some increase in the cost of both, but not in the composite cost.

At some point, as debt is further increased, risk is added to the enterprise as a result of an unbalanced capital structure. Then the rate on debt and common will rise to such an extent as to cause an increase in the overall cost-of-capital. The amount of debt which each company should carry will depend on a variety of circumstances.

This second school seems most sensible in that it follows sound principles of finance. It takes a long-range point of view within the realm of practicality.

Short Range—High Leverage Unsound

There are those who erroneously believe that the cost-of-capital can be reduced by piling on all the debt the traffic will bear. They contend that debt, with the interest deductible for tax purposes, is cheap, and common is expensive; therefore, using all the debt possible will result in a decrease in the overall cost-of-capital. The proponents of this third school tend to ridicule bond quality ratings and see no ill effects from having a company's bond rating fall to Baa and lower. They fail to consider the greater risk to both the debt and the common stock and the fact that the rate on both debt and common will increase so as to cause an increase in the overall cost.

In the short run, during a bull market when investors are not worrying about adverse developments, it may be possible to disregard temporarily the disadvantages and danger of too much debt. Of course, security holders who advocate this policy have in the back of their minds that they will sell their common stock before the company encounters adversity. Fine for them, but not for all the stockholders in the long run.

Management that follows this policy may have in mind retiring before adversity hits, may be the high-pressure promoter type and throw sensible caution to the winds or may be so naive as to believe that adversity will never be encountered.

From the long-range point of view of the stockholders, the short range approach must be assiduously avoided. The company does not have the mobility of a security holder who can sell out if he expects trouble. A company will have to consider the effect on cost-of-capital when adversity is encountered. There are many reasons why it is best for a company in the long run to keep its debt within the high grade category.

These three different schools of thought on the effect of capital structure mix on cost-of-capital are shown in the diagram in Exhibit 15-14 as they might apply to a large, well-situated industrial company. The figures, bond ratings, etc., are for illustrative purposes only and are not supposed to represent true numerical relationships.

What evidence can be advanced to prove the above conclusions? Because of the many factors which affect security prices, adequate statistical proof is not available to show the effect of differences in debt ratio on cost-of-capital. It is impossible to obtain adequate samples during good years and bad in which the effect of debt ratio alone is isolated from all the other factors which bear on security prices. Those efforts at statistical proof which have been based on price-earnings ratios are wrong because they do not measure the common cost properly.

We must rely on logical reasoning as explained above, based on sound assumptions, to arrive at a conclusion.

Hypothetical Example

Since adequate market evidence cannot be found which would screen out all other effects on cost-of-capital except differences of capital structure mix, you may obtain some idea of the magnitudes involved by setting up various hypothetical examples. Shown in Exhibit 15-15 are three different capital structures as they might apply to an industrial company. Ratings are assigned to the different amounts of debt in order to help you visualize the quality of the securities.

These examples indicate the advantages of leverage and the fact that interest is deductible for tax purposes. However, when the quality of debt and common falls below good quality, it does not appear that the added return on common offsets the added financial risk with lack of financial flexibility, the disadvantages of a strained credit, possible effects on dividend payments, etc. Furthermore, it can be visualized that over the long run the composite cost might even be increased with excessive leverage.

For the To Investor Rate in Columns III and IV, we assign debt cost rates and calculate the common costs so as to make the composite come out the same 10.75% figure for the three capital structures. We note that the common rate is 11.45%, 12.00% and 12.23% respectively for the three capital structures. Undoubtedly, the 12.23% common rate is far too low with the BBB-rated debt, so that the BBB would result in a higher overall cost-of-capital.

In the last two columns, we give effect to the tax savings from interest. We assume the same composite cost for the three capital structures—that is, 9.875%—and then note what this would do to the common cost. It went from 11.02% to 12.00% and 13.04% as the debt was increased. With the added leverage for BBB, the common would undoubtedly require a higher rate than 13.04%, so the BBB capital structure would have the highest overall cost-of-capital. To help your thinking in this area you may wish to shadowbox with some capital structures of your own with various assumptions as to the cost rates.

What we have just discussed—that is, varying the debt ratio for a particular company—is quite different from different debt ratios for companies with different risk. With different risk, companies might have different debt ratios and the same bond rating. For example, debt representing 25% of total long term capital might mean an A grade bond for an industrial; whereas, a finance company might have 85% debt and have the same rating.

The lower the business risk the greater the amount of senior securities that can be used. This is illustrated in Exhibit 15-16 for three types of businesses which have marked differences in risk. Industrial companies in the past have been more risky than electric utility companies, and they are both more risky than finance companies.

Exhibit 15-14

DEBT RATIO EFFECT ON COST OF CAPITAL FOR AN INDUSTRIAL COMPANY

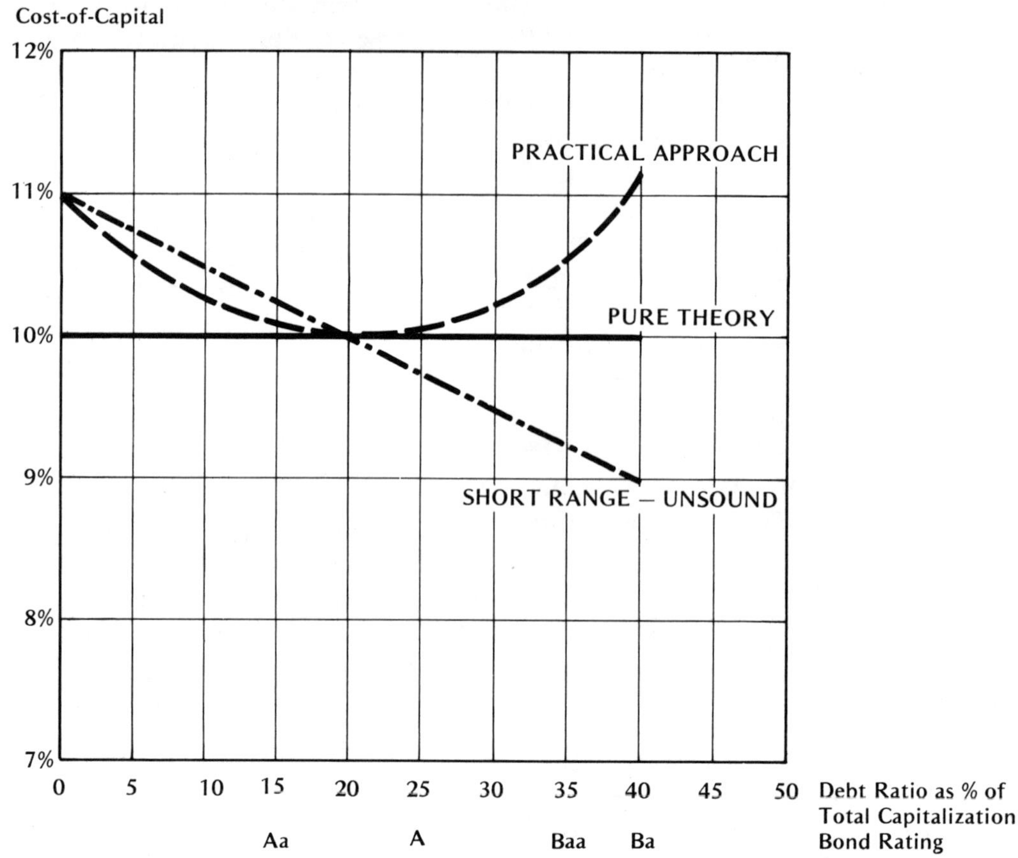

Also shown are the experienced returns on total long term capital and common equity. Returns on capital are not one and the same as cost-of-capital. However, the figures do illustrate an important principle. For large companies, if debt is used only up to the point where the debt has good quality, the risk to the common stockholders tends to be equated. For example, if an industrial company has 25% debt and its bonds are rated A, the common stockholders should be willing to accept the same return on the common of a finance company if it had 85% debt and its bonds were also rated A. The lower debt ratio of the industrial company tends to equate the risk to the stockholder with the higher debt in the finance company. This, of course, assumes that both companies' earnings are satisfactory.

Note that while the returns on the common equities are relatively equal, the businesses with lower risk and larger amounts of senior securities have lower returns on long term capital. Thus, a company can lower its overall cost-of-capital by using debt appropriately up to the point where the debt has good quality and a financial risk is not added.

It is, of course, possible for the risk of a business to be so great that the risk to the common stockholders could not be equated out by lowering the debt ratio. This would apply particularly to smaller companies, and

Exhibit 15-15

HYPOTHETICAL EXAMPLE OF EFFECT OF CAPITAL STRUCTURE MIX ON COST-OF-CAPITAL, ASSUMING A 50% CORPORATE INCOME TAX

Column	I	II		III	IV	V	VI
				To Investor Rate Total Composite Rates the Same–10.75%		After-Tax Equivalent Rate Total Composite Rates the Same–9.875%	
Line	Bond Rating	Capital Structure		Rates	Composite Cost	Rates	Composite Cost
1	Aa	Debt	15%	6.80%	1.02%	3.40%	0.510%
2		Common	85	11.45	9.73	11.02	9.365
3		Total	100%		10.75%		9.875%
4	A	Debt	25%	7.00	1.75	3.50	0.875
5		Common	75	12.00	9.00	12.00	9.000
6			100%		10.75%		9.875%
7	BBB	Debt	35%	8.00	2.80	4.00	1.400
8		Common	65	12.23	7.95	13.04	8.475
9		Total	100%		10.75%		9.875%

Exhibit 15-16

RATES OF RETURN AND CAPITAL STRUCTURES FOR BUSINESSES WITH DIFFERENT RISKS

	All Manufacturing Companies*	Electric Utility Companies†	Finance Companies**
Long Term Capital			
Debt	25%	53%	86%
Preferred and common equity	75	47	14
Total	100%	100%	100%
Return on total long term†† capital after taxes	11.3%	7.8%	7.4%
Return on common equity after taxes	12.4%	10.8%	10.4%

**Quarterly Financial Report for Manufacturing Corporations*–4th Quarter, 1973. Federal Trade Commission–Securities and Exchange Commission. This report covers the 12 months ended December, 1973. Included in the figures are all manufacturing corporations except newspapers.

†Privately Owned Electric Utilities–*Edison Electric Institute Statistical Year Book*, 1974 Edition.

**Average of Commercial Credit Company and Dial Financial Corporation December 31, 1973. Senior debt rated A.

††Return is after taxes but before interest on long term debt.

very risky businesses. Investors tend to regard companies with less than $100 million in sales or assets as small companies, and consequently more risky investments. The size factor depends to some extent on the type of industry.

There are many other subjects which are either a part of or related to cost-of-capital and profit goals which remain to be covered. We will have to discuss them to answer questions such as:

How to treat deferred taxes.
The effect of lease financing.
The importance of understanding various aspects of risk.
A fair return for the regulated industries.
How return on sales is related to return on investment.
How to reduce the cost-of-capital.
The effect of inflation on cost-of-capital.
How the press has failed to report earnings meaningfully.

Deferred Tax Treatment

To the extent that taxes are deferred, the government provides capital without charge. The purpose of allowing for fast depreciation of assets which results in deferred taxes is to induce business to expand by making expansion more profitable.

In Chapter 16 it is explained how to calculate the profitability rate for a capital expenditure. The basis for the calculation is the cash flow after taxes actually paid. The deferrals will result in a greater cash flow at the beginning of the project and a smaller flow towards the end as the tax expense increases. Thus, for a particular project, the tax deferral provides more immediate cash, which has a definite value. This is illustrated in Exhibit 15-17, Part I.

If a company normalizes its financial reports, the income statement for book purposes provides for taxes with depreciation on a straight line basis with the tax deferral making up the difference between taxes actually paid and taxes accrued. The liability side of the balance sheet includes the accruals. For example, a balance sheet with deferred taxes might look as shown in Exhibit 15-17, Part II.

Financial analysts will study the deferred taxes, but there does not seem to be any uniformity as to how they will treat them for capital structure purposes. For a growing industry, the argument may be made that the reserve will continue to grow and that it is a form of capital which protects the senior capital. This seems questionable, because it is a definite liability and not equity in any sense of the word: in liquidation accrued taxes are certainly a liability. In studying capital structure ratios, deferred tax accruals can either be shown separately as a part of total long term capital or they can be left out and weight given to them separately on the basis of judgment. We prefer the latter treatment.

Similarly, for cost-of-capital calculations, we prefer to leave out deferred tax accruals and only consider the long-term capital provided by investors. And also, in figuring the return on total long term capital, we prefer to take the net income after normalized taxes and interest, add back interest on long term debt and then divide by total long-term capital, excluding deferred tax accruals.

In using assets as a base for calculating return on investment, allowance does have to be given to the deferred tax accruals. In the example above, Long Term Capital $100 plus Deferred Taxes $1 provides a total of $101. The $101 provides Working Capital $51 (Current Assets $101 less Current Liabilities $50) and Plant, Net $50. In order to be consistent with the above comments, a 10% return on a $100 Long Term Capital in the balance sheet above is equivalent to a 10% return on assets based on the following approach:

Current assets	$101
Less: Current liabilities	50
Working capital	51
Plant, Net	50
Total	$101
Less: Deferred taxes	$ 1
Assets provided by Long Term Capital	$100

Exhibit 15-17

TAX DEFERRAL EFFECT

PART I

INCOME STATEMENT ITEMS

ASSUMING 50% TAX RATE

Column		I	II	III	IV
		Using Straight Line Depreciation for Books and Fast Depreciation for Taxes		Using Straight Line Depreciation for Both	
Line		Reported Book Figures	For Tax Purposes	Reported Book Figures	For Tax Purposes
1	Income before taxes and depreciation	$26	$26	$26	$26
2	Depreciation	6	8	6	6
3	Net income before taxes	$20	$18	$20	$20
4	Taxes	9	9	10	10
5	Deferred taxes	1			
6	Income after taxes and depreciation	$10	$ 9	$10	$10
7	Cash Flow				
8	Depreciation	$ 6		$ 6	
9	Deferred taxes	1			
10	Income after taxes and depreciation	10		10	
11	Total	$17		$16	

PART II

BALANCE SHEET ITEMS

Assets		Liabilities		
Current Assets	$101	Current Liabilities		$ 50
Plant, Net	50	Deferred taxes		1
		Long Term Capital		
		Debt	$ 0	
		Common Equity	100	
		Total		$100
Other Items	0	Other Items		0
Total	$151	Total		$151

This gives effect to the fact that the deferred taxes do provide some of the assets.

If a company does not normalize its financial reports, income will be increased to the extent that taxes are decreased. There will be no tax deferral item in the balance sheet.

Consequently, the return on long term capital will be distorted to the extent of the tax reduction.

Leases Unless Capitalized Produce a False Effect

The danger of focusing on the cost of the specific financing for a project is clearly illustrated by the misinterpretation that can occur with leases.

In order to determine a capital structure which is representative of a company's financial policy, leases which are a form of long term financing should be capitalized. This may present problems if there is lack of information or if the leases are complicated in nature. Since approximations are perfectly satisfactory, it is generally possible to come up with a figure which will serve the purpose. The leased asset would then go on the asset side of the balance sheet. We can explain what happens if this is not done by using a simple example of the effect on return on capital.

Assume that we are dealing with a type of company which can keep its securities high grade with debt representing 50% of long term capital. We have two plants, each costing $10 million and each having a ten-year life. To start with, we finance one with bonds at an assumed 5% interest and the other with common stock. For illustrative purposes, assume that the common cost is 10%. Then the composite cost-of-capital would be 7 1/2%. Each plant should earn at least this rate. The simplified balance sheet, assuming current assets equalled current liabilities, and selected items from the income statement, would be as shown in Exhibit 15-18, Part I. Total return (interest $500,000 plus earnings for common $1 million) would represent 7 1/2% on total long term capital of $20 million.

Let us switch to financing Plant A with lease financing. We sell the plant for $10 million and lease it back. We use the proceeds from the financing to pay off the bonds. Now the balance sheet and selected items from the income statement would be as shown in Exhibit 15-18, Part II.

If we forget Plant A, which has disappeared from the balance sheet, it looks as though the return on total long term capital has been increased to 10%; that is, $1 million of income applicable to $10 million of long term capital.

Something is wrong! What happened to Plant A?

We do not own Plant A any longer since it was financed with a lease. Depreciation of $1 million has dropped out of the income statement and also, since we paid off the $10 million of debt with the proceeds from the sale and lease back, the $500,000 of interest has dropped out.

But, what has been added and where? We have to make lease payments. Raising capital through the sale of property and then leasing it back is a form of debt financing. We saw above that the proceeds from the sale of the property were used to pay off the debt. If we leased Plant A in the first place, we would have been using lease financing as an alternative to financing the plant with debt and owning it.

The lessor generally expects to get back the principal which he put up to buy the property and also interest on the amount of the unpaid principal. Since the property owned by the lessor will be fully depreciated in ten years on our assumption as above, the lessor would want to get back the equivalent of $1 million of principal each year for ten years. If we assume that the lessor would be satisfied with a 5% interest rate, he would expect to receive $500,000 in interest on his principal during the first year. Thus, the lease payments in the first year would total $1,500,000.

Generally, leases call for payments of varying amounts of principal and interest each year with the two combined being equal in amount each year. We have used the above assumptions to simplify the explanation.

In the first year, depreciation on Plant A and interest on the bonds are dropped from

Exhibit 15-18

EFFECT OF LEASES ON RETURN ON CAPITAL

PART I

FINANCIAL STATEMENTS

Balance Sheet

Assets		Liabilities		
Current Assets	$ 5,000,000	Current Liabilities		$ 5,000,000
		Long Term Capital		
Plant A	$10,000,000	Bonds	$10,000,000	
		Common	10,000,000	
Plant B	$10,000,000	Total		20,000,000
Other Items	0	Other Items		0
Total	$25,000,000	Total		$25,000,000

Income Statement Items

Depreciation Plant A	$1,000,000
Depreciation Plant B	$1,000,000
Income Before Interest and Taxes	$2,500,000
Interest	$ 500,000
Income Taxes (50% Rate)	$1,000,000
Earnings for Common	$1,000,000

PART II

FINANCIAL STATEMENTS RECAST

Balance Sheet

Assets		Liabilities	
Current Assets	$ 5,000,000	Current Liabilities	$ 5,000,000
Plant B	10,000,000	Long Term Capital	
		Common Equity	10,000,000
Other Items	0	Other Items	0
Total	$15,000,000	Total	$15,000,000

Income Statement Items

Depreciation Plant B	$1,000,000
Income Before Taxes	$2,000,000
Income Taxes (50% Rate)	$1,000,000
Earnings for Common	$1,000,000

the income statement, as mentioned above. By selling and leasing back the plant, we add \$1,500,000 in lease payments above the line in operating expenses. Selected items in the income statement would be as shown in Exhibit 15-19, Part I.

We have swapped the depreciation on Plant A and interest on the bonds for a like total of lease payments. On the basis of our assumptions, we would come out the same at the end of ten years whether we owned Plant A and financed it with debt or leased it, except for two possible differences:

1. Under the lease, we might have to pay some renewal rental charge if we wished to continue to use the property.
2. At the expiration of the lease, we would not own the fully depreciated plant; consequently, we might lose the residual value to the lessor.

But the picture looks a lot different on the surface. With the lease financing, we apparently have long term capital consisting only of common equity, amounting to \$10 million and showing a 10% return.

Right before your eyes something happened! But was it so dramatic? We merely swapped one form of debt for another. With lease financing we are in effect using \$10 million of a debt type of financing. Thus, the common is leveraged to the extent of the lease financing and it should earn 10%.

In other words, with debt financing we earned 7 1/2% on total capital of \$20 million with 10% on the common. With the lease financing, we substituted lease charges for a similar amount of charges on the debt. The common earnings come after the lease charges, and the 10% return on the remaining long term capital consisting only of common stock represents no improvement.

We can make the two situations comparable by capitalizing the lease and putting Plant A back on the balance sheet with an equivalent amount of debt on the liability side as shown in Exhibit 15-19, Part II.

Now to figure the return, we would take the interest part of the lease payment of \$500,000 and add it to the income for common of \$1 million to get a total of \$1,500,000. The long term capital, with leases capitalized, would amount to \$20 million. The return on long term capital would be 7 1/2%—the same as the return with Plant A owned.

Thus, if a company has used a large amount of lease financing, the return calculated on the long term capital as shown on the balance sheet may be very misleading. A true picture of the return on total long term capital can only be obtained by capitalizing leases and figuring the return so as to eliminate leverage effect of the lease financing.

Risk Varying from Project to Project

A company will first wish to determine the risk for the business as a whole through the cost-of-capital approach. However, the company may be involved in various businesses which have different risks, and it should establish different rates for the different parts of the business. It may be possible to find other companies similar to each separate business to use as a source of information on which to assess these different risks. More than likely, however, it will be necessary to rely on judgment.

If a company expands its existing business it can use the figure which has been developed for the company as a whole. However, if the expansion is in a different field it should use a figure based on the risk in that particular field.

For example, if a company has a composite cost-of-capital of 10% and it goes into a project which has a 12% risk, it should use the 12% figure as the basis for setting its goal rather than 10%. After the project is completed and it becomes a part of the company, the overall risk of the company will change in proportion to the extent to which the new investment is related to the total investment of the company. Conversely, if the risk in the new project is 9%, that figure should be used as the basis for a goal rather than the 10% company figure. After the project is com-

Exhibit 15-19

EFFECT OF LEASES ON RETURN ON CAPITAL

PART I

INCOME STATEMENT ITEMS

	With Plant A Owned	With Plant A Sold and Leased Back and Debt Paid Off
Depreciation Plant A	$1,000,000	0
Depreciation Plant B	$1,000,000	$1,000,000
Lease Payments		$1,500,000
Income Before Interest and Taxes	$2,500,000	$2,000,000
Interest	$ 500,000	0
Income Taxes	$1,000,000	$1,000,000
Earnings for Common	$1,000,000	$1,000,000

PART II

LEASES CAPITALIZED

BALANCE SHEET

Assets		Liabilities		
Current Assets	$ 5,000,000	Current Liabilities		$ 5,000,000
Plant A Leased	10,000,000	Long Term Capital		
		Lease Capitalized	$10,000,000	
Plant B	10,000,000	Common Equity	10,000,000	
		Total		$20,000,000
Other Items	0	Other Items		0
Total	$25,000,000	Total		$25,000,000

pleted and the earnings realized, the total earning rate of the company will decrease, but so will the risk so that the investors will not be hurt.

A small company will generally be viewed by investors as having more risk than a large one, even though a moderate-sized company may be better able to compete in some businesses than a very large one. At what size the risk starts to increase from the investors' point of view will depend to some extent on the nature of the business. There is no clearly defined dividing line. We suggest as a rough bench mark $100 million of total assets or sales, whichever is larger.

If a large company acquires a small one, it will have to consider the risk of the business being acquired. However, it may eliminate the risk element due to the small size because the company being acquired will receive the benefits of the larger size when it is merged.

Alternative Opportunities

It is sometimes suggested that capital decision making should be based on alternative opportunities. In other words, if there are four opportunities available with profitability prospects of 4%, 11%, 12% and 13%, the company should choose the one providing the highest return. Stated in this way the idea may be quite incorrect. Each prospective return must be evaluated in terms of the risk involved. This is consistent with the basic principles of investing in any form. For example, suppose the prospective returns and risks for these four opportunities are as shown in Exhibit 15-20.

Alternatives 3 and 4 might produce losses in the long run. If they were the only ones available, the company would be better off keeping the money in government bonds, where the return equals the risk, or returning the money to its investors. In our example, alternative 2 is available and it is the only one which should be accepted in spite of the prospects of higher returns for 3 and 4. Alternative 1 would preserve capital if no other acceptable opportunity were available.

Undoubtedly, managements will make mental assessments of the returns in relation to the risks in considering alternative opportunities, but the lure of the high returns can easily court disaster. A formal procedure should be used so as to avoid such a bias.

Factors That Affect Risk

In assessing risk we must think in terms of how it is appraised by the investors who provide the capital. As we have stated previously, sometimes managements forget this idea and think only in terms of how they personally look at the risk. They are too close to the situation and often underestimate the risk. They have a tendency to think that a new project is a sure thing, while investors taking a broad view might feel quite differently. Furthermore, capital has to be obtained from investors and it is their appraisal which determines the cost rates for capital.

Exhibit 15-20

ALTERNATIVE OPPORTUNITIES

Alternatives	Prospective Return	Risk
1. Government bonds	4%	4%
2. Expansion in U.S.	11	10
3. Diversification in U.S.	12	13
4. Foreign expansion	13	15

Risk is not susceptible to precise measurement. Some risks which affect the company as a whole are suggested below.

- A new type of investment.
- The size of the company—a small company is more vulnerable to adverse developments.
- Sales to one customer—for example, an automobile parts manufacturer selling to one automobile company as compared to another selling to three different companies.
- A company producing a product which is a fad, or a high-style business.
- A company dependent on the skills of one or two individuals.
- An industry in which there are many small operators who do not know their costs.
- A company engaged in a field where entry by newcomers is relatively easy—where the capital costs and skills required are moderate and the return on investment at the particular time is inviting.
- An industry in which government pressure or control may make it difficult to adjust prices when costs increase.
- A company with a high wage factor.
- A raw material which is a large element of cost of the final product and which may be subject to quick price increases causing a profit squeeze.
- An extractive industry in which the source of supply of the product is uncertain.
- A company which is dependent on government contracts, particularly those requiring large amounts of capital.
- A company which has a large investment in fixed assets which cannot be liquidated readily or used for another purpose and for which there is a possibility of obsolescence, as compared with a company which has a relatively large amount of assets in current form, liquidatable at reasonable prices.
- A company in an industry going through major changes in technology.
- A company which is subject to major acts of Nature, such as a company which

would be adversely affected by a hurricane.
- A company requiring large and special research and development expenditures.
- A company with important interests in foreign activities with unstable governments or soft currencies.

Foreign Investment

Foreign investment may have strong appeal; the grass may look greener because the return seems higher than in this country. To the extent that the risk is correspondingly higher, there is no gain.

Foreign investment may carry three additional risks not present in this country:

1. Currency

Devaluation–loss in value of earnings and investment because of inflation and devaluation of the currency in terms of American dollars.

Inconvertibility–a dollar of earnings in this country is worth a dollar, but earnings abroad are worth dollars only if they can be turned into dollars.

2. Political

The attitude towards business in general and outside capital in particular, including the possibility of expropriation.

3. Operating Conditions

Including law and legal systems, government controls, taxes, labor, marketing methods, financing, accounting techniques, etc., which are unlike those in this country and with which management may have less experience.

These risks will vary widely in degree from country to country, but informed investors add substantially to their appraisal of risk for a company which has large foreign investment, depending on surrounding circumstances.

It is interesting to observe the thinking of some companies toward foreign investment. A company which has little foreign investment may anxiously seek more. On the other hand, a company with large foreign investments may strive to build more business in this country to offset the prejudices of investors against its large proportion of foreign investments.

These remarks merely suggest that management should weigh carefully the possible added earnings versus the greater risk as viewed by investors. Investors will take careful account of the nature, extent and location of foreign investments. If the company does not produce sufficient earnings abroad to compensate for investors' appraisal of the additional risk, the prices of securities will suffer. A publicly owned company cannot afford to use yardsticks for foreign investments that vary too widely from those used in the securities market.

How do you assess the risk from country to country? This is a difficult question. If there were active markets in this country for a large number of bonds and stocks of foreign companies, we could appraise the risk by the cost-of-capital approach. Adequate data is not available. We must look for the answers primarily on the basis of judgment, since there is scant evidence to view.

The bulk of foreign securities in this country for which market quotations are available consists of government bonds payable in American dollars. Obviously, they do not represent the cost-of-capital for an industrial company, but they may help to direct our thinking. The figures may have some significance when compared to the yield on United States Government bonds.

Given in Exhibit 15-21 are a few of the foreign government issues payable in American dollars.

The exhibit shows the higher yield on the foreign bonds based on quotations in the United States. They are not strictly comparable for a number of reasons:

1. The maturity and coupons are not the same.
2. They are spot figures for two periods. A thorough study should use average figures over a period of years.

3. Quotations of foreign securities are tricky to understand. They may not represent investors' true appraisal of the risk involved for many reasons:
    - The market may be very thin.
    - Special taxes may affect the yield.
    - There may be a special demand for foreign exchange purposes, etc.

    You would do well to consult an expert in foreign securities in order to avoid using misleading data.

Exhibit 15-21

COMPARISON OF YIELDS ON U.S. GOVERNMENT BONDS WITH BONDS OF CERTAIN FOREIGN COUNTRIES PAYABLE IN U.S. DOLLARS.

	Increase in Yield of Foreign Bonds Over U.S. Bonds	
	1967	1974
Canada 2 3/4s of 1974	14%	
" 6 7/8s of 1988		32%
Australia 5's of 1983	20	
" 5½s of 1985		19
Norway 5½s of 1977	28	
Japan Dev. 6s of 1978	42	
Denmark 6s of 1976		14
Finland 6s of 1976	48	
Mexico 6½s of 1979	48	
" 8½s of 1987		64
Venezuela 6¼s of 1980	49	

However, they are adequate for illustrative purposes. And they show a return for most of the issues considerably higher than in U.S. government bonds.

This sample, which covers only debt securities, in no way shows the difference in risk for an industrial company for the following reasons:

- The bonds are payable in American dollars, whereas earnings of an industrial company would be in terms of the local currency.
- The bonds are government obligations and do not reflect the risks of domestic operations abroad that industrial companies would face.

However, even if these percentages alone were used to increase a Profit Goal established in this country, it shows that substantial increases would be necessary for use in foreign investment.

If you are interested in pursuing this approach for any particular country, you will wish to review all possible sources of security information which might be available, including both industrial and government securities quoted in the United States. It may be of some interest to consider the returns that investors require in the foreign country itself, but it should be emphasized that this does not take into account the risk of American investors.

To take an entirely different attack on the problem, an approximate way of looking at the return from a foreign investment might be as follows: A dollar of after-tax earnings in this country is worth a dollar, but the return from an investment in a foreign corporation only consists of the income received in this country. In other words, the transferable income from foreign investment might be considered as equivalent to earnings of a company in this country. On this basis, if a company in this country earned 10%, a foreign investment paying out 50% of its earnings in dividends would have to earn 20% to be on an equivalent basis. Admittedly, this is rough figuring and leaves out the appreciation in principal and amount of earnings that could be transferred, but it is only for the purpose of broad thinking.

In some countries in which the political situation is unstable, the risk is akin to that of venture capital situations in this country. Venture capital was discussed in Chapter 7. Depending on the circumstances, an investor in a venture capital situation in this country may only be interested if the original investment has a possibility of being multiplied five to ten times in a few years.

Another approach to assessing risk in foreign investments is explained in several brief excerpts from an article by Millard H. Pryor, Director of Corporate Planning for the Singer Company:[6]

> Political risks are much greater abroad than in the United States. The danger that either war losses or expropriation will result in partial or complete loss of investment is far from remote. . . . To compensate for such risks, the return in any foreign country should be greater than the return in the United States by an amount at least equal to the cost of war risk and confiscation insurance.
>
> Loss of investment and earnings due to currency inflation represents a significant risk in many areas of the world.
>
> The costs of managing an international operation are usually greater than those in a corporate domestic business. . . .
>
> As a result of the potential risks in international operation, it is desirable to establish what can be called long-range "compensatory" financial goals for operations outside the United States. For example, if an appropriate long range goal for activities in the United States is 12% return on invested capital, long range compensatory goals for an international company's activities in three different countries could be established in the manner shown in Exhibit 15-22.

[6]"Planning in a Worldwide Business," *Harvard Business Review,* January-February 1965, Volume 43, Number 1.

Information on profit results of the foreign investments of domestic corporations may not be strictly comparable. And the profitability varies considerably from industry to industry. However, the figures in Exhibit 15-23 clearly show that the grass is not greener abroad and that the returns in no way compensate for the added risk. The high profit outside the U.S. in year 1973 was largely due to translation of foreign exchange into U.S. dollars.

Note that these returns are on net worth and not total capital. Some foreign investing is done on a highly leveraged basis through borrowing in the local country in order to reduce the amount of United States' investment. It should be recognized that the high debt adds to the risk of the common, and the return should be high because of this factor alone.

Regulated Companies and a Fair Return

An industry which, of necessity, is knowledgeable about cost-of-capital is the utility industry. Since the industry operates as a monopoly, its return is regulated. Regulation is supposed to operate as a substitute for competition. A fair return should provide some allowance above cost-of-capital, just as a

Exhibit 15-22

HYPOTHETICAL INTERNATIONAL LONG-RANGE "COMPENSATORY" GOALS

(In Terms of Percentage Return on Investment)

Column	I	II	III	IV
	U.S. Operations	Country A Operations	Country B Operations	Country C Operations
U.S. financial goal	12%	12%	12%	12%
Compensation for political risk	––	––	2	5
Compensation for currency risk	––	1	2	25
Absentee management factor	––	1	––	2
Compensatory financial goal	12%	14%	16%	44%

Exhibit 15-23

PROFITABILITY OF U.S. CORPORATIONS FROM OPERATIONS INSIDE U.S. AND OUTSIDE*

	Return on Equity	
	Inside U.S.	Outside U.S.
1973	12%	18%
1972	14	12
1971	11	13
1970	10	13
1969	13	12
1968	15	12
1967	13	11
	12.6%	13.0%

*Weekly Report, July 12, 1974. Business International Corporation, One Dag Hammarskjold Plaza, New York, N.Y. 10017.

profit goal is established for a company in competitive industry.

Competitive industry has very little understanding of the problems the utility industry has in maintaining an adequate return. Competitive industry seems to believe that utilities have a guaranteed income and all they have to do is apply for a rate increase when their return falls behind. In the first place, the income is not guaranteed. If the industry loses its economic strength, regulation can't generate earnings. Regulation can only give the industry the opportunity to earn if it is economically able to do so.

When earnings are increasing because of cost reductions with growth, which has happened in the history of utilities, the companies prosper. They can reduce rates and this keeps everybody happy. But when costs go up and rate increases are needed, it is a losing battle to try to achieve a fair return. Then, investors tend to turn their backs on the industry.

Regulation faces a difficult task when rate increases are needed. The need is never understood by the consumers and as a consequence it is a heaven sent opportunity for some elements to prey on the consumer's ignorance and use the utilities as whipping boys.

By now, you should appreciate how difficult the subjects of cost-of-capital and a fair return are. Imagine the problem regulators face of sifting through the conflicting testimony of the various witnesses that come before regulation in a full-blown rate case, and then granting an adequate increase in the face of all the consumer and political pressures.

The record of the various regulatory authorities in granting rate increases to permit utilities an adequate return to raise capital has varied widely. Some commissions have acted in a thoroughly statesmanship way in spite of all of the pressures. They have realized that at times rate increases are necessary to keep the industry financially healthy so that it will be able to raise capital and provide good service to the customers.

However, there is one area in which regulation has yet to find a solution; that is, the problem of regulatory lag. If a commission grants the proper rate increase, which theoretically would provide the company a fair return, the actual results generally prove to be inadequate because it takes so long after the request for an increase to be put into effect. By the time the decision is made, the utilities' expenses have already increased still further so that the company never earns the return which regulation has deemed to be proper. Some commissions are trying to solve this problem by using such means as a year-end rate base and by taking a forward look. Another approach which could be most helpful would be to allow a fair return which would compensate for regulatory lag. For example, if regulation felt that a company should earn a fair return equal to 14% on common equity it might have to allow a 15% rate in a decision so that a company could achieve 14%.

It is not only the job of the commission to establish a return which is fair but to grant sufficient rate increases to make it possible for the company to earn that return.

Utility companies generally use a large amount of debt because of their stable nature. When the industry ran into earnings problems in the 1970's, the companies were not only adversely affected by poor returns on common, but also by the erosion of protection for the bondholders by a decrease to a dangerous level of the number of times interest charges were covered. This endangered the quality of their debt and numerous companies had their bond ratings downgraded. Some companies had their earnings coverage fall so badly that they were unable to sell debt because they couldn't meet the minimum coverage for interest in their indenture. Therefore, it became vital for regulation to consider the necessity of rate increases to permit the industry to do bond financing.

A major consideration in determining the earnings for a regulated company is to make allowance for the change in value of the dollar in the rate base. No unregulated company would sell its plant at original cost, and since regulation is a substitute for competition, regulation should recognize the inflationary situation in the rate base. However, many regulatory authorities have chosen to ignore this problem because it would mean further rate increases. That does not justify an economically unsound principal.

Return on Sales Tied to Investment—The So-Called DuPont Formula

We have emphasized the importance of looking at return on capital rather than return on sales. However, so many people are oriented to return on sales, that it is important to show the relationship between the two.

Two ratios are used to tie these factors together as a management tool. Combined, they are often referred to as the duPont formula because the E.I. duPont de Nemours Company is known to make use of them. They are:

$$\text{Earnings as a Percent of Sales} = \frac{\text{Earnings}}{\text{Sales}}$$

$$\text{Turnover} = \frac{\text{Sales}}{\text{Investment}}$$

Combined they produce return on investment.

$$\frac{\text{Earnings}}{\text{Sales}} \times \frac{\text{Sales}}{\text{Investment}} = \frac{\text{Return}}{\text{Investment}}$$

The formula as presented by duPont is in much more detail in Chapter 17. These two simple ratios clearly emphasize the part which investment plays. If the management team can be trained to understand these relationships, they will help to point the way to better utilization of investment and consequently a better return.

On existing investment, management is interested in increasing the return on capital employed. An increase in income or a reduction of the amount of investment will produce the desired result. Increasing income may be accomplished by improving sales or lowering expenses.

Examples of Return on Sales and Return on Total Long Term Capital

The percent return on sales which is sufficient to provide an adequate return on capital depends on the amount of sales that can be generated with a certain amount of capital. This varies from industry to industry depending on the nature of the business. These figures for three industries are shown in Exhibit 15-24.

Reducing the Cost-of-Capital

Reducing the cost-of-capital means reducing the risk to the investor. This has been discussed throughout the book, but to bring them together at this point, they are:

1. Take a long range view in policy making and don't jump at short range gimmicks in finance.

2. Use senior securities judiciously with a well-reasoned financial policy which will provide good quality securities and simple capital structure.
3. Avoid high-cost incentive type securities.
4. Provide a dividend policy which will produce the best price for your stock.
5. Use methods of financing which will be attractive to security holders, such as the use of rights offerings of common when appropriate.
6. Have investor relations program based on *credibility*.
7. Make proper capital management decisions so that capital will not be wasted.
8. Have an independent board of directors who will have enough guts to truly represent the stockholders and not let poor management persist in running the company into the ground.

Cost-of-Capital and Inflation

Some economists contend that one of the reasons for the high interest rates which materialized in the 1960's is inflation. They contend that buyers of debt securities require higher rates to take care of inflation. Others contend that the higher rates are a matter of heavy demand for debt capital, particularly by the utility industry, and the Federal Reserve System trying to tighten the money supply in order to prevent inflation. The latter argument seems to fit the facts better. Regardless of the reason for high interest rates, what about the effect on the common cost rate? If it was 12% when inflation was at a 3% annual rate and interest rates were low, shouldn't investors require a substantially higher rate with interest rates and inflation more than double?

A company which has had as its profit goal to earn 14% on its common book value may ask whether it should increase the rate substantially to allow for inflation?

It would seem to make sense for investors to increase the return they require because of inflation. However, a company has to look to the competitive capital market to get its cost rates. It is not what investors should do, but what they actually do. It does appear from market evidence that common stock investors have certainly increased the rate they require.

With high interest rates, investors should be more interested in debt securities. When investors switch from stocks to bonds, the rates

Exhibit 15-24

SALES PER DOLLAR OF CAPITAL, RETURN* ON SALES, AND RETURN ON TOTAL YEAR-END LONG TERM CAPITAL† FOR CERTAIN TYPES OF BUSINESS

	Sales per $1 of Total Year-End Long Term Capital	Return on Sales	Return on Total Year-End Long Term Capital
Electric Utility Companies**	$0.39	26%	7.6%
All Manufacturing Companies††	2.0	5.7	11.3
Super Market (The Kroger Co. 1973)	4.0	1.9	7.8

*Return is income after taxes before interest on long term debt. For Kroger, leases were capitalized and interest estimated on the leases.

†Total long term capital includes long term debt and equity. For Kroger, minimum lease rentals were capitalized.

**Privately Owned Electric Utilities–Edison Electric Institute, *Statistical Year Book,* 1973 Edition.

††*Quarterly Financial Report for Manufacturing Corporations*–4th Quarter, 1973. Federal Trade Commission Securities and Exchange Commission. This report covers the 12 months ended December 1973. Included in the figures are all manufacturing corporations except newspapers. Interest on long term debt is estimated.

required on stocks would go up. This transition may take place slowly because there does not seem to be great fluidity between stock and bond investment for the great mass of capital. However, management should realize what it means when investors do require a sufficient return on common to fully compensate them and should be ready to act to increase their profit goals for capital investment decision making.

Maintenance of the Integrity of the Dollar

With regard to inflation, we also have to consider the investment base.

As a simple example, let us suppose that a company had $100 in capital and that its goal was 10% after taxes. Then, if it earned $10 on this capital, it would achieve its goal. But let us suppose that the price level doubled and it still only earned $10. Then the poor investor would only be able to buy one-half as much with his return as he did before inflation. After all, money is only a medium of exchange and the investor is interested in maintaining his ability to buy goods. Therefore, the goal should be applied to the $100 of capital revalued after inflation at $200. Ten percent on this figure produces $20, which would be worth the same, in terms of goods, as $10 before inflation. This would be keeping the investor whole. This is what is meant by maintaining the integrity of the dollar.

If there have been great technical advances in an industry so that its old plant has become more obsolete than is covered by depreciation, then the investors will have to take their losses. That is a capital risk which they should have evaluated before they put up their money. However, they should be allowed a chance to protect themselves against a change in the value of the dollar. Therefore, if properly applied as a test to see how much a company should earn on the existing plant to meet its cost-of-capital goal, the assets should be valued on a reproduction cost new basis less depreciation. This would take care of changes in the value of the dollar as well as wear and tear, obsolescence and other causes of depreciation.

This problem, of course, does not arise when using cost-of-capital as a goal in deciding on whether to go into new projects, because new projects are built at the current price level. Since we have been concerned primarily with setting the goal for new projects, we have left this subject until now. Furthermore, while an important factor, it was felt that it would add to your confusion to discuss it earlier. It is of importance for industrial companies in Return-on-Investment analysis. Relating current earnings to past investments on the basis of balance sheet figures may reflect very misleading results.

The subject is particularly important in the utility industry as we have discussed.

The same idea, of course, applies to the matter of the proper allowance for depreciation in order for it to replace the equivalent property and not just a dollar amount. Bookkeeping depreciation allocates the cost of the property to periods of time. During inflation, provision for such depreciation does not provide sufficient dollars to replace the economic power of the original investment. That raises the question of whether a profit exists, in a real sense, without the full recovery of the equivalent economic power. This intriguing subject, termed economic depreciation, is a study in itself. We will not attempt to go into it, but this is not to suggest that its importance should be minimized.

Bad Profit Reporting by the Press

Before we conclude, we have to say a word about how earnings are reported by the press.

People may be led to believe that corporate earnings have been increasing. How else would they interpret the following often-observed newspaper headline?

Corporate Earnings Show 5% Increase
Over Last Year

An article following such a headline generally elaborates on the increase in earnings rather than explaining the significance of the figures.

Earnings are only meaningful in terms of capital invested. If capital increased 5%, the investors would be getting no increase in the rate of profit.

To look at it another way, suppose you buy a $1,000 bond and get $50 in interest, which represents a 5% return. Next year you continue to receive $50 in interest on your investment, but interest rates change and you buy another $1,000 bond and earn only $40 on your new investment so that your total interest is $90. Your wife might comment, "Aren't we fortunate—an increase in income from $50 to $90." You would probably blow your stack, and rightly so. You might then try to explain that the return on the savings should be related to the amount of capital invested and that it fell from 5% to 4 1/2% ($90 in interest divided by $2,000 investment).

By the same token, union leaders would be justified in criticizing a newspaper story about wage increases which emphasized an increase in the total wages if the total increased only because labor worked longer hours and there was no increase in the rate of pay.

The capital of corporations increases from sale of securities and retention of earnings after dividends. Lack of information about the added investment may be responsible for making the public think that increases in earnings are unjustified.

Furthermore, an increase in earnings over a prior period may be emphasized without any recognition as to whether the earnings in the previous period were abnormally low.

An equally erroneous impression is created by the press relating profits to sales without explaining the amount of capital required to generate the sales. In an article about American Telephone and Telegraph, the profit margin was referred to as—"the highest among U.S. industrial grants." The margin was compared with IBM, G.M. and G.E. Such a comparison is totally meaningless without capital turnover figures. The figures in 1971 at the time of the article are shown at the bottom of this page.

Some difference when you look at the facts!!!

There is another significant factor in interpreting increases in earnings. Labor is interested in receiving real wage increases. If prices go up more than wages, there is a decrease in labor's purchasing power. Likewise, changes in corporate earnings should be interpreted in terms of the change in the value of the dollar. Perhaps we cannot expect newspapers to do this kind of reporting. Yet, it is a point that should be kept in mind in interpreting earnings when consumer prices rise.

One would think that at least corporate managements would point out that profit increases alone are misleading. How many annual reports show the relationship between increases in profits and capital investment? Perhaps this is being unfair to managements, because in annual reports they naturally wish to make the record look good to stockholders, who are interested in the raw increase in earnings per share.

Our free press, the newspapers and magazines, which do so much to help preserve our democratic way of life by telling the public the facts, could help preserve our free enterprise system by telling a fuller story in reporting profits.

	AT & T Consolidated	IBM	GM	GE
$\frac{\text{Sales}}{\text{Long Term Capital}}$	$0.38	$1.13	$2.48	$2.63
$\frac{\text{Return}}{\text{Sales}}$	19%	14%	7.1%	6.07%
$\frac{\text{Return}}{\text{Long Term Capital}}$	7.3%	16%	18%	16%

Comparison of Companies Which Follow Sound and Unsound Financial and Capital Investment Policies

By way of concluding this chapter we have prepared exhibits which show how a company, with poor financial and capital investment policies, can create *the same earnings per share* for a number of years as a company with sound capital investment policies, by steadily increasing debt.

The financial results are shown for two hypothetical industrial companies, designated A and B, which are alike in all respects except for the financial and capital investment policies. Company B is also shown revised with policies it should have followed.

Exhibit 15-25 shows the principal figures for each company. In Exhibit 15-26, three key figures are shown in chart form. The figures on which these exhibits are based are shown in Appendix 15-A.

The period of time is compressed into five years in order to simplify the picture. The first four years show good earnings. The rates of return are kept relatively low in the first four years in order to help compress the illustration in a short period. In the fifth year trouble is encountered, and return on long term capital is reduced to 5.9%. Ordinarily, such a financial picture would be stretched out over a greater time period.

Exhibit 15-25

COMPANY A, COMPANY B AND COMPANY B REVISED

Year	0	1	2	3	4	5
PART I Co. A						
Earnings per Share	$0.83	$0.88	$0.93	$0.98	$1.04	$0.52
Dividend	$0.41	$0.44	$0.47	$0.49	$0.52	$0.52
Return on Total Long Term Capital	10%	10%	10%	10%	10%	5 .9%
Debt Ratio	25%	25%	25%	25%	25%	25%
Interest Coverage Before Tax	10.4x	10.7x	10.3x	10.5x	10.4x	5.7x
Bond Rating	A	A	A	A	A	A
PART II Co. B						
Earnings per Share	$0.83	$0.88	$0.93	$0.98	$1.04	$0.40
Dividend	$0.41	$0.44	$0.46	$0.49	$0.52	$––
Return on Total Long Term Capital	10%	9.8%	9.5%	9.3%	9.2%	5.9%
Debt Ratio	25%	32%	37%	42%	46%	46%
Interest Coverage Before Tax	10.4x	7.8x	6.3x	5.3x	4.6x	2.2x
Bond Rating	A	A	A	BBB	BBB	BB
PART III Co. B Revised						
Earnings per Share	$0.83	$0.88	$0.93	$0.98	$1.04	$0.52
Dividend	$0.41	$0.44	$0.47	$0.49	$0.52	$0.52
Return on Total Long Term Capital	10%	10%	10%	10%	10%	5.9%
Debt Ratio	25%	25%	25%	25%	25%	25%
Interest Coverage Before Tax	10.4x	10.7x	10.3x	10.3x	10.4x	5.7x
Bond Rating	A	A	A	A	A	A

Exhibit 15-26

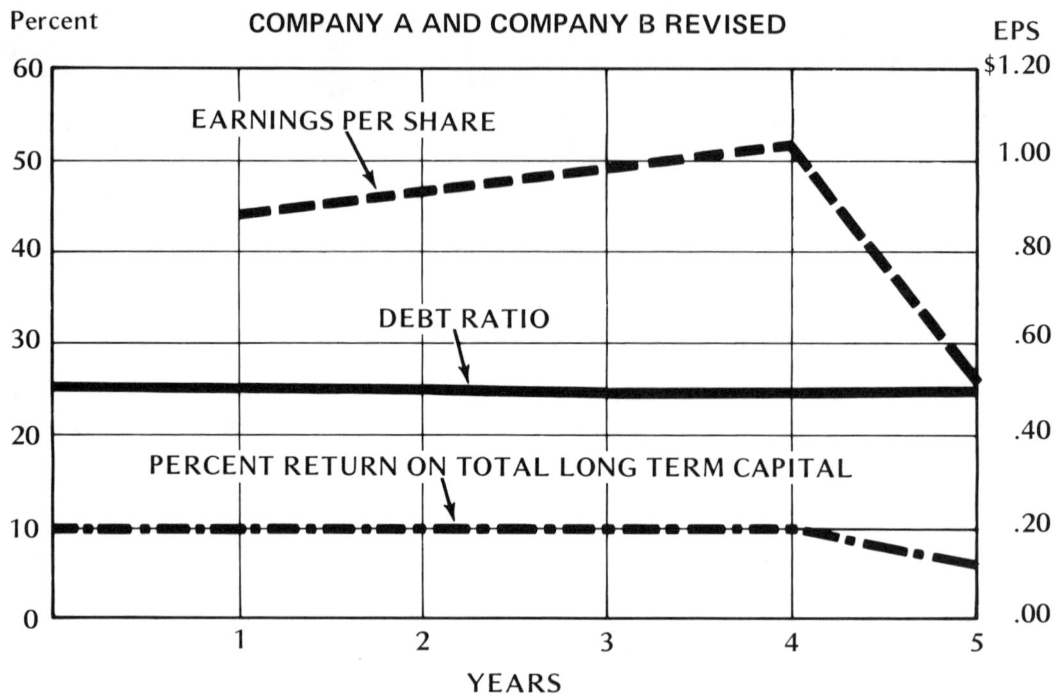

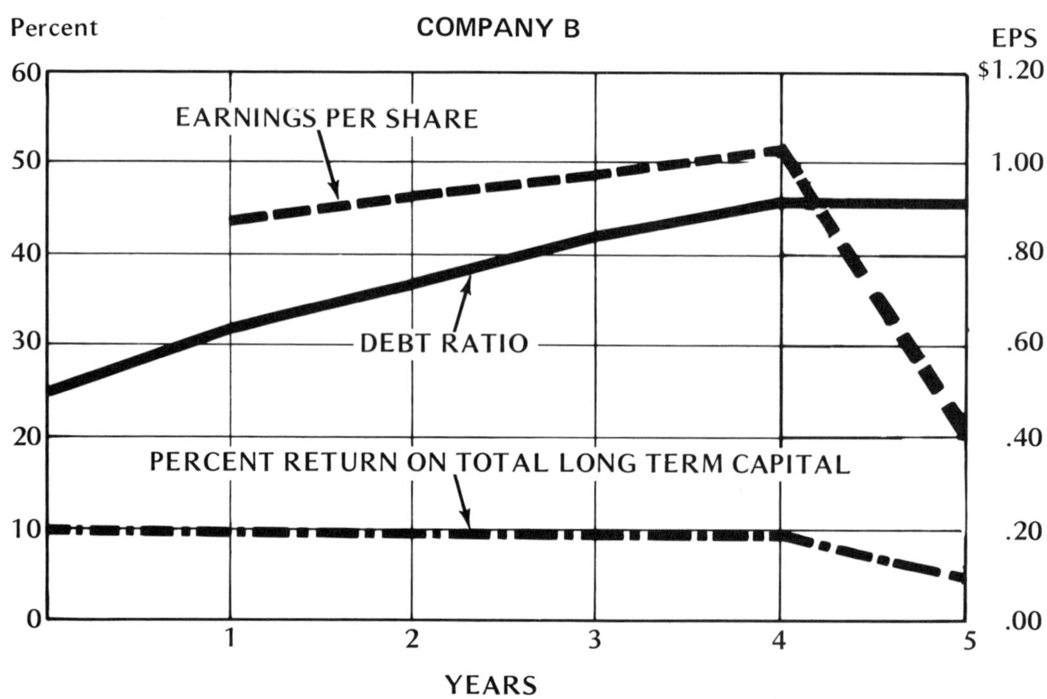

Company A keeps its capital structure in balance and makes capital investments which provide a satisfactory return. Company A maintains its A grade bond rating and never has to cut its common dividend.

Company B has the same earnings per share as Company A during the first four years and has the same 50% dividend payout policy. But it does so by increasing its debt ratio while accepting capital investments with an inadequate return because it can't find sufficient projects with a high return. Its A grade bond rate slips to BBB even in good years. And in the fifth year of bad earnings, its rating falls to BB. It has to cut its common dividend, and consequently the market price of its stock would become badly depressed compared to that of Company A.

Exhibit 15-25, Part III, shows how Company B could have maintained sound financial and capital investment policies if it had been willing to slow down its expansion program and only accept projects with an adequate return. It would have been smaller than Company A, but its financial position would have been equally as strong. And the market price of its stock would have held up like that of Company A.

Conclusion

So we conclude this chapter by emphasizing that the concept of cost-of-capital is basic to capital expenditure decisions. Understanding and applying this concept will result in wide benefit:

- Companies will not cause over-expansion and excessive competition that depresses prices and profits.
- A company's stockholders will be saved from being hurt by the market value of their stock declining below the book value represented by the money the stockholders actually provided the company.
- Management will not be inhibited in capital expenditure decisions by the mistaken belief that the existing return on capital is a determining factor. Regardless of the earnings on the existing investment, the stockholders will benefit, providing the return realized on the new project is above the cost-of-capital for that particular project.
- Capital will tend to be used where it can be most beneficial to our economy, and goods will not be produced that are not really needed. This will reduce the possibility that capital may be wasted and assure the highest possible standard of living for our nation.

Appendix 15-A

Detailed Data for Exhibits 15-24 and 25

COMPANY A

SOUND FINANCIAL AND CAPITAL INVESTMENT POLICIES

Balance Sheet	Base Year	Year 1	Year 2	Year 3	Year 4	Year 5
Current Assets	100					
Plant	50					
Total Assets	150					
Current Liabilities	50					
Capital–Debt	25 (25%)	29.1 (25%)	33.6 (25%)	38.6 (25%)	44.0 (25%)	44.0 (25%)
–Equity	75 (10 shares)	87.4 (11 shares)	100.9 (12 shares)	115.7 (13 shares)	131.9 (14 shares)	131.9 (14 shares)
	100	116.5	134.5	154.3	175.9	175.9
Total Liab. & Cap.	150					
Income Statement						
Sales						
Interest–7%	1.75	2.0	2.4	2.7	3.1	3.1
Tax	8.25	9.7	11.2	12.8	14.6	7.3
Net Income	8.25	9.7	11.2	12.8	14.6	7.3
Dividends (50% Payout)*	4.10	4.85	5.6	6.4	7.3	7.3
Amount Retained	4.10	4.85	5.6	6.4	7.3	—
Earnings per Share	.83	.88	.93	.98	1.04	.52
Dividends per Share	.41	.44	.47	.49	.52	.52
Return on L.T. Cap.	10%	10%	10%	10%	10%	5.9%
Return on Common	11	11	11	11	11	5.5
X Int. Earned–Bef. Tax	10.4x	10.7x	10.3x	10.5x	10.4x	5.7x
Bond Rating	A	A	A	A	A	A

*50% payment, except for year 5.

COMPANY B

SAME EARNINGS PER SHARE AS COMPANY A IN GOOD YEARS BUT FOLLOWS UNSOUND FINANCIAL AND CAPITAL INVESTMENT POLICIES. ITS STOCK WOULD SUFFER IN ADVERSE CONDITIONS IN FIFTH YEAR.

Balance Sheet	Base Year	Year 1	Year 2	Year 3	Year 4	Year 5
Current Assets	100					
Plant	50					
Total Assets	150					
Current Liabilities	50					
Cap.–Debt	25 (25%)	37.1 (32%)	50.4 (37%)	65.3 (42%)	81.7 (46%)	81.7 (46%)
–Equity	75 (10 shares)	79.4 (10 shares)	84.1 (10 shares)	89.0 (10 shares)	94.2 (10 shares)	96.6 (10 shares)
	100	116.5	134.5	154.3	175.9	178.3
Total Liab. & Cap.	150					
Income Statement						
Sales						
Interest†	1.75	2.6	3.5	4.6	5.7	6.5%
Tax	8.25	8.8	9.3	9.8	10.4	4.0
Net Income	8.25	8.8	9.3	9.8	10.4	4.0
Dividends (50% Payout)*	4.10	4.4	4.6	4.9	5.2	—
Amount Retained	4.10	4.4	4.7	4.9	5.2	4.0
Earnings per Share	.83	.88	.93	.98	1.04	.40
Dividends per Share	.41	.44	.46	.49	.52	—
Return on L.T. Cap.	10%	9.8%	9.5%	9.3%	9.2%	5.9%
Return on Common	11	11	11	11	11	4.1%
X Int. Earned–Bef. Tax	10.4x	7.8x	6.3x	5.3x	4.6x	2.2x
Bond Rating	A	A	A	BBB	BBB	BB

*50% payout, except for year 5.

†Because of the company's deteriorating credit, the interest rate would have to be increased. Adjustment for this factor was only made in year 5 when the rate was increased from 7% to 8%.

COMPANY B REVISED

BY ACCEPTING ONLY CAPITAL INVESTMENTS WHICH PROVIDE AN ADEQUATE RETURN AND FOLLOWING SOUND FINANCIAL POLICIES, COMPANY B REVISED IS SMALLER. BUT ITS COMMON STOCK IS EQUALLY ATTRACTIVE AS COMPANY A.

Balance Sheet	Base Year	Year 1	Year 2	Year 3	Year 4	Year 5
Current Assets	100					
Plant	50					
Total Assets	150					
Current Liabilities	50					
Capital–Debt	25 (25%)	26.4 (25%)	27.95 (25%)	29.65 (25%)	31.35 (25%)	31.35 (25%)
–Equity	75 (10 shares)	79.4 (10 shares)	84.05 (10 shares)	88.95 (10 shares)	94.15 (10 shares)	94.15 (10 shares)
Total Liab. & Cap.	150	105.8	112.00	118.60	125.50	125.50
Income Statement						
Sales						
Interest–7%	1.75	1.8	2.0	2.1	2.2	2.2
Tax	8.25	8.8	9.3	9.8	10.4	5.2
Net Income	8.25	8.8	9.3	9.8	10.4	5.2
Dividends (50% Payout)*	4.10	4.4	4.65	4.9	5.2	—
Amount Retained	4.10	4.4	4.65	4.9	5.2	—
Earnings per Share	.83	.88	.93	.98	1.04	.52
Dividends per Share	.41	.44	.47	.49	.52	.52
Return on L.T. Cap.	10%	10%	10%	10%	10%	5.9%
Return on Common	11	11	11	11	11	5.5%
X Int. Earned–Bef. Tax	10.4x	10.7x	10.3x	10.3x	10.4x	5.7x
Bond Rating	A	A	A	A	A	A

*50% payout, except for year 5.

CHAPTER 16

Capital Investment Analysis and Acquisition Pricing

Strides have been made in capital budgeting, but to say that all companies use sound policies in this area would be a misstatement of fact. Some companies have a procedure to follow, but it may be either inadequate or poorly applied. Serious errors in capital investment analysis will show up in poor earnings performance. Acquisitions are a part of capital investment, and the decisions some managements make in acquisition pricing are ridiculous.

The problem really starts with the top management. If top management doesn't understand the basic principles involved, capital will be misdirected no matter how much groundwork is done. The principles include many of the ideas covered in the previous chapter on profit goals: the importance of earning more than the cost-of-capital, of not using earnings per share as a guide, of relating rate of return and risk and of not allowing the source of capital to affect the rate required.

You find managements represent two extremes in capital decision making.

There are those who use inadequate tools for calculating return on a project such as payback. They contend that anything more complicated would not be understood by the company's division managers. That is a slim excuse for using a poor method, and avoids an opportunity to upgrade the division managers' capability.

At the other extreme, there are those who know all the fancy techniques of risk analysis and get so tied up in computer calculations that they lose sight of what has gone into the calculations in the first place. And their final figures may be so many steps from the original input that the top management who have to make the final decision cannot relate the figures to the important factors which will determine success or failure.

A proper approach to capital investment analysis should lie somewhere in between these two extremes—as simple an analysis as possible with a list of questions which will determine the success or failure of the project.

In this chapter we will discuss how to calculate return on investment for a project, how to apply it and how to price an acquisition.

In the first place, it is vital to use the right goal rate related to the right base. We started out determining a profit goal by calculating the cost-of-capital on long term capital. When you do capital decision making you will have to be sure of the assets that are included and how that base compares with total long term capital. If the base is different from long term capital, the rate will also have to be changed in order to meet the profit goal on long term capital.

When you calculate the income resulting from a project, it will be after taxes with no interest in expenses. Therefore, the goal rate you use will have to be an After-Tax Equivalent Rate.

Forecasting

Return on investment for a capital investment analysis cannot be calculated without a forecast. This book does not cover forecasting, but a few words about its significance is a necessary introduction to the subject.

In the first place, you must be sure to include all expenses and investments which are connected with the project. You must also include a fair share of overheads and corporate level investments which will support the project or you must increase the goal rate to take care of them.

Some people seem to have little faith in forecasts and feel the same way about a profitability rate based thereon. Believe it or not, the management of one company stated that since they had never made a correct forecast they had decided not to make any more. The quick answer to that statement is that the stockholders needed new management to save them from reliance on pure luck.

Those who try to shun forecasts may argue that a company spends millions on pure research without explicitly forecasting the profits resulting from these expenditures. Companies must, at least, evaluate the overall results of pure research. Because of the nature of the expenditure, the evaluation may have to be on a post-audit basis. However, the limitation of forecasts for research expenditures in no way argues against profit forecasts which can be used as the basis for judgment in deciding on other types of capital expenditures.

Each capital decision in fact involves a forecast—the forecasting process is employed even though a forecast is not put down on paper. In effect, if no written forecast is made, the management is saying that it expects, or mentally forecasts, that profits on the proposal will be satisfactory. The purpose of a written forecast is to provide a background on which to base judgment and aid management in its mental processes. It is the best kind of discipline to force thinking about all the elements which will affect profits. It provides a basis for post-audit appraisal.

A financial forecast is an attempt to describe future events in numerical terms. Its accuracy is limited proportionately with our ability to see into the future—like a man peering into a haze, the farther we try to see, the less certain we are about what is out there. This is no argument for abandoning forecasts. All the tools at your disposal must be used in order to improve the vision; even a hazy picture of the future is better than no picture at all.

However, it is important to know how much weight to give to your forecast in making a decision. What are the chances that the forecast is seriously wrong? One way to try to answer this question is to bracket your forecast with two others—one if everything goes right and another if all the problems you are worrying about in fact occur. These bracketing forecasts give some idea of what happens if the central forecast is wrong.

If certain items which are key to the success of a project are hard to foretell, various forecasts might be made with the key items varied within a realistic range in order to show possible effects.

There are sophisticated techniques that can be used to test the reliability of forecasts and to show how important each assumption is to the final outcome. For the technician they may be helpful, but they would be of little value for presentation to top management; the raw forecast figures would mean more.

Most important in reviewing a forecast is to critically analyze the relationship of the key figures, such as inventories and receivables to sales, sales per dollar of capital, profit margins and rates of return on capital. Are these relationships realistic?

When forecasting is mentioned, someone may ask "For how many years should the forecast be made?" If ten years is suggested, there may be some cynical comment such as: "I defy you to show me someone who has made a correct forecast in my industry for more than three years." This, of course, is no answer and only indicates that the person has missed the point. Even if definite figures cannot be established, projections can be made on the basis of reasonableness, or should we say within the range of possibility. If these figures are translated into a profitability rate which can be compared with a Profit Goal, they can be the basis of a reasoned decision of go or no-go.

No definite figure can be given as to how many years the forecast should be extended. This will depend upon the circumstances. In the case where an entire company is acquired, the forecast may be projected for as long as 20 years based on possible percentage growth rates.

A forecast should represent a basis for you to use in coming to a final decision by sitting back and asking yourself the question: From a practical point of view, is it within the realm of reasonableness for one to make these figures come true in view of the obstacles that may be encountered?

As will be explained, the forecast should give cash flows. These cash flows can be picked out of the forecast income statements and balance sheets.

Common Measures

Each part of the capital decision making process should be perfected as far as possible so as to arrive at correct decisions. Granted that forecasting is the key to the whole investment decision and that it may include errors, we see no reason why the profitability rate itself should compound the errors by being calculated incorrectly.

Let's consider several ways of determining a profitability rate for Project A, shown in Exhibit 16-1. This project will require a $100,000 initial investment and is expected to increase annual corporate profits, after depreciation and income taxes, by $10,000 during its estimated four-year economic life. The proposed $100,000 investment involves the purchase of machinery which will be depreciated on a straight-line basis at $25,000 annually; the machinery is expected to have no salvage value at the end of its four-year life.

Exhibit 16-1

THREE COMMONLY EMPLOYED INVESTMENT MEASURES

PROJECT A

Column	1	2	3	4
Year	Investment	Profit After Tax	Depreciation	Cash Flow
0	$100,000	—	—	—
1		$10,000	$ 25,000	$ 35,000
2		10,000	25,000	35,000
3		10,000	25,000	35,000
4		10,000	25,000	35,000
Total	$100,000	$40,000	$100,000	$140,000

Payback Method

$$\text{Payback Period} = \frac{\text{Total Investment}}{\text{Annual Cash Flow}} = \frac{\$100{,}000}{\$\ 35{,}000} = 2.9 \text{ years}$$

Accounting Methods

$$\text{Return on Total Investment} = \frac{\text{Annual Avg. Profit After Taxes}}{\text{Total Investment}} = \frac{\$\ 10{,}000}{\$100{,}000} = 10\%$$

$$\text{Return on Average Investment} = \frac{\text{Annual Avg. Profit After Taxes}}{\text{Average Investment}} = \frac{\$10{,}000}{\$50{,}000} = 20\%$$

The exhibit includes three commonly employed measures to appraise the profitability of this investment.

The payback method shows the number of years it takes a project to pay back its initial capital outlay from cash flows produced by profits and depreciation. In our example, it will take about 2.9 years to recover the $100,000 initial investment from the $10,000 annual profit and the $25,000 annual depreciation.

To calculate payback if the cash flows are not constant, deduct the net cash flow each year from the initial investment until the remaining initial investment is less than one year's cash flow. Then determine the proportion of that year's cash flow required to complete the repayment of the initial investment. The cash flows should be net after any additional investment. If there are negative net cash flows in any year, due to losses or investments greater than cash flow incomes during the year, they should be deducted from the positive cash flows in calculating the payback period.

The return on total investment simply divides the expected $10,000 in annual earnings by the $100,000 total investment. If there is an additional investment during the period, it must be added. Replacements are not added since they do not add to total book value.

The return on average investment relates the expected $10,000 in annual average earnings to the average net investment outstanding over the life of the project. In the case of Project A, with straight line depreciation, the average investment is $50,000; that is, the $100,000 initial investment plus the $0 ending investment, divided by two to get the average.

The most straightforward method of making this calculation is to total the net book investment for the beginning of each year and the end of the last year and then divide by the number of years plus one.

Each of these three measures is widely used in industry today. Which is a valid profitability rate? Which can be compared with a Profit Goal to determine whether the investment is worthwhile? Unfortunately, to use any of them may lead to unsound investment choices.

The correct profitability rate is actually 15%. It can be determined by discounted cash flow procedures to be described later.

Why Common Measures Are Inadequate

Because the three profitability measures discussed above—payback period and both accounting methods—are so widely employed, it is worthwhile to point out just why they may produce unreliable profitability rates. First, we must admit that both the payback period and accounting methods are easy to compute and easy to understand.

Payback Method

The method which industry uses most often to rank capital investment proposals is payback. As a measure of risk, it actually is useful. It is easy to see that the faster your initial capital outlay is recovered, the less time your capital is at risk.

However, payback does not measure profitability. A payback evaluation ignores all of the cash flows expected after the payback period; these post-recovery cash flows can be of vital importance to a project's profitability.

For example, suppose we are considering two projects, each of which requires a $100,000 initial capital outlay. Each will generate $50,000 cash each year for the first two years. Both projects will obviously have an equal payback period—two years. But suppose the cash flows from Project One cease after those first two years, while Project Two continues to produce cash flows at the rate of $50,000 annually for another two years. In this extreme example it is easy to see that the payback method offers the decision-maker no assistance at all in evaluating the post-recovery income.

Another major objection to payback is that it fails to consider the time value of money.

Suppose we add Project Three to the example above and assume that it also requires an initial $100,000 capital outlay. Its cash flows, however, will be $75,000 the first year, $25,000 the second year and then $50,000 for the next two years. The cash flows of these three projects are shown in Exhibit 16-2.

Payback will indicate that Project Three has the same two-year capital recovery period as the other two projects; it thus seems equally desirable. However, it is actually more desirable than Project Two, since the extra $25,000 return in the first year can be put to work earning more income in the second year.

Despite these two major objections we do not recommend dropping payback computations completely, but we do suggest that payback is helpful only in measuring risk by showing how soon we will get our money back. It is certainly not a valid profitability rate.

Accounting Methods

Neither of the so-called accounting return on investment methods provides a valid profitability rate. In the capital investment process, they are useful only as very quick and crude profitability indicators for preliminary evaluations. For some proposals they may come fairly close to a true profitability rate, but for others they may be very misleading. The basic faults of the accounting methods are two: one, they focus upon accounting income figures rather than upon cash flows; and two, they fail to consider the time value of money.

Cash Flows

Why is it important to look at cash flows rather than at expected income in evaluating capital investments? Very simply because it is not until we actually spend cash that we have incurred any monetary sacrifice; conversely, it is only when we receive cash—not income as accounting measures it—that we have received something which can be put back to work to earn more money.

For correct decision-making in the case of Project A, shown in Exhibit 16-1, the profitability measure should focus upon the $35,000 annual cash receipts that we expect—not on the $10,000 annual accounting income figures. It is these $35,000 cash flows that can be put back to work earning more money. The accounting return on investment methods focus upon the $10,000 expected income, not upon the $35,000 cash flows which are more significant for decision making purposes.

This may sound as though we are interested in the return *of* capital rather than the return *on* capital. Actually, the cash flows include both the return of capital and the return on capital. The return of the capital reduces the investment base on which the earnings are figured to produce a true profitability rate on capital. We will explain this idea shortly.

Time Value of Money

The concept of time value of money is central to the whole approach of determining a correct profitability rate. Both the payback and accounting methods fail to consider properly the time value of money.

Just what do we mean when we say money has a time value? It means that a dollar due in the future is worth less than a dollar we have in hand today. Why? Because today's dollar can be put to work to earn more money between now and that future date.

Put another way, if someone owes you $1 and offers to pay either $1 today or $1 a year from now, which would you choose? You would choose today even if you do not need the money right away, because you could put it into a savings account or some other investment. A year later, that dollar would have grown to $1.04 if the savings account paid interest at an annual rate of 4%. In its most basic form, then, this is the meaning of time value of money—a dollar today is worth more than a dollar received at a future date; how much more depends on how much you could earn with today's dollar between now and that future date.

Exhibit 16-2

THREE PROJECTS WITH THE SAME PAYBACK IN TWO YEARS

Cash Flows = Profit, After Tax, Plus Depreciation

Year	Investment	Project One Cash Flow	Project Two Cash Flow	Project Three Cash Flow
0	$100,000			
1		$50,000	$50,000	$75,000
2		50,000	50,000	25,000
3			50,000	50,000
4			50,000	50,000

Our aim, then, is to develop a method of measuring the profitability rate of a proposed project in a way that correctly handles the time value of money. The projects we are considering will almost always extend over more than one year; if an investment does not affect more than one year, it is probably more of an operating decision than a capital budgeting decision.

Compounding

This leads us into the effects of compounding. In case it has been a number of years since you thought about compound interest, here is a one-sentence refresher: Compound interest means that each year we compute interest earned on that year's invested principal and then add the interest earned to the principal amount; this compound sum—that is, interest plus principal—then becomes the new principal for computing the interest earned the next year. In other words, in the second year you earn interest on the initial principal, plus interest on earnings of the first year.

We will use annual compounding because it is easy to use in explaining principles. In actual practice, of course, interest can be compounded more than once a year, once a quarter, monthly or for whatever period you choose.

It is certainly not practical to assume that all your corporation's income will come on the last day of each year. Even so, annual compounding will give reasonably accurate results. If further refinement is necessary, the details of more frequent compounding into monthly or even continuous compounding rates can be left to your financial analysis group.

We will use a simple example to further illustrate compounding. Suppose you put $10,000 in a savings bank that offers annual interest of 4%. If you left it there for two years, you should be quite unhappy if it had earned only $400 the first year and $400 the second year. The second year your deposit should have earned $416—4% on the initial $10,000 plus 4% on the $400 earned the first year. At the end of the second year, then, your $10,000 has grown to $10,816.

Instead of going through these several multiplications each time, it is much simpler to consult tables which show the amount to which $1 will grow at a certain interest rate; multiplying that amount by the actual dollars invested will give us the same answer much more rapidly.

Exhibit 16-3 shows a sample of such a table. To illustrate: the figure of 1.082, which is shown in the 4% column for period 2, multiplied by the $10,000 initial investment in the example above, indicates that you will have a sum of approximately $10,820 at the end of two years if you invested $10,000 at an interest rate of 4% compounded annually.

Tables carried to more decimal places are available which will give the more precise $10,816 result we obtained in the previous paragraph. Three or four decimal places are usually adequate for capital budgeting purposes.

Exhibit 16-3

SAMPLE TABLE OF COMPOUND INTEREST FACTORS*

The future worth of $1 invested today, at compound interest; or amounts to which $1, invested today, will grow in the future, at compound interest.

i / n	4%	6%	8%	10%	15%
1	1.040	1.060	1.080	1.100	1.150
2	1.082	1.124	1.166	1.210	1.323
3	1.125	1.191	1.260	1.331	1.521
4	1.170	1.262	1.360	1.464	1.749

FORMULA: $f = (1 + i)^n$

f = Compound interest factor
n = Number of compounding periods
i = Interest rate per period

*One of the most complete sets of tables is the Financial Compound Interest and Annuity Tables, Fifth Edition. Publication No. 376 (1970) of the Financial Publishing Company, Boston (Price $30). This book contains almost 1,000 pages of tables. The tables cover rates of interest ranging from 1/12% to 100%, with different compounding periods. Each table contains factors to 10 decimal places compounding and discounting and four other types of value computations. The book also contains some auxiliary tables and many examples of applications.

Also for continuous compounding see tables available in *Principles of Engineering Economy*, Fifth Edition, 1970, revised by Eugene L. Grant and W. Grant Ireson, Ronald Press, New York City, Appendix 4 (Price $13.95).

Discounting or Present Value—The Other Side of the Coin

Now let us just turn the compounding approach around. This will produce discount or present value factors. In compounding, we derived the amount to which $1 will grow at compound interest. Discount factors answer the question, "What amount do I have to invest today, in order to have $1 at the end of 'n' years, assuming 'i' interest rate 'compounded'?"

Another way of saying it is that the discount factors give the present value of a sum due at a future date at a certain rate of interest. Exhibit 16-4 is a sample table of discount or present value factors.

Exhibit 16-4

SAMPLE TABLE OF DISCOUNT OR PRESENT VALUE FACTORS

The present worth of $1 due in the future at compound interest; or amounts which will grow to $1 in the future, at compound interest.

i / n	4%	6%	8%	10%	15%
1	0.962	0.943	0.926	0.909	0.870
2	0.925	0.890	0.857	0.826	0.756
3	0.889	0.840	0.794	0.751	0.658
4	0.855	0.792	0.735	0.683	0.572

FORMULA: $f = \frac{1}{(1 + i)^n}$

f = Discount or present value factor
i = Interest rate per period
n = Number of compounding periods

To illustrate the use of Exhibit 16-4, suppose we want to know what amount will grow to $1 by the end of two years, if we invest at 4% compound interest. The table shows $0.925 would be the answer. The proof of this is as follows: First year, adding investment of $0.925 to interest of $0.037 results in $0.962 at the first year end, which will earn $0.038 during the second year, for a total of $1.

A discount factor is the reciprocal of the corresponding compound interest factor. For example, the compound interest factor for 4%

for two years is 1.082. The discount factor for 4% for two years is 1/1.082 or 0.925.

The amounts in Exhibit 16-4 can be multiplied by amounts other than $1 to determine the present value of such other amounts. For example: What would need to be invested at 10% compound interest to have $10,000 at the end of two years? From the exhibit, in the column for 10% on the line for two periods, we read the factor 0.826; multiplying $10,000 times 0.826 gives us $8,260—the amount which we would have to invest now in order to have $10,000 two years hence.

The time value of money is a key concept in all correct capital budgeting techniques, because it enables us to convert all the cash flows pertaining to a proposed project into their equivalent values at a single point in time.

The single point in time is referred to as the "zero point" in time. This permits us to make a correct comparison between the investment and the expected return.

There are various techniques which take into effect the time value of money. Let us look at the technique which we recommend for capital budgeting—the "Time Value Profitability Rate" technique.

You may see this technique, in other authors' writings, called "Internal Rate of Return," the "Investors' Method" or the "Discounted Cash Flow" technique. "Discounted Cash Flow" is probably the most widely used term, but it is somewhat misleading; all three of the correct capital budgeting techniques actually use the principle of discounting cash flows, so to entitle just one as the "Discounted Cash Flow" technique is confusing. Therefore, we suggest the title "Time Value Profitability Rate" as the best descriptive term.

By comparing this rate to your profit goal, you have a way of evaluating how desirable the project is expected to be. For Project A, which we used as an example at the beginning of this chapter, we stated that the correct profitability rate, by which we meant the Time Value Profitability Rate, was 15%; whereas, the two accounting methods showed 10% and 20%—quite a difference.

Time Value Profitability Rate Technique

To determine the Time Value Profitability Rate for a project, the technique finds, by trial and error, the rate which makes the present value of the future cash flows, at the "zero point" in time, equal to the value of the initial investment.

Basically, the Time Value Profitability Rate technique employs what Operations Research people call an "iterative" approach. This high-flown title merely means "trial and error." In other words, this technique starts out with some trial rate. If this first rate does not provide the answer, another higher or lower second rate, depending on the results of the first rate, is chosen and the computations performed again. This process continues until the correct rate is found.

As an example, to make that statement clearer, we will use Project A referred to in the first part of this chapter. Project A called for an investment of $100,000 and had an expected economic life of four years. For simplicity, we assumed that the investment is fully depreciable and will be depreciated on a straight-line basis; this resulted in an annual depreciation charge of $25,000. The forecast showed a profit after tax of $10,000 annually. The first four columns of Exhibit 16-5 show this information.

Suppose we select a trial rate of 10% for Project A. In Column 5 of the exhibit, we write the present value factors for 10% taken from the table in the previous exhibit. Each year's Net Cash Flow in Column 4 is then multiplied by that year's factor, and the multiplication results are written down in Column 6. Column 6 is totaled, for the four years, excluding the initial $100,000 investment. This total is $110,930; it means that if Project A required a $110,930 initial investment and we expected to receive four annual cash flows of $35,000, we would be earning 10% on our investment. But the proposal we are evaluating does not require an initial investment of $110,930; it requires only $100,000. Because the $110,930 exceeds the required $100,000 capital outlay, the proposal's correct profitability rate must exceed 10%.

We therefore select a second trial rate—say 15%—and repeat the process. Column 7 sets forth the present value factors for 15%. Now each year's $35,000 net cash flow is multiplied by the 15% present value factor for that year, and the results are shown in Column 8. The resulting total in column 8 is $99,550 which is nearly $100,000, the amount of the proposal's initially required capital outlay. Therefore, the project's Time Value Profitability Rate is approximately 15%.

All very well, but just what does this 15% Time Value Profitability Rate mean? Actually, it is the rate of profit which is expected to be earned each year on the unrecovered capital investment in the project. This is illustrated in Exhibit 16-6.

Exhibit 16-5

ILLUSTRATION OF TIME VALUE
PROFITABILITY RATE TECHNIQUE

Project A

Column / Year	1	2	3
		Expected Cash Flows	
	Investment	Profit After Depreciation and Taxes	Depreciation Add-Back
0	$(100,000)		
1	--	$10,000	25,000
2	--	10,000	25,000
3	--	10,000	25,000
4	--	10,000	25,000
Total	--	$40,000	$100,000

Column / Year	4 (1 + 2 + 3)	5	6 (4 x 5)	7	8 (4 x 7)
		Expected Cash Flows Discounted			
		Discounted at 10%		Discounted at 15%	
	Net Cash Flow	Factor	Amount	Factor	Amount
0	$(100,000)	1.000	$(100,000)	1.000	$(100,000)
1	35,000	.909	$ 31,820	.870	$ 30,040
2	35,000	.826	28,910	.756	26,460
3	35,000	.751	26,290	.658	23,030
4	35,000	.683	23,910	.572	20,020
Total	$ 140,000		$ 110,930		$ 99,550

At the beginning of the first year, $100,000 is invested. Part of the first year's $35,000 cash flow is first applied to the $15,000 earnings expected ($100,000 by 15%); the $20,000 balance of the cash flow ($35,000 – $15,000) then goes to reduce the investment to $80,000 at the beginning of the second year. In the second year the earnings on the $80,000 unrecovered investment are $12,000 ($80,000 by 15%) and the balance of the $35,000, or $23,000, goes to reduce the investment. The same steps occur in the third and fourth years; the fourth year's reduction of investment reduces the unrecovered investment to zero.

The Exhibit shows that the principle of the Time Value Profitability Rate is this: Each year part of the net cash flow is first applied to annual earnings at the applicable rate on the unrecovered investment; then the balance of the cash flow represents a recovery of the capital originally invested in the project.

On the earlier inflows, more goes for earnings, but in later years larger proportions of each payment are applied to reducing the principal of the investment.

If there is inadequate cash flow to provide income in any year, the process allocates income to that year by adding the amount of unrecovered income to the investment to be recovered in subsequent years.

In other words, the Time Value Profitability Rate method assumes that the initial investment will be recovered. In addition, it answers the question, "What return will be earned on the unrecovered investment each year?"

Is the Time Value Profitability Rate Technique Really Complex?

A question that often arises in discussing the Time Value Profitability Rate technique is whether the increase in accuracy obtained by this technique is really worth all that complexity. At first, it appears to be complicated and hard to understand.

There are two answers to this accusation of complexity. First of all, part of the problem is that its use is unfamiliar and therefore seems much more confusing than it really is. Close scrutiny will show that it is actually only the computations which are really different—the basis forecasts are already essential to proper capital budgeting, even if one of the inadequate methods such as payback is used.

Exhibit 16-6

MEANING OF TIME VALUE PROFITABILITY RATE

Project A

Column / Year	1 Unrecovered Investment (at Beginning of the Year)	2 Total Cash Flow	3 Where Cash Flow Goes: Annual Earnings (15% of Unrecovered Investment)	4 Where Cash Flow Goes: Reduction of Investment (2-3)
1	$100,000	$ 35,000	$15,000	$ 20,000
2	80,000	35,000	12,000	23,000
3	57,000	35,000	8,550	26,450
4	30,550	35,000	4,450*	30,550
5	–0–			
Total		$140,000	$40,000	$100,000

*Rounded because rate is not exactly 15%.

So it is only the computations that bear the brunt of the complexity allegation. But are they very complex? Not really. When computations are required, they are readily reduced to routine. In fact, many companies now utilize computer programs which will perform the mechanics of trial and error to derive the rate.

The second answer to the complexity question is that the amount of time and effort required is more than counterbalanced by the importance of capital budgeting. Given the fact that capital investment decisions often have more impact on the company's future than many of management's other decisions, it seems logical to present management with as reliable a guide as possible. This is particularly appropriate when necessary computations can be performed by clerical or computer time, thus affording a better rationing of top management's time and effort.

Is the Time Value Profitability Rate Technique Always Worthwhile?

The spectrum of capital projects to which the Time Value Profitability Rate technique can be applied is quite broad. This is not to say, however, that it is worthwhile for every project.

If the financial outcome is exceedingly uncertain, a rate of return analysis may be of very little practical value. We have already suggested as an example corporate expenditures on fundamental research. Although financial forecasts of the possible benefits from these expenditures may be worthwhile, risk considerations and experienced management judgment are probably more important to the decision than are detailed profitability rate analyses.

Other proposals may be so clearly attractive or unattractive that no analysis is necessary. Clearly undesirable projects can be rejected without detailed analysis. Others may be so obviously desirable that detailed profitability calculations are superfluous—for example, expenditures for emergency repairs to assembly line facilities to assure a continued production flow.

Still other capital investments may be so small that the work involved in making detailed analyses is unwarranted. To provide a suitable segregation of such proposals, management may set a level of investment below which the analysts need not make detailed supporting analyses.

The answer to the question, then, is that the Time Value Profitability Rate technique is not always worthwhile, but it can be very valuable for a great majority of capital investments. It is a straightforward analytical tool which considers all of the relevant facts included in the forecast.

Applications of Time Value Profitability Rate

We will show how to apply the time value profitability rate to a plant opening and a division liquidation.

Plant Opening

The management of Dairy Products Company is considering opening a new plant to provide additional production capacity for the company's new product line of pre-mixed formulas. It is estimated that this will require an initial investment of $1,550,000 comprising the following:

Working Capital	$ 550,000
Land	200,000
Building (Estimated 40-year life)	600,000
Fixtures (Estimated 10-year life)	200,000
	$1,550,000

Forecasts of growth in sales volume indicate that an additional $150,000 working capital investment will be required at the end of the fifth year. It is estimated that, on the average, plant fixtures will require complete replacement every ten years. For both book and tax purposes, the company uses the sum-of-the-digits method in computing depreciation. Estimates of expected sales and profit results are shown in Columns 3-5 in Exhibit 16-7.

Management estimates the company's After-Tax Equivalent Cost-of-Capital at approximately 9% and that this new investment would have about the same risk. Accordingly, management wishes to assess whether or not the new plant will generate a return sufficiently above this Cost-of-Capital to justify the undertaking.

If the expansion is successful, sales and earnings are expected to continue for an indefinite period of time—certainly for more than 20 years. However, for evaluation purposes a 20-year economic life is arbitrarily assumed. This assumption produces satisfactory results provided the remaining value of plant investment at the end of 20 years is estimated and considered in the profitability evaluation. In this case, it is estimated that the residual value of the investment at the end of 20 years, after considering applicable income taxes, will comprise the following:

Working Capital	$ 700,000
Land and Building (After Taxes on Gain from Disposal)	509,000
	$1,209,000

This amount is considered in the cash flow analysis as a cash receipt at the end of the twentieth year.

If it is felt that other terminal values should be estimated, additional calculations should be made. In principle, the terminal value should be the higher of these two figures: the liquidating value of the investment (net of taxes), or the value of the investment to the company on a going concern basis at the chosen terminal date.

An alternative evaluation procedure would consist of forecasting cash flows from the plant for an indefinite life, whereupon the above terminal value estimate would not be required. However, computational simplicity results from considering the investment to have a 20-year life. Ordinarily, negligible differences in Time Value Profitability Rates obtain under either method of analysis. Because of the discounting procedure, relatively little weight is assigned to cash flow estimates made for more than 20 years in the future. The effect of the terminal value on the rate, of course, depends on its relative size and the chosen terminal date.

By trial and error, the prospective Time Value Profitability Rate is found to be 9.5%. Relevant computations are shown in Column 8-11 and in the calculations at the bottom of the table. This return is slightly above the 9% Cost-of-Capital for the proposal.

Also shown in the Exhibit is the fact that the returns on the two accounting methods are 9.2% and 12.1%. The extent of the possible error in the use of one of the accounting methods is 2.6%—a significant amount in a close case like this one, and the spread may be substantial with a different set of figures.

One of the company's top officers suggests that there are risks inherent in this proposed expansion and that further analysis appears desirable before proceeding.

He specifically mentions two risks: First, changing technology in the preparation of pre-mixed formula may make present equipment obsolete at the end of, perhaps, ten years; and second, the sales and profit projections used in deriving the 9.5% Time Value Profitability Rate may prove unduly optimistic, especially considering the possible introduction of similar product lines by competitors. Accordingly, he suggests that the proposal's Profitability Rate be estimated under two alternative assumptions concerning economic life and estimated future profits.

The plant's Time Value Profitability Rate is computed, assuming premature liquidation of operations at the end of ten years with an estimated residual value of the plant of $1,322,600 after considering applicable income taxes. The proposal's Time Value Profitability Rate under this pessimistic assumption is found to be 7.5%, an amount below the Cost-of-Capital.

Another Time Value Profitability Rate is calculated under conservative assumptions

Exhibit 16-7

ANALYSIS OF PROPOSED NEW PLANT.
EVALUATION OF EXPECTED OPERATION
CASH FLOW SCHEDULE

(Dollars in Thousands)

COL. / LINE	1	2	3	4	5	6	7 (2 + 5 + 6)	8	9 (7 x 8)	10	11 (7 x 10)
		EXPECTED CASH FLOWS						EXPECTED CASH FLOWS DISCOUNTED			
								Discounted at 8%		Discounted at 10%	
	Year	Investment	Sales	Profit (% of sales)	Profit after depreciation and taxes	Depreciation	Net cash flow	Factor	Amount	Factor	Amount
1	0	$(1,550)[a]					$(1,550.0)	1.000	$(1,550.0)	1.000	$(1,550.0)
2	1	–	$2,000	– %	$ (10)	$65.7	$ 55.7	.926	51.6	.909	50.6
3	2	–	2,500	2.0	30	61.2	91.2	.857	78.2	.826	75.3
4	3	–	2,750	4.0	55	56.9	111.9	.794	88.8	.751	84.0
5	4	–	3,000	5.0	75	52.5	127.5	.735	93.7	.683	87.1
6	5	$ (150)[b]	3,250	6.0	97.5	48.1	(4.4)	.681	(3.0)	.621	(2.7)
7	6	–	3,500	8.0	140	43.8	183.8	.630	115.8	.564	103.7
8	7	–	3,750	8.0	150	39.4	189.4	.583	110.4	.513	97.2
9	8	–	4,000	10.0	200	35.0	235.0	.540	126.9	.467	109.7
10	9	–	4,000	10.0	200	30.7	230.7	.500	115.4	.424	97.8
11	10	$ (200)[c]	4,000	10.0	200	26.3	26.3	.463	12.2	.386	10.2
12	11	–	4,000	10.0	200	58.4	258.4	.429	110.9	.350	90.4
13	12	–	4,000	10.0	200	53.9	253.9	.397	100.8	.319	81.0
14	13	–	4,000	10.0	200	49.6	249.6	.368	91.9	.290	72.4
15	14	–	4,000	10.0	200	45.3	245.3	.340	83.4	.263	64.5
16	15	–	4,000	10.0	200	40.8	240.8	.315	75.9	.239	57.6
17	16	–	4,000	10.0	200	36.5	236.5	.292	69.1	.218	51.6
18	17	–	4,000	10.0	200	32.1	232.1	.270	62.7	.198	46.0
19	18	–	4,000	10.0	200	27.7	227.7	.250	56.9	.180	41.0
20	19	–	4,000	10.0	200	23.4	223.4	.232	51.8	.164	36.6
21	20	$ 1,209[d]	4,000	10.0	200	19.0	1,419.9	.215	305.3	.149	211.6
22					$3,137.5				$ 1,788.7		$ 1,465.6

[a] Initial investment.
[b] Additional working capital.
[c] Replacement of fixtures.
[d] Residual value.

CALCULATIONS

Time value profitability rate: $8\% + 2\% \times \frac{(\$1{,}788.7 - 1{,}550.0)}{(\$1{,}798.7 - 1{,}465.6)} = 9.5\%$

Return on average book value: $\frac{\$3{,}137.5/20}{\$1{,}294.2} = 12.1\%$

Return on total book value: $\frac{\$3{,}137.5/20}{\$1{,}700} = 9.2\%$

concerning future sales and earnings. It results in a 7.1% return and measures the lower limit of expected earning power.

Equipped with these estimates—9.5%, 7.5% and 7.1%—of the project's anticipated profitability, management must decide whether or not to open the plant. In this case, the only forecast which shows a return even slightly above the Cost-of-Capital is the optimistic one. Since a Profit Goal should be above the Cost-of-Capital, management decided against opening the plant.

Note in this example that the Time Value Profitability Rate is computed on working capital plus fixed assets, rather than on the total current and fixed assets. This is because the corporate Cost-of-Capital we used is computed on long term capital which provides plant and working capital. As we have said many times, profitability rates, to be comparable, should be computed on the long term capital invested in projects, or appropriate adjustments should be made in the rate.

Division Liquidation

Dairy Products Company has one division which has been showing poor earnings. Returns on this division's total book investment for the last three years have been 1.3%, 1.1% and 1.0% respectively. Management attention has been directed toward improving the situation, but detailed studies suggest that little can be done. Accordingly, management wishes to evaluate the desirability of closing the division. It is believed that closing this division would have little, if any, effect upon the profitability of the remaining divisions. If a division closing does affect the profits or expenses of other divisions, these effects must be included in the evaluation of the profitability of the division under consideration.

First, estimates are made of the income which may be expected from continuing to operate the division for a reasonable number of years. It is expected that the division, after depreciation and taxes, can at best be expected to earn the amounts set forth in Exhibit 16-8, Column 3, over the next seven years. These projected earnings will produce an apparently unattractive annual return on a $725,000 total book investment of less than 1%.

However, the book value of the permanent capital invested in the division is not a valid measure of the economic investment in the division. The economic value of the capital invested in the division is its value in best alternative use. Typically, this is its liquidating value since sale of the investment is typically its best alternative use. In a few cases, however, when facilities can be diverted to some other corporate use, the value of the investment for such purpose may be higher than resale value. Dairy Products Company would liquidate divisional assets if the division were shut down and thus prepared divisional balance sheets on both a book and a liquidating basis, as shown in Exhibit 16-9.

The liquidating value of the division is estimated to be considerably less than its book value. Upon liquidation, it is expected that accounts receivable collection losses will mount, that inventory losses will be suffered and that prepaid items will have a zero value.

The Time Value Profitability Rate which could be earned on the $365,000 economic investment in the division by continuing operations is computed in Exhibit 16-8. The resulting 9.1% rate is the appropriate measure of financial worth to use in deciding upon whether or not to liquidate the division. If this is above the company's cost-of-capital and the risk of the division is the same as that for the company, continuing to operate the division is slightly more profitable than liquidating it. This is true despite the fact that the division's prospective rate of return on total book value is less than 1.0%. However, management estimates that the risk of this division is somewhat greater than the risk of the business as a whole. On the basis of this judgment, cost-of-capital of 9% for the com-

Exhibit 16-8

ANALYSIS OF POSSIBLE DIVISIONAL LIQUIDATION.
EVALUATION OF PROFITABILITY OF CONTINUED OPERATION
CASH FLOW SCHEDULE

COL. / LINE	1	2	3	4	5 (2 + 3 + 4)	6	7 (5 x 6)	8	9 (5 x 8)
		EXPECTED CASH FLOWS				EXPECTED CASH FLOWS DISCOUNTED			
						Discounted at 8%		Discounted at 10%	
	Year	Investment	Profit after depreciation and taxes	Depreciation[b]	Net cash flow	Factor	Amount	Factor	Amount
1	0	$(365,000)[a]			$(365,000)	1.000	$(365,000)	1.000	$(365,000)
2	1	—	$ 7,000	$ 31,500	$ 38,500	.926	$ 35,651	.909	$ 34,997
3	2	—	7,000	31,000	38,000	.857	32,566	.826	31,388
4	3	—	7,000	31,000	38,000	.794	30,172	.751	28,538
5	4	—	6,500	31,000	37,500	.735	27,563	.683	25,613
6	5	—	6,500	30,500	37,000	.681	25,197	.621	22,977
7	6	—	6,000	30,500	36,500	.630	22,995	.564	20,586
8	7	$ 325,000[c]	5,500	30,500	361,000	.583	210,463	.513	185,193
9			$45,500	$216,000	$ 586,500		$ 384,607		$ 349,292

CALCULATION

$$\text{Time value profitability rate} = 8\% + 2\% \times \frac{(\$384{,}607 - \$365{,}000)}{(\$384{,}607 - \$349{,}292)} = 9.1\%$$

[a] Equivalent investment.
[b] Depreciation is based on stated book value of the investment.
[c] Residual value.

Exhibit 16-9

DIVISIONAL BALANCE SHEET

	Book Value	Liquidating Value
Current Assets:		
Cash	$100,000	$100,000
Accounts Receivable	150,000	120,000[a]
Inventory	175,000	120,000[a]
Prepaid Expenses	25,000	------------[a]
Total	$450,000	$340,000
Less Current Liabilities	200,000	200,000
Working Capital	$250,000	$140,000
Property, Plant and Equipment:		
Land	$200,000	
Plant and Equipment ($1,000,000 less $725,000 accumulated depreciation)	275,000	
Total	$475,000	$225,000[a]
Permanent Capital	$725,000	$365,000[a]

[a]Amounts are after adjustment for applicable tax credits.

pany as a whole should be increased to at least 10% for this division. Thus liquidation is appropriate.

Other Correct Techniques

We now discuss briefly two other correct capital budgeting techniques. They are the Excess Present Value Method and the Annual Excess Value Method.

Excess Present Value

Of the three correct capital budgeting techniques, Excess Present Value is probably the simplest to complete. Two steps are required once a proposal's initial investment and expected cash flows have been estimated.

First, the investment's projected cash flows are discounted, at the Profit Goal Rate, back to the present "zero point" (or discounted or compounded to some "zero point" other than the present). Secondly, the investment required at the "zero point" (usually the initial investment) is subtracted from the sum of discounted cash flows to determine the dollar excess (or deficiency) in present value. An excess present value signals a profitable investment; a deficiency in present value indicates an investment which fails to meet the Profit Goal.

For illustration purposes, we will use the same Project A that we used to illustrate the Time Value Profitability Rate. That project required an initial investment of $100,000 and was expected to generate four annual cash returns of $35,000 each, with no salvage value left at the end of its four-year economic life. Assume that management has established a Profit Goal of 10% for this type of investment.

Exhibit 16-10 is in the form that might be used for the necessary computations. Column 1 shows the net cash flows; Column 2 gives the factors for 10% from a discount table; and

Column 3 is filled in by multiplying Column 1 by Column 2 for each year. Column 3 is then totaled; the sum is $110,915. Comparing this sum to the $100,000 initial investment, shown at the "zero point" in time in the Exhibit, we see that Project A's proposal has a $10,915 Excess Present Value—the sum of Column 3 is $10,915 higher than the $100,000 initial investment. This means that the proposed investment is expected to return more than the 10% profit goal that management has set for this type of project. Therefore, all other things being equal, this proposal should be accepted. If the proposal's total present value had been below $100,000, then the deficit present value figure would have indicated that the project failed to meet the 10% Profit Goal, and the investment would not be desirable.

Excess Present Value Index

In actual use for capital budgeting decision-making, the raw $10,915 Excess Present Value is not as useful as the ratio of the total Present Value to the initial investment; that is, $110,915 divided by $100,000 which equals 1.11. This ratio of 1.11, usually called the "Excess Present Value Index," enables decision-makers to rank projects with different initial investment.

To explain, we might assume another project which has the same raw $10,915 Excess Present Value—but which requires an initial investment of $1 million or ten times as much. While the Excess Present Value is the same, the second project's Excess Present Value Index is only 1.01 ($1,010,915 divided by $1 million).

The Excess Present Value Index, therefore, correctly ranks the second project as having a lower profitability rate. So long as a proposal shows an Excess Present Value Index greater than 1.00 however, the proposal's return exceeds the Profit Goal and is economically desirable, all other things being equal. But an Excess Present Value Index of less than 1.00 would indicate a project which fails to meet the 10% Profit Goal.

Annual Excess Value

The third of the three correct capital budgeting techniques is the Annual Excess Value Method. To explain this technique, we will again use Project A. Its Excess Present Value amounted to $10,915; dividing by four gives $2,729 per year for the four-year life of the project. However, this $2,729 simple annual figure is not an adequate measure of the annual excess value. It fails to consider that the Excess Present Value could be invested at interest so that over the four years of the project life, it could return an aggregate amount of more than the $10,915 principal amount. In fact, if the $10,915 is invested at the project's 10% Profit Goal Rate, it will produce $3,438 per year for four years. This $3,438 Annual Excess Value is the annual amount that will return $10,915 over a four-year period plus a return of 10%.

In other words, the Excess Present Value of $10,915 represents the excess above the Profit Goal at the "zero point" in time; the Annual Excess Value of $3,438 represents the annual amount which would return the $10,915 over the four-year project life at the Profit Goal rate.

To put it in still another way, the present value of the Annual Excess Present Value at the Profit Goal Rate is equal to the Excess Present Value.

To calculate the Annual Excess Value, first calculate the Excess Present Value. Then multiply by a factor similar to interest and discount factors, which gives the annual amount that the Excess Present Value will produce so as to return the principal amount and income at the applicable rate. These factors are known as annuity factors or Capital Recovery Factors. A sample of annuity factors is shown in Exhibit 16-11. For example, at a 10% rate for four years, the factor is 0.315. This means that an annual receipt of $0.315 for four years would return to an investor his initially invested $1 amount plus an annual return of 10% on his unrecovered principal. Multiplying the $10,915 Excess

Exhibit 16-10

EXCESS PRESENT VALUE
TECHNIQUE ILLUSTRATION

PROJECT A

Column	1	2	3
Year	Net Cash Flow	10% Discounts Factors	Present Value (1 x 2)
0	$(100,000)	1.000	$(100,000)
1	$ 35,000	.909	$ 31,815
2	35,000	.826	28,910
3	35,000	.751	26,285
4	35,000	.683	23,905
Total	$ 140,000		$ 110,915
Excess Present Value			$ 10,915

Excess Present Value Index $= \frac{\$110,915}{\$100,000} = 1.11$

Present Value for Project A by the 0.315 factor gives $3,438, Project A's Annual Excess Value.

The Annual Excess Value method is also referred to as the Equivalent Uniform Annual Cost Technique. To explain the method more fully, we will explain it in the same way as do those who refer to it by this latter term.

In its simplest form, for a project with equal annual net cash flows, this technique merely subtracts one year's capital charge from one year's Net Cash Flow. If the remainder is positive, the investment meets the Profit Goal established; if the remainder is negative, however, the investment should not be made. The capital charge in the Annual Excess Value or Equivalent Uniform Annual Cost Technique is that uniform, annual amount which will both amortize the initial investment and also provide a return at the Profit Goal rate. This capital charge can be determined by referring to annuity factors described above.

To illustrate, we will again use Project A. Each year's Net Cash Flow was $35,000. The economic life was four years. From annuity tables we have just noted that the capital charge for $1 is 0.315 for a 10% return over four years. Since Project A requires an investment of $100,000, its capital charge is therefore $31,500 each year. The equivalent Uniform Annual Cost Technique would be applied to the project as shown in Exhibit

Exhibit 16-11

SAMPLE TABLE OF ANNUITY FACTORS

Annual amounts, including principal and interest, which will be provided by $1 invested today at compound interest.

i / n	4%	6%	8%	10%	15%
1	1.040	1.060	1.080	1.100	1.150
2	.530	.545	.560	.576	.615
3	.360	.374	.388	.402	.438
4	.275	.288	.302	.315	.350

Formula: $f = \frac{i}{1-(1+i)^{n}}$

f = Annuity factor
n = Number of compounding periods
i = Interest rate per period

16-12. The fact that there is an equivalent uniform annual remainder of $3,500 left, after the annual capital charge, signifies that this project more than meets the Profit Goal of 10%.

Exhibit 16-12

ANNUAL EXCESS VALUE
FOR PROJECT A

Annual Net Cash Flow	$35,000
Equal annual payments required to amortize $100,000 initial investment over 4-year life and return 10% on unrecovered balance	31,500
Equivalent uniform annual revenue (or Annual Excess Value)	$ 3,500[a]

[a]This $3,500 would be equal to the $3,438 as previously calculated from the Excess Present Value if the factors used in making the calculations were carried out more decimal places. The figure by both methods would then be $3,453.

All four of the annual net cash flows in our example conveniently are equal, which makes the application of the technique with this method of calculation quite simple. In actual evaluations, this uniformity is somewhat rare. The calculation can be done this way even with unequal cash flows, but the preferable method of calculation is, as explained above, to determine the Excess Present Value at the "zero point" in time and then convert it to the Annual Excess Value by applying annuity factors.

Comparison of the Three Correct Techniques

There are numerous variations[1] and modifications of the three techniques described above, but these three are basic.

The Time Value Profitability Rate, as the title suggests, solves for the rate that a project is expected to return.

The Excess Present Value technique solves for the excess present dollar equivalent, or a ratio of the total present value dollar to the initial investment, that the project will return above the Profit Goal.

The annual Excess Value Technique solves for the excess dollars per year that the project will return above the Profit Goal.

Correctly applied, all three techniques will give correct answers. That is, they will properly combine all three of the factors which basically determine the financial worth of the project—1) the initial investment, 2) the net cash flows and 3) the timing of the net cash flows. Why, then, do we recommend the Time Value Profitability Rate?

The Time Value Profitability Rate is preferable for most companies because it has two practical advantages in assisting top management in formulating capital budgeting decisions. First, it is the only one of the three techniques which supplies an answer in terms of a rate. Usually this is easier for management to comprehend. For example, if management has set a Profit Goal of 12% it is easy to grasp the significance of a 15% Time Value Profitability Rate for a proposed project.

The second advantage is that the technique does not require the pre-establishment of the appropriate Profit Goal. A proposal's Time Value Profitability Rate can be calculated by staff analysts before the proposed project is presented to the capital budgeting decision-makers. The decision-makers can then compare the Time Value Profitability Rate against that Profit Goal they believe necessary to allow for risk. In each of the other two correct techniques, a pre-established Profit Goal must be used in arriving at the final answer. If the decision-makers decide the pre-established goal was inappropriate for the project's risk, it is necessary to redo the calculations.

The principal advantage of Excess Present Value is that it is simple to compute. In the Time Value Profitability Rate, the trial-and-

[1]For example, a variation on the Annual Excess Value technique, developed by the Machinery and Allied Products Institute and known as "the MAPI System," offers a very structured method of deriving an "urgency rating" for equipment replacement and (as revised in 1958) for more unsophisticated capital budgeting proposals. Although very simple to apply, the system is difficult to understand. This often leads to mechanical applications of the system to project analyses, which may be undesirable in any but the simplest proposals.

error work necessary in the calculation is more arduous than the original calculations for Excess Present Value. If the forecast figures change, it is much less time consuming to recalculate the result for the Excess Present Value. New figures can be added or subtracted after discounting at the Profit Goal Rate used in the original calculation. This makes it possible readily to test the sensitivity of project profitability to changes in expected revenues, costs and required investment. Furthermore, if a company wishes its division managers to perform the calculations, it can furnish just one table with discount factors for the Profit Goal the company has established for that division. These can be applied directly to the cash flows. These advantages, however, may be outweighed by the two disadvantages mentioned above—the necessity of pre-establishing Profit Goals for each project, and the difficulty of grasping the significance of, say, a $10,915 Excess Present Value or even of a 1.11 Excess Present Value Index.

The same advantages and disadvantages generally apply to the Annual Excess Value technique, although it requires one more step in calculation than the Excess Present Value method. The technique can be used wherever the other methods can be used, and some people prefer this one for all purposes.

You should understand that there are two additional objections to the Time Value Profitability Rate. Neither of these objections apply to excess present value or annual excess present value. The objections are:

1. The "implied reinvestment rate assumption" when the method is used to make a choice between mutually exclusive projects.

   Briefly, the implied reinvestment rate assumption does not suggest that the Time Value Profitability Rate is incorrect. But if a company had to make a choice between two projects, the choice would be affected by the rate at which the company could reinvest the cash flows that the projects generate. If the cash flows are unequal, then the result of reinvesting the cash flows would be different. In a direct comparison of two projects based on the Time Value Profitability Rate, there is an assumption that the cash flows resulting from return of the investment would be reinvested at the Time Value Profitability Rate for each project.

2. The multiple rate problem.

   The multiple rate problem arises for an investment which has cash flows of both positive and negative amounts. In such a situation, there can be more than one Time Value Profitability Rate.

It is well worthwhile to understand these two problems of the Time Value Profitability Rate. They are covered in Appendix 16-A. However, if you are too bogged down with figures at this point, go ahead and use the Time Value Profitability Rate knowing that it has these drawbacks, or switch to the excess present value which avoids them. With a good computer program, the calculations are duck soup so long as you get the right cash flows.

ACQUISITION PRICING—HOW TO FOOL YOURSELF, AND PUT A MONKEY ON YOUR BACK

When some managements make acquisitions, they act like they are just as clever as hell—like they are making a great deal, getting a bargain and putting something over on someone.

Ten years later their company isn't doing so well and they are not just sure what happened, or what sinister force beyond their control stepped out of the woodwork and bit them.

The answer, of course, lies in the fact that it was the monkey they put on their back ten years ago. The method they used to determine whether they should have made the acquisition was wrong.

The acquisition craze which started in the 1960's brought to the surface some of the worst in American management. Acquisition-minded managements could be divided into four groups:

1. The financial manipulators
2. The sheep

3. The scared ones
4. The doers

The financial manipulators were the ones who played the game of increasing current earnings per share. They boosted their price-earnings ratio by every means possible in order to buy lower price-earnings ratio companies and further extend their false high price-earnings ratio. They may have used all kinds of complicated securities with excessive leverage. The only ones who benefited in this game in the long run were the management promoters. Our economy did not benefit in any way, and the poor investors ultimately paid the price.

The sheep were the poor innocents who were in the game because it was the thing to do. They feared that they would be looked down on if they were not in the action.

The scared ones were those unfortunates who were vulnerable to being taken over—perhaps through their own fault; perhaps not. They got almost panicky to grab someone else in order to add interest to their company and increase their price-earnings ratio in order to stave off a tender offer.

The doers were the only ones who were constructive. Their approach was to improve the companies they took over in order to provide better products and thus earn more money. This helped our economy and everyone concerned, provided the anti-trust laws were not violated and the acquisitions made sense from a long-range managerial point of view.

Conflicting Goals

Some companies set conflicting and meaningless goals for acquisitions. One company which had a dividend payout policy of 50% had the following goals:

Earn 10% on sales after taxes
Earn 15% on common book value
Growth rate in earnings per share of 15% per year

We have already explained why percent on sales is meaningless unless the capital intensity of the business is also defined. The 15% return on common book value and a 15% growth rate in earnings per share with a 50% payout in dividends is inconsistent. With a 15% return on common book value as well as a fixed dividend payout, the growth rate in earnings per share would be 7 1/2% (15% earned on common book value multiplied by 50% of earnings retained). If the management expected to achieve a permanent 15% growth in earnings per share with a 50% payout, the return on common equity goal would have to be 30%.

As far as the return on common book value is concerned, the leverage or proportion of debt in the capital structure makes a major difference, and the amount of debt depends on the risk of the business. A return on common book value of 15% for a highly leveraged company is nothing to brag about. Thus, in establishing a return on common, it is also necessary to define the percentage of senior securities in long term capital; it may be preferable to use a return on long term capital.

The company which set the above goals should probably have been acquired rather than doing the acquiring. Anyone has to be daydreaming to believe that successful companies are readily available for purchase at a reasonable price.

Increasing Earnings per Share as an Acquisition Test

The effect of an acquisition on earnings per share of the acquiring company is a dangerous approach to acquisition decision making. It would only work in an ideal situation as follows:

1. If the acquired company had a well-balanced capital structure with good quality securities, it earned the acquiring company's goal rate, and the growth rate in earnings per share was due entirely to plowback with a constant payout ratio.
2. The acquiring company was in exactly the same situation and the acquisition was financed so that after the acquisition

the acquiring company had a balanced capital structure.

3. The risk of the acquired company was the same as that of the acquiring company, or if there is a difference in risk there is a corresponding difference in capital structures.

In such a situation, if the acquisition resulted in equalling or improving future earnings per share, then the acquisition could be justified. However, consider the many factors that could affect the future combined growth rate in earnings per share from an acquisition:

1. The method of financing.
2. Growth in earnings per share due to an increase in rate of return, or other transitory way in which earnings per share increase.

The common cost rate depends on investor expectations and not on a company's forecast. For example, suppose the price of a company's stock was at a high price because investors expected the growth rate in earnings per share to be 8%. However, the company's forecast rate was 6%. If it acquired a company which maintained the 6% growth rate, the stock would fall as soon as investors found out that they were wrong in expecting an 8% growth rate.

If a company used as its guide to increase earnings per share that which investors expected, it would just be earning the common cost rate.

The Problems of Paying a Premium

Let's explain with a simple example how a company buying another company at a substantial premium may get itself behind the eight ball. The figures are shown in Exhibit 16-13.

Company A decides to make a tender offer for the stock of Company B at 15% over the market price, or at a price of $83. Since the price of the stock of Company A is $133, it would offer 0.62 shares of its stock for each share of the stock to be acquired. (Price of Company B stock with 15% premium–$83, divided by price of Company A stock–$133, equals 0.62.) For each share originally outstanding, Company A will have outstanding 1.62 shares and combined earnings of $14.50, or earnings per share of $8.95. This would produce an 11% increase in earnings per share.

But what really happened?

Company B was earning $6.50 on a beginning book value of $50 or 13%. Company A made a capital investment of $83 which consisted of an investment in tangible book value of $50, and $33 in intangibles. The return on the total investment was only 7.8%, a very poor return, below any reasonable cost-of-capital rate.

If the acquisition is going to earn the cost-of-capital, it would have to earn more than 11% on the $83 capital investment or $9.13. This represents a return of 18% on the tangible assets of Company B of $50. That means that Company A has got to do magic with Company B just to make it a breakeven on the price it paid–probably no way! The acquiring company only has the fixed assets of the acquiring company to use to produce a profit. If it expects to earn a high return on the investment it made, it will be forced to earn a super high return on the assets it has to work with. If Company A wanted to earn the same rate on the price it paid for B, as it was earning on its book value of 16%, it would have to earn 27% on the book value of Company B–a rather hopeless task.

It is a totally ridiculous assumption that you can acquire a company in the market at a premium over the market and make a great deal, even though it increases your company's current earnings per share. In the first place, if investors in the stock estimate the future potential of the company correctly, and are satisfied with a return equivalent to the common cost, then it has to follow that if the acquisition is made at market, the investment would provide a return on the price the acquiring company paid equivalent to the common cost. And if the acquiring company paid a premium over market, the return it will get on its investment is going to be less than the common cost, which is a bad investment.

Exhibit 16-13

DATA USED TO SHOW EFFECT OF A PREMIUM ON AN ACQUISITION

	Acquiring Company A	Acquired Company B
Beginning Common Book Value	$50.00	$50.00
Return on Beginning Common Book Value	16%	13%
Earnings per Share	$ 8.00	$ 6.50
Price-Earnings Ratio	16.7	11.1
Dividend Pay-Out Ratio	50%	50%
Dividend	$ 4.00	$ 3.25
Market Price	$133	$72
Dividend Yield	3.00%	4.50%
Growth Rate in Earnings per Share from Plowback	8.00%	6.50%

So for a company to win at this game, it has to be for one or more of the following reasons:

1. The market price underestimates the potential for the company and you get a bargain.
2. The acquiring company can run the acquired company more efficiently and increase the return on the investment.
3. The acquisition gives the acquiring company sufficient opportunity to invest new capital at a rate above the cost-of-capital so as to overcome the premium it paid.

We will use another example to show the effect of the opportunity to invest more capital at a high rate. Suppose you can acquire Company A with $100 million book common equity earning 30% on the book value after taxes. Your goal is to earn 15% on the price you pay.

First, let us assume that Company A provides absolutely no opportunity to invest any new capital. Company A remains exactly the same size by depreciation being reinvested, but with no opportunity to even reinvest retained earnings. Then you would pay $200 million for Company A or a 100% premium.

Company A would earn $30 million or a 30% return on the book value of $100 million. The return you would earn on your investment of $200 million would be 15%.

These calculations assume that Company A would go on forever. If after a period of years, Company A came to an end, then the value at the end of the period would affect how much you would pay. If it was worth less than $200 million at the end, you could not pay $200 million and still earn your goal of 15%.

Now let's assume that the acquisition of Company A gave you the opportunity to immediately double the size and make a new division exactly like Company A in all respects so that you could spend $100 million and earn 30% or $30 million on the new investment. That investment would be worth $200 million to you, because it would provide a 15% return.

If we assume that Company A and the new investment continued on indefinitely, but did not provide any further opportunity to reinvest more capital, you would be willing to pay $300 million for Company A as follows:

$200,000,000	For Company A.
$100,000,000	Premium for the opportunity to reinvest another $100,000,000 at a 30% return.
$300,000,000	Total acquisition price.
100,000,000	New capital investment.
$400,000,000	Total investment.

In other words, you would be willing to pay a premium of $200 million to acquire

Company A or a total of $300 million. On the basis of this price, you would only show a 10% return from the $30 million of earnings generated by Company A before you made the new investment. This would be below your goal of 15%. The new investment would increase earnings to $60 million, which would represent 15% on the $400 million investment.

Many companies get caught in buying companies in glamorous fields which appear to have good prospects, but the opportunity to invest new money at high rates is not sufficient to ever overcome the premium that they paid.

If you pay a premium over book value of common equity, the premium may be termed goodwill, but it might be viewed as some form of expenditure such as for research and development, a patent, an exclusive franchise, a start-up cost for a new business, etc. If a company has a valuable pattern or franchise on which its earnings are dependent, and which does not show up on the balance sheet at its true worth, the market price of the stock may show no significant relationship to book value. However, if you are certain that the book value represents a sound present value of the assets, you might ask yourself these five questions regarding the premium:

1. Is the premium a reasonable amount to pay for research and development, a patent, an exclusive franchise, a start-up cost for a new business or whatever definition is most appropriate to apply?
2. As an alternative, could you start the business from scratch, spend the money for assets and something less than the premium over book value in start-up costs, advertising, etc. and have as good earning prospects as acquiring the company at the asking price?
3. Is it reasonable to expect that you could earn a satisfactory percentage return on the purchase price of the acquisition, including the premium over book, under competitive conditions in which your competitors would only be seeking to earn a satisfactory return on their investment in assets with no goodwill?
4. What would be the return on the book assets necessary for you to earn adequately on the total purchase price? Is the return so high as to create vulnerability from competition?
5. What opportunity does the acquisition give you to invest more capital at a high rate?

Two Separate Decisions—What It Is Worth and How It Should Be Financed

There is no way you can come out correctly in acquisition decision making unless as a first step you separate completely two decisions—the way the acquisition is financed and the price you are willing to pay. The decision made on the basis of how your company will look with the acquisition combined can be very misleading. That approach completely obscures the facts. Of course, before you make the acquisition you should combine the company with yours, to see how it would look, but that comes last, not first.

The reason the two must be separated is because the method of financing affects the impact on your company's earnings per share. For example, if you buy a company with cash you are holding in a demand deposit, earnings per share will be increased even if the company you buy is a complete dog with poor earnings. And if you buy a company with stock, you can buy every company in the country with a lower price-earnings ratio and increase current earnings per share. This proposition was illustrated in Chapter 14 in which it was shown how a high price-earnings ratio company purchasing a low price-earnings ratio company increases current earnings per share.

Two Prices—What Has to Be Paid and What It Is Worth

There are two prices in any acquisition: What has to be paid and what the acquisition is worth. Generally, only the first is considered even by the acquiring company. What has to be paid for an acquisition depends on the demand and supply for the type of company being acquired. If there is a seller's market, the price that has to be paid may well be out of line. The price will probably be stated in terms of a price-earnings ratio for the common as compared to price-earnings ratios of similar stocks, with allowances for differences in the companies being compared.

There has been much controversy over the way an acquisition is accounted for—pooling or purchase. The method of accounting does not determine the price to be paid. It will affect the timing of the bookkeeping earnings per share, but not the true return on invested capital. In fact, if an acquisition makes sense from the point of view of return on investment, it may be even better with purchase accounting than with pooling treatment, because purchase accounting may provide an added tax benefit from the write-up and subsequent redepreciation of some of the assets. However, because some managements erroneously use earnings per share as a guide for decision making, pooling may appear indispensable in acquisition decision making.

Acquisition Pricing—What It Is Worth

What is it that is going to determine whether you should acquire a company at a certain price?

You will be investing capital to obtain a return just as you do when you make a capital expenditure. We have illustrated how to determine the profitability of a capital expenditure. To obtain an answer we needed to know:

- The earnings, cash flows and timing.
- The terminal value and timing.

An acquisition similarly represents a capital investment. There are, of course, differences between a capital investment and an acquisition. Most important, an acquisition represents a going concern so that there are earnings immediately available. However, we should want to know the return on the investment in order to make a decision. Therefore, it is necessary to make a forecast just as we did for a capital expenditure. There is no way that this can be avoided.

However, we run into a problem. A capital expenditure does have a finite life; whereas, if we buy a company, we might hope that it would go on forever. On this basis, we would have to make an analysis in perpetuity. This, however, is impractical because a forecast after a certain time becomes meaningless. So we have to struggle with the terminal value problem at the end of a certain number of years. That raises a difficult problem because how do we decide what it will be worth at the end of a specified period? At this point, we will not try to answer this question. However, in order to value an acquisition, it is essential to start out by knowing what we should do in order to come up with an answer. Let's repeat the necessary elements:

1. The earnings, cash flows and their timing.
2. A terminal value at some time in the future in order to eliminate the problem of making an analysis in perpetuity.

Various methods for analyzing acquisitions have been proposed. Some of them seem to avoid some of the problems we have suggested, particularly the problem of terminal value. They cannot, however, avoid any of these problems because they are the fundamentals of capital investment. They merely mask the problems and make you think that the problems have been eliminated, which is false.

Then how can meaningful figures be developed to help management make a decision as to whether or not to pay a certain price for an acquisition?

You can price an acquisition the same way we described for a new plant analysis—that is, using discounted cash flow. If you use this method of pricing, you might use various terminal values such as a book value, liquidating value, an estimated appraisal of assets or a capitalized earnings value.

We will suggest another approach, which may be easier for management to understand. It does not avoid terminal value, since there is no way to avoid terminal value. It assumes that the company will be worth the book value plus premium throughout the analysis.

Our approach is based on developing a forecast in such a way that you will be able to view return on common equity with a sound capital structure. A similar approach can just as well be developed on the basis of return on total capital. However, many managements might not have as good a feel for such a rate as they would for the return on common equity, since the latter is closer to earnings per share.

We will suggest the steps to take, and use some simple figures to illustrate each step.

1. *Establish the purchase price you expect to pay.* If you buy it for cash, that amount will be the purchase price. If the acquisition is made with stock, the purchase price is the number of shares you have to give for the company times the market price.

   3,000,000 shares times market price of $50 per share = purchase price $150,000,000.

   From here all figures will be shown with six zeros omitted.

2. *Deduct excess assets from the purchase price.* Examine the assets that can be liquidated which are not needed to carry on operations and determine their present after-tax value. Deduct this amount from the purchase price to get the net purchase price.

Assets		Liabilities		
Current assets	$100	Current liabilities		$ 50
		Long term capital		
Extra cash	5	Debt	$ 30	
Plant, net	45	Common	70	
	$150			$100
				$150

The balance sheet shows extra cash of $5. Deduct this from the purchase price:

Purchase price	$150
Less: Extra cash	5
	$145

The balance sheet, excluding extra cash, would then be as shown below. That is what we are buying for $145.

Current assets	$100	Current liabilities		$ 50
Plant, net	45	Long term capital		
		Debt	$ 30	
		Common	65	
		Total		$ 95
Total	$145			$145

3. *Review the balance sheet items.* Go over the balance sheet with a fine-tooth comb and determine a sound valuation of all the assets. This will require checking receivables, inventories, etc. Make a pro-forma balance sheet based on a sound appraisal of all assets.

   In our example we will assume no adjustments are necessary.

4. *Pro-forma the long term capital.* Pro-forma the long term capital so as to include all appropriate items. If short term bank loans in current liabilities are rolled over, they should be moved down into long term debt. Finance leases should be capitalized and added to long term debt.

   Lease payments amounting to $1.25 annually, capitalized at eight times, would mean $10 added to long term debt and $10 added to assets. So our balance sheet further adjusted would be as follows:

Current assets	$100	Current liabilities		$ 50
Plant, net	45	Long term capital		
Leased plant	10	Debt	$ 30	
		Leases	10	
		Common	65	
		Total		$105
Total	$155			$155

5. *Substitute the net purchase price for book common equity.* Substitute the net purchase price you paid for the company in place of the common equity, and include the intangibles as goodwill.

Current assets	$100	Current liabilities		$ 50
Plant, net	45	Long term capital		
Leased plant	10	Debt	$ 30	
Goodwill	80	Leases	10	
		Common	145	
		Total		$185
Total	$235			$235

6. *Establish sound capital structure for company.* Establish what should be the average debt ratio for long term capital so that the debt would have a good-quality bond rating of A or AA depending on the nature and size of the company. This percentage should be established with the goodwill excluded.

   Adjust the long term capital in the balance sheet to conform to that standard.

   We will assume that without goodwill, total long term capital should be as shown below for the company's debt to be rated A.

Debt	25%
Common	75
	100%

   The long term capital in the balance sheet before adjustment is as follows:

	Without Goodwill		With Goodwill
Debt	$ 30	38%	$ 30
Leases Capitalized	10		10
Common	65	62	145
	$105	100%	$185

   Adjust the capital structure to conform to our standard for an A grade bond. This would mean that the long term capital should be as follows:

	Without Goodwill		With Goodwill
Debt	$ 26	25%	$ 26
Common	79	75%	159
	$105		$185

   Reduce the debt and increase the common in the balance sheet so as to have a sound long term capital. The balance sheet would then be as follows:

Current assets	$100	Current liabilities		$ 50
Plant, net	45	Long term capital		
Leased plant	10	Debt	$ 26	
Goodwill	80	Common	159	
		Total		$185
Total	$235			$235

7. *Assess the quality of the earnings.* Go over each item in the income statement to see if the earnings are over- or understated. Carry the historical earnings figures down to income after depreciation, before taxes and interest.

8. *Adjust the earnings to conform to adjustments in the balance sheet.* Adjust the interest to conform to the amount of debt in the balance sheet and also adjust income taxes. In our example, the extra cash was eliminated to get the net purchase price. If it was invested in short term investments, this part of non-operating income would have to be eliminated.

   Now we have a sound balance sheet with the price we paid for it in the common stock position, and a sound income statement. Goodwill is included, but the amount of debt is stated at a figure which will give an A rating.

9. *Make a forecast.* Make a forecast income statement and balance sheet, adding to debt and common equity as capital is needed in order to keep the debt at 25% of long term capital excluding goodwill. The goodwill will be included in the balance sheet but the amount of debt will be determined without the goodwill.

   The forecast should take into account how the company will be operated as a part of the acquiring company including additional earnings that may result from the combined operation.

   Do not write off goodwill in the income statement for these calculations regardless of how it is purchased.

   Figures for our simple example would be as shown in Exhibit 16-14.

These calculations are not simple. Tax questions may be knotty and various special factors may arise. The effect of changes in critical expense items and critical capital expenditures must be tested. It may be advisable to make two or three forecasts with different assumptions.

How to Use the Forecast

Now we will explain how to use the forecast for acquisition pricing. At the start of the forecast, the net purchase price is plugged into the balance sheet. The question we will

Exhibit 16-14

EXAMPLE OF FINANCIALS FOR FORECASTING

Income Statement	Latest Figures Available	Forecast Years 1	2	3	4	5	6
Sales	$200						
Operating expenses	178						
Income before interest and taxes	22						
Interest @ 8%	2						
Taxes	10						
Income for common	10						
Balance Sheet							
Current assets	$100						
Net plant	45						
Leased plant	10						
Goodwill	80						
Total assets	235						
Current liabilities	50						
Long term capital							
Debt	26						
Common	159						
Total liabilities	235						
Return on common,							
excluding goodwill	12.7%						
including goodwill	6.3%						

seek to answer is whether the forecast will provide an adequate return to justify the net purchase price.

Merely for illustration, we will assume that for the company with a sound capitalization, a return on the common stock of 11% will just cover the common cost. Our approach will be to determine from the forecast how many years it will take to earn the 11%.

The return on common is calculated on common equity including and excluding goodwill.

The return on common equity including goodwill is the critical return, because it shows the relationship of earnings to the net purchase price plus subsequent additions.

The return on common equity excluding goodwill is also important, because it shows the return that will have to be earned on tangible assets in order to achieve the return with goodwill included.

If at the start of the forecast, the return on the common book value with goodwill included is 11% or more, we know that the net purchase price will, at least, earn the common cost rate.

However, in all likelihood, the return at the start will be below 11%. Any deficit below 11% in any year has to be made up subsequently by earnings above 11%. In order to take into account the time value of money, any earnings deficit below 11% is compounded each year at the 11% figure and carried forward. This is illustrated in Exhibit 16-15.

In the Exhibit, the breakeven point is year 5. But note the returns which would be required on the tangible book value excluding

Exhibit 16-15

BREAKEVEN POINT FOR ACQUISITION–YEAR IN WHICH INCOME SUFFICIENT TO COVER COMMON COST

Year	1	2	3	4	5
Forecast income available for common	$ 12.00	$ 17.00	$ 20.00	$ 24.00	$ 30.00
Common book value,					
Excluding intangibles	$ 79	$ 87	$ 97	$107	$120
Including intangibles	$159	$167	$177	$187	$200
Return on common book value,					
Excluding intangibles	15.2%	19.5%	20.6%	22.4%	25.0%
Including intangibles	7.5%	10.1%	11.3%	12.8%	15.0%
Income requirements to earn 11% on common book value, including goodwill	$ 17.49	$ 18.37	$ 19.47	$ 20.57	$ 22.00
Annual income deficit or excess	$ –5.49	$ –1.37	$ +0.53	$ +3.43	$ +8.00
Income deficit compounded at 11% and cumulated		$ –7.46	$ –7.75	$ –5.17	$ +2.26

Calculation of deficit compounded at 11% and cumulated:

Year 2 –\$5.49 –\$5.49 X 11% –\$1.37 = \$–7.46
Year 3 –\$7.46 –\$7.49 X 11% +\$0.53 = \$–7.75
Year 4 –\$7.75 –\$7.75 X 11% +\$3.43 = \$–5.17
Year 5 –\$5.17 –\$5.17 X 11% +\$8.00 = \$+2.26

goodwill. It shows that returns will have to be over 20%. This should raise a question in management's mind whether such returns are achievable and would call for a more realistic forecast.

Because such forecasts may have to be for a number of years ahead, it may appear that the forecasts are of little value. Before you throw up your hands in disbelief at the value of such forecasts, you should consider their purpose. Their primary purpose is to provide a picture of figures that might unfold so that the management can ask themselves whether the figures are within the realm of possibility in view of such factors as: the premium over sound asset value which has to be paid, the new capital which has to be added, the sales which have to be generated, the size of the major expense items, the profit margin on sales, etc.

In using this method of analysis, the management has to answer the question, can it afford to wait until the breakeven point. That depends on what the potential will be after the breakeven point. That should be apparent in the growth in earnings that took place during the forecast years and whether they can be expected to grow as fast in the future. If management is interested, the forecast can be carried out further to see what happens to the return figures.

These calculations have used the cost-of-capital rate. This approach can also be used to determine the time required to earn the profit goal rate on the common including goodwill.

The advantage of this technique of acquisition pricing lies in the fact that management can readily see how the picture would unfold in the future in terms of significant return figures.

However, it does not avoid the terminal value problem. It assumes the terminal value to be the same as the balance sheet figures at the end of the period. You should now raise the question whether that terminal value makes sense. Ask yourself the following questions:

1. Are the earnings reasonably attainable at the end of the period?
2. Is the terminal value reasonable in relation to the earnings?

If your estimate of the terminal value is less than common book value plus intangibles, this means that you would not achieve your goal. If you estimate the terminal value to be more than book value plus intangibles, discount it back to year 1 at the goal rate. This is the amount the acquisition is worth, more than the goal rate. If the terminal value is estimated to be less than the book value, discount it back to year 1 at the goal rate and subtract from the purchase price.

Finally, you have all the figures to do a discounted cash flow analysis. Try it with different terminal values equal to:

1. Book value less intangibles.
2. Other reasonable estimates of terminal value.
3. Scrap value to find out how you would come out if it turned out to be a turkey.

Another View of Acquisition Pricing

We can illustrate the premium that might be paid by looking at an acquisition as an investment in a stock the way in which an individual might evaluate a stock. This approach assumes a knowledge of the method of pricing a stock as explained in Chapter 18. You should turn to that chapter to see if you are familiar with the technique. Our illustration is shown in Exhibit 16-16.

The figures show how it takes a high return to justify a high premium. And how even with a high return, it takes many years for the return on the investment to equal the goal rate with high premium.

In this exhibit two factors are controlling:

1. New capital investment is just equal to the retained earnings.
2. The same rates of return on old and new investment continue indefinitely.

These are very limiting factors.

The Combined Effect of an Acquisition

After you have decided to buy a company because you think the price is right, you should combine the balance sheet and income statement with your company so that you can see the effect on earnings per share and on the capital structure of your company. If your company has a high debt ratio and the one you are acquiring has an even higher debt ratio, it may not be a good idea for you to take the financial risk.

If you acquire a company with common stock, the price of your common will have an effect on the resulting earnings per share. The higher the price of your stock, the better off you will be. However, this does not mean that you should change your ideas as to price. That, as we have said, is a separate question.

If your stock is high priced, it would only remain high priced as time goes on if you made an acquisition so that the return on the price you paid will maintain the price of your stock.

The Chinese Money Question

If a company's stock is selling at a relatively high price, does that necessarily mean that it can pay a higher price for another company through an exchange of stock?

In this discussion, we are assuming that while the stock is over-priced, the price represents a fair figure at which new stock could be offered. It is possible for the market price to be artificial in that the quoted price would not permit the raising of any reasonable amount of capital at that price. This is more of a case of a price representing froth, and we are not talking about that situation.

The question of over-valued stock is often referred to as the Chinese Money Question, the idea being that over-valued stock is like Chinese money and has a false value. In Exhibit 16-17, Part I (page 568) companies A and B both have a cost-of-capital based on the risk of the business of 10%. Neither one actually has any growth prospects, and present earnings represent their future earning power.

Exhibit 16-16

ILLUSTRATION OF P/E TO PAY FOR AN ACQUISITION DEPENDING ON ITS RETURN ON BOOK INVESTMENT

PART I

EARNINGS DATA FOR VARIOUS COMPANIES

Company	Book Value	Return on Book Value	Earnings per Share Year 1	Dividend Payout Ratio	Growth Rate in Earnings per Share from Plowback
A	$100	20%	$20	35%	13.00%
B	"	18	18	"	11.70
C	"	16	16	"	10.40
D	"	15	15	"	9.75

PART II

PREMIUM THAT COULD BE PAID

		← 15% Return	→			
Company	Return Goal of Acquiring Company	Return from Market Appreciation Assuming Constant Price-Earnings Ratio	Dividend Yield to Make Total Return 15%	Price-Earnings Ratio*	Price of Acquisition	Premium
A	15%	13.00%	2.00%	17.5	$350	$250
B	"	11.70	3.30	10.6	191	91
C	"	10.40	4.60	7.8	125	25
D	"	9.75	5.25	6.7	100	0

PART III

RETURN ON PRICE PAID IN FIRST YEAR, AND NUMBER OF YEARS IT WOULD TAKE FOR EARNINGS TO PROVIDE A 10% AND 15% RETURN ON BOOK VALUE PLUS PREMIUM

Company	Return of Earnings on Price Paid Year 1	Year in Which Return of Earnings on Book Value Plus Premium Equals 10%	Year in Which Return of Earnings on Book Value Plus Premium Equals 15%
A	5.7%	8	17
B	9.4	1	14
C	12.8	--	13
D	15.0	--	1

*Price-earnings ratio equals dividend payout percentage divided by dividend yield.

Investors, however, expect growth, and they have bid up the stocks excessively so that they are both equally over-valued.

Company A acquires Company B on a 1-for-1 basis. Then the results would be as shown in Exhibit 16-17, Part II.

Ultimately investors will come to realize that they made a mistake in expecting growth, and the market price will collapse to \$40 per share on the basis of a price-earnings ratio of ten times. This is in line with the 10% cost-of-capital based on the risk.

If Company A had not acquired Company B, the stock of Company A would likewise ultimately have collapsed to \$40 per share when investors realized their mistake. Thus, as a result of the merger, Company A issued more shares but it gained nothing. We will demonstrate that there was an alternative available which would have been preferable.

The point we make is that any time a company has capital, or raises capital, no matter what the security medium or its price, it should never expand or make an acquisition below the cost-of-capital commensurate with the risk. In this case, the company issued one share of stock which could have been sold in the market for \$100. It is this amount of capital which Company A actually invested in Company B. It should not have done so unless the return on the \$100 was equivalent to the risk of the business. Actually, the return was only 4% since the earning power of Company B was only \$4 per share; it should have been \$10 or 10%.

If Company A had sold the share of stock in the market and retained the cash until it found a similar investment which would provide a 10% return commensurate with the risk, it would have obtained additional earnings of \$10. This \$10 combined with Company A's \$4 would produce total earnings of \$14 or \$7 per share.

After investors' false hopes had vanished, the stock would sell at ten times earnings or \$70 per share. Thus, the stockholder in Company A would have his stock fall from \$100 per share to \$70 rather than to \$40 as happened when Company B was acquired. The only depreciation in value that the stockholder would suffer would be due to his own mistake of over-valuing the stock of Company A. There would be no additional loss due to the fact that Company A improperly invested the proceeds from the issuance of the new share of stock below the rate commensurate with the estimated risk.

If Company A cannot find any place to invest the proceeds from the sale of a share of stock at \$100, it always has the alternative of putting the money in high-grade short term bonds. We will assume that it invests in tax-free bonds which provide a return of 4% or \$4. This return would be in line with the risk of those securities—or in line with the lack of risk. Exhibit 16-17, Part III shows what would have happened if Company A had followed that policy.

Now Company A's earnings are still \$4 per share, but note that the overall risk factor has changed from 10% to a combination of 10% and 4%. This would represent a weighted average risk of 5.71%[2] and a price-earnings ratio of 17 1/2 times. Thus, ultimately, the price of the stock would be \$4 x 17 1/2 or \$70.

To recapitulate, in the above example, we started with two companies which had stocks equally over-valued. Then, after the acquisition, when the market woke up to the true picture of earnings in the future and when the air went out of the balloons, investors suffered a loss because of their foolishness in over-valuing Company A's stock. There was a similar loss due to the acquisition of Company B, because Company A acquired Company B at such an inflated value. We pointed out that if it had invested the money in short term bonds until it found a chance to make an investment above the cost-of-capital, it

---

[2](\$40 x 10% + \$100 x 4%) ÷ \$140 = 5.71%.

Exhibit 16-17

CHINESE MONEY ILLUSTRATION

PART I

ASSUMPTIONS

Column	I	II	III	IV	V
	Shares	Book Value	Present Earnings per Share	Present Price Earnings Ratio	Present Market Price
Co. A	1	$40	$4	25	$100
Co. B	1	$40	$4	25	$100

PART II

IMMEDIATE EFFECT OF COMPANY A AND B COMBINED

Column	I	II	III	IV	V
	Shares	Total Present Earnings	Present Earnings per Share	Present Price-Earnings Ratio	Present Market Price
Co. A + B	2	$8	$4	25.	$100

PART III

COMPANY A INVESTS $100 OF NEW CAPITAL FROM SALE OF 1 SHARE IN HIGH GRADE BONDS

Column	I	II	III	IV
			Present Earnings	
	Book Value	Shares	Total	Per Share
Co. A–Old Share	$ 40	1	$4	$4.00
Co. A–New Share	$100	1	$4	$4.00
Total		2	$8	$4.00

would have prevented that part of the loss which resulted from the acquisition. A company always has this alternative.

If the acquiring company is more over-priced than the company to be acquired, when the day of reckoning arrives and the market reflects the true value commensurate with the risk, the deflation will be less drastic for the acquiring company. The extent of the ultimate deflation depends on the extent to which the stocks are over-priced, both absolutely and relatively.

The ideas which we have just expressed might be viewed in another way as follows. If an investor owns a stock which is too high and sells it, he should not reinvest the cash in another stock if he thinks it is over-priced. He should put the money in government bonds.

The two situations are analogous, and the whole idea is just as simple as that.

Managements which at least understand the importance of obtaining an adequate return on capital in an expansion program where money is invested directly in plant, seem to change their standards of valuation when there is an acquisition or merger through stock-swapping.

As an example, a certain company wished to acquire another company through a stock-swap. The fair book value of the common stock of the company to be acquired was $1,300,000, the estimated earning power was $200,000 and the risk of the business appeared to require a return of about 10%. The acquiring company observed that similar stocks sold at 15 times earnings, and therefore felt it could afford to give enough of its shares on the basis of market value to pay $3 million—until the following was suggested: "Suppose you had owned the assets of this company from its beginning and invested $1,300,000 in the plant and another $1,700,000 for start-up costs to get the plant operating efficiently so that it would earn $200,000. The total investment would be $3 million. Then the return on your total outlay would have only been 6 2/3%. Would you have considered this a good project?" The answer was: "Absolutely not!" The fact that the acquisition was going to be made with stock clouded management's thinking. The acquisition could have been justified only on the basis of forecast profits which would produce a substantially higher rate.

You may feel that we have given too little weight to the realities of the securities market in this chapter. We used one example in which earnings per share decreased when the proceeds from the sale of stock were invested in government bonds. Although the market price for the stock might show an immediate decline due to the reported decrease in earnings per share, ultimately the price of the stock should hold up because the risk in the earnings decreased proportionately.

The picture might be summarized as follows: Management should avoid acquisitions, mergers and expansion programs which will have an adverse effect on the company's long-range earning power, in spite of the fact that temporarily it might improve earnings.

Once you accept the principle that all capital has a cost, you will have no difficulty in seeing that investing capital below cost will ultimately result in a loss. Equally serious results follow no matter what the source of capital; the only difference is that management errors do not become immediately apparent and investors are currently led to misinterpret the picture.

Because investors are influenced by the reported earnings per share figure, management has them at its mercy. Maneuvers which produce temporary earnings improvement provide an opportunity for management which wishes to jazz up the common stock for a few years for stock option purposes, to make a good showing before retiring, or to justify becoming a bigger company.

An amusing incident occurred at a management meeting of a company which had acquired a number of other companies. The presidents of the acquired companies were now presidents of divisions. The purpose of the meeting was to set goals for return on investment. In one of the discussions, a division president spoke up and said:

> I certainly can meet your goal on the asset value of my company, but you can't expect me to meet it on the price you paid.

That thought is a good finale for this chapter.

Appendix 16-A

Time Value Profitability Rate Problems–The Implied Reinvestment Rate Assumption and Multiple Rates

Chapter 16 covered methods of calculating the profitability of a project. In the Time Value Profitability Rate Method, it was briefly explained that there were two problems with regard to the use of this rate. They are discussed in detail in this Appendix.

Implied Reinvestment Rate Assumption–Unequal Cash Flows

In directly comparing one project with another on the basis of Time Value Profitability Rates, an assumption concerning the profitability of cash throwoff reinvestments is always made. If there is no specific different assumption made, profitability conclusions drawn from rate comparisons are based upon the assumption that each project's cash flows will be reinvested at the same rate that is shown for the project itself. By this we do not mean that Time Value Profitability Rate calculation itself includes any such assumption for any project. What we are saying is that in deciding on which of two projects to accept, a straight rate comparison assumes that the cash available for reinvestment will be invested at the project rate. For projects which have unequal cash flows, a straight rate comparison presents a problem for this reason.

In some writings on the subject, the term "implicit" rate is used to describe the reinvestment rate assumption if no other rate is specifically applied. If some other rate is applied for the reinvestment, it is referred to as the "explicit" reinvestment rate.

Suppose that a choice must be made between Project M and Project N, both of which have the same $100,000 initial investment and Time Value Profitability Rate of 50%, but which have different cash flows as shown in Exhibit 16-A1.

Exhibit 16-A1

TIME VALUE PROFITABILITY RATES FOR UNEQUAL NET CASH FLOWS. THE IMPLIED REINVESTMENT RATE PROBLEM

Year	Project M	Project N
0	($100,000)	($100,000)
1	150,000	54,800
2		54,800
3		54,800
4		54,800
5		54,800
6		54,800

Which project is more attractive depends upon the rates at which cash flows can be reinvested. Project M would be the more attractive if all cash flows were reinvested at greater than a 50% rate because we would get the money back quicker to reinvest at the higher rate. Conversely, it would be less attractive if the reinvestment rate were less than 50%. The inference that the proposals are equally attractive because each has a 50% rate is valid only if indefinite cash flow reinvestments at 50% rates are presumed.

To illustrate, assume a 10% reinvestment rate. If Project M's $150,000 cash throwoff were reinvested at 10%, a capital sum of $241,577 would accumulate six years after the project's adoption. This amount is derived by multiplying the $150,000 by the compounding factor of 1.610510 for 10% for the remaining years, which equals $241,577.[3]

If Project N's cash flow were reinvested at 10%, a capital sum of $422,815 would accumulate six years after the project's adoption. This amount is derived by multiplying each $54,800 amount by the compounding factor for 10% for the period remaining. $54,800 x 1.610510 + $54,800 x 1.464100 + $54,800 x 1.331000 + $54,800 x 1.210000 + 54,800 x 1.100000 + 54,800 = $422,815. It can also be obtained by multiplying the $54,800 annual cash flow by the factor 7.715610. This is the factor which shows how much $1 deposited for each of six annual periods at 10% compound interest will grow.[4]

Considering the two projects over a six-year period and taking into account the 10% reinvestment rate, the Time Value Profitability Rate for the projects can be determined to be 16% for Project M and 27% for Project N as shown in Exhibit 16-A2.

Recognizing the need for making some reinvestment rate assumption is of particular practical importance in evaluating conflicting, or mutually exclusive, projects. Such proposals are alternative to one another so that the acceptance of one automatically triggers the rejection of the other(s). For example, a company considering whether to make or buy an item is confronted with two conflicting proposals. Direct profitability comparisons among conflicting projects are essential; thus, the reinvestment rate assumption is important.

While precision in forecasting reinvestment rates is admittedly impossible, management may, in comparing conflicting proposals, wish to make reinvestment rate assumptions different from those implicitly made in direct Time Value Profitability Rate comparisons. For example, management may have definite expectations concerning the profitability of projects that it believes are feasible for the near future. These expectations may be substituted for the rate which the project shows as the Time Value Profitability Rate. An alternative approach is to calculate the Time Value Profitability Rate for conflicting projects using the Company's Profit Goal rate as the reinvestment rate.

In evaluating independent projects—those which are not conflicting or mutually exclusive—it is generally impossible, even with the best of forecasts, to estimate the profitability of cash flow reinvestments on an individual project basis. This is because cash flows available for reinvestment at any point in time are typically derived from numerous projects and constitute a homogeneous pool of capital at management's disposal. Identification of specific segments of this pool with individual investments is possible only on an arbitrary basis. Thus, in appraising most independent proposals, the reinvestment assumption at the project's own rate is unimportant in making project decisions. Ignoring the reinvestment assumptions, a company will accept, after due consideration to risks and intangibles, all projects with Time Value Profitability Rates equal to or greater than the company's Profit Goal. This course of action will lead to best results from the shareholder viewpoint.

However, in certain appraisals of independent projects, the reinvestment assumption at

---

[3]The formula is $S \times (1 + i)^n$, or $\$150{,}000 \times (1 + 0.10)^5 =$ $241,577.

[4]Formula: $S \times \frac{(1 + i)^n - 1}{i}$ or $\$54{,}800 \times \frac{(1 + 0.10)^6 - 1}{10}$ = $422,815.

Exhibit 16-A2

TIME VALUE PROFITABILITY RATES FOR UNEQUAL CASH FLOWS ADJUSTED FOR REINVESTMENT RATE

	PROJECT M				PROJECT N			
			Cash Flow Discounted at 16%				Cash Flow Discounted at 27%	
Yr.	Investment	Cash Flow with 10% Reinvestment Rate	Factor	Amount	Investment	Cash Flow with 10% Reinvestment Rate	Factor	Amount
0	$100,000		1.0000	($100,000)	$100,000		1.0000	($100,000)
1								
2								
3								
4								
5								
6		$241,577	.4104	$99,143		$422,815	.2383	$100,757

the project's own rate may be important and lead to incorrect decisions. For example, the feasibility of certain foreseeable future projects may be contingent on adopting certain present alternatives. For example, a plan to construct a plant one year hence may require the present reservation of liquid capital. Account should be taken of this fact in determining the Time Value Profitability Rate for the present alternative.

The point to note is that while management may be satisfied with the assumption that the reinvestment rate is the same as the project rate in many cases, in other cases this assumption may be unsatisfactory. In such situations, a more appropriate assumption should be made.

Implied Reinvestment Rate Assumption—Unequal Initial Investment

In a comparison of one project with another on the basis of Time Value Profitability Rates, a problem of the implied reinvestment rate assumption also arises when the initial investments are unequal. Here, again, the problem is important only when conflicting proposals are being evaluated. For example, Project X, shown in Exhibit 16-A3 with a 10% rate, cannot directly be compared with the 15% rate for Project Y if the projects require initial investments of $100,000 and $60,000 respectively.

Which project is more attractive depends upon the rate that would be earned upon the differential $40,000 that would be available if Project Y were accepted. Only if this differential rate were 6% would the two projects be equally profitable. And this is true only if the cash flows from each project were reinvested at the particular project's rate. This is illustrated in Exhibit 16-A4.

The Time Value Profitability Rate can be adapted satisfactorily to evaluate such conflicting proposals by means of the "incremental added investment method." This procedure involves comparing all of a set of conflicting proposals that show Time Profitability Rates higher than the Profit Goal in order of size, from the smallest to the largest, in the following two steps.

1. Determine the Time Value Profitability Rate for the proposal requiring the smallest initial investment.
2. Compute the Time Value Profitability Rate implied by the incremental original capital and the incremental cash flows needed to adapt the proposal requiring the next largest investment. If the resulting rate exceeds the Profit Goal, drop

Exhibit 16-A3

TIME VALUE PROFITABILITY RATES FOR UNEQUAL INITIAL INVESTMENTS
THE IMPLIED REINVESTMENT RATE PROBLEM

	PROJECT X				PROJECT Y			
			Cash Flow Discounted at 10%				Cash Flow Discounted at 15%	
Yr.	Investment	Cash Flow	Factor	Amount	Investment	Cash Flow	Factor	Amount
0	$100,000		1.000	($100,000)	$60,000			($60,000)
1		$40,000	.909	36,360		$25,000	.885	22,125
2		$40,000	.826	33,040		25,000	.783	19,575
3		$40,000	.751	30,040		25,000	.693	17,325
				$ 99,440				$59,025

Exhibit 16-A4

TIME VALUE PROFITABILITY RATE FOR
UNEQUAL INITIAL INVESTMENTS WITH
DIFFERENTIAL INVESTMENT DISCOUNTED AT
RATE TO MAKE PROJECTS COMPARABLE

			Cash Flow Discounted at 6%	
Year	Differential Investment	Differential Cash Flow	Factor	Amount
0	$40,000			($40,000)
1		$15,000	.943	14,145
2		15,000	.890	13,350
3		15,000	.840	12,600
				$40,095

the first project from further consideration. Using the second project as a new standard, repeat this incremental approach until only one proposal remains. This is financially the most attractive.

This adaptation of the Time Value Profitability Rate analysis is straightforward and can serve satisfactorily to evaluate such conflicting investment opportunities. Care, however, is required in measuring the differential cash flows expected from successive incremental investments. This can be a somewhat complicated process involving initially a recognition of the appropriate alternatives to include within a set of conflicting proposals.

Multiple Rate Problem

Some incremental investments and, less frequently, some individual proposals can have more than one Time Value Profitability Rate. Appropriate reinvestments assumptions must be made in developing usable rate measures in these instances.

An investment expected to produce cash flows of both positive and negative amounts can have more than one Time Value Profitability Rate; the maximum number of rates is equal to the number of sign changes in the total net cash flows, including the initial investment. For example, Project Z requires a $10,000 initial outlay (a negative cash flow) and will produce three cash flows as follows: Year 1, $60,000; Year 2, $110,000 (negative) and Year 3, $60,000. This project has three rates (0%, 100% and 200%)—the maximum number possible since there are three reversals of cash flow signs. This is shown in the figures in Exhibit 16-A5 by applying discount rates for 0%, 100% and 200% to the cash flows.

Manifestly, this illustrative proposal does not have three different valid indexes of profitability. Valid rate measures can be developed for projects with multiple rates by initially assuming appropriate reinvestment rates. To illustrate, the proposal cited above has a 4 1/2% rate if a 10% reinvestment rate is assumed. The cash flows reinvested at a 10% rate would be as follows: $60,000 x 1.210 – $110,000 x 1.1 + $60,000 = $11,600. With an initial investment of $10,000, this $11,600 at the end of the three-year period would produce a Time Value Profitability Rate of 4 1/2%.

With an assumed 50% reinvestment rate, the project has a 44% rate of return. The cash flows reinvested at a 50% rate would be as follows: $60,000 x 2.250 – $110,000 x 1.500 + $60,000 = $30,000. With an initial investment of $10,000, this $30,000 at the end of the three-year period would produce a Time Value Profitability Rate of 44%. These resultant rates are valid profitability indexes. If projected cash flows alternate between positive and negative amounts, care must be taken to use a specific reinvestment rate in solving for the profitability rate. However, individual proposals with multiple rates of return are relatively rare.

We have tried to indicate in this technical discussion that the problems involved with the Time Value Profitability Rate should not be viewed as hurting its effectiveness. These problems were included for the purpose of presenting a complete picture. When a management reaches the point of choosing a method for profitability analysis of projects which includes the time value of money technique, it will have to choose the one best suited to its particular situation. The technique chosen should be the one which permits management to grasp the results most readily, and it should be consistent with the way in which they are most accustomed to consider capital expenditures.

In a project analysis which involves evaluating conflicting or mutually exclusive projects, the simplest approach might be to use the Time Value Profitability Rate without making adjustments for the unequal cash flows and unequal initial investment problems, and also use the Excess Present Value Technique. And where there are changes in signs of cash flows, use only the Excess Present Value Technique.

Exhibit 16-A5

TIME VALUE PROFITABILITY RATE

MULTIPLE RATE PROBLEM

Year	Net Cash Flows	Discounted at 0%		Discounted at 100%		Discounted at 200%	
		Factor	Amount	Factor	Amount	Factor	Amount
0	($10,000)	1	($10,000)	1.000	($10,000)	1.00000	($10,000)
1	60,000	1	60,000	.500	30,000	.33333	20,000
2	–110,000	1	–110,000	.250	–27,500	.11111	–12,222
3	60,000	1	60,000	.125	7,500	.037037	2,222

CHAPTER 17

Division Performance Standards

This chapter is primarily concerned with division performance standards. However, at the start of the chapter we will discuss return on investment as an analytical tool to improve corporate profits. And before we finish the chapter, we will explain how divisional performance standards can be used for long range planning.

Return on Investment as an Analytic Tool

The first use of return on investment is to assist management in fully comprehending the factors which make for successful profit performance. For this use the "duPont" formula is quite helpful. It was included in Chapter 15 as shown below.

$$\frac{\text{Return}}{\text{Investment}} = \frac{\text{Earnings}}{\text{Sales}} \times \frac{\text{Sales}}{\text{Investment}}$$

The essence of this formula is to separate return on investment into its two components: profit margin and asset turnover. Thus, comparisons among companies are possible and guides may be obtained concerning whether profit problems relate to profit margins being too low or to turnovers not being at a satisfactory level. Some companies have found it helpful to analyze their returns on investment in detail as set forth in Exhibit 17-1.

Exhibit 17-2 shows a schematic which may be helpful in assessing ways of improving return on assets employed. Set forth in the Exhibit are the returns actually experienced in one fiscal year for the company, showing the individual assets and income statement elements going to make up the return. Also shown is the company's proposed profit plan for the succeeding year broken down in a similar fashion. To the extent that the pro-

Exhibit 17-1

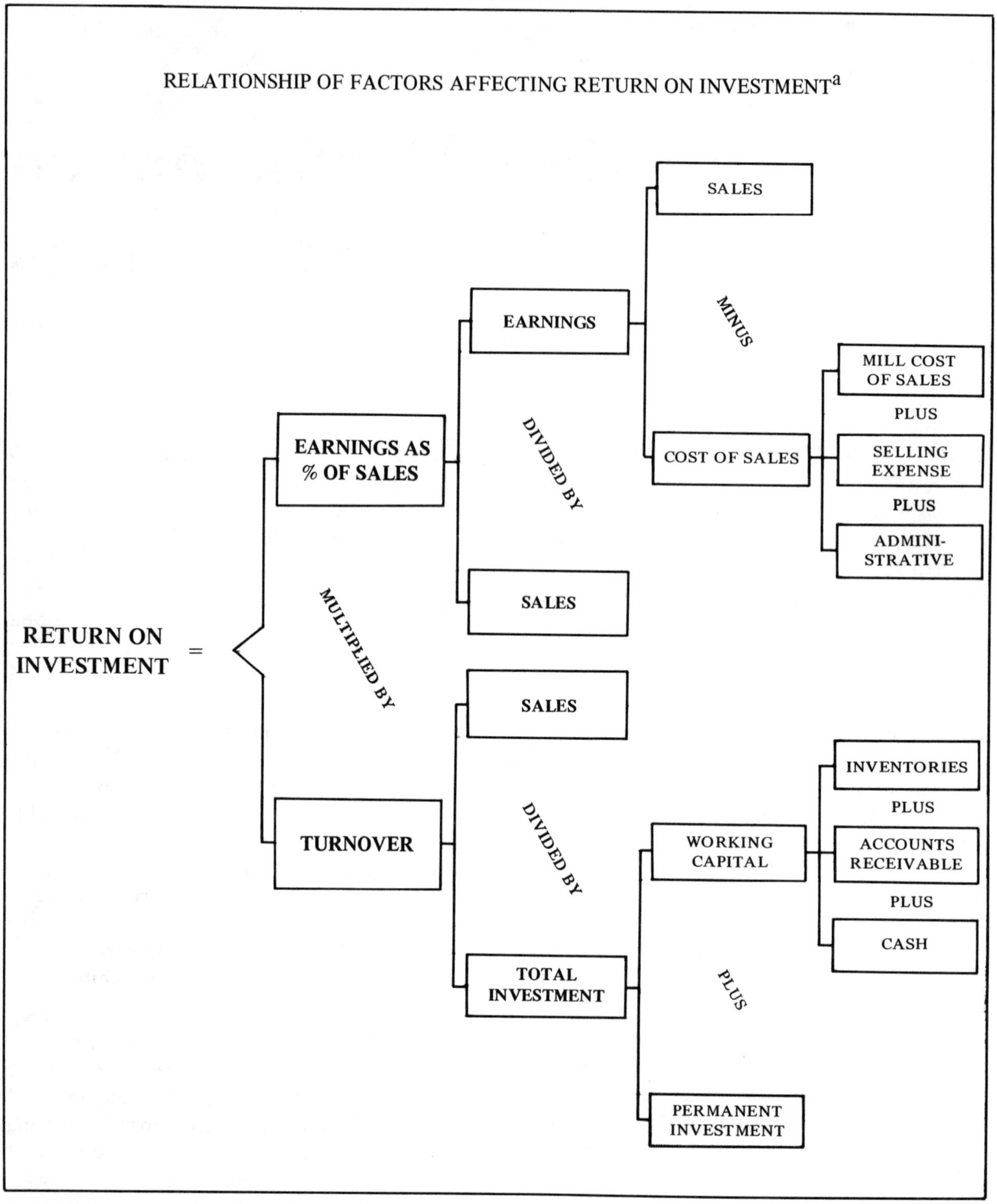

[a]Reprinted by permission of E.I. du Pont de Nemours & Co., Inc., Wilmington, Delaware 19898, from its publication *Executive Committee Control Charts.*

Exhibit 17-2

RETURN ON INVESTMENT WITH COMPONENT BREAKDOWN

P–Proposed Profit Plan
L–Latest Reported Year

Figures Are Presented in Boxes for Each Year for Each Item

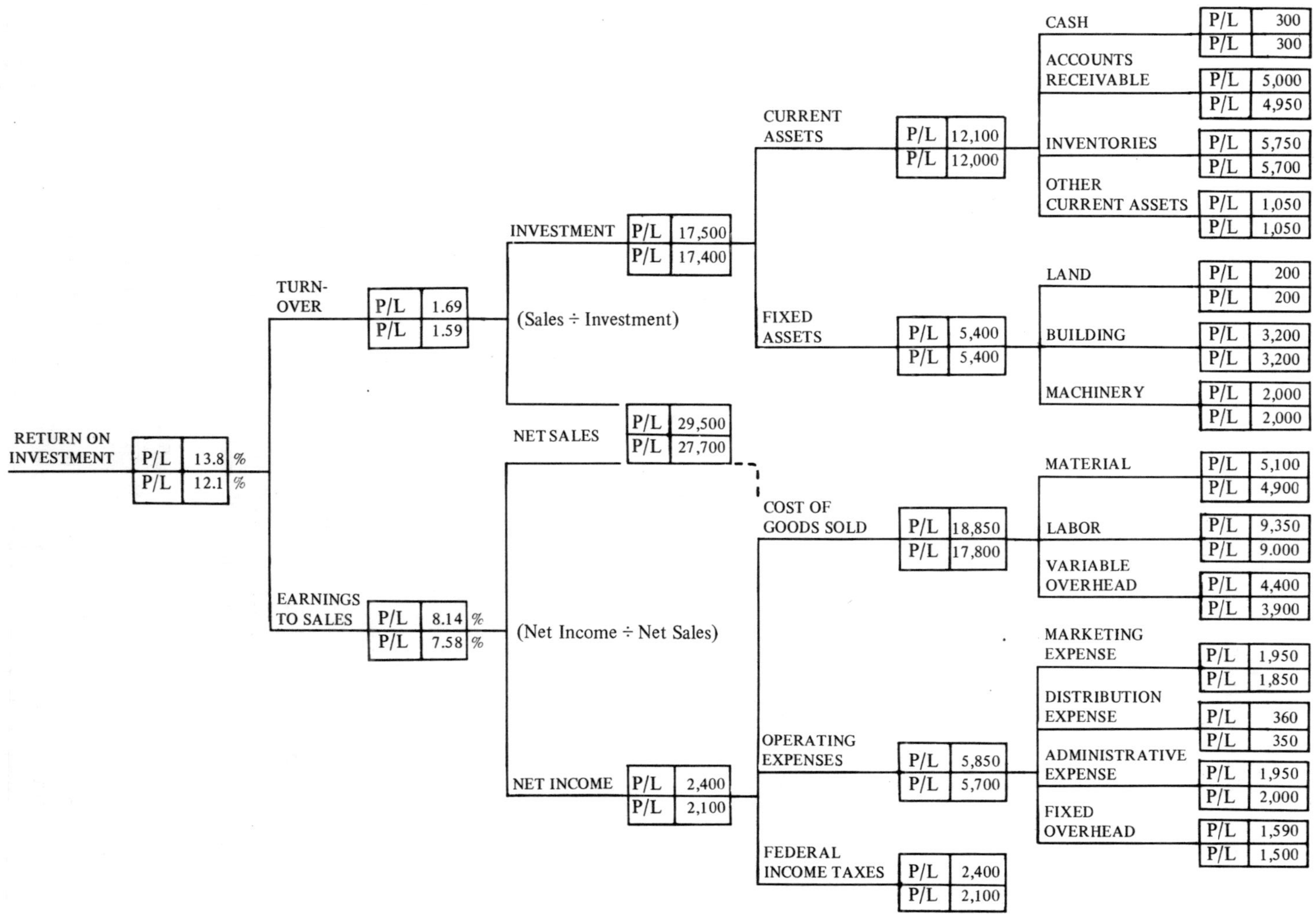

posed profit plan yields an unsatisfactory return on investment, management has the ability through the schematic to assess the impact of changes in various elements of sales, costs and asset components upon the final measure of corporate success—return on investment. Where a company breaks down its organization by profit centers, each division can be analyzed on a similar basis, either with the "duPont" formula or as shown in Exhibit 17-2.

Divisional Profit Performance Standards

Top corporate management is concerned with achieving a satisfactory return on the total corporate investment. Attaining this objective is facilitated if each responsible subordinate level executive focuses on the same criterion.

As a performance standard, return on investment is helpful in two ways. First, it can test whether or not the proposed profit plan set forth by a division manager is satisfactory. Secondly, it can tell whether the individual division manager is doing an excellent, a satisfactory or a poor job.

How useful return on investment is as a top management tool depends upon the basic organizational structure of the company and the particular responsibilities assigned to subordinate level executives.

Defining Profit Centers

Return on investment is primarily helpful as a performance standard in those companies which are organized into profit centers, where each profit center manager has a certain investment entrusted to his care and is responsible for producing a satisfactory return on that investment. This profit center concept is widely employed in American business. Many, if not most, large corporations, and quite a few of those of medium and small size, are organized divisionally on this basis.

The return on investment measure is most meaningful if it relates to a particular responsible manager who has full control over both the income and investment base associated with his profit center. The more control the profit manager has over his center's revenues, its costs and its investment, the more effective is return on investment both as a measure of the manager's historical and planned performance and as a device to stimulate him to seek added profits.

Of course, in defining profit centers, corporate management customarily does not give profit center managers full autonomy to control all factors bearing on their returns on investment. This is because it is essential to overall corporate success to assure that actions taken at the divisional or profit center level are consistent with total corporate objectives. Exactly how much control the divisional manager must retain over the factors bearing on his return on investment for the measure to be meaningful is a matter of judgment requiring resolution in each individual case.

One problem frequently encountered by companies wishing to employ the return on investment concept as a divisional performance standard relates to the question of how to price goods transferred among divisions. In some cases, one division transfers all or substantially all of its production to another division of the company. In such cases it seems questionable as to whether the transferring division can meaningfully be considered a profit center at all, and therefore it is questionable whether return on investment is useful as the divisional performance standard. This is because the division manager does not in any meaningful sense "sell" his product to the receiving divisions; he thus has virtually no control over his revenues.

Other multi-divisional companies have divisions which transfer a significant, but not dominant, portion of their production to other corporate divisions. In these cases, meaningful prices must be set defining the value at which one division "sells" to other divisions if the profit center concept is to be introduced. Different pricing concepts such as market prices, negotiated prices or cost-plus prices may be appropriate depending upon the individual corporate circumstance. It is generally essential, however, for corporate management, as distinguished from divisional management, to retain final control over the pricing mechanism by which interdivisional transfers are made. This is to assure that divisional decisions are made on a basis consistent with total corporate welfare.

Another problem relates to the responsibility of the division manager over the investment. For example, a national retailing chain can fairly well identify the return on assets related to its autonomous store groups. As the return on investment concept is applied to the next lower level—to appraise individual store performance—certain difficulties arise. Specifically, identifying cash, accounts receivable and inventories to particular stores sometimes becomes difficult. Any method of allocating these assets to individual stores must be arbitrary. As the concept is applied to still the next lower level—to the individual departmental level—identifying the investment base accurately is usually impossible except for the investment in inventory. Accordingly, to appraise departmental performance, a return measure which relates departmental margins with departmental inventories and investment in floor area is more appropriate than a measure attempting to relate net allocated income to allocated total assets employed.

Using the Profit Performance Standard

Properly designed, and based upon meaningful profit center definitions, return on investment can be one of top management's most effective control tools.

A number of companies have successfully linked division management compensation with the management's ability to meet or surpass the targets established in return on investment terms by top management.

A word of caution is in order. Return on investment cannot be utilized as the sole measure of divisional success. Other factors such as share of market enjoyed, funds expended on research and development and the number of new products introduced, all of which bear upon the long-term return on assets employed, must also be taken into account in evaluating performance.

Experience suggests that it is all too easy for a division manager to improve upon his return on investment for a year or two at the expense of long-term corporate success. Thus, for example, a division manager can postpone certain expenses, thereby improving his return in the short term. However, long-term success of the division may thereby be impaired. Therefore, in a divisional review of return on investment, top management should also cover the factors which will make for long term as well as short term success.

At least four questions arise in deciding upon how to use return on investment as an effective divisional profit performance standard:

1. How to define the investment on which the return on investment measure is computed.
2. What elements of income should be included for individual divisions or profit centers?
3. The usefulness of the measure in cases where capital is not the important income producing factor.
4. How a satisfactory return on investment goal should be computed for specific divisions.

Investment Base

Used to appraise divisional performance, return on investment can probably best be measured as the relationship between division income and the total *assets employed* by that divisional unit. Assets employed is preferable to either equity or long term capital as the investment base. Since division managers have typically little control over the sources of outside capital, it seems logical that the base to use in measuring their performance should be the total of the assets under their direction, regardless of the sources from which these funds were derived.

Differences of opinion exist concerning whether the asset base on which the rate of return is calculated should be the gross asset figure or the net figure after allowances for depreciation, or whether the figure should represent replacement cost of assets. There is, furthermore, the question as to whether leased facilities should be reflected for rate of return calculation purposes as if they were owned.

A number of companies use the gross value of assets—that is, original book value—in order to inject a rough equalization factor between older assets which are substantially depreciated and new assets. On the other hand, net book value figures are commonly used as the asset base so that the base agrees with reported balance sheet asset figures. A number of variations concerning how the investment base should be measured are in existence.

Those who argue in favor of adjustments to the net book figures contend that the divisions can be put on a more equal basis. To the extent that adjustments can be meaningfully made, this is all to the good. But it should be recognized, as will be pointed out subsequently, that developing investment bases among divisions so that direct comparisons can be made is virtually impossible. Circumstances will differ from one division to another, and making adjustments to reflect assets on an equal basis may be a cumbersome and time-consuming process. Further, it may tend to cause confusion among executives looking at the asset figures as adjusted and then trying to relate these figures to the asset figures appearing on the balance sheet.

Companies beginning to use return on investment as a performance tool would be well advised to use the net book values as reflected on the financial statement as the investment base. Finance leases should be capitalized and the asset included as part of the investment base.

Divisional Income

The question of what income should be assigned to divisional units is directly related to the question of what assets are assigned to these units and how these assets are measured. The principle involved is that income should be identified with those assets involved in producing that income. Thus, for example, if the investment base includes fixed assets at net book value, then depreciation should be related to those assets in computing the income derived from their use.

On the other hand, if it is decided to value fixed assets at their gross book value, then depreciation should not be assigned to the assets in deriving an income figure on which to compute return on assets employed. Similarly, if it is decided that corporate marketable securities should not be assigned to individual divisions since divisions have no control over the size of the corporate marketable securities investment, then interest income derived from these securities should not be assigned to individual divisions.

Pre-tax operating income is sometimes a worthwhile measure. Removing income tax considerations from the measure is helpful because different items may be handled differently from a tax viewpoint among divisions. Comparability is thus sometimes better achieved.

Where Capital Is Not a Significant Income Factor

There are certain cases where return on assets employed is not a prime performance standard, because capital is not a significant income producing factor.

Such situations arise in service organizations. For a law firm or an accounting firm, the scarce resource is not capital but competent individuals. In a similar fashion, there are some profit centers or units within large corporations where return on assets employed is not a meaningful measure because the limiting factor is not capital. In such cases, special treatment must be accorded these segments of the organization in order to get meaningful return on assets employed comparisons among the organizational units.

Setting Divisional Profit Standards

There are at least two fairly common fallacies involved in applying return on assets employed as a performance standard. One of these might be called the "higher the better" philosophy or fallacy. This states that the higher a division's return, the better is the performance of the division manager. Accordingly, a division manager should strive to maximize the return on his assets employed.

Some reflection will illustrate the fallacy of this approach in setting a goal. To achieve the highest return, a division manager might try to eliminate the investment in accounts receivable and reduce inventory to a bare cash-and-carry minimum, ignoring the question of customer service. Further, he might allow his investment in equipment to wear out, thus further reducing the investment base. All of these actions, obviously absurd from a corporate point of view, will have the short term effect of increasing divisional return on assets employed.

What corporate management desires, of course, is for subordinate managers to continue to make investments until the point where the additional investment will earn a return just equal to the company's Profit Goal. In this fashion, divisional and corporate profit maximization is assured. But this result is not obtained if divisional management is urged constantly to increase its return on assets employed.

Another common top management fallacy is to attempt to compare the returns on assets employed from one division to another. Certain comparisons are inevitable. However, the goal established for an individual division should reflect corporate expectations concerning what that particular division should do. Short term comparisons from one division to another can lead to inequitable and disruptive situations. This is so for several reasons.

First, as mentioned previously, it is almost impossible to assure that the way in which assets are measured from one division to another is such as to produce strictly comparable investment bases. For example, the manager of Division A may be dealing with a plant exactly similar to that of Division B. However, Division B had its plant built two years after that of Division A, and at that point in time construction costs were significantly higher. Thus, Division B has a higher asset base, however measured.

Second, the importance of capital as an income producing factor can vary from one division to another, as suggested above. Commonly, management would expect a higher return on that division with a lower required capital base than on the one where capital was a more important income producing element.

Third, it is unrealistic in any one year to expect that all divisions will earn approximately equal returns. In today's diversified corporations, inevitably one division will find itself in a different phase in either the growth cycle or the economic cycle. Thus, corporate management should establish divisional goals to reflect what can reasonably be expected.

Profit Performance Standards and Long Range Planning

Divisional returns on assets employed should be tested against top management's reasonable expectations as to what the division should do in light of its products' positions in the economic environment and in light of its stage in the growth cycle. Effectively implementing this comparison against plan implies that a meaningful long term plan for each divisional segment has been constructed.

A number of companies which have given serious thought and study to the development of long-range corporate plans have found the use of return on assets employed effective as a device to summarize the results of this planning. In abbreviated form, Exhibit 17-3 illus-

Exhibit 17-3

Z CORPORATION

FIVE-YEAR PLAN OF ASSETS EMPLOYED AND EXPECTED RETURNS

(000,000's Omitted)

Year	1	2	3	4	5
DIVISION					
A	$100 10%	$100 10%	$100 10%	$100 10%	$100 10%
B	230 12.4%	225 11.3%	210 11.8%	195 9.9%	190 9.0%
C	50 15%	75 20%	100 20%	130 22%	140 24%
Corp.	20 —	20 —	20 —	20 —	20 —
	$400 11.5%	$420 12.0%	$430 12.5%	$445 13.0%	$450 13.5%

trates such a presentation for Z Corporation's long-range financial plan for five years.

Z Corporation has three major divisions. Additionally, there are certain amounts of assets employed which are not specifically identifiable with any one division but rather are corporate in nature.

In columnar form for each year are shown the amount of assets employed and also the anticipated returns on assets employed for each of the individual divisions.

Such a format focuses management's attention on both the amount of asset investment and the earnings expected on these divisional investments over time. This permits management to explore the consequences on total corporate return on assets employed of different rationing schemes by assigning assets to various divisions in the future. The earnings rates represent the appropriate earnings goals by which to measure divisional performance on a year-to-year basis.

Compared with Profitability Rate

Chapter 16 explained the use of profitability rate in appraising the economic worth of new investments. In this chapter, we have discussed the use of a related return on investment concept as a device for both appraising subordinate level performance and for long range planning.

We now hasten to point out that the two measures are not directly comparable one to the other. There are at least three reasons for this.

First, Time Value Profitability Rate is developed for an individual proposed new project. Return on assets employed is related to the performance of the total organization or a particular segment of the organization; each organizational segment consists of a number of individual projects.

Secondly, profitability rate depicts the average annual earnings rate for a proposed new project over its entire economic life. Return on assets employed, on the other hand, depicts an earnings rate for a particular time period, usually a year.

Thirdly, profitability rate is correctly computed on a cash flow basis. Return on assets employed, on the other hand, depicts the relationship of accrual—not cash—earnings to book assets.

This lack of comparability over the long run is not important. If a division manager continues to accept only those new investments which meet the corporate criterion of the correct Profit Goal, he will also, over time, achieve a return on assets employed which will also achieve the corporate Profit Goal.

For example, let us suppose a division manager of a highly profitable division, earning a very large return on assets employed, is being encouraged to improve still further on this percentage return. As we have already suggested, this manager would be extremely reluctant to accept any new investment which would have the effect of reducing his return, particularly if he were evaluated for compensation or otherwise on the basis of whether he improved on last year's return. Specifically, let us suppose that the corporate Profit Goal is 15%. The division manager is presently earning a 30% return on assets employed. He is considering a new project which has a prospective profitability rate of 20%. From the corporate viewpoint, the project is desirable since 20% exceeds the 15% Profit Goal. The division manager, however, understandably would be reluctant to accept the 20% project if he is told to improve upon his already high 30% return on assets employed. His required return on assets employed must be tempered by corporate management to encourage him to accept this sort of project.

A similar problem may arise in the case where a proposed new investment has a very high profitability rate, say 25%, over its entire project life but has negative earnings in the first year or two of its life because of heavy start-up costs. Corporate management must expect its performance standards for a particular division to be lowered for the first two years of a new project of this type if it anticipates a division manager's accepting such a new project.

Coping with these short term problems requires intelligent administration of the rate of return control mechanism. This implies intelligent setting of the performance standards for particular organization segments and an educational process so as to assure that divisional managers, in appraising new investments, will take actions consistent with total long-range corporate welfare.

How the Rates Tie Together

First, it is necessary to establish a profit goal for the company as a whole, and then this must be translated in terms of the base and income that will be used for division performance standards. We will use a simple example for illustrative purposes.

Our company has decided that its profit goal on a To Investor Rate Basis should be 11 1/2% on total long term capital as follows:

Debt	25%	7%	1.75%
Common	75	13%	9.75
Total	100%		11.50%

The company's balance sheet is as follows:

Current assets	$100	Current liabilities		$ 50
Plant, net	50	Long term capital		
		Debt	$25	
		Common	75	
		Total		$100
Total	$150	Total		$150

It has decided to use total depreciated assets as the investment for division performance standards.

Its income statement would look as follows if it just earned its profit goal:

Sales	$200.00
Expenses and Depreciation	178.75
Income Before Interest and Taxes	21.25
Interest	1.75
Income After Interest Before Taxes	19.50
Taxes (50% Rate)	9.75
Income Available for Common	9.75

It has decided to use a pre-tax rate for division performance standards. To meet the profit goal rate of 11.50% on long term capital on a To Investor Rate Basis would require a pre-tax rate of 21.25% on the same base. Relating this rate to total depreciated assets would result in a pre-tax profit goal rate of 14.2%.

There are other numerous adjustments which may have to be made:

If any assets are included in corporate level, then they have to be allocated to the divisions or the rate has to be adjusted accordingly. Assume that $10 million of assets of the company are at the corporate level so that total assets of the divisions would amount to $140 million. This $10 million has to be allocated to the divisions or the rate has to be increased accordingly. Our 14.2% on total depreciated assets would be increased to 15.2% if the investment is not allocated.

If certain expenses and overheads are included in the income statement but not in the division statements, these expenses have to be allocated to the divisions or the profit goal rate increased accordingly. For example assume that interest on short-term seasonal bank borrowings amounts to $500,000 annually and that overheads amount to $500,000. This total of $1 million which is reported at the corporate level has to be allocated to the divisions or the profit goal rate increased accordingly. If we increase the rate, which is now at 15.2% on the $140 million asset base, to take care of $1 million of expenses not shown in division statements, the rate would be increased to 15.8%.

After the appropriate investment base and profit goal rate are developed for the divisions, then it may be necessary to adjust the rate for the divisions to the extent that there is a difference in risk between divisions, and also for the many reasons previously discussed in this chapter.

Other Techniques

Like all management techniques return on investment has its drawbacks as discussed above, and there are those[1] who recommend other techniques. For example, one approach focuses on residual income after an interest cost of capital so that divisional managers are induced to maximize the dollar income for the corporation. If management wishes to go into the subject of division performance standards in detail, it may wish to refer to other methods and choose the one most suited. In any event, management must have its division managers oriented in some way with performance in terms of return on investment where it has meaning. Otherwise, the division managers may function at cross-purposes with the goals of the company. No purely mathematical formula can take into account all factors—and properly applied, return on assets is probably the easiest to use and understand in most situations.

Above all, division performance standards cannot be used mechanically. They will function in direct relationship to the amount of education the top management employs to explain how division performance standards must be meaningfully applied, and how they should function to meet the overall company goal.

---

[1]Dearden, John, "The Case Against ROI Control," *Harvard Business Review,* May-June, 1969.

Salomons, David, Division Performance: Measurement and Control. Financial Executives Research Foundation, 1965.

CHAPTER 18

A Fair Return for Investors and a Reasonable Price for Your Stock—Completing the Cycle

Everything Has to Tie Together

A thorough understanding of the capital management story requires that you see how all the parts tie together into one ball of wax, from raising the capital from investors to putting it to work, and then returning a fair return to investors. This is the big concept you should have in order to do a good management job.

First let's make a quick review:

1. You set a profit goal by first determining the composite cost-of-capital for long term capital on a To Investor Rate Basis. We will assume that you estimated the rate that investors require to induce them to provide common equity capital is 12%. This has to be adjusted for financing costs by dividing by 90%. This gives a common cost rate of 13%. We estimate that with satisfactory earnings, your company could have a debt ratio of 25% and have good quality of securities, and that a cost rate for the debt is 7%. You decide that your profit goal should be 100% above cost-of-capital. This would produce a profit goal on a To Investor Rate Basis as shown on the next page.

Long Term Capital	Amount	Rate	To Investor Rate
Debt	25%	7%	1.75%
Common equity	75%	13%	9.75
Total	100%		11.50
Allowance above cost			1.00
Profit goal on long term capital			12.50

2. You convert your profit goal to an After-Tax Equivalent Rate to use as a cut-off point for capital investments. Assuming a 50% tax rate, the rate you would use would be calculated as follows:

Long Term Capital	Amount	Rate	After-Tax Equivalent Rate
Debt	25%	3 1/2%	0.875%
Common	75%	13	9.75
Total	100%		10.625
Allowance Above cost			1.000
Profit Goal for Project Analysis			11.625%

You have to be sure to have the right asset base in making a project forecast, and you have to determine the return on a project by allowing for the time value of money. Then the resulting earnings will produce the right rate on long term capital over the long run. You have to vary the rate for projects which are different in risk from that for your company.

3. When earnings materialize, you determine whether your company is doing a good job by computing the return on long term capital on a To Investor Rate basis and comparing it with your profit goal.

We will assume that you earn your profit goal on your old investments and that you have achieved the After-Tax Equivalent on working capital and plant for new projects so that the return on Total Long Term Capital on a To Investor Rate basis is 12.50%. This will produce the following return on beginning common book value as follows:

Return on Total Long Term Capital	12.50%
Less: Interest	1.75
Available Return for Common	10.75%
Beginning Common Equity	75%
Return on Beginning Common Equity	= 10.75% / 75%
	= 14.33%

4. The return on beginning common equity of 14.33% combined with the dividend policy, which we will assume is 35%, will provide a growth rate in earnings per share from plowback of 9.31%.

A Fair Return to Investors

We started out by obtaining the cost-of-capital rate by determining what investors considered a fair return. We decided that investors wanted a return of 12% to induce them to provide common equity money. Now to tie everything together, the resulting earnings should provide a fair return to the stockholders. Thus, we are at the point of considering what should be the market price of the stock in relation to earnings in order to provide investors a 12% return. And there is a corollary question of the relationship of market price to book value.

If managements truly believe that investors deserve a fair return, managements should have a constructive attitude towards the price of their stock. Managements almost universally cheer when the price of their stock goes up, thinking that this is a boon to their stockholders, and, of course, incidentally, if management owns stock they may be thinking about the benefit to themselves. However, if new stockholders are paying too high a price, as time goes on, they will receive less than a fair return. Thus, while management should not attempt to control the market price, it should be concerned when their stock sells at too high a price as much as when it sells too low. The ideal situation should be for the price-earnings ratio to remain constant at a figure which will provide a fair return to investors in keeping with the return the company earns. As earnings per share grow from plowback of earnings, the market price of the stock will appreciate.

Management may also be interested in the price of the stock because there will be occasions when management may wish to consider whether the stock is over- or underpriced: when the company is contemplating the sale of new stock, when it is considering purchasing its stock or when it is planning to use its stock for acquisition purposes. Also, some idea as to what its stock is worth may help management tell whether its investor relations program is getting across a complete story about its operations.

In the short run, investors may vary in their preference for stocks in different companies or different industries. Each period in the stock market has its glamour stocks which are in vogue while stocks of other companies with fine basic performance may be ignored. And the whole market does get way out of line at times because of excessive optimism or pessimism. Our approach will offer a long-range frame of reference independent of market excesses.

In discussing the market price of your stock, we will take a long range view.

When we talk about growth in earnings per share, we will assume that it is due to plowback of earnings since this is the only way that earnings per share can show continuous growth. This was explained in the chapter on dividend policy and again in the chapter on how earnings per share grow. If you need a refresher be sure to review it, otherwise we will lose you.

What Price for Your Stock if All Earnings Were Paid Out in Dividends?

Let's start off very easy. To do that we will use as an example Company A, which has a book value per share of $100 and earns $12 per share or 12% on book value.

Most companies only pay out part of their earnings in dividends and retain a part. We will assume that Company A pays out 100% of its earnings in dividends so that its dividend per share is $12.

Since Company A retains no earnings, it will have no growth in earnings per share from plowback. It keeps on earning $12 and paying it all out in dividends.

What should be the market price of its stock? That depends on the yield that would satisfy investors. If investors wanted a 12% return on their money to induce them to buy the stock, then the market price should be $100. These figures are shown in Exhibit 18-1.

Suppose another Company B had a book value per share of $100 and earned $24 per share or 24% on book value, and paid a dividend of $24. If investors wanted a 12% return, the market price of the stock would be $200. These figures are also summarized in Exhibit 18-1.

If all companies paid out all their earnings in dividends, determining the market price of a stock would be easy. Investors would only have to figure out what return they wanted and what the dividends were expected to be.

Unfortunately, it isn't that easy, because most companies don't pay out all their earnings in dividends.

All earnings for the common stock belong to the stockholder, but as we have said, part are paid out in dividends and part retained by the company. How might you evaluate the two parts in order to determine a market price for your company's stock. As a first step, you would have to decide how much return you might want from both the parts. So far in the examples above, we have assumed that investors wanted a total return of 12%.

Before we go any farther, we should point out that investors might take a different attitude towards the two parts. Cash dividends are a bird in the hand and have no risk once they are received; whereas, the value of the retained earnings depends on what the company does with them—that is certainly more risky than cash. If we ignore the distinction in some of the discussion which follows, it is only to make it a little easier to understand. You should remember that there is this inherent risk difference.

Aside from this difference in risk, why aren't the two parts the same as far as the investor is concerned? Simply because the value of the earnings retained depends on

Exhibit 18-1

PRICE OF STOCK FOR COMPANIES WHICH PAY OUT ALL THEIR EARNINGS IN DIVIDENDS

	Company A	Company B
Book value per share	$100	$100
Return on book value	12%	24%
Earnings per share	$ 12	$ 24
Dividend Payout Ratio	100%	100%
Dividends per share	$ 12	$ 24
Return wanted by investors	12%	12%
Market price of stock	$100	$200

what the company is able to do with them. How much can the company earn on the earnings that are retained? That is the important point!

Going back to Company A and B, suppose each paid out 50% of their earnings in dividends. Company A which earned 12% in its book value would have an earnings per share growth of 6% because it would earn 12% on the retained earnings. Company B, which earned 24% in its book value, would have an earnings per share growth of 12% because it would earn 24% on the retained earnings. Investors would pay more for Company B's stock because the dividend was greater, and also substantially more because it would earn more on the retained earnings.

We should point out that to the extent that earnings are paid out in dividends, the company has less capital on which to increase earnings per share. And no allowance is made for a return on the dividends the investors receive, so the two parts of earnings are treated quite differently.

When we assumed that investors required a 12% return, we are saying that investors feel that such a return is just enough to satisfy them in view of the risk of the business. Therefore:

> If the company earns less than 12% on its common book value, it should not retain any earnings—it would be wasting investors' capital.
>
> If it earns 12% it would be just meeting investors' requirements.
>
> If it earns more than 12% investors would be benefited by the retained earnings.

So we now arrive at the point of trying to explain how to evaluate the price of a stock which does not pay out all of its earnings in dividends.

Return from Market Appreciation and Dividend Yield

Stockholders get their return from dividends and appreciation in the market price of their stock.

Market price appreciation can occur because of a change in earnings per share and the price-earnings ratio. The price-earnings ratio can go up and down, but it can't go in either direction indefinitely. Over the long run, the price-earnings ratio should settle down at an average figure so that investors get a fair return in relation to the company's earnings. For our explanation we will assume that the price-earnings ratio remains constant. If it does remain constant, then the percent return the investors get from market price appreciation will be the same as the percent increase in earnings per share. For example, if the earnings per share increased 10% from

$10 to $11 and the price-earnings ratio remained constant at ten times, the market price would appreciate 10% from $100 to $110.

In our example, in the first part of the chapter, we expected earnings per share to grow at 9.31% per year because the return on common book value was 14.33% and the payout was 35%. Therefore, stockholders will get 9.31% from market appreciation with a constant price-earnings ratio.

Dividend Yield. We have assumed that common stockholders expected to get a return of 12%. If they get 9.31% from market appreciation, the balance of the return must come from dividend yield which is obtained by subtraction: 12% total return less 9.31% market appreciation requires a dividend yield of 2.69%.

With a constant dividend payout ratio, the dividends would grow at the same rate as the earnings grow. Since we have assumed a constant price-earnings ratio, the market price of the stock would grow at the same rate as the earnings and dividends and the yield would remain constant.

Thus, for a company which has constant figures for the price-earnings ratio, and dividend payout ratio, the total return to investors is equal to the growth rate in earnings per share plus the dividend yield.

Applying this idea to the figures we developed in the first part of the chapter, the results would be as follows:

Market appreciation with a constant price-earnings ratio is the same as the growth rate in earnings per share.	9.31%
Dividend yield remains constant if the payout is constant and the market price appreciates at the same rate as the earnings.	2.69
Total return to common stock holders.	12.00%

Price-Earnings Ratio and the Price of Your Stock

In order to obtain the price-earnings ratio, we use the formula given below, the derivation of which is shown in Exhibit 18-2, Part I.

$$\text{Price-Earnings Ratio} = \frac{\text{Payout}}{\text{Yield}} = \frac{35\%}{2.69\%} = 13$$

In order to get the price of the stock, we would apply this price-earnings ratio to the company's earnings. In all of these calculations, we are talking about long range averages and not spot figures. Short range earnings, which are either inflated or depressed, could not be used to obtain a reasonable price.

All of these figures are tied together in Exhibit 18-3.

To summarize, a company should have a good idea of the growth rate in earnings per share which would provide a similar market appreciation for the stock with a constant price-earnings ratio. It should know what return investors require to induce them to put up common equity capital—this is the common cost rate. Subtraction of the rate of market appreciation from the total return common stockholders want gives the dividend yield, assuming the payout remains constant. Division of the yield into the payout gives the price-earnings ratio.

It should be emphasized that the market price of a stock depends not on what a company earns but on what investors expect it will earn. In the short run, there may be a wide difference in the two earnings rates. It would be hoped that in the long run there will be some reasonable relationship between what investors expect and what a company earns.

Market Price of Common Related to Book Value per Share

We mentioned at the beginning of this chapter that there was a corollary question: the relationship of market price of a stock to its book value.

The stated book value as shown on the balance sheet may not be representative of the book value based on true value of the assets. There may be fictitious items on the

Exhibit 18-2

FORMULAS FOR DETERMINING PRICE-EARNINGS RATIO AND MARKET PRICE DIVIDED BY COMMON BOOK VALUE

PART I

DETERMINATION OF PRICE-EARNINGS RATIO FROM DIVIDEND PAYOUT RATIO AND DIVIDEND YIELD

Since

$$\text{Dividend Payout Ratio} = \frac{\text{Dividends per Share}}{\text{Earnings per Share}}$$

$$\text{and Dividend Yield} = \frac{\text{Dividends per Share}}{\text{Market Price}}$$

Then

$$\frac{\text{Dividend Payout Ratio}}{\text{Dividend Yield}} = \frac{\left(\dfrac{\text{Dividends per Share}}{\text{Earnings per Share}}\right)}{\left(\dfrac{\text{Dividends per Share}}{\text{Market Price}}\right)}$$

$$= \frac{\text{Dividends per Share}}{\text{Earnings per Share}} \times \frac{\text{Market Price}}{\text{Dividends per Share}}$$

$$= \frac{\text{Market Price}}{\text{Earnings per Share}}$$

$$= \text{Price-Earnings Ratio}$$

PART II

DETERMINATION OF MARKET PRICE DIVIDED BY COMMON BOOK VALUE FROM RETURN ON COMMON BOOK VALUE AND PRICE-EARNINGS RATIO

Since

$$\text{Return on Common Book Value} = \frac{\text{Earnings per Share}}{\text{Common Book Value}}$$

$$\text{and Price-Earnings Ratio} = \frac{\text{Market Price}}{\text{Earnings per Share}}$$

Then

$$\text{Return on Common Book Value x Price-Earnings Ratio} = \frac{\text{Earnings per Share}}{\text{Common Book Value}} \times \frac{\text{Market Price}}{\text{Earnings per Share}}$$

$$= \frac{\text{Market Price}}{\text{Common Book Value}}$$

asset side of the balance sheet or the assets may be undervalued based on current value. However, we will assume that the book value which we used for return on common book value represents true value.

The relationship between market price and

Exhibit 18-3

RETURN TO COMMON STOCKHOLDERS FROM MARKET APPRECIATION AND DIVIDEND YIELD

Company Earns 14.33% on Common Book Value, Pays Out 35% of Earnings in Dividends and Produces a 9.31% Growth Rate in Earnings and Dividends per Share from Plowback. No Other Factors Affect Growth in Earnings per Share.

PART I

MARKET APPRECIATION WITH CONSTANT PRICE-EARNINGS RATIO

Column	I	II	III	IV	V
Year	Earnings per Share	Growth Rate in Earnings per Share	Price-Earnings Ratio	Market Price Common	Appreciation in Market Price
0	$14.33		13	$186	
1	15.66	9.31%	"	204	9.31%
2	17.12	"	"	223	"

PART II

DIVIDEND YIELD WITH CONSTANT DIVIDEND PAYOUT AND PRICE-EARNINGS RATIO

Column	I	II	III	IV	V	VI
Year	Earnings per Share	Dividend Payout Ratio	Dividends per Share	Price-Earnings Ratio	Market Price Common	Dividend Yield
0	$14.33	35%	$5.02	13	$186	2.69%
1	15.66	"	5.48	"	204	"
2	17.12	"	5.99	"	223	"

PART III

TOTAL RETURN TO COMMON STOCKHOLDERS

Market appreciation	9.31%
Dividend yield	2.69
Total return	12.00%

PART IV

PRICE-EARNINGS RATIO

$$\text{Price-earnings ratio} = \frac{\text{Payout}}{\text{Yield}}$$

$$= \frac{35\%}{\$2.69} = 13$$

PART V

MARKET PRICE DIVIDED BY BOOK VALUE

Percent Return on Common Book Value x Price-Earnings Ratio = 14.33% x 13 = 186%

common book value is determined by the following formula, the derivation for which is shown in Exhibit 18-2, Part II.

Market Price Divided by Common Book Value	=	Return on Common Book Value x Price-Earnings Ratio
	=	14.33% x 13
	=	186%

In our example, the return to investors is 12% on market price while the company earns 14.33% on common book value. This difference is due to the fact that the market price is above book value.

If the market price is sufficiently above book value so that after allowing for financing costs, new stock could be sold at least for book value, the investors would be saying that the earnings they expect the company will earn in the future will provide them a break-even fair return. For a company to be financially healthy and assure its ability to finance readily with common stock, it should earn a sufficient return so that its stock will sell at an additional premium. For a really profitable company, the stock should sell at a further premium above book value.

Furthermore, in a highly inflationary environment the market price should be related to the real book value, not merely the nominal book value.

When new shares of stock are sold by a company, the market price and book value are the same for those particular shares because the proceeds from those shares are transferred into book value at the time of the sale.

Limitations of the Formulas

The formulas for price-earnings ratio and market price divided by common book value are primarily for the purpose of illustrating that there has to be a tie-in between what the company earns and a fair return to investors. Unfortunately, we now have to tell you that the formulas have definite limitations as follows:

1. They assume constant figures for price-earnings ratio, dividend payout ratio and increase in earnings from plowback. The figures for return on common book value, price-earnings ratio and dividend payout ratio are not constant for a particular company.
2. They do not differentiate between return from dividends and market appreciation. Dividends are far more certain than the prospects of market appreciation. A lower overall return may be acceptable to some investors if a substantial portion of it comes in the form of dividend yield.
3. They cannot be used at all for a company which pays no dividends. In such a situation, no matter what the price-earnings ratio, the return to investors from market appreciation would be equal to the growth rate in earnings per share provided the price-earnings ratio remained constant.
4. The price-earnings ratio is overly sensitive when the price-earnings ratio is high and the dividend yield low. We can illustrate this problem by the following two figures for dividend payout policy:

Growth Rate in Earnings per Share (14.33% x 65%)	9.31%
Dividend Yield to Make Return to Investors 12%	2.69
Total Annual Return Expected by Investors	12.00%
Price-Earnings Ratio	$= \frac{35\%}{2.69\%}$
	= 13

Now increase the growth rate to 10.75% by dropping the payout ratio to 25% and the results would be as follows:

Growth Rate in Earnings per Share (14.33% x 75%)	10.75%
Dividend Yield to Make Return to Investors 12%	1.25
Total Annual Return Expected by Investors	12.00%
Price-Earnings Ratio	$= \frac{25\%}{1.25\%}$
	= 20

This approach would suggest that the price-earnings ratio ought to increase from 13 to 20, with a reduction in payout ratio from 35% to 25%. This is clearly unrealistic.

It may be noted that as the payout decreases the growth rate in earnings per share increases. As we previously explained, this is due to the fact that retained earnings grow at the rate the company earns while there is no allowance for a return on the dividends the investors receive. This, however, has nothing to do with the operation of the formula.

5. The price-earnings ratio is also sensitive to assumptions made about the return required by investors. This is illustrated in the figures below.

year might be high in anticipation of improved earnings in the next year. Also, if such a company ran into a period of adverse earnings and then reversed the trend so that the return on the common book value increased in subsequent years it would produce a high growth rate in earnings per share and possibly a high price-earnings ratio, depending on how investors interpreted the growth rate. However, these would be short range variations around a basic norm.

We should caution that a high return on common book value should not necessarily be assumed to produce a high price-earnings ratio. If the high return is accompanied by high risk due to the nature of the business or excessive leverage, then investors in the long run will require a higher return than such a figure as 12%.

Column		I	II
Return on Common Book Value		14.33%	14.33%
Dividend Payout Ratio		35%	35%
Growth Rate in Earnings per Share (13.67% x 65%)		9.31%	9.31%
Dividend Yield		2.69%	1.69%
Total Annual Return Acceptable to Investors		12.00%	11.00%
Price-Earnings Ratio	=	$\frac{35\%}{2.69\%}$	$\frac{35\%}{1.69\%}$
	=	13	21

The estimate of what the right price-earnings ratio ought to be goes up from 13 to 21 times if it is assumed that investors will accept an 11% return rather than 12%.

In view of all these reservations about the validity of this approach, you may ask whether it is worthwhile. Interpreted with understanding, it can be helpful to management in viewing the connection between a company's basic earning ability and market price. For example, a company which reaches an average return of 12% on its beginning common book value would be foolish to think in terms of a high price-earnings ratio in the long run. The common stock of such a company could sell at a high price-earnings ratio under some circumstances. For example, in a year of poor earnings, the price-earnings ratio in that

The Price of Your Own Stock—Illustrated with the Dow-Jones Industrial Common Stock Average

Now let's see how these relationships might tie together for a company over a ten-year period. For illustrative purposes, we will use the Dow-Jones Industrial Common Stock Average. There is some criticism of this average as an index of stock prices, but it can be used to show how the various figures might tie together for a particular company. Furthermore, the average is of interest because it is so widely quoted.

The figures for the Dow-Jones are shown in Exhibit 18-4. They are tied together in Exhibit 18-5. It shows that investors would have received about 11.8% return on the

Exhibit 18-4

DATA FOR DOW JONES INDUSTRIAL COMMON STOCK AVERAGE

Line		Average	Est. 1974*	1973	1972	1971
1	Earnings per share ($)		95.00	86.17	67.11	55.09
2	Year-to-year growth rate in earnings per share (%)	8.05	10.3	28.4	21.8	8.0
3	Dividends per share ($)		38.50	33.44	32.27	30.86
4	Payout ratio (%)	52	41	39	48	56
5	Yield (%)	3.7	5.1	3.6	3.4	3.5
6	Average high-low market price ($)		756	920	963	874
7	Price-earnings ratio	14.5	8	11	14	16
8	Beginning common book value per share ($)		696	643	608	573
9	Return on beginning common book value (%)	11.7	13.7	13.5	11.0	9.6
10	Year-to-year change in return on beginning common book value (%)	2.4	1.3	17.1	14.6	2.1
11	Market price–divided by beginning common book value (%)	167	109	143	158	153

Line		1970	1969	1968	1967	1966	1965
1	Earnings per share ($)	51.02	57.02	57.96	53.77	57.68	53.67
2	Year-to-year growth rate in earnings per share (%)	(10.5)	(1.6)	7.8	(6.8)	7.5	15.6
3	Dividends per share ($)	31.53	33.90	31.34	30.19	31.89	28.61
4	Payout ratio (%)	62	59	54	56	55	53
5	Yield (%)	3.7	3.9	3.5	3.5	3.7	3.2
6	Average high-low market price ($)	855	869	905	865	870	905
7	Price-earnings ratio	17	15	16	16	15	17
8	Beginning common book value per share ($)	542	521	477	476	453	417
9	Return on beginning common book value (%)	9.4	10.9	12.2	11.3	12.7	12.9
10	Year-to-year change in return on beginning common book value (%)	(13.8)	(10.7)	8.0	(11.0)	(1.6)	18.3
11	Market price–divided by beginning common book value (%)	158	167	190	182	192	217

*Based on data through September, 1974.

Exhibit 18-5

DOW JONES INDUSTRIAL COMMON STOCK AVERAGE*
RELATIONSHIP BETWEEN RETURN ON COMMON BOOK VALUE,
RETURN TO INVESTORS, PRICE-EARNINGS RATIO
AND MARKET PRICE DIVIDED BY COMMON BOOK VALUE

10-Year Average 1964-1973
(Line References Are to Exhibit 18-4)

Line				
	Growth rate in earnings per share from:			
	Plowback			
	Return on beginning common book value	Earnings retained (100%-55% paid out)		
1	11.7% (see line 9) x	48% (see line 4)	=	5.6%
2	Increase in return on beginning common book value†			2.4 (see line 10)
3	Other factors (this is a balancing figure to equate the total to 8.1)			+0.1
4	Total growth rate in earnings per share			8.1 (see line 2)
5	Dividend yield			3.7 (see line 5)
6	Total return to investors if price-earnings ratio had remained constant			11.8%
7	Price-earnings ratio		=	Payout / Yield
8			=	52% / 3.7%
9			=	14.1% (see line 7)
10	Market price of stock divided by common book value		=	Return on common book value x price-earnings ratio
11			=	11.7 x 14.1%
12			=	165% (see line 11)

*Includes the following stocks: Allied Chemical, Aluminum Co. of America, American Brands, American Can, American Telephone & Telegraph, Anaconda, Bethlehem Steel, Chrysler, DuPont, Eastman Kodak, Esmark Inc., Exxon, General Electric, General Foods, General Motors, Goodyear, International Harvester, International Nickel, International Paper, Johns-Manville, Owens-Illinois, Proctor & Gamble, Sears Roebuck, Standard Oil of California, Texaco, Union Carbide, United Aircraft, U.S. Steel, Westinghouse Electric, Woolworth.

†The increase in return to the common stockholder from the increase in return on book value is only fully beneficial if there is no change in the leverage which would add risk to the earnings.

average if the price-earnings ratio had remained constant at 14.1 times.

Why did the Dow sell at an average of 14 times? Should it have sold there? On the basis of the 8.1% average growth rate, the 14 times price-earnings ratio might be justified. But is 8.1% representative of the growth rate in earnings per share for the long-range earning power of the Dow? It would not seem to be. The average return on beginning common book value of 11.7% with an average payout of 52%, produced a 5.6% growth rate from plowback. The other principal growth rate factor was an average increase in rate of return of 2.4%; that type of growth is transitory.

What do you think the long range return on beginning book value for the Dow will be? Let's use 12% and a dividend payout of about 50%. That would provide a long-range growth rate of earnings per share of 6% from plowback. If other factors provided 0.5% growth rate, the total growth in earnings per share would be 6.5%. Let's assume investors are willing to accept an 11% return, then the yield would have to be 4.5%. To get the price-earnings ratio, we divide the yield of 4.5% into the payout of 50% and arrive at an 11-times price-earnings ratio. In 1973 the Dow sold at 11 times. Perhaps this is a more realistic figure if investors only had more sense. On the basis of our assumptions, the market price divided by book value would be 132%. (Return on book value 12%, times the price-earnings ratio 11.)

Exhibit 18-6 shows the actual price range for the Dow and what it might have sold at if it had sold for 11 times earnings, with a line fitted to the average yearly figures.

Unfortunately, the market is highly influenced by short range changes in earnings per share. And the return on beginning book value has varied from a low of 9.4% to a high of 13.7% in the last ten years. This will cause wide fluctuations in earnings per share. Furthermore, the market will be subject to even wider fluctuations due to over-optimism or pessimism.

The high interest rates in current years, and particularly 1974, make a return of 11% to investors in common stocks totally inadequate. Therefore, in evaluating what the Dow should sell for, we would have to use a substantially higher rate for the return to investors. If we assumed that investors wanted 14%, then a price-earnings ratio for the Dow might be as follows:

Plowback		
Return on beginning common book value	Earnings retained	
12%	50%	6.0%
Other factors		0.5
Total		6.5
Dividend yield		7.5
Total return to investors		14.0

$$\text{Price-earnings ratio} = \frac{\text{Payout}}{\text{Yield}} = \frac{50\%}{7.5\%} = 7$$

In Exhibit 18-6, the lower lines show what the Dow would have sold for at seven times earnings with a line fitted to the yearly figures. As long as interest rates stay where they are, it would appear that the level of the market reached in 1974 made some sense.

You can develop similar figures as suggested above for your company and use the same method of reasoning to get some idea of a reasonable price for your company's stock in the long run.

When we look at the historical results for a particular company in terms of these parameters, it should be kept in mind that the total return on common book value is not necessarily equivalent to common cost, because investors may have expected something quite different from what they received. The market price for a common stock is a result of what investors expected in terms of earnings per share rather than what actually occurred. Investors may get market prices out of line when their expectations are not realistic.

Why Do Stock Prices Get so Far Out of Line?

Most analysts act like sheep or lemmings. They look for hot stocks which will show an increase in near-term earnings per share. The hotter a stock gets the more they rush in and push it up. During a boom this action is particularly evident in the emphasis put on market appreciation rather than dividend yield. As the boom grows hotter, the interest in yield fades away. When the boom busts, the analysts all run for shelter. Thus, we have the irrational booms and busts in the stock market.

Even the performance of the fund managers has been poor, no matter how you measure it. Standard and Poor's 500 stock index outperformed 89% of the mutual funds

Exhibit 18-6

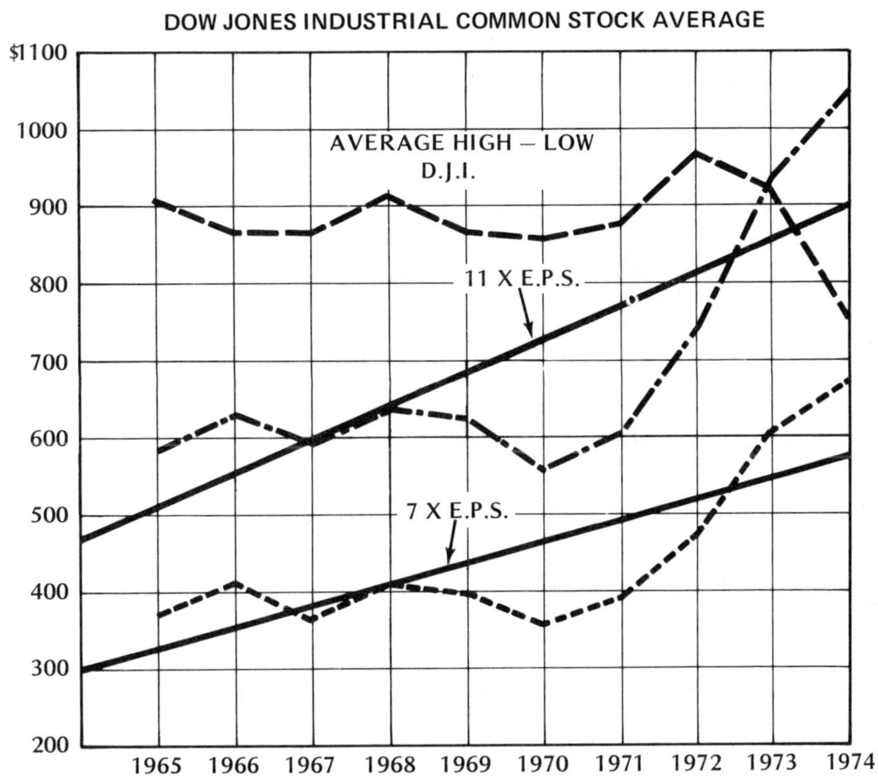

in the ten years ended December 31, 1973 as compiled by Lipper & Co. In 1973, the index outperformed 78% of the funds. The index outperformed 300 pension fund managers in an approximately similar manner on the basis of figures compiled by A.G. Becker & Co.

There are a few fundamental analysts who look for value in terms of the long-range earning power of a company. These poor fellows suffer badly in the short run, because the market may ignore such values. They should come out ahead in the long run.

If all analysts looked at long-range earning power, the booms and busts in the stock market would be leveled out as well as the extreme range in prices for stocks which were hot and cold. Furthermore, if all analysts followed such a policy, stocks in the long run would sell at a somewhat lower level in relation to company earnings so that investors would come out with a better return. This would be healthy for our entire economy.

As management, you can't do anything about this deplorable situation, but it is important that you appreciate how irrational the market price of your stock, at times, may be. All you can do is console yourself with an understanding that these are the facts of life.

Directors—The Stockholders' Representatives

It seems appropriate to finish up the book and this chapter about return to the stockholders with a few words about the directors.

They play a very crucial role. They should represent the stockholders' best interests. And they are the only ones who can pass on the top management if it is doing a poor job. However, directors seem to be the weakest link in the management team.

Directors are picked by the president or chairman and they are in most instances his buddies. They rubber stamp what he does. It is an honor and looks good in *Who's Who,* so most directors don't have the guts to speak up and do the job they are supposed to do.

There is much controversy over the method of electing directors, which revolves around non-cumulative or cumulative voting. Cumulative voting is required by the law in some states for companies incorporated therein; it is permissible in some and not allowed in others.

The difference between non-cumulative and cumulative voting can best be explained by a simple example. Assume that three directors are to be elected, and a stockholder has 100 shares of stock. If the voting is non-cumulative, he can cast his 100 shares for each of three directors, or just one or two as he sees fit, but in no event will his vote count in favor of one director for more than 100 shares. In cumulative voting, each stockholder gets the number of votes equivalent to his number of shares multiplied by the number of directors to be elected. He can divide these votes between directors as he wishes. In other words, in cumulative voting, when three directors are to be elected, he can split up his 300 votes among the directors, or he can cast them all for one director. Minority stockholders, by concentrating their votes on one or a few directors, may get representation on the board.

The effectiveness of cumulative voting is dulled by staggering the terms of directors so that only a few are elected at a time. For example, if there is an 11-man board and all 11 are elected at the same time, a holder of 10% of the stock would have slightly more than enough votes to elect a director. It works this way. Assume that there are 100,000 shares outstanding, and that a minority stockholder owns 10,000 shares. He would have 110,000 votes; the other stockholders would have 990,000 votes. If they spread their votes in an effort to try to elect the entire board, that would mean 90,000 votes apiece. The minority stockholder could easily elect one director. If there were a staggered election, the effectiveness of the minority stockholder would be progressively diluted as the number of directors elected at one time became less. If only one director were elected, cumulative voting would have no effect.

Cumulative voting is a hot issue between some managements and stockholder groups. It is contended by some managements that cumulative voting makes possible raids on companies by outside elements trying to obtain a voice in the management for their own benefit and to the detriment of the holders of the majority of the stock. On the other hand, small stockholder groups contend that without cumulative voting they are totally ineffective in obtaining any representation on the board. Enough has been written on this subject, both pro and con, that if one wishes to make a study of the matter, there is ample literature available.

The principal job of directors is to remove the top management if it is mediocre or incompetent. Directors should not try to manage. However, directors must take enough interest in the company and devote sufficient time to determine whether management is doing a good job. This is not an insurmountable task for a person skilled in management. By studying reports, talking to members of the management team, visiting operations, noting how the company is doing in relation to competitors, etc., a good director should be able to tell whether management is competent.

This, of course, takes some time. But a director should be willing to give the time if he takes on the assignment.

Some points with regard to directors are as follows:

1. The number of inside directors should be limited to the chairman and the president. Any officer of the company has to take orders from the chairman of the board and can't be expected to throw him out.

   The number of directors should not be so few that the management on the board controls the situation, nor so many that it is unwieldy. Around 11 is a reasonable number, with not more than two places being taken up by officials of the company. Of course, regardless of who he is, if a person owns a large amount of stock, he has a right to be on the board. A company which only has a small amount of stock publicly held, may very well have a number of insiders on the board for this reason.

2. Conflict of interest should be avoided meticulously. The management of the company should be free from pressure by directors which will in any way restrict the officers from making contracts, etc., on the best available basis. This applies in all matters.

   Nepotism may deaden the spirit of an organization. When a family-owned company becomes publicly owned, this should be guarded against. And for a company which is all publicly owned, there is an obligation to avoid any such possibility.

   If an investment banker is on the board, his firm should not be the lead in any financing. At the least, a member of the board should eliminate himself from having anything to do with the financing. A commercial banker might do business with the company, but he should not be the lead bank, and all banking services should be priced with other banks before the banker on the board is given any business.

   To obtain a knowledgeable, active, ideal board of directors as measured by all possible tests is not an easy matter. There may be exceptions where there is value in having some directors on the board even though they may have personal axes to grind. Therefore, one of the most important tests is those men's standards of business ethics. A director holds a position of highest trust, and his every action should be performed as if all the stockholders were looking over his shoulder.

   A good board of directors cannot be assured by a company's charter or resolutions, but some provisions may be of assistance. The provisions of some companies governing the boards of directors are rather ancient, and revision may be needed.

   Each year the auditors should certify to the Audit Committee of the Board that there was, in fact, no conflict during the year.

3. There should be a definite retirement age.
4. Directors should insist that they be kept adequately informed about the company's operations. If directors get the impression that they are being given only favorable information and bad news is being withheld, it is time for a change in top management—and directors should act. If a company wants to do so, keeping directors fully informed is not a difficult task.

   One way for directors to keep informed is through the auditors. There should be an audit committee of the board made up of outside board members. It should insist that the auditors keep the committee fully informed. If the auditors do not do so, the board should insist on the appointment of new auditors.

   The audit committee should meet regularly with the outside auditors. The outside auditors should be responsible for giving the directors a thorough insight as to the company's position. The audit committee should solicit all outside directors for questions they may want to ask the auditors.

5. There are various other committees of the board such as the salary committee. These committee assignments should be taken seriously and should not be dictated to by management.
6. Directors may meet monthly or less often. But quarterly meetings might be too infrequent if the company has many problems. The meetings should not be perfunctory. They should be substantial, with the management giving a comprehensive report on its stewardship. Any director who attends short meetings should realize that if there was any occasion for him being sued, he would be in a very embarrassing position.

7. The operations of the board should be handled with a definite program. Each new member should be presented with a notebook giving the background of the company, how it is organized, its bylaws and an explanation of the liability of a director. There should be a specific orientation program, including plant and management visits for a new director.

   The regular directors' meetings should be formalized with a regular agenda and a program established which will keep the directors completely informed with verbal presentations and written material.

   A very important part of a program should be for the outside directors to meet alone once a year, with no management people present, to discuss among themselves how the management is performing. Otherwise, if some directors want to discuss the subject, they have to do it behind management's back, and then management usually hears about it and tension builds up. Management ought to understand that the directors want to discuss among themselves how management is doing.
8. A director should make a major contribution to a company, in one way or another, and should not continue to be on the board just for his satisfaction or benefit.

The subject of directors is not an integral part of financial policy, so we won't dwell on the subject any longer; but since financial policies are passed on by the directors, there is actually a close relationship. Furthermore, directors have a major responsibility in preserving our system of private capital by establishing sound and fair policies. Anyone who takes on this responsibility for a publicly owned company should study thoroughly not only the legal aspects, but also the scope of the position, and the ethical standards required. A board member who allows himself to be a rubber stamp for management's policies lacks sufficient character for the position. To do a good job as a director, a person must understand many phases of business and keep up on the dynamic changes which are ever taking place in our fast-growing society.

We can end the book here with a fervent hope that boards will do a better job so that companies will have the type of management that the stockholders, employees and customers deserve.

INDEX

E

F

G

I

J

L

S

T

U